KV-387-074

NURMA SMURFIT
NATIONAL COLLEGE
OF IRELAND

WITHDRAWN FROM STOCK

# BUSINESS LAW

*General Editor*
Denise Collins

OXFORD
UNIVERSITY PRESS

# OXFORD
UNIVERSITY PRESS

Great Clarendon Street, Oxford OX2 6DP

Oxford University Press is a department of the University of Oxford.
It furthers the University's objective of excellence in research, scholarship,
and education by publishing worldwide in

Oxford New York

Auckland Cape Town Dar es Salaam Hong Kong Karachi
Kuala Lumpur Madrid Melbourne Mexico City Nairobi
New Delhi Shanghai Taipei Toronto

With offices in

Argentina Austria Brazil Chile Czech Republic France Greece
Guatemala Hungary Italy Japan Poland Portugal Singapore
South Korea Switzerland Thailand Turkey Ukraine Vietnam

Oxford is a registered trade mark of Oxford University Press
in the UK and in certain other countries

Published in the United States
by Oxford University Press Inc., New York

© Law Society of Ireland 2009

The moral rights of the authors have been asserted

Database right Oxford University Press (maker)

Crown Copyright material is reproduced under Class Licence
Number C01P0000148 with the permission of HMSO
and the Queen's Printer for Scotland

First published 2009

All rights reserved. No part of this publication may be reproduced,
stored in a retrieval system, or transmitted, in any form or by any means,
without the prior permission in writing of Oxford University Press,
or as expressly permitted by law, or under terms agreed with the appropriate
reprographics rights organization. Enquiries concerning reproduction
outside the scope of the above should be sent to the Rights Department,
Oxford University Press, at the address above

You must not circulate this book in any other binding or cover
and you must impose this same condition on any acquirer

British Library Cataloguing in Publication Data
Data available

Library of Congress Cataloging in Publication Data
Business law/Denise Collins, general editor.—4th ed.
p. cm.—(Law Society of Ireland manual)
Includes bibliographical references and index.
ISBN 978–0–19–921234–7
1. Business law—Ireland. 2. Commercial law—Ireland. I. Collins, Denise.
KDK175.B87C66 2009
346.41507—dc22

2008051887

Typeset by Laserwords Private Ltd, Chennai, India
Printed in Great Britain
on acid-free paper by
Ashford Colour Press Ltd, Gosport, Hampshire

ISBN 978–0–19–921234–7

1 3 5 7 9 10 8 6 4 2

## Disclaimer

While every care has been taken in the production of this book,
no legal responsibility or liability is accepted, warranted or implied by the
authors, editors, publishers or the Law Society in respect of any
errors, omissions or mis-statements.

# PREFACE

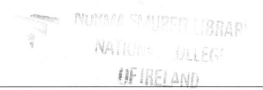

WITHDRAWN FROM STOCK

This textbook is designed to support the teaching of the Business Law module on the Law Society's Professional Practice Course. The book aims to equip trainees with a knowledge of those aspects of business law areas most likely to be encountered at the outset of their legal careers. The text is not designed to be a comprehensive exposition of business law. It is hoped, however, that the work will be of interest to all who find that business law touches upon their practice, whether in the public or private sector.

The book covers: Chapter 1: Partnership Law (Dr Michael Twomey); Chapter 2: Company Formation and Secretarial Management (Michael M. Moran); Chapter 3: Company Law Enforcement (Aillil O'Reilly); Chapter 4: Shareholders Agreements (Stephen Keogh); Chapter 5: Buying and Selling a Business (Brendan Heneghan and Stephen Keogh); Chapter 6: Irish Merger Control (Denise Collins); Chapter 7: Irish Competition Law (Denise Collins); Chapter 8: Regulation (Denise Collins); Chapter 9: Consumer Law (Howard Linnane); Chapter 10: Intellectual Property (Carol Plunkett); Chapter 11: Information Technology (Rob Corbet and Philip Nolan); Chapter 12: Commercial Lending (Kevin Hoy); Chapter 13: Insolvency (Fergus Doorly); Chapter 14: Dispute Resolution (Michael Carrigan); Chapter 15: Vertical Agreements (Agency, Distribution, Franchising) (Denise Collins); Chapter 16: Commercial Drafting (Jeanne Kelly).

This book aims to reflect the law as of 1 March 2008.

While every effort has been made to ensure that this text is accurate, neither the authors, the editors, nor the Law Society of Ireland accept legal liability for any errors, omissions or mis-statements of law. Any comments or queries on the contents of this manual should be sent to the general editor at the Law Society.

Special thanks to Zoe Donnelly for her assistance in compiling this edition.

Denise Collins, Editor
October 2008

v

WITHDRAWN FROM STOCK

Barcode No:39006010285338
Dewey No: 346.41707
Date Input: 11/02/09
Price: € 51.20

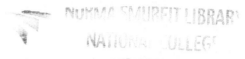
NORMA SMURFIT LIBRARY
NATIONAL COLLEGE
OF IRELAND

# AUTHORS

**Michael Carrigan** is a partner in Eugene F. Collins, Solicitors. He practises extensively in the area of commercial property and is a practising arbitrator. He is Chairman of the Arbitration Committee of the Law Society of Ireland and is the author of *Handbook on Arbitration Law in Ireland* published by the Law Society in 1998. He is a Fellow of the Chartered Institute of Arbitrators and was Chairman of the Chartered Institute of Arbitrators—Irish Branch in 1991–1992. He is the member for Ireland of the ICC International Court of Arbitration and is a member of the International Roster of the American Arbitration Association. He is a former Chairman of the Society of Young Solicitors in Ireland and a Past President of the Association Internationale des Jeunes Avocats.

**Denise Collins** qualified as a Solicitor in 1996. Denise holds an LLB from Trinity College Dublin and a Master's Degree in European Law from the Université Libre de Bruxelles. She practised EU and Competition Law in Brussels, London and Dublin for eight years. Between 2005 and 2007 Denise was responsible for the Law Society Business Law courses. She has lectured in competition law for several years.

**Rob Corbet** is a partner of the Technology Unit at Arthur Cox. He qualified in 1999 and joined Arthur Cox in 2000. His clients include established and start-up companies engaged in technical innovation. He has lectured and published extensively on information technology law. Rob has lectured and tutored in the area of business law at the Law Society.

**Fergus Doorly** is a partner in William Fry, Solicitors. He practises in all aspects of insolvency, corporate recovery and commercial litigation. He has extensive experience in advising liquidators, receivers, examiners and others in all aspects of insolvency law.

**Brendan Heneghan** is a partner in William Fry, Solicitors. He practises in the area of mergers and acquisitions with particular focus on transactions involving listed companies, including public takeovers and venture capital investments. Brendan has lectured in the area of business law and takeovers and mergers at the Law Society. He is also the author of a number of publications, including the Irish chapter in *A Practitioner's Guide to the Acquisition of Private Companies in the European Union*.

# AUTHORS

**Kevin Hoy** is a partner in Mason Hayes and Curran, Solicitors, where he leads the financial services unit. His work includes acquisition financing, development financing and project financing. Kevin is the internal examiner for the Law Society final examination—Part I Contract Law, and has lectured in the area of business law at the Law Society.

**Jeanne Kelly** is a partner in Mason Hayes and Curran, Solicitors. Jeanne studied law at University College Dublin and at the Université de Haute Normandie, Rouen, France. She joined Mason Hayes and Curran, Solicitors from the Intellectual Property and Information Technology Unit of another leading Irish firm. She advises both public and private clients in relation to data protection, contract, communications, information technology and intellectual property issues. Jeanne is actively involved in the Licensing Executives Association (LES) and the Society for Computers and Law (Irish branch) and is a board member of both bodies. She is also a member of INTA, the International Trade Mark Association. In addition to this edition of *Business Law*, Jeanne has also co-authored a book on *Irish Information, Technology Law* by Cavendish and a book on *Data Protection Law* in Ireland published by Thompson Round Hall in 2004. Jeanne is a lecturer in commercial drafting and information technology at the Law Society.

**Stephen Keogh** is a partner in William Fry, Solicitors. He practises in the Corporate Department where he specialises in mergers and acquisitions, venture capital investments and also advises on a range of other commercial and company law matters. Stephen has tutored in the area of business law at the Law Society.

**Howard Linnane** is a solicitor and former barrister and has worked predominantly as a professional support lawyer in research, know-how, information and training. He has also worked in legal education, both academic and professional, particularly in the area of company/commercial law which he has taught part-time at University College Dublin and Dublin Institute of Technology and full-time on a law degree course at Portobello College. In 1999–2000 he was course coordinator at the Law Society's Law School where he was responsible for all company/commercial law modules and their transfer from the old-style courses to the first new-style PPC1 course which commenced in October 2000. He has written extensively on company law and commercial law topics and has had numerous articles published in Irish and UK law journals. He has lectured and tutored in the area of business law at the Law Society.

**Michael M. Moran** is a practising in-house solicitor and a Community Trade Mark Attorney, with Deloitte and Touche, Chartered Accountants and is a past Chairman of the Irish Branch of the Chartered Institute of Arbitrators and the Law Society Arbitration and Mediation Committee. Michael practises inter alia in company law and company secretarial practice and procedure and has lectured on these subjects at the Law Society.

**Philip Nolan** is a partner in the Commercial Department of Mason Hayes and Curran, Solicitors. He graduated with a BCL from University College Dublin in 1996 having spent a year studying at De Paul University Law School in Chicago as an exchange student. Having completed a BCL Masters in Law at the University of Oxford in 1997 specialising in commercial and competition law, he joined Mason Hayes and Curran in the same year, and thereafter completed his apprenticeship with the firm. As an apprentice, he was a founding member of the *Hibernian Law Journal* and represented the Law Society at

NORMA SMURFIT LIBRARY
NATIONAL COLLEGE
OF IRELAND

the finals of the Jessup Moot Court Competition in Washington, DC. As a partner in the Commercial Department at Mason Hayes and Curran, Solicitors, he advises both public and private clients in relation to telecommunications law, information technology law, intellectual property law and competition law. He contributes regularly to numerous law journals and other industry publications. Philip has lectured and tutored in the area of business law at the Law Society. He lectures on contract law at Trinity College Dublin.

**Aillil O'Reilly** is a practising barrister, focusing on company and insolvency law. He read Classical Civilisation and French at Trinity College Dublin. He commenced an MLitt under Trinity's Department of Russian in 1996, at the same time as studying for the Irish Bar. He graduated from the Honorable Society of King's Inns in 1999 with a degree of barrister-at-law. He contributes to Irish law journals on topics related to his areas of practice. In 2002, he was asked to join the Drafting Committee of the Company Law Review Group and has assisted in the formation of the heads of the Companies Bill 2004. Aillil has tutored in the area of business law at the Law Society.

**Carol Plunkett** is a partner in William Fry, Solicitors. She practises in intellectual property law and has acted in many of the patent, copyright, trade mark and passing-off cases which have come before the courts in recent years. Carol has lectured in the area of business law at the Law Society.

**Dr Michael Twomey** is the author of Twomey, *Partnership Law,* (Butterworths, 2000). He practises exclusively in partnership law and his practice consists of advising law firms on their own behalf and on behalf of their clients in relation to all aspects of partnerships. He previously lectured in partnership law at Trinity College Dublin and currently lectures at the Law Society of Ireland. He is a member of the Business Law Committee of the Law Society of Ireland and the Association of Partnership Practitioners (UK).

NURMA SMURFIT LIBRARY
NATIONAL COLLEGE
OF IRELAND

# OUTLINE CONTENTS

**OUTLINE CONTENTS**

**PART 4   BUSINESS AGREEMENTS**

# DETAILED CONTENTS

**DETAILED CONTENTS**

**DETAILED CONTENTS**

## PART 2  BUYING AND SELLING A BUSINESS

**DETAILED CONTENTS**

## DETAILED CONTENTS

**DETAILED CONTENTS**

## DETAILED CONTENTS

# TABLE OF CASES

## TABLE OF CASES

# TABLE OF CASES

# TABLE OF LEGISLATION

NORMA SMURFIT LIBRARY NATIONAL COLLEGE OF IRELAND

# UK Legislation

## *Statutes*

## *Statutory Instruments*

# European Legislation

## *Treaties*

# International Legislation

# PART 1

# ESTABLISHING AND OPERATING A BUSINESS

# CHAPTER 1

# PARTNERSHIP LAW

## 1.1 Nature of Partnerships

### 1.1.1 IMPORTANCE OF PARTNERSHIP LAW

#### 1.1.1.1 General

Partnerships occupy an important part of Irish business life for a number of reasons. First, partnership is the default form of business organisation in the sense that any time two or more people carry on a business venture without forming a company, they will invariably be partners. This point is highlighted by the case of *Joyce v Morrissey* [1998] TLR 707 which involved The Smiths, the 1980s rock band. A dispute arose about the sharing of the band's profits between, on the one side, the lead singer (Morrissey) and lead guitar player (Johnnie Marr) and, on the other side, the drummer and bass guitarist. Although the four may never have thought that they were creating a partnership when they formed the band, it was held that they were carrying on business as partners and therefore the rules in the Partnership Act, 1890 (the '1890 Act') about the division of profits applied to them. In that case, it meant that all four were entitled to share the band's profits equally and the court rejected Morrissey's and Marr's claim that as they were the main creative force behind the band, they were entitled to a greater share of the profits.

In most cases, any time two or more people carry on business together without doing it through the medium of a registered company, they constitute a partnership and are subject to partnership law. Indeed, even where two or more companies are involved in business together, they will be subject to partnership law if they do not form a special purpose joint venture company for the project.

The second reason partnerships are important is that they form an integral part of Irish business life because there is a large section of Irish business which is effectively required to use partnerships to operate. This is because professionals such as lawyers, doctors, dentists, vets and accountants are not allowed to incorporate. Thus, any time two or more such professionals carry on business together, they will invariably be partners.

The final reason why partnerships occupy an important role in Irish business life is because they provide significant tax, accounting, and disclosure advantages over companies. For example, in a company, both corporation tax and income tax are paid in respect of the profits of the enterprise, i.e. corporation tax is paid on the company's profits and income tax is paid on the company's dividends paid to shareholders. However, a partnership is 'see-through' for tax purposes and therefore there is only one point at which tax is payable on the enterprise's profits, i.e. income tax is paid by the partners on the share of the profits received by them and no tax is paid by the partnership. As regards disclosure and accounting advantages, partnerships do not generally have to file their accounts publicly while companies do and it is considerably easier and cheaper for partners to subscribe and withdraw capital from a partnership than it is for shareholders in a limited company, thus making partnerships popular venture capital vehicles.

For the foregoing reasons, it follows that a solicitor, whether in a large corporate practice or a general practice, will encounter clients who either consciously or unconsciously are in business partnerships and who will require advice on the applicable law. In addition, the solicitors themselves may be partners in a law firm, since approximately one out of every four solicitors is a partner in a law firm. Perhaps the most important aspect of partnership law is the fact that the Partnership Act, 1890 implies standard terms into every partnership unless the parties agree otherwise. Since many of these implied terms are inappropriate for modern partnerships, it is imperative that every partner and his legal adviser be aware of those terms and have a written partnership agreement which replaces them with more appropriate terms.

### 1.1.1.2 Partnership versus company

It is useful at this juncture to compare partnerships with the main form of business association in Ireland, the registered company. A partnership, unlike a company, is not a separate legal entity from its members, thus explaining why a company is taxed separately from its owner shareholders while a partnership is not taxed but the partners are taxed. Similarly, it is to be noted that partnerships are not required to go through any registration process to be formed, while companies have to be registered in the Companies Registration Office. On the other hand, the main advantage that limited companies have over partnerships is that the shareholders have limited liability while partners have unlimited liability. Yet it should be remembered that partners may themselves be limited liability companies and in this way have an effective cap on their liability. In addition, in many companies (particularly in small businesses), limited liability is largely illusory because of the common requirement for directors and often their spouses to provide personal guarantees to banks and other creditors.

In addition, as is noted hereunder (see **1.6** below), there are two other types of partnerships in which some of the partners have limited liability, namely the limited partnership and the investment limited partnership. In this section, however, we concentrate on ordinary partnerships.

### 1.1.1.3   Why is it important to determine whether a partnership exists?

In this section, we look at the rules for determining whether a partnership has come into existence as well as some of the formalities for the operation of partnerships. The question of whether a partnership exists is important, because a partner is liable for the losses which his co-partner causes in carrying on the partnership business, even though he had no knowledge of his co-partner's activities and this includes situations where the co-partner has defrauded clients of the business. On the other hand, a partner is also entitled to an equal share of the partnership profits and for this reason, in a profitable business, it would be an advantage to be a partner. Another situation where it is important to establish whether a partnership exists is where a potential plaintiff is faced with a penniless defendant. If the defendant is carrying on business with a richer business colleague, it would be useful to establish that his richer business colleague is his partner and therefore jointly liable for the damages suffered by the potential plaintiff. Clearly, in these types of situations the question of whether a partnership exists will be of importance.

## 1.1.2   RELEVANT LAW

Much of the law relating to partnerships is to be found in the Partnership Act, 1890. The 1890 Act was a codification of the law of partnership as it had developed up to 1890. However, it is important to note that the Act does not provide a complete code of partnership law, and indeed s 46 specifically provides that:

> *The rules of equity and of common law applicable to partnership shall continue in force except so far as they are inconsistent with the express provisions of this Act.*

Therefore, regard must always be had to the case law from both before and after the 1890 Act.

## 1.1.3   DEFINITION OF PARTNERSHIP

### 1.1.3.1   General

The definition of a partnership is to be found in s 1(1) of the 1890 Act which states: 'Partnership is the relation which subsists between persons carrying on a business in common with a view of profit'. Where people carry on business in common through the medium of a company, they are specifically excluded from being partners by s 1(2) of the 1890 Act. It should be noted that a written partnership agreement is not a prerequisite for the existence of a partnership since the court will have regard to the true contract and intention of the parties as appearing from the whole facts of the case.

To satisfy the definition of partnership, two or more persons must actually be carrying on a business. It follows from this that an agreement to run a business in the future does not constitute an immediate partnership, nor does the taking of preliminary steps to enable a business to be run. Similarly, two or more people cannot agree that they were partners retrospectively unless they were actually carrying on business at the relevant time. In *Macken v Revenue Commissioners* [1962] IR 302, the parties signed a partnership agreement in the month of April, but it provided that the partnership 'shall be deemed to have commenced' in January of that same year. The High Court held that the partnership did not commence until the parties actually started carrying on business together which was in the month of April.

The definition of partnership in s 1(1) also requires the parties to be carrying on business with a 'view of profit'. In *McCarthaigh v Daly* [1985] IR 73, the respondent, a prominent Cork-based solicitor, was involved in a rather clever tax loophole which has since been closed off by the Revenue Commissioners. Under that scheme, Mr Daly agreed to contribute capital of £50 to a limited partnership connected with the Metropole Hotel in Cork in the tax year 1977–78. However, the arrangement was completely uneconomical and was clearly designed to make a loss, rather than a profit, which loss was to be used to reduce the income tax of Mr Daly on his personal income as a solicitor. Mr Daly sought to set off his share of the losses of the limited partnership which amounted to £2,000 against his personal income tax as a solicitor. O'Hanlon J in giving his decision was constrained by procedural rules. It is clear that, if it were not for the constraints of these procedural rules, O'Hanlon J would not have held that this arrangement constituted a partnership because of the absence of the 'view of profit'.

In addition to the definition of partnership in s 1(1) of the 1890 Act, s 2 of the 1890 Act lays down certain rules for determining the existence of a partnership. These rules include the following:

> (a) *joint or common ownership of property 'does not of itself create a partnership' even where profits from the property are shared (s 2(1));*

> (b) *the sharing of gross returns does not of itself create a partnership (s 2(2)). The difference between gross returns and net profits is illustrated by the example of a person who sells goods on commission for another. Such a person will receive a percentage of the gross sales or gross returns of the business. However, if he was to receive a percentage of the profits, this would involve the additional step of calculating the costs and overheads which would have to be deducted from the gross returns to calculate the profits, if any, of the business. Thus, a percentage of the gross returns could be valuable while a percentage of the net profits might be nothing; and*

> (c) *the receipt of a share of profits is prima facie evidence of partnership (s 2(3)), but it does not of itself make the recipient a partner.*

### 1.1.3.2 Co-ownership agreements

An important issue in recent times has been the question of the status of co-ownership agreements between investors in property and whether these are in fact partnerships.

The very act of simply co-owning property with another person or company does not of itself constitute the co-owners as partners. Indeed, this principle is enshrined in s 2(1) of the Partnership Act, 1890.

> *Joint tenancy, tenancy in common, joint property, common property, or part owner-ship does not of itself create a partnership as to anything so held or owned, whether the tenants or owners do or do not share any profits made by the use thereof*

However, a considerable amount of confusion has been caused regarding property investments in this country in the past few years because of undue reliance on this section. But s 2(1) of the Partnership Act, 1890 must not be looked at in isolation. Even the section itself does not state that co-owners of property cannot be partners. It simply says that co-ownership does not *of itself* lead to partnership. This means that to prove a partnership exists. It is not suf-ficient simply to show that two or more people own property jointly. That is what s 2(1) means; it does *not* mean that an investment *is prevented* from being a partnership because the investors happen to co-own the property which is the subject of the investment.

To determine whether a partnership exists between people who happen to co-own property, s 2(1) is only a small part of the equation. The most impor-tant thing to consider is whether the property project satisfies the definition of partnership in s 1(1) of the Partnership Act, 1890. As we have seen at **1.1.3.1**, this simply requires two or more people to be carrying on business in common with a view to profit. The fact that the arrangement or investment may be termed a 'co-ownership' rather than a partnership is irrelevant. In the words of Lord Halsbury in *Adam v Newbigging* (1888) 13 AC 308 at 315:

> If a partnership in fact exists, a community of interest in the adventure being carried on in fact, no concealment of name, no verbal equivalent for the ordinary phrases of profit or loss, no indirect expedient for enforcing control over the adventure will prevent the substance and reality of the transac-tion being adjudged to be partnership . . . and no phrasing of it by dextrous draftsmen . . . will avail to avert the legal consequence of the contract.

We have noted that s 2(1) means that co-ownership of property is not suf-ficient in itself to make the co-owners partners. Therefore, something more is required than simple co-ownership of property for there to be a partnership. However, very little more is required to establish that people who enter a prop-erty investment together with a view to making a profit are in fact carrying on a business for the purposes of s 1(1) so as to be partners.

The real aim of s 2(1) is to establish that those people who become co-owners almost by chance are not partners just because they happen to be co-owners of property. For example this would apply to people who become co-owners through an inheritance and who are not carrying on any business with the property—the very fact of co-ownership does not make them partners. However, where the property is simply the means by which two or more peo-ple carry on business or an investment together, s 2(1) does not grant them immunity from being partners.

It follows that most co-ownership agreements which are being entered into by investors in the current climate *are* in fact partnership agreements. As such, the default partnership agreement in the Partnership Act, 1890 with all its implied terms (referred to at **1.1.8** below) will apply to them, unless their agreement contracts out of those terms.

### 1.1.3.3 Distinction between partner and lender

The case of *AIB Group (UK) plc v Martin and Another* [2002] 1 All ER 353 is a co-ownership case that provides a salutary lesson to the increasing number of individuals who are involved in property partnerships. It involved a Mr Gold who bought investment property with Mr Martin and signed a standard form bank mortgage with Mr Martin as part of the purchase. The mortgage provided, inter alia, that:

The mortgagor herby covenants with . . . the bank . . . that it will on demand pay or discharge to the bank . . . all sums of money . . . advanced to the mortgagor by the bank . . .

Clause 1 of the mortgage contained an interpretation section that provided an expanded definition of the term 'mortgagor' to adapt the mortgage where it was executed or used by more than one person. In such a case, Clause 1 provided that the expression 'mortgagor'

shall be construed as referring to all and/or any one of those persons and the obligations of such persons hereunder shall be joint and several.

On this basis and to Mr Gold's horror, the AIB Group successfully argued that Mr Gold undertook to pay on demand all monies which had been advanced by AIB Group not just to Mr Gold himself, or to himself and Mr Martin jointly, but also any sums which had been advanced by AIB Group to Mr Martin separately.

### 1.1.3.4 Distinction between partner and lender

At this juncture, it is appropriate to consider the distinction between a partner and a lender since it has been noted that s 2(3) provides that a person who receives a share of the profits of a partnership is prima facie a partner. Obviously, this distinction is important in view of the unlimited liability of a partner for the debts of the partnership whereas the lender only stands to lose the money invested if the business fails. It is not unknown for some lenders/investors to wish to avoid the consequences of being a partner but at the same time share in the profits of the borrower's business.

Subsections (a) to (e) of s 2(3) of the 1890 Act provide for this and other such scenarios by stating that:

(a)  *a person does not become a partner merely because a debt is paid to him by instalments out of profits;*

(b)  *an employee does not become a partner merely because his remuneration varies with profits;*

(c)  *a widow or child of a partner is not a partner merely because a proportion of profits is paid to that person as an annuity;*

(d)     *a lender who receives a share of profits is not automatically a partner if the contract is in writing and signed by all the parties; and*

(e)     *a vendor who receives payment for his business varying with profits is not automatically a partner.*

However, there remains a risk that anyone who receives a share of profits may be held to be a partner and therefore personally liable for debts. For this reason, it is important for a lender who does not wish to take on the risk of unlimited liability to ensure that he does not become a partner, e.g. by avoiding any suggestion that he has a right to take part in management and by having a written agreement setting out the terms of his involvement with the firm as required by s 2(3)(d). It will often occur that the same fact situation will fall within more than one of the subsections of s 2(3). This was the case in *Re Borthwick* (1875) ILTR 155 which concerned the payment of a share of the profits of a partnership business to an employee, Kirkpatrick, who was also a lender to the business. In that case, Kirkpatrick advanced £800 to Borthwick, a general merchant in Belfast. This sum was to be used to purchase Irish flax for the business. Under the terms of their agreement, Kirkpatrick was to receive repayments of interest and principal at a rate of half of the profits derived from the sale of the flax.

On the bankruptcy of Borthwick, it was alleged by his assignees in bankruptcy that Kirkpatrick was a partner of Borthwick's and therefore should have his debt deferred to the other creditors of Borthwick (see further in relation to the deferral of a partner's debts on the bankruptcy of his partner, Twomey, *Partnership Law* (Butterworths, 2000) paras 27.153 *et seq.*). Harrison J held that Kirkpatrick, although the recipient of a debt out of the profits of Borthwick's business, was not his partner but his employee.

## 1.1.4    NUMBER OF PARTNERS

The Companies Act, 1963, s 376 prescribes that the maximum number of persons who may be members of a partnership is twenty. However, pursuant to s 13 of the Companies (Amendment) Act, 1982 solicitors and accountants are not subject to this limitation. In addition, two orders have been made under s 13(2) of the Companies (Amendment) Act, 1982 (i.e. SI 54/1988 and SI 506/2004) exempting limited partnerships from this twenty-partner limit if they are formed for the purpose of thoroughbred-horse breeding and exempting limited partnerships which have no more than fifty partners that are formed for venture capital purposes.

## 1.1.5    CAPACITY

Like any other contract, any person including a minor is legally capable of entering into a partnership contract. Yet, the minor will not, during his minority, incur liability to his co-partners or to third parties for the debts of the firm or the acts of his co-partners (*Lovell and Christmas v Beauchamp* [1894] AC 607). In addition, the contract is voidable at the instance of the minor.

Companies, as well as individuals, may enter into a partnership with other companies or with individuals, provided that the companies have the power to do so under their objects clause.

In marital disputes, it is sometimes overlooked that spouses may be partners in relation to a family business or investments. Thus, there is no reason why one spouse would not be able to rely on the terms of the 1890 Act regarding the equal division of profits and assets on a dissolution of the partnership, which dissolution will invariably occur on the breakdown of a marriage.

## 1.1.6 TYPES OF PARTNERSHIPS AND PARTNERS

Every partnership is either a partnership at will (informal partnership) or a formal partnership (or, as it is sometimes called, a fixed-term partnership). A partnership at will is one which may be dissolved by any one partner at any time by notice (see 1890 Act, ss 26(1) and 32(c)). Every partnership is presumed to be a partnership at will unless there is an express or implicit agreement to the contrary between the partners (*Murphy v Power* [1923] 1 IR 68). Where there is an express or implicit agreement to exclude the right of a partner to dissolve the partnership by notice, the resulting partnership is known as a formal partnership (fixed-term partnership).

The exclusion of this right is often achieved implicitly, e.g. by the agreement that the partnership will last for a fixed term and the majority of formal partnerships are such fixed term partnerships.

In addition to there being different types of partnerships, there may also be different types of partners. Two types of partners are worthy of specific mention, i.e. a dormant partner and a salaried partner. A dormant partner is a partner who plays no active role in the business of the partnership. However, the term has no legal significance since a dormant partner has the same rights and liabilities as any other partner and so he is entitled to an equal share of the profits of the firm, he is equally liable for the losses of the firm and he is entitled to take part in the management of the firm.

The term 'salaried partner' is in fact a contradiction in terms, since he is not a partner but an employee. A salaried partner is a person who normally operates in the middle rank of professional partnerships between true partners and salaried employees. The salaried partner is held out to the world as a partner yet he receives a salary and sometimes a bonus by way of remuneration, but he does not receive a share of the profits like a normal partner. In addition, he is not entitled to the other rights of partnership, e.g. to vote at partners' meetings, to dissolve the firm etc. However, as regards outsiders who deal with the firm, the salaried partner is as good as a partner. This is because he is held out to be a 'partner' and thus will be liable to third parties who relied on the fact that he was a partner under the principle of holding out as a partner, which is considered below (see **1.3.4**). For this reason, it is advisable for a salaried partner to receive an indemnity from the partners in respect of such potential liabilities to third parties.

### 1.1.7 BUSINESS NAME OF PARTNERSHIP

Partnerships commonly trade under a name other than the names of the partners. This has implications under the Registration of Business Names Act, 1963 since if the business of a partnership is carried on under a name which does not consist solely of the surnames of all the partners, then the firm must register this name as a business name (Registration of Business Names Act, 1963, ss 3(1)(a) and 4) and it must publish the true names of the partners on the stationery of the firm (Registration of Business Names Act, 1963, s 18). The case of *Macken v Revenue Commissioners* [1962] IR 302 highlights that, although the filing in the register of business names may appear to be troublesome red tape, it may be important at a subsequent date in establishing that a certain person had become, or had ceased to be, a partner.

There, the High Court held that no partnership existed between a father and his two children who traded under the name 'Patrick Macken & Son'. One of the factors in the court's decision that the children were not partners was that they had not registered that name as a business name. They would have had to do this if it was a partnership, since the name 'Patrick Macken & Son' was not the name of the three purported partners.

### 1.1.8 WHY A WRITTEN PARTNERSHIP AGREEMENT IS ESSENTIAL

The effect of the 1890 Act for partnerships is like the effect of Table A of the Companies Act, 1963 for companies. This is because, like Table A, the 1890 Act sets out certain basic terms of the partnership agreement which will apply to every partnership, save in so far as they are modified or excluded by the partners. In this sense, the 1890 Act may be viewed as a default partnership agreement whose terms apply to every partnership if they are not excluded. For this reason, it is crucial for partners and their advisers to be aware of all of the rights and duties which are implied by the 1890 Act and then to decide which of them are appropriate for the partnership and which of them should be modified by the terms of the partnership agreement.

Unlike Table A, where the majority of the terms of Table A are appropriate for most companies, it is fair to say that the majority of the terms of the 1890 Act are wholly inappropriate for most partnerships. It is for this reason that it is crucial that most partnerships have a written partnership agreement and that such a partnership agreement expressly provides terms which are contrary to those contained in the 1890 Act. A few examples will illustrate how inappropriate the 1890 Act is for most partnerships.

(a) There is no right under the default partnership agreement to expel a partner. Thus, no matter how unprofessional or negligent or belligerent a partner is, his co-partners may not expel him from the partnership in the absence of a right of expulsion.

(b)   In every partnership at will, regardless of the number of partners in the firm, be it two or thirty-two, any one partner in the firm may dissolve the partnership by simply arriving at a partners' meeting and giving notice orally that the firm is dissolved.

(c)   If a partner dies, the firm will automatically dissolve under the terms of s 33 of the 1890 Act and may be wound up at the wish of any one partner. There is no general right in law to acquire a deceased partner's share, so if the surviving partners want the firm to continue, they have to enter negotiations with the deceased partner's estate to purchase this share. Therefore, a written partnership agreement should provide that the death of a partner will not dissolve the firm but instead that the deceased partner's share may be purchased by the surviving partners pursuant to an agreed valuation mechanism.

(d)   There is no general power to retire under partnership law. Thus, the only possibility for a partner who wishes to retire in the absence of a retirement provision is for him to dissolve the partnership. This is a drastic solution and accordingly it is important to have a provision allowing a partner to retire.

These are but four examples of why a carefully drafted partnership agreement is necessary to avoid the full rigours of the 1890 Act (see further Twomey, *Partnership Law*, paras 21.03 *et seq.*). The only way to ensure against these and other rights which may be inappropriate in a partnership is to have a carefully drafted provision in the partnership agreement excluding those rights.

Finally, in considering the application of the terms of a partnership agreement to the day-to-day running of a firm, it is important to bear in mind the terms of the 1890 Act, s 19. Section 19 provides that the rights of partners may be varied by express or implied consent. For this reason, in some circumstances, it may be prudent for a partner who is conducting himself contrary to his express rights under the partnership agreement to clarify in writing that such action is not to be construed as an implied variation of the terms of the partnership agreement.

## 1.2   Partners' Rights *Inter Se*

### 1.2.1   INTRODUCTION

Once it is established that a partnership is in existence, the next step is to determine the respective rights of the partners *inter se*, and in this section consideration is given to these rights. It has been noted that the 1890 Act operates for partnerships in much the same way that Table A of the Companies Act, 1963 operates for companies, since in the absence of any other agreement between the partners, the terms of their partnership agreement may be found in the 1890 Act. It has also been seen that some of these default rules are inappropriate for modern partnerships and therefore the partners may wish to have a written partnership agreement which excludes them. Reference has already been made to one of those default rules, namely the right of any one partner to dissolve the partnership by giving notice. Reference will now be made to the other important default rules in the 1890 Act regarding the internal operations of a partnership.

## 1.2.2 MANAGEMENT OF THE PARTNERSHIP

Section 24(5) of the 1890 Act states that, subject to contrary agreement, express or implied, '[e]very partner may take part in the management of the partnership business'. If the management structure of a particular partnership is to be different from the equality of partners presumed by s 24(5), then express agreement should be made. For example, in the large professional partnerships, it is usual for the partnership agreement to provide for the management of the firm to be delegated to a management committee.

### 1.2.2.1 Decisions of the partners

Section 24(8) of the 1890 Act says that (subject to contrary agreement, express or implied):

> *any differences arising as to ordinary matters connected with the partnership business may be decided by a majority of the partners, but no change may be made in the nature of the partnership business without the consent of all the partners.*

It should be noted that the expression 'majority of the partners' means a majority in number and not on the basis of capital contribution, profit-share or otherwise. It follows that under the default partnership agreement, a simple majority of the partners is required to take a decision regarding ordinary partnership matters. If the partners desire a different voting system, an express term must be put in the partnership agreement. In the case of *Highley v Walker* (1910) 26 TLR 685, the taking on of one of the partner's sons as an apprentice in the partnership business was regarded as an ordinary matter within the terms of s 24(8) and therefore it only required a decision of the majority of the partners and not a unanimous decision of the partners. If there is an equality of votes between the partners, the law provides that a decision is deemed not to be taken and the status quo is preserved (*Clements v Norris* (1878) 8 Ch D 129).

### 1.2.2.2 Restrictions on majority rule

There are two main limitations imposed on the ability of the majority of the partners to bind the whole firm.

First, partners are under a fiduciary duty to each other and so must exercise their powers for the benefit of the firm as a whole. For example, in *Heslin v Fay (No 1)* (1884) 15 LR Ir 431, the partnership agreement for a grocery store in North King Street in Dublin gave one partner, Fay, the power to increase the capital of the firm if it was necessary for carrying on the business of the firm. The agreement also entitled each partner to withdraw the amount of any surplus capital paid by him to the partnership. When one of the partners, Heslin,

**13**

called on his co-partners to repay the surplus capital which he had paid to the firm, Fay responded by raising the capital of the firm, so as to reduce the amount of the surplus owed to Heslin. It was held that Fay had no right to use his power of increasing the capital for the purpose of resisting Heslin's demand for a return of his surplus capital and, for this reason, Heslin was granted a dissolution of the partnership. Thus, a partner owes a fiduciary duty to his fellow partners and an important aspect of this is the requirement to show the utmost good faith in his dealings with them much like the duty a trustee owes to a beneficiary. This aspect of a partner's fiduciary duty is considered further below at **1.2.4**.

The second main type of limitation on the majority rule is to be found in the following provisions of the 1890 Act:

(a) Section 24(8) requires unanimity for a change in the partnership business. This is because a partner who has decided to invest in one particular type of business may not be forced to invest in something else against his wishes.

(b) Section 24(7) provides that: 'No person may be introduced as a partner without the consent of all the existing partners'. Such a rule is vital to the running of a small partnership where each partner will wish to ensure that his fellow partners cannot force him to go into partnership with someone of whom he disapproves. In large firms, it is common to exclude this default rule by allowing for a new partner to be admitted by a vote of 75 per cent or more of the partners.

(c) Section 25 prevents expulsion of a partner by a majority of the partners unless all the partners have expressly agreed to such a power being conferred. Since there is no right of expulsion under the default partnership agreement, one reason for having a written partnership agreement is to provide the partners with such a right.

Finally, another limitation on majority rule in partnerships is the general common law principle that, like any contract, a partnership contract may not be amended without the consent of all the signatories, although it is possible for an amendment to the partnership agreement to be inferred from a course of dealings by all the partners.

## 1.2.3 OTHER PROVISIONS OF THE 1890 ACT AFFECTING PARTNERS' RIGHTS *INTER SE*

Other provisions of s 24 which affect the relationship between the partners are as follows:

Section 24(2) gives a partner a right to be indemnified by the firm in respect of payments made and personal liabilities incurred 'in the ordinary and proper conduct of the business of the firm or in or about anything necessarily done for the preservation of the business or property of the firm'.

Section 24(9) gives all the partners a right to inspect and copy the partnership accounts.

### 1.2.4    A PARTNER'S FIDUCIARY DUTY TO HIS CO-PARTNERS

#### 1.2.4.1    Generally

The existence of a partner's fiduciary duty to his co-partners has long been recognised by the courts. It is because they trust one another that they are partners in the first instance and therefore the partners are required not to abuse this trust and this duty between fiduciaries is the primary control of partners' behaviour *inter se*. In the case of *Williams v Harris* [1980] ILRM 237, McWilliam J in the High Court recognised the existence of a partner's fiduciary duty and he noted that 'the mere existence of a partnership creates a fiduciary relationship between the partners'. In addition to this general common law duty, the 1890 Act recognises a number of aspects of the duty in ss 28–30.

#### 1.2.4.2    1890 Act, s 28

Section 28 provides that:

> *Partners are bound to render true accounts and full information of all things affecting the partnership to any partner or his legal representative.*

The Scottish case of *Ferguson v MacKay* 1985 SLT 1994 provides a good example of this fiduciary duty. It concerned a solicitor who was retiring from his firm and who was negotiating the terms of his retirement package with his partners. Before finalising these terms, his partners failed to disclose that three substantial conveyancing instructions had been received by the firm. After the retirement package was agreed, the retiring partner discovered that his co-partners had been less than frank in relation to these lucrative instructions. The court held that his co-partners had breached their fiduciary duty to give him full information on all things affecting the partnership and granted damages to the retiring partner for this breach.

#### 1.2.4.3    1890 Act, s 29

Section 29 provides that a partner must account to the firm for any profits made from partnership property in the following terms:

> *(1)    Every partner must account to the firm for any benefit derived by him without the consent of the other partners from any transaction concerning the partnership, or from any use by him of the partnership property, name or business connection.*

> *(2)    This section applies also to transactions undertaken after a partnership has been dissolved by the death of a partner, and before the affairs thereof have been completely wound up, either by any surviving partner or by the representatives of the deceased partner.*

The principle in s 29 to account for private profits made by partners applies also to 'partnership opportunities' so that if a transaction was entered into by a partner where the opportunity came to him as a result of the partnership and which might have been used to benefit the partnership, he will have to account to his partners for the benefit he derived therefrom unless his partners have consented to the transaction following full disclosure of the circumstances. The

**15**

concept underlying this principle is that these opportunities are regarded as partnership property and therefore may not be appropriated by one partner for his exclusive benefit.

### 1.2.4.4    1890 Act, s 30

Section 30 of the 1890 Act provides that:

> *If a partner, without the consent of the other partners, carries on any business of the same nature as, and competing with that of the firm, he must account for and pay over to the firm all profits made by him in that business.*

In *Lock v Lynam* (1854) 4 Ir Ch R 188, the parties had agreed to enter a partnership for the purpose of obtaining contracts for the supply of meat to British troops based in Ireland. During the operation of this partnership, Lynam entered into similar arrangements with third persons, whereby he was to share in the profits of similar contracts, if obtained by them. Lock sought an account of the profits of these contracts which Lynam had with third parties. Lynam argued that there was no agreement with Lock that he would not enter into similar contracts with third parties. Nonetheless, Lord Chancellor Brady held that such conduct by Lynam was a breach of his duty of good faith to his partner and he ordered that an account of those contracts be taken.

It remains to be observed that there is overlap between s 30 and s 29(1), since a partner who continues as a partner but at the same time sets up a new business may be held accountable to his partners, because he is competing with his firm *or* because he is using 'the partnership property name or business connection' for his own benefit.

### 1.2.4.5    No common law restriction on former partner competing with firm

A related issue concerns the position of a former partner. It should be noted that a partner's fiduciary duty to his co-partners does not prevent a *former* partner from competing with his former firm in the absence of an agreement to that effect. Thus, a party to a partnership agreement governed only by the default terms of the 1890 Act who leaves the partnership and sets up a competing business and who does not use the partnership property, name or business connection is not liable to his partners in any way under the 1890 Act. For this reason, it is common for written partnership agreements to have non-compete clauses. Any such restriction must however, comply with the Competition Act, 2002. In the Competition Authority decision No 333 in *Doyle v Moffit*, 10 June 1994 the agreement between two vets provided for Moffit to gradually acquire Doyle's partnership share over the life of the partnership and their partnership agreement restricted Doyle, for five years from the date of his retirement and within twenty miles of the practice, from acting as a vet for any clients of the firm. The Competition Authority held that in terms of geographic coverage (twenty miles) and subject matter (veterinary surgeon) the restriction was reasonable but in terms of duration (five years) it was excessive since, in general, non-compete clauses of more than two years are longer than necessary to secure the transfer of the goodwill and therefore offend against s 4(1) of the Competition Act, 1991. The 1991 Act has now been repealed and replaced by the Competition Act, 2002 but the new Act contains identical wording to s 4(1) of the 1991 Act.

## 1.2.5 FINANCIAL RIGHTS AND DUTIES OF PARTNERS

### 1.2.5.1 Capital

The capital of a partnership is the cause of more confusion than most other areas of partnership law. This is caused in part by the confusion between the assets or other property of a partnership on the one hand, and its capital on the other hand. This confusion will be avoided if the capital of a firm is thought of as the sum which is contributed by the partners to establish the firm. The capital of a partner may be contributed in the form of cash or in the form of property (including, for example, business premises or the goodwill of an existing business).

### 1.2.5.2 Division of profits and sharing of losses

Section 24 of the 1890 Act lays down a number of rules as to division of profits. These rules are default rules since they may be varied by an express or implied agreement of the partners. Nevertheless, even if the default rules are to apply, the partnership agreement should state the ratios in which profits and losses of income and profits and losses of capital are to be divided between the partners, in order to avoid any confusion. The main default provision is to be found in s 24(1) of the 1890 Act which provides that:

> *All the partners are entitled to share equally in the capital and profits of the business, and must contribute equally towards the losses whether of capital or otherwise sustained by the firm.*

Thus, s 24(1) provides as regards the sharing of profits that they are to be shared equally. The contribution of capital in unequal shares does not give rise to the implication that profits are not to be shared equally. If a partner is to receive more than an equal share of profits because of his capital contribution or the work he does or for any other reason, this must be specifically agreed to and should be expressly stated in the partnership agreement.

As regards the sharing of losses, s 24(1) states that the default rule is that losses are shared equally. However, if the partners share profits unequally (because of an express or implied agreement to do so), then losses of capital or of income will also be shared in the same proportion unless there is an agreement to the contrary. This principle is clear from s 44(a) and s 44(b)(4) of the 1890 Act and also from the case of *Robinson v Ashton* (1875) LR 20 Eq 25.

### 1.2.5.3 Redistribution of capital contributions and sharing of capital losses and profits

Section 24(1) states that 'all the partners are entitled to share equally in the capital'. Particular care should be taken with this phrase since it does not mean that the capital which was contributed unequally by partners is treated as an aggregate fund to be divided between the partners in equal shares. Rather, this reference to 'capital' must be read as being first subject to the requirement in s 44(b)(3) of the 1890 Act that capital contributions are repaid to the partners rateably according to the amount of their respective contributions. The effect of this part of s 24(1) is that once the capital contributions have been repaid, the partners share equally in the capital profit or divide the capital losses equally, unless they have agreed a different sharing ratio. If there is no specific agreement regarding capital profits and capital losses, then if the profits or losses of income have been agreed by the partners to be shared unequally, the profits and losses of capital, in the absence of a specific agreement, will be shared in that proportion (1890 Act, s 44(a) and (b)(4) and *Robinson v Ashton* (1875) LR 20 Eq 25). The partners are, of course, free to agree to any form of division they like and, for example, they may decide that capital profits should be divided in the same ratio as capital was contributed by the partners.

### 1.2.5.4 Interest on capital

Section 24(4) provides that in the absence of contrary agreement 'A partner is not entitled . . . to interest on capital'. Where capital is contributed unequally, it may be considered appropriate to make provision in the partnership agreement for interest on capital to be paid to the partners so as to compensate the partner who has contributed more. In such a case, the partnership agreement should specify the rate of interest to be paid. At the end of the firm's financial year, the net profit of the firm is determined and the partners' first entitlement will be to interest on capital and then the remaining net profit will be allocated in accordance with the agreed profit-sharing ratio.

### 1.2.5.5 Interest on loans

Section 24(3) also provides a default rule in respect of loans by a partner to his firm. It provides that, in the absence of contrary agreement, a loan by a partner to the partnership carries interest at the rate of 5 per cent. It should be noted that this rate of interest is paid only on 'actual payments or advances'. Interest is not payable under s 24(3) on a share of profits which is simply left in the business in the shape of undrawn profits of a partner. The partners are, of course, free to agree that interest will be paid on undrawn profits if they wish.

### 1.2.5.6 Remuneration of partners

Another important default rule regarding partners' financial rights and duties is contained in s 24(6) which provides that: 'No partner shall be entitled to remuneration for acting in the partnership business'. In some partnerships, it may be appropriate to override this default rule, e.g. where the division of work between the partners is unequal and the partners agree that some of them are to be paid compensation for the extra work which they do. As with interest on capital, such a sum payable to a partner is merely a preferential appropriation of profit. It is important not to confuse such a partner who receives a preferential appropriation of profit with a 'salaried partner'. The latter is simply an employee of the firm who is held out to the world as a partner. He is not a partner since he is not 'carrying on business in common' with the partners but is employed by them.

**1.2.5.7    Drawings**

The amount of money which represents a partner's share of the profits of the firm will not be known until the profit and loss account of the firm has been drawn up after the end of the partnership's financial year. For this reason, it is usual for a partnership agreement to provide that the partners have the right to take a specified amount of money on account of their anticipated profits, known as 'drawings'. If at the end of the year the partner has taken less than he was entitled to, he may draw the balance. If he has taken more than his entitlement, the partnership agreement should provide for him to pay back the excess to the firm. Sometimes, the partnership agreement may provide that each partner is to leave undrawn in the business a proportion of his entitlement to profit. This is because businesses normally need to retain funds to meet increased costs of trading and to fund any future expansion.

## 1.2.6    PARTNERSHIP PROPERTY

In every partnership, it is important to determine which property is owned by the partnership and which property, although it may be used by the partnership, is the property of a partner or partners individually or of some third party. This is because partnership property, unlike the personal property of a partner which is used by the firm, must be used for the purposes of the partnership and so, for example, any increase in its value will accrue to the firm and not to an individual partner. In the case of the personal property of a partner, that partner will be entitled to use it as he wishes and on the bankruptcy of the firm or on his bankruptcy, the property is available for the benefit of his separate creditors, in priority to the firm's creditors.

This crucial question of whether property is partnership property is determined by the agreement and intention of the partners, be that express or implied. If the partners intend that property is to be partnership property, then the fact that it happens to be vested in one partner's name will be irrelevant to a finding that the property belongs to the firm. For this reason, each case must be determined according to its own set of circumstances. However, the 1890 Act assists in this enquiry by providing two rebuttable presumptions regarding the status of property as partnership property. Thus, it is presumed that property which is acquired for the purposes of, and in the course of, the partnership business is partnership property since s 20(1) of the 1890 Act provides that:

> *All property and rights and interests in property originally brought into the partnership stock or acquired, whether by purchase or otherwise, on account of the firm, or for the purposes and in the course of the partnership business, are called in this Act partnership property, and must be held and applied by the partners exclusively for the purposes of the partnership and in accordance with the partnership agreement.*

It is also presumed that property which is purchased with partnership funds is partnership property, since s 21 of the 1890 Act provides:

> *Unless the contrary intention appears, property bought with money belonging to the firm is deemed to have been bought on account of the firm.*

Yet, one must not lose sight of the overriding importance of the intentions of the partners and these presumptions may therefore be rebutted in appropriate circumstances. *Murtagh v Costello* (1881) 7 LR Ir 428 illustrates that courts do not take a restrictive approach to determining whether property was acquired 'for the purposes of and in the course of the partnership business' as required by s 20(1) of the 1890 Act. In that case, the partnership agreement provided for the parties to become partners as flour merchants and 'in all other matters in which the majority of them should agree to trade or deal'. During the course of the partnership, the partners acquired two pieces of freehold land in Athlone, which were purchased using partnership money and were conveyed into the name of two of the partners in trust for the firm. One piece of land was farmed by one of the partners, and the second piece of land was occupied by tenants. The profits from the farming and the rent from the tenants were brought into the profit and loss account of the firm. It was argued that neither piece of land was partnership property since farming and renting of property were not part of the trade of flour merchants. This argument was rejected by Chatterton VC who held that both properties were partnership property since the improvements thereon were paid for out of partnership money; the profits therefrom were entered into the profit and loss account and the lands themselves were entered in the balance sheet. It is clear therefore that the term 'partnership business' as used in s 20(1) of the 1890 Act is not to be interpreted restrictively but rather includes a situation where property is not strictly within the description of partnership business as set out in the partnership agreement, provided that it is held for the benefit of, or on behalf of, the partnership business.

To avoid a situation where a court has to decide the intention and agreement of the partners regarding the status of property, the question of which property is partnership property should be clarified where practicable in the partnership agreement. Indeed, sometimes of equal importance is a provision indicating which property is not partnership property. In the High Court case of *Barr v Barr*, 29 July 1992, High Court (unreported), a wholesale grocery partnership in Donegal stored some of its goods in a garage which adjoined the home of one of the defendant partners. The garage appeared in the balance sheet of the firm and was held to be partnership property. However, the other partners claimed that the defendant's home was also partnership property. While the report does not indicate what evidence supported such a claim, it was rejected by Carroll J. Such problems could have been avoided by a provision in the partnership agreement clearly delineating which property was and which property was not partnership property.

## 1.3    Relations between Partners and Third Parties

### 1.3.1    INTRODUCTION

In the course of carrying on the partnership's business, the partners will invariably incur debts and other obligations. In this section, we look at the nature of the partners' liabilities for these obligations as well as the extent to which an individual partner may bind the partnership as a whole. We will then go on to look at whether it is possible for individuals who are not in fact partners at the time the debt or obligation was incurred to be liable for that debt or obligation (whether because they have been held out as partners or because they are admitted to the partnership subsequently).

## 1.3.2 NATURE OF LIABILITY OF PARTNERS TO THIRD PARTIES

Partners are liable for the debts and obligations of the partnership without limitation (1890 Act, ss 9 and 10). Their liability is joint in the case of contractual obligations and joint and several in the case of tortious obligations. However, the significance of this distinction between joint and joint and several obligations was much reduced by the Civil Liability Act, 1961 which now allows proceedings to be brought successively against persons jointly liable even where there has been an earlier judgment against other persons who were jointly liable for that obligation. Where a firm is unable to pay its debts out of partnership property, the creditor of that firm is entitled to obtain payment from the private estates of the partners. Special rules apply in such cases, so as to attempt to do justice both to the creditors of the firm and to the separate creditors of the individual partners. These rules are contained in the Bankruptcy Act, 1988, s 34. It is not intended to deal with these rules in detail (see further Twomey, *Partnership Law*, paras 27.01 *et seq*.). However, they may be summarised as follows:

(a)  partnership property is used to pay partnership creditors in priority to the personal creditors of each partner;

(b)  personal property of each partner is used to pay his personal creditors in priority to partnership creditors;

(c)  if the personal creditors of a particular partner are paid in full from his personal property, then the partnership creditors may resort to the balance of that partner's personal property; and

(d)  if the partnership creditors are paid in full from partnership property, the personal creditors of a partner may resort to the balance of his share of the partnership property.

## 1.3.3 AUTHORITY OF PARTNER TO BIND FIRM

### 1.3.3.1 Generally

The relationship between partnership law and the law of agency is very close and some of the rules regulating the relationship between a partnership and the outside world may be explained purely in terms of particular applications of agency principles and, in particular, from examining the nature of a partner's authority to bind the firm. In general terms, the partnership as a whole is bound by a partner acting within the scope of his authority. This authority of a partner may arise in three ways, i.e. express authority, implied authority and ostensible authority.

(a)     Express authority is where the authority of the partners is specifically agreed upon by the partners.

(b)     Implied authority is implied either from a course of dealings between the partners (which amounts to an actual agreement) or because the authority is a natural consequence of an authority actually given to the partner.

(c)     Ostensible authority arises from the fact that a person dealing with a partner is, in certain circumstances, entitled to assume that the partner has authority to bind the firm.

The first two types of authority are categories of actual authority (in the sense that the partner has in fact authority to do the act in question), which distinguishes them from ostensible authority where there is no actual authority but, for the protection of third parties, the partner is deemed to have authority to do the act in question.

### 1.3.3.2    Express authority

The scope of express authority depends on the agreement between the parties. The partnership agreement may specify what powers the partners individually are to have and may specify that some partners are to have greater powers than others. The extent of express authority is not, in practical terms, of great significance to a person dealing with a partner. This is because, whether or not there is express authority, the third party will usually be able to rely on the ostensible authority of the partner. The outsider need only rely on express authority where the partner has done something which the law does not consider to be within the ostensible authority of a partner.

### 1.3.3.3    Implied authority

It has been noted that the authority of a partner to do an act may be implied from a course of dealing involving the partners or because the authority is a natural consequence of an authority actually given to the partner. This is called implied authority. The implied powers of partners in a trading partnership are more extensive than the powers of partners in a non-trading partnership. This is because the court recognises the need of the partners and the persons dealing with them to rely on normal trading practices.

Examples of powers assumed to be available to partners in all partnerships include the power to:

(a)     bring or defend legal proceedings in the firm name or the joint names of all of the partners;

(b)     open a bank account in the name of the firm;

(c)     sign cheques on behalf of the firm;

(d)     enter contracts on behalf of the firm within the ordinary course of business of the firm;

(e)    sell goods belonging to the firm; and

(f)    take on employees for the purposes of the partnership business and dismiss such employees.

A partner in a trading partnership will be assumed to have all the above powers and also the power to grant security for borrowings and to draw, accept or endorse a bill of exchange or promissory note.

### 1.3.3.4    Ostensible authority

The scope of ostensible authority is not always easy to establish or describe. Such authority may be said to arise from the fact that the partner who is acting of behalf of a firm *appears* to have authority to bind the firm and it is, therefore, reasonable for the outsider to assume such authority. It is for this reason that it is sometimes referred to as apparent authority. The principle underlying ostensible authority is to be found in the 1890 Act, s 5 which provides that:

> *Every partner is an agent of the firm and his other partners for the purpose of the business of the partnership; and the acts of every partner who does any act for carrying on in the usual way the business of the kind carried on by the firm of which he is a member bind the firm and his partners, unless the partner so acting has in fact no authority to act for the firm in the particular matter, and the person with whom he is dealing either knows that he has no authority, or does not know or believe him to be a partner.*

The easiest way to understand the scope of the section is to examine each of the qualifications on a partner's authority which the section recognises. First, it should be noted that the section does not say that *anything* which a partner does binds the firm; rather, to bind the firm the following requirements must be satisfied:

(a)    the act must be done by a partner;

(b)    the act must be done *qua* partner; and

(c)    the act must be within the ordinary course of business of the firm.

The first and second requirement are generally easy to establish, while the requirement that the act be within the firm's ordinary course of business has caused the most difficulty.

#### Act must be done by a partner

Before a firm is bound by the act of its partner, it is perhaps self-evident that the act must be that of a partner and the fact that the partner in question is a dormant partner or a junior partner does not in any way reduce his power to bind his partners (*Morans v Armstrong* (1840) Arm M & O 25). In cases where a partner in a firm does not have the authority to do acts within the ordinary course of business of a firm, the third party must believe that he is dealing with a partner. This is because, under s 5 of the 1890 Act, if the partner does not have authority to do an act which is within the firm's ordinary business, the firm will nonetheless be bound by that act, *unless* the third party did not know or believe that he was a partner. Where the third party does not believe that he is dealing with a partner, he must then be taken to know that the first requirement for the firm to be bound has not been satisfied. If the partner is a partner, with the authority but the third party does not know he is a partner, then the firm will still be bound provided that each of the requirements above is satisfied.

### Act must be done qua partner

The second requirement to be satisfied for a firm to be bound by the actions of a partner is that the act in question must be done by the partner qua partner. It is important to distinguish between this requirement and the fact that the act must be done within the ordinary course of business of the firm. Thus, the act of a partner in an accountancy firm who becomes a company director of his family company, may not be binding on his firm since, although done by a partner and constituting an act which is within the ordinary course of business of an accountancy firm, it may not have been done by him qua partner. A good example of a case in which a partner was held not to be acting *qua partner* is *British Homes Assurance Corporation Ltd v Paterson* [1902] 2 Ch 404. In that case, the plaintiff instructed a solicitor, Atkinson, to act on its behalf in relation to a mortgage. At that time, Atkinson practised under the name of Atkinson and Atkinson. Soon after, he entered partnership with Paterson and he informed the plaintiff that he would in future carry on business under the name of Atkinson and Paterson. The plaintiff ignored this and continued to deal with the solicitor as Atkinson and Atkinson and, on completion of the transaction, sent a cheque to him in the name of 'Atkinson and Atkinson or order'. When Atkinson absconded with this money, the plaintiff sued Paterson for the return of the money. It was held that the defendant was not liable for the default since the plaintiff had intentionally contracted with Atkinson as an individual and not qua partner.

### Act must be within the firm's ordinary course of business

The third and final condition to be satisfied for a firm to be bound by the acts of its partners is the one which has received the most attention from the courts, namely that the act be within the ordinary course of business of the firm. The classification of a particular act as being within the 'ordinary course of business of the firm' is crucial since in most cases the question of the liability of the firm for the acts of a partner is determined by this fact. For example, a firm of doctors would be liable for the damage caused by the negligent driving of one of the partners where he is involved in a car accident on the way to see a patient. This is because the negligent driving of the partner is an act which is committed by the partner while acting in the ordinary course of business of the firm. On the other hand, the firm of doctors will not generally be liable for the damage caused by one of the partners where, on his way to see a patient, he decides to take a detour and assault an innocent third party. This assault would not be regarded as being 'within the ordinary course of business of the firm' since the partner is acting in a completely unusual manner for his own purposes and not in order to benefit the firm.

In the context of the ordinary course of business of a solicitors' partnership, in *United Bank of Kuwait v Hammond* [1988] 1 WLR 1051 an undertaking, given by a solicitor to the bank as security for a loan by the bank to his client, was held to be within the ordinary course of business of a solicitor. Accordingly, the firm in this case was held liable when the undertaking given by one of the partners was not honoured. In contrast, in the nineteenth-century case of *Plumer v Gregory* (1874) LR 18 Eq 621, a partner borrowed money from a client without the knowledge of his co-partners, saying to the client that the firm wanted it to lend to another client. The borrowing of money from a client for lending to another client was held not to be within the ordinary course of business of a solicitors' firm and the firm was held not to be liable for the loss to the client.

Finally, a partner who makes a contract with an outsider without authority will be personally liable to the outsider for breach of warranty of authority where the partnership as a whole is not made liable on the contract. However, where a contract made without authority is ratified by the partnership, it becomes binding on the partners as well as on the outsider. In addition, where the partner's authority to do acts within the ordinary course of business of the firm is restricted, s 8 of the 1890 Act provides that an outsider is not prejudiced since it provides that the third party is not affected by any restriction placed on the powers of the partner unless he has notice of it.

### 1.3.4 PERSONS HELD OUT AS PARTNERS

So far we have only considered the liability of actual partners vis-à-vis outsiders. A person who holds himself out as a partner or who 'knowingly suffers himself to be represented as a partner' is liable to anyone who 'on the faith of such representation' gives credit to the firm as if he were a partner (1890 Act, s 14). The most common example of the application of this rule is where a 'salaried partner' (who is in fact an employee of the firm, rather than a partner) allows his name to be used by the partnership (e.g. on notepaper), and it is worth noting that in the most recent Law Society survey, it was estimated that 8 per cent of law firms had salaried partners. In view of the potential liability under s 14(1), it is advisable for salaried partners to obtain an indemnity from the 'true' partners in relation to this potential liability. A person cannot be held liable under s 14(1), unless he has in some way contributed to the mistake made by the person giving credit to the firm, for example, by allowing his name to be given as a partner. This is illustrated by the English case of *Tower Cabinet Co Ltd v Ingram* [1949] 2 KB 397. In that case, a partner retired from his firm and due to carelessness on his part omitted to destroy the headed notepaper of the firm which contained his name. It was held that this carelessness did not constitute him knowingly suffering himself to be held out as a partner, as he did not know that the notepaper was used by the firm after his retirement. Clearly, if he had known this fact, he would have been held to have knowingly suffered a holding out and would have been liable to the creditors who relied on him being a partner.

Section 14(1) only applies where 'credit is given' to the firm by the third party on the basis of the misrepresentation that a person was a partner in the firm.

This term is construed widely so that, for example, the apparent partner is liable where goods are delivered, as well as where cash is lent to the firm. In *Nationwide Building Society v Lewis* [1993] 3 All ER 143 it was noted that, as s 14(1) was simply an example of the wider doctrine of estoppel by conduct, the precise language of s 14(1) ('given credit to the firm') was not important once there was a reliance or an acting on the faith of the representation.

## 1.3.5 LIABILITY OF NEW PARTNERS

Section 17(1) of the 1890 Act provides that 'a person who is admitted as a partner into an existing firm does not thereby become liable to the creditors of the firm for anything done before he became a partner'. This provision ensures that an incoming partner is not liable to the existing creditors of the firm merely because he has become a partner in a firm which has a large number of obligations and debts. As between himself and the existing partners, the incoming partner may agree to pay a share of debts owed to existing creditors. This does not make him directly liable to the existing creditors as they are not privy to the contract. The new partner may become directly liable to existing creditors by a novation (that is, a tripartite contract between the old partners, the new partner and the creditor whereby the existing contract between the old partners and the creditor is discharged and replaced by a contract between the new firm, including the new partner, and the creditor). However, this will not be a regular occurrence in modern partnerships because it would necessitate an agreement between a partnership and its creditors every time a partner joins the firm.

## 1.3.6 LITIGATION INVOLVING PARTNERSHIPS

Order 14, r 1 of the Superior Court Rules (SI 15/1986) provides that a partnership may sue or be sued in its firm name. There is no need to set out in the proceedings the names of the individual partners since the use of the firm name means that the partners are sued individually as definitively as if they had their names set out. Order 14, r 1 states:

> *Any two or more persons claiming or being liable as co-partners and carrying on business within the jurisdiction, may sue or be sued in the name of the respective firms, if any, of which such persons were co-partners at the time of the accruing of the cause of action . . .*

However, it is crucial to bear in mind that this procedural rule is simply that, i.e. a rule of procedure which allows partnership litigation to be conducted as if the firm was a separate legal entity. It does not alter the fundamental nature of a partnership as an aggregate of its members and this issue will remain of relevance in the conduct of any such litigation. A consequence of this aggregate nature of partnerships is the fact that although the same firm name may be used in litigation by or against a firm, with each change in the membership of the firm, a new partnership is created. It follows that one must 'look through' the firm name to see who is ultimately liable for the partnership obligation being litigated, namely those persons who were partners in the firm at the time of the accrual of the cause of action. It is for this reason that the Rules of Court also allow a party in partnership litigation to apply to court for a statement of the names of the partners in the firm at the time of the accrual of the cause of action. It follows that parties to an action against a firm may not dispense with the need to identify the correct parties to their action, since it is only these parties against whom a judgment may be executed.

Where an action is brought against a partnership in the firm's name, the proceedings may be served:

(a)   on any one or more partner; or

(b)   at the principal place of business of the partnership within the State, on the person having control or management of the partnership business there.

A person who has a judgment against a partner for the partner's personal liability may enforce that judgment against the partner's share of partnership property by means of 'a charging order' (1890 Act, s 23(2)). He may not enforce such a judgment against the partnership property by means of execution proceedings (s 23(1)). Where a charging order is made, the other partners may discharge it by paying off the judgment debt or, if a sale of the partner's interest in the firm is ordered, they may purchase that partner's interest. A charging order gives the other partners a right to dissolve the partnership if they wish (s 33(2)).

### 1.3.7   GUARANTEES

Section 18 of the 1890 Act is a very important provision and one which should be borne in mind by lawyers acting for a bank receiving a guarantee from a partnership in respect of its loan. Section 18 provides that a continuing guarantee is revoked by any change in the firm whose liabilities are being guaranteed. Accordingly, it is very important to have a provision in such a guarantee to the effect that the terms of the guarantee will continue after any change in the firm. Otherwise s 18 will ensure that the guarantee is automatically revoked by any retirement of a partner in the firm or any admission of a new partner into the firm.

## 1.4   Actions between Partners

### 1.4.1   INTRODUCTION

Disputes between partners may involve a wide variety of potential actions ranging from a claim for damages to an application for the appointment of a receiver to the firm. However, regardless of the form of action, two important characteristics of the partnership relationship should be borne in mind as these two characteristics will commonly influence the outcome of the litigation.

First, one of the grand characteristics of a partnership is the fact that it is not a separate legal entity, but an aggregate of all the partners. For this reason, the partners are not treated as debtors or creditors of the firm while the partnership continues, since to do so would involve the concept of a person owing himself a debt. It is only on a final settlement of accounts between the partners on the firm's dissolution that they are regarded as debtors and creditors. It is for this reason that the courts are reluctant to facilitate a partner in suing his co-partners in respect of a single partnership obligation. Instead, the courts lean in favour of all partnership obligations being determined as part of the general settlement of accounts on the dissolution of the firm.

The second important characteristic of the partnership contract is that it requires a high degree of confidence and trust between the partners. It is, therefore, understandable that the courts would be reluctant to compel an unwilling person to be another person's partner. For this reason, the specific performance of partnerships, while not unheard of, are certainly not granted as a matter of course. For the same reason, the courts favour granting other remedies such as injunctions and appointing receivers/managers as part of the dissolution of partnerships rather than during the life of partnerships. This judicial attitude may be easily justified since the very fact that a court application is being made in the first place indicates that the degree of trust and confidence necessary for the partnership to continue may be absent. Thus, any order which is intended to apply during the life of the partnership may turn out to be futile and clearly the court does not wish to involve itself in making such orders.

In this section, we look at the remedies available to a partner which include dissolution of the partnership, appointment of a receiver and other remedies which may be available under the terms of the partnership agreement itself. (For further remedies, see Twomey, *Partnership Law*, paras 20.01 *et seq.*)

## 1.4.2 DISSOLUTION BY THE COURT

### 1.4.2.1 Generally

Dissolution of a partnership may occur automatically (e.g. on the death of a partner) by notice (e.g. any partner may give notice dissolving a partnership at will) or by court order (e.g. in the case of permanent incapacity of a partner). The various circumstances in which dissolution takes place are considered at **1.5.** In this section, we intend to consider only those types of dissolution which provide a remedy in a dispute between partners, i.e. under s 35(c) (order of dissolution where a partner is guilty of misconduct), s 35(d) (order of dissolution where a partner breaches the partnership agreement) or s 35(f) (order of dissolution where it is just and equitable to dissolve the partnership).

In a formal partnership (i.e. where the partners have excluded the right of a partner to dissolve the partnership by notice), the partners usually agree to remain in partnership together for a fixed term (for this reason, they are sometimes referred to as fixed-term partnerships). It will often occur that some of the partners may wish to bring the partnership to a premature end for a variety of reasons ranging from personality clashes to the wrongful conduct of a partner. Unfortunately, there is no automatic right under the 1890 Act for the partners to expel a partner guilty of misconduct and for this reason, these types of situations often result in an application to court for a dissolution of the partnership under the 1890 Act, s 35. The only other option open to the partner(s) wishing to end the partnership with a difficult partner is to attempt to terminate the partnership in breach of the partnership agreement which is obviously an unsatisfactory solution.

A number of general aspects of s 35 are worthy of mention at this juncture. This section provides for the dissolution of a partnership in six separate instances (as to which see **1.5.2.4**). The court has an absolute discretion to order a dissolution in any of the six cases listed in s 35. If for no other reason, this fact should encourage potential litigants to make every effort to resolve their differences amicably since there is no requirement on a court to order or not to order a dissolution, regardless of the conduct of the partners. However, since the courts generally lean against ordering the specific performance of a partnership agreement between unwilling partners, the result of an application to dissolve a partnership often, but not always, is a court dissolution. In addition, partnership disputes usually end up in dissolution because a court in a partnership dispute, unlike the situation in a company dispute, does not have a statutory power to order the expulsion of a partner or the sale of one partner's share to his co-partners. It follows that the parties to a partnership dispute have the added knowledge that a dissolution is more likely than not to result from an application to court under s 35 with the likelihood that the practice or business of the partnership will have to be sold and the consequent loss of goodwill. In general terms therefore, there is a very great incentive for partners to attempt to agree to dissolve amicably without incurring the costs of going to court to obtain an order to dissolve the partnership.

Although s 35 has six separate headings under which a dissolution of a partnership may be claimed, more often than not, a dissolution will be sought under s 35(f) on the grounds that it is just and equitable for the court to order the dissolution of the partnership. Such an application obviates the need for the petitioner to satisfy the preconditions of the other subsections of s 35 such as incapacity, breach of partnership agreement etc.

### 1.4.2.2    Conduct prejudicial to the business (s 35(c))

Section 35(c) provides that a partner may apply to the court for dissolution

> *when a partner, other than the partner suing, has been guilty of such conduct as, in the opinion of the court, regard being had to the nature of the business, is calculated to prejudicially affect the carrying on of the business.*

This subsection may be relied upon even though the prejudicial conduct has nothing directly to do with the partnership. Thus, a partner's criminal actions may have been committed completely separate from his partnership, but yet may fall within the terms of s 35(c). The use in s 35(c) of the phrase 'guilty of such conduct . . . as is calculated to prejudicially affect' connotes a strong degree of culpability on the part of the partner. Accordingly, it is thought that the conduct in question must be done with the intention of causing harm to the partnership and not simply that it has a possibility of harming the partnership business.

### 1.4.2.3 Breach of partnership agreement (s 35(d))

Section 35(d) provides that a partner may apply to the court for dissolution

*when a partner, other than the partner suing, wilfully or persistently commits a breach of the partnership agreement, or otherwise so conducts himself in matters relating to the partnership business that it is not reasonably practicable for the other partner or partners to carry on business in partnership with him.*

This subsection contemplates that the trust between partners has broken down. If this breakdown results from persistent breaches of the partnership agreement or conduct in relation to the business, then the court may order dissolution. *Heslin v Fay (No 1)* (1884) 15 LR Ir 431 provides an example of a case where a dissolution order was made as a result of the wilful breach of the terms of the partnership agreement. There, the partnership deed for a grocery partnership in North King Street in Dublin provided that each partner was entitled to withdraw any surplus capital in the firm which had been advanced by him. When Heslin called on his partners to repay him his surplus capital, they refused to do so and instead falsely claimed that they had raised the capital of the firm by admitting another partner and this had the effect of swamping Heslin's surplus capital. Accordingly, it was held by the Irish Court of Appeal that the decision by the other partners to refuse to return the capital was a wilful breach of the partnership agreement which justified an order for the dissolution of the partnership.

### 1.4.2.4 Just and equitable dissolution (s 35(f))

Section 35(f) provides that a partner may apply to the court for dissolution 'whenever in any case circumstances have arisen which in the opinion of the court render it just and equitable that the partnership be dissolved'. This provision is the equivalent of s 213(f) of the Companies Act, 1963 which applies only to companies but the cases decided under that section are likely to be relevant to s 35(f). One such case is *Re Vehicle Buildings* [1986] ILRM 239 which concerned a quasi-partnership. (A quasi-partnership is an entity, which is in form a company, but in substance a partnership, such that it is appropriate to apply the principles of partnership law to it.) It involved a private company which was a partnership in all but name, since it was owned by a Ms Fitzpatrick and a Mr Howley in equal proportions and in which they were the sole directors. The relationship between the two broke down leading to a state of deadlock in the management of the company. Murphy J granted an order for the winding-up of the company on just and equitable grounds under s 213(f) of the Companies Act, 1963 on the basis that treating it as a partnership, it would be appropriate to dissolve it under s 35(f) of the 1890 Act.

### 1.4.3 APPOINTMENT OF RECEIVER/MANAGER

The court may appoint a receiver or manager in all cases in which it appears to be just and convenient to so do on the application of any partner or other persons interested in the preservation of the firm's assets, such as the personal representative of a deceased partner. It is important to distinguish between the two officers: a receiver takes the assets of the partnership under his protection and in this way, the assets remain under the protection of the court; while a manager has the additional role of carrying on the partnership business under the direction of the court. For this reason, it is perhaps more useful for a manager to be appointed. However, it should be noted that the court is particularly reluctant to make an appointment of a manager or receiver in the case of a professional partnership in view of the damage to the professional reputation of the firm (*Floydd v Cheney* [1970] 2 WLR 314).

### 1.4.4 MEDIATION AND ARBITRATION

'Partnership actions always take a long time and, indeed, are one of the most expensive and unsatisfactory types of action which we have' *per* Kenny J in *O'Connor v* Woods, 22 January 1976, High Court (unreported). This view of partnership disputes was reiterated by the Supreme Court, albeit in the context of quasi-partnerships, when Murphy J observed that they were similar to matrimonial proceedings in that:

> [Partnership disputes and family law disputes] both involve an examination of the conduct of the parties over a period of years and usually a determination by them to assert rights rather than solve problems. It may well be that the disparate forms of litigation are frequently fuelled by a bitterness borne of rejection: matrimonial or commercial. In neither discipline can the courts persuade the parties that it is in their best interests to direct their attention to solving their problems rather than litigating them. (*Re Murray Consultants Ltd* [1997] 3 IR 23)

By repeating the observations of the Irish judiciary on the subject of partnership disputes, it is hoped to persuade some partners and their legal advisers to try and solve their problems by mediation or other non-adversarial methods and in particular to include a compulsory mediation clause in their partnership agreement and, failing resolution by mediation, it is suggested that the parties seek to resolve their differences by arbitration. A typical mediation clause along the following lines is recommended:

> All disputes and questions whatsoever which shall either during the term of the Partnership or afterwards arise between the Partners or their representatives or between any Partners or Partner and the representatives of any other deceased Partner touching this Indenture or construction or application thereof or any clause or thing herein contained or any amount valuation or division of assets, debts or liabilities to be made hereunder or as to any act, deed or omission of any Partner relating to the Partnership or as to any other

matter in any way relating to the Partnership business or the affairs thereof or the right duties or liabilities of any persons hereunder shall be referred first to a single mediator to be nominated by all the persons in dispute or in default of agreement by the President for the time being of the Law Society. Failing a resolution of the dispute through such mediation to the satisfaction of all the parties, the dispute shall be referred to a single arbitrator to be nominated by all the persons in dispute or in default of agreement by the President for the time being of the Law Society in accordance with and subject to the provisions of the Arbitration Acts, 1954 to 1998 or any statutory modification or re-enactment thereof for the time being in force.

## 1.4.5    EXPULSION OF A PARTNER

We have seen in this section that it is possible for a partnership to be dissolved by the court as a way of giving the plaintiff partner a remedy against his co-partners. However, the circumstances of the dispute within the partnership may be such that some partners would prefer to get rid of one or more of their co-partners without fully dissolving the partnership. This section, therefore, considers the expulsion of a partner from a partnership.

### 1.4.5.1    Need to expressly provide for expulsion in partnership agreement

There is no right under the 1890 Act to expel a partner. Indeed, the contrary is expressly stated by s 25 which reads 'no majority of the partners can expel any partner unless a power to do so has been conferred by express agreement between the partners'.

The absence of a right under general partnership law to expel a partner is an important reason for having a written partnership agreement incorporating such a right, since no matter how unprofessional, negligent or belligerent a partner becomes, the other partners are not entitled to expel him from the firm in the absence of such a right. The desire of the partners in a firm to expel their co-partner, in the absence of a right to expel, may lead to a general dissolution of that firm. This is because the only recourse for the 'innocent' partners is to apply to court under the 1890 Act, s 35 for a general dissolution of the partnership on the grounds of the partner's misconduct.

Where an expulsion clause is included in the agreement, it will normally state that specific activities (such as fraud) or breaches of certain terms of the partnership agreement (such as requiring a partner not to compete with the partnership or to devote the whole of his time to the business) will justify expulsion. As noted at **1.5.2.3** below, bankruptcy of a partner is a ground for the automatic dissolution of the whole partnership (under the default rules contained in s 33(1) of the 1890 Act), but in order to avoid the consequences of dissolution it is common for the partnership agreement to override this default rule and provide that a bankruptcy of a partner will not cause dissolution, rather that it will justify expulsion.

**1.4.5.2    Exercise of expulsion clause**

If an expulsion clause is included in the partnership agreement, then the power must be exercised strictly in accordance with the agreement and in a bona fide manner and for the benefit of the partnership as a whole (*Blisset v Daniel* (1853) 10 Hare 493). The exercise of a power of expulsion will have serious repercussions for the expelled partner and may often lead to a loss of livelihood. For this reason, a court will strictly construe the right to expel a partner and any conditions which have to be met to exercise that right. Yet the courts will take a practical approach to the interpretation of expulsion clauses, as is illustrated by *Hitchman v Crouch Butler Savage Associates Services Ltd* (1983) 127 SJ 441. There, an expulsion clause which required the senior partner in a firm to sign all expulsion notices, was interpreted by the English Court of Appeal as not requiring his signature, when it came to his own expulsion notice.

# 1.5    Dissolution of a Partnership

## 1.5.1    GENERAL DISSOLUTION vs TECHNICAL DISSOLUTION

An important distinction must be made between the general dissolution of a partnership and its technical dissolution. If a partnership is subject to a general dissolution, the partnership will come to an end and its business is wound up. A technical dissolution is where there is a change in the membership of the partnership but no winding-up of the 'old' partnership since the business of the partnership continues as before the change in membership, such as where a partner leaves the firm or a partner joins the firm. The same events lead to the technical and general dissolution of a partnership, thus the death of a partner 'dissolves' the partnership that existed between the partners, and thereafter the surviving partners may continue the partnership business as before (in which case there would be a technical dissolution) or they may decide to sell the partnership assets and wind up the business (in which case there would be a general dissolution). In this section, we consider the legal consequences of the occurrence of both a general and a technical dissolution since it is only with the benefit of hindsight (i.e. was the firm wound up or did it continue in business) that one may determine whether a particular event led to the general or the technical dissolution of the firm.

As noted below at **1.5.2.3**, unless the partnership agreement provides otherwise, the death of bankruptcy of a partner results in the automatic dissolution of the partnership (1890 Act, s 33(1)), and at that stage any partner may demand that the partnership is wound up, in which case the partnership will go into general dissolution (1890 Act, s 39). General dissolution is such an extreme step that an important reason to have a written partnership agreement is to provide expressly that dissolution is not to occur automatically on the occurrence of the death or bankruptcy of a partner.

## 1.5.2 DISSOLUTION OF A PARTNERSHIP

### 1.5.2.1 Dissolution by notice

Under the 1890 Act, ss 26 and 32(c) and in the absence of any express or implied contrary agreement, any one partner may, at any time, give notice to their fellow partners to dissolve the partnership. This notice takes effect from the date specified in the notice (subject to the fact that the date of dissolution may not be before the date of receipt). If the notice is silent on the point, it takes effect from the date when the notice is received. Once the firm is dissolved under s 26 or 32(c), any partner is entitled under s 39 of the 1890 Act to demand the sale of the partnership assets in order for the liabilities of the firm to be paid off and in this way to force the general dissolution of the firm. In most cases, this will have disastrous consequences for the partnership business. It is important, therefore, to bear in mind that ss 26 and 32(c) may be overridden if the partnership agreement contains provisions to the contrary.

As a result many partnership agreements exclude these default rights completely or require a majority vote or a minimum period of notice to be given before the partnership is dissolved. Commonly, the right of a partner to dissolve a partnership is excluded by implication, namely by an agreement between the partners that the partnership shall last for a fixed term.

### 1.5.2.2 Dissolution by agreement

The partnership agreement may specify circumstances which cause the partnership to be dissolved, such as the occurrence of a particular event. The agreement may also specify the manner in which the partnership will be dissolved.

### 1.5.2.3 Automatic dissolution

A number of events cause partnerships to dissolve automatically under the terms of the 1890 Act.

#### Bankruptcy or death

The death or bankruptcy of a partner causes the partnership to be automatically dissolved, unless the partnership agreement contains provisions to the contrary (1890 Act, s 33(1)). A good example of the automatic dissolution of a partnership by death is provided by *McLeod v Dowling* (1927) 43 TLR 655. In that case, McLeod posted a notice of dissolution to his sole partner, Dowling, that as and from the date of the notice, namely 23 March, the partnership was dissolved. The notice was received by Dowling on 24 March at 10 a.m., but McLeod had died at 3 a.m. on that same day. Accordingly, the English High Court held that the partnership was dissolved not on the purported effective date (23 March), nor at the time that it was received (at 10 a.m. on 24 March), but at the time of death of McLeod, at 3 a.m. on 24 March since a partnership is dissolved automatically on the death of a partner, in the absence of contrary agreement.

Dissolution is a serious matter, as it allows any one partner to demand the general dissolution of the partnership under s 39 and for this reason, many partnership agreements provide that, instead of causing automatic dissolution, the death or bankruptcy of a partner shall give rise to the same consequences as a retirement, i.e. the deceased partner's share or the bankrupt partner's share is sold to the continuing partners (see **1.5.4.1**). This highlights again the importance of having a well-drafted partnership agreement to override the default rules in the 1890 Act, which are in many ways inappropriate for modern professional firms, since most firms intend to continue in spite of the death or bankruptcy of a partner.

### *Illegality*

Partnerships formed to carry out an illegal activity or which are contrary to public policy are automatically dissolved. A change of circumstances (including a change in the law) may make illegal a partnership initially formed for a legal purpose. Section 34 of the 1890 Act provides that a partnership is dissolved on the happening of an event which makes the business unlawful (for example, the date the change in the law takes effect). A provision to the contrary in the partnership agreement will not override s 34. Two illegal partnership cases are of particular interest to lawyers. The first is the case of *Hudgell Yeates & Co v Watson* [1978] 2 All ER 363 which concerned a partnership in breach of the English equivalent of s 59 of the Solicitors Act, 1954 (the provision that solicitors may only enter partnership with other solicitors). The case involved an action by the plaintiff law firm against one of its clients for unpaid fees. The defendant argued that the action against him should be struck out because of one partner's inadvertent failure to renew his solicitor's practising certificate for a period of seven months. On this basis, the defendant alleged that it was an illegal partnership and he claimed that the firm was automatically dissolved as required by s 34 of the 1890 Act. Although the failure by the partner to renew his practising certificate was accidental, the Court of Appeal was left with no option but to uphold the defendant's claim that the firm was illegal and dissolved automatically on the failure of this partner to renew his practising certificate. This case highlights that professionals, who are prohibited by statute from acting in partnership with unqualified persons, should ensure that their practising certificates are renewed on a timely basis. The failure to do so will render their partnership automatically dissolved, even where the failure is inadvertent.

The second case is the eighteenth-century decision in *Everet v Williams* (1893) 9 LQR 197. In this case, an account of partnership dealings by one partner against his co-partner was sought. However, despite the partners' best efforts to conceal the purpose of the partnership, the court rejected the application on the grounds that it was an illegal partnership. The bill in equity which was filed by the plaintiff stated that he was experienced in commodities such as rings and watches and that it was agreed that he and the defendant would provide the necessary tools of their proposed trade together, namely horses, saddles and weapons. They also agreed to share equally in the costs of the venture, i.e. the expenses involved in staying at inns, alehouses and taverns. The bill stated that they had successfully 'dealt with' a gentleman for a gold watch and other goods and the plaintiff sought an account of these dealings. The court surmised that the partnership was between highwaymen and the action was dismissed on the grounds that it was an illegal partnership. To add insult to injury, the costs were ordered to be paid by the counsel who signed the bill and the solicitor for the plaintiff was attached and fined.

### By expiration

Under s 32(a) and (b) of the 1890 Act, a partnership is dissolved:

(a)  if it was entered into for a fixed term, upon the expiration of that term; and

(b)  if it was entered into for a single adventure or undertaking, upon the completion of that adventure or undertaking.

A provision to the contrary in the partnership agreement overrides s 32(a) and (b). If the agreement is silent and the partnership continues despite the expiry of the term or the completion of the adventure, the 1890 Act, s 27 provides that a partnership at will, dissolvable by notice, is brought into existence. Such a partnership is subject to the terms of the original agreement to the extent that these terms do not conflict with the incidents of a partnership at will.

## 1.5.2.4    Dissolution by the court

Finally, a partner may apply to the court for dissolution of the partnership provided one of the statutory grounds for dissolution by the court exists. This is only really an option when an easier method of dissolution is not available, either under the 1890 Act or under any partnership agreement. Section 35 of the 1890 Act sets out grounds for dissolution by the court. Those grounds which give the partners a remedy in the event of a dispute between the partners (that is to say, s 35(c), (d) and (f)) have been considered earlier at **1.4.2**. The full list of s 35 grounds is as follows:

### Partner of unsound mind (s 35(a))

A court may dissolve a partnership under s 35(a) when a partner is of permanently unsound mind. It seems that s 35(a) must be interpreted as requiring not just mental incapacity of the partner, but also that the incapacitated partner is incapable of performing his part of the partnership contract. In most cases, this will be easy enough to establish. However, where the partner is a dormant partner, his mental incapacity may have no such consequence since he will have no duties to perform in the partnership. For this reason, it is contended that the mental incapacity of a dormant partner may not lead to the firm's dissolution. Support for this view is to be found in the Scottish case of *Eadie v McBean's Curator Bonis* (1885) 12 R 660. There, the court refused to order the dissolution of the partnership where the insane partner had no active duties in the management of the firm but had merely provided the capital and the curator bonis of the insane partner opposed the application.

### *Partner incapable of performing partnership contract (s 35(b))*

A partnership may be dissolved by the court when a partner, other than the partner suing, becomes permanently incapable of performing his part of the partnership contract. Whether or not a partner has become permanently incapable is a question of fact. In *Whitwell v Arthur* (1865) 35 Beav 140 an attack of paralysis prevented a partner from performing his partnership duties. However, since medical evidence indicated that the paralysis might only be temporary, the petition for the dissolution of the partnership was refused.

### *Partner's behaviour prejudicially affecting business (s 35(c))*

A court may dissolve a partnership when a partner, other than the partner suing, has been guilty of such conduct as, in the opinion of the court, regard being had to the nature of the business, is calculated to affect prejudicially the carrying on of the business (see **1.4.2.2**).

### *Partner in breach of partnership agreement (s 35(d))*

A court may dissolve a partnership when a partner, other than the partner suing, wilfully or persistently commits a breach of the partnership agreement, or otherwise so conducts himself in matters relating to the partnership business that it is not reasonably practicable for the other partner or partners to carry on the business in partnership with him (see **1.4.2.3**).

### *Business running at a loss (s 35(e))*

A court may dissolve a partnership when the business of the partnership can only be carried on at a loss. In order for s 35(e) to be invoked, the circumstances must be such as to make it a practical impossibility for the partnership to make a profit. If the partners who find themselves in this position cannot agree to bring the partnership to an end, this may be a valuable right if a delay in terminating the partnership will increase the amount of the loss, for which all the partners will be personally liable.

### *Just and equitable (s 35(f))*

A court may dissolve a partnership whenever, in the opinion of the court, it is just and equitable that the partnership be dissolved (see **1.4.2.4**).

## 1.5.3 CONSEQUENCES OF A DISSOLUTION

### 1.5.3.1 Generally

The occurrence of one of the events leading to the automatic dissolution of a partnership (see **1.5.2.3**) will cause the partnership to be 'dissolved'. Whether this results in the technical or general dissolution of the firm depends on whether the right to wind up the firm under s 39 of the 1890 Act has been

NORMA SMURFIT LIBRARY
NATIONAL COLLEGE
of IRELAND

excluded by the partners and, if not, whether a partner wishes to force the general dissolution of the firm by exercising this right under s 39 of the 1890 Act. Section 39 provides:

*On the dissolution of a partnership every partner is entitled, as against the other partners in the firm, and all persons claiming through them in respect of their interests as partners, to have the property of the partnership applied in payment of the debts and liabilities of the firm, and to have the surplus assets after such payment applied in payment of what may be due to the partners respectively after deducting what may be due from them as partners to the firm; and for that purpose any partner or his representatives may on the termination of the partnership apply to the Court to wind up the business and affairs of the firm.*

The most common way in which the right under s 39 is excluded is by the partners having a partnership agreement which provides that when a partner leaves the firm, his share shall be purchased by the continuing partner.

Where the firm goes into general dissolution, s 38 provides that, after the dissolution, the authority of each partner to bind the firm (as well as the other rights and obligations of the partners) continues despite the dissolution but only to the extent necessary to wind up the affairs of the partnership, and to complete transactions begun but unfinished at the time of the dissolution.

### 1.5.3.2 Realisation of partnership assets on general dissolution

Once the firm has been dissolved and the general dissolution begins, the value of the assets owned by the partnership will be ascertained, as will the extent of the debts and liabilities owed to creditors. In so far as it is necessary, the assets will be sold to raise the funds to discharge the debts. These assets will include the 'goodwill' attaching to the business. Goodwill has been defined by Lord Macnaghten in *Trego v Hunt* [1896] AC 7 as:

the whole advantage, whatever it may be, of the reputation and connection of the firm, which may have been built up by years of honest work or gained by lavish expenditure of money.

Where goodwill is sold, the purchasers will want to protect their investment against the loss of custom arising from the former owners setting up in competition in the same vicinity. Accordingly, the purchaser may wish to include a restrictive covenant in the sale agreement to guard against this possibility (see **1.2.4.5**).

### 1.5.3.3 Distribution of partnership assets on general dissolution

Once the liabilities of the partnership have been met, any surplus is distributed to the partners. Section 44(b) of the 1890 Act provides that, in the absence of any contrary agreement, on a general dissolution, the assets of the firm shall be applied in the following order:

(a)  debts of the firm to third parties;

(b)  repayment of advances made by the partners to the firm;

(c)   repayment of the capital contribution made by the partners to the firm; and

(d)   balance is divided in the same manner as the profits are divided amongst the partners.

Section 44(a) of the 1890 Act provides that if the partnership has made losses (including losses of capital), in the absence of any contrary agreement, these shall be met on the general dissolution of the firm in the following order:

(a)   from profits;

(b)   from capital; and

(c)   from the partners in the proportion in which profits are divisible.

Both parts of s 44 are subject to contrary agreement. In particular, the partners may agree to share surplus assets and to contribute to losses in a ratio different from their normal profit sharing. However, the requirement that creditors are paid off first is not subject to variation by the partners.

### 1.5.3.4    Sharing of losses on general dissolution

Under s 44(a) and (b), any loss or residue, whether of capital or profits, will be shared between the partners in the proportion in which they share the profits, in the absence of contrary agreement. These subsections are traps for the unwary, as this sharing of the capital losses or capital profits applies irrespective of the manner in which the partners have contributed to the capital of the firm but rather in proportion to the rate at which profits are shared. (See also 1890 Act, s 24(1); *Ex parte Maude* (1867) 16 LT 577; *Re Weymouth Steam Packet Co* [1891] 1 Ch 66; and *Re Wakefield Rolling Stock Co* [1892] 3 Ch 165.) Therefore, a partner who contributes all the capital of the firm and shares the profits of the firm evenly with his partner, will, in the absence of any agreement to the contrary, share evenly in any capital profit or capital loss on the winding-up of the firm. In some cases, this may come as a surprise to the partner who contributes all the capital and accordingly the terms of the sharing of capital residues or losses require careful consideration in such partnerships.

An example will highlight this issue. A, B and C contributed capital of €2,000 in the following proportions: €1,000, €500 and €500 respectively, the partners sharing profits and losses equally. On a winding-up there is residual capital of only €1,000, thus leaving a capital loss of €1,000. Under the general rules governing the sharing of capital losses, these are shared in the same proportion as the profit shares (1890 Act, s 44(a)) so that A, B and C are required to contribute a third each, i.e. each notionally contribute €333 giving a notional capital of €2,000. This is because such a shortfall in the capital is as much a loss as any other shortfall and is made up in the same way, namely by being shared between the partners. The notional capital is then repaid to the partners in accordance with their capital contributions, since s 44(b) requires the capital to be repaid to partners 'rateably'. Therefore, they will notionally receive the €2,000 divided in proportion to their capital contributions, i.e. 2:1:1 so that A will notionally receive his €1,000 back and B and C will receive back €500 each. To get the actual amount received by A, deduct his notional contribution of €333 from the notional amount of capital he should receive (€1,000) to give €667 which he actually receives. Similarly for B and C, deduct their notional contribution of €333 from the notional amount of capital, which they were to receive (€500), to give €167, which they will each receive. So, in respect of A's initial capital contribution of €1,000, he gets back €667, and thus he makes a loss of €333. While in respect of B's and C's capital contributions of €500, they get back €167 and thus they also make a loss of €333 each. The same result could have been achieved by dividing the capital loss of €1,000 equally between A, B and C.

### 1.5.3.5    Notification of the dissolution

Under s 36(1) of the 1890 Act, outsiders dealing with the firm after a change in the membership of the firm are entitled to treat all apparent members of the firm as still being members until the outsider has notice of the change (see **1.5.4.3**). In order to protect themselves from liability for obligations incurred after the dissolution, the partners in the dissolved firm are entitled to publicly notify the fact of the dissolution (1890 Act, s 37) and s 36(2) of the 1890 Act provides that persons who had no dealings with a firm prior to a change in the membership of the firm are deemed to be on notice of a change in the firm which is advertised in Iris Oifigiúil.

Section 36(2) only provides that *new* customers of the firm are on notice of the change advertised in Iris Oifigiúil. It does not apply to existing customers of the firm.

To obtain protection from liability for obligations incurred with *existing* customers after the dissolution, the former partners should give notice individually to each of these customers. In the case of a technical dissolution (i.e. where the business of the partnership continues after the departure of a partner), this will be an important issue since the partnership business will continue as before. In practice in larger firms, the former partner may opt to rely on an indemnity from the continuing partners in respect of such liabilities rather than attempting to notify all the clients of the firm that he is no longer a partner.

## 1.5.4    DEPARTURE OF A PARTNER FROM A FIRM

### 1.5.4.1    Generally

Partnership agreements can, and should, contain provisions dealing with the departure of a partner from the firm. This is because the 1890 Act does not specifically deal with retirement. Under the 1890 Act the only option available to a partner who wishes to leave a firm is to give notice to dissolve the partnership under s 26, if it is a partnership at will. If a s 26 notice is given the partnership will be dissolved (see **1.5.2.1**); the section does not permit a partner to depart, ie retire, without having to dissolve the partnership. To avoid this, suitable provisions must be included in the agreement entitling a partner to leave the firm and usually providing for the continuing partners to purchase his share in the partnership. This section considers the position of a former partner, regardless of how he leaves the firm, whether by retirement or expulsion. The position of a partner who dies is considered at **1.5.5**.

### 1.5.4.2 Obligations incurred before departure

The mere fact that a partner leaves a firm does not release him from obligations incurred by the firm while he was a partner. Section 17(2) of the 1890 Act provides that a 'partner who retires from a firm does not thereby cease to be liable for partnership debts or obligations incurred before his retirement'. For this reason, it is common for the former partner to be indemnified by the continuing partners. In the absence of such an indemnity, the former partner is fully liable for all obligations incurred while he was a partner, subject only to the relevant rules on the barring of claims under the Statute of Limitations.

### 1.5.4.3 Obligations incurred after departure

The general rule is that partners are only liable for debts incurred by the partnership while they are members of the firm. Therefore, ceasing to be a partner prevents the *former* partner becoming liable on future debts as the retirement terminates the agency relationship. However, this general rule is subject to the very important exception in s 36(1) of the 1890 Act which is considered below.

#### Section 36(3)

Section 36(3) is in keeping with the general rule that a former partner is not liable for obligations incurred after his departure. This section provides that a deceased partner's estate, a bankrupt partner or a retiring partner (who was not known to have been a partner by the person dealing with the firm), is not liable for obligations incurred after the date of death, bankruptcy or retirement. The subsection was considered in *Tower Cabinet Co Ltd v Ingram* [1949] 2 KB 397. In that case, A and B were in partnership. A retired and B continued the business under the old name. After A's retirement, the business ordered goods from a new supplier and failed to pay. The supplier sought to enforce judgment against A. The only knowledge the supplier had of A's connection with the firm was that A's name appeared on headed notepaper which, contrary to A's express instructions, had not been destroyed. The court found that, as the customer had no knowledge prior to A's retirement that A was a partner in the firm, A was completely protected by s 36(3). (A further question arose of A's possible liability under s 14(1) which is considered at **1.3.4**.)

#### Section 36(1)

In cases where creditors know of the partner's connection with the firm before the former partner departs, s 36(3) is of no assistance. In this regard, s 36(1) provides the important exception to the general rule that a former partner is not liable for obligations incurred by a firm after his departure. It provides that:

> *where a person deals with a firm after a change in its constitution, he is entitled to treat all apparent members of the old firm as still being members of the firm until he has notice of the change.*

It is important to note that s 36(1) only applies to existing customers of the firm and not to those persons who only began dealing with the firm after the former partner departed.

If the former partner wishes to be absolutely protected from liability for future debts, he should give the existing customers formal notification of his retirement. Although the matter is not beyond dispute, it is thought that actual notice is not required under s 36(1). Thus, it is suggested that some reasonable limits will be placed by the courts on the requirement of notice and this is likely to be done by interpreting 'notice' as including situations where from all the circumstances the third party should have been aware that the former partner was no longer a partner in the firm, i.e. constructive notice (see further Twomey, *Partnership Law,* paras 11.62 *et seq.*).

### Section 14(1)

A former partner may also be liable for obligations incurred after his departure from the firm under the doctrine of holding out. This concept applies to all persons (whether they are former partners or not) who allow themselves to be held out as partners in a firm when in fact they are not partners: see also **1.3.4**). Section 14(1) of the 1890 Act provides that:

> *Every one who by words spoken or written or by conduct represents himself, or who knowingly suffers himself to be represented, as a partner in a particular firm, is liable as a partner to any one who has on the faith of any such representation given credit to the firm, whether the representation has or has not been made or communicated to the person so giving credit by or with the knowledge of the apparent partner making the representation or suffering it to be made.*

Therefore, even if no liability arises under s 36(1), the former partner may be liable to any person (whether they had previous dealings with the firm or not) who has given 'credit' to the firm on the faith of a representation that the former partner is still a partner. In *Tower Cabinet Co Ltd v Ingram* [1949] 2 KB 397, it was also alleged that the former partner had allowed himself to be held out as a partner. However, since the former partner had not authorised the use of the old notepaper, he had not 'knowingly' allowed himself to be held out as an 'apparent' partner and so no liability under s 14(1) arose.

In order to reduce the likelihood of a former partner being liable for obligations incurred after his retirement, he should ensure that the partnership agreement is amended to reflect the fact that he is no longer a partner from the date of his departure, he should remove his name from the headed notepaper of the firm, from the firm's signs and from the register of business names (if the firm name is registered as a business name, see **1.1.7**). If there is a dispute about when he left the firm, these actions will have the additional benefit of supporting the claim that he left on a certain date and is not liable for liabilities incurred after that date.

### 1.5.4.4   Post-dissolution profits of a firm

Once a partner has left a firm, the partnership agreement should provide for his share in the firm to be purchased by the continuing partners. If there is no agreement, the default right in s 39 of the 1890 Act will apply and the former partner may force the winding-up of the partnership under s 39.

In addition, s 42(1) of the 1890 Act provides for the situation where a member of a firm ceases to be a partner (including by death) and the continuing partners carry on the business of the firm without any final settlement of accounts as between the firm and the outgoing partner or his estate. Under this section, the outgoing partner or his estate is entitled, subject to contrary agreement, at the option of himself or his personal representatives to claim:

(a)   such share of the profits made since the dissolution as the court may find to be attributable to the use of his share of the partnership assets; or

(b)   interest at the rate of 5 per cent p.a. on the amount of his share of the partnership assets.

Thus, in either case, it is necessary to determine the former partner's share of the partnership assets. The approach to be taken in determining this issue was considered by the Supreme Court in *Meagher v Meagher* [1961] IR 96. The case involved three brothers, who carried on the business of buying houses, renovating them and selling them at a profit. On the death of one brother, the other two brothers continued to carry on the business. The value of the assets of the partnership had increased considerably since the date of death of the first brother, due to a general increase in property prices in Ireland at that time. In considering the deceased partner's estate's claim, for his share of the profits made since the dissolution attributable to his share of the partnership assets under s 42(1), the question arose as to whether the value of a deceased partner's share in the houses was to be calculated on the date of death or on the date these partnership assets were realised. The deceased's personal representative claimed that the deceased partner's share in the partnership should be valued on the basis of the prices received for the houses when they were sold, which was a number of years after the death. The Supreme Court held that the value of a partner's share of the partnership assets is the value of those assets on dissolution, but as a general rule, this is to be taken as the price realised on the sale of the assets, whenever that may be, unless there is a plausible case that the value at dissolution varied appreciably from that realised by sale. In this case, the post-dissolution profits were due primarily to an increase in the value of the partnership assets (i.e. houses) which had increased in value while they remained unsold. For this reason it seems that the Supreme Court did not make any attempt to ascertain what share of the post-dissolution profits were attributable to the use of the former partner's share of the partnership assets, but rather appears to have assumed that his share of the revalued partnership assets included his share of the post-dissolution profits.

Any amount due from the continuing partners to the former partner under this section is a debt accruing at the date of the death (1890 Act, s 43). Raising a large capital sum to pay a former partner or his estate will put a large financial strain on the resources of many partnerships. For this reason, it is common for the partnership agreement to provide a method for valuing the former partner's share in the firm and by providing for this capital sum to be paid by instalments.

### 1.5.5 DEATH

As noted at **1.5.2.3**, death causes the automatic dissolution of a partnership. In order to avoid inconvenience to the surviving partners, it is common to provide in the partnership agreement that, instead of leading to the general dissolution of the partnership, the surviving partners will continue the partnership business and usually the agreement provides for the deceased partner's share to be purchased by them. In this way, the right of a partner to wind up the partnership under the 1890 Act, s 39 is excluded.

#### 1.5.5.1 Liability of partner's estate for debts

It has already been noted that under the 1890 Act, s 9 every partner is jointly liable for debts and obligations of the firm incurred while he is a partner. In addition, s 9 provides that the estate of a deceased person is severally liable for such debts and obligations so far as they remain unsatisfied but subject to the prior payment of the deceased partner's personal debts. A partnership creditor may, therefore, proceed against the estate of a deceased partner in respect of partnership debts (even after obtaining a judgment against the other partners) provided some part of the debt is unsatisfied. However, partnership creditors are postponed to the deceased partner's own creditors. It has been noted at **1.5.4.3** that s 36(3) of the 1890 Act provides that the deceased partner's estate is not liable for partnership debts contracted after the death.

## 1.6 Partnerships with Limited Liability

### 1.6.1 INTRODUCTION

The main type of partnership in Ireland is the ordinary partnership, which is the main focus of this text. However, there are two other types of partnership under Irish law, the limited partnership and the investment limited partnership, each of which will be considered in turn.

### 1.6.2 LIMITED PARTNERSHIPS

#### 1.6.2.1 Generally

The legislation governing this type of partnership is the Limited Partnerships Act, 1907 and this provides that the general law of partnership applies to limited partnerships save as provided by the express terms of the 1907 Act. Therefore, all of the principles of general partnership law which we have considered above are equally applicable to limited partnerships, unless inconsistent with the terms of the 1907 Act.

A limited partnership must consist of at least one general partner and at least one limited partner. The general partner has unlimited liability like a partner in an ordinary partnership. It is worth noting that there is nothing to stop a limited company being a general partner and in this way effectively limiting the liability of the general partner. The limited partner has limited liability since his liability is limited to the amount of capital contributed by him to the firm. In return for the Limited Partnerships Act granting the limited partner the protection of limited liability, he forsakes the normal rights of a partner to take part in the management of the firm. In many ways, the role of the limited partner is like a shareholder in a limited company because his liability is limited to the capital he has contributed and he has no role in the management of the firm. Unlike an ordinary partnership, a limited partnership must be registered in the Companies Registration Office and only comes into existence on the issue of the certificate of registration.

## 1.6.2.2    Popularity of limited partnerships

### Tax avoidance vehicles

Limited partnerships became popular tax avoidance vehicles during the 1970s because, like all partnerships, they are tax-transparent in the sense that unlike a company (in which the company and its shareholders are two taxable entities) in a partnership, the partnership itself is not taxed, but only the individual partners. Thus, instead of having two levels of tax (i.e. corporation tax on the company and income tax on the dividend received by the shareholders) the profits of an enterprise which is organised as a partnership are subject to just one level of tax, namely income tax on the profits paid to the partners. In addition, the limited partnership gives the added bonus of limited liability for the limited partners in the venture. Limited partnerships remain popular vehicles in tax-based ventures for these reasons (e.g. film financing).

However, in the 1970s the limited partnership had the added bonus of facilitating the reduction of a partner's personal income tax bill by allowing him to use large losses in his role as a limited partner. As a see-through vehicle for tax purposes, the losses of the partnership were passed on to the limited partners and used by them to offset profits on their other income. If these losses were in excess of the amount of capital contributed by the limited partner, as they usually were, then the limited partner only lost his capital but was able to set off a much larger amount against his personal income tax. This practice has been eliminated by the Revenue, which now restricts the amount that may be set off against a limited partner's personal income to the amount of capital, which he has contributed to the partnership.

### Venture capital vehicles

Limited partnerships are popular today as venture capital vehicles since they allow for the easy withdrawal of capital by investors in the limited partnership. The limited partners take no part in the management of the firm's money (which suits most venture capitalists) and instead the money invested in the partnership is managed by the general partners. The limited partnership structure has the advantage over limited companies of not requiring an application to be made to court for the capital of a limited partnership to be repaid to the investors.

### 1.6.2.3 Loss of limited liability by limited partner

The protection of limited liability for the limited partners may be lost in certain circumstances under the terms of the 1907 Act. Since the *raison d'être* for limited partnerships is, in many cases, the presence of limited liability for the limited partners, it is important to bear in mind that the protection of limited liability will be lost in a number of situations, including if the limited partner takes part in the management of the firm or if there is a failure to properly register the firm or any change in the details of the firm, e.g. as happened in the case of *McCarthaigh v Daly* [1985] IR 73. This case involved a prominent Cork solicitor in the tax loophole referred to already at **1.1.3.1** which has since been closed off by the Revenue Commissioners. The respondent agreed to contribute capital of £50 to a limited partnership formed for the purpose of leasing assets to the Metropole Hotel in Cork in the tax year 1977–78. He sought to set off his share of the losses of the limited partnership which amounted to £2,000 against his personal income tax as a solicitor. Mr Daly was successful in having this amount set off. However, s 5 of the Limited Partnerships Act provides that if there is a failure to properly register a limited partnership in accordance with the terms of the Act then every limited partner is deemed to be a general partner with unlimited liability. In that case, the limited partnership was formed in December 1977 and the following February the form LP1 (the form to be completed and filed for the registration of a limited partnership) was filed in the Companies Office containing details of the £50 contributed by the limited partners. The certificate of registration of the limited partnership was issued by the registrar of companies on 16 February 1978.

It transpired that the £50 was not actually contributed by the limited partners until April 1978. For this reason, the form LP1 was incorrect when it stated that the limited partners had contributed £50. In the High Court, O'Hanlon J held that the limited partnership was an ordinary partnership since the partnership had not been properly registered. The lesson to be learnt from this case is that special care should be taken to ensure that any filings, which are required to be made under the 1907 Act, are accurately and properly made in order to avoid the intended limited partners failing to obtain limited liability.

## 1.6.3 INVESTMENT LIMITED PARTNERSHIPS ACT, 1994

The third and final type of partnership under Irish law is the most recent creation. It is the investment limited partnership which was introduced into Irish law for the first time by the Investment Limited Partnerships Act, 1994. It is important to bear in mind that although this is an investment 'limited' partnership, it is not governed by the Limited Partnerships Act, 1907 but by the general principles of partnership law as set out by the Partnership Act, 1890, the case law thereunder and by the Investment Limited Partnerships Act, 1994 itself.

### 1.6.3.1 Purpose and nature of an investment limited partnership

In 1986, legislation was enacted in Ireland to encourage the establishment of an International Financial Services Centre in the Custom House Docks area. As the limited partnership is a popular investment vehicle in the US, it was decided to introduce this concept into the Irish funds industry in order to further encourage investment in the IFSC from other jurisdictions such as America, the Cayman Islands, and Bermuda where such vehicles have been popular for many years.

The investment limited partnership is a collective investment scheme which has the Irish Financial Services Regulatory Authority as its regulatory authority and the general partner must have a minimum paid-up share capital of €125,100. Section 5 of the Investment Limited Partnerships Act, 1994 defines an investment limited partnership as a partnership consisting of at least one general partner and one limited partner having as its principal business the investment of its funds in property of all kinds. Like the position with limited partnerships formed under the Limited Partnerships Act, 1907, a general partner in an investment limited partnership has unlimited liability for the debts and obligations of the firm, while a limited partner is not liable for the debts and obligations of the firm beyond the amount of his capital contribution. However, having one general partner and one limited partner is not sufficient for a partnership to constitute an investment limited partnership since an investment limited partnership is defined as 'a partnership which holds a certificate of authorisation' from the Central Bank. Thus, an investment limited partnership only comes into existence on the receipt of this certificate of authorisation. As these partnerships are only of interest to sophisticated investors in the Irish funds industry, it is not proposed to go into the detailed regulation of these partnerships, much of which is to be found in the Central Bank Notices issued pursuant to the Investment Limited Partnerships Act, 1994.

### 1.6.3.2 Limited partner

As with limited partnerships under the 1907 Act, a limited partner under the Investment Limited Partnerships Act is not liable for the debts or obligations of the investment partnership beyond the amount of capital which he has contributed. An individual, body corporate or a partnership may be a limited partner.

### 1.6.3.3 General partner

The general partner will normally be the fund manager and, like a partner in an ordinary partnership, he will be personally liable for all debts of the investment limited partnership. An individual and body corporate, and it seems a partnership, may be a general partner. Thus, there is nothing to stop a limited company being a general partner and in this way to effectively limit the liability of the general partner.

## 1.6.4 LIMITED LIABILITY PARTNERSHIPS

Although not in existence in Ireland yet, this new type of partnership is in existence in Great Britain and Northern Ireland. Nonetheless, this type of partnership is worth referring to, since it may be introduced to Ireland in the near future. However, while called a 'partnership', the UK limited liability partnership ('LLP') is in many ways more accurately described as a company, which is taxed as if it was a partnership. This is because under the statute which establishes the LLP (the Limited Liability Partnerships Act 2000 in Britain and the Limited Liability Partnerships Act (Northern Ireland), 2002 in Northern Ireland), it is formed as a body corporate with an existence separate from its members/partners and the members/partners in the LLP, are subject to the extensive body of British company law by adaptation, i.e. the regulations issued under that Act provide that everywhere there is a reference to a provision applying to a director of a company, that provision will be deemed to apply to a partner in an LLP. In addition, the UK LLP is subject to filing accounts in the same way as if it was a company. Two of the main advantages of the partnership structure (i.e. not being subject to company law and not being required to file accounts) do not therefore apply to an LLP. The LLP does, however, have the advantage of being taxed as a partnership, so that it does not pay corporation tax. The other main advantage of the LLP is that it offers limited liability protection to the partners for the negligence of their co-partners. This is achieved by providing that the LLP is a body corporate separate from its members and in this way actions are taken against the body corporate and its assets, rather than against the personal assets of the partners.

The only exception to this is that the personal assets of an individual partner are available to third parties in the event of that partner being personally negligent.

LLPs have also been introduced in the United States and Canada. However, it is suggested that the form of LLP in both these countries is preferable to the UK LLP. This is because in Canada and the US, LLPs were introduced, not by creating a brand new body corporate, but by simply amending the existing partnership law (and thereby retaining the aforementioned advantages of the partnership structure) to provide a protection for the personal assets of a partner in the event of the negligence of his co-partner.

### Further reading

Twomey, *Partnership Law* (Butterworths, 2000)

**CHAPTER 2**

# COMPANY FORMATION AND SECRETARIAL MANAGEMENT

## 2.1 Introduction

### 2.1.1 TYPES OF COMPANY

One of the principal ways of carrying on business is by way of a company. In Ireland, the usual form of entity that is used to conduct business is a private company limited by shares. The membership may simply consist of one person, as in the case of a single member company; but usually it consists of at least two persons, which is the prescribed minimum for all other types of private companies. There is a maximum limit of fifty members in private companies (not including employee members). Public limited companies (which may or may not be quoted on a Stock Exchange) may be used where there is a need to have a larger membership (i.e. more than fifty) and to raise money from the public to finance the business. An example is the case of the flotation of Eircom plc. Another type of company, namely a company limited by guarantee and not having a share capital, is very commonly used where the purpose is a charitable one or involves the promotion of sport. The principal difference is that in this type of company the members do not have to subscribe for shares but instead agree to contribute a specified amount if there are insufficient funds to meet the company's liabilities on a winding-up.

### 2.1.2 ADVANTAGES OF INCORPORATION

The advantages of incorporation are that a company:

(a) has a separate and distinct legal personality from that of its members;

(b) has perpetual succession until it is either wound up or struck off the Register of Companies; and

(c) is liable for its own debts and may be sued by creditors and may itself sue debtors. Financial institutions usually prefer to lend money to a company rather than to individuals and a company, unlike an individual, may give a floating charge as security.

As against these favourable criteria, there is a requirement that every company (except an unlimited one, where members have unlimited liability for its debts) file its financial statements with the Registrar of Companies on an annual basis. These are available for public inspection on payment of the prescribed fee. Sole traders and partnerships are only obliged to file their financial records with the Revenue Commissioners and they are not available for public inspection.

## 2.1.3　COMPANY LAW

### 2.1.3.1　Statutory regulation

Companies are principally governed by the Companies Acts, 1963–2006. Semi-state companies, e.g. An Post and Aer Lingus, are also governed by their own legislation, e.g. Postal and Telecommunications Services Act, 1983, which should be read in conjunction with the Companies Acts. In addition to primary legislation in the form of Acts of the Oireachtas, secondary legislation in the form of statutory instruments also regulates companies, e.g. European communities (Single-Member Private Limited Companies) Regulations, 1994 (SI 275/1994). Most of the statutory instruments relating to company law have been drafted to implement EU Directives. The EU is involved in an ongoing process of updating and harmonising company law in the Member States.

The impact of judicial decisions is very important in the interpretation of the Companies Acts; there are hundreds of reported cases which provide authoritative interpretations of the legislation. In addition, judicial decisions of other common law jurisdictions, especially in the United Kingdom, are of persuasive authority in Ireland.

The Companies (Amendment) (No 2) Act, 1999 ('C(A)(No 2)A 1999') introduced new provisions regarding Irish companies:

(a) A company will not be registered unless the Registrar of Companies is satisfied that when registered it will carry on an activity in Ireland, being an activity referred to in its memorandum of association (C(A)(No 2)A 1999, s 42). A declaration is required to this effect, and it forms part of the revised Companies Registration Office Form A1.

(b) A company is obliged to have at least one director resident in Ireland, unless a bond in the prescribed form to the value of €25,395 has been entered into by the company (C(A)(No 2)A 1999, s 43). The purpose of the bond is to meet any fine imposed under the Companies Acts, 1963–2003, or the Taxes Consolidation Act, 1997 or a penalty under the latter Act in respect of any offences committed by the company. An alternate director will not constitute a director for the purposes of s 43.

(c) The requirement that a company must have an Irish resident director or, alternatively, give a bond may be dispensed with if the Registrar of Companies grants to a company, on application in the prescribed form, a certificate stating that the company has a real and continuous link with one or more economic activities that are being carried on in Ireland.

(d)  C(A)(No 2)A 1999, s 45 imposes an upper limit of twenty-five on the number of directorships a person may hold. There are a number of exceptions to this rule, e.g. directorships of public limited companies and of groups of companies are excluded from calculation.

### 2.1.3.2  The Companies (Auditing and Accounting) Act, 2003

The Companies (Auditing and Accounting) Act, 2003 provides for inter alia:

(a)  The establishment of The Irish Auditing and Accounting Supervisory Authority to supervise the regulation and monitoring by prescribed accountancy bodies of their members, promote adherence to high professional standards across the accountancy profession, monitor compliance with the Companies Acts, 1963–2006 of companies and provide specialist advice to the Minister for Enterprise, Trade and Employment, on auditing and accounting related matters.

(b)  The establishment of 'Audit Committees'.

(c)  The requirement that all companies, with the exception of private companies, where the balance sheet total for the year does not exceed €7,618,428 (or other prescribed amount) and the annual turnover does not exceed €15.2 million (or other prescribed amount) to complete and publish a Directors Compliance Statement which will contain the information regarding the company as set out in s 45(3) of the above Act.

### 2.1.3.3  Capital of a company

Since 1 January 2002, the capital of Irish companies is designated in Euros. The capital of companies expressed in Irish pounds prior to this was automatically redenominated into the Euro currency but required to be renominalised (a procedure whereby figures are adjusted to produce even amounts) into a suitable unit of currency and this required an ordinary resolution if the amount was renominalised downwards to €1.25 with the difference between that and the redenominated amount being transferred to a Capital Conversion Account. If the amount was renominalised upwards to €2.00 this would have required an ordinary resolution and the injection of further capital. There were transitional provisions which allowed a company to renominalise its capital which were available for a period of eighteen months from 1 January 2002 (see s 25 of the Economic and Monetary Union Act, 1998). Since 1 July 2003, adjustments involving an increase or a reduction in the issued share capital of a company will require an injection of fresh capital (in the event of an increase) or the approval of the court in case of a reduction.

It is also possible for a company to have its capital expressed in another currency such as the US dollar or the Japanese Yen. Indeed, it is possible to have a capital expressed in various currencies such as the Euro, US dollar and Japanese Yen.

### 2.1.3.4 Taxation of companies

The Taxes Consolidation Act, 1997, and subsequent Finance Acts, in particular the Finance Act, 1999, are relevant in the context of the taxation of Irish companies. Under the Taxes Consolidation Act, 1997, every company incorporated in Ireland is obliged to furnish certain information to the Revenue Commissioners within thirty days from the date of incorporation on a Form 11 F CRO. The Finance Act, 1999 contains provisions to deal with the taxation of Irish registered companies. The Irish government deemed it necessary to introduce these provisions to curb abuses which had arisen regarding the use of Irish non-resident companies. A dividend withholding tax was introduced with effect from 6 April 1999 in respect of dividends paid by companies resident in the State. All companies deemed to be Irish resident under the Act are subject to the new dividend withholding tax rules. The Finance Act, 1999 provides that a company incorporated in Ireland will be tax-resident in Ireland. The general rule is, however, subject to a number of exceptions, e.g. if the company is quoted on a stock exchange or is resident in another country under a double tax treaty between Ireland and that other country.

Companies must also comply with the general law of the State.

## 2.1.4 PRE-INCORPORATION CONTRACTS

Individuals incorporating their business as a company are often called promoters. A promoter may enter into a contract on behalf of a company which is about to be incorporated. The Companies Act, 1963 ('CA 1963') recognises such contracts in s 37. Once the company has been incorporated, it may then ratify and take over the contract from the promoter and assume all rights and obligations under it but, until such time, the promoter or promoters will remain personally liable under the contract and the company is not bound by it.

## 2.1.5 ULTRA VIRES

At common law, unless the activity or contract entered into by a company was within its principal objects clause as specified in the memorandum of association, such activity or contract would be void. This doctrine was somewhat modified by the CA 1963, s 8 and further modified by the European Communities (Companies) Regulations, 1973 (SI 163/1973), reg 6 which implemented the EC First Company Law Directive.

Essentially, as a result of these changes an outsider who enters into a transaction unaware of the contents of the memorandum and articles of association is now able to enforce the transaction against the company even though it was ultra vires.

## 2.2 A Company's Constitutional Documents

A company has two main constitutional documents: the memorandum of association and the articles of association.

### 2.2.1 MEMORANDUM OF ASSOCIATION

The memorandum of association sets out the purposes for which the company is being established. The memorandum of a limited company is divided into the following parts:

(a) the name of the company;

(b) the objects and powers of the company;

(c) a statement that the liability of the members of the company is limited;

(d) the authorised share capital of the company, which is the number of shares the company may issue; and

(e) the 'association' clause, whereby the initial subscribers agree to come together to form the company.

In the case of a public limited company, the words 'public limited company' or its Irish language equivalent 'cuideachta phoiblí teoranta' or their respective abbreviations 'plc' or 'cpt' must be included as the last word of the name. A private limited company must usually have the word 'Limited' in its name, or the Irish word 'Teoranta', or their abbreviations 'Ltd' or 'Teo'.

Slightly different provisions apply to an unlimited company in that heads (c) and (d) above are not inserted. In the case of a company limited by guarantee and not having a share capital, a statement that liability is limited is inserted as at head (c) above but instead of a statement as to capital, a clause is inserted to the effect that the members of the company will guarantee the liabilities of the company up to a specified sum which may be as low as €1.00 or as high as the members so decide.

The principal objects are set out in the memorandum of association. Usually, the principal objects are set out in the first three paragraphs or so and the remaining paragraphs contain the powers which will enable the company to carry out the principal objects such as the power to acquire real and personal property, to apply for intellectual property rights, to lend and borrow and give guarantees, to mention but a few. It is important when drafting the main objects and powers of the company to ensure that they are comprehensive and cover the activities which the company proposes to do.

Where a company is seeking charitable status or exemption as a sporting entity, additional special clauses should be included in the memorandum of association to comply with Revenue Commissioner requirements.

## 2.2.2   THE ARTICLES OF ASSOCIATION

The articles of association establish how the business of the company will be carried on. CA 1963 contains model articles of association in the form of Tables A, C, D and E, which are suitable for the different types of company. For example, Table A, Part I is suitable for a public limited company, whilst Table A, Part II is suitable for a private limited company. The difference between Table A, Part I and Table A, Part II is that Part II contains alterations to the provisions of Part I, to make it suitable for a private limited company. In reality the articles set out in Table A, Part I and Table A, Part II are almost always modified to make them more suited to the conduct of business by modern companies.

One of the main provisions of Table A, Part I is article 1 which deals with directors' powers to allot shares (subject to Companies (Amendment) Act, 1983 ('C(A)A 1983'), s 20 authority).

The provisions of Table A, Part II which modify Table A, Part I are as follows:

(a)    Article 2 provides for a statement that the company is private and stating the principal consequences (required by CA 1963, s 33). The most important consequences are that the right to transfer shares freely is restricted, the number of members is limited to fifty and any invitation to the public to subscribe for shares is restricted.

(b)    Article 3 gives the directors an absolute right to refuse to register a transfer (as contrasted with the more limited right under Table A, Part I, article 24 which is excluded).

(c)    Article 4 stipulates different notice periods for the calling of meetings (Table A, Part I, article 51 is excluded).

(d)    Article 5 fixes the quorum for members meetings at two unless the company is a single member company in which case the quorum is one irrespective of a contrary provision in the articles (Table A, Part I, article 54, which is excluded, specifies three).

(e)    Article 6 gives power to allow members' resolutions to be made in writing rather than at an actual meeting.

(f)    Article 7 gives the directors the right to vote on matters in which they are interested (in contrast with the more limited rights under Table A, Part 1, articles 84 and 86). Section 194 of CA 1963 as amended by Companies Act, 1990, s 47 requires directors to declare their interests.

(g)    Article 8 gives the directors authority to vote as they think fit in respect of shares in any other company held or owned by the company.

(h)    Article 9 allows alternate directors to be appointed.

The articles of association of a company form a contract between a company and its members and deal with the internal regulation of a company. They may be very straightforward and adopt the relevant Table A in the appropriate form or they may be amended to deal with a particular company's rights, especially where there are different classes of shareholders.

In practice, when preparing a set of articles of association for a private limited company many modifications are made to the standard format set out in Table A, depending on the company's requirements. It may be necessary to insert details of offer round provisions to override the power of the directors to refuse to register a transfer as provided in Table A, Part II, article 3. It may also be necessary to provide in detail for how the directors of the company are to be appointed and to be removed instead of adopting the Table A provisions for retirement by rotation. In addition, the share capital of the company may be divided into different classes with different rights attaching to the various classes of shares which rights are usually set out in detail in the articles of association.

It is quite common to provide that the provisions of Table A, Part I and/or Part II as appropriate, will apply subject to certain stated exceptions. The articles which have been removed will be replaced with paragraphs setting out the new variables. It is a useful practice to attach a copy of Table A, Parts I and II to a set of articles of association, where they have not been reproduced in full, so that shareholders who are unfamiliar with the content of Table A may refer to them in conjunction with the specified articles of association which apply in a particular case.

### 2.2.3 EFFECT OF MEMORANDUM AND ARTICLES OF ASSOCIATION

Section 25 of CA 1963 provides that the memorandum and articles of association bind the company and its members as if they had been signed and sealed by each member and contain covenants on the part of each member to observe the provisions. When a member sues to enforce a personal right given to him by the articles, he may do so by way of personal action. (The rule in *Foss v Harbottle* has no application in the case of an infringement of a member's personal rights.)

### 2.2.4 PREPARING MEMORANDUM AND ARTICLES OF ASSOCIATION

The Solicitors Act, 1954, s 58 and CA 1963, s 397 provide that, with certain exceptions, it is illegal for any person other than a solicitor of the Court of Justice in Ireland to perform the act of drawing or preparing a memorandum or articles of association for the purposes of the Companies Acts, 1963–2003.

## 2.3    Incorporation

### 2.3.1    TYPES OF COMPANIES WHICH MAY BE INCORPORATED

#### 2.3.1.1    Companies limited by shares

The overwhelming majority of all companies are private companies limited by shares. The members of such a company are those who have agreed to become members and whose names have been entered on the register of members. Their liability to creditors is limited to paying the full amount payable on their shares.

#### 2.3.1.2    Single member companies

Prior to October 1994, it was not possible to have a limited liability company with a single member. Section 36 of CA 1963 provides that where a company carries on business with less than the required minimum number of members (two in a private company and seven in a public company) for more than six months, each member is personally liable for the payment of the debts of the company at that time. With the introduction of the European Communities (Single Member Private Limited Companies) Regulations, 1994 on 1 October 1994, it is now permitted to form, or convert existing companies into, single member private limited companies with only one shareholder.

It is important to note, however, that all companies must have a minimum of two directors and the 1994 Regulations do not dispense with the requirement to file an annual return or accounts in the case of single member companies.

All the powers exercisable by a company in general meeting may be exercised by the sole member without the need to hold any meeting for that purpose except the powers contained in CA 1963, s 160(2)(b), (5) and (6), being the power to remove an auditor from office. In that situation, it is necessary to hold the requisite meeting.

#### 2.3.1.3    Public limited company

A public limited company may be listed or 'quoted' on a Stock Exchange or remain unquoted. It must have at least seven members, and a nominal and issued share capital of at least €38,092.00 of which at least 25 per cent must be paid up together with the entire premium.

#### 2.3.1.4    Unlimited companies

Members of an unlimited company have unlimited liability to contribute to the company's assets in the event of the company being unable to pay its debts. However, such members do not have personal liability to creditors.

### 2.3.1.5 Companies limited by guarantee and not having a share capital

Companies limited by guarantee and not having a share capital are often used for clubs and charities which are not trading and do not need capital and where members may pay an annual subscription and undertake to pay a further amount (the guarantee) specified in the memorandum of association in the event of insolvency. All companies of this type are public (as private companies must always have a share capital (CA 1963, s 33)).

### 2.3.1.6 Private company limited by guarantee and having a share capital

The liability of a private company limited by guarantee and having a share capital is limited to the amount the members have undertaken to contribute to the assets of the company in the event of its being wound up, in addition to the amount, if any, unpaid on shares held by them. In practice, such companies are rarely used.

### 2.3.1.7 External companies

Until the introduction of the European Communities (Branch Disclosures) Regulations, 1993 (SI 395/1993), any foreign company which established a place of business within Ireland was required to register with the Registrar of Companies, as an external company under CA 1963, Part XI.

Under the 1993 Regulations, there are different requirements as to registration imposed on a company incorporated in a Member State and companies incorporated in other countries. The regulations apply where a foreign company has established a 'branch' in the State. If the foreign company has established a 'place of business', it must continue to register under CA 1963, Part XI. The Regulations contain no definition of 'branch', but it may be taken that a branch is regarded as a place of business, which is permanent and carries on business with a management team, and is not merely a postal address.

## 2.3.2 COMPANY NAMES

Generally speaking, a new company name or a change of name for an existing company will not be registered if:

    (a)    it is identical to a name already on the register of companies;

    (b)    in the opinion of the Registrar of Companies it is offensive; or

    (c)    it would suggest State sponsorship.

Every company name should be unique. Consequently CA 1963, s 23(2) provides that if, through inadvertence or otherwise, a company is registered by a name which is too similar to that of an existing company, then the second company may be ordered by the Registrar of Companies to change its name. An objection to a name pursuant to s 23(2) must be received within six months of the registration of the name.

Section 21 of CA 1963 provides that no company may be registered by a name which, in the opinion of the Registrar, is undesirable. In general, the following types of name are regarded as undesirable:

(a)  names which are identical, or confusingly similar to names already on the register;

(b)  names that could be regarded as deceptive or misleading, i.e. could imply State sponsorship;

(c)  names which include a year date are not acceptable.

For a private limited company, 'Limited' or 'Teoranta' (or their respective abbreviations 'Ltd' or 'Teo') must be the last word in the name. If the company's objects are the promotion of commerce, art, science, education, religion or charity, a licence to omit the word 'limited' may be obtained from the Registrar under CA 1963, s 24 as amended by s 87 of the Company Law Enforcement Act, 2001 ('CLEA 2001'). If the word 'bank' is to be used in a company name, a licence must be obtained from the Central Bank. This would apply even in the case of a name such as 'Hollybank Construction Limited'.

The word 'insurance' may only be included if the company is to engage in the business of insurance and has been licensed by the Minister for Enterprise, Trade and Employment to do so. If the company carries on the business of insurance broking, then the words 'insurance' or 'insurance broking' may be used. The word 'co-operative' may not be used in a company name. This is to avoid confusion between entities registered in the Registry of Friendly Societies and limited companies. The word 'Society' may be used if permission has been obtained from the Registrar of Societies.

A dissolved company may be restored to the register under CA 1963, s 310 within a two-year period of its dissolution. A company struck off the register under CA 1963, s 311 may be restored within a period of twenty years. Consequently, these names may not be reused until these time limits have expired.

A company trading under a name other than its own is obliged to register under the Registration of Business Names Act, 1963. This Act is in the course of being replaced by new legislation on business names.

Registration of a business name confers no protection of the name and there is no cross-check between the Business Names Register and the Company Register. In certain cases, it may also be necessary to carry out a search of the Register and Pending Register of Trade Marks maintained pursuant to the Trade Marks Act, 1996 to ensure that no intended trade mark or service mark is already registered or pending registration and thus avoid any action for possible infringement. In exceptional cases, a search of the Trade Marks Register and Pending Register maintained by the Office for the Harmonisation of the Internal Market in Alicante, Spain, may be necessary. Care should also be taken not to infringe domain names and the necessary searches of the relevant domain registry may also have to be made.

## 2.3.3 DOCUMENTS LEADING TO INCORPORATION OF PRIVATE LIMITED COMPANY

The main documents required to incorporate a private limited company are set out below.

### 2.3.3.1 Memorandum and articles of association

It is necessary that the memorandum and articles of association be signed by at least two subscribers (one in the case of a single member company) and in the case of the memorandum, each of the subscribers set opposite their respective names the number of shares which they are going to take up with a minimum of one share each. This must be expressed in words. The signature of a subscriber must then be witnessed by an independent person and dated.

### 2.3.3.2 Company registration form A1

A Form A1 has to be completed by the directors and the secretary with a consent by each of these persons to act as directors or secretary. (At least one director should be resident in Ireland; alternatively, a bond for €25,395.00 in the prescribed form may be lodged instead.) Directors must be natural persons but a secretary may also be a body corporate or a firm as well as being a natural person. The form must also be signed on behalf of the subscribers and have the company's capital duty section completed by a director or secretary. In addition, it must state the address of the registered office of the company.

In addition to the statutory declaration that all the requirements of CA 1963 have been met, C(A)(No 2)A 1999, introduced new provisions which require the declarant to state the classification of the activity of the company in accordance with the NACE Rev 1 (which is the common basis for statistical classifications of economic activities within the EU) and to describe the general nature of the activity of the company or, where it is not possible to classify the activity, to describe the activity. The declarant goes on to further declare the place or places in Ireland where it is proposed to carry on the activity and where the central administration of the company will normally be carried on.

The declaration must be completed by a director, secretary or by a practising solicitor before a commissioner for oaths, a practising solicitor, a notary public or a peace commissioner.

### 2.3.3.3 Registration fees

The Registrar's fees for the incorporation of a company under the Companies Acts, 1963–2006 can be obtained from the Companies Registration Office website (www.cro.ie).

## 2.3.4   PROCEDURE FOR INCORPORATION OF A COMPANY

In relation to the incorporation of new companies, there are two systems at present in operation in the Companies Registration Office.

### 2.3.4.1   Fé Phráinn

The Fé Phráinn system is restricted to private limited companies, unlimited companies and companies limited by guarantee and not having a share capital. The system is available to all applicants who use a standard form of memorandum and articles of association which has been approved by the Companies Registration Office. All copies of the memorandum and articles of association submitted under this system must be printed. Only certain information needs to be inserted such as: the company's name, principal objects clause (which must be restricted to not more than twenty words) and nominal share capital. If the documentation furnished is correct and complete, a company will be incorporated within ten days from the date of lodgement at the Companies Registration Office.

A modification of the Fé Phráinn scheme is CROdisc. The information on the Form A1 is recorded on a computer disk and submitted with the hard copies of Form A1 (signed and declared) together with the standard memorandum and articles. If the documentation is in order, incorporation will take place within five working days from the date of lodgement in the Companies Registration Office.

### 2.3.4.2   Ordinary List

The Ordinary List comprises companies which do not belong to the Fé Phráinn scheme and public limited companies. A time scale for the incorporation of companies on the Ordinary List is between three and four weeks. The principal difference from the Fé Phráinn Scheme is that hard copies of the documentation, which may include memoranda and articles of association that have not received the approval of the Companies Registration Office, are lodged with the Companies Registration Office. Such documentation is then manually checked to ensure that it complies with the Companies Acts, 1963–2006.

## 2.3.5   CERTIFICATE OF INCORPORATION

When all the documents and fees have been lodged in the Companies Registration Office and the Registrar is satisfied that all formalities have been completed, a certificate of incorporation is issued for the company which is conclusive evidence that the company has been properly incorporated.

### 2.3.5.1   Post formation

The company must keep certain statutory books and have a common seal. The company may trade under a different name which must be registered under the Registration of Business Names Act, 1963.

The subscribers become members on incorporation. Even if they are nominees, their names should be entered on the register of members and then they should transfer their shares. Alternatively, they may renounce their rights to take shares (without ever becoming shareholders) in favour of the persons to whom it is intended to allot the shares.

The directors should order notepaper as soon as possible so as to be sure that they comply with the provisions of the Companies Acts, 1963–2006 as regards letterheads etc.

### 2.3.5.2 Nameplate

A nameplate must be affixed outside every office or place in which the company carries on business. The plate(s) must be affixed in a conspicuous position and the name must be shown in letters that are easily legible.

### 2.3.5.3 Company letterheads etc.

Every company is required to have the following particulars on its letters and order forms:

(a) the place of and number of registration of the company;

(b) the address of its registered office;

(c) in relation to a company exempted from the requirement to add 'Limited' or 'Teoranta' to its name, the fact that it is a limited company;

(d) the full name of the company (note that the only permissible abbreviation is Ltd for Limited or plc for Public Limited Company or their Irish language equivalents, Teo or cpt respectively); and

(e) the names and any former names of the directors and nationality, if not Irish: CA 1963, s 196.

The Companies (Amendment) Act, 1983 ('C(A)A 1983'), s 47(9) requires public investment companies as defined by s 47(3) of that Act to include the expression 'investment company' on their letters and order forms.

With effect from 1 April 2007, the disclosures rules with respect to company particulars on certain hard-copy company documentation (e.g. letterheads) was extended to company websites and e-mails as a result of the European Communities (Companies)(Amendment) Regulations, 2007.

### 2.3.5.4 Company seal

An embossed seal must be obtained and, when required, affixed to documents. When a company carries on business abroad, and if the articles of association of the company so permit, it may have a seal for use abroad. The only difference is that the name of every territory, district or place where it is to be used must be added to the name of the company on the common seal.

## 2.4 Meetings and Resolutions

### 2.4.1 CALLING AND CONDUCT OF MEETINGS AND PASSING OF RESOLUTIONS

The day-to-day business of a company is conducted by the board of directors of that company.

It is occasionally necessary for the members to be consulted regarding the business of a company. This may occur where it is proposed, e.g. to amend the memorandum and articles of association, or increase the authorised share capital or for a number of other purposes. At least once in each year, apart from the company's first year of existence, the members must meet for an Annual General Meeting.

A minimum of three (in the case of a public limited company) or two (in the case of a private company other than a single member private limited company) shareholders of a company may pass resolutions.

For a resolution to be valid, it must be passed by the requisite majority of those persons who are entitled to attend and vote and who do vote in person or by proxy (where permitted by the articles of association) at a meeting where a quorum is present and of which notice has been duly given.

### 2.4.2 ANNUAL GENERAL MEETING

Every company is obliged to hold an Annual General Meeting (AGM) of its shareholders:

(a) it must be held once in each calendar year, and not more than fifteen months after the previous one (CA 1963, s 131);

(b) provided the first AGM is held within eighteen months of incorporation, one need not be held in the year of incorporation or the following year;

(c) if an AGM is not held, the High Court may order it to be held either on its own motion or on application by a director of the company or any member who is entitled to vote at the meeting.

(d) twenty-one clear days' notice of the AGM must be given unless all entitled to attend and vote agree to accept shorter notice;

(e) the only business which must be dealt with at the AGM is the laying before the meeting of the balance sheet, profit and loss account, auditors' report and directors' report on the state of the company's affairs for consideration by the shareholders. However, the articles of association may provide that the following matters are dealt with also at the meeting as ordinary business:

(i)    the declaration of a dividend,

(ii)   the election of directors in place of those retiring,

(iii)  the re-appointment of the retiring auditor, and

(iv)  the fixing of the remuneration of the auditors.

Under the standard form of articles in Table A any business save that deemed as 'ordinary business', which is usually the above four items along with the presentation of the accounts and reports, transacted at the AGM or at an Extraordinary General Meeting (EGM) is treated as 'special business' e.g. the fixing of the remuneration of the directors (article 53, Table A). The auditors' report must be read at the meeting and must be open to inspection by any of the members (CA 1990, s 193(2)). (For provisions on AGMs see CA 1963, s 131 as amended by C(A)A 1982, Sch 1.)

## 2.4.3   TIMETABLE FOR THE AGM

The timetable leading up to the AGM is as follows:

(a)   Determine the financial year end of the company.

(b)   As soon as practicable after the financial year end, the auditors will commence the audit.

(c)   Auditors submit draft accounts to the directors, who review them and agree any adjustments with the auditors.

(d)   A directors' meeting is called to sign the accounts, and prepare the directors' report and instruct the secretary to convene the AGM. The chairman considers preparing his speech. The directors may recommend the declaration of a dividend.

(e)   The secretary sends out notice convening the meeting to members, accompanied by the accounts, the chairman's address and the auditors' report.

(f)   The secretary must make sure to give twenty-one days' clear notice, and thus this will usually mean sending out the notice at least twenty-four days in advance of the meeting. He will have booked the room in advance, and may have notified the press if necessary. Some public limited companies use their annual accounts as a form of advertisement to attract new investments and they will therefore contain extra information about the company.

(g)   Hold the AGM and prepare minutes of the meeting as soon as practicable after its conclusion.

(h)   File the annual return within twenty-eight days of the Annual Return Date together with the appropriate financial statements.

## 2.4.4   EXTRAORDINARY GENERAL MEETING

Any meeting of the shareholders of a company, other than the AGM, is an Extraordinary General Meeting (EGM).

Unless all entitled to attend and vote agree to accept shorter notice, fourteen clear days' notice is required for an EGM in the case of a public limited company, seven clear days' notice in the case of a private company to pass an ordinary resolution and twenty-one clear days if a special resolution is to be passed. The articles may provide for longer periods of notice of meetings.

The EGM may be convened by the directors (see Table A, Part 1, article 50). In addition, the members may require the directors to convene such meetings. The directors must convene an EGM on a requisition of a member or members holding at the date of the requisition not less than one-tenth of the paid-up capital which carry a right to vote at a general meeting. This provision may not be excluded by the articles (CA 1963, s 132).

## 2.4.5   TYPES OF RESOLUTION

### 2.4.5.1   Special

A special resolution requires twenty-one clear days' notice regardless of the type of meeting and three-quarters majority; a special resolution is necessary in any case where the Companies Acts, 1963–2006 or the articles so specify, e.g. change of name, objects, articles.

The Acts specify that a special resolution is required as follows:

(a)   to change the name;

(b)   to permit the giving of financial assistance for the purchase of its shares;

(c)   to reduce the share capital;

(d)   to alter the memorandum and/or articles of association; or

(e)   to wind up the company.

### 2.4.5.2   Ordinary resolution

The required notice depends on the type of meeting: a simple majority of the members present must vote in favour of the resolution for it to be adopted. An example of an ordinary resolution is where there is an increase in the authorised share capital of the company.

Certain ordinary resolutions must be filed which relate to attaching, restricting or varying rights on shares.

Extended notice (twenty-eight days minimum) must be given for certain ordinary resolutions, i.e. resolutions removing a director or auditor.

## 2.4.6   CONTENTS OF NOTICE

A notice of a general meeting must contain:

(a)   The date, time and place of meeting (Table A, Part 1, article 51).

(b)   A statement that every member entitled to attend and vote is entitled to appoint a proxy, who need not be a member. (This may be excluded by the articles of association of a company limited by guarantee and not having a share capital.)

(c)   The general nature of any special business, which should be sufficiently specified so that members may decide whether or not they wish to attend. (All business at an EGM is special and all business at an AGM is special other than declaring a dividend, the consideration of accounts, balance sheets and the reports of directors and auditors, the election of directors in place of those retiring, the reappointment of the retiring auditors and the fixing of the remuneration of the auditors.)

(d)   The exact wording of special resolutions.

## 2.4.7   VOTING

Resolutions are decided by a show of hands unless a poll is demanded. Except on the question of adjourning the meeting or electing a chairman, the articles of association may not exclude the right to demand a poll by the following (CA 1963, s 137):

(a)   the chairman;

(b)   five or more voting members or their proxies;

(c)   a member or members holding one-tenth of the total voting rights; or

(d)   a member or members holding shares representing at least one-tenth of the total paid-up capital conferring a right to vote.

See Table A, Part 1, articles 59 and 62.

Note that the chairman may have a casting vote (see Table A, Part 1, article 61). Voting is usually on a show of hands unless a poll is demanded (before or on the declaration of the result of the show of hands). If a poll is duly demanded it must be taken in such manner as the chairman directs. On a show of hands, one vote per member is counted; while on a poll each share is accorded the number of votes to which it is entitled under the articles or terms of issue. This allows for the use of weighted votes and a member with a large number of shares can influence the vote (see articles 59–67, Table A, Part I).

Any member of a company entitled to attend and vote at a meeting of the company is entitled to appoint another person (whether a member or not) as his proxy to attend, speak and vote instead of him. A proxy so appointed has the same right as the member to speak at the meeting and to vote on a show of hands and on a poll (CA 1963, s 136(1)).

The instrument appointing a proxy and the power of attorney or other authority, if any, under which it is signed must be deposited, not less than forty-eight hours before the meeting, at the appropriate venue specified for that purpose in the notice convening the meeting (Table A, Part I, article 70) unless the articles specify otherwise.

The chairman must conduct the meeting and must accord the members a reasonable opportunity to express their views. He must also proceed through the agenda efficiently.

## 2.4.8 AFTER THE MEETING

Printed copies of special and certain ordinary resolutions passed at a meeting or written resolutions which have effect as special or ordinary resolutions must be sent within fifteen days for filing to the Registrar of Companies (CA 1963, s 143). Minutes of the proceedings of general meetings and meetings of directors must be entered in books kept for that purpose (CA 1963, s 145).

## 2.4.9 WRITTEN RESOLUTIONS

Where the articles of association provide, it is possible in most cases to pass the relevant resolution by all the members entitled to attend and vote at general meetings, consenting in writing to the passing of the resolutions. The written resolution is not effective until the last signatory has signed it. It is not possible to transact the business of an AGM by way of written resolution and such a meeting must actually take place. Similarly, where there is a serious loss of capital, an extraordinary general meeting must take place as provided in C(A)A 1983, s 40.

## 2.4.10 SINGLE MEMBER COMPANIES

In the case of a single member company, resolutions may be replaced by written decisions of the sole member.

## 2.5 Administrative Records of Private Limited Company

Every company is obliged to maintain statutory registers and minute books pursuant to the Companies Acts, 1963–2006.

## 2.5.1 REGISTER OF APPLICATIONS AND ALLOTMENTS

A company is not required by law to maintain a register of applications and allotments, but a register has proved to be a useful link in the company's records, as it provides a continuous visual diary of the movement of the company's share capital. The cross-referencing in the headings in this register also becomes a useful index to the several operations relating to share transactions. The directors may not exercise any power to allot shares unless duly authorised under C(A)A 1983, s 20. Pre-emption rights in favour of existing holders of shares must be observed unless excluded: (C(A)A 1983, s 23).

In the context of the allotment and issue of new shares, the 'pre-emption (i.e. right of first refusal) provisions' referred to in s 23 mean that before any 'equity securities' as defined in the section are allotted and issued to any third party, they must first be offered to the existing shareholders on a 'pro rata' basis, i.e. in proportion to their existing shareholdings.

## 2.5.2 REGISTER OF TRANSFERS

Similarly, a company is not required by law to keep a register of transfer of shares, but such a register has proved to be a very useful and necessary adjunct to the records of a company and will assist in the preparation of annual returns. The register provides a continuous visual diary and indicator of share transfers. The cross-referencing in the headings on the register also becomes an index to the several related operations.

## 2.5.3 REGISTER OF MEMBERS

The register of members contains details of each member in the company. If the register is kept at a place other than the registered office of the company the Registrar of Companies *must be notified* within fourteen days of the place, or any change in the place, where the register is kept. Form B3 is used for this purpose (CA 1963, s 116(5)–(8)).

Save for the subscribers to the memorandum of association, a person does not become a member in a company until he has agreed to become a member and his name has been entered in the register of members, or cease to be a member until a like entry has been made transferring out his shares. The secretary should therefore ensure that all duly authorised changes in membership are recorded promptly in the appropriate registers, subject to the prior stamping of the relevant instrument.

The register must be open to the inspection of any member of the company without charge for not less than two hours daily during business hours and likewise to any other person on payment of not more than six cent (CA 1963, s 119).

A copy of the register or any part of it must be furnished within ten days of a request by a member or any other person on payment of 3 cent per 100 words or part of 100 words copied (CA 1963, s 119(2)).

## 2.5.4 REGISTER OF DIRECTORS AND SECRETARIES

The register of directors and secretaries contains details of directors to include their full names, residential addresses, nationality (if not Irish), date of birth, details of directorships held worldwide during the preceding ten years and particulars of appointment and retirement/removal. A director must be an individual—bodies corporate may not be directors.

The register must be open to the inspection of any member of the company without charge for not less than two hours daily during business hours, and likewise to any other person on payment of the appropriate fee (CA 1963, s 195(10)).

It is not necessary for particulars to be recorded in the register of 'other directorships' held by a director (CA 1963, s 195(3)):

(a)  in companies of which the company is the wholly-owned subsidiary, or

(b)  in companies which are the wholly-owned subsidiaries, either of the company or of another company, of which the company is the wholly-owned subsidiary.

The expression 'company' for this purpose includes any body corporate incorporated in the Republic of Ireland and a body corporate shall be deemed to be the wholly-owned subsidiary of another if it has no members except that other and that others' wholly-owned subsidiaries and its or their nominees.

Section 174 of CA 1963 states that every company must have at least two directors. Any changes of directors or in the particulars in this register must be notified to the Companies Registration Office on Form B10 within fourteen days of the occurrence (CA 1963, s 195 as amended by C(A)A 1982, s 8).

The register of directors and secretaries contains details of the secretary or joint secretaries and includes the full name of the secretary/joint secretaries and address. A secretary may be either an individual or a body corporate or a partnership.

Generally, where all the partners in a firm are joint secretaries, the name and the principal office of the firm may be stated in the register instead of the detailed particulars and the names etc. of those partners (CA 1963, s 195(4)(b) and (5)).

Anything required or authorised to be done by or to the secretary may, if the office is vacant or there is for any other reason no secretary capable of acting, be done by or to any assistant or deputy secretary or, if there is no assistant or deputy secretary capable of acting, by or to any officer of the company authorised generally or specially in that behalf by the directors (CA 1963, s 175(2)).

Any changes of secretary or joint secretaries or in the particulars in this register must be notified to the Companies Registration Office on a Form B10 within fourteen days of the occurrence (CA 1963, s 195 as amended by C(A)A 1982, s 8).

### 2.5.5    REGISTER OF INTERESTS

The register of directors' and secretaries' interests contains particulars of directors, secretaries and connected persons, e.g. spouses and minor children's interests in shares and debentures in the company. If the company's register of members is kept at its registered office, then the register of interests must also be kept there. Alternatively, if the register of members is not so kept, then the register of interests must be kept either at the company's registered office or at the place where the register of members is kept. The company must notify the Registrar of Companies of the place where the register is kept and of any change in that place.

The register must be available for inspection during business hours (subject to such reasonable restrictions as the company in general meeting may impose, so that not less than two hours in each day be allowed for inspection) by any members of the company without charge and by any other person on payment of €1.27 for each inspection. The company must maintain an index of names entered on the register to enable the information kept therein to be readily accessible (Companies Act, 1990 ('CA 1990'), s 60).

CA 1990, s 53 applies to directors, secretaries, shadow directors and their respective families. It provides that any such person who is interested in shares in, or debentures of, the company or any other body corporate, being the company's subsidiary or holding company or a subsidiary of the company's holding company, must notify such interest in writing to the company within five days of the event. Any subsequent change in that interest must also be notified and the company must maintain a register of such interests.

### 2.5.6    REGISTER OF CHARGES

Every company is obliged to keep a copy of every instrument creating a charge which is required to be registered with the Registrar of Companies, under CA 1963, Part IV, at the registered office.

Copies of such instruments may be inspected during normal business hours by any creditor of the company free of charge.

### 2.5.7    REGISTER OF SEALINGS

A company is not required by law to keep a register of sealings, but such a register is a useful adjunct to the records of a company.

Every company must have a common seal with its name engraved on it in legible characters. The seal should be kept in safe custody at all times and be used only with the authority of the directors.

It should be affixed only in the manner allowed by the articles of association of the company, which commonly provide that documents to which the seal is affixed shall be attested by two directors, or by a director and the secretary, or a director and one other authorised person. Every care should be taken to ensure that the description of the document sealed will be sufficient to identify that document beyond doubt. As an added precaution against substitution it is advisable to endorse the document with the consecutive number of the entry in the sealings register.

Entries should always be made and authenticated at the time of affixing the seal. When a company transacts business abroad it may, if its articles allow, have an 'official' seal for use abroad but with the addition on its face of the name of every territory, district or place where it is to be used (CA 1963, s 41(1)).

A company may in writing under its common seal empower any person, either generally or otherwise, as its attorney, to execute deeds on its behalf in any place outside Ireland (CA 1963, s 41(3)).

## 2.5.8 MINUTES

Every company must keep minutes of proceedings at general meetings of the company and meetings of its directors (CA 1963, s 145(1)).

The minutes are the permanent record of business transacted at a meeting and must be absolutely impartial. They must record the decisions reached at a meeting and be expressed in clear and unambiguous terms. Special care should be taken to record relevant dates and figures.

Minutes, when signed by the chairman of the meeting, or by the chairman of the next succeeding meeting, are prima facie evidence of the proceedings (CA 1963, s 145(2)). Looseleaf minute books are permissible, but for security reasons precautions must be taken to guard against falsification and to facilitate discovery (CA 1963, s 378(2)). As an added precaution, each page of the minutes should be initialled at the foot of the page.

It is preferable to keep the minutes of general meetings separated from those of directors' meetings, because members have a right to inspection only of the former. The minutes of proceedings of all general meetings must be kept at the registered office of the company and be open to inspection by any member (CA 1963, s 146(1)) without charge for not less than two hours daily during business hours (CA 1963, s 146(1)).

Copies of any minutes of general meetings must be supplied within seven days after a request by a member at a charge of not more than six cent for every 100 words (CA 1963, s 146(2)).

### 2.5.9 SHARE CERTIFICATE

Every member of a company is entitled to a certificate specifying the shares held by him and such certificate issued under the seal of the company shall be prima facie evidence of the title of the member to the shares. The company must have the certificate ready for delivery to the shareholder within two months of allotment of the shares or the lodgement of a properly completed transfer (CA 1963, ss 86 and 87).

Share certificates should be completed with the full name(s) of the shareholder(s) and it should be ensured that the details on the certificate correspond exactly with the entry in the register of members. The certificate should be sealed and the sealing witnessed as provided by the articles of association of the company. On the issue of a certificate, the counterfoil should be completed and kept by the company. Appropriate cross-references should be made to the register of allotments or transfers and to the register of sealings.

### 2.5.10 LOCATION OF STATUTORY BOOKS

The statutory books of the company must be kept at the registered office of the company or at such other address in Ireland that has been certified to the Registrar of Companies on Form 113 (CA 1963, s 146). The minute book of general meetings of the company must be kept at the registered office.

### 2.5.11 COMPUTERISATION OF RECORDS

Section 4 of the Companies (Amendment) Act, 1977 introduced provisions to allow the statutory records of a company other than minute books of directors and general meetings to be kept on a computer. However, such records must be able to be reproduced in a legible written form.

## 2.6 Shares

### 2.6.1 GENERAL

A shareholder in a company has a statutory right to transfer his/her shares, in the 'manner provided by the articles of the company' (CA 1963, s 79). A private company is a company which *inter alia* restricts the right to transfer its shares (CA 1963, s 33(1)(a)).

The articles of association of a private company usually provide that the directors have a power to refuse to register a transfer either for certain reasons or a general power, without the necessity to state any reasons; for instance article 3, Part II, Table A provides that:

The directors may, in their absolute discretion and without assigning any reason therefore, decline to register any transfer of any share, whether or not it is a fully paid share.

Three principles govern the construction of this type of clause:

(a)    If the company refuses to register a transfer, it must send a notice of refusal to the transferee within the period of two months from the date the transfer is lodged with the company (CA 1963, s 84(1)). If the notice is not given in two months, then unless there are special circumstances, the right to veto will be deemed to have lapsed.

(b)    The courts will, where a clause has more than one potential meaning, take the narrowest construction.

(c)    Where the directors have discretion to refuse, they must exercise their power bona fide in what they consider the best interests of the company (*Clark v Workman* [1920] 1 IR 107). In practice, it is difficult to prove that directors were not acting bona fide and in the best interests of the company, especially if they do not have to state their reasons for refusing to register the transfer.

Alternatively, the articles of association of a private company may contain pre-emption (right of first refusal) provisions. Under these provisions, a prospective transferor would first have to offer his/her shares to the remaining members of the company.

There are also statutory pre-emption provisions contained in C(A)A 1983, s 23. These relate to the allotment of shares and not their transfer. C(A)A 1983, s 23(10) allows a private company to exclude the relevant s 23 provisions by a provision contained in either the memorandum or the articles of association of the company. Alternatively, where the directors have been authorised to allot shares, the provisions of C(A)A 1983, s 23 may be disapplied by special resolution passed pursuant to C(A)A 1983, s 24.

## 2.6.2    TRANSFER FORM

Registered securities may be transferred by means of an instrument under hand in the prescribed form. The prescribed form is that set out in the First Schedule to the Stock Transfer Act, 1963 as amended by the Stock Transfer (Forms) Regulations, 1996 (SI 263/1996). The form must set out:

(a)    particulars of consideration;

(b)    description of security;

(c)    number, or amount of security;

(d)    name and address of transferor; and

(e)    name and address of transferee.

The transfer form must be signed by the transferor (Stock Transfer Act, 1963, s 4(1)). However, the form need not be attested. Further, the form need not be signed by the transferee provided that the share is fully paid. However, in an unlimited company the transferee must sign.

If the share being transferred is only part paid, then the standard transfer form must be amended to provide for signature by the transferee. A form common or usual before the commencement of the Stock Transfer Act, 1963 will be valid if it complies with the requirements as to execution and contents which apply to a stock transfer.

A 'transfer in blank' is a transfer on which the name and address of the transferee have not been inserted. In practice, it is not uncommon for nominee shareholders to execute share transfers in blank, and these transfer forms are handed over to the client. While this is perfectly in order, it is an offence for the transferee or the person(s) acting on his/her behalf to part with possession of the transfer form until the name(s) of the transferee(s) have been inserted (Stock Transfer Act, 1963, s 4(1)). This offence is punishable by a fine and the transferee or anyone acting on his/her behalf must also pay the unpaid stamp duty.

Section 81 of CA 1963 provides that it shall not be lawful for a company to register a transfer of shares in or debentures of the company unless a proper instrument of transfer has been delivered to the company. If a secretary or registrar of a company receives a transfer form on which any of the details referred to above have been omitted, he will be entitled to refuse to register the transfer. Section 81(1) of CA 1963 shall not prevent the company registering as shareholder or debenture holder a person to whom the right to any shares has been transmitted by operation of law (CA 1963, s 81(2)).

A person may become entitled to shares in a company by operation of law, e.g. the personal representative of a deceased shareholder is entitled to be registered as the holder of the shares without production of an executed share transfer form. That person would, however, have to produce to the registrar or secretary of the company evidence of their right to be registered as owner of the shares, e.g. a grant of probate.

## 2.6.3   STAMP DUTY ON TRANSFERS

Stamp duties are a form of tax levied on documents used to transfer property. The Revenue Commissioners are charged with the assessment and collection of this tax. Stamp duty is imposed on the market value or the consideration, whichever is greater, and not the nominal value of the shares transferred.

Duty, generally, is levied at one of two rates:

(a)   under the head 'Conveyance or Transfer on Sale' transfers in which a beneficial interest passes attract *ad valorem* duty. This is calculated at the rate of one per cent of the market value or the consideration (whichever is greater) of the shares; or

      (b)    under the head 'Any Case other than a Sale' transfers or securities in which no beneficial interest passes (e.g. transfer of subscriber shares, nominee shares); such transfers no longer attract a duty.

A registrar or secretary of a company has a duty to satisfy himself that the correct stamp duty has been paid on the transfer before registering the transferee as a member of the company. It is the responsibility of the transferee to lodge the instrument, but under the Stamp Duties Consolidation Act, 1999, s 129, the secretary is liable to a fine if she/he registers or records any instrument not duly stamped. However, it appears that the transfer is valid if registered, notwithstanding the fact that it is not properly stamped.

A person/company may hold shares in a company through a nominee. The nominee is registered as the owner of the shares, but in fact he holds these shares 'in trust for' some other person/company (the beneficial owner). On transfer to the nominee by the legal owner, no beneficial interest will pass and stamp duty is levied on the transfer form at the nominal rate. Where shares are held by a nominee, that person/company executes a declaration of trust *in* favour of the beneficial owner. The declaration of trust is itself no longer stampable even at the nominal rate.

In passing, it should be noted that under CA 1963, s 123, a registrar or secretary of a company is not permitted to receive notice of or register the existence of a trust and must register the trustee as the shareholder.

In certain transactions, before a transfer form may be stamped, it must first be adjudicated. An example of a transaction in which this arises is a company reconstruction or amalgamation qualifying for relief from stamp duty under the Stamp Duties Consolidation Act, 1999, s 80.

A transfer form, which has not been stamped or which has been improperly stamped, is still a legal transfer of the security to which it refers. However, the transfer document itself is not producible as evidence in court, unless correctly stamped or not chargeable for duty except in criminal cases or in civil proceedings by the Revenue Commissioners (Stamp Duties Consolidation Act, 1999, s 127).

### 2.6.4    COLLECTION AND ENFORCEMENT OF STAMP DUTY

The Finance Act, 1991 introduced new provisions regarding the collection and enforcement of stamp duty. These sections brought stamp duty into line with the collection and enforcement provisions of other taxes and have now been reproduced in Part 2 and Part 10 of the Stamp Duties Consolidation Act, 1999.

The payment of stamp duty is now mandatory and must be made within thirty days of the date of execution of the stampable instrument, regardless of where execution took place, e.g. if the stampable instrument is executed in France, it must be stamped in Ireland within thirty days. Failure to have an instrument properly stamped within the prescribed period will result in penalties, interest and surcharges being payable. Surcharges are also payable if the consideration on the instrument is understated. Where an instrument is lodged for adjudication and stamp duty is assessed, it must be paid within fourteen days of the issuance of an assessment.

The register of members will be prima facie evidence of any matters directed or authorised to be contained in it (CA 1963, s 124). A person wishing to have a name removed from the register, or, alternatively, added to the register, may apply to the court (under CA 1963, s 122(1)) to have the register rectified. The transferee of shares in a company has a right, subject to anything contained in the memorandum or articles of association of the company, to be entered on the register as a member of the company.

Where a contract to sell shares is in existence, then, in the absence of an express stipulation to the contrary, there is an implied undertaking on the part of the transferor that he will do nothing to prevent or delay registration of the transferee as a member. There is, however, no implied term that the transferee will be registered.

## 2.6.5 SHARE CERTIFICATES

CA 1963 provides that:

(a)  a share certificate under the common seal of a company specifying the shares held by a member shall be prima facie evidence of the title of the member to the shares (CA 1963, s 87(1));

(b)  the date that a share certificate has been issued and the number of the share certificate is recorded in the register of members;

(c)  a purported transfer of shares in respect of which a share certificate has been issued will not be accepted for registration unless the relevant share certificate is presented with the transfer form;

(d)  if a share certificate is lost, a duplicate may be obtained from the company on the terms provided in the company's articles of association. The company will usually require that an indemnity in respect of the lost certificate be given to the company.

## 2.6.6 DIVIDENDS

The payment of dividends mechanism is usually set down in the memorandum and articles of association. A fundamental principle of company law is that dividends must be paid out of 'distributable profits' and may not be paid out of capital of the company since this would effectively be an unauthorised reduction of the company's capital.

The procedure in regard to the declaration of dividends is usually set down in the company's articles. The company in general meeting may declare dividends, but no dividend should exceed the amount recommended by the directors (Table A, Part I, article 116).

The directors are allowed to declare such interim dividends as appear to them to be justified by the profits of the company (Table A, Part I, article 117).

Additionally, the directors are entitled to set aside certain of the profits of the company to a reserve.

It is also possible at the general meeting declaring a dividend, to make a distribution of paid-up shares in lieu of a dividend (Table A, Part I, article 122).

The EC Second Directive on Company Law, which was implemented by C(A)A 1983, made specific regulations regarding the distribution of profits. Previously, the only definitions in company law of distributable profit (other than in a company's memorandum or articles) were to be found in case law. Distributions are now restricted to those permitted by C(A)A 1983, Part IV subject to any further restrictions which may be included in a company's articles of association or in case law.

The rules of distribution may be summarised in the following terms. The definition of 'profits available for distribution' is by reference to the excess of realised profits over realised losses as shown in the accounts (C(A)A 1983, s 45(2)).

There is an additional restriction for public limited companies. A public limited company may not allow a distribution to reduce its net assets below the amount of its called-up share capital and undistributable reserves (C(A)A 1983, s 46(1)).

A public limited company which is an investment company as defined (principally a listed investment trust) may, as an alternative to the foregoing, distribute the excess of its realised revenue profits over its realised and unrealised revenue losses but may not let the distribution reduce the value of its assets below one and one half times its liabilities (C(A)A 1983, s 47(1)).

## 2.6.7   MERGERS CLEARANCE

A further matter to be considered under the heading 'share transfers' is that of mergers clearance.

The Competition Act, 2002, has replaced the Competition Acts, 1991 and 1996 and the Mergers and Takeovers (Control) Acts, 1978–1996. Certain mergers and takeovers require consideration under the Competition Act, 2002 or European merger control. This issue is considered in detail in **chapter 6**.

## 2.7    Division of Powers

### 2.7.1    DIRECTORS

#### 2.7.1.1    Generally

The articles usually delegate to the directors the exercise of all the powers of the company not required by the articles or by the Companies Acts, 1963–2006 to be exercised by the company in general meeting (Table A, Part 1, articles 80–90). The directors' powers may be usurped by a court-appointed examiner by way of application to the court pursuant to C(A)A 1990, s 9. The general rule is that powers given exclusively by the articles to the directors may not be altered by the members in general meeting except by changing the relevant article by special resolution under CA 1963, s 15. However, the power to dismiss directors may not be taken away from the members by any provision in the articles (CA 1963, s 182). The powers granted to directors enable them to conduct and manage the day-to-day business of the company and would include such powers as borrowing money, using the company seal, recruiting employees and entering into contracts.

#### 2.7.1.2    Appointment and removal of directors

The first directors of a company must be named in a statement delivered to the Registrar of Companies (C(A)A 1982, s 3). Any subsequent directors of the company must be appointed in the manner set out in the articles of association. If no format of appointment is set down, directors must be elected by the members in general meeting. The election of more than one director by a single resolution may not be proposed unless by prior unanimous resolution of the members (CA 1963, s 181). It is normal that the directors have the power to fill casual vacancies in their number (Table A, Part I, article 98).

The manner of appointment of subsequent directors will depend upon the articles (see Table A, Part I, articles 98–100).

The company must keep a register of directors and secretaries and must notify the Registrar of Companies of all changes (Form B10). The articles may prescribe a maximum number of directors. There is no statutory maximum. The articles may also require directors to hold qualification shares. Table A, Part I, article 77 provides that no shareholding qualification is required unless and until so fixed by the company in general meeting.

A person may be disqualified from acting as a director either under the general law or under the articles. An undischarged bankrupt may not act as a director (CA 1963, s 183 as substituted by CA 1990, s 169).

The court may disqualify persons from acting or being appointed as, inter alia, directors, auditors or managers for a five-year period, or such other period as the court may order, if they are convicted of any indictable offence in relation to a company or an offence involving fraud or dishonesty or their conduct makes them unfit to be involved in managing a company (CA 1990, s 160(2) as amended by CLEA 2001, s 42).

### 2.7.1.3 Restriction of directors

For disqualification under the articles, see Table A, Part I, article 91.

The articles may provide that directors must retire by rotation (see Table A, Part I, articles 92–97).

The articles of association adopted by a company may include a special article facilitating the removal of a director. This would apply for instance in the case of a subsidiary company, where the holding company may be entitled to appoint or remove a director by notice in writing to the secretary or by leaving notice at the registered office.

### 2.7.1.4 Removal of directors

The directors of a company may be removed by an ordinary resolution of the company in general meeting (CA 1963, s 182). Unless the directors are directors of a private company holding office for life, this provision may not be altered by the articles of association. At least twenty-eight days' notice must be given of a resolution proposing to remove a director and a director must have an opportunity to speak at the meeting and must receive a copy of the notice of the resolution. The director whose removal is being sought is allowed to make representations in writing to the company upon receipt of the notice of the resolution.

Removal under s 182 does not deprive the director concerned of right to damages etc., irrespective of any claim under employment protection legislation.

The articles of association may be modified to confer loaded voting rights on a director where it is proposed to pass a resolution to dismiss him, thus enabling the director to remain in office (*Bushell v Faith* [1970] AC 1099).

### 2.7.1.5 Powers of directors

The directors' powers will be conferred on them by the articles or by resolution of the company (see Table A, Part 1, articles 79 and 80).

Directors' powers are exercisable by them collectively by resolution at board meetings. The conduct of board meetings will be laid down by the articles (see Table A, Part 1, articles 89 and 101–109).

### 2.7.1.6 Delegation of powers by directors

Directors may not delegate their powers unless the articles so permit (see Table A, Part I, article 105).

In particular, articles invariably enable directors to appoint a managing director (see Table A, Part 1, article 110). The managing director is often given powers co-extensive with the powers of the board as a whole (see Table A, Part I, article 112).

The board of directors may delegate any of its powers to committees consisting of such member or members of the board as it thinks fit (see Table A, Part I, articles 105–108).

Special articles may be inserted to provide for the appointment of alternate directors who act as a substitute director for the appointing director when the latter is absent from the meetings of directors.

### 2.7.1.7  Statutory and fiduciary limitations on powers of directors

A director owes his duty to the company, not to the individual shareholders (*Percival v Wright* [1902] 2 Ch 421).

A director must not make a personal profit out of his position (*Cook v Deeks* [1916] AC 554) and must account to the company for any personal profit as a result of a transaction, which he would not have entered into but for his directorship (*Regal (Hastings) Ltd v Gulliver* [1942] 1 All ER 378). Directors must exercise their powers for the benefit of the company.

A director must exercise a duty of skill and care in accordance with the following criteria:

(a)  directors are only required to perform their duties with the degree of skill which may be reasonably expected from persons with their particular knowledge and experience;

(b)  directors need not give continuous attention to the affairs of the company. Directors may delegate their functions to other officials in the absence of suspicious circumstances (subject to there being power to do so in the articles);

(c)  in exercising their duties to the company, directors are now under a duty to have regard to the interests of the company's employees in general (CA 1990, s 52), as well as the interests of its members.

### 2.7.1.8  Statutory provisions concerning directors

To prevent them from abusing their position, directors are subject to a considerable number of statutory controls.

#### *Remuneration*

Accounts laid before the company in general meeting must disclose aggregate amounts of directors' emoluments, aggregate amounts of directors' or past directors' pensions and aggregate amounts of compensation in respect of loss of office (CA 1963, s 191).

#### *Compensation for loss of office*

A company may not pay compensation for loss of office gratuitously to a director, unless disclosed to and approved by members (CA 1963, s 186).

#### *Register of directors' and secretaries' interests*

There must be maintained a separate register of the interests of directors, their spouses and minor children and of 'connected persons', in the company's shares (CA 1990, s 59).

### Substantial property transactions involving directors and loans to directors

CA 1990, ss 29 and 31 regulate certain 'substantial property transactions' and the giving of loans or other similar financial benefits by a company to its directors. A director includes 'shadow director' and 'connected person'. Section 78 of the CLEA 2001, which repeals and substitutes a new s 34 CA 1990, reduces the severity of the s 31 prohibition by permitting companies to enter into guarantees and provide security in respect of loans, quasi loans or credit transactions made by a third party to a director if the validation procedure laid down in the new s 34 is followed. This issue is considered in further detail in **chapter 12**.

### Interest in contracts

A director who is interested, directly or indirectly, in a contract or proposed contract with his company must declare the nature of his interest at a board meeting (CA 1963, s 194). This rule also applies to a shadow director, who must declare his interest by written notice to the directors (CA 1990, s 27(3)).

### 2.7.1.9 Meetings of directors

The management of a company is vested in its board of directors. It is at meetings of the board that many decisions which affect the company must be formally taken. The articles of association of the company set down the regulations pertaining to the holding of directors' meetings. Directors may meet together as and when they think fit. A director is entitled to and the secretary, if requested by a director, must at any time summon a meeting of directors (Table A, Part I, article 101). The quorum for the transaction of the business of directors is fixed by them and unless so fixed is two (Table A, Part 1, article 102).

Every director is entitled to reasonable notice of a meeting of directors save that it is normal to provide that a director who is abroad does not have to receive notice of the meeting if the directors so resolve (Table A, Part 1, article 101). Where due notice is not given of a meeting or a quorum is not present, it is an irregular meeting and its decisions are not valid (although the 'indoor management' rule may apply in the case of an outsider without notice).

It is a matter of choice as to whether the chairman is given a casting vote at directors' meetings. Article 101 of Table A, Part I provides that the chairman has a casting vote and therefore care should be taken in the event of Table A articles being used in companies in which there is likely to be any contention in this matter. A casting vote of the chairman will arise where there is an equal number of votes in favour of and against a resolution. To break the deadlock the chairman (if authorised by the articles of association) is given a second or casting vote.

It is also normal for a provision to be set down in the articles of association that a resolution in writing signed by all the directors entitled to receive notice of a meeting is as valid as a resolution passed at a duly convened meeting of directors. Such a provision is particularly helpful for a company where many of the directors are overseas (Table A, Part 1, article 109).

It should be noted that the use of the company seal is dependent upon the authority being given by the directors, or a committee of the directors, and it is normal for the articles to set down the signing requirements attaching to the sealing of a document, e.g. under article 115, Table A, Part I, two directors, a director and secretary or a director and a person duly authorised by the board of directors for that purpose.

As regards directors' meetings, most solicitors will be called upon to be present at the first directors' meeting of a company. This meeting will usually deal with the following matters:

(a)    approval of the company's seal;

(b)    formal approval of the registered office of the company;

(c)    opening a bank account and signing of mandate;

(d)    appointment of auditors pending the first AGM;

(e)    appointment of solicitors;

(f)    issue of shares;

(g)    disclosure of directors' interests;

(h)    formal ratification of the board of directors;

(i)    formal ratification of the appointment of the secretary; and

(j)    approval of transfer of subscriber shares.

### 2.7.1.10    Disclosure in the company's accounts

CA 1990, s 41 increases both the details of disclosure necessary and the range of persons to whom disclosure should be made in regard to certain transactions by requiring same to be disclosed in the company's accounts, e.g. disclosure of directors' loans, quasi loans etc.

### 2.7.1.11    Inspection of directors' service contracts

CA 1990, s 50 requires that a company must keep at either its registered office, the place where its register of members is kept if other than its registered office, or its principal place of business:

(a)    in the case of each director whose contract of service is in writing, a copy of that contract;

(b)    in the case of each director whose contract of service with the company is not in writing, a written memorandum setting out the terms of that contract;

(c)    in the case of each director who is employed under a contract of service with a subsidiary of the company, a copy of that contract or, if it is not in writing, a written memorandum setting out the terms of that contract; and

(d) a copy or written memorandum, as the case may be, of any variation of any contract of service, referred to in sub-paragraphs (a), (b) and (c) above. Members of the company may inspect such documents during normal business hours by virtue of s 50(6). Section 50(7) provides for a range of penalties if these provisions are breached.

These requirements do not apply to the unexpired portion of the term of the service contract if that is less than three years, or where the company may, within the next three years, terminate the contract without payment of compensation.

## 2.7.2 SECRETARY

Every company must have a secretary. Any act required to be done by or to a director and a secretary may not be performed by the same person acting in both capacities.

The secretary is the principal administrative officer of the company, with apparent authority to enter into contracts connected with the administrative side of the company's business (*Panorama Developments (Guildford) Ltd v Fidelis Furnishing Fabrics Ltd* [1971] 2 QB 711).

The secretary is an officer of the company and therefore shares, with the directors, the responsibility of ensuring compliance with all those provisions of the Companies Acts, 1963–2006 where a penalty for non-compliance is imposed on an officer.

## 2.7.3 AUDITORS

### 2.7.3.1 Generally

Every company must have a duly qualified independent auditor. CA 1990, s 187 (as amended by the Companies Act 1990 (Auditors) Regulations, 1992) lists those who are not qualified for appointment as auditor of a company. These include: a present officer or servant of the company or a person who has been an officer or servant of the company within a period in respect of which accounts would fall to be audited by him; a parent, spouse, brother, sister or child of an officer of the company; a person who is a partner or in the employment of an officer of the company; or a person who is disqualified from appointment as auditor of any other body corporate that is a subsidiary or holding company of the company. If, during his term of office as auditor of a company, a person becomes disqualified under the Companies Acts, 1963–2003 for appointment to that office, he must immediately vacate his office, giving notice in writing to the company.

The auditors' primary duty is to make a report to the members on the accounts examined by them and to state whether they give a 'true and fair view' of the company's financial position and whether they have been prepared in accordance with usual accountancy standards and procedures. As a result the auditors can be appointed and removed by the members and it is the members to whom they owe their primary duty.

Auditors now have a duty to report to the Director of Corporate Enforcement (whose office was established by the CLEA 2001) any of the indictable offences which have been committed.

### 2.7.3.2    Appointment of auditors

The first auditors of a company may be appointed by the directors at any time before the first AGM of the company. If the directors fail to do so, the Minister for Enterprise, Trade and Employment may do so instead. Normally the auditors will be appointed at each AGM and hold office until the next AGM and the auditors' remuneration must also be fixed. There is now provision that an auditor may be removed and replaced by an ordinary resolution at an EGM of a company as well as at an AGM. Extended notice (which means at least twenty-eight days) of such a resolution is required and notice of the removal must be filed in the Companies Registration Office.

Under CA 1963, s 160 a company may remove an auditor by ordinary resolution before the expiry of his term of office. Pursuant to CA 1990, s 184 shareholders of a company are now accorded the option of being able to appoint new auditors if a casual vacancy should arise. Previously, only the board of directors could fill such a vacancy.

### 2.7.3.3    Removal of auditors

Extended notice being at least twenty-eight days' notice must be given of a resolution at the AGM or EGM proposing the appointment of someone other than the retiring auditors as auditor of the company. An auditor has a right to attend and to be heard at any general meeting at which it is proposed to remove him from office and also at the AGM at which his term would have expired. He is entitled to receive all notices and other communications relating to any such meeting which are sent to members of the company.

### 2.7.3.4    Resignation of auditors

CA 1990, s 185 allows auditors of an Irish company to resign or decline to be reappointed, if they so wish. The auditors are entitled to require an EGM to be convened to consider the situation (CA 1990, s 186). If they consider that their reasons should be brought to the notice of the shareholders and creditors, they must state these reasons in writing and forward a copy to the Registrar of Companies and the company must forward a copy to each shareholder. If the auditors require an EGM to be held, the directors on receiving such a notice from the auditor are bound within fourteen days to convene a general meeting of the company for a day not more than twenty-eight days after such notice. The auditors, of course, have the right of audience at such meetings and are entitled to receive all notices and communications relating to such a meeting.

### 2.7.3.5 Removal of statutory requirement for an audit for small companies

Part III of C(A)(No 2)A 1999 introduced new provisions, which allow small private limited companies to claim exemption from the requirement to have their accounts audited. The company must satisfy certain criteria to avail of this exemption and must have:

(a) turnover not exceeding €7,300,000 per annum (effective in respect of accounting periods beginning on or after 1 July 2004);

(b) balance sheet total not exceeding €3,650,000;

(c) number of employees not exceeding fifty persons; and

(d) the company is a company to which C(A)A 1986 applies.

The exemption is not available if the company is a parent company or subsidiary, or holds a bank licence, insurance licence or is one of the companies listed in the Second Schedule of that Act.

The annual return of the company must be furnished to the Companies Registration Office in compliance with the requirement of CA 1963, s 127(1), that is that the return must be completed *within 28 days of the Annual Return Date and forwarded to the Registrar of Companies*.

Unless the financial year, in respect of which the exemption is being claimed, is the first financial year of the company, the company must also have satisfied all the conditions set out in s 32(3) in respect of the preceding financial year (s 32(1)(b)).

This means, for instance, that where a company has failed to file its annual return on time either during the preceding financial year, or it fails to file its return on time during the financial year in respect of which it wishes to claim the exemption, that company is not entitled to the exemption from the requirement to have its accounts audited, notwithstanding that it may satisfy all of the remaining conditions.

If the exemption is available, the appointment of an auditor may be terminated for so long as the exemption may be claimed.

A company which has claimed the exemption will still have to prepare annual accounts and submit them to the members at the AGM and file them in the Companies Registration Office with the annual return.

### 2.7.3.6 Qualifications

Basically, persons undertaking company audit work in Ireland must possess qualifications as accountants. Usually they will be a member of a body of accountants recognised by the Minister for Enterprise, Trade and Employment or have an accountancy qualification from a body of accountants which, in the opinion of the Minister, is of a similar standard to that required for membership of a recognised body of accountants.

The Minister is given wide powers in relation to the recognition or authorisation of bodies of accountants as to their qualifications as auditors. The Minister may attach such terms and conditions to his recognition or authorisation as he believes necessary and may at any time, by notice in writing, revoke or suspend such recognition and may further require the recognised body of accountants to prepare and submit for his approval a code of professional conduct and standards (CA 1990, s 192).

### 2.7.3.7 Statutory report

The auditors duty to report to the members arises under s 193(1). 'The auditors of a company shall make a report to the members on the accounts examined by them, and on every balance sheet and profit and loss account, and all group accounts laid before the company in general meeting during their tenure in office'.

The contents of the auditors' report are now set out in CA 1990, s 193. CA 1990, s 193(6) states that an auditor is under a general duty to carry out audits with professional integrity. The 1990 Act does not state what this consists of, but it will presumably entitle the company to take action against the auditor if he fails to observe the appropriate standard. The auditor is now entitled to require, from the officers, any information within the knowledge of the directors etc., which he thinks necessary for the performance of his duties. In the report itself, the auditors must state whether they are satisfied that proper books of accounts have been kept by the company and that proper returns adequate for their audit have been received from branches of the company not visited by them.

### 2.7.3.8 Subsidiary companies

The auditor of a holding company is empowered to request information and explanations from the subsidiary company. The subsidiary and its auditors must give information and explanations, as may reasonably be required by the auditors of the holding company, for the purposes of their duties as such. It is the duty of the holding company, if required by its auditors to do so, to take all such steps as are reasonably open to it to obtain from the subsidiary the information required (CA 1990, s 196(1)). If the subsidiary company or its auditor fails to comply within five days of the making of the requirement, the company and every officer in default or the auditor shall be guilty of an offence (CA 1990, s 196(2)).

### 2.7.3.9 Book of accounts

The company has a duty to provide accurate information to enable auditors to keep proper books of accounts.

An officer of a company who knowingly or recklessly makes a statement, which is misleading, false or deceptive is guilty of an offence. It is also provided that an officer must, within two days, provide the auditor with any information which the auditor requires as an auditor of the company and which is within the knowledge of, or may be procured by, the officer (CA 1990, s 197). This puts an onus on the officers in question to provide accurate information at all times.

Every company must, on a continuous and consistent basis, keep proper books of accounts which correctly record and explain the transactions of the company and at any time will enable the financial position of the company to be determined with accuracy (CA 1990, s 202). If a company is being wound up and is unable to pay all its debts and has not kept proper books of accounts and the court considers that such contravention has contributed to the company's inability to pay all its debts, or has resulted in a substantial uncertainty as to the assets and liabilities of the company or has impeded the ordinary winding-up of the company, every officer of the company who is in default is guilty of an offence (CA 1990, s 203).

The court, on the application of a liquidator or any creditor or contributory of the company, may declare that any one or more of the officers or the former officers who is or are in default in relation to this matter shall be personally liable, without any limitation of liability, for all or such part as may be specified by the court of the debts and other liabilities of the company (CA 1990, s 204).

## 2.7.4 POWERS OF MEMBERS

The members of a company are:

(a) the subscribers to the memorandum provided they have not transferred their shares;

(b) those others who have agreed to become members, having taken shares from the company (on allotment), from another member (by transfer) or on a transmission by operation of law (e.g. personal representatives) and whose names are entered on the register of members.

The members' powers comprise those powers of the company which have not been or cannot be delegated to the directors. Members can exercise their powers at general meetings, which have been duly convened (see below). In general terms, a member may vote in relation to his shares in whatever manner he wishes. However, there is authority to the effect that he must exercise his powers 'bona fide for the benefit of the company as a whole' and that any exercise of the powers is subject to equitable considerations which may make it unjust to exercise (them) in a particular way (*Ebrahimi v Westbourne Galleries Ltd* [1973] AC 360, quoted in *Clemens v Clemens Bros Ltd* [1976] 2 All ER 268).

## 2.7.5 ANNUAL RETURNS

It should also be noted that every company must make an annual return (CA 1963, s 125(1)). The return must be completed, signed by a director and the secretary of the company and be forwarded to the Companies Registration

Office. The return is made up to a date which is designated as an Annual Return Date ('ARD').

The ARD is a date fixed by law and is determined by reference to the date of the filing of the previous Annual Return and Financial Statements.

To find what the ARD of a company is, a check should be made at the Companies Office website (www.cro.ie) via the online services by entering the name or number of the company. The ARD may be shortened or lengthened by up to six months (in the case of lengthening the ARD this can only occur once every five years). This new date becomes the ARD. In the case of a new company, an Annual Return without Financial Statements is made up to a date six months after incorporation and this becomes the ARD for future years unless altered.

An Annual Return must be filed within 28 days of the ARD. Failure to do so will result in fines and penalties for late filing.

A shortened form annual return (Form B 1 S) is also available.

All companies must attach to the annual return a certified copy of the profit and loss account, balance sheet, auditors' report and directors' report as required by CA 1963, ss 128 and 157 and C(A)A 1986, s 16 unless an exemption is granted. See C(A)A 1986, ss 10–12 or the exemption in respect of subsidiaries provided by the 1986 Act, s 17 (as amended) is availed of and see s 128 of the Companies Act, 1963.

Section 128 is amended by s 47 of the Companies (Auditing and Accounting) Act, 2003, which requires a copy of the Auditor's Report confirming that they audited the accounts for the relevant year. This should be certified by a director and by the company secretary to be a true copy of that report and must be attached to the annual return of the types of company set out in s 47.

It is now possible to file an annual return in advance of the ARD, but still maintain the existing ARD. This can be done by ticking the appropriate box on the annual return.

## 2.7.6 COMPANIES (AMENDMENT) ACT, 1986

C(A)A 1986 as amended by the European Communities (Accounts) Regulations, 1993 (SI 396/1993), reg 4 introduced new accounting formats and disclosure requirements for all companies. It created the concept of small and medium-sized companies and imposed disclosure requirements accordingly.

The level of detail required to be included in a company's financial statements varies depending on the classification of a company as large, medium or small. Section 8, as amended, sets out the definitions as follows:

### 2.7.6.1 Small companies

A small company is a private company which complies with at least two of the following three conditions:

(a)   its balance sheet total for the year does not exceed €1,904,607;

(b)   its turnover for the year does not exceed €3,809,204; or

(c)   the average number of people employed by the company for the year did not exceed 50.

In the case of a small company, the abridged accounts will include a special auditors' report and the balance sheet together with notes to the balance sheet which are required so that the abridged financial statements show a true and fair view.

### 2.7.6.2   Medium companies

A medium company is a private company which complies with at least two of the following three conditions:

(a)   its balance sheet total for the year does not exceed €7,618,438;

(b)   its turnover does not exceed €15,236,856 for the year; or

(c)   its average number of employees for the year does not exceed 250.

In the case of a medium-sized company, the abridged financial statements will be similar to the full accounts, except that the profit and loss account will commence with gross profit but is not required to include turnover or costs of sales.

### 2.7.6.3   Subsidiaries

Where a private company is a subsidiary of a parent company established under the laws of a Member State of the EU, the company shall, as respects any particular financial year of the company, be exempted from the provisions of C(A)A 1986, s 7 (other than subsection (1)(b); i.e. the need to annex a copy of its accounts to the annual return) if the following conditions are fulfilled:

(a)   every person who is a shareholder of the company, on the date of the holding of the next AGM of the company after the end of that financial year, shall declare his consent to the exemption;

(b)   there is in force, in respect of the whole of that financial year, an irrevocable guarantee by the parent company of the liabilities of the subsidiary company in respect of that financial year and the company has notified in writing every shareholder of the guarantee;

(c)   the annual accounts of the company for that financial year are consolidated in the group accounts prepared by the parent company and the exemption of the parent company, under C(A)(A) 1986, s 17 is disclosed in a note to the group accounts;

(d)   a notice stating that the company has availed of the exemption in respect of that financial year and a copy of the guarantee and notification referred to in paragraph (b) of C(A)(A) 1986, s 17(1), together with a declaration by the company in writing that paragraph (a) of C(A)A

1986, s 17(1) has been complied with in relation to the exemption, is annexed to the annual return for the financial year made by the company to the Registrar of Companies;

(e) the group accounts of the parent must be drawn up in accordance with the requirements of the Seventh Council Directive (No 83/849 EEC), and the group accounts of the parent company are annexed to the annual return as aforesaid and are audited in accordance with art 37 of the Seventh Council Directive.

## 2.8 Compliance

There is now an emphasis on compliance, by companies and their officers, with the provisions of the Companies Acts, 1963–2006 and the secondary legislation relating to companies in the form of statutory instruments. This was given impetus by the enactment into law of the CLEA 2001, whose main provisions flow directly from recommendations in the Report of the Working Group on Company Law Compliance and Enforcement which was published in March 1999.

The principal provisions of CLEA provide for the establishment of the post of Director of Corporate Enforcement and the transfer to the Director of the functions of the Minister for Enterprise, Trade and Employment relating to the investigation and enforcement of the Companies Acts, 1963–2006. CLEA also recognises the need for ongoing review of company legislation to deal with changes in the commercial world and provides for the establishment of a statutory Company Law Review Group to monitor, review and advise the Minister for Enterprise, Trade and Employment on matters relating to company law. The onus on directors to comply with company legislation is increasing and directors will be required to formally state that they acknowledge that they have legal duties and obligations under the Companies Acts, 1963–2003, as well as under the general law of the land and at common law.

## 2.9 Future Developments

There are also further far-reaching developments such as the creation of a 'European company' and the consolidation of the Companies Acts, 1963–2006 into a single Act in the same way as the consolidation of the tax legislation into the Taxes Consolidation Act, 1997. The role of technology will also be very important in both compliance, by way of electronic filing, and the exchange of information such as the availability of forms and legislation on the internet. The Companies Registration Office is introducing new measures to encourage the filing of Annual Returns online. This will be more important in view of the proposed transfer of the Companies Registration Office to Carlow from

Dublin. The Company Law Review Group have published the General Scheme of Companies Consolidation and Reform Bill in two separate publications. The first, entitled Pillar A, deals with private limited companies, whilst the second publication deals with public limited companies and all other types of legal entities. The General Scheme of the new Companies Bill is available to view online at www.clrg.org.

**CHAPTER 3**

# COMPANY LAW ENFORCEMENT

## 3.1 Introduction

The enforcement of (compliance with) company law has different aspects and is not limited to the powers of the various State agencies involved. The Companies Acts, 1963–2006 (the Companies Acts) are a large body of laws and include 400 criminal offences. Their enforcement has a public and a private aspect, divided according to the subject matter and the laws in question. Corporate regulation (i.e. the enforcement by the State of company law) is limited in scope and serves the public interest, not any private one. Regulation does not cover all of the possible instances of enforcement, many of which will remain matters of private law. Companies remain subject to the law contained in the Companies Acts and their Statutory Instruments. Officers of all companies are under a general obligation to ensure that their companies comply with those laws. Companies and their officers may be forced to comply with the Companies Acts: companies via the general body of laws themselves; their officers via s 371 of the Companies Act ('CA') 1963. Some situations will allow additional obligations to be brought to bear but these are the basic obligations for all compliance.

This chapter is divided between public and private enforcement.

Shareholders appoint directors to manage and direct a company. In private companies (most of the companies registered in Ireland), the shareholders and the board of directors tend to be the same people, but wearing different hats. Trading as a company, regardless of its type, brings responsibilities for *the company* and for its officers (the board of directors). It is important to remain precise about the specific duties of the players (shareholders, directors and the company itself).

Do not confuse company law enforcement with the rules designed to fight organised crime and terrorism. Anti-money-laundering rules force certain undertakings to report information to the Gardaí. That obligation is a cumulative one and is in addition to any rules covered in this chapter.

Company law serves many masters. It must operate within Constitutional norms, which include thereby the law of the European Community. It must be interpreted in accordance with the European Convention on Human Rights. Its overarching aim is commerce and it tries to provide basic rules for the operation of companies. These laws include those designed to curb excesses and to protect creditors and investors from avoidable loss. Some of these laws may only be enforced by private parties. Those rules, which relate to loss and insolvency, were for many years the most visible form of enforcement. Since the commencement of the Company Law Enforcement Act 2001 (the 'CLEA'), the Office of the Director of Corporate Enforcement (the 'ODCE') and the Companies Registration Office (the 'CRO') have attracted attention for enforcement actions (restriction and disqualification of directors and striking-off of companies). Private parties retain their *locus standi* but are no longer at the forefront of enforcement.

The instruments of regulation are: (i) the ODCE; (ii) the Director of Public Prosecutions (the 'DPP'); (iii) the CRO; (iv) the Irish Auditing and Accounting Supervisory Authority ('IAASA'); and (v) Private Parties.

## 3.2    Public Enforcement

All of the exercise of the powers of the ODCE, the DPP, the CRO and IAASA are governed by public law (although IAASA is slightly more complicated). Any unauthorised exercise of those powers is subject to judicial review by the High Court. While the ultra vires rule of company law will shortly be repealed, administrative law of necessity requires strict compliance by a public body with the grant of its power.

The two most visible types of enforcement are the prosecution of Companies Acts offences and the collection of information by the State bodies via mandatory reporting rules. Applications for restriction (s 150 CA 1990) are properly part of insolvency and disqualification (s 160 CA 1990), while applications more closely related to enforcement is best dealt with as part of the treatment of restriction.

### 3.2.1    CRIMES

The Companies Acts criminalise a large number of breaches of company law. Indictable offences under the Companies Act are all those whose penalties exceed a €1,904.61 fine or twelve months' imprisonment. Pursuant to s 240 CA 1990, the maximum term of imprisonment for an offence under the Companies Acts is five years, although nothing precludes consecutive sentences giving a longer effective term of imprisonment.

Section 12(1)(a) CLEA permits the Director of Corporate Enforcement (the Director) to enforce any breach of the Companies Acts by summary criminal proceedings. The Director is entitled under s 109(1) CLEA to impose fines to be paid before a twenty-one-day notice of intention to prosecute expires. If the fine is paid and the default remedied, the Director will not prosecute. This section provides a means whereby the Director may, without the institution of court proceedings, levy fines in respect of summary offences in order to avoid the need to prosecute without denying the person accused of the offence the right to be heard in court.

Section 240(5)(a) CA 1990 states that the time limit for the prosecution of a summary offence is three years from the date of commission. This time limit may be extended if the accused person was outside the jurisdiction, or if the information describing the offence came to the attention of the authorities, after the expiry of the time limit. There is no time limit for the prosecution of indictable offences but, in exceptional circumstances, prosecutorial delay may result in an accused being denied the opportunity of a fair trial.

The requirements for the formation of an offence committed by an officer of the company in s 383 CA 1963 were altered in the CLEA. The new section makes no reference to acting 'knowingly and wilfully' and creates the presumption that an officer of a company has permitted the default in question unless proven otherwise.

The venue for the prosecution of a summary offence under the Companies Acts may be either the court area in which the offence is charged, the court area in which the accused is arrested or resides, the court area in which the registered office of the company is situated, or a court area specified under s 15 of the Courts Act 1971.

Summary offences are defined as those incorporating a fine of less than €1,904.61 or twelve months' imprisonment. Indictable offences are those carrying a higher tariff. Offences are enforceable by summary prosecution or on indictment at the option of the prosecutor. The Director may prosecute all summary offences under the Companies Acts. The DPP may prosecute all indictable offences. Section 104 CLEA applies the Criminal Justice Act 1984 to all indictable offences under the Companies Acts, permitting the Gardaí to arrest and detain a suspect, without a warrant, for up to twelve hours. Section 4 of the Criminal Justice Act 1997 also provides for circumstances in which a civilian may effect an arrest of a person suspected of having committed an indictable offence carrying a sentence of five years' imprisonment.

## 3.3 Functions of the Regulators

Each regulator has a different focus and statutory bailiwick. It is not uncommon for a given client issue to span a number of regulators. All situations remain subject to general obligations (on the company) to comply and (on its officers) to ensure compliance.

### 3.3.1 THE OFFICE OF THE DIRECTOR OF CORPORATE ENFORCEMENT

The Office of the Director of Corporate Enforcement (ODCE) was created by s 7 CLEA. Section 12(1) CLEA defines the functions of the Director: he may enforce and encourage compliance with the Companies Acts, investigate suspected company law offences, and, where relevant, supervise receivers and liquidators. It also empowers him to do such acts or things as are necessary or expedient for the discharge of his functions under the Act and that he may perform those functions through the staff of the office.

Section 12 CLEA states that Gardaí seconded to the Director shall remain vested with their usual powers and duties as Gardaí, in addition to any powers that they may exercise as officers of the Director. Clients should be made aware of this issue when dealing with a Garda member of the ODCE, especially as regards general powers of arrest, entry, search and seizure.

The Director may refer cases to the DPP (*per* s 12(1)(d)) where he considers that an indictable offence under the Companies Acts has been committed. The Director may refer a case to the DPP, prosecute summarily himself or impose an instant fine to be paid before the expiry of a notice of intention to prosecute.

The Director has brought disqualification applications under s 160 CA 1990. He may relieve a liquidator of his obligation to bring restriction applications against directors of an insolvent company under s 150 CA 1990. These sections penalise transgressions of company law but are more properly dealt with in **chapter 13** on Insolvency.

The Director has the power to seek an order restraining an officer of a company from removing from the State, his, or the company's, assets or reducing them where so ever located. The Director may apply to the High Court to compel a company or officer to make good a failure to comply with the Companies Acts or to repay or restore assets in cases of misfeasance.

In addition, *in a winding-up*, the Director may seek from the court an order to obtain records, to examine an officer, or to arrest an absconding contributory or officer.

Pursuant to ss 150 and 160 CA 1990, respectively, the Director may apply to have a person restricted or disqualified from acting as a director. The CLEA compels a liquidator of an insolvent company to apply to have the directors of that company restricted, unless relieved of his duty after making a report under s 56 CLEA.

## 3.3.2    THE DIRECTOR OF PUBLIC PROSECUTIONS

The Director of Public Prosecutions was created by the Prosecution of Offences Act 1974 and has authority to prosecute all indictable offences under the Companies Acts. The question of whether the Attorney General retained a residual constitutional right to prosecute (as suggested by Walsh J in *State (Collins) v Ruane* [1984] IR 105) probably does not arise. The DPP has no special role to play other than to decide whether to prosecute on foot of evidence prepared for him.

### 3.3.3 THE COMPANIES OFFICE

The Joint Stock Companies Act 1844 established the Registrar of Companies. It operates the filing and registration requirements of the Companies Acts. Its role is to provide essential information about registered companies, to enforce the provisions of company law in relation to filing obligations and to register the creation of a company in the certificate of incorporation. The Registrar is empowered to prosecute companies summarily for registration offences, to impose fines to be paid before the expiry of a notice of intention to prosecute and to strike companies off the register of companies.

### 3.3.4 THE IRISH AUDITING AND ACCOUNTING SUPERVISORY AUTHORITY

The Irish Auditing and Accounting Supervisory Authority (IAASA) was established in accordance with the provisions of Part 2 of the Companies (Auditing and Accounting) Act 2003. IAASA, pursuant to s 8 of the C(AA)A 2003, supervises prescribed accountancy bodies, whether the accounts of certain classes of companies (private companies meeting certain turnover or balance sheet thresholds and plcs) comply with the Companies Acts and whether companies governed by the laws of the EU that are listed on regulated markets (i.e. certain stock exchanges) have published accounts that comply with the International Financial Reporting Standards ('IFRS') as adopted for use by the European Union.

## 3.4 Reporting

By creating a flow of information to the State bodies the Oireachtas intends to support enforcement. Officers of a company, auditors, liquidators and receivers each have different obligations to make reports to some or all of the State bodies. Those obligations crystallise according to each section creating the requirement. They are dealt with below. These reports are mandatory.

### 3.4.1 DUTIES ON AUDITORS, LIQUIDATORS, RECEIVERS, AND EXAMINERS

There is a general obligation to comply with the law, including the provisions of the Companies Acts. There are extra duties imposed on certain designated persons. The duties consist of reports that must be made to those statutory bodies. There is an extra duty in the case of a liquidator, who must bring s 150 CA 1990 restriction proceedings against all the directors of a company in liquidation. This is dealt with in **chapter 13** on Insolvency.

NORMA SMURFIT LIBRARY
NATIONAL COLLEGE
IRELAND

## 3.4.2 AUDITORS' DUTIES

An auditor's responsibility is to report to the shareholders on the truth and fairness of the financial statements presented at the annual general meeting. By amending s 194 CA 1963, the CLEA forces an auditor to report all indictable offences arising from the Companies Acts believed to have been committed by the company, or its agents, to the Director. The obligation does not affect legal or professional privilege but client confidentiality (or other legal duty) may be breached. The CLEA makes it clear that an auditor cannot be held liable for damage caused by compliance with the Act.

An auditor's responsibility has been described as onerous but according to Lopes LJ (in *Re Kingston Cotton Mill Co (No 2)* [1896] 2 Ch 279 at 288), the law regards an auditor as 'a watchdog, not a bloodhound'. This statement should be used with care. Accounting standards have developed greatly since that century and even prior to the CLEA the standard required, while remaining that of a careful and competent auditor, included investigation of suspected non-compliance with the Companies Acts.

Section 194(5) CLEA provides as follows:

> *Where, in the course of, and by virtue of, their carrying out an audit of the accounts of the company, information comes into the possession of the auditors of a company that leads them to form the opinion that there are reasonable grounds for believing that the company or an officer or agent of it has committed an indictable offence under the Companies Acts (other than an indictable offence under section 125(2) or 127(12) of the Principal Act), the auditors shall, forthwith after having formed it, notify that opinion to the Director and provide the Director with details of the grounds on which they have formed that opinion.*

The obligation arises 'in the course of, and by virtue of' an audit. The use of the conjunctive 'and' between 'in the course of' and 'by virtue of' in s 194 could mean that the duty does not arise if the accountant is carrying out non-audit work solely. If an auditor forms a belief, after the discharge of his duties that allows him to form a view that an offence has been committed, he does not appear to be obliged to report it. If the information indicates *post facto* that the audit is not a 'true and fair' view of the books and records, then the audit 'sign-off' should be withdrawn at that point. If it indicates that an indictable offence has been committed, but that the audit itself remains a true and fair view, then arguably the duty to report the evidence to the ODCE does not arise as the audit was completed. If the offence was such that it required a withdrawal of the audit sign-off, then it seems likely that the ODCE should be informed. If the audit is withdrawn and the auditor proceeds to recast the report in the light of new information, the CLEA may require him to report all indictable offences as he is again 'in the course of' the audit. An auditor should be mindful that failure to report is an offence. A strict reading of the subsection suggests that the duty ends when the report is delivered, subject to the exceptions suggested above.

When a firm forms the requisite opinion in the course of non-audit work and subsequently is appointed to carry out an audit, it would be illogical if the auditor were aware that an indictable offence had been committed but did not act on his knowledge unless he rediscovered the information during the audit. Statutes should be interpreted in a fashion that does not fly in the face of common sense. In such a situation, subsection (5) would oblige an auditor to check whether there are reasonable grounds for forming that opinion and act accordingly. His obligation to enquire should arise as soon as he was appointed.

The Director goes slightly further than the Companies Acts and offers an explanation for 'audit'. This, it is suggested in his Decision Notice 1(5), is an examination of the financial statements of a company performed by an auditor. The basic accounting standard requirements of an audit are set out and it is acknowledged that auditors are required to comply with the standards set by the Auditing Practices Board.

The IAASA may intervene in the disciplinary process of prescribed acountancy bodies and conduct its own review of suspected breaches of the standards of registered auditors pursuant to s 25 C(AA)A 2003.

### 3.4.3    EXAMINERS' DUTIES

Examinership is the protection afforded by the court while it appoints an examiner to investigate a company's affairs and to report on its commercial prospects of survival. An examiner is subject to regulation by the ODCE to the extent that an examiner is subject to the Companies Acts.

### 3.4.4    LIQUIDATORS' DUTIES

A liquidator is a person appointed to the company to wind it up and cause it to be dissolved. His duties are to gather in and realise the assets of the company and then distribute them to the creditors in accordance with priority.

Under s 56 CLEA, a liquidator appointed to an insolvent company is obliged to report to the Director on the conduct of the directors. This obligation is articulated in SI 324/2002, which provides a detailed form for the report. The report is designed to assist the Director in the performance of his functions.

Liquidators appointed to all insolvent companies are required to bring an application pursuant to s 150 CA 1990 to restrict the directors of that company. The court is asked to enquire whether the directors acted honestly and responsibly in relation to the affairs of the Company and that there is no other reason why it would be just or equitable that they be made subject to the restrictions. The ODCE is entitled, if he so chooses, to relieve the liquidator of this obligation if he receives a favourable report from the liquidator.

Where a liquidator in a voluntary winding-up believes that any past or present member or officer of the company has been guilty of a criminal offence, that liquidator is obliged to report his belief and the grounds for it to the ODCE (as well as the DPP). Section 299(2A) CA 1963 requires the liquidator to furnish such information, and facilitate access or such copies for the ODCE as he may require. Section 299(1A) CA 1963 requires a court-appointed liquidator to make an identical disclosure when directed by the High Court. A failure to make a report in a voluntary winding-up permits an interested party to apply to the High Court to require the liquidator to do so.

On request from the ODCE, a liquidator must provide his books for inspection. Liquidations that have been completed more than six years ago are exempted from this requirement. The liquidator must also answer any queries or provide such reasonable assistance as required.

A liquidator is also required to make certain filing returns to the CRO.

### 3.4.5 RECEIVERS' DUTIES

A receiver is a person appointed on foot of a debenture (or sometimes by a court order) who is responsible for gathering in the charged assets, realising their value and applying the proceeds to discharge the debt. He has no general duty to inform the company of how business is going. After a receiver has ceased to act, he must send to the CRO a statement of opinion as to whether the company is solvent. Section 319(2A) CA 1963 requires the CRO to forward that statement to the ODCE.

Pursuant to s 323A CA 1963, the ODCE may request a receiver to produce his books for inspection. The receiver faces an identical compulsion to a liquidator and must provide his books for inspection. Receiverships that have been completed for more than six years are exempt from this requirement. The receiver must answer any queries or provide such reasonable assistance as required.

Section 179 CA 1990 requires that where a receiver believes that any past or present member or officer of the company has been guilty of a criminal offence, that receiver is obliged to report his belief and the grounds for it to the ODCE (as well as the DPP). Section 299(2A) CA 1963 requires the liquidator to furnish such information, and facilitate access or copies for the Director he may require.

## 3.5 Information Gathering

A company inspector may be appointed by the ODCE or the court. Strictly speaking, he is not a part of any regulatory body, but he is subject to the supervision of the High Court. He is best seen as an intrusive form of information gathering. When dealing with the statutory power to investigate company law abuses, the courts have repeatedly pointed to the privilege conferred by incorporation and the need to protect creditors and the general public. Murray J (in *Dunnes Stores Ireland Co v Ryan* [2002] 2 IR 60) described the purpose of the powers of inspection as being:

> to ensure, *inter alia*, that companies who have availed of the right to incorporate and register under the Acts and the advantages which such incorporation

confers, do not abuse those advantages to the detriment of their shareholders, creditors and, in particular, the public interest. (p. 17)

A company inspection is not required to accord with the rules of natural and constitutional justice until it reaches a point at which adverse *conclusions* are to be drawn against a person. Murphy J in *Chestvale v Glackin* ([1993] 3 IR 35) speaks of the entry of a verdict against an investigated party as a condition precedent to the procedural rights identified in *Re Haughey*. Shanley J followed this logic when ruling on the legality of the process of inquiry adopted in *Re National Irish Bank (No 1)* ([1999] 3 IR 145). The learned judge decided that a mere information-gathering exercise did not attract rights of natural justice.

Kelly J in *Re National Irish Bank and National Irish Bank Financial Services* ([1999] 3 IR 190) further analysed the inspection process, and confirmed that the making of an allegation under oath does not elevate an information-gathering process unless the inspectors admit such allegation as evidence or if its admission as evidence may give rise to adverse conclusions being drawn against the accused party.

As made clear by Barrington J in *Re National Irish Bank (No 1)* in the Supreme Court, the privilege against self-incrimination did not apply to officers or agents of the company being examined under oath by the inspector.

There are two types of company inspectors. The first is appointed by the ODCE to determine the true ownership or control of a company or its shares. The second is appointed by the court to investigate and report on the affairs of a company.

### 3.5.1    INSPECTORS APPOINTED BY THE ODCE

Section 14(1) CA 1990 gives the ODCE power to appoint an inspector to discover the 'true persons' who are financially interested, or able to materially influence the policy of a company. In order to make the appointment, the ODCE must satisfy himself that the inspection is necessary either for:

(a)    *the effective administration of law relating to companies;*

(b)    *for the effective discharge of the Director of his functions under any enactment; or*

(c)    *in the public interest.*

Section 17 CA 1990 applies s 14 to all bodies incorporated outside the State that are, or were, carrying on business as if they were registered under CA 1963. Section 15 CA 1990 allows the ODCE, for reasons identical to s 14, to investigate the ownership of shares or debentures of a company.

Section 19 CA 1990 allows the ODCE to give directions that a body, of a type specified in that section, produce specified books or documents once he has certified his opinion that the following circumstances exist with regard to the that company:

*(a)* *it is necessary to examine the books and documents of the body with a view to determining whether an inspector should be appointed to conduct an investigation of the body under the Companies Acts; or*

*(b)* *that the affairs of the body are being or have been conducted with intent to defraud—*

    *(i)* *its creditors,*

    *(ii)* *the creditors of any other person, or*

    *(iii)* *its members; or*

*(c)* *that the affairs of the body are being or have been conducted for a fraudulent purpose other than described in paragraph (b); or*

*(d)* *that the affairs of the body are being or have been conducted in a manner which is unfairly prejudicial to some part of its members; or*

*(e)* *that any actual or proposed act or omission or series of acts or omissions of the body or on behalf of the body are or would be unfairly prejudicial to some part of its members; or*

*(f)* *that any actual or proposed act or omission or series of acts or omissions of the body or on behalf of the body are or are likely to be unlawful; or*

*(g)* *that the body was formed for any fraudulent purpose; or*

*(h)* *that the body was formed for any unlawful purpose.*

Section 66 CA 1990 permits the Director to appoint an investigator in respect of share dealings where a breach of s 30, 53 or 65 CA 1990 is suspected.

O'Hanlon J held in *Desmond v Glackin (No 2)* ([1993] 3 IR 67) that the warrant of appointment of the inspector under s 14 need not state the reasons for the appointment. The width of the discretion conferred on the Director's predecessor, the Minister for Enterprise, in declaring that something was 'in the public interest' could only be defeated by evidence that the appointment was made *mala fides* or unreasonably (in the *Wednesbury* sense).

Blayney J in *Lyons v Curran* ([1993] ILRM 375) stated in reference to the power to appoint an inspector under s 14(1) CA:

> In my opinion the correct construction of this subsection is that an inspector appointed under it to investigate a particular company has the duty and power to investigate the membership of the company for the purpose of determining who are or have been financially interested in the success or failure of the company. An investigation of the membership is not simply for the purpose of ascertaining who the members are. It is for the purpose of determining who are the true persons financially interested in the success or failure of the company. That would clearly cover ascertaining the identity of the beneficiary, where shares are held by a person or persons as trustees, or by a corporate trustee, but in my opinion it also covers ascertaining the identity of the persons entitled to the shares of a corporate member. Otherwise it would be necessary to conclude that where an inspector had ascertained

that some or all of the shares in the company he was investigating belonged to another company, he had finished his investigation; he had determined the true persons financially interested in the success or failure of the company. In my opinion that could not be so. I am satisfied that the phrase 'the true persons' means the real individuals who are financially interested, and cannot refer to a company. So, where an inspector finds a company as shareholder in the company he is investigating, he must go further and seek to determine the persons who are the beneficial owners of that company.

Thus, the identification of the 'true persons' entitles an inspector to investigate companies not named on the warrant of appointment in order to determine the identity of those true persons. Blayney J went on to state that where an investigator merely thought, but did not know, that the investigation of a body corporate not named on his warrant of appointment was necessary to perform his duty, then he would require separate authorisation for that company under s 9 CA 1990. Thomas Courtney in *The Law of Private Companies,* 2nd edn (Butterworths, 2002) at p. 861 has considered this judgment as providing a significant advantage for an inspector looking to extend the scope of his investigation to companies that are not strictly related to the investigated company.

McCarthy J in *Desmond v Glackin (No 2)* approved the statutory power to lift the veil of incorporation to determine those financially interested in the ownership of a company so as to investigate possible breach of duties to the company.

## 3.5.2 INSPECTOR APPOINTED BY THE HIGH COURT

Section 7 CA 1990 permits the court, of its own motion or on application, to appoint an investigator to inquire into the affairs of the company. Application may be made by the company, a director, creditor, not less than 100 members, or those representing 10 per cent of the paid-up share capital, or not less than one-fifth of the register of members in a company not having share capital. No reason or criteria are offered to govern the exercise of the High Court's discretion. The power of the court to investigate the affairs of a company may be exercised even if the company is being wound up.

Section 8 permits the court to appoint an investigator to inquire into the affairs of the company, on the application of the ODCE. Before acceding to his request, the court should be satisfied that there are circumstances suggesting:

(a)   *that its affairs are being or have been conducted with intent to defraud its creditors or the creditors of any other person or otherwise for a fraudulent or unlawful purpose or in an unlawful manner or in a manner which is unfairly prejudicial to some part of its members, or that any actual or proposed act or omission of the company (including an act or omission on its behalf) is or would be so prejudicial, or that it was formed for any fraudulent or unlawful purpose; or*

(b)   *that persons connected with its formation or the management of its affairs have in connection therewith been guilty of fraud, misfeasance or other misconduct towards it or towards its members; or*

> (c)   *that its members have not been given all the information relating to its affairs which they might reasonably expect.*

The meaning of 'affairs' of the company has not been analysed by an Irish court. Judicial precedent from the UK suggests a broad meaning to the term. Giving the word its plain meaning in the statute, s 8 suggests a wide inspection.

With the approval of the court, an enquiry by a court appointed inspector may be extended to a related company, including a company that only has a commercial relationship with the company under inspection.

### 3.5.3   POWERS OF INSPECTORS

Section 10 CA 1990 gives an inspector, howsoever appointed, power to require the production of documents, to examine a person on oath and to certify to the court any refusal to comply with requests for documents or to attend before the inspector. An inspector appointed by the court may require the production of books and documents relating to directors' bank accounts.

The duty to cooperate with an inspector is imposed on 'all officers and agents' of the company and 'any other body corporate whose affairs are investigated'. 'Officers and agents' includes past officers and agents, and all persons employed by the company as professional advisers such as bankers, solicitors, auditors or accountants.

Where the inspector considers some other person to be 'in possession of any information concerning [the company's] affairs' it shall be the duty of that person to provide all reasonable assistance, without prejudice to any lien on books or documents. A lien claimed on documents, the production of which is required under s 10 CA 1990, conforms to a similar provision in respect of documents under s 19 CA 1990. A lien is a right over a debtor's property to protect a debt charged on that property. Where a person claims a lien over documents required by an inspector, the statutory protection of that lien will facilitate their production and limit the scope for objection to their production on the part of the person in possession of them.

Failure to provide 'reasonable assistance' may be considered by the court. Following the judgment of the Supreme Court in *Desmond v Glackin*, pursuant to s 10(5) CA 1990, in cases of non-compliance with the requests of an investigator, the matter may be referred to the court which can direct that the person concerned comply with the requests or, if it sees fit, can direct that the person need not comply with the requests but it cannot treat such person as being guilty of contempt of court by virtue only of a refusal to comply with the request of the inspector. Failure to comply with a court order is contempt of court.

'Agents' for the purposes of this section includes accountants, bookkeepers and taxation advisers, bankers, solicitors and auditors of the company or body corporate under investigation.

Section 18 provides that answers to questions put on oath to an officer, agent or other person by an inspector in exercise of his powers may be used in subsequent civil proceedings and/or perjury proceedings.

Certification to the court that a party has refused or failed to assist the inspectors permits the court to, inter alia, make an order directing that the party produce the relevant document, answer the relevant question or stating that he does not have to do so.

Both types of inspector must make a report at the end of the enquiry. All reports must be furnished to the Director, and the report is a privileged document pursuant to s 23(3) CA 1990.

## 3.6 Private Enforcement

Private parties may participate in enforcement to the extent that they possess *locus standi*. High Court litigation for non-compliance is commonly not justified by the bulk of instances of non-compliance. As stated above, a member, creditor or director may apply through s 371 CA 1963 to enforce compliance with the Companies Acts by that company.

Section 205 CA 1963 oppression suits can include a comparison of the corporate compliance sins of the various litigants. Examples of compliance breaches may establish that the powers of a company are being exercised in an oppressive fashion, but the mere fact that an action is illegal does not render it an act of oppression. The corollary is true of legal act, which is not necessarily benign merely because it is permitted by the Companies Acts. On hearing an oppression suit, the High Court may make such order 'as it thinks fit', which can encourage litigants to identify non-compliance so as to detract from the merits of the other party's argument.

Keep in mind the limits of any derivative action (a company should sue for wrongs committed against it (*Foss v Harbottle* [1843] 2 Hare 461)). A derivative action may be taken if an illegal act is perpetrated; if more than a bare majority is required to ratify the wrong complained of, if the members' personal rights are infringed, where a fraud has been perpetrated on a minority or where the justice of the case permits it.

Insolvency-type situations are not strictly relevant here. They tend to move into a search for missing assets and knowledge where compliance is only of relevance if it facilitates asset recovery, either by providing information, or by making available the funds of persons responsible for the losses.

### 3.6.1 ENFORCEMENT OF DUTY TO COMPLY WITH THE COMPANIES ACT

Section 371 CA 1963 states:

*(1)    If a company or any officer of a company having made default in complying with any provision of this Act fails to make good the default within 14 days after the service of a notice on the company or officer requiring it or him to do so,*

> *the court may, on an application made to the court by any member or creditor of the company or by the Director or by the registrar of companies, make an order directing the company and any officer thereof to make good the default within such time as may be specified in the order.*

> *(2) Any such order may provide that all costs of and incidental to the application shall be borne by the company or by any officers of the company responsible for the default.*

> *(3) Nothing in this section shall be taken to prejudice the operation of any enactment imposing penalties on a company or its officers in respect of any such default as aforesaid.*

Members, creditors and the ODCE have *locus standi*. The section envisages a request to a company, or an officer thereof, to remedy a breach of the provisions of the CA 1963. The Companies Acts may be construed as one Act and accordingly this provision applies to all the Companies Acts. If the default remains uncorrected for a further fourteen days, application may be made to the High Court.

No rules are provided for the application. In such circumstances, application may be made by way of a motion. It should be noted that the minimum period required to bring such an application is fifteen ordinary days; being the service of the notice plus the fourteen subsequent days stated in the Act. Unless otherwise stated, 'a day' means an ordinary solar day. The court appears to have jurisdiction to make an order once a valid notice is served and failure to remedy the default complained of has been adduced. Presumably the fourteen-day notice must identify the section, the nature of the default alleged and the time limit. Thereafter, as commentators have observed, the court has no guidance as to the operation of its discretion. Such an application is pursuant to statute rather than any inherent or equitable jurisdiction of the High Court.

No existing litigation is needed to invoke this section, which in those circumstances would proceed by way of originating notice of motion.

## 3.6.2 PRIVATE CRIMINAL PROSECUTIONS FOR BREACH OF THE COMPANIES ACT

On the criminal side, jurisdiction exists for a private party (not a company) to prosecute summary offences as a 'common informer'. The continuation of this jurisdiction as 'an important common law right that has survived the Constitution' was reaffirmed by the Supreme Court in *Cumann Luthchleas Gael Teo v Windle* ([1994] 1IR 525).

# CHAPTER 4

# SHAREHOLDERS AGREEMENTS

## 4.1  Introduction

The Companies Acts, 1963–2006 (the 'Companies Acts') provide relatively few protections for minority shareholders in a company, especially minorities holding less than 25 per cent (who, accordingly, cannot block the passing of a special resolution). Principal amongst these protections include the right to receive the company's annual accounts and the right to seek the protection of the courts if they are being oppressed. Largely because of the limited benefit of these protections, as a matter of convention, a minority shareholder in a company (for example, a financial investor) will often seek the additional protection of a contract with the other shareholders, establishing certain additional rights. This contract is a shareholders agreement.

Larger shareholders may also benefit from the existence of a shareholders agreement, as it will govern the conduct of all shareholders in the company, establish a framework for the operation and management of the company and thus provide greater certainty for everyone. A joint venture relationship may be an example of this. On the other hand, a majority shareholder may feel that, as it controls the composition of the Board (because directors are appointed by ordinary resolution of the shareholders of the company) it is thus in a position to control the actions of the company and that, accordingly, the existence of a shareholders agreement creating rights for other shareholders may not be in its interest. These pros and cons should be carefully weighed up before taking any decision to enter into a shareholders agreement or what provisions to include in it.

There is no legal requirement for all shareholders in a company to be party to a shareholders agreement. In many cases, however, this will be considered desirable as it will ensure that all shareholders are bound by the terms of the agreement. In other cases, it may be preferred to exclude some shareholders from the shareholders agreement in order to avoid creating any additional rights in favour of such shareholders.

While the company itself is often a party to a shareholders agreement, care should be taken to avoid infringing the principles stated by the House of Lords in 1992 in *Russell v Northern Bank Development Corporation*. The Board of Directors of a company must not unlawfully fetter its discretion when it comes to making decisions in the best interests of the company and any attempt to do so may be unenforceable. Care should be taken to use language whereby the shareholders agree to procure that a certain action is taken (through the manner in which they exercise their voting rights), rather than language that imposes direct obligations on the company itself.

The articles of association of the company also govern the relationship between all of the shareholders and to some extent there is an overlap between what could be included in the articles and what could be included in a shareholders agreement. The articles tend to deal with the regulations applicable to share issues, share transfers and shareholders' and directors' meetings. It should be borne in mind that anything included in the articles will be in the public domain (as articles must be filed in the Companies Registration Office) and for commercially sensitive provisions. In these instances, however, care should be taken to ensure that all necessary shareholders are party to the shareholders agreement, so that they are bound by these provisions.

## 4.2 Subscription

Shareholders agreements are frequently entered into at the same time as a new investment is made in the company. In these cases, in addition to the provisions dealing with how the company is to be run, the shareholders agreement will contain provisions dealing with the investment.

### 4.2.1 PRECONDITIONS

In the same way that a share purchase may be subject to preconditions, a share subscription may also be agreed to be subject to certain preconditions. For a fuller discussion on this subject, see **chapter 5** on Buying and Selling a Business.

### 4.2.2 MECHANICS

These clauses will specify the amount being paid by way of subscription for new shares in the company and the number and class of shares being issued. The parties will agree that upon receipt of payment, a Board meeting is to be held authorising the issue of the new shares (and possibly the appointment of new directors, see further below).

### 4.2.3 WARRANTIES

In the same way that a purchaser of existing shares will normally require warranties to be given by the seller in respect of the company, an investor subscribing for new shares will frequently require the company and/or existing shareholders in the company (perhaps the main promoters of the company) to provide warranties in respect of the company (to be qualified as necessary by a disclosure letter from the warrantors). For a fuller discussion on this subject, see **chapter 5** on Buying and Selling a Business. It is worth bearing in mind that not all warranties, or limitations on warrantor liability, that are appropriate to a share purchase (where control of the company is usually passing and the consideration is being received by selling shareholders) will necessarily be appropriate to a share subscription (where often only a minority interest is being acquired and the consideration is being received by the company rather than its shareholders).

### 4.2.4   OTHER MATTERS

The following other matters will also frequently need to be considered in connection with the subscription for new shares:

(a)   whether the Board has a current s 20 authority from the shareholders to issue new shares as required by the Companies Act, 1983;

(b)   whether the company has sufficient authorised share capital to issue the shares;

(c)   whether any directors are being issued shares, in which case s 53 notices will be required to be served on the company pursuant to the Companies Act, 1990;

(d)   whether the existing shareholders should be simultaneously confirming that they have no outstanding claims against the company (or waiving any such claims);

(e)   whether pre-emption rights in the company apply (either because the statutory pre-emption provisions in s 23 of the Companies (Amendment) Act, 1983 have not been disapplied or because different pre-emption rights have been adopted under the articles or a pre-existing shareholders agreement), in which case the existing shareholders will need to waive their pre-emption rights on the new issue of shares (either in stand-alone pre-emption waiver letters or by virtue of a dedicated clause to this effect in the shareholders agreement).

## 4.3   Main Provisions

In addition to a possible section dealing with share subscription, a typical shareholders agreement is usually divided into some or all of the following sections.

### 4.3.1   COVENANTS CONCERNING SHARES IN THE COMPANY

Some or all of the following provisions can equally be dealt with in the company's articles of association.

#### 4.3.1.1 Lock In

It is sometimes the case that one or more shareholders agree not to sell any (or no more than an agreed proportion) of their shares in the company for a period of time or indefinitely without the consent of one or more other shareholders. This is to protect an investor from being 'abandoned' in the company by the main promoters.

#### 4.3.1.2 Offer round

It is often the case that shareholders will agree that they may not sell shares to a third party without first offering them at the same price to the other share-holders. This protects shareholders from finding themselves co-shareholders with an undesirable party.

It is commonplace to exempt intra-group transfers (where the shareholder is a corporate entity) from this. Sometimes more contentious shareholders who are individuals might seek exemption for intra-family transfers—although the other shareholders might be more wary of this. If such exemptions are agreed, it is important to stipulate that the transferee must agree to be a party to the shareholders agreement (normally by signing a deed of adherence). In the context of intra-group transfers, it is also important to state that should the transferee company cease to be in the same group as the transferor, it must offer to sell its shares under the offer-round process.

#### 4.3.1.3 Tag Along

This describes an arrangement whereby if a shareholder wishes to sell to a third party he must first procure an offer for one or more of the other shareholders on the same terms (this can become difficult if some or all of the consideration is not in cash). As with the Lock In, this is to protect an investor from being 'abandoned' in the company by the main promoters.

#### 4.3.1.4 Drag Along

This describes an arrangement whereby if one or certain shareholders wish to sell their shares they can compel the other shareholders also to sell their shares, on the same terms. This is to overcome one of the main disadvantages in investing in a private company—ultimately realising the investment. A Drag Along clause makes it easier to achieve an exit as the entire company can be offered for sale. Note that if all shareholders will not be party to the sharehold-ers agreement, the Drag Along clause should be included in the articles so as to ensure that the provision binds all shareholders.

#### 4.3.1.5 Former employee compulsory sales

It is sometimes provided in a shareholders agreement that if an employee shareholder ceases to be an employee he must transfer some or all of his shares to the company or the other shareholders. The price payable for these shares, as well as the proportion of shares to be sold, is sometimes dependent on the circumstances in which employment ceased (e.g. was it by mutual agreement, was the employee dismissed etc.). These are often called 'good leaver/bad leaver' provisions.

## 4.3.2 COVENANTS CONCERNING THE OPERATIONS OF THE COMPANY

### 4.3.2.1 Board

An important protection for a minority shareholder is the right to appoint one or more representatives to the Board of directors. This can be expressed as a general right or a right to appoint a named person as a director (which may be more acceptable to the other shareholders). A certain level of directors' fees (or at least an entitlement to expenses) is often also provided for.

Some shareholders agreements will also provide for the establishment of committees of the Board, for example a remuneration committee to deal with salary, bonus and share option grants for staff or an audit committee to deal with audit and accounting matters concerning the company. A minority shareholder, particularly one who is not a company executive, will frequently seek to have the right to appoint a representative to these committees.

Some shareholders prefer to try to avoid the responsibilities that go with being company directors and instead seek 'observer' rights, i.e. the right to attend but not vote at Board meetings. Care should be exercised in this regard, as the observer by his actions may in fact be acting as a shadow director of the company.

The shareholders agreement will usually state that regular Board meetings should be held with reasonable notice given and a detailed agenda circulated with the notice.

### 4.3.2.2 Information

To supplement the Companies Act right to annual accounts, it is common to set out additional information rights in the shareholders agreement, such as the right to receive the annual accounts as soon as they have been approved by the Board and the auditors, monthly and/or quarterly management accounts (which will often be the key source of current financial information concerning a company), annual budgets and business plans, and any other information that a shareholder might reasonably request. The company's management will be concerned to ensure that the obligation to produce this level of information is not unduly burdensome.

### 4.3.2.3 Vetoes

One of the primary sources of protection in a shareholders agreement is the vetoes section. This sets out a list of transactions which may not be undertaken without the consent of the protected shareholder (often with the intention of protecting a shareholder's investment in the company). Examples can include:

(a) issuing new shares;

(b) amending the company's memorandum or articles of association;

(c) altering the nature of the company's business;

(d) hiring or firing senior employees;

(e) increasing levels of remuneration;

(f) paying dividends;

(g) engaging in litigation;

(h) material asset disposals or acquisitions;

(i) incurring new borrowings;

(j) giving security over the company's assets etc.;

(k) any other action that a shareholder might consider significant enough to require restriction in this way.

### 4.3.2.4  Deadlock

In the case of a company having only two shareholders holding 50 per cent each, failure to agree on any proposed course of action will result in stalemate. The parties may wish to anticipate this scenario in the shareholders agreement, and provide for some form of deadlock resolution process. This will often either involve one party buying out the other (with different possible mechanisms to determine price and to determine who the buyer is and who the seller is) or both parties agreeing to sell or wind up the company.

All of these are quite drastic solutions and for this reason parties sometimes prefer not to provide for this in the shareholders agreement and instead hope that some commercial agreement can be reached between the parties should a deadlock situation arise.

## 4.3.3  NON-COMPETE COVENANTS

To protect the value of a shareholder's holding in a company, it is usual to include a non-compete restriction in a shareholders agreement, that prevents all of the shareholders (or possibly just management shareholders) from competing with the company for so long as they remain shareholders (and often for a stated time period afterwards). As with all non-compete clauses, care should be taken to ensure that they do not offend against the rules governing enforceability. Areas typically covered are:

(a) non-competition with the company's business;

(b) non-solicitation of the company's staff;

(c)    non-solicitation of the company's customers;

(d)    non-solicitation of the company's suppliers.

For a fuller discussion of non-compete clauses generally, see **chapter 7** on Irish Competition Law.

A related area that is often covered in a shareholders agreement is to provide that any intellectual property created by an employee shareholder while an employee of the company and relating to the business of the company, belongs to the company not the employee and that the employee must cooperate in assigning such intellectual property to the company on request.

### 4.3.4    OTHER PROVISIONS

#### 4.3.4.1    Termination of old agreements

If some or all of the shareholders have previously entered into a shareholders agreement concerning the company, it is usually appropriate that this be terminated by the new agreement, which will replace it. Exceptions to this may arise, where for a specific reason it is desirable to leave an existing agreement in situ and have two shareholders agreements in respect of the company effective at the same time. If this is the case, care needs to be taken to ensure that there are no mutually inconsistent provisions in the two shareholders agreements.

#### 4.3.4.2    Loss of rights

Consider whether some or all of the above rights (for example, the right to Board representation) should be expressed to fall away if the shareholder's percentage ownership of the company falls below a certain minimum level.

#### 4.3.4.3    Assignment

Consider whether the shareholders should be able to assign their rights under the agreement to a third party who acquires their shares. If this is permitted in principle, beware of creating a situation where a shareholder can sell portions of its shareholding to multiple buyers and each time be allowed to transfer full rights to each of those buyers.

#### 4.3.4.4    Confidentiality

Shareholders agreements will normally contain a confidentiality clause imposing a duty of confidentiality in respect of company information given to a shareholder.

#### 4.3.4.5    Costs

It is sensible to record what the parties have agreed with respect to the costs of preparing the agreement, normally either that the company will pay the investor's costs (which is specifically permitted by s 60 Companies Act, 1963) or that each party will pay its own costs.

### 4.3.4.6    Arbitration

As with many other types of contract, the parties may choose to include a provision that requires any disputes to be settled through arbitration or mediation rather than litigation (the main benefit being that the dispute will hopefully be resolved in private rather than in public).

### 4.3.4.7    No partnership

To avoid the undesired consequences arising were a partnership to be found to exist between some or all of the parties to a shareholders agreement, it is common to include a clause specifically stating the parties' agreement that no such partnership arises.

### 4.3.4.8    Conflict with articles

Given the potential for a conflict to arise inadvertently between provisions agreed in a shareholders agreement and the provisions of the company's article of association, it is often stated in the shareholders agreement that in the event of such a conflict, the provisions of the shareholders agreement will apply (on the assumption that the parties have considered the terms of this document in more detail and therefore it is more likely to express their true intention). The parties give effect to this by agreeing to amend the articles as necessary to conform them to the provisions of the shareholders agreement. A view exists that such a clause of itself may create an obligation to file the shareholders agreement in the Companies Registration Office as it impacts on the articles. In practice this is rarely done.

## 4.4    Articles

Very often when a shareholders agreement is being entered into, the parties will want to amend the company's articles of association simultaneously in order to (1) eliminate any inconsistencies between what has been agreed in the shareholders agreement and the current version of articles—for example concerning shareholders' meetings and directors' meetings (such as specific quorum requirements); and, (2) deal with certain other matters, such as:

(a)    those items that it has been decided to set out in the articles, rather than the shareholders agreement—for example, those matters set out above at **4.3.1**; or

(b)    to provide for pre-emption rights on the issue of new shares by the company (in a different manner than statutory pre-emption under s 23 Companies (Amendment) Act, 1983).

# PART 2

# BUYING AND SELLING A BUSINESS

# CHAPTER 5

# BUYING AND SELLING A BUSINESS

## 5.1 Introduction

The purpose of this chapter is to explain the principal features of transactions under which businesses are purchased and sold. In the case of share purchase (i.e. where a company is being acquired) the following pages assume that what is being purchased is 100 per cent of a company ('the target company' or 'target') and that accordingly a normal share purchase agreement is being drawn up. The features discussed in this chapter are the standard features of a share purchase agreement for the entire issued share capital of the target company.

It is of course possible to effect a share purchase on the basis of a much simpler form of agreement, and indeed in many instances the formal agreement may be dispensed with in its entirety, particularly in the purchase of a small shareholding where the most basic form of a share purchase agreement, a share transfer form, is all that is completed.

The format of the share transfer form is prescribed by the Stock Transfer Act, 1963. It has been possible since 1996, however, to transfer shares pursuant to the Companies Act, 1990 (Uncertificated Securities) Regulations, 1996 (SI 68/1996) without requiring an instrument in writing at all. This facility allows for the operation of the CREST system (see further **chapter 12** at **12.5.3.7**), in the context of publicly listed companies and allows for a paperless format for share transfers.

## 5.2 Structuring of Transactions

### 5.2.1 GENERAL CONSIDERATIONS

When a transaction is first proposed, careful consideration needs to be given as to whether the transaction is best structured as a purchase of the shares of a target company or the purchase of the assets and liabilities of that target company. In most, but not all cases, having considered the factors involved, the decision would be taken to proceed by way of share purchase. However, this is an issue which should be considered at the outset of every transaction. The salient concerns are shown overleaf.

## 5.2.2 CHOICE OF ASSETS AND LIABILITIES

The advantage of being able to choose certain assets and liabilities is probably the most common reason for a purchaser electing for an asset purchase rather than share purchase. This choice, in particular, may be taken where the company has uncertain liabilities, such as a pending legal claim. The purchaser will require only the assets and will not want to take on liabilities which could turn out to be substantial. In such an instance, the purchaser will always be conscious that if the liability is subsequently not met by the company, the creditor may seek to challenge the transaction. Therefore, it is important that the transaction be carried out at arm's length and that the price be demonstrably fair. Careful thought is also required as to how the sale proceeds will be disbursed because, if a purchaser is in any way complicit in an arrangement where a creditor is being prejudiced, they may have difficulty if the transaction is subsequently challenged. The choice might also be made if there are assets in the target company which the purchaser does not want and it is not possible to extract those assets from the target company in advance of completing the transaction without creating excessive tax liabilities. In these circumstances, it is usually a question of assessing whether the taxation liabilities are more onerous if the assets are extracted or if the assets and relevant liabilities are sold by the target company.

*General considerations: salient concerns*

| Share purchase | Asset purchase |
| --- | --- |
| All assets and liabilities pass to purchaser | Purchaser has flexibility to choose assets and liabilities |
| Stamp duty is levied at a rate of 1 per cent | Stamp duty is leviable at rates up to 9 per cent (although intellectual property may be exempt) |
| Tax losses pass, subject to anti-avoidance legislation | Difficult to secure tax losses |
| Employees pass automatically | May be some flexibility not to take employees, but this is rendered difficult by European Communities (Protection of Employees on Transfer of Undertakings) Regulations, 2003 (SI 131/2003) |
| Consideration paid to vendor shareholders | Consideration paid to target company |

### 5.2.3 STAMP DUTY

It is provided by the Stamp Duties Consolidation Act, 1999 that stamp duty at a rate of 1 per cent is payable on the transfer of shares. Consequently, a share purchase attracts stamp duty at a rate of 1 per cent. On a transfer of assets, the rate of stamp duty depends very much on the assets which underlie the business. For example, the Finance Act, 2004 provides that the transfer of certain types of intellectual property (including patents, trademarks, copyright and directly attributable goodwill) shall be exempt from stamp duty. However, in a business which consists substantially of items such as property, goodwill or book debts, stamp duty is payable usually at the rate of 9 per cent on those assets. This usually results in the stamp duty being significantly greater for the purchaser on an asset purchase. On the other hand, assets such as stock and loose plant and machinery may, if the transaction is properly structured, pass by delivery and it is theoretically possible (but unlikely) that an asset purchase may be cheaper if the entire assets of the target company are of this type. It is always necessary to check the stamp duty rates currently in force when assessing the benefits of an asset purchase over a share purchase.

### 5.2.4 TAX LOSSES

If a target company which has ongoing tax losses is acquired, it may be possible for the share purchaser to utilise those tax losses in the future trading of the target company. There are some restrictions on this imposed by the Taxes Consolidation Act, 1997, s 401 which prevents significant changes in the nature of the business. It is conversely regarded as extremely difficult to transfer tax losses when a business is acquired by way of an asset purchase. The issue of transfer of tax losses is becoming less significant with the reduction in corporation tax rates to the 12.5 per cent level. Nevertheless, if a business has very significant tax losses, this might remain a relevant consideration.

### 5.2.5 CONSIDERATION

If a person carries out a transaction by way of a share purchase, the proceeds of sale are paid to the holders of the shares in the target company and they are subject to taxation if they have made a gain on those shares. On the other hand, if the assets are purchased from the target company, the target company receives the proceeds and is the chargeable entity rather than its shareholders. If the target company then wishes to pass the sale proceeds to its shareholders, there will be tax payable by those shareholders on what they have obtained from the target company. There are, therefore, two possible tax events on an asset purchase, whereas the share sale will involve only one taxable event. An added complication with an asset purchase is that the target company, depending on its trading position, may be prohibited by financial prudence requirements from immediately handing over the sale proceeds to its shareholders. Thus, for example, if there are significant liabilities in the target company which are unquantified, it may be appropriate to await quantification of those liabilities before the target company distributes the proceeds out to its shareholders.

### 5.2.6   EMPLOYEES

If the shares in a target company are purchased, the legal status of the employees of the target company will be unaffected as they will remain employed by the target company (albeit indirectly for the purchaser). In an asset purchase scenario, under the European Communities (Protection of Employees on Transfer of Undertakings) Regulations, 2003, there is an automatic transfer of the rights and obligations of the target company towards its employees to the purchaser on a transfer of an undertaking or business. There are, however, possible situations where the regulations do not apply; for example, if the assets being purchased form part of a distinct business within the target company, it may be permissible to take only those employees who relate to that business. This is a specialist area on which there is a considerable volume of case law.

### 5.2.7   NAME

If the target company's shares are purchased, the name of the target company is automatically acquired. If, on the other hand, the transaction is conducted by way of asset purchase through a shelf company or other vehicle of the purchaser and it is intended to continue trading under the target company's name, it would be necessary for the purchase vehicle to change its name and for the target company to change its name to something different. This is not a very difficult procedure where the parties are in agreement, but it is an inconvenience and may give rise to practical difficulties with issues such as bank accounts.

## 5.3   Heads of Agreement

When the parties have reached agreement on the basic principles of the deal (such as structure and price), it is common to record these in a short document sometimes called a Heads of Agreement (or Term Sheet, Letter of Intent, Memorandum of Understanding etc.). This is designed to ensure that the fundamental terms are indeed agreed, in advance of devoting resources to due diligence (see below) and negotiation of the purchase agreements.

Heads of Agreement are generally stated to be non-binding save in respect of any confidentiality provisions and any exclusivity provisions (where the vendor agrees not to negotiate with anyone else for a limited period).

## 5.4    Due Diligence

### 5.4.1    GENERALLY

When instructed in relation to a business acquisition, one of the first items which needs to be attended to by a purchaser, is the carrying out of a number of investigations on the assets or company being acquired, usually referred to as due diligence. This should usually include some or all of the following:

(a)    accounting due diligence;

(b)    general legal due diligence;

(c)    Companies Registration Office/statutory books review;

(d)    investigation of title;

(e)    actuarial due diligence;

(f)    insurance review;

(g)    environmental review;

(h)    areas specific to the target company.

The level of detail into which these investigations will go depends on the nature of the target. As a general principle, the level of investigation will be greater where the purchase price is greater, but this principle would not always apply. For example, a company acquired for €1 may have very significant liabilities and a very extensive investigation to quantify these may be appropriate. When the investigations are complete, the purchaser's advisers will sometimes compile the results in a formal due diligence report.

Due diligence is often initiated by way of a general due diligence checklist prepared by the purchaser's lawyer, for completion by the vendor and its advisers. In some cases, vendors will seek to facilitate the process by collating the relevant documentation in a Data Room, either physical (e.g. at its solicitor's office) or virtual (on a website). Sometimes, particularly if there is more than one potential purchaser, the vendor will even instruct its own advisers to complete the due diligence report, which is then shared with the purchaser. This is known as 'vendor due diligence'.

### 5.4.2    ACCOUNTING DUE DILIGENCE

It is important that every acquisition of a target company be the subject of some form of accounting review. This is usually carried out by a financial adviser to the purchaser. In a simple case, this may involve reviewing the last few sets of audited accounts and reviewing projections for a future period. In a more complex situation, a very detailed accountants' report would be prepared pointing out any accounting deficiencies of the target company and very detailed work would be done on the future position. The scope of this work is largely outside the territory of the legal adviser, but it is critical that a legal adviser should advise the client to make sure that this matter is attended to as it is likely to be the most fundamental review that requires to be carried out. The accounting review should also cover the tax affairs of the target company, in particular where the target company is a member of a group, as leaving a group often crystallises tax liabilities.

## 5.4.3   GENERAL LEGAL DUE DILIGENCE

It is good practice, at an early stage in an acquisition, to look for a copy of all significant legal documentation which has been entered into by a target company. Apart from areas specifically dealt with below, this would include a review of employment contracts, distribution/agency agreements, agreements relating to trademarks, patents and other intellectual property rights, hire purchase/leasing agreements and conditions of sale. Given the increasing importance of technology and the increasing frequency with which technology companies are acquired, particular attention needs to be paid to intellectual property rights. It is critical to establish that the target company either owns or has proper licences for all of its intellectual property to avoid litigation by third parties alleging breach. Furthermore, in a company that supplies technology, there must be a full understanding of the basis on which that technology is made available to others, with particular focus on arrangements where exclusive licences have been agreed or where the licence arrangements permit the customer to sub-licence the technology or a product incorporating same.

## 5.4.4   COMPANIES REGISTRATION OFFICE/STATUTORY BOOKS REVIEW

When advising on the acquisition of a target company, the legal adviser should at an early stage conduct a Companies Registration Office search against the target company and its subsidiaries. Consideration should also be given to searching against any company with a similar name, as this may disclose potential passing-off problems or issues being raised about the name of the target company. Obviously, this is only practical where a name is somewhat unusual. It may also be appropriate to check domain names and trade mark registrations. The Companies Registration Office search gives the purchaser's solicitor useful information at an early stage such as a list of registered charges, a list of the directors as filed in the Companies Registration Office and information as to when the last annual return is made up to. This may indicate deficiencies in paper work. It is useful at an early stage also to obtain a copy of the memorandum and articles of association of the target company and its subsidiaries. This will highlight issues which may need to be dealt with in the course of the acquisition such as the waiver of pre-emption rights on share transfers. The due diligence in this regard should also cover a review of the statutory books of the target company and its subsidiaries. This is often left until the last moment, but in practice should be conducted as early as possible in the transaction, as clearly the entries in the statutory books should mirror details in the share purchase contract and in the Companies Registration Office.

### 5.4.5 INVESTIGATION OF TITLE

Where valuable lands and buildings are being acquired (either directly or within a target company), it is critical that some form of title investigation is carried out. The most usual format of investigation involves raising requisitions on title and enquiries in the same way as if the property itself is being bought and getting various documents on completion in the same way as the completion of a property transaction. A possible (but less common) alternative is to have the vendor's solicitors certify the title. A certificate of title may be the only practical way to proceed if there are a significant number of properties and there is a commercial urgency in completing the transaction. A less satisfactory alternative to investigation or certificate of title is to rely on the warranties given by the vendor as part of the share purchase agreement. This is sometimes done when the properties are comparatively insignificant in value compared to the target company as a whole or where there are a lot of properties, none of which individually is particularly material, and where the purchaser has some degree of confidence that they have been acquired and managed in a competent fashion. As in a property transaction, it is of course always advisable that a purchaser should conduct a survey of the property. A purchaser should always be advised that this is an appropriate course of action. It is a commercial decision for a purchaser to then weigh up the cost of the survey as against the benefits.

### 5.4.6 ACTUARIAL DUE DILIGENCE

If a target company has set up a pension scheme, it is important that some form of investigation (usually known as an actuarial investigation) be carried out into the pension scheme. This will specifically focus on whether the assets of the pension scheme are sufficient to meet its liabilities. If it is found that a pension scheme is inadequately funded, there is often an adjustment in the purchase consideration to reflect this. There are two different types of schemes: defined benefit schemes (where the members are promised a definitive amount based on their salary when they retire, e.g. one-half of final salary) and defined contribution schemes (where the members receive whatever their aggregate contributions will buy at the time of retirement). Defined benefit schemes are usually more problematic and generally require more thorough investigation than defined contribution schemes, but both would need to be reviewed by specialists in the area. The review should also encompass any promises that have been made to employees in relation to their pension. A recent trend has been for nearly all new schemes to be defined contribution schemes and for some existing defined benefit schemes to be converted into defined contribution schemes. The mechanics of such a conversion (including whether beneficiary consent is required) can be very complex and it is an area to be focussed on during the actuarial due diligence review.

### 5.4.7 INSURANCE REVIEW

The purchaser should review the insurances put in place by a target company because if the purchaser completes the purchase, and the insurance turns out to be inadequate, it is the purchaser who will suffer the loss. This task is usually carried out by handing over a schedule of insurance policies to the purchaser's insurance brokers. The review needs to cover property and public liability insurance, employers' liability, product liability and directors' and officers' insurance.

### 5.4.8 ENVIRONMENTAL REVIEW

Given the increasing legislative importance that is being placed on care of the environment, it may be important, particularly with a target company which has a significant environmental impact, that an environmental assessment be carried out. This may involve a thorough review (similar to a survey) carried out by appropriately qualified personnel. The focus would be on whether the target company causes air, water, noise or other pollution, how waste products are disposed of and compliance with any existing licences which the company has. Particular attention may need to be paid as to whether the land on which the company operates has been historically contaminated as this may give rise to problems in the future which could be expensive to remedy. While not specifically an environmental area, thought should also be given to issues concerning the safety of employees as the internal environment may give rise to as many problems as the external environment.

### 5.4.9 OTHER ISSUES

While the above headings enumerate the principal issues which need to be looked at as a part of due diligence, thought should always be given to the particular circumstances of the target company. Depending on the business the target company is engaged upon, there may be further issues that require consideration. For example, if a company is heavily involved in the processing of data, compliance with the data protection legislation becomes enormously relevant; if a company is involved in mineral exploration, compliance with appropriate legislation and with mining licences is critical. The purchaser should be readily able to identify the areas that are likely to require focus, based on the specifics of the target company.

## 5.5 Pre-conditions to a Purchase Agreement

### 5.5.1 GENERALLY

In a number of cases where the commercial details of a purchase agreement are agreed, it is not possible for the parties to proceed immediately to complete the matter because of the necessity to get the consent of one or more third parties (often a State entity). The device which is used in these circumstances to enable the parties to commit to their agreement (under the heads of agreement (see above) which are generally non-binding) is the insertion in the purchase agreement of a number of pre-conditions. This enables the parties to sign and therefore be bound by their agreement subject only to these appropriate pre-conditions (for example such consent being forthcoming) being satisfied.

A technical distinction should be drawn between conditions precedent to an agreement and conditions precedent to completion of the agreement. In the case of conditions precedent to an agreement, no contract exists and no contractual obligations on the parties arise if the conditions are not fulfilled. No contract is even deemed to have existed until the conditions are fulfilled. In the case of conditions precedent to completion, a contract exists but the parties have the right to rescind on the terms of the contract if the pre-conditions are not fulfilled. The parties may, therefore, incur contractual obligations to each other even though the contract is never completed. The more common types of pre-conditions tend to be conditions precedent to completion.

### 5.5.2 STANDARD CONDITIONS PRECEDENT

The most common issues giving rise to conditions precedent are the need to obtain:

(a) consent of shareholders;

(b) consent of a grant authority such as Enterprise Ireland, Shannon Development, Udaras Na Gaeltachta;

(c) consent of bankers to or other parties having a contract with the target company; or

(d) clearance under the Competition Act, 2002.

These are discussed in detail below at **5.5.5**.

### 5.5.3 'NEGATIVE' CONDITIONS PRECEDENT

If conditions precedent, of the type listed above, are being inserted into a contract, there will inevitably be a time delay between signing and completion. Accordingly, consideration needs to be given to the insertion of other conditions precedent, which broadly consist of events which should not occur during the period while the substantive condition is being fulfilled. Examples of the types of 'negative' conditions that would be included would be a condition that no substantial damage should occur to the assets of the company by reason of fire, explosion or other similar hazard and a condition to the effect that there should be no substantial breach of warranty between the date of signing and completion. Clearly, a purchaser faced with the situation where a premises has burnt down or substantial litigation against a target company has been initiated, at some stage between signing and completion, will want to be able to decide not to proceed with the contract. Therefore, the insertion of such pre-conditions will normally be required by the purchaser (although if the company carries on its trade from a number of premises, a more suitable pre-condition may be that not more than one of the premises has been damaged). Purchasers may also seek to insert conditions concerning a due diligence process, such as a condition to the effect that they should be satisfied with the due diligence process in general or certain aspects thereof. This, however, is normally resisted by the vendor as it gives the purchaser too much room to decide not to proceed with the contract.

## 5.5.4    END DATE

If a contract contains pre-conditions, there is a possibility that third parties who have to give the relevant consents/approvals may take some considerable length of time to do so, or indeed may never do so. It is also possible that by the time they get around to issuing their approval or consent, circumstances will have radically changed. It is, therefore, common practice to include a latest date by which all of the conditions are to be satisfied (which may normally be extended by agreement). This means that either of the parties is free not to proceed with the contract if the pre-conditions are not satisfied within a reasonable time period. While there is no set practice for the length of time involved, normally a reasonable estimate as to how long it is going to take to fulfil the conditions will be made and a period of approximately one month added to this to allow for slippage.

## 5.5.5    SUBSTANTIVE CONDITIONS PRECEDENT

### 5.5.5.1    Competition Act, 2002

The Competition Act, 2002 consolidated the competition legal framework by repealing existing legislation and replacing it with the new Act. In doing so, jurisdiction over mergers control (both investigations and decision making) was largely transferred from the Minister for Enterprise, Trade and Employment to the Competition Authority.

The transaction may require prior clearance from the Competition Authority before it can be completed. This is an important consideration as it can affect the timetable for completion. In addition, if the transaction raises serious competition issues, there may be a risk that the Authority will prohibit the transaction or clear it only subject to conditions (e.g. requiring the purchaser to divest of a competing business). This issue is considered in detail in **chapter 6** on Irish Merger Control.

### 5.5.5.2 Consent of grant authority

Many Irish companies, particularly those in the manufacturing sector, will have received grant assistance from grant authorities. The most usual grant authorities encountered are Enterprise Ireland, Shannon Development (which administers grants in the midwest region) and Udaras Na Gaeltachta (which administers grants in Irish-speaking areas). The grant agreements used by these bodies typically provide that the controlling interest in a grant-aided target company will not change hands without the grant authority's consent or else the grant will be recalled. Therefore, it is necessary on a share purchase to get a prior written consent from the authority involved. This is a fairly simple procedure which involves liaising with the authority concerned, usually by the target company or the vendor. However, it is prudent to make an application for this as early as possible in the acquisition process, as the matter may require formal board approval of the grant authority and this may take several weeks.

### 5.5.5.3 Banking consent

If the target company has banking facilities, it is quite possible that the bank may have provided, in its banking facilities, that its consent is required to a change of control and if it is not obtained that this amounts to an event of default. It is important in these circumstances that bank consent is obtained as, even if the bank is aware of the situation, it is unsatisfactory to create technical defaults. The purchaser should make enquiries into this matter at an early stage in the transaction. Obviously, if a search as part of the due diligence process indicates there is a charge registered by a bank against the target company, an enquiry should immediately be made as to whether bank consent is required.

In a way similar to banks, other persons who contracted with the target company may impose a condition which allows that party to take certain action if control of the company changes. For this reason, it is prudent to establish that none of the important contracts to which the company is a party, is subject to such a change of control clause. This is often done by way of warranties, which will then be disclosed against (see below at **5.7**). Again if there is such a change of control clause, the necessary consent should be obtained and this may be included in a pre-condition to the contract.

### 5.5.5.4 Consent of shareholders

In some cases, the consents of the shareholders of the vendor and/or the purchaser will be required. This in particular arises:

(a) in large transactions for publicly quoted companies as required by the Stock Exchange rules; and

(b) where the purchaser or the vendor is a director or connected with a director, in which event it may be required by the Companies Act, 1990, s 29 or by Stock Exchange rules.

## 5.6 Warranties

### 5.6.1 GENERALLY

Warranties are statements by a vendor concerning the company or assets it is selling. By far the most substantive part of a typical purchase agreement is the section, usually contained in the main body of the agreement, providing for the giving of warranties by the vendors and accompanied by a schedule to the agreement setting out a very detailed list of warranties. For example, in the Dublin Solicitors Bar Association specimen share purchase agreement (2003 edition) the substantive agreement at clauses 6 and 7 includes provisions relating to warranties and this is accompanied by a schedule extending to over thirty pages. The warranties tend to be the aspect of the agreement which gives rise to the most discussion between the parties and accordingly they should be regarded as being of great significance.

### 5.6.2 WHY SHOULD A PURCHASER SEEK WARRANTIES?

If a purchaser purchases a target company or target assets without the benefit of a purchase agreement containing warranties, the principle of *caveat emptor* applies. Thus, for example, if it emerges after completion that a target company is subject to a substantial undisclosed litigation claim which arose before the transaction was concluded, the purchaser has no recourse to the vendor. It is accordingly commonplace, in most purchase transactions, that the purchaser will seek fairly extensive statements in relation to the target, the substantive effect of which is a series of promises to the effect that the target is virtually perfect. Exceptional situations do arise where, as a matter of contractual negotiations, no warranties are given. In particular, this can arise in:

(a) situations where one shareholder in a target company is buying the shares of other shareholders;

(b) management buyouts (because management already has sufficient knowledge of the company's affairs);

(c) share purchases for very nominal consideration (although in these instances, the purchaser ought to be conscious of the possibility that there could be very substantial liabilities); and

(d) an acquisition of a listed or quoted company where, because of the large number of shareholders in the target, it is impractical to get warranties.

It is sometimes argued by vendors that, where a very extensive due diligence process has been carried out, warranties should not be given or should be significantly watered down. This is usually resisted by a purchaser, as no matter how extensive the due diligence process is, it is no substitute for warranties from those people who know the target best.

### 5.6.3    WHO SHOULD GIVE THE WARRANTIES?

In most situations, the vendor or, if there are more than one, all of the vendors will give the warranties. However, care should be taken to ensure that the warranties are not being given by a 'man of straw' as no matter how technically perfect the warranties are, they are of no benefit if they are not given by someone with sufficient means to satisfy a warranty claim.

Particular care should be taken when acquiring from a vendor which is a member of a group of companies. Ideally in these circumstances, the most appropriate warrantor may be the holding company within the group, although it may be prudent to get warranties from the vendor company and perhaps other group companies with substantial assets.

If there is more than one vendor, the purchaser will normally seek to have warranties given on a joint and several basis. This means that the purchaser may make his warranty claim against every vendor and may choose to enforce against any (or all) of them. Conversely, vendors will sometimes seek to have liability established on a several basis only, which means that each particular vendor is liable only for a proportion of a claim. This is unsatisfactory from a purchaser's viewpoint, as it may mean that the purchaser may only recover part of their claim, in the event that some of the warrantors turn out to be difficult to locate or of inadequate means.

While this chapter is primarily concerned with purchase agreements, warranties may also arise in the context of a subscription for new shares. In such circumstances, the warranties are often given by the company whose shares are being subscribed for. It would clearly be inappropriate to do this in a share purchase as the purchaser will end up owning the vehicle giving the warranties. In the case of a subscription, the person investing in the company may well accept this after negotiation, but they should, however, at least look for warranties from other shareholders as well.

### 5.6.4    MEASURE OF DAMAGES

The measure of damages which may be obtained, should there be a breach of warranty in relation to a target company, is a matter which gives rise to much debate. The prevailing view is that a court is required to look at the market value of the shares held in the target company by the purchaser, in the light of what has happened in breach of warranty, and compare this with what their market value would have been had the position been as it was warranted. This is quite a difficult exercise and, from the point of view of the purchaser, the damages recovered will not necessarily be enough to put the target company in the position that it would have been in, had the breach of warranty not taken place. In some instances, to cover this point, the purchaser may seek a provision that the measure of damages should be sufficient to effect restitution—however, this would usually be resisted by vendors as effectively amounting to an indemnity.

### 5.6.5 SUBJECT MATTER OF WARRANTIES SOUGHT

The subject matter of warranties is discussed in greater detail below at **5.6.8–5.6.12**. In relation to a target company, the subject matter will usually cover every conceivable aspect of the target company's affairs, ranging from its accounts and its taxation affairs to matters relating to its employees, its assets and debtors and any litigation against the company. A considerable number of warranties have the function of eliciting detailed information in relation to the target company through the Disclosure Letter (discussed at **5.7** below), rather than seeking to represent that there are no issues which may result in substantial liability.

### 5.6.6 PREPARATION FOR POTENTIAL WARRANTY CLAIM

If a purchaser has some concern that warranty claims may arise, there are a number of possible further steps that should be taken. One possibility is for the purchaser to seek to retain a portion of the purchase price which is only to be paid over in the future if no warranty claims have been asserted by a certain point in time. This is sometimes referred to as 'retention for warranties'. It may also be possible to get insurance cover against warranty claims (although this is rare). This is normally something which is obtained by a vendor and involves giving a copy of the agreement and the underlying disclosure letter to the insurer who is then in a position to assess the premium payable for taking the risk.

### 5.6.7 LIMITS ON WARRANTIES

If a vendor or vendors give warranties, he or they are potentially exposed to risk of being sued for breach of warranty for as long as the Statute of Limitations, 1957 permits. In addition, they could be exposed to a claim for an amount greater than they received for the target company or they could be subjected to trivial claims being asserted by a purchaser, usually for ulterior motives. For this reason, it is usual for a vendor to seek to negotiate limits on warranties. Typical variations which a vendor will seek are set out below.

(a) A vendor may seek a provision that any warranty claim must be notified in writing to the vendor by the purchaser within an agreed time scale. It is common practice in this area to distinguish between claims relating to tax and other claims. In the case of tax claims, the time limit agreed is usually somewhere between three and seven years. Section 17 of the Finance Act, 2003 limits the Revenue Commissioners' entitlement to seek arrears for four years from the relevant period of account. In the case of non-tax claims, a vendor will usually seek a shorter period of liability and in this instance periods in the order of one year to three years are common. From a purchaser's point of view, it is often considered that two separate audits which are finished after completion should be sufficient to bring to light any warranty claims and in negotiating a limiting period, a purchaser may therefore seek sufficient time to complete two full audits post completion.

(b) A vendor will usually seek to cap the aggregate liability which may arise on foot of the warranties. Quite frequently, the cap is the purchase consideration. The purchaser should, however, always be advised that in extreme circumstances their loss may be considerably greater than the purchase price and they will obviously lose the benefit of an alternative use to which they could have put the money. Care should also be taken by purchasers when the purchase price is relatively low. If there are provisions for increasing or varying the consideration, this should be considered when agreeing any limit.

(c) The vendor will usually seek to negotiate a minimum threshold for claims to exceed before they may be brought. This is often known as a 'de minimus' provision and the level will vary from transaction to transaction. A vendor will sometimes seek to have this amount constitute an excess, so that if a claim arises this amount will be a matter for the purchaser. This is not normally acceptable to a purchaser. The vendors will also sometimes seek to rule out any individual claim which falls below a certain amount. From a purchaser's point of view, this practice is dubious as it is possible that there could be a very large number of very small claims which, in the aggregate, would have a significant financial effect.

(d) Where there is more than one vendor, the vendors may seek to apportion liability on a several basis. This is discussed at **5.6.3** above.

(e) The vendor may seek to avoid responsibility for claims which arise due to a change in the law after completion. This is normally acceptable.

(f) The vendor may seek to be relieved of liability if the warranty claim arises as the result of any action by the purchaser after completion. The purchaser will often resist this and try and confine it, if agreed, to actions outside the normal course of business.

(g) The vendor will try and exclude matters which are covered by a provision or reserve in the company's accounts. To the extent that something is specifically provided for or reserved, this should be acceptable.

(h) The vendor will try and exempt liability for anything which is covered by a policy of insurance maintained by the company; again this is normally acceptable, although the insurance premium may increase as a result of the insurance claims being made.

(i) A vendor will sometimes seek to reduce its level of exposure in a warranty, by giving the warranty 'to the best of their knowledge, information and belief' or 'so far as the vendor is aware'. The qualification of warranties by these words is often the subject of considerable debate in the context of a purchase transaction but is generally resisted by a purchaser except for fairly trivial warranties.

(j)    The limits are often expressly disapplied in case of fraud or wilful concealment by the vendor.

If the English decision of *Eurocopy plc v Teesdale* [1992] BCLC 1067, is followed by the Irish courts, a purchaser may not have a remedy for a breach of warranty, if it knew of the circumstances giving rise to the breach before it signed the share purchase agreement. The further English decision of *Infiniteland Ltd and John Stewart Aviss v Artisan Contracting Ltd* [2005] EWCA Civ 758 suggests that courts may adopt different approaches to actual knowledge, constructive knowledge and imputed knowledge that a purchaser may possess.

## 5.6.8    FINANCIAL MATTERS

Warranties which may be sought on financial matters related to a target company include those set out below.

(a)    A warranty that the latest set of audited accounts comply with all applicable laws and with generally accepted accounting principles ('GAAP') and that they give a true and fair view of the assets and liabilities and financial position of the target company may be sought. This is commonly regarded as the most essential warranty obtained on any share purchase, and if this warranty is obtained, it may well give coverage against the bulk of claims which are likely to arise even in the absence of any other warranties. If a company has a trading record, it is important to focus on whether accounts are consistent with previous accounting periods and if not, why not.

(b)    It is usual to seek some comfort that apart from transactions in the ordinary course of business, there have been no material changes since the date to which the last audited accounts have been made up. This is a particularly important matter to cover if the last audited accounts are relatively old. In addition, if the last audited accounts are quite old, the vendor may be asked to warrant management accounts.

(c)    Extensive provision is usually made in warranties to deal with taxation. These warranties principally focus on whether the company has paid all of its tax which has become due prior to the date of completion. They also focus on whether the company is registered for all taxes for which it is liable and whether it has made returns on time. The warranties frequently focus on points of detail within the tax code, for example, whether the company has claimed roll-over relief under the capital gains legislation and whether it has ever incurred balancing charges. For trading companies with employees, the warranties should focus very clearly on VAT, PAYE and PRSI, as non-payment of these taxes may, quite quickly, give rise to very substantial financial liability.

(d)    Warranties are usually given as to the borrowing facilities available to the company, whether these are guaranteed or otherwise secured by the vendor, and the level of borrowing which has been incurred up to completion.

(e) It is not unusual to seek a warranty to the effect that the net assets of the company are not less than a stated figure. If such a warranty is given at completion of the transaction, it acts as an assurance that there have not been any major negative changes since the end of the last audited accounting period.

## 5.6.9    CONSTITUTION OF TARGET COMPANY

Warranties relating to the constitution of a target company include warranties:

(a) that the memorandum and articles of the target company are as supplied;

(b) as to the identity of directors and secretary;

(c) as to filing and returns to the Companies Registration Office;

(d) as to who owns the share capital;

(e) that proper records including statutory books are being kept by the company;

(f) that no petition has been presented to wind up the company;

(g) as to dividend payments; and

(h) as to whether there have been any breaches of the Companies Acts, 1963–2006, particularly investigations under Part II of the Companies Act, 1990 or the Company Law Enforcement Act, 2001 and disclosure issues under Part IV of the Companies Act, 1990.

## 5.6.10    ASSETS OF TARGET COMPANY

The various warranties described below focus on matters relating to assets:

(a) Warranties are frequently sought as to the ownership of intellectual property (e.g. trademarks, patents and copyrights) used by a target company. In a target company which is substantially dependent upon intellectual property, material issues to consider include whether it has the right to use all the intellectual property which it is using. If the target company is selling a product which incorporates intellectual property, it is important to ensure that the target company's right to use the intellectual property covers the right to incorporate that intellectual property in the product sold. It is also important to ascertain that such a company has not given any exclusive licence to one party, which would preclude the company from providing the product to other parties.

(b)   The warranties will focus on whether a target company is party to any unusual agreements such as long-term contracts or guarantees.

(c)   The warranties will focus on whether a target company owns all of its assets and whether they are subject to lease, hire purchase etc.

(d)   Warranties will often focus on the state of the assets and whether they are in good repair or are likely to require replacement. These warranties are often resisted by a vendor who might require purchasers to take their own view on assets.

(e)   A warranty is usually sought that stock in trade is in good condition and, somewhat more controversially, that stocks are not excessive or slow moving or obsolete.

(f)   A warranty is frequently sought that the book debts of a target company will be collected in the normal course and within a set time period after completion. This is frequently the subject of debate between vendor and purchaser, as the vendor will not want to guarantee their collectability.

(g)   It is not unusual that extensive warranties would be given in relation to the properties occupied by a target company. This would normally focus on the target company having good and marketable title to the property and any encumbrances which may exist. The warranties would also cover the planning on the property and any notices which have been served affecting the property.

(h)   There is usually a warranty as to whether the assets include amounts owed to a target company by the vendor or its associates. These will usually be collected at completion.

(i)   A warranty is usually sought that a target company has all the licences it needs to carry on its business.

(j)   A warranty will be sought as to distribution and agency agreements to which a target company is party.

(k)   Warranties are usually sought as to the insurance held by a target company. This is frequently disclosed against by producing all of the insurance policies and requiring the purchaser to take its own view as to the appropriateness of same.

## 5.6.11   LIABILITIES OF TARGET COMPANY

Warranties will also address liabilities of a target company. Examples are set out below:

(a)   A warranty will usually focus on any litigation to which the target company may be subject. Issues addressed include:

(i)   whether there is any litigation in which the target company is involved or litigation which is contemplated;

     (ii)   whether the target company has been in breach of any environmental law, in particular those relating to air pollution, water pollution, noise and waste; and

     (iii)  whether it has sold defective products.

(b)    There is usually a warranty to the effect that the target company has complied with its statutory obligations generally without any specific statute being averted to.

(c)    There is usually a warranty seeking to establish whether the target company has any grants. If this is the case, there may be a liability to repay if there is default (e.g. a change of control).

(d)    There is sometimes a warranty focusing on whether customers or suppliers have indicated that they are going to cease dealing with the target company or are winding down their level of dealing.

(e)    There is usually a warranty seeking to ascertain whether the target company owes any money to the vendors or persons associated with them. If there is a disclosure against this, the money is often discharged at completion.

## 5.6.12   EMPLOYEE-RELATED MATTERS

This section of the warranties usually focuses on the status of employees. This would include a warranty:

(a)    containing a list of employees and details of their benefits, including salary;

(b)    that no one is entitled to a significant period of notice;

(c)    that there are no liabilities or claims pending for unfair dismissal or redundancy;

(d)    that there are no trade disputes;

(e)    that all employee safety legislation has been complied with; and

(f)    that there are pension schemes in place for employees and that they are properly funded.

## 5.6.13   OTHER ISSUES

There is usually concern on the part of the purchaser that, notwithstanding the details of all of the specific warranties set out above, there are issues which they ought to be aware of as a purchaser. For this reason, it is not unusual to find a warranty to the effect that the vendor has disclosed to the purchaser any matter which would render any information otherwise given as untrue or misleading, or any matter which ought to be disclosed to an intending purchaser of shares in the company. The inclusion of this type of warranty is sometimes resisted by the vendor. This type of warranty may be useful if there are personal circumstances connected with the vendor or senior officers of the vendor or the target company which cause difficulty at a subsequent stage.

## 5.6.14 CONCLUSION

The warranties which are typically given vary to some extent from transaction to transaction. While most legal advisers to a purchaser tend to have their own typical list of warranties, thought should always be given to whether additional warranties are needed in the context of the transaction. For example, if a target company's assets largely consist of intellectual property, it may be prudent to expand the intellectual property warranties over and above those which appear in a standard type of list of 'off the shelf' warranties. If a target company has substantial involvement with data, it may be appropriate to look carefully at legislation such as the Data Protection Acts, 1988 and 2003 and draft specific warranties to ensure compliance.

# 5.7 Disclosure Letter

In every share purchase transaction where there are warranties, the net effect of those warranties is to state that the company is 'perfect'. Clearly no company will reach the state of perfection required by warranties and the vendor is therefore given an opportunity to set out, clearly in a letter, where the company deviates from 'perfection'. This is known as the disclosure letter. This is an extremely important document from the vendor's point of view and must be prepared with enormous care. The preparation of the letter involves the vendor being brought through each of the warranties and being asked whether there are any matters associated with the target company which would be a deviation from those warranties. Specialist areas such as tax warranties and pension warranties are usually referred to the target company's tax and pension advisers for their comment.

While this list can only be regarded as being indicative, typical disclosures would include:

(a)   banking facilities available;

(b)   Companies Registration Office filings not being up to date;

(c)   litigation by or against the company;

(d)   details of all of the company insurance policies;

(e)   disputes concerning employees;

(f)    assets which are leased by the company;

(g)    details of the company's pension affairs;

(h)    issues with title to property;

(i)    non-compliance with legal obligations;

(j)    arrears of taxation or past occasions when taxation was discharged late; and

(k)    areas where there might be a doubt as to the tax payable.

It is normal that the disclosure letter be prefaced by a number of general disclosures. These may be quite contentious (as between vendor and purchaser) as some standard general disclosure may be construed as putting the purchaser on notice of matters that he could ascertain by inspection. Therefore, disclosures of Companies Registration Office records and statutory registers which are actually given to a purchaser would be regarded as acceptable. However, a disclosure of everything which might be ascertained by inspecting the premises and records of the target company is normally regarded as inappropriate as this, would put a purchaser on notice of everything that might be in the company's filing cabinets or anything that might be found out about the property as a result of a survey.

The disclosure letter is usually written by the vendor to the purchaser. It is occasionally written on behalf of the respective clients by the firms of lawyers involved, in which event it should be clearly stated by the vendor's lawyers that it is based on instructions from their client and that they themselves disclaim the contents.

## 5.8    Consideration Payable under Share Purchase Agreement

### 5.8.1    GENERALLY

There are a number of ways in which the consideration payable under a share purchase agreement may be discharged. The principal methods of consideration are as follows:

(a)    cash;

(b)    allotment of shares in the purchaser company;

(c)    discharge of loan;

(d)    payment of dividend by target company; and

(e)    loan notes.

## 5.8.2    PAYMENT IN CASH

Payment in cash is the simplest and most common form of consideration and it applies in most transactions.

## 5.8.3    ALLOTMENT OF SHARES IN PURCHASER

Allotment of shares in the purchaser company is somewhat unusual but it arises in a few cases. It most often arises where the purchaser is a public limited company, particularly one which has a listing or quotation for its shares. It is settled law that a company must not issue its shares at a discount. However, historically this has not created any particular problem where a purchaser was issuing shares because, except in the most extreme of circumstances, shares in the target company would represent sufficient consideration to pay up the shares being allotted. However, the Companies (Amendment) Act, 1983 introduced an important qualification to this principle which is particularly important for the vendor to appreciate. Section 30 of that Act severely regulates the circumstances in which a public limited company may allot shares paid up otherwise than in cash. Subject to an exception, which is dealt with below, a public limited company may not generally allot shares without a valuation of the consideration for those shares from a person qualified to be the auditor of the company. A valuation report must be made to the company during the six months immediately preceding the allotment of the shares and a copy of that report must be sent to the proposed allottee. If the allottee does not receive a report or, to the knowledge of the allottee, there is some other contravention, the allottee is liable to pay the company the nominal value of the shares together with any premium and interest at 5 per cent per annum. This is quite a draconian sanction. If, for instance, a vendor was allotted shares in the purchaser company deemed to be worth €1 million (including premium) at the time of an acquisition, the vendor could find itself liable to the purchaser for the sum of €1 million plus interest. Thus it is extremely important to comply with s 30 of the Companies (Amendment) Act, 1983.

An important exception to the provision is contained in s 30(2). This provides that, the procedure does not apply where there is an arrangement providing for the allotment of shares in a company, on terms that the whole or part of the consideration for the shares allotted is to be provided by the transfer to that company of all or some of the shares of a particular class in another company. However, the arrangement to take newly allotted shares must be available to all the holders of the shares in the target company. Thus, if a purchaser is acquiring the shares in a target company from six vendors and the arrangement to take shares is available only to one of them, the exception would not apply. Given the draconian nature of the provision, it is critical that the vendor satisfies itself that the exception applies. In case of any doubt, it is recommended that valuation procedures be followed, although they are rather cumbersome.

The acquisition of a target company for shares in the purchaser company may be attractive because it may qualify for stamp duty and capital duty relief under the Stamp Duties Consolidation Act, 1999, ss 80 and 119 respectively. It may also qualify for roll-over capital gains tax relief.

### 5.8.4    DISCHARGE OF LOAN

It is often the case that a target company owes money to the vendors or to persons associated with the vendors. It is usually a good idea to obtain a warranty that there are no such sums outstanding, or a warranty which results in the disclosure of the amounts outstanding and the arrangements for repayment. This is a matter which should always be looked at. Clearly if a target company owes money to the vendors post the transaction, there should be a clear-cut basis on which this is to be repaid.

### 5.8.5    DIVIDEND

If the target company is entitled to pay dividends (and in this regard, the technical provisions of the Companies (Amendment) Act, 1983, Part IV need to be carefully considered), there may be scope to discharge part of the consideration by paying dividends from the target company rather than the purchaser paying consideration. The attractiveness of this route has been much reduced with various tax changes surrounding dividends, but it may be still be appropriate in particular circumstances.

### 5.8.6    LOAN NOTES

A possible method of paying consideration, otherwise than by cash, is by way of loan notes. Recent tax changes, which have denied capital gains tax roll-over relief for such transactions, have made this method less attractive than in the past. The vendors need to focus on whether the loan notes are secured or unsecured and whether they are guaranteed by a relatively financially stable third party such as a bank.

### 5.8.7    OTHER RELEVANT FACTORS RELATING TO THE CONSIDERATION

#### 5.8.7.1    Deferred consideration

A device which is commonly used in share purchase transactions is to defer the payment of part of the consideration. Frequently, the amount which is deferred is uncertain and is computed by reference to future events, most notably the financial performance of the target company (called an 'earn-out'). If a vendor agrees to payment of deferred consideration, which is dependent upon the financial performance of the target company, considerable thought needs to be given to controls placed on the purchaser in relation to the target company's behaviour during the period, by reference to which the deferred consideration is computed. The vendor would want to ensure that profits are calculated on a basis consistent with past practice. The vendor is also likely to insist on a right to have an independent review of the basis on which the calculation is made and a right to appeal to a third party, in the event that they are dissatisfied with the results as produced by the purchaser's auditors. Deferred consideration is also somewhat unsatisfactory from the point of view of the vendor, in that it may seem convenient to the purchaser to withhold payment of deferred consideration if there is any issue of warranty claims arising. For this reason, there are sometimes extensive negotiations if the vendor looks for a specific assurance from the purchaser in the agreement, that payment will not be withheld on account of pending warranty claims. As a further comfort to vendors, deferred consideration is sometimes paid on completion into an escrow account under the joint control of the purchaser and the vendor (or their respective advisers) and subject to strict rules concerning withdrawals.

### 5.8.7.2    Form CG50A

Section 980 of the Taxes Consolidation Act, 1997 contains provisions intended to stop the avoidance of capital gains tax on the disposal of land in Ireland and on the disposal of certain other assets. If land in Ireland is being disposed of, it is necessary for the purchaser to either get a clearance (known as a Form CG50A) of the vendor from capital gains tax or, alternatively, to withhold 15 per cent of the purchase price at source.

Clearly, it would be easy to avoid this particular provision by putting land into a company and then selling the shares in the company. The Revenue has, therefore, extended this principle to shares in a company, the value of, or the greater part of whose value is, derived from land situated in Ireland and also from certain other assets, most notably mineral and exploration rights. The Revenue Commissioners have a fairly liberal interpretation of what constitutes 'deriving the greater part of the value of shares in a company from land'. It is therefore necessary to look very closely at the target company's accounts to determine whether this requirement applies. If in doubt, the purchaser should insist on a CG50A certificate. In practice, any target company which owns substantial lands is one to which the provision may apply and it is usually prudent to seek a CG50A clearance. This should be obtained by the vendor. It is usually dealt with fairly quickly by means of an application, in the appropriate form, to the inspector of taxes who deals with the vendor's affairs (although complications arise with foreign vendors).

If a transaction is completed in which a Form CG50A ought to have been obtained and was not, the purchaser may subsequently be called upon by the Revenue to pay over 15 per cent of the sale proceeds to the Revenue Commissioners. It is therefore a serious problem for a purchaser not to obtain such a certificate when one is required. As a result of an anti-avoidance measure introduced in 1995, it is also necessary to get this clearance even where something other than cash is paid for land. This procedure does not apply to small transactions, with the current threshold being fixed at €500,000 (by the Finance Act, 2002).

### 5.8.7.3    Companies Act 1963, s 60

Section 60 of the Companies Act, 1963 prohibits a target company from giving financial assistance in connection with the purchase of, or subscription for, its own shares. This does not give rise to any particular problem where a purchaser is proposing to fund a purchase entirely from within its own resources. However, if the purchaser intends in some way to use the financial resources of the target company to fund the purchase, the provisions of s 60 will require consideration. Section 60 renders it unlawful for a company to give, whether directly or indirectly, and whether by means of a loan, guarantee, the provision of security or otherwise, any financial assistance for the purpose of, or in connection, with a purchase or subscription made, or to be made, by any person of, or for, any shares in the company.

The section most commonly arises in practice where the purchaser is taking a bank loan to fund the purchase and the bank proposes to secure the facilities, not only on the purchaser and its assets, but also on the assets of the target company or companies. The security being given by the target company or companies would constitute financial assistance and is unlawful unless the procedure for derogating from s 60 is carried out. In general terms, this procedure involves the swearing of a statutory declaration as to solvency by the directors and the passing of a special resolution permitting the financial assistance by the members. If s 60 is an issue, it should be flagged early in the transaction as the derogation procedure will require cooperation from the vendor. The derogation procedure is not available to public limited companies or companies with a restricted director on their Board.

It was noted above that consideration may include the payment of dividends or the discharge of indebtedness to the vendor. Neither of these is caught by s 60, as s 60(12) specifically allows for the payment of a dividend properly declared by a company or the discharge of a liability lawfully incurred by the company.

It is critical for the vendor to satisfy itself that s 60 is not breached, as any transaction in breach of the section is voidable by the company as against a person who had notice of the facts which constitute the breach. It is extremely likely that the vendor would have notice of such facts and would be so caught.

Section 60 is dealt with in more detail in **chapter 12** on Commercial Lending.

## 5.9    Restrictive Covenants

A share purchase agreement usually includes a clause restricting the vendors from competing with the company. The validity or otherwise of this is governed by s 4(1) of the Competition Act, 2002. The former notification procedure whereby parties could seek advance clearance from the Competition Authority (or instead rely on previous relevant decisions of the Authority) is no longer operative. Parties must now take a view as to whether the restrictions are prohibited by s 4(1) (bearing in mind the civil and criminal consequences of infringement). Guidance on the extent of the restrictions which a purchaser can impose upon vendors could formerly be found in s 6 of the Competition Authority Notice, Decision No N/02/001 'Notice in Respect of Agreements Involving a Merger and/or Sale of Business'. This has since expired and not been replaced by the Competition Authority, although further guidance from the European Commission is contained in Commission Notice on restrictions directly related and necessary to concentrations (OJ C56 of 5 March 2005 (p. 24)). As a general principle the Competition Authority holds the view that where the agreement involves the sale of the goodwill of the business such restrictions are not in breach of the Competition Act and should therefore be enforceable. This is provided that the restrictions are limited in terms of duration, geographical coverage and subject matter, to what is necessary to secure the adequate transfer of goodwill. This topic is discussed at **chapter 6**.

## 5.10 Signing and Completion of Share Purchase Agreements

### 5.10.1 INTRODUCTION

One of the common practical difficulties with share purchase agreements is the concept of the signing of a share purchase agreement and the concept of completion of such an agreement. While the distinction may be difficult to grasp, from a lawyer's point of view it is similar to the concept, which arises in a property transaction, where a contract is signed on one day and some time later there is a completion. However, in many share purchase transactions, and particularly where no pre-conditions are involved, the signing will take place contemporaneously with completion.

### 5.10.2 SIGNING

The central feature of signing for a share purchase agreement is that a document has been agreed that contains all of the relevant commercial details. This would cover not only the share purchase agreement, but also ancillary documents such as the disclosure letter, a deed of indemnity and documents dealing with other issues such as distribution agreements, employment agreements etc. Usually at the time of signing, the share purchase agreement and the disclosure letter are signed by the parties. It is common practice that documents, such as a deed of indemnity and the ancillary documents mentioned above, would be in agreed form at the time of signing but would not in fact be signed until completion takes place.

### 5.10.3 COMPLETION

If completion of a transaction is to be delayed for some time, there are a number of matters with which the purchaser and, to a lesser extent, the vendor must concern themselves. These matters are considered below.

#### 5.10.3.1 Completion date

A firm completion date must be set or, alternatively, a date by which completion must take place. If this is not met, it is usually provided that either party may walk away from the transaction. This is important, for the reasons outlined in more detail under pre-conditions at **5.5.4** above, as the parties would not want to be bound to a course of action for an indefinite time while waiting for pre-conditions to be fulfilled.

#### 5.10.3.2 Business between signing and completion

If there is to be a gap between signing and completion, it is critical, from the purchaser's point of view, that between signing and completion the company operates strictly in the ordinary course of business. Consequently, the purchaser will usually seek to insert a clause insisting that it must agree any course of action other than trading in the normal course of business. These clauses would usually restrict the target company from issuing new shares, paying dividends, making acquisitions or disposals, hiring and firing an employee, granting mortgages, incurring significant capital expenditure and entering a number of other unusual types of transactions. The inclusion of such a provision is important from the point of view of a purchaser because, if the owners of the target company were free to take all manner of actions between signing and completion, the purchaser may find that the target company (and its financial position) had radically changed over a short period of time.

#### 5.10.3.3 Repetition of warranties

If there is a gap between signing and completion, it is critical from the purchaser's point of view that the warranties should be repeated at completion. If the vendor accepts this, the vendor is likely to want the ability to add extra disclosure items to the disclosure letter because issues, could arise between signing and completion which would have been included in the disclosure letter had they arisen before signing. If this is agreed by the purchaser, it is usually on the basis that they have the right to walk away from the transaction should they not like the particular additional disclosures. This is a matter which should always be considered when there is a gap between signing and completion.

### 5.10.4 FORMALITIES OF COMPLETION

In practice, completion generally involves a meeting between the purchaser and vendor. The purchaser will arrive at a completion meeting with a cheque or bank draft for the purchase price and the vendor will arrive at the meeting with a set of papers, which are handed over to the purchaser.

The set of completion papers will vary from transaction to transaction but will include the following:

(a) share transfer forms for the shares in the target company and the appropriate share certificates (if a share certificate is lost an indemnity in place of the lost certificate will usually suffice);

(b) any necessary pre-emption waivers in relation to these transfers;

(c) if there is a group of companies involved in the target, all shares in subsidiaries which are not owned by other group companies should be covered by a share transfer form and appropriate share certificate;

(d) a copy duly executed by the vendor and the target company of ancillary documents such as the deed of indemnity and ancillary contracts;

(e) the statutory books and registers of the target company;

(f) the directors' minute book of the target company;

(g) the seal of the target company;

(h) the certificate of incorporation of the target company;

(i) title documents to any properties owned by the target company (although if these are mortgaged to a bank and the mortgage is being left in place, they may not be presented at a completion);

(j) a certificate of title in relation to properties (if this has been agreed);

(k) any letters of consent required from third parties such as grant-aiding authorities, banks, mergers consent etc. (these are discussed in more detail in relation to pre-conditions above);

(l) CG50A clearance (if this is required);

(m) a certified copy of the memorandum and articles of association of each target company;

(n) mandates that have been put in place for the target company (there may be a need to amend the mandates at completion and having a copy of the mandates enables the necessary changes to be identified and made);

(o) letters of resignation of the directors and secretary (if it is agreed that they should resign. The letters of resignation should ideally include a confirmation that they have no outstanding claims against the target company. If this is not done, there is a danger from the purchaser's point of view that a claim could be asserted by such people);

(p) repayment of loans between target company and the vendor/his associates; and

(q) any other documents that may be required depending on the circumstances.

## 5.10.5 BOARD MEETING

A second important component of the completion of a transaction, which needs to be organised by the vendor, is the holding of board meetings of each target company, duly convened in accordance with all applicable requirements. Handing over the above documents it is not sufficient to complete the transaction. Some of them must be processed and approved by the board of the target company. In particular, the following must be dealt with:

(a)  transfer forms must be approved for registration;

(b)  resignations of directors must be approved and new directors appointed;

(c)  resignation of the secretary must be approved and a new secretary appointed;

(d)  the resignation of the auditors must be noted and new auditors appointed;

(e)  changes to the bank mandates should be effected; and

(f)  if the registered office is to be changed, a resolution to this effect must be adopted.

With regard to the transfer of shares, the board of the target company should satisfy itself that it has an absolute power to register the transfers without any consent being required from any shareholder. Alternatively, if shareholders have some form of pre-emption rights on the transfer of shares, these pre-emption rights should have been properly waived. In the context of the appointment of new directors, the target company should obtain the consent of the new directors in the form of the usual Companies Office Form B10 (it is desirable but not strictly necessary to deal with this at completion).

Once the various documents required are handed over to the purchaser and the board meetings are held, the purchaser then completes the transaction by formally handing the consideration over to the vendor.

## 5.10.6 ITEMS TO BE ACTIONED POST-COMPLETION

There are a number of matters which must be attended to after completion takes place. In particular, the issues outlined below must be considered.

### 5.10.6.1 Stamping

All share transfers must be presented for stamping within thirty days of completion of the transaction. Stamp duty is levied at the rate of 1 per cent of the consideration. Where the consideration is other than for cash or the transaction is not at arm's length, it may take some considerable time for the Stamps

Adjudication Office to finalise the stamp duty. Generally, and particularly in those circumstances where stamping will take a long time, it is appropriate to include in the terms of the share purchase agreement a provision under which the vendor agrees to cooperate with the purchaser in voting the shares in whatever way the purchaser wishes. This is because it is not permissible to enter the name of the purchaser onto the register of members until stamping is completed. Thus, for example, if stamping is to take six months and an AGM of the target company takes place four months after completion, the persons strictly entitled to be represented at the AGM are the outgoing vendors. The purchaser should get sufficient powers of attorney, under the share purchase agreement, to enable itself to represent the vendor and control the votes on the shares at the AGM.

### 5.10.6.2   Companies Office returns

Various returns to the Companies Registration Office need to be made. The introduction of the Company Law Enforcement Act, 2001 signalled a greater emphasis on enforcing the various filing requirements of the Companies Acts, 1963–2006. It is not necessary to return particulars of the new shareholders to the Companies Registration Office, although this detail will in due course be included in the next annual return. However, if there are changes concerning company officers or the company's, registered office, then particulars of the changes should be filed within fourteen days from completion. A new bank mandate should be given to the bank as soon as possible.

### 5.10.6.3   Directors' interests

There is a requirement, under Part IV of the Companies Act, 1990, for directors and the secretary to notify the acquisition and disposal of shareholdings in a company for which they are officers. This should be done within five business days of the acquisition or disposal occurring. If the vendor is a director, or an entity controlled by a director, the target company should be notified of the disposal. If the purchaser is a director, or a party connected with a director, a notice should also be given to the target company of the acquisition of the shareholding interest. Failure to give this notice in the case of an acquisition may result in any right or interest, of any kind, in respect of the shares not being enforceable directly or indirectly by action or legal proceedings (Companies Act, 1990, s 58). It is also an offence to fail to comply with such a requirement.

### 5.10.6.4   Tax returns

The vendor may be required to file a capital gains tax return following completion.

### 5.10.6.5   Name change

If a target company is a member of a group or has a name which identifies it with the vendor, it will almost certainly be provided in the agreement that the target company must change its name. Again, this is a matter which must be actioned post completion. It is often the case that if this arises, a special resolution providing for the change of name will be adopted at the time of completion, and it is therefore a matter of processing this through the Companies Registration Office following completion.

### 5.10.6.6 Access to records

The vendor may need access to the records of the target company after completion and may seek the inclusion of such a clause in the share purchase agreement. This may be acceptable to the purchaser, but should be subject to a stringent confidentiality obligation, which only allows for disclosure of information if it is required by law.

# 5.11 Analysis of Typical Share Purchase Agreement

A typical share purchase agreement consists of the following components:

(a)  parties;

(b)  recitals;

(c)  definitions;

(d)  pre-conditions;

(e)  consideration provision;

(f)  warranties;

(g)  restrictive and other covenants;

(h)  completion;

(i)  miscellaneous provisions; and

(j)  schedules (including schedule of warranties).

## 5.11.1 PARTIES

It is standard to set out the names and addresses of the parties at the front of the document. If any of the parties are companies, it may be useful to list their registered numbers as no matter how many times a company changes its name, it can always be identified by reference to the registered number.

## 5.11.2 RECITALS

It is standard in a commercial contract, such as a share purchase agreement, to set out recitals. These broadly set out brief details of the target company, including its registered number and issued share capital, and then recite that the vendor has agreed to sell the shares and that the purchaser has agreed to purchase the shares. Recitals are useful in that they set out the broad parameters of the target company up front and give an idea as to the broad subject matter of the agreement.

### 5.11.3 DEFINITIONS

It is conventional in a share purchase agreement, as with other commercial documents that terms which are frequently used are defined for all purposes of the agreement. This section may appear in different parts of the agreement, but usually, it is found at the opening section of the agreement. However, it may appear at the end of the main body of the agreement or sometimes in a schedule. A few terms, which are frequently included in this, are worth mentioning.

(a) Definitions will normally include a definition of the 'accounts'. The purchaser will want this to cover accounts of each company involved in a group and also to include consolidated accounts for the group as a whole. This definition should also include the directors' and auditors' reports and relevant notes as these form a very important part of the accounts.

(b) Terms are sometimes defined for the purposes of restrictive covenants. It is extremely important, in this context, to clarify that the territory to which they extend and the business which is covered are commercially acceptable to the parties involved, and that they do not infringe the principles of common law and competition law applicable to restrictive covenants.

If there is to be a difference between the vendors and the people who are giving the warranties, it is conventional to insert a separate definition of the term 'warrantors'.

### 5.11.4 PRE-CONDITIONS

This section of the agreement covers the matters which are referred to in detail in 'Pre-conditions to a Purchase Agreement' at **5.5**. Specifically the section will identify:

(a) the substantive conditions precedent;

(b) relevant 'negative' conditions precedent; and

(c) an end date.

This section typically provides that the vendor and the purchaser will use their best efforts to secure the satisfaction of the pre-conditions.

### 5.11.5 CONSIDERATION PROVISION

This provision is the operative provision, which provides that the purchaser will purchase and the vendor will sell the shares in question. It is important that the provision makes it clear that they are being sold free from all encumbrances and with the benefit of all rights attaching to them, otherwise there is a possibility that the purchaser will be deemed to have acquired the shares subject to whatever encumbrances may be attached to them such as equities, options, mortgages, charges, reservation of title, etc.

This provision also sets out the consideration, which is actually payable. This is fully discussed in 'Consideration Payable under Share Purchase Agreement' at **5.8**.

### 5.11.6   WARRANTIES

It is usual to include, in a share purchase agreement, the provisions which govern the detailed terms of the warranties. Typical items, which are included in this section, are as follows:

(a)   a warranty that the parties have full power and authority to enter into and perform the share purchase agreement;

(b)   a warranty that the shares being sold constitute all of the shares in the capital of the company and are not subject to encumbrance;

(c)   a provision that the warrantors warrant the terms set out in a schedule to the document;

(d)   a provision that the warrantors waive any rights which they may have to sue the target company, or its employees, or agents for any inaccurate information given to them in connection with the preparation of the disclosure letter (if this were not done, a warrantor on being sued by the purchaser might seek to join an employee or agent of the target company who in turn would probably have a right to join the target company. If this were to occur, it would defeat the purpose of getting the warranty, and the target company might end up funding the ultimate award to the purchaser);

(e)   agreed limits on warranties (although it is also common to include these in a separate schedule). The types of provisions are reviewed in 'Limits on Warranties' at **5.6.7**.

### 5.11.7   RESTRICTIVE AND OTHER COVENANTS

The agreement normally provides for restrictive covenants, which bind the vendor. The details of what would be included in such covenants are discussed in **chapter 6**. Such a section may also include other covenants such as covenants concerning a change of name of the target company or the vendor and covenants concerning ancillary agreements.

### 5.11.8   COMPLETION

A section of the agreement usually provides for the formalities of completion. This will include: the list of documents to be handed over at completion; the agenda for the board meeting to take place at completion; and a covenant that the purchaser will pay the purchase price on completion. If there is to be a gap between signing and completion, it may be appropriate, at this point of the agreement, to make provision to address the issues that arise.

The relevant issues are discussed in 'Signing and Completion of Share Purchase Agreements' at **5.10**. This section may also deal with matters to take place post completion such as stamping of share transfers.

## 5.11.9 MISCELLANEOUS PROVISIONS

It is usual that the last clause of a share purchase agreement consists of general provisions sometimes referred to as 'boilerplate clauses'. Matters typically dealt with in these clauses include: a prohibition on the making of any public announcement, except by agreement between the parties; a provision dealing with the assignment of warranties; a provision dealing with who will bear expenses; and a provision dealing with the service of any notices required under the agreement. This usually provides for notices to be served by hand or by post and specifies a time limit after which they are deemed to have been given. It may also provide for methods of communication, such as fax or e-mail. There is usually a clause providing that a once-off waiver by a party of a liability will not be construed as a general waiver and further that an acquiescence in a breach will not be deemed to be a general waiver.

It is often provided, particularly where there are a number of parties involved, that the original agreement may be signed in more than one counterpart. This facilitates signing where parties are in a number of different locations.

It is sometimes provided that the share purchase agreement and identified ancillary documents constitute the entire agreement between the parties. This is helpful, particularly from a vendor's point of view, as it prevents a purchaser from arguing that there are unwritten warranties or representations which form the basis on which they entered into the agreement.

The general clauses at the end will usually deal with the governing law of the contract. If all of the parties are clearly located in Ireland, this should not give rise to a problem if it is omitted. However, if there are parties from different jurisdictions, the omission of a governing law clause may give rise to difficulties and consequently it is important that something should be included. For foreign parties, it may also be appropriate to include a clause under which they submit to the jurisdiction of an Irish court.

## 5.11.10 SCHEDULES

It is usual to include matters in schedules to cover the detail of items such as warranties, the members of the board of the target company and details of its properties.

# CHAPTER 6

# IRISH MERGER CONTROL

## 6.1    Introduction

This chapter considers the Irish merger control regime. All mergers involving a business with sales in Ireland, even mergers between small businesses or mergers with little impact on competition, require consideration under the regime.

Mergers can have beneficial effects for the economy and consumers. A merger can facilitate the efficient development of new products resulting in the reduction of production and distribution costs and the promotion of product innovation, through the combination of complementary skills. The net effect of a merger may be a more competitive market with higher quality goods at lower prices. This ultimately benefits consumers. However, a merger can also have negative effects on competition. Some mergers may reduce competition due to the high market power of the merging businesses and high barriers to potential competitors entering the market. This is likely to harm consumers through higher prices, reduced choice and less innovation. The objective, therefore, of merger control is to consider the proposed future impact of a merger on the market in order to prevent harmful effects on competition and ultimately consumers.

### 6.1.1    MERGER CONTROL JURISDICTION: EU OR IRISH?

Mergers may fall within the scope of either the European merger control regime, or the Irish merger control regime. European merger control is considered in the Law Society manual on *European Law*.

There has been a system of European merger control in place since 1990. Since then, EU Member States have enacted systems of merger control that are gradually becoming harmonised with the European regime. The European regime is based on the concept of exclusive jurisdiction. A merger, which qualifies under the relevant legislation for notification, is *either* reviewed by the European Commission *or* by one or more national competition authorities.

If the annual combined turnover of the undertakings concerned in a merger exceeds certain thresholds, then the transaction comes within the scope of the European Commission's jurisdiction under Council Regulation (EC) No 139/2004 (the 'ECMR').

The ECMR thresholds are as follows:

(a) the combined aggregate worldwide turnover of all of the undertakings concerned is more than €5,000 million; and

(b) the combined aggregate Community-wide turnover of each of at least two of the undertakings concerned is more than €250 million,

unless each of the undertakings concerned achieves more than two-thirds of its aggregate Community-wide turnover within one and the same Member State (Art 1(2)).

A merger which does not meet the above thresholds still has a Community dimension where:

(a) the combined aggregate worldwide turnover of all of the undertakings concerned is more than €2,500 million; and

(b) in each of at least three Member States, the combined aggregate turnover of all of the undertakings concerned is more than €100 million; and

(c) in each of at least three Member States included for the purpose of para (b), the aggregate turnover of each of at least two of the undertakings concerned is more than €25 million; and

(d) the aggregate Community-wide turnover of at least two of the undertakings concerned is more than €100 million,

unless each of the undertakings concerned achieves more than two-thirds of its aggregate Community-wide turnover within one and the same Member State (Art 1(3)).

If the merger falls below the turnover thresholds in the ECMR then national competition authorities may apply their respective legislation to mergers falling within their jurisdiction.

In Ireland, the Competition Authority (the 'Authority') has competence to review mergers under the Competition Act, 2002 (the '2002 Act').

## 6.2 Irish Merger Control

The Authority's merger control function under the 2002 Act is to determine the competitive impact that a merger may have on competition in Ireland. The Authority will assess a merger to determine whether it is likely to 'substantially lessen competition' in Ireland. The Authority will then issue a determination either:

(a) permitting the merger;

(b) permitting the merger subject to certain conditions (such as a divestment of a particular line of business); or

(c) prohibiting the merger.

Prior to the enactment of the 2002 Act, the test for merger control was a public interest test. Under the 2002 Act, the test is a pure competition test, unless the transaction constitutes a 'media merger' (within the meaning of s 23), in which case a public interest test may be used. Media mergers are considered at **6.3.4** below.

The Authority has provided guidance on the merger control terms in the 2002 Act. This is contained in the Authority's amended (12 December 2006) Notice in respect of certain terms used in Part 3 of the 2002 Act (N/02/003). Not every merger control concept is explained in this Notice. For further guidance it is appropriate to refer to the European Commission Consolidated Jurisdictional Notice under Council Regulation (EC) No 139/2004 on the control of concentrations between undertakings, with the exception of the following parts:

Section B (concerning the concept of concentration);

Section C I (concerning thresholds); and

Section C III (concerning the relevant date for establishing jurisdiction).

It is appropriate to rely on the European Commission Notice because the substantive concepts underlying European and Irish merger control are the same. The Authority, however, has made it clear on its website that it is only appropriate to rely on the European Commission's Notice pending the adoption by the Authority of further guidance notices.

## 6.2.1 DEFINITION OF A MERGER

Under the 2002 Act (s 16(1)), a merger or acquisition will occur if:

(a) there is a merger between two or more previously independent undertakings;

(b) one or more undertakings acquire direct or indirect control of the whole or part of another undertaking (including the creation of a joint venture performing indefinitely all the functions of an autonomous economic entity); or

(c) one undertaking acquires the assets of another undertaking as a result of which the first undertaking can replace (or substantially replace) the second undertaking in the business concerned.

In other words, the 2002 Act covers: mergers: the acquisition of 'control'; asset acquisitions; and 'joint ventures', provided they meet certain criteria.

The concept of an 'undertaking' is discussed in **chapter 7** on Irish Competition Law. The concepts of 'control' and joint ventures' are considered in more detail below.

## 6.2.2    CONTROL

The acquisition of 'control' can result in a 'merger' within the meaning of the 2002 Act. This test is used because it is the undertaking that ultimately controls the business that can control its competitive behaviour on the market.

The 2002 Act, provides that control is acquired if, by securities or any other means, decisive influence is capable of being exercised with regard to the activities of the undertaking being acquired, and in particular, by:

(a)    ownership of, or the right to use all or part of, the assets of an under-taking; or

(b)    rights or contracts which enable decisive influence to be exercised with regard to the composition, voting or decisions of the organs of an undertaking.

In essence, this means that an undertaking may be acquired through legal means or through circumstances (i.e. de facto control). Legal control may be acquired through rights conferring control in a contract. An example of de facto control is a situation where a minority shareholder controls the board and the shareholder meetings of a company because the rest of the shares are diluted.

Control is defined in the 2002 Act as the capability of exercising decisive influence with regard to the activities of an undertaking. A majority shareholder may not be capable of exercising decisive influence over an undertaking whereas a minority shareholder may have that capability. The capability of exercising decisive influence is determined by the ability to control the strategic commercial behaviour of the undertaking. The undertaking that controls the board and/or controls key business decisions (such as decisions in relation to the budget, the business plan, the appointment of senior management or the making of major investments) controls the strategic commercial behaviour of the undertaking.

A company may be under sole or joint control. Joint control normally concerns a situation where the shareholders must reach agreement on major decisions concerning the company. Sole control normally involves the acquisition of a majority of the voting rights of an undertaking.

The issue of control is an important consideration for transactions involving venture capital companies. Venture capital companies are primarily concerned with investment. They rarely get involved in the day-to-day operations of companies, in which they invest, but they may insist on having contractual rights to control key businesses decisions, in order to protect their business investments. These rights may confer 'control' from a competition law perspective, thus triggering a mandatory notification requirement.

The issue of control is also relevant when considering the question of competitive overlap between the purchaser and the target undertaking. At first glance, it may appear as though the purchaser is not active in the target's market however, further analysis of the purchaser's portfolio of investments may reveal that the purchaser is in fact active in the target's market. This will impact on the level of detail and competition analysis to be provided in the notification to the Authority. It may also raise competition concerns that require detailed analysis and resolution.

## 6.2.3 JOINT VENTURE

A joint venture constitutes a 'merger' for the purposes of the 2002 Act, if the joint venture (created by the transaction) can perform, on an indefinite basis, all the functions of an autonomous economic entity. In essence, this means that the joint venture must be fully functional and it must operate indefinitely on the market. The rationale for including these sorts of joint ventures in the definition of 'mergers and acquisitions' is that they can have an impact on the competitive dynamic of the market, therefore they should be subject to merger control. For the same reason, a joint venture that has been established purely as a holding company on a temporary basis is not subject to the merger control regime.

## 6.2.4 EXCEPTIONS

Certain types of mergers and acquisitions are specifically excluded from the scope of the 2002 Act (s 16(6)).

The first exception concerns situations of insolvency. If an undertaking becomes insolvent, then the acquisition of control by a receiver, liquidator, underwriter or jobber is not considered to be a merger for the purpose of the 2002 Act. The rationale for the exclusion is that the acquisition is unlikely to impact on the competitive dynamic of the market and it is also likely to be temporary.

The second exception relates to intra-group transfers. The rationale for the exclusion is that there will be no ultimate change in control of the undertaking (i.e. the corporate group as a whole) as a result of the transaction.

The third exception concerns testamentary dispositions. Where control of an undertaking is acquired solely as a result of a testamentary disposition, intestacy or due to the right of survivorship under a joint tenancy, this does not constitute a merger under the 2002 Act.

The fourth exception concerns acquisitions by financial undertakings (such as banks, other credit institutions and insurance companies) that hold shares on a temporary basis with a view to disposal of that undertaking within a year of control being acquired. In order to qualify for this exception, the acquisition of voting rights must not be exercised for the purpose of determining the way in which any activities of the undertaking are carried on and which could affect competition in the State.

## 6.3    Mandatory Notification

There is a mandatory requirement to notify a merger or acquisition to the Authority in the following circumstances:

(a)    where certain turnover thresholds are exceeded by the 'undertakings involved' in the merger or acquisition (s 18(1)); or

(b)    where the merger falls within a class of merger designated by the Minister for Enterprise, Trade and Employment.

Media mergers constitute a class of mergers that have been so designated by the Minister for Enterprise, Trade and Employment (s 18(5)). Media mergers must be notified to the Authority if one of the 'undertakings involved', in the merger or acquisition, carries on a media business in Ireland. Media mergers are discussed at **6.3.4** below.

### 6.3.1    'UNDERTAKINGS INVOLVED' IN THE MERGER OR ACQUISITION

In order to apply the criteria outlined above, it is necessary to first identify the 'undertakings involved' in the transaction.

Where two undertakings merge then both undertakings will clearly be 'undertakings involved' for the purpose of the 2002 Act. In the case of an acquisition, however, the undertakings involved are not always obvious. In the case of the purchaser, the 'undertaking involved' may appear to be the party signing the agreement, however from a competition law perspective, the 'undertaking involved' is the undertaking that ultimately controls the purchaser. This is because the undertaking that ultimately controls the purchaser, is the undertaking that can influence the purchaser's competitive activity on the market.

With regard to the vendor, it is that part of the undertaking being acquired that is the 'undertaking involved' and not the vendor. This is because after the transaction has completed, the vendor will no longer control the competitive behaviour of the business it has sold.

Further guidance on the meaning of this term is contained in the Competition Authority Notice in respect of certain terms used in s 18(1) of the Competition Act, 2002 (N/02/003).

### 6.3.2    TURNOVER THRESHOLDS

It is only the turnover of the 'undertakings involved' that is taken into account to determine whether the mandatory notification requirements have been met.

The turnover thresholds are as follows:

(a)  the worldwide turnover of each of two or more of the undertakings involved in the merger is not less than €40 million;

(b)  each of two or more of the undertakings involved in the merger carries on business in any part of the island of Ireland (i.e. including Northern Ireland); and

(c)  the turnover in the State, of any one of the undertakings involved in the merger is not less than €40 million.

Turnover does not include any payment in respect of value added tax on sales or excise duty (s 18(2)(a)).

The turnover thresholds relate to the most recent financial year-end of the 'undertakings involved' in the transaction (s 18(1)).

The term 'turnover in the State' is understood by the Authority to comprise sales made or services supplied to customers within the State (Notice (N/02/003)).

For asset transactions, it is the turnover generated from the assets, the subject of the transaction that is taken into account (s 18(2)(c)).

The European Commission Jurisdictional Notice contains useful guidance on the concept of turnover. This is particularly useful in the case of banks and other financial institutions whose turnover does not comprise sales in the traditional sense of the meaning of turnover.

Having established the turnover of the undertakings involved, it is necessary to determine whether at least two of those undertakings carry on business in any part of the island of Ireland.

### 6.3.3  'CARRIES ON BUSINESS IN ANY PART OF THE ISLAND OF IRELAND'

The Authority used to adopt quite a broad interpretation of the term 'carries on business in any part of the island of Ireland'. In a recent amendment to Notice N/02/003, the Authority revised its position. According to the amendment, the Authority understands the term to mean that the undertaking involved has a physical presence on the island of Ireland (including a registered office, subsidiary, branch, representative office or agency) and makes sales and/or supplies services to customers on the island of Ireland. Alternatively, the undertaking involved must have made sales on the island of Ireland in its most recent financial year of at least €2 million. It should be noted, however, that the Notice merely reflects the Authority's interpretation of the 2002 Act. What is required is an amendment to the 2002 Act. This amendment has been recommended to the Minister for Enterprise, Trade and Employment by the Authority as part of a review of the 2002 Act.

### 6.3.4  MEDIA MERGERS

Media mergers can also trigger the mandatory notification requirement.

The Minister for Enterprise, Trade and Employment (the 'Minister') may specify a class of merger that must be notified to the Authority, irrespective of the turnover of the undertakings involved in the merger. Media mergers have been specified by the Minister as a class of merger that always requires notification. The reason for the designation is that it enables the Minister to regulate plurality of the media in Ireland. Since all media mergers must be notified and a copy of the notification sent to the Minister, the Minister has an opportunity to review media mergers. The Minister considers the merger, not only from a competition perspective, but also from a public interest perspective. The relevant criteria are set out in s 23(10) and include: diversity of ownership; strength of indigenous media; and cross-ownership of different forms of media. It is therefore possible that a merger may be investigated and/or prohibited on the basis of the criteria set out in s 23 rather than on the basis of competition concerns.

The definition of a media merger was revised in 2007 by way of statutory instrument (SI 122/2007). A media merger is now defined as a merger where two or more of the undertakings involved in the transaction carry on a 'media business'. A 'media business' is defined in s 23(10) of the 2002 Act as:

*a business of the publication of newspapers or periodicals consisting substantially of news and comment on current affairs;*

*a business of providing a broadcasting service; or*

*a business of providing a broadcasting services platform.*

Each of the above concepts are expanded upon in s 23 of the 2002 Act.

The amendment to the definition of a 'media merger' is welcome. The definition used to require that only one of the undertakings involved in the transaction carry on a 'media business' in the State. In practice, this provision caught a lot of mergers that had little or no impact on an Irish market. Twenty-two media mergers were notified to the Authority during 2006. None of those mergers were investigated or prohibited by the Minister. The number of media mergers notified to the Authority has been greatly reduced as a result of the amendment to the definition of a 'media merger'.

There is a difference in the statutory review procedure when the transaction constitutes a 'media merger', within the meaning of the 2002 Act.

A media merger has a longer statutory timetable for clearance than other mergers. In addition, the Minister has the ability to consider the transaction.

When the Authority receives notification of a media merger it has an obligation within five days of receipt of the notification to forward a copy of the notification to the Minister; and notify the undertakings involved that it considers the transaction to be a media merger.

If the Authority clears the transaction without the need to conduct a full investigation (generally referred to in the Authority's determinations as a 'Phase 1 preliminary investigation'), it must inform the Minister who has ten days within which to direct the Authority to carry out a full investigation (generally referred to as a 'Phase 2 full investigation').

If the Authority clears the transaction following a Phase 2 investigation, the Minister has thirty days within which to clear the merger, clear it with conditions or prohibit the merger. The Minister makes his or her decision on the basis of public interest criteria (set out in s 23(10)).

## 6.4     Voluntary Notifications

It is possible to make voluntary notifications under s 18(1)(3) of the 2002 Act in respect of mergers that do not come within the scope of the mandatory filing requirements.

The Authority's guidelines for merger analysis (N/02/004) (the 'Merger Guidelines') set out a general rule for voluntary notification as follows:

(a)     consider notifying the Authority if the post merger market share is above 40 per cent on any reasonable definition of the relevant market (see **chapter 7** on Irish Competition Law for a discussion of the relevant market);

(b)     do not notify if post merger the market is not very concentrated, i.e. if it falls within Zone A of the merger guidelines (discussed below); and

(c)     for in-between cases, or cases where the assessment relies critically on market definition, or cases where a foreign entrant is involved, informal pre-notification discussions with the Authority are encouraged.

There are two principal advantages to making a voluntary notification. First, there is the advantage of legal certainty. If a merger (that has not been notified) raises competition concerns under s 4 or s 5 of the 2002 Act, the Authority may conduct an investigation to determine whether there has been an infringement of those provisions. A notified merger that has been cleared by the Authority is statutorily excluded from the prohibitions in s 4 and s 5 of the 2002 Act. Section 4(8) and s 5(3) of the 2002 Act provide that s 4 and s 5 do not prohibit the putting into effect of a merger or acquisition that has been cleared by the Authority in accordance with Part 3 of the 2002 Act. Secondly, the merger will be dealt with within a statutory timetable. There is no statutory timetable for s 4 or s 5 investigations. Therefore, if the Authority decides to investigate a merger that it suspects may raise competition concerns, this may result in:

(a)     a delay in the completion of the merger transaction;

(b)     the merger being unravelled; and

(c)     the usual penalties for breach of s 4 and s 5 of the 2002 Act.

In practice, voluntary notifications are rare. Between January 2003 (when the Authority took over responsibly for mergers under the 2002 Act) and December 2007, the Authority issued determinations in respect of only one voluntary notification received in 2003, one in 2006 and one in 2007.

MICHAEL SMURFIT LIBRARY NATIONAL COLLEGE OF IRELAND

## 6.5    The Substantive Test

The test used by the Authority to assess notified mergers is whether the proposed transaction would substantially lessen competition in Ireland (s 20(1)(c)).

The Authority's guidelines for merger analysis (N/02/004) (the 'Merger Guidelines') provide useful elaboration on this concept. According to the Merger Guidelines, the Authority considers that the test of 'substantially lessening competition' should be interpreted in terms of consumer welfare. Consumer welfare depends on a range of variables including: price; output; quality; variety and innovation. However, in most cases the effect on consumer welfare is measured by whether the price in the market will rise (or output will fall). This differs from the traditional test under the ECMR, which was whether a merger would create or strengthen a dominant position. The current test under the ECMR is whether the transaction will significantly impede competition in the common market or a substantial part of it, as a result of the creation or strengthening of a dominant position. This is effectively a combination of the old ECMR test and the Irish test for merger control.

In order to apply the Irish 'substantial lessening of competition' test, the Authority considers, inter alia, the following:

(a)    the market definition, by reference to the product and geographic markets and substitution of products (see **chapter 7** for a discussion of this concept);

(b)    the effect of a merger on market structure;

(c)    an analysis of the immediate competitive effects of a merger; and

(d)    a consideration of other competitive effects such as market entry and efficiencies created by the merger.

### 6.5.1    MARKET STRUCTURE

For each relevant market identified, the Authority will consider the effect of the proposed transaction on market structure. One element of market structure is the level of concentration in the market.

Where a transaction involves a merger between competitors (referred to as horizontal mergers), the Authority will calculate the level of concentration between the merging parties and assess the effect of the merger on the level of rivalry amongst existing competitors in the market.

A concentrated market is one with a small number of firms with a large market share. An un-concentrated market is one with a large number of firms with a small market share.

Market concentration is assessed by reference to the Herfindahl Hirshcmann Index ('HHI'). This is explained in detail in the Merger Guidelines. In essence, market share figures (or estimates thereof) for all market participants are used to calculate the HHI. The HHI is calculated by first, adding the sum of the squares of all the market participants before the merger (this will give proportionately greater weight to the market shares of the larger undertakings). The sum of the squares of the entire market participants post merger is then calculated. The change in market concentration before and after the merger is known as the delta. By reference to possible changes in the delta the Authority uses three zones (A, B and C) to decide whether to intensify its analysis of effects on competition.

The zones are as follows:

| Zone | Definition | |
| --- | --- | --- |
| | HHI | Delta |
| A | Less than 1,000 | Any |
| | Between 1,000 and 1,800 | Less than 100 |
| | Above 1,800 | Less than 50 |
| B | Between 1,000 and 1,800 | Greater than 100 |
| | Above 1,800 | Between 50 and 100 |
| C | Above 1,800 | Greater than 100 |

According to the Merger Guidelines, mergers in Zone A are less likely to have adverse competitive effects. Mergers in Zone B may raise significant competitive concerns and Zone C mergers occur in already highly concentrated markets and are likely to raise competitive concerns.

If figures for the HHI are not available then the four firm concentration ratio can provide an indication of market concentration. This ratio is calculated by adding the market shares of the four largest firms in the market. If the sum of the market shares of the four largest firms is more than 40 per cent, then the market is generally considered to be concentrated.

If the transaction does not involve competitors (i.e. if there is no overlap of competing products) then the merger will not result in a change in the level of market concentration. Such a merger is less likely to raise competition concerns than horizontal mergers.

A merger between undertakings at different levels of the supply and distribution chain is known as a 'vertical merger'. The term 'conglomerate merger' is used to describe the remaining set of mergers, for example a merger between two retailers selling products that do not compete. The issues considered by the Authority in reviewing vertical and conglomerate mergers include a consideration of whether the integration of functions may result in foreclosure (for example, because integration covers such a high share of the market that an entrant to one market must also enter the second market in order to compete in the first market). The Authority will also consider portfolio effects, i.e. the theory that market power is created as a result of the merger because the firm is better able to leverage its products by tying, bundling or other means. These issues are considered in further detail in the Merger Guidelines.

## 6.5.2   ANALYSIS OF COMPETITIVE EFFECTS

Because the test under the 2002 Act is whether the merger will substantially lessen competition, the Authority will investigate the likely effect of the merger on competition. The starting point is an assessment of market concentration and the market share of the merged entity. However, although market share might suggest a negative impact on competition it is not the determining factor for this test.

The Authority will analyse the likelihood of the exercise of market power by the merged entity (known as unilateral effects) and whether increased collusive behaviour between competing undertakings would restrict competition (coordinated effects). The Authority will consider how difficult it is for a new competitor to enter the market as this may prevent the merged entity from exercising market power. The Authority will also analyse any likely pro-competitive benefits to the market of such a merger (i.e. any potential efficiency gains) and the 'failing firm defence' (this defence is rarely pleaded and is very difficult to establish. It is discussed in the Merger Guidelines at p. 26).

Other elements of market structure to be considered include vertical integration, cost and technology factors and product differentiation.

In practice, the determining factor used by the Authority in assessing the impact of a merger on competition appears to be whether prices will rise as a result of the merger. In order to make a determination on this issue, the Authority will:

(a)   conduct a quantitative analysis of economic evidence;

(b)   consider internal documents of the parties; and

(c)   consider customer evidence.

The impact on prices for customers is important. Customer evidence is therefore very valuable. This was evident in the IBM/Schlumberger determination (Determination M/04/032), the first prohibition determination under the 2002 Act.

## 6.5.3   PROHIBITION DETERMINATION

The first prohibition determination, under the 2002 Act, was taken on 28 October 2004. The determination concerned the proposed acquisition by IBM Ireland Limited ('IBM') of Schlumberger Business Continuity Services (Ireland) Limited ('Schlumberger') (M/04/032). The economic sector concerned was IT products and services and in particular business continuity/disaster recovery services. Following a detailed Phase II investigation the Authority concluded as follows:

(a)     The relevant market is the market for the supply of business recovery hot site services in the State. The conclusion concerning the competitive effects of this transaction, however, is not dependent upon the finding with regard to the definition of the relevant market.

(b)     The merging parties are the two largest providers of business recovery hot site services in the State, and compete directly and closely against each other.

(c)     Neither of the other two providers of business recovery hot site services in the State, Synstar and Network Recovery, nor the combination of both of them, would exert sufficient competitive pressure to discipline the combined market power of the merging parties.

(d)     There is an identifiable group of customers in respect of whom in-house provision of business recovery services would not exercise a sufficient competitive constraint upon the parties' ability to increase price.

(e)     There is an identifiable group of customers in respect of whom general service IT companies, teaming specialists and aggregators who supply some aspects of business recovery services would not exercise a sufficient competitive constraint upon the parties' ability to increase price.

(f)     There is no evidence that entry to the market would occur in sufficient time and scale to limit any increase in price.

(g)     Taking all potential sources of competitive constraint together, there exist identifiable customers for whom the merger would be likely to result in an increase in price. This effect is reinforced by the ability of suppliers to set different prices for individual customers with observable demand characteristics, so that customers negatively affected by the merger would not be protected by customers who would be able to switch more easily.

Due to the lack of competitive restraint on the merged entity, either from competitors or customers, coupled with the lack of potential market entry, the Authority concluded that the merged entity would be likely to result in increased prices for customers. This appeared to be the main reason for the prohibition of the merger.

The second prohibition determination was issued in 2006. The determination concerned the proposed acquisition of Leanort Group ('Xtratherm') by Kingspan Group plc ('Kingspan') (M/06/039). The economic sector concerned was building materials and insulation materials in particular. The relevant market was the market for PU/PIR insulation materials. Following a detailed analysis, the Authority decided to prohibit the merger. The principal concerns of the Authority are set out below.

The market structure was not conducive to competition as it was characterised by the following:

(a)    a homogeneous product;

(b)    high concentration;

(c)    a high market share by the proposed merged entity;

(d)    limited growth potential in the market;

(e)    limited competition from imports; and

(f)    sufficient excess capacity among industry operators to prevent entry.

The merging parties were the two largest providers in the State of PU/PIR insulation materials and they competed directly and closely against each other.

The target business, Xtratherm, had taken considerable market share from Kingspan, the prospective purchaser, since its entry to the market in 2002.

The merger would lead to a significant lessening of competition through the removal from the market of a vigorous competitor to Kingspan. The merger would create a market participant with a market share in excess of 80 per cent.

Kingspan had unsuccessfully attempted to increase its prices in 2004 and 2005 due to input prices. One of the reasons that the price increase had been unsuccessful was the competition from Xtratherm.

The main competitor to the merged entity would be unlikely to constrain the market power of the merged entity. It is not in the interests of market participants to compete vigorously on price where there are only two major suppliers, the price is homogeneous, and there is limited potential growth in the market. If the merged entity were to raise its prices, the most profitable strategy for the main competitor would be to match the price increase and increase its output. The merged entity would be unlikely to reduce its price as it would still find it profitable to accept some loss of market share. Eventually, a new equilibrium would be reached where the prices would be higher and output would be reduced.

Entry to the market would be unlikely, given the level of excess capacity in the market held by the merged entity and its main competitor. Imports would be unlikely to act as a competitive constraint on any exercise of market power by the merged entity, given the considerably higher prices in Great Britain.

In summary, the Authority concluded that the merger would lead to a significant lessening of competition for the following reasons: a vigorous competitor to the purchaser would be removed from the market; and the remaining competitor would be likely to accommodate price increases by the merged entity.

## 6.5.4    CONDITIONAL DETERMINATIONS

The Authority has issued a number of conditional determinations since it commenced its merger control function under the 2002 Act. In addition, a number of transactions have been cleared without conditions being imposed as a result of the parties offering commitments to the Authority at the preliminary stage of its investigation.

The IBM/Schlumberger determination can be contrasted with the Authority's determination of 6 January 2005 in relation to Grafton's acquisition of Heiton (Determination M/04/051). In that case, notwithstanding the high market share of Heiton and Grafton, the Authority issued a conditional determination, permitting the merger. One of the critical factors that led to this conclusion was that entry and expansion of rivals had already had a significant pro-competitive effect in the industry. The Authority's investigation demonstrated that there would be continued entry and expansion throughout the country (Competition Authority Press Release of 6 January 2005).

The Authority's clearance determination was conditional. First, the parties were required to notify the Authority in advance of any future mergers in the sector and notify the mergers to the Authority. Secondly, pursuant to s 22(6) of the 2002 Act, the parties were required to complete the transaction within twelve months of the making of the determination. The conditions imposed on the parties were not as onerous as in some other cases. Given the high turnover and high market share of the parties, it is likely that future mergers would require a mandatory notification or merit a voluntary notification. The second condition is a statutory obligation. This can be compared with a situation where the parties are required to divest of a profitable business.

The conditions imposed by the Authority in the purchase of FM104 by Scottish Radio Holdings (Determination M/03/033) were somewhat more onerous. The market affected was defined as the market for radio advertising. The Authority considered that there were two areas of overlap in the parties' activities, namely national advertising on Today FM and FM 104; and local (i.e. Dublin) advertising on Today FM and FM 104. The owners of FM 104 also held 8.89 per cent of News 106 Limited, trading as Newstalk 106 FM. Scottish Radio Holdings owned and controlled Radio Ireland Limited which broadcasted as Today FM.

The Authority imposed conditions to alleviate its concerns that structural links between the parties could, through exchange of information and commonality of interest, lead to coordinated behaviour with adverse effects for consumers. The Authority therefore required, inter alia, that following completion of the transaction the parties would:

(a)   divest all ownership interests in Newstalk 106 FM to a buyer agreeable to the Authority by 31 December 2004;

(b)   not participate on the Board of News 106 Ltd;

(c)   not vote in respect of, or participate in, the operations of the business of Newstalk 106; and

(d)   if the ownership interests in Newstalk 106 were not divested by 31 December 2004, ownership interests should be transferred to a trustee nominated by the parties and subject to the approval of the Authority.

FM 104 was also prevented from renewing a certain sales agency contract.

In 2005, the Authority issued a determination imposing an unprecedented nineteen conditions in its decision to clear a merger. This was the first merger raising significant 'cross-ownership' concerns. In other words, concerns that directors of the merged entity also had interests in its competitors and/or suppliers. The merger concerned the acquisition of MS Irish Cable Holding BV (trading as NTL Ireland) by UPC Ireland PV (M/05/024 of 4 November 2005). UPC Ireland was ultimately owned by Liberty Global Inc, which also owned the Irish cable provider, Chorus. In this case, the Authority had concerns regarding the cross-ownership interests held by a number of directors of Liberty Global, including one who was the leading shareholder in Liberty Global. The Authority was particularly concerned about cross-ownership interests that linked Liberty Global to News Corporation and BSkyB.

The issue of most concern to the Authority was the cross-shareholding of the Chairman and controlling shareholder of Liberty Global and the cross-management of persons on the Boards of Liberty Global and Liberty Media Corporation. The concern arose from the fact that Liberty Media Corporation owned a significant indirect stake in BSkyB, which was both the principal competitor to NTL and Chorus in the pay-TV market and also supplied premium 'must have' content to each of them. In addition, the Authority was concerned about a number of common directors on the Boards of the companies through which the Chairman held his interests in Liberty Global and BSkyB. The key issue was the impact on competition between the merged entity and BSkyB, as well as the terms of the provision of premium 'must have' content by BSkyB to the merged entity. In order to address these concerns, the Authority imposed nineteen conditions on its clearance determination. The conditions included a requirement that there be a separate holding company to manage the day-to-day running of Liberty Global's Irish operations and that final decisions on negotiations with BSkyB relating to premium content and retail pricing of video services be taken by the Irish holding company Board alone. Various conditions designed to prevent the 'common directors' from participating in decisions relating to the merged business were also imposed. A reporting condition was also imposed by the appointment of a named independent director (a partner in the law firm that represented Liberty Global in relation to the merger) to oversee the implementation of the various conditions and to report to the Authority on an ongoing basis regarding compliance with those conditions.

No conditions were imposed on determinations of the Authority during 2006 and 2007.

## 6.5.5    COMMITMENTS

The 2002 Act provides that the Authority may enter into discussions with the undertakings involved (and interested parties) with a view to identifying measures that would 'ameliorate' any effects of a proposed transaction on competition in Ireland (s 20(1)(b)). The Authority may accept binding commitments from the undertakings involved to remove potential anti-competitive effects. Where commitments are offered the Authority has an additional fifteen days in which to issue a determination on the merger (s 21(4)).

## 6.6    Investigations

According to its 2003 Annual Report, the Authority investigated a number of non-notifiable mergers when the merger control regime under the 2002 Act first came into force. As a result of these investigations, the Authority issued a notice in respect of the review of non-notifiable mergers and acquisitions (N/03/001). The Authority's notice makes it clear that many mergers do not give rise to any competition concerns. However, a small number, including some that do not meet the notification thresholds, may have the potential to substantially lessen competition in the relevant market or markets. According to the Notice, it is the Authority's policy to seek to prevent the implementation of any merger that has not been notified and that would substantially lessen competition in any market in the State. Where such a merger has already been implemented, the Authority may seek to have it reversed. It is therefore important to consider the likely impact of a merger on competition (even where it does not meet the mandatory notification thresholds) to determine whether a voluntary notification is advisable in the circumstances.

If the Authority considers that the transaction may raise competition concerns, it will contact the undertakings involved, to determine whether they wish to notify voluntarily. If the parties intend to notify upon conclusion of the agreement, the Authority will ask for confirmation in writing. The matter will then rest in abeyance until the transaction has been notified.

If, having been contacted by the Authority, the parties do not volunteer to make a notification; the Authority may open a s 4 or s 5 investigation. The Authority may issue proceedings seeking an injunction to prevent the implementation of the merger. The parties may opt to notify the transaction at any time during this procedure and such a notification will cause the investigation to cease. The transaction will be analysed from that point onwards in accordance with the provisions of Part 3 of the 2002 Act.

A detailed enquiry into the State's two largest mushroom producers in 2003 resulted in such an investigation, albeit prior to the publication of the Notice. The transaction was ultimately cleared on the basis that there was not a sufficient likelihood of anti-competitive effects, arising as a result of the merger, that would give rise to a breach of either s 4 or s 5 (Decision No E/04/001).

During 2006, the Authority carried out an investigation of a merger that fell below the turnover thresholds. The investigation was subsequently closed on the basis that there were no serious competition issues arising from the merger (see further Authority Annual Report 2006, p. 36).

## 6.7 Ancillary Restrictions/Restrictive Covenants

A share (or asset) purchase agreement usually makes provision to restrict the vendor from competing with the business being sold. These restrictions are referred to as 'ancillary restrictions' (i.e. restrictions that are ancillary to a merger) or 'restrictive covenants'.

Mergers and acquisitions usually involve the transfer of the 'goodwill' of the vendor to the purchaser. The general principle is that restrictions on the vendor, which are necessary to protect 'goodwill', are permissible, provided they do not go beyond that which is necessary to secure the adequate transfer of goodwill being acquired.

It should be noted that, in most transactions involving the sale of a business, there is no clause in the relevant agreement specifically transferring goodwill. The purchaser generally acquires the goodwill when it acquires the assets, business and reputation of the company.

### 6.7.1 APPLICATION OF SS 4 AND 5, 2002 ACT TO ANCILLARY RESTRICTIONS

The validity or otherwise of ancillary restrictions comes within the scope of the 2002 Act. Section 4(8) and s 5(3) of the 2002 Act provide that s 4 and s 5 do not prohibit the putting into effect of a merger or acquisition that has been cleared by the Authority in accordance with Part 3 of the 2002 Act or 'any arrangements constituting arrangements which are directly related and necessary to the implementation of the merger or acquisition and which are referred to in the notification'. Consequently, unless a restriction has been specifically referred to in the notification, it may not benefit from this provision. Where no reference is made in a notification to ancillary restrictions, or indeed where the parties do not notify a merger or acquisition to the Authority, then the parties need to assess whether any ancillary restrictions in the agreements contravene s 4 or s 5 of the 2002 Act.

The Authority issued a notice in respect of agreements involving a merger and/or sale of business (N/02/001) in 2002. The Notice was only effective until 31 December 2002 but it still provides guidance on the Authority's approach to ancillary restrictions. According to the Notice, in order for such a restriction to be enforceable the restriction must not:

(a) exceed two years from the date of completion of the sale;

(b) apply to any location outside the territory where the products concerned were manufactured, purchased or sold by the vendor at the time of the agreement; and

(c) apply to goods or services other than those manufactured, purchased or sold by the vendor at the time of the agreement.

A five-year restriction (from the date of completion) may be possible if the business involves the use of technical know-how, defined as a body of technical information that is secret substantial and identified in an appropriate form. The restriction must cease to apply once such know-how is in the public domain. The Notice makes it clear that knowledge concerning a particular line of business does not constitute technical know-how.

Restrictions on the vendor using or disclosing confidential information regarding the business, for an unlimited period of time, are permissible

In addition to the above, it is possible to have restrictions on vendors and shareholders in certain circumstances. First, where, following completion, the vendor remains engaged in the business as a shareholder, director or employee, the vendor may be prevented from competing with the business, soliciting customers and/or employees of the business. The restriction may apply for so long as he or she remains engaged in the business whether as a shareholder, director or employee.

Secondly, where a vendor, has retained a shareholding, of not less than 10 per cent, in the business following completion of the sale agreement, then the vendor may be prevented from competing with the business, soliciting customers and/or employees of the business for a period of up to two years from the date of any future sale of such shares.

The Authority tends to follow the general principles set out in its Notice when considering notified restrictions. The Authority adopted this approach when Musgrave acquired Express Checkout in 2003 (M/03/001). The agreement restricted the vendor from competing with the purchaser anywhere in Ireland for a period of two years post completion, however, the Authority considered that the geographic reach of the restriction was too broad, as it extended to the whole island of Ireland. The restrictions were therefore limited to narrower geographic areas.

The European Commission Notice, on the application of competition law to ancillary restrictions, contains further guidance on the subject ((2001) OJ C188/5).

## 6.8    The Procedure

In February 2006, the Authority published a document outlining its revised procedures for the review of mergers and acquisitions (the 'Procedural Guidelines'). This useful document is available on the Authority's website. This part of the chapter considers the procedure involved in making a notification to the Authority.

### 6.8.1    OBLIGATION TO NOTIFY

If a merger or acquisition qualifies for mandatory notification under the 2002 Act, then each of the undertakings involved has an obligation to notify the Authority 'within one month' of the 'conclusion of an agreement or the making of a public bid' (s 18(1)).

In an amendment to its Notice (N/02/003) in December 2006, the Authority clarified its understanding of the phrase 'within one month after' as used in s 18(1) and s 21(2) of the 2002 Act. The Authority is of the view that where that phrase is used in either section, the month will be calculated by including the date after which the month is expressed to run. Therefore, where notification must be made 'within one month after' the date on which an agreement has been concluded, the date of conclusion of the agreement will be counted as the first day of the calendar month. The month will then expire on the day before the corresponding date in the following month.

The Authority has issued a notification form that provides a framework for supplying the Authority with the information required to review the merger or acquisition. The notification form (effective since 1 September 2005) is available on the Authority's website.

It is not necessary to complete section 4 of the Notification Form in relation to overlapping products and/or services of the parties where there is no overlap (either horizontal or vertical) between the activities of the undertakings involved on the island of Ireland (see p. 3 of the Notification Form). This is because such mergers do not raise significant competition issues, therefore the information required by the Authority in such cases is less comprehensive.

## 6.8.2  JOINT OR SEPARATE NOTIFICATIONS

The Authority encourages all parties to a proposed transaction to make a joint notification, though they are not legally obliged to do so.

The principal consequences of notifying separately are as follows:

(a)  the date of commencement of the statutory review period of the proposed transaction (the 'appropriate date' as defined in s 19(6) of the 2002 Act) is the date of receipt of the latest notification;

(b)  each notifying party must separately comply with the entire information requirements specified on the form;

(c)  each of the notifying parties must pay the Authority's filing fee of €8,000 (only one filing fee is payable where a joint notification is made and the parties often agree to share the cost of the filing fee).

In practice, the undertakings involved rarely elect to notify separately. The most common example of separate notification occurs in the case of a hostile bid, where the target company may wish to delay the process by making its notification at the last possible statutory date.

In the case of a joint notification, each party must separately complete that part of the form relevant to their business and an authorised representative of each notifying party must sign the declaration at the end of the form.

### 6.8.3 THE NEED FOR A CORRECT AND COMPLETE NOTIFICATION

If any of the information provided (or statement made in response to a request for further information from the Authority) is false or misleading, in a material respect, then the notification is invalid and any determination issued on foot of such notification is void (s 19(12)). If the issue arose during the notification process, it could delay completion of the transaction as the parties would be required to submit a new notification and the statutory timetable for consideration of the notification would commence on the date of receipt of the new notification (or receipt of further information requested by the Authority). If this issue arose after the Authority had issued a determination then, arguably, the transaction would be void, since the determination would be void. Section 19(2) of the 2002 Act provides that a merger is void if it is put into effect before the Authority has issued either a positive determination; a conditional determination; or the statutory time limit for clearance has elapsed.

### 6.8.4 PRE-NOTIFICATION DISCUSSIONS

The Authority encourages pre-notification discussions with its mergers division in cases of doubt concerning jurisdictional and other legal issues.

The Authority will only meet at the stage when an agreement has been concluded or where the parties can satisfy the Authority that they have a bona fide intention to proceed with the transaction. The Authority generally accepts any of the following documents as proof of such intention:

(a) signed heads of agreement;

(b) signed memorandum of understanding; or

(c) a letter of intent signed by all the parties.

### 6.8.5 FEES

A filing fee of €8,000 is payable to the Authority (SI 623/2002). The Authority accepts one filing fee for joint notifications.

### 6.8.6 TIMING

Both the signing and completion of an agreement are significant events in the notification process.

As discussed above, under s 18(1) of the 2002 Act, there is an obligation on the undertakings involved in a proposed merger or acquisition to notify the Authority within one month of the conclusion of an agreement or the making of a public bid. The Authority understands 'the conclusion of an agreement' to mean the signing of an agreement. In practice, the Authority may accept (at its discretion) a memorandum of understanding or letter of intent signed by all the parties. This is a matter for discussion with the Authority.

Notification can impact on the transaction timetable because notification to the Authority has a suspensory effect. In other words, if a merger has been notified to the Authority, the notifying parties must wait until the Authority has issued its determination before they complete their transaction. If they complete prior to the Authority issuing a determination; contrary to a prohibition decision; or prior to the statutory time period for the Authority to make a determination then the transaction will be void.

The timing of completion may also be affected by factors such as regulatory clearances, clearance in other jurisdictions, or approval from the Irish Take-over Panel (in the case of a public listed company). The Authority indicated in 2004 that it would issue a guidance notice on the relationship between Irish merger control and the Irish take-over code. To date, no such guidance notice has been issued.

## 6.8.7 REVIEW PROCESS

There is a two-step process for the assessment of mergers by the Authority. A preliminary (or Phase I) investigation and a full (or Phase II) investigation. It is only those mergers that raise competition concerns (and certain media mergers) that are subject to a Phase II investigation.

### 6.8.7.1 Phase I

In Phase I, the Authority has one month after receipt of the notification (or after the receipt of any further information requested by the Authority) to reach a decision. The end date of this period is referred to as the 'appropriate date'. If any of the notifying undertakings makes proposals for commitments, with a view to securing clearance, the one-month period is extended to forty-five days. If the Authority fails to reach a decision within that time frame then the merger may be put into effect (s 19(1)).

The Authority failed to make a determination in the Topaz/Statoil merger (M/06/044) within the prescribed time period under s 19(1) and the parties were therefore legally permitted to complete the merger. However, this was as a result of an error rather than inaction on the part of the Authority. In its 2006 Annual Report, the Authority explains how the error occurred (pp. 28–31).

At the end of Phase I, the Authority must inform the notifying undertakings (and any other persons who have made submissions in relation to the notification) either:

(a)    that the merger may be put into effect because it will not substantially lessen competition in Ireland; or

(b)    that it has decided to carry out a Phase II investigation.

The transaction must be put into effect within twelve months of the date of the determination (s 19(3)).

In practice, the average time period to obtain a Phase I determination is three weeks to one month.

### 6.8.7.2    Phase II

Phase II is an additional three-month period which enables the Authority to conduct a detailed examination of the transaction (s 22). In effect this means that the Authority has four months from the date of receipt of a notification (or receipt of further information requested by the Authority) to issue a determination on the merger. The end date of this period is referred to as the 'appropriate date'.

The Authority's Procedural Guidelines outline its Phase II procedure. The procedure is summarised briefly below.

### 6.8.7.3    Initiation of the investigation

The Authority informs the notifying undertakings (and any other parties who have made submissions) within one month of the appropriate date (or within forty-five days where commitments have been offered in accordance with s 20(3)) of its intention to carry out a Phase II investigation.

The Authority issues a press release on the date of its determination to initiate the investigation and invites submissions from third parties within a specified time frame (generally three weeks).

Within eight weeks of its determination to carry out a Phase II investigation, the Authority will either:

(a)    issue a clearance determination;

(b)    issue a conditional clearance determination; or

(c)    furnish a copy of its assessment to the notifying parties. The assessment will outline the nature of the Authority's concerns regarding the effect of the proposed transaction on competition.

### 6.8.7.4    The assessment

If the Authority does not clear the transaction or clears the transaction subject to conditions after eight weeks, it will issue an assessment to the undertakings involved in the transaction. The assessment will outline the nature of the Authority's concerns regarding the effect of the proposed transaction on competition.

The undertakings involved may reply to the Authority's assessment in writing within three weeks of its receipt. According to the Authority's Procedural Guidelines, failure by any one of the notifying parties to respond within the time frame provided may be deemed to constitute a waiver of that party's right to contest the issues set out in the assessment. Failure of all notifying parties to respond within three weeks may authorise the Authority, without further notice, to adopt a final determination on the basis of the facts set out in the assessment (para 3.11).

### 6.8.7.5    Access to the file

If the investigation proceeds to the stage where the Authority furnishes an assessment to the notifying parties, then they will have the right of 'access to the file'. In essence, this means that the notifying parties will have the right to review the Authority's file on the investigation.

In accordance with the criteria set out in the Authority's 'Procedures for Access to the File in Merger Cases' (February 2006), the notifying parties will not be entitled to have access to all documents on the Authority's file, including in particular:

(a)    minutes of meetings between the Authority and the parties or third parties;

(b)    information that qualifies as business secrets; and

(c)    confidential information.

Further details are set out in Article 8 of the Authority's 'Procedures for Access to the File in Merger Cases' (February 2006).

### 6.8.7.6    Oral submissions

The notifying parties may make oral submissions. If they wish to do so, they must notify the Authority in writing within one week of the assessment being furnished. Third parties who have furnished submissions may also be invited to make oral submissions at the sole discretion of the Authority.

It should be noted that the Authority has the power (under s 31) to summon witnesses to be examined on oath. The Authority can also require those witnesses to produce any document in their power or control. In practice, the Authority does issue witness summonses in merger investigations. The consequences of failing to comply with a witness summons, refusal to take an oath or refusal to produce requested documentation, is liability to fines of up to €3,000 and/or imprisonment of up to six months.

### 6.8.7.7    Discussion and proposals

The Authority may enter into discussions with undertakings involved with regard to the manner in which the merger may be put into effect and the undertakings involved may make proposals of measures that would ameliorate negative effects of the merger on competition. This must occur no later than three weeks after the assessment has been issued (Procedural Guidelines, para 3.14).

**6.8.7.8    Determination/putting the merger into effect**

On completion of the Phase II investigation, the Authority will issue one of the following determinations:

(a)    that the merger may be put into effect;

(b)    that the merger may be put into effect subject to certain conditions; or

(c)    that the merger is prohibited.

The transaction must be put into effect within twelve months of the date of the determination (s 19(3)).

The transaction may be put into effect if the Authority has failed to make one of the above determinations within four months of the appropriate date (i.e. the date of receipt of the last notification or the date of receipt of further information requested by the Authority) (s 19(1)). The transaction must be put into effect within sixteen months of the appropriate date (s 19(5)).

# 6.9    Confidentiality/Publication of Merger Information by the Authority

The confidential nature of a merger is often a sensitive issue. Clients may not want the merger to be made public before their public announcement because they want to inform their employees in advance of the announcement, or because they are concerned that it might affect the share price in the case of a public bid.

The practice of the Authority is to keep pre-notification discussions confidential, however, the Authority has certain statutory obligations to publish certain information. The Authority generally publishes this information on its website.

The Authority has a statutory obligation to publish the fact of the notification within seven days of receipt (unless publication is contrary to the public interest) (s 20(1)). The reason for publication is to prompt third parties (especially customers, suppliers and competitors) to comment on the proposed merger. In practice, the Authority may, at its discretion be prepared to defer publication until the last of the seven days.

The Authority has an obligation to inform the notifying undertakings (and any other individual or undertaking that has made a submission) of its Phase I determination. The determination must be published by the Authority with due regard for commercial confidentiality within two months of its making (s 22(3)). Again, the Authority may, at its discretion, be prepared to defer publication until the end of that period.

Any Phase II determination must be published within one month of its issue and must include reasons for the Authority's determination. The practice of the Authority is to issue a press release on the commencement of a Phase II investigation and on the issuance of a Phase II determination. The Authority will publish the written determination on its website after allowing the undertakings involved an appropriate period to indicate whether certain information should be redacted on the basis that it constitutes a business secret (Procedural Guidelines, para 4.4).

There is a general confidentiality obligation in s 32 of the 2002 Act in respect of confidential information that comes into the possession of the Authority under its powers. This obligation does not apply to communications made by a member of the Authority, a member of staff or an authorised officer in the performance of its functions under the 2002 Act, where such communication is necessary for the performance of any such function. It is possible for third parties to seek documents from the Authority under the Freedom of Information Act, 1997 but commercially confidential information should not be disclosed (unless disclosure is in the public interest).

## 6.10    Appeals

There is a statutory right of appeal to the High Court (s 24) against a determination of the Authority to either prohibit a merger or to permit it subject to conditions. There is no statutory right to appeal a clearance determination of the Authority.

An appeal may be made by any of the undertakings that made the notification. The appeal must be made within one month of the date on which the Authority informs the undertaking concerned of the determination. In the case of media mergers, the date runs from ten days after a determination has issued in Phase I or thirty days after a determination has issued in Phase II.

The High Court is obliged, in so far as it is practicable, to hear and determine an appeal under s 24, within two months of the date on which the appeal is made.

The High Court may annul the determination, confirm the determination or confirm the determination subject to modifications. An appeal to the Supreme Court against any decision of the High Court made under s 24 may only be made on a question of law.

## 6.11    Enforcement

### 6.11.1    FAILURE TO NOTIFY

If the undertakings involved in a merger (that qualifies for mandatory notification under the 2002 Act) do not notify the merger, then the persons in control of those undertakings are liable to fines.

Section 18(11) defines a 'person in control of an undertaking' as follows:

(a) in the case of a body corporate, any officer of the body corporate who knowingly and wilfully authorises or permits the contravention;

(b) in the case of a partnership, each partner who knowingly and wilfully authorises or permits the contravention;

(c) in the case of any other form of undertaking, any individual in control of that undertaking who knowingly and wilfully authorises or permits the contravention.

The penalties are, on summary conviction, fines of up to €3,000 or on conviction on indictment, fines of up to €250,000 (s 18(9)). There is a fine for a continuing contravention of €300 on summary conviction or €25,000 on conviction on indictment (s 18(10)). These penalties also apply in a similar manner where a transaction has been notified and the notifying parties do not provide the information requested by the Authority.

## 6.11.2  COMPLETING WITHOUT CLEARANCE OR 'GUN-JUMPING'

Any merger that is completed prior to the issuance of a determination of the Authority, contrary to a prohibition decision of the Authority, or prior to the expiry of the legislative time period for the Authority to make a determination, is void.

In May 2003, the Authority investigated a transaction to determine whether a purchaser had acquired the target company prior to the mandatory waiting period. On the basis of the information supplied to the Authority, the Authority found no breach. The Authority nonetheless issued a press release, on 13 May 2003, warning merging parties against 'gun-jumping' or putting a merger into effect prior to the expiry of the mandatory waiting period. The press release made it clear that the Authority is concerned to ensure that merging parties maintain separate and independent operations until the Authority has made its determination. If the parties were allowed to behave as if a merger had already occurred before the Authority had made its assessment, there could be a negative effect on the market and ultimately on consumers.

The Authority also considered this issue in relation to the acquisition of Newstalk 106 by 98 FM (Determination M/04/003). The Authority was of the view that the merger had been put into effect prematurely and was therefore void under s 19(1). However, the Authority considered that it could still review the merger, and having issued a positive determination that the merger could be put into effect. The Authority took the following view:

Section 19(2) does not state whether a merger or acquisition which contravenes Section 19(1)(a) is rendered void for all time, or merely until such time as the Authority makes a determination. Based on a reading of all the pertinent provisions, the Authority is of the view that the section is designed to protect the Authority's right of review and is not intended to render a merger or acquisition void indefinitely. . . . The Authority takes the view that any other interpretation would result in an absurdity: namely, that a completed merger would be void for all time. (para 8)

### 6.11.3 FAILURE TO COMPLY WITH A COMMITMENT, DETERMINATION OR ORDER

The Authority, or any third party, may apply to the High Court, under s 26, for an order to enforce compliance with a commitment, determination or order.

Section 26(4) provides that it is an offence to contravene the provision of a commitment, determination or order with penalties on indictment of up to €10,000 and or two years' imprisonment. ·

## 6.12 The Relationship between Irish and European Merger Control

There are some aspects of the European merger control regime which merit brief consideration in this chapter as they concern the relationship between Irish and European merger control.

### 6.12.1 ARTICLE 9 PROCEDURE

Article 9 of the ECMR legislates for the referral of a merger, notified to the European Commission, back to a national competition authority. In other words, even though a merger may qualify for mandatory notification to the European Commission under the ECMR (thereby excluding the jurisdiction of the national competition authority), a Member State may request jurisdiction. The Commission has discretion to grant jurisdiction to the national authority if:

(a) the transaction threatens to significantly affect competition in a market within that Member State, which presents all the characteristics of a distinct market; or

(b) the transaction affects competition in a market within that Member State which presents all the characteristics of a distinct market and which does not constitute a substantial part of the common market.

The European Commission has an obligation to send a copy of every merger notification to the national competition authorities. Within fifteen days of a notification, a Member State may request to have jurisdiction of the case under Art 9 of the ECMR.

If the European Commission were to accede to such a request by Ireland, then the notification made to the Commission would constitute a notification under the 2002 Act. The date of receipt by the Authority of the Commission's decision is deemed to be the date of the notification (s 19(14)). Obviously this will extend the time frame within which the parties can complete the transaction, as the Authority will have up to four months from the date of receipt of the notification (or receipt of other information requested by the Authority) to issue its determination. It is therefore advisable to brief the Authority on transactions that are likely to raise an Art 9 issue, in advance of notifying the Commission. This will help to avoid unnecessary delays in the timing and execution of the transaction.

To date, the Authority has not yet made an Art 9 request since the 2002 Act came into force, although it did consider making an Art 9 request when the Royal Bank of Scotland acquired First Active in 2003. The Authority ultimately decided not to make a request (Competition Authority Press Release dated 26 November 2003). The reason for the Authority's concern was not obvious, as the transaction did not result in any significant increase in the market power of the parties post merger and it qualified for a simplified procedure under the ECMR. The Authority's concern can possibly be explained by the fact that the case arose at a time when the Authority was conducting a study into the banking sector in Ireland. The existence of a study into an industry is a factor to bear in mind for cases that raise an Art 9 issue.

## 6.12.2   ARTICLE 4(4) PROCEDURE

Under Art 4 of the ECMR, the notifying parties may request the European Commission, in advance of notification, to refer the notification to a national competition authority. The basis for the referral is a reasoned submission from the notifying parties, that: 'the concentration may affect competition in a market within a Member State which presents all the characteristics of a distinct market and should therefore be examined, in whole or in part, by that Member State' (Art 4(4)). The Commission must take its decision within twenty-five working days of the receipt of submissions.

This approach can expedite the notification process by avoiding an Art 9 reference procedure. The disadvantage is that it requires the notifying parties to identify, at the outset, the competition issues arising from the transaction.

## 6.12.3   ARTICLE 22 PROCEDURE

Under Art 22 of the ECMR, one (or more) Member States may request the European Commission to examine a transaction that falls within its (or their) jurisdiction and not the ECMR. The Commision may grant such a request where the transaction affects trade between Member States and threatens to significantly affect competition within the territory of the Member State or States making the request.

Ireland made an Art 22 request, together with several other national competition authorities, in 2003 in a transaction concerning General Electric and Agfa (Comp/M 3136).

### 6.12.4   ARTICLE 4(5) PROCEDURE

Article 4(5) of the ECMR provides that where a merger falls outside the scope of the ECMR, but is capable of being reviewed under the national competition laws of at least three Member States, then the notifying parties may request the European Commission to take jurisdiction of the case. The advantage of this procedure is that it can avoid multi-jurisdictional filings.

### 6.12.5   ARTICLE 21 PROCEDURE

Article 21 of the ECMR enables a Member State to object to a merger on grounds other than its effect on competition. Therefore a Member State may take measures to protect legitimate interests other than competition. Article 21(4) provides that public security, plurality of the media and prudential rules shall be regarded as legitimate interests. Any other public interest criteria may be communicated to the Commission, by the Member State concerned. The Commission will assess its compatibility with the general principles of Community law before the measures may be taken. The Commission has an obligation to inform a Member State within twenty-five working days of that communication.

## 6.13   Practical Approach to Merger Control

The following checklist may be useful to practitioners advising on the merger control aspects of a merger or acquisition:

(a)   Does the transaction constitute a 'merger'?

(b)   Does the transaction come within the scope of the ECMR?

(c)   Are the turnover thresholds in the 2002 Act exceeded?

(d)   Does the transaction involve a 'media business'?

(e)   Does the likely competitive impact of the merger on the market mean that a voluntary notification to the Authority is advisable?

If there is an affirmative reply to any of the above questions, then a notification should be made either to the European Commission or the Authority, as appropriate. The client will require advice on the procedure and the likely outcome of the merger process. In complex cases raising serious competition concerns, it may be advisable to engage an economist to advise on competition issues.

A suitable condition precedent should be inserted into the share purchase (or other relevant) agreement, as the transaction may not complete without prior clearance from the European Commission or the Authority (depending on who has jurisdiction).

## 6.14    Review of Irish Merger Control

The Minister for Enterprise, Trade and Employment has undertaken a review of the 2002 Act as it has been in force for over five years. The Minister issued a public consultation on the issue inviting responses from the public by the end of 2007. The Authority's proposed legislative reforms to the merger control provisions of the 2002 Act are available on the Authority's website (www.tca.ie).

# PART 3
# SELECTED BUSINESS LAW ISSUES

# CHAPTER 7

# IRISH COMPETITION LAW

## 7.1 Introduction

This chapter provides an overview of Irish competition law, excluding Irish merger control, which is covered in **chapter 6**.

The underlying objective of competition law is to ensure that businesses operate in a competitive market as this will ultimately benefit consumers. The economic theory behind this objective is that when businesses operate under competitive conditions they are likely to compete on price, quality and innovation to the benefit of consumers. Anti-competitive behaviour generally inhibits the natural competitive process, resulting in less choice and higher prices for consumers. Anti-competitive behaviour may take the form of agreements between businesses or independent action taken by a business that is powerful on a particular market. Competition law seeks to prevent anti-competitive behaviour and regulate mergers that may reduce competition.

Irish competition law is largely based on EC competition law, however there are some important differences. First, EC competition law requires that there be a potential effect on trade between EU Member States, secondly, the Irish regime carries criminal sanctions (unlike the European regime) and thirdly, Ireland does not have a State aid regime. EC competition law is considered in the Law Society manual on *European Law*.

In order to fully understand the application of Irish competition law, it is useful to first consider the relationship between Irish and EC competition law.

## 7.2 The Relationship between Irish and EC Competition Law

Irish competition law is largely modelled on EC competition law. Other than the requirement in EC competition law that there be a potential effect on trade between EU Member States, the substantive rules are largely the same. A business arrangement or practice in Ireland may infringe both Irish and EC competition law if it has the potential to affect trade between EU Member States.

The Competition Authority and the Irish courts have the power to enforce Irish competition law and the substantive EC competition rules. The substantive rules are the prohibition on anti-competitive arrangements, contained in

Article 81 of the EC Treaty (Art 81), and the prohibition on abuse of dominance contained in Article 82 of the EC Treaty ('Art 82'). The Irish Competition Act, 2002 contains penalties for infringement of both Irish competition law and Arts 81 and 82.

## 7.2.1 THE MODERNISATION REGULATION

Council Regulation (EC) No 1/2003 (the 'Modernisation Regulation') came into force on 1 May 2004. The Modernisation Regulation resulted in both the modernisation and decentralisation of competition law. The Modernisation Regulation harmonises and modernises the substantive law and provides for its decentralised application. Decentralisation involves a system of parallel competences in the application of EC competition law by the European Commission and national competition authorities. Therefore the European Commission, a national authority or various national authorities acting in parallel, can deal with a competition case affecting trade between EU Member States. The objective of this approach is to allow the European Commission to concentrate its resources on important cases. It also aims for greater enforcement of EC competition law throughout the EU.

EU Member States were required, under the Modernisation Regulation, to designate national authorities with responsibility for the application of Arts 81 and 82. In Ireland, both the Competition Authority and the courts have been so designated (European Communities (Implementation of the rules on competition laid down in Art 81 and Art 82) Regulations 2004 (SI 195/2004)). The designation includes the District Court, the Circuit Court, the High Court, the Court of Criminal Appeal and the Supreme Court. In practice, this means that the Competition Authority and the courts may take the following decisions in competition law cases (as set out in Art 5 of the Modernisation Regulation):

(a) require that an infringement be brought to an end;

(b) order interim measures;

(c) accept commitments; and

(d) impose fines, periodic penalty payments or any other penalty provided for by national law.

## 7.2.2 COOPERATION BETWEEN EUROPEAN COMPETITION AUTHORITIES

One of the main challenges, arising from the decentralised application of EC competition law, is the need to ensure the consistent application of EC competition law throughout the EU. As a result, the Modernisation Regulation requires that the European Commission and the national competition authorities apply the EC competition rules in close cooperation. The national competition authorities and the European Commission together, form a network of public authorities that cooperate closely in order to protect competition. The network, known as the European Competition Network ('ECN'), is a forum for discussion and cooperation in the application and enforcement of EC competition policy. Further details on the ECN are contained in a European Commission Notice on cooperation within the Network of Competition Authorities ((2004) OJ C101/43).

The European Commission has also produced a notice concerning cooperation between the Commission and the courts of the EU Member States, when the latter apply Arts 81 and 82 ((2004) OJ C101/104). Where the national court is acting in its capacity as a designated competition authority, then both this notice and the ECN notice cover cooperation with the court.

## 7.2.3    EFFECT ON TRADE BETWEEN EU MEMBER STATES

Article 3 of the Modernisation Regulation provides that national courts and competition authorities must apply EC competition law when they apply competition law to a situation where trade between EU Member States is affected. If the prerequisite condition of 'trade between Member States' is not fulfilled, then the case must be determined under national law. The European Commission Notice on the effect of trade ((2004) OJ C101/81) separates the concept into the elements of: the concept of 'trade between Member States'; the notion of 'may affect'; and the concept of 'appreciability'.

The 'effect on trade' concept was considered by the High Court in a case taken by the Competition Authority against the Irish League of Credit Unions (High Court judgment of 22 October 2004) (the 'ILCU case'). The Authority initially adopted the position that there was no inter-state trade issue. In the light of subsequent evidence, the Authority adopted the position that there was, as a matter of probability, the potential that inter-state trade might be affected to an 'appreciable' extent. The possibility arose due to the existence in Northern Ireland of credit unions affiliated to the ILCU. The High Court held that the simple fact that the agreement or practice at issue applied to more than one EU Member State was sufficient to establish the notion of 'trade between Member States'. Under the established jurisprudence of the Community, any form of cross-border activity is sufficient to establish community law jurisdiction. The court considered that, even though there was no immediate effect on inter-state trade, the potential or capability for such an occurrence is sufficient for the application of Arts 81 and 82. With regard to the question of appreciability, the court considered that the ILCU, with 80 per cent market share in the island of Ireland, had market power and that the negative definition of appreciability would not apply. As a result of this finding, the case came within the scope of the Modernisation Regulation.

Where a case comes within the scope of the Modernisation Regulation, the court has the powers and obligations set out therein. For example, the court is obliged to refer its draft judgment to the European Commission for comment.

When a national competition authority is acting under Art 81 or 82 it has an obligation, under Art 11 of the Modernisation Regulation, to inform the European Commission in writing before (or without delay after) commencing the first formal investigative measure. The information may also be made available to the ECN, however there are safeguards in place to protect confidentiality. The national competition authority also has an obligation to inform the European Commission, no later than thirty days before the adoption of a decision requiring: that an infringement be brought to an end; accepting commitments; or withdrawing the benefit of a block exemption regulation. This information may also be made available to the ECN. The national competition authority may also consult the European Commission on any case involving the application of Community law. These powers and obligations also apply to the courts where they are acting in their capacity as 'competition authorities'.

## 7.3    Institutional Framework

There are several administrative and judicial institutions with responsibility for competition law in Ireland.

### 7.3.1    THE COMPETITION AUTHORITY

The Competition Authority (the 'Authority') is the institution with primary responsibility for the administration and enforcement of competition law in Ireland. The Authority is an independent statutory body.

The powers and functions of the Authority are set out in the Competition Act, 2002 (the '2002 Act'). The principal functions of the Authority are to enforce competition law, to regulate mergers and to fulfil an advocacy function. The advocacy function is to advise the government, to study and analyse any practice or method of competition, to influence the legislative process and to inform the public about issues concerning competition (s 30).

As discussed above, the Authority cooperates with other European competition authorities through the ECN. At a national level, the Authority has entered into various cooperation agreements with sectoral regulatory bodies. The purpose of these agreements, as set out in s 34 of the 2002 Act, is:

(a)    to facilitate cooperation between the sectoral regulatory bodies and the Authority in the performance of their functions;

(b)    to avoid duplication of activities; and

(c)    to ensure consistency between their decisions.

The Authority has entered into cooperation agreements with the Broadcasting Commission of Ireland, the Commission for Aviation Regulation, the Commission for Communications Regulation, the Commission for Energy Regulation and the Office of the Director of Consumer Affairs.

As a result of these agreements, the Authority may refer complaints (received under the 2002 Act) to the appropriate sectoral regulator for consideration (see, for example, the Authority's press release of 19 March, 2004 concerning the referral of a complaint to the Commission for Communications Regulation).

### 7.3.2 THE MINISTER FOR ENTERPRISE, TRADE AND EMPLOYMENT

The Minister for Enterprise, Trade and Employment has overall responsibility for competition policy and legislation. Under s 30(2) of the 2002 Act, the Minister may request the Authority to carry out a study or analysis of any practice or method of competition affecting the supply and distribution of goods or the provision of services. The Minister also has a function, under Part 3 of the 2002 Act, in the regulation of media mergers in Ireland (this function is discussed in **chapter 6**).

### 7.3.3 THE COURTS

Under the Community law principle of direct effect and Art 6 of the Modernisation Regulation, national courts have the power to apply Arts 81 and 82. The courts also have an obligation, under Art 3 of the Modernisation Regulation, to apply EC competition law where they are applying national competition law (other than national merger control) to a situation where trade between EU Member States may be affected.

When the courts are acting in their capacity as a competition authority, in the application of Arts 81 and 82, they have the powers and functions outlined in the Modernisation Regulation. The first case in which an Irish court acted in such a capacity was in the ILCU case. Because the case came within the scope of the Modernisation Regulation, the High Court was obliged to refer its draft judgment to the European Commission for comment. The Commission did not exercise its right to comment in that case. As part of this process, the court received an undertaking that confidentiality would be maintained and that no information with regard to the content of the decision would be made available to the competition authorities of other EU Member States (including the Authority who was the plaintiff in the case).

The court was also obliged, under Art 15 of the Modernisation Regulation, to send a copy of the final written judgment to the European Commission. The judgment was added to a European Commission database of judgments of EU national courts concerning the application of Community competition law (available on DG Competition's website: www.europa.eu.int/comm/competition/index_en.html).

Article 15 of the Modernisation Regulation provides for cooperation between the Commission and the national courts. There is a facility for the Authority and the Commission to submit observations to a national court on issues relating to Arts 81 and 82. Further details on these interventions (known as '*amicus curiae*' or 'friend of the court') are set out in the European Commission Notice on the cooperation between the Commission and the courts of the EU Member States in the application of Arts 81 and 82 ((2004) OJ C101/104).

## 7.4 The Relevant Market

In order to apply competition law to the commercial behaviour of a business, it is necessary to understand the market in which it operates. By defining the market, it is possible to understand with whom a business competes and the conditions under which it operates on the market. The concept of the 'market' is not always easy to define. From a client's perspective, market definitions may vary for the purpose of marketing or business strategy. For competition law purposes, the market is divided between the product market and the geographic market. The analysis of the 'relevant market' can be complex. In cases where the market definition is critical to the case it may be necessary to consult an economist.

### 7.4.1 MARKET DEFINITION

There are three principal issues to be considered when defining the relevant market:

(a)   the products or services that the consumer would consider to be an alternative to that offered by the business;

(b)   the geographic area in which the business operates and in which competing products are supplied by competing businesses; and

(c)   additional factors that may affect the competitive behaviour of the business, i.e. the market dynamics.

### 7.4.2 PRODUCT AND GEOGRAPHIC MARKET

Guidance on the concept of market definition can be found in a European Commission Notice on the definition of relevant market for the purposes of Community competition law ((1997) OJ C372/5).

According to the European Commission's Notice (para 7), the relevant product market comprises all those products and/or services which are regarded as interchangeable or substitutable by the consumer, by reason of the products' characteristics, their prices and their intended use.

According to the European Commission's Notice (para 8), the relevant geographic market comprises the area in which the undertakings concerned are involved in the supply and demand of products or services, in which the conditions of competition are sufficiently homogeneous and which can be distinguished from neighbouring areas because the conditions of competition are appreciably different in those areas. The geographic market can be considered on a preliminary basis by taking broad indications as to the distribution of market shares between the parties and their competitors. A preliminary analysis of pricing and price differences, between geographic areas, may indicate a different geographic market. Different regulatory regimes may also be relevant to the analysis.

In an Irish context, it is often necessary to consider whether the relevant market is the island of Ireland or the State. Alternatively, markets may be local or regional, for example a grocery market may be local from a consumer's perspective, as he or she will not travel more than fifteen–thirty minutes for groceries.

The market is defined having consideration to both demand substitutability and supply substitutability in both a product and geographic context. From an economic point of view, the first is more important since: 'demand substitution constitutes the most immediate and effective disciplinary force on the suppliers of a given product in particular in relation to their pricing decisions' (para 13).

Demand substitutability relates to the products, which are considered by consumers to be substitutable for each other. A method of determining the substitutability of a product is by postulating a hypothetical small but permanent price increase (between 5 and 10 per cent). If the price increase results in consumers changing to another product, thus rendering the price increase unprofitable because of the resulting loss of sales, then the substitute products should be included in the market definition (para 17). This is also known as the 'SSNIP' test (i.e. small but significant and non-transitory increase in price). In other words, if a consumer wanted to buy pears for example, but the price had gone up 10 per cent, would the consumer buy apples instead of the pears? If the consumer bought the apples as a substitute for the pears, then it is arguable that apples and pears are in the same market.

Supply substitution concerns those suppliers who are able to switch production to the relevant market in the short term, without incurring significant additional costs or risks, in response to small and permanent changes in relative prices. The additional production that is put on the market will have a disciplinary effect on the competitive behaviour of the companies involved (para 20), therefore those firms can be considered as suppliers to the relevant market.

### 7.4.3   MARKET DYNAMICS

Once the product and geographic markets have been established, potential competition can be considered, i.e. whether new suppliers would enter the market if prices were increased by existing suppliers. In other words, would a potential competitor be likely to take the opportunity to enter the market and offer a cheaper product in response to the higher prices. The potential competition represented by the new competitor should be taken into account in the evaluation of the structure of the market. According to the Commission's notice: 'If required, this analysis is only carried out at a subsequent stage, in general, once the position of the companies involved in the relevant market has already been ascertained, and when such position gives rise to concerns from a competition point of view' (para 24). Concerns from a competition law perspective are most likely to arise where the market definition results in a small number of businesses having a large share of the market. This is because competition law places certain constraints on businesses with market power. Although market share does not necessarily equate to market power, it is an indication of market power.

If the market can be defined quite widely, on any reasonable definition of the market, then it may well dilute the market share and arguably the market power of the undertaking involved. Behaviour that might be considered problematic when engaged in by a company with a considerable degree of market power, is not problematic if the company does not have market power. If it appears that the undertaking concerned has market power, then it may be necessary to conduct a more detailed economic analysis of the competitive behaviour. The evidence used to define markets usually includes evidence of substitution in the past, views of customers and competitors and barriers to entering and exiting a market (see further, paras 36–52).

Defining the relevant market is important to determine whether any of the undertakings that are party to an agreement have market power. It is also relevant in applying the various Authority declarations and European Commission block exemption regulations (considered further below), as both the declarations and block exemption regulations contain market-share tests.

The Authority Notice, in respect of Guidelines for merger analysis, also contains useful guidance on the concept of the relevant market (N/02/004).

### 7.4.4 EXAMPLES OF MARKET DEFINITION

In competition law cases, a plaintiff, a competition regulator or a prosecutor will wish to define the market narrowly, as this will enhance the market power of the defendant and the constraints that may apply to the defendant under competition law. The defendant will naturally seek to argue for a broader market definition, as it will reduce its market share and also arguably its market power. There are two useful examples to illustrate this, one concerning beer and the other chocolate.

The first example concerns the case of *Ballina Mineral Water v Murphy Brewery* (High Court, unreported judgment of Mr Justice Kearns of 31 May 2002). In that case, the High Court overturned a finding by the Circuit Court that Heineken was dominant in the market for draught lagers. The High Court considered that the relevant product market was the beer market, rather than the narrower market for draught lager. The court considered the degree of substitutability between lagers, but considered that there was also a sufficient degree of substitutability between lagers, stouts and ales. Heineken had a market share of 18 per cent in this wider market. The court also considered the narrower possible market definition of the lager market and considered that Heineken had a market share of approximately 37 per cent. The plaintiff had attempted to define the market very narrowly so that Heineken would be found dominant in that narrow market definition. However, the broader market definition adopted by the High Court led to the conclusion that Heineken was not dominant. The plaintiff was therefore unsuccessful in its claim that Heineken had abused a dominant position.

The second example is found in a decision of the Authority concerning agreements between Cadbury and its retailers (Decision No 590, 23 June 2001). The decision concerned the legality of a standard loan agreement, notified to the

Authority under the Competition Act 1991 (when it was possible to notify the Authority for a licence confirming that an agreement was compatible with the Act). Cadbury argued that the relevant market in which it sold confectionary was the market for 'snack products'. Cadbury argued that, according to market research, ten products were 'acceptable alternatives' to 'chocolate and sugar'. The alternatives included: ice cream, yoghurts, crisps and nuts, biscuits, fresh fruit, and noodles/nachos/pizza (i.e. 'snack products'). Cadbury argued that suppliers of confectionary competed in a market with suppliers of these products (para 6). The Authority, however, adopted a narrower approach. The Authority considered that the relevant market was the market for 'impulse confectionary', which (although no market shares were given in the decision) would obviously have given Cadbury a higher market share than if the market were defined more broadly as the market for snack products.

## 7.5 Competition Act, 2002

The principal piece of legislation regulating competition in Ireland is the 2002 Act. The 2002 Act came into force on 1 July 2002 (other than the merger control provisions which came into force on 1 January 2003).

Since then, the Authority has developed its practice and procedure and issued various declarations and guidance notices. Given the similarities between Irish and EC competition law, the Authority has indicated (on its website) that it is appropriate to refer to European Commission notices for guidance on certain issues, provided that they are consistent with the application of the 2002 Act.

Part 2 of the 2002 Act contains the two basic prohibitions, i.e. the prohibition on anti-competitive arrangements and the prohibition on abuse of dominance. Part 3 of the 2002 Act contains the provisions that govern the Irish merger control regime. Part 4 of the 2002 Act sets out the powers and functions of the Authority.

## 7.6 Anti-competitive Arrangements

Section 4 of the 2002 Act prohibits anti-competitive arrangements. Section 4 is modelled on Art 81. Unlike Art 81, there is no requirement that there be a potential effect on trade between EU Member States, rather it is only necessary that the arrangement negatively affect competition 'in trade in any goods or services in the State or in any part of the State'.

Section 4(1) contains a general prohibition on anti-competitive arrangements and also provides that prohibited agreements are void. Section 4(2) and (5) provide for exceptions to the rule in s 4(1).

Section 4(1) provides as follows:

> *Subject to the provisions of this section, all agreements between undertakings, decisions by associations of undertakings and concerted practices which have*

*as their object or effect the prevention, restriction or distortion of competition in trade in any goods or services in the State or in any part of the State are prohibited and void, including in particular, without prejudice to the generality of this subsection, those which—*

*(a) directly or indirectly fix purchase or selling prices or any other trading conditions;*

*(b) limit or control production, markets, technical developments or investment;*

*(c) share markets or sources of supply;*

*(d) apply dissimilar conditions to equivalent transactions with other trading parties thereby placing them at a competitive disadvantage;*

*(e) make the conclusion of contracts subject to acceptance by the other parties of supplementary obligations, which by their nature or according to commercial usage have no connection with the subject of such contracts.*

Many aspects of the prohibition in s 4 are complex and require elaboration. The concepts are discussed below.

## 7.6.1 UNDERTAKINGS

The prohibition in s 4 concerns arrangements between two or more 'undertakings'. An agreement (decision or concerted practice) will not come within the scope of s 4 unless there are at least two separate 'undertakings' involved.

An 'undertaking' is defined in the 2002 Act as: 'a person being an individual, a body corporate or an unincorporated body of persons engaged for gain in the production, supply or distribution of goods or the provision of a service' (s 3).

The concept of 'engaged for gain' was considered by the Supreme Court in *Deane v VHI* [1992] 2 IR 319, albeit under the Competition Act, 1991. The Supreme Court found that the VHI, a mutual non-profit making insurer, constituted an undertaking for the purposes of the Competition Act, 1991. The Supreme Court declined to adopt an interpretation of the words 'for gain' as equating with 'for profit' and stated that:

> the true construction . . . is that the words 'for gain' connote merely an activity carried on or a service supplied . . . which is done in return for a charge or payment . . .

The position under EC competition law is not dissimilar. There is no statutory definition of 'undertaking' in EC competition law. According to the jurisprudence of the EU courts, the definition turns on 'economic activity' regardless of the entity's legal status or the way in which it is financed. Any activity consisting in offering goods and services on a given market is considered to be an economic activity, it is not necessary that the entity make a profit (Case C–475/99, *Amulanz Glockner* [2001] ECR 8089 and Joined Cases C–180/98 to C–184/98, *Pavlov and Others* [2000] ECR I–6451).

Section 4 also applies to an association of undertakings. In the ILCU case, referred to at **7.2.3** above, the High Court considered that a trade association itself could be considered to be an 'undertaking'.

It appears that the basis for this finding was that the provision of a savings protection scheme was an economic activity with an economic objective.

Section 4 does not apply to so-called 'intra-group' transactions because, from a competition law perspective, there is only one 'undertaking' involved in the transaction. In other words, agreements or contracts between companies within the same corporate group will not fall within the scope of s 4(1) if the relationship between the companies is so close that economically it would be realistic to regard them as a single economic entity. Whether a transaction is wholly intra group for this purpose will depend on whether the relevant companies are under common control. The concept of control is discussed at **chapter 6**.

An agreement between an employer and an employee will not normally be considered to be an agreement between two undertakings, as an employee is not normally considered to be an undertaking. Agreements between employers and employees do not therefore fall within the scope of s 4 or Art 81. Restrictive covenants in employment agreements should be analysed under the common law doctrine of restraint of trade.

The Authority had considered this issue in a Notice published in September 1992 on 'Employment Agreements and the Competition Act'. The Authority's view as expressed in that Notice was that employees are not normally undertakings, however, if an employee were to set up a business in his own right, then the employee would at that point become an undertaking and the agreement between him and his employer would become an agreement between undertakings. In January 2007, the Authority revoked this Notice to reflect its revised position that a contract of employment cannot become an 'agreement between undertakings' and those contracts will therefore never come within the scope of s 4 of the 2002 Act. Restrictive covenants in employment agreements should therefore be assessed under the common law doctrine of restraint of trade and not s 4 of the 2002 Act.

Under the common law doctrine of restraint of trade, a non-compete clause must be reasonable if it is to be enforceable. Whether it is reasonable will depend on the circumstances of the case. The non-compete clause must be limited in scope to the business of the company and limited in its geographic scope to the area in which the company carries on its business. The time limit must be reasonable and this will vary depending on the circumstances of the case (see further *Petrofina (Great Britain) Ltd v Martin* [1966] Ch 146, *John Orr Ltd v Orr* [1987] ILRM 702 and V. Power, *Competition Law and Practice* (Tottel, 2001) p. 354).

## 7.6.2 AGREEMENTS, DECISIONS AND CONCERTED PRACTICES

The prohibition in s 4 covers anti-competitive agreements, decisions of associations of undertakings and concerted practices. The concept covers both legally enforceable contracts and oral or 'gentlemen's agreements' (Case 41/69, *ACF*

*Chemiefarma NV v Commission* [1970] ECR 661). The concept also covers coordination between independent undertakings, for example through the medium of a trade association, through complex cartels or where there is a concerted practice between competitors.

### 7.6.2.1 Agreements

An agreement will generally be deemed to exist whenever one undertaking agrees (directly or indirectly) with another undertaking to limit its freedom of action so as to restrict competition in the marketplace.

This broad definition of the concept of 'agreement' means that mere contact or communication between undertakings regarding their competitive behaviour is problematic.

### 7.6.2.2 Decisions by associations of undertakings

Competitors often communicate through the medium of a trade association. Constitutions, byelaws, articles of association, rules, recommendations, codes of conduct or other basic documents of a trade association may amount to a decision by an association of undertakings. If the decision has an anti-competitive object (for example, to fix prices) or effect (for example, to boycott a supplier), then it will come within the scope of s 4 and/or Art 81 of the EC Treaty. In some cases, it may be easier to establish the existence of a decision of an association of undertakings than to prove the existence of individual agreements or a concerted practice. The question of whether an association itself is party to an agreement is a question of fact to be decided in each case. Minutes, agenda, circulars and other documentation may evidence the decision. If a decision by an association of undertakings is held to breach s 4/Art 81, both the association and its individual members may be liable to fines.

### 7.6.2.3 Concerted practice

The concept of a concerted practice is complex. In *Dyestuffs* (Case 48/69 [1972] ECR 619, [1972] CMLR 557), the European Court of Justice ('ECJ') defined a concerted practice as:

> a form of co-ordination between undertakings which, without having reached the stage where an agreement properly so-called has been concluded, knowingly substitutes practical co-operation between them for the risks of competition.

In *Polypropylene*, the ECJ stated that each undertaking, by its participation in meetings, had taken part with its competitors in concerted action, which had the purpose of influencing conduct on the market generally. The Court was influenced by the fact that the parties had disclosed to each other the course of conduct which each contemplated adopting on the market.

Unilateral behaviour therefore falls outside the scope of Art 81 and s 4 of the 2002 Act as there is no agreement with another undertaking (although the behaviour could possibly infringe Art 82/s 5 if the undertaking concerned has a dominant position).

### 7.6.3   OBJECT OR EFFECT

Section 4 prohibits agreements that have as their *object* or *effect* the prevention, restriction or distortion of competition in trade in any goods in Ireland or in any part of Ireland. Therefore, if an arrangement has an anti-competitive object, even though it has no such effect it will be prohibited and void unless it complies with the conditions in s 4(5).

It is the objective intention of the arrangement and not the subjective intention of the parties that is relevant, i.e. the purpose of the agreement considered in the economic content in which it is to be applied.

### 7.6.4   PERMISSIBLE SECTION 4(1) ARRANGEMENTS

If on a preliminary analysis, an arrangement falls within the scope of the prohibition in s 4(1), the next stage is to consider whether the arrangement:

(a)   satisfies the conditions in s 4(5); or

(b)   benefits from a declaration issued by the Authority.

### 7.6.5   SECTION 4(5) CONDITIONS

In proceedings for a breach of s 4(1), it is a good defence to prove that the agreement, decision or concerted practice did not contravene s 4(1) because it complied with the efficiency conditions set out in s 4(5) or a declaration issued by the Authority. Section 4(5) is similar to Art 81(3). In the case of Art 81(1) offences, s 6(4) provides that it is a good defence to show that the arrangement benefited from an exemption under Art 81(3).

The conditions in s 4(5) are as follows:

> . . . *the agreement, decision or concerted practice or category of agreement, decision or concerted practice, having regard to all relevant market conditions, contributes to improving the production or distribution of goods or provision of services or to promoting technical or economic progress, while allowing consumers a fair share of the resulting benefit and does not:*
>
> *(a)   impose on the undertakings concerned, terms which are not indispensable to the attainment of those objectives;*
>
> *(b)   afford undertakings the possibility of eliminating competition in respect of a substantial part of the products or services in question.*

In other words, although the agreement contains restrictions, the agreement ultimately benefits consumers. The restrictions must not eliminate competition or go beyond the scope of the objective of the agreement.

## 7.6.6 DECLARATIONS AND NOTICES

The Authority has the power (under s 4(3) of the 2002 Act) to issue declarations that, in its opinion, certain categories of agreements comply with the efficiency conditions set out in s 4(5).

Section 4(2) of the 2002 Act provides that an agreement, decision or concerted practice shall not be prohibited if it complies with certain conditions or comes within the scope of a declaration issued by the Authority. A declaration is an opinion of the Authority that a category of agreement, or practice, complies with the efficiency conditions in s 4(5) and consequently is not prohibited under s 4. In essence this means that, even if the agreement falls within the scope of the prohibition in s 4(1), it may qualify for exemption. A declaration, issued by the Authority, is similar to an exemption under Art 81(3).

Under the Competition Act, 1991 (which was repealed by the 2002 Act) there was a procedure in place to notify the Authority to determine the compatibility of an agreement with the legislation. There is no such procedure under the 2002 Act (other than in respect of mergers discussed in **chapter 6**). Practitioners therefore need to rely on the Authority's declarations or guidance notices, to assess the competitive effects of arrangements or, in their absence, rely on European Commission exemptions, by analogy.

When the 2002 Act came into force, the Authority issued a statement to the effect that existing category licences (similar to declarations but issued under the Competition Act 1991) would continue for the rest of their term (unless they were first revoked) as though they were declarations. Since then, various declarations have been issued. There is one remaining category licence in relation to motor fuels (Competition Authority Decision No 25). It concerns long-term exclusive purchasing arrangements for the resale of petroleum products in service stations.

Given the abolition of the former notification system, practitioners and businesses have to assess the compatibility of arrangements or commercial practices without the comfort of an individual decision from the Authority. It is worth noting, however, that the Authority has issued almost 600 decisions in respect of notifications under the old regime that still provide guidance on the Authority's approach to certain agreements. In addition, the Authority has published various enforcement decisions under the 2002 Act and various guidance notices, published in accordance with s 30(1).

It is advisable, when considering the application of s 4 to an arrangement, to first consider whether the Authority has issued any declarations in respect of the category of agreement or practice concerned. If no such declaration exists, consider whether the European Commission has issued any exemptions or notices on the subject. Given the similarities between s 4 and Art 81, the European Commission exemptions set out the general principles which are generally applicable in an Irish context.

## 7.7 Horizontal and Vertical Agreements

From a competition law perspective, agreements are often categorised as either 'horizontal' or 'vertical' agreements. Horizontal agreements are agreements between undertakings at the same end of the supply and distribution chain, i.e. competitors. Vertical agreements are agreements between undertakings at different ends of the supply and distribution chain, for example suppliers and distributors.

The rationale for the distinction between horizontal and vertical agreement is that, in general, vertical agreements pose a low risk of anti-competitive effect unless one of the participating undertakings has a high degree of market power. On the contrary, horizontal agreements involve cooperation between competitors, therefore they pose a high risk of anti-competitive effect unless they are limited to issues that are unlikely to have such an effect.

### 7.7.1 HORIZONTAL AGREEMENTS

Cooperation between competitors to restrict competition through price fixing or market sharing is clearly unlawful. These practices are known as 'hard-core offences' and are subject to more severe penalties than other offences (see **7.9** below). Competitors often cooperate in this way as a cartel. The detection and prosecution of anti-competitive cartels has been identified as a top priority for both the Authority and the European Commission.

There is an Irish cartel immunity programme that has been adopted by the Authority and the Director of Public Prosecutions (the DPP). Provided certain criteria are met, an individual or business may be able to obtain immunity from prosecution for cartel offences under the 2002 Act for being the first to report the crime and cooperating with the Authority in its investigation of the cartel. Any person or undertaking implicated in an activity that violates the 2002 Act may apply for immunity. If an undertaking qualifies for a recommendation for full immunity, all past and present directors, officers and employees who admit their involvement in a cartel as part of the corporate admission and who comply with the conditions in the notice also qualify for immunity. Application for immunity should be made to the Authority in accordance with a notice on its website, however only the DPP can grant immunity. Subject to the requirements in the notice, the Authority will make a recommendation to the DPP to grant immunity.

Cooperation between competitors is not always negative. Cooperation may result in an improvement in the production or distribution of goods or may promote technical or economic progress, to the benefit of consumers. Agreements relating to research and development and specialisation are an example of such agreements. The Authority has not issued specific guidance on horizontal agreements, therefore it is necessary to turn to EU jurisprudence for guidance on the issue.

The European Commission has adopted various block exemptions in relation to horizontal agreements (Commission Regulation (EC) No 2659/2000 in relation to research and developments agreements and Commission Regulation (EC) No 2658/2000 in relation to specialisation agreements). The Commission has also issued guidelines in respect of horizontal agreements ((2001) OJ C3/2). The guidelines consider six types of agreements, namely: research and development, production, purchasing, commercialisation, standardisation and environmental agreements. The guidelines make it clear that horizontal cooperation agreements may lead to competition problems where the parties agree to fix prices, limit output or share markets or where cooperation enables the parties to maintain, gain, or increase their market power, thereby causing negative effects with respect to prices, output, innovation or the variety and quality of products. It is acknowledged however, that substantial economic benefits can flow from horizontal cooperation such as sharing risk, improving know-how and launching innovation. The benefit to small and medium-sized enterprises is particularly noted. Market structure and market share is important in any analysis. In general terms, the larger the market power of the cooperating undertakings the harder it is to justify the need for cooperation.

## 7.7.2 VERTICAL AGREEMENTS

In general, vertical agreements pose a low risk of anti-competitive effect unless one of the participating undertakings has a high degree of market power. There is a general exemption for vertical agreements under both EC and Irish competition law. Both legal instruments set out the restrictions in vertical agreements that infringe s 4/Art 81. Both legal instruments also contain a market-share test. Although market share does not equate to market power, it is a good indicator of the relative strength of a business on a market. The market-share test ensures that business with a small market share can benefit from the exemption set out in these legal instruments, provided they meet the rest of the relevant criteria. Businesses with a high market share need to analyse their situation carefully to determine whether restrictions in their agreements are prohibited under s 4/Art 81. This topic is considered in detail in **chapter 15** on Vertical Agreements.

## 7.8 Abuse of Dominance

Irish and EU law prohibit businesses in a dominant position from abusing their dominance. A dominant business has market power. The reason competition law places constraints on businesses with market power is because the law seeks to protect weak competitors from abusive behaviour by large competitors. If businesses with market power were to operate without constraint, there is a risk that the market would be less competitive to the ultimate detriment of consumers.

Section 5 of the 2002 Act contains the Irish prohibition on abuse of dominance. Section 5 is based on Art 82. Article 82 requires that the abuse occur within the common market, or a substantial part of the common market and that it may affect trade between EU Member States. Section 5 requires that the abuse occur in the State or in any part of the State.

Section 5(1) provides that:

> *Any abuse by one or more undertakings of a dominant position in trade for any goods or services in the State or in any part of the State is prohibited.*

Unlike s 4, s 5 is an absolute prohibition and no exemption is possible. Many aspects of the prohibition in s 5 are complex and require elaboration. The concepts are discussed below.

## 7.8.1    DOMINANCE

Undertakings in a dominant position have a responsibility to ensure that their behaviour does not constitute an abuse of dominance. In other words, dominant companies have a special responsibility to ensure that the way they do business does not prevent competition and does not harm consumers. It is not the existence of dominance that is prohibited, but rather the abuse of dominance.

There is no definition in the 2002 Act of the concept of a 'dominant position' or 'dominance'. The ECJ has formulated the test as being whether the undertaking enjoys:

> a position of economic strength . . . which enables it to prevent effective competition being maintained on the market by affording it the power to act to an appreciable extent independently of its competitors, customers and ultimately consumers.

This is the definition that was adopted by the ECJ in Case 27/76, *United Brands v Commission* [1979] ECR 207, p. 227.

In essence, the test is whether the undertaking has sufficient market power to be able to act to an appreciable extent independently of others in the market-place. There is no single market share figure beyond which one is dominant, but consistent market shares in excess of 40 per cent can raise concerns.

In *Ballina Mineral Water v Murphy Brewery* (see above) disregarding the plaintiff's arguments regarding brand strength, Justice Kearns described dominance in the following terms:

> the development of a strong brand image . . . is nothing more than a vehicle or a means whereby one achieves market share. It is not an end in itself . . . it may add value and it may help with advertising and promotion and so on to have a strong brand image, but at the end of the day, the markers for dominance essentially resolve around market share and the capacity, to put it bluntly, to throw one's weight around in terms of price adjustment

and so on without fear of consequence or suffering loss of market share as a result of steps one takes. It is perfectly clear from the evidence in this case that if Heineken were to put a foot wrong, that the main competitor and its larger competitor would stop in overnight to hoover up the slack that would be left by any ill-advised price adjustments or hikes or anything of that sort with a ready supply of products to take the place of Heineken.

Essentially the Court considered the degree of market power held by Heineken and whether it could act independently of its competitors or whether they would react to a price rise and thus constrain any potentially abusive behaviour by Heineken.

The Authority adopts a similar approach to the assessment of dominance. In a decision concerning allegations of predatory pricing (Decision No E/05/001), the Authority made it clear that market share is only one factor in determining dominance. Relying, largely on EU jurisprudence, the Authority considered that a number of factors should be considered in determining whether or not a firm is dominant. These include:

(a)   the market shares of the allegedly dominant firm relative to its competitors, both current and past levels;

(b)   barriers to entry;

(c)   barriers to expansion;

(d)   customer switching costs;

(e)   the ability of the allegedly dominant firm to act independently of its competitors; and

(f)   countervailing buyer power.

According to the decision, these factors should not be viewed solely as a checklist, but rather as a means of understanding and characterising the dynamics of a market and thus coming to a view about dominance. The Authority concluded that (notwithstanding the high market share of the company concerned) in the case at hand, market share was not indicative of dominance. According to the decision:

> this reaffirms the view that market share should only be used as an initial screening device for situations where there may be competition concerns and not as a definitive test for determining dominance. (para 2.51)

The factors identified in this decision are considered below. These factors help to determine whether a business is dominant in a market. The starting point in the analysis should be first to define the relevant market (see **7.4** above). It is only when the market has been defined that it is possible to determine the market share of the business as well as the dynamics of the market.

### 7.8.1.1   Market share

A high market share is an indication of dominance and it is a useful starting point in any analysis of dominance. There is no single market-share figure, which indicates dominance, but consistent market shares in excess of 40 per cent can raise concerns. Once a consistently high market share has been established it is necessary to consider the additional factors that determine whether or not the undertaking concerned has sufficient market power to act independently on the market. In other words, these factors help to determine dominance.

### 7.8.1.2 Barriers to entry and expansion

Barriers to entry are barriers that prevent or dissuade potential competitors from entering the relevant market. Barriers to expansion are barriers that prevent or dissuade existing competitors from expanding and increasing their output in order to compete in the relevant market.

Barriers to entry and expansion can take a number of forms. Legal barriers would include a legislative framework that limits the number of market participants through licences. Barriers can also arise due to capacity constraints, for example if a competitor has to commit large sunk investments in order to expand capacity, which it would not recover if it were to exit the market. Barriers can also take the form of essential infrastructure such as a port or an airport, which are difficult or impossible to replicate for reasons of cost or planning limitations.

Where barriers to entry or expansion exist on a market, a dominant undertaking is not constrained in its behaviour by the threat of potential competition from new entrants or increased competition from existing competitors. This is an important factor in the assessment of whether an undertaking has market power.

### 7.8.1.3 Economies of scale

Economies of scale or scope refer to a situation where an undertaking's average total costs fall as their customer base and output grow. This can give an undertaking an advantage over smaller competitors.

'Scale and scope economies result from the spreading of fixed costs over larger output or a broader set of products, leading to a reduction of average costs' (see DG Competition, Discussion paper on the application of Article 82 of the EC Treaty to exclusionary abuses, Brussels, December 2005 (para 40) available at: http://ec.europa.eu/comm/competition/index_en.html).

### 7.8.1.4 Customer switching costs

Customer switching costs may be a factor in enhancing the market power of an allegedly dominant undertaking. If there is a cost involved for a dominant supplier's customer switching to alternative suppliers, then this may be a factor in enhancing the market power of the dominant supplier. For example, there may be a punitive break clause in the contract between the dominant supplier and its customer that acts as a disincentive for the customer to switch supplier, even where the dominant supplier raises its prices:

> The reactions of customers to a potential price increase must therefore be analysed. If customers have alternative sources of supply and there are low costs associated with sourcing their demands elsewhere, it will undermine the ability of an undertaking with a large market share to profitably increase its prices. (Authority Decision No E/05/001, para 2.49)

#### 7.8.1.5  Countervailing buyer power

Buyers with market power may be in a strong bargaining position with a dominant supplier. The large supermarket chains are an example of strong buyers. Strong buyers can respond to a price increase by a supplier by seeking an alternative supplier. The buyers can effectively find alternative suppliers and easily switch suppliers. The Authority considered this issue in an enforcement decision concerning TicketMaster Ireland (Decision No E/06/001, 26 September 2005).

#### 7.8.1.6  Independence

The ability to act independently can arise from a culmination of the factors described above. By taking the above factors into account, it should be possible to determine whether the undertaking concerned has the ability to act independently of its competitors, customers and ultimately consumers and thus to exercise market power in the relevant market.

### 7.8.2  COLLECTIVE DOMINANCE

The prohibition in s 5 covers an abuse by 'one or more undertakings'.

One or more undertakings may be collectively dominant and together they may abuse that collective dominant position. The EU jurisprudence in this area is set out in the Law Society manual on *European Law*. The issue of collective dominance has yet to be considered in detail by the Irish courts.

The leading EU case in this area is the judgment of the European Court of First Instance (the 'CFI') in Case T-342/99, *Airtours plc v Commission* (ECR 2002, p. II–02585). According to the court, the essence of collective dominance is tacit coordination. This can be summarised as follows: first, dominant undertakings adopt a common policy on the market; second, in order to adopt that policy there must be sufficient transparency in the market for the dominant undertakings to monitor the common policy; third, the situation must be sustainable over time and there must be an incentive not to depart from the common policy (i.e. that highly competitive action by one undertaking would provoke identical action by the others, so that it would derive no benefit from its initiative). Finally, in order to prove the existence of a collective dominant position to the requisite legal standard, it is necessary to also establish that the foreseeable reaction of current and future competitors, as well as of consumers, would not jeopardise the results expected from the common policy.

### 7.8.3 OBJECTIVE JUSTIFICATION AND PROPORTIONALITY

In order to establish a breach of s 5 and/or Art 82, it is necessary to demonstrate first that the undertaking concerned is dominant, and, second, that its conduct constitutes an abuse of dominance. The conduct is not abusive if it is objectively justified and proportionate to the legitimate aim.

In accordance with EU jurisprudence, the concepts of 'objective justification' and 'proportionality' are generally used to distinguish abusive behaviour from legitimate behaviour (*Centre Belge d'Étude de Marché Télémarketing v CLT*, Case 311/84 [1985] ECR 3261, [1986] 2 CMLR 558 and *Eurofix-Bauco v Hilti*, OJ [1988] L65/19, [1989] 4 CMLR 677). These concepts are equally applicable in the application of s 5 of the 2002 Act. The Authority has described the concepts in the following terms:

> If the conduct arises as a result of the application of objective (e.g. technical) rather than anti-competitive criteria that are uniformly applied in all its commercial dealings, this may be considered legitimate behaviour. Where it is established that the dominant undertaking's conduct is objectively justified it must then be established that the conduct is proportional, i.e. does not go beyond what is necessary for the attainment of those objectives. (Decision No E/05/001 para 2.4)

### 7.8.4 EXAMPLES OF ABUSE OF DOMINANCE

Some of the principal examples of abuse of dominance are discussed below. For a more indepth discussion on these issues, the reader is referred to the Law Society manual on *EU Law*. It is also worth noting that the European Commission is conducting a review of the EU jurisprudence in this area with the aim of issuing guidelines on the application of Art 82. In December 2005, the Commission published a paper for discussion with the public. The paper describes a general framework for analysing abusive exclusionary conduct by a dominant company. The most important topics raised by the replies to this paper were discussed at a public hearing in June 2006. Both the paper and the public response to the paper are available at: http://ec.europa.eu/comm/competition/antitrust/art82/index.html. The guidelines are useful in an Irish context. The guidelines will be consulted upon within the ECN, therefore the Authority will have an input on the document that is ultimately produced.

Section 5(2) contains the following examples of abuse of dominance:

(a) *directly or indirectly imposing unfair purchase or selling prices or other unfair trading conditions;*

(b) *limiting production, markets or technical development to the prejudice of consumers;*

(c) *applying dissimilar conditions to equivalent transactions with other trading parties, thereby placing them at a competitive disadvantage;*

(d) *making the conclusion of contracts subject to acceptance by the other parties of supplementary obligations, which, by their nature or according to commercial usage, have no connection with the subject of such contracts.*

### 7.8.4.1 Abusive pricing

Section 5(2)(a) of the 2002 Act provides that it may be an abuse of dominance to impose unfair purchase or selling prices. In practice this arises where prices are excessively high, prices are discriminatory or where prices are unfairly low (amounting to 'predatory pricing').

In *United Brands*, the ECJ held that prices set by a dominant undertaking are excessively high where they bear no resemblance to the economic value of a product. This is a difficult test to apply and in practice there have been relatively few cases on excessive pricing.

Section 5(2)(c) provides that it can be an abuse of dominance to apply dissimilar conditions to equivalent transactions with other trading partners. The issue of discriminatory pricing was also considered in the *United Brands* case. In essence, a dominant undertaking cannot charge a different price to two comparable customers unless it can justify the difference in price.

The ECJ formulated a test for predatory pricing in Case 62/82, *AKZO Chemie v Commission* [1991] ECR 3359. The ECJ held that a dominant undertaking would be guilty of abusing its dominant position if were to sell its product at a price that did not allow it to recover its costs. It drew a distinction between below-cost selling, where most but not all of the costs are recovered (i.e. sales below average total cost), and even lower selling prices, where even less of the costs are recovered (i.e. sales below average variable cost). As it can be difficult to determine recovery of costs, it is also necessary to consider whether the below-cost selling is part of a wider plan to eliminate a competitor.

The Authority considered the question of predatory pricing in a case concerning the alleged predation by the Drogheda Independent Company Limited in the market for advertising in local newspapers in the greater Drogheda area (Decision No E/05/001).

The Authority found that even if the Drogheda Independent Company Limited were dominant, its conduct did not constitute an abuse of dominance. The Authority described predatory pricing as follows:

> Predatory pricing refers to a situation whereby a dominant undertaking strategically reacts to the entry or presence of a competitor by pricing so low that it deliberately incurs losses so as to expel the competitor from the market in order to charge above the competitive level in the future. While consumers benefit in the short run from low prices, ultimately consumers suffer as a result of higher prices and reduced choice in the long term following the exit from the market of the undertaking subject to predation. Thus, predation has two purposes: to induce exit from the market and to deter future entry by establishing a reputation for fighting entry. (para 2.54)

According to the decision, the Authority follows a structured rule of reason approach when investigating predatory pricing allegations. This approach involves a consideration of the following issues:

(a) the plausibility of the alleged predation (i.e. whether the alleged predation made economic sense and whether the market facts are consistent with the alleged predation);

(b) whether there is business justification for the behaviour;

(c) the feasibility of recouping losses (i.e. predatory pricing requires that there is a reasonable expectation that short-term losses can be recovered through charging higher prices in the medium to longer term. Recovery of losses depends on entry conditions in the relevant market: the higher the barriers to entry, the greater the chance of recovery);

(d) whether or not pricing below cost has taken place.

### 7.8.4.2 Exclusionary abuses

In its current review of the EU jurisprudence on abuse of dominance, the Commission has divided abuse of dominance into two main categories, namely exclusionary abuses and exploitative abuses. Exclusionary abuses are those which exclude competitors from the market. Exploitative abuses involve exploitation of a dominant position by, for example, charging excessive prices or discriminating between customers. The Commission's current review focuses on the first category as it is the most common.

The following are examples of exclusionary abuse:

(a) predatory pricing, i.e. pricing below cost as part of a plan to eliminate a competitor and deter entry to the market (considered above);

(b) single branding, i.e. where purchasers are required contractually or by inducement to purchase all or almost all of their requirements from the dominant supplier;

(c) loyalty rebates, i.e. discounts which induce a purchaser to purchase all or almost all of its requirements from the dominant supplier;

(d) tying and bundling, i.e. where the dominant supplier leverages its market power from one market to another market by selling a dominant product together with a non-dominant product; and

(e) refusal to supply, i.e. where a dominant supplier refuses to supply in order to limit competition on a (secondary) market in which it is active.

This conduct is 'exclusionary' in that it enhances the market power of a dominant supplier and limits the remaining competitive constraints on that dominant undertaking. The approach of both the Authority and the Commission to assessing such cases is to determine the *effect* of any allegedly abusive behaviour on competition and consumers.

### Single branding and loyalty rebates

Both single branding and loyalty rebates (also referred to as fidelity rebates) are methods used by suppliers to induce customers to purchase all or almost all of their requirements from that supplier. When these practices are engaged in by a dominant undertaking, they can foreclose the market to competitors and thus constitute an abuse of dominance. In other words, the restriction can limit a market, contrary to s 5(2)(b) and Art 82(b).

Single branding is an obligation on a buyer to purchase all, or practically all, of its requirements from a single supplier. This is also referred to as exclusive dealing or exclusive purchasing or a 'non-compete obligation' (as defined in Commission Regulation (EC) No 2790/1999 on the application of Art 81(3) to categories of vertical agreements and concerted practices (1999) OJ L336/21).

The general principle is that this type of restriction on a seller where the supplier has market power can result in foreclosure of the market to competing suppliers. Where the buyer is a retailer selling to final consumers, the restriction can also result in a loss of in-store inter-brand competition (see further paras 138–160, Vertical Restraints Guidelines (2000) OJ C291/1). As a result, competitors of the dominant supplier cannot compete to gain the business of the buyer. For example, if a dominant baker enters into an exclusive arrangement with a supermarket, whereby the supermarket commits to purchase bread only from the dominant baker, then the baker's competitors cannot supply the supermarket. The system is aggravated if the baker enters into similar arrangements with several supermarkets, as it may completely cut out its competitors from the market.

For the reasons outlined above, dominant undertakings may not impose exclusive purchasing obligations on their customers. However, it is possible that dominant undertakings may seek to achieve the same end through their rebate system. These sorts of rebates, also known as 'loyalty' or 'fidelity' rebates constitute an abuse of dominance. Essentially, the rebate system is structured so that the customer gets rewarded for loyalty. The reward takes the form of a discount where the customer purchases all (or a substantial percentage) of its requirements for a particular product, from the dominant supplier. This will prevent the customer from switching to a competitor of the dominant undertaking.

Volume rebates (i.e. rebates granted based on the quantity of products purchased) are generally considered to be objectively justifiable; therefore, they do not constitute an abuse of dominance. The Commission has described the distinction between legitimate rebates and loyalty rebates as follows:

> a dominant supplier can give discounts that relate to efficiencies, for example discounts for large orders that allow the supplier to produce large batches of product, but cannot give discounts or incentives to encourage loyalty, that is for avoiding purchases from a competitor of the dominant supplier (Virgin/ British Airways, OJ [2000] L30/1, [2000] 4 CMLR 999, para 101).

*Tying and bundling*

Section 5(d) provides that it can be an abuse of dominance to:

> *make the conclusion of contracts subject to acceptance by the other parties of supplementary obligations, which, by their nature or according to commercial usage, have no connection with the subject of such contracts.*

Tying and bundling products can lead to significant savings in production, distribution and transaction costs. Companies may also engage in tying to ensure quality, reputation and good usage of their machinery. However, tying and bundling when engaged in by a dominant company may result in foreclosure, price discrimination and higher prices. In particular, tying or bundling can cause a problem where it enables a dominant supplier to leverage market power from one market into an ancillary market in which the dominant undertaking is not dominant. This can result in foreclosure in the ancillary market as it limits potential customers in the secondary market. It may also raise barriers to entry. In addition, if the ancillary market is closely related to the tying market, it may also strengthen the market power of the dominant supplier as more customers opt to purchase the tied or bundled product, thus raising barriers to entry and expansion in that market. Therefore, it can be an abuse of dominance to make the sale of one product subject to the purchase of another unrelated product (see further *Hilti* [1991] ECR II–14239 and DG Comp DG Competition discussion paper on exclusionary abuses, paras 177–183).

The approach of the Irish courts to this issue was tested in the ILCU case. In May 2007, the Supreme Court overturned an earlier High Court judgment that the ILCU had abused its dominant position by tying the provision of a savings protection scheme to the purchase of its credit union representation services. The Court held that no unlawful tying had occurred as the scheme did not constitute a distinct product from the bundle of services that the ILCU had provided to its own members. As the scheme and the representation services were not distinct products in distinct markets, the case for tying as an abuse failed (*Competition Authority v O'Regan and Others*, Supreme Court, unreported judgment, 8 May 2007).

*Refusal to supply*

When a dominant undertaking refuses to supply a customer, it can, in certain circumstances, constitute an abuse of dominance contrary to s 5(2)(b) and Art 82(b). This general principle is controversial for a number of reasons. First, it is a generally accepted principle of contract law that companies should be free to choose with whom they wish to enter a contract. Second, dominant companies often argue that obligations to allow competitors access to their facilities or proprietary information is both an unjustified attack on private property rights and a disincentive to innovation and capital investment. The main aim in forcing supply is to improve competition on a downstream market. This aim has to be balanced against the fact that the incentive for a dominant undertaking to invest or innovate may be negatively affected if competitors can free ride on their investment, rather than making the investment themselves.

There are two scenarios when the issue of refusal most frequently arises in practice. First, the issue can arise where an undertaking requires access to certain information in order to compete in a related market. The dominant undertaking may refuse access on the basis that the information is protected by intellectual property rights (see Case C–241/91, *RTE and ITP v Commission (Magill)*, [1995] ECR I–743 and Case C–418/01, *IMS Health and NDC Health*, OJ C118, 30.04.2004, p. 14). Second, the issue can arise when an undertaking requires access to a particular facility in order to compete in a related market. This often arises in regulated sectors where companies require access to an essential facility such as a port, an airport, telephone or electricity infrastructure, in order to compete in a related market. The legislation governing the regulated sector will normally legislate for access but it is worth remembering that competition law also mandates access in certain circumstances (see *Oscar Bronner v Mediaprint*, Case C7–97 [1998] ECR 1–7791).

Both the Authority and the European Courts have made it clear that it is difficult to establish a refusal to supply as an abuse of dominance and that there are a number of factors to be considered. In particular, it is necessary to consider whether:

(a)   the refusal prevents the emergence of a new product for which there is potential consumer demand;

(b)   the refusal is not justified by objective considerations; and

(c)   the refusal is such as to exclude any competition on a secondary market.

In December 2005, the Authority issued a guidance note on refusal to supply (available on www.tca.ie). The guidance note explains that the Authority is concerned with cases that have a negative impact on competition and consumers. It is not concerned about disputes between a seller and supplier that do not impact on competition. Of the numerous complaints received annually on this topic, very few merit action (see p. 3). The Authority has set out a list of the information that should be included in a complaint for cases which do raise an issue (p. 14).

## 7.8.5   ABUSE OF DOMINANCE ANALYSIS

In order to analyse a potential abuse of dominance (where certain behaviour has been identified as being potentially abusive), it may be helpful to adopt the following approach:

(a)   consider whether the behaviour is engaged in by an 'undertaking' or undertakings;

(b)    define the relevant market;

(c)    consider whether the undertaking has a dominant position in the relevant market;

(d)    consider whether the behaviour constitutes a potential abuse of dominance;

(e)    consider whether there is objective justification for the conduct; and

(f)    if there is objective justification for the conduct, whether it is proportionate to that legitimate aim.

## 7.9    Penalties for Infringement

One of the important distinctions between EC competition law and the 2002 Act is that the 2002 Act legislates for so-called 'hard-core offences', which are subject to more severe penalties than other offences.

### 7.9.1    HARD-CORE OFFENCES

Hard-core offences concern s 4(1) arrangements between competing undertakings. There is a presumption under s 6(2) that agreements between competitors to:

(a)    fix prices (in relation to the provision of goods or services to third parties);

(b)    limit output or sales; or

(c)    share markets or customers

have the object of preventing, restricting or distorting competition.

The liability for hard-core offences on summary conviction, is fines of up to €3,000 and/or six months' imprisonment. The liability for hard-core offences, on conviction on indictment, is fines of up to the greater of €4 million or up to 10 per cent of worldwide turnover and/or up to five years' imprisonment.

### 7.9.2    OTHER OFFENCES

For breaches of s 4 and/or Art 81 and s 5 and/or Art 82, other than hard-core offences, the liability to fines is the same as for hard-core offences, but there are no prison sentences.

In addition, under s 14(7), where an undertaking is found to have breached s 5(1) of the 2002 Act, a court may order that the dominant position be discontinued or adjusted, for example, by ordering a sale of the assets of the undertaking.

### 7.9.3 PERSONAL LIABILITY

Clients should be advised that breach of the 2002 Act could result in personal liability.

Section 8 provides that where an offence has been committed by an undertaking, and the doing of the acts that constituted the offence has been authorised, or consented to, by an officer of the undertaking, that person as well as the undertaking, is guilty of an offence.

The 2002 Act also provides for vicarious liability. For the purpose of determining liability, there is a presumption that any act done by an officer or an employee of an undertaking for the purposes of or in connection with, the business of the undertaking shall be regarded as an act done by the undertaking (s 8(7)).

Shareholders may also be liable where its members manage the affairs of a body corporate (s 8(8)).

Section 160 of the Companies Act, 1990 provides that where a person is convicted on indictment of any indictable offence in relation to a company, he is disqualified from acting as a director or other officer of a company for five years or such other period as the court may order. Therefore, if a person is convicted of an indictable offence under the 2002 Act, then he may also be disqualified from acting as a director or other officer of a company.

## 7.10 Enforcement

Competition law in Ireland is enforced through both civil and criminal means.

The Authority, the Minister for Enterprise, Trade and Employment and any 'aggrieved person' can take a civil action to enforce the 2002 Act. The Authority and the Director of Public Prosecutions (the 'DPP') can institute criminal proceedings to enforce the 2002 Act.

Enforcement is made effective through complaints, investigations and litigation. In addition, the Authority is informed of infringements through 'whistle blowing'.

### 7.10.1 COMPLAINTS

An aggrieved person may make a complaint to the Authority, however the Authority has a discretion to investigate the complaint. According to its annual reports, the Authority pursues investigations that create a precedent and/or that are of public interest (e.g. the investigation is in the public domain, and the issue has been subject to considerable debate and discussion).

The Authority has introduced a complaint screening system in order to focus resources on the most substantive cases, while ensuring that complaints that have little or no supporting evidence are disposed of quickly. As the complaints procedure can often be a long drawn out affair, it is important to understand where a complaint lies in the process. According to the Authority's 2004 Annual Report, out of a total of 293 complaints, 212 were resolved following preliminary screening, twenty-five were resolved following detailed evaluation, forty-two were added to current investigations and fourteen resulted in new investigations.

## 7.10.2   INVESTIGATIONS

The Authority has extensive powers of investigation. It has the power to carry out 'dawn raids' and issue witness summons in order to fulfil its functions under the 2002 Act.

### 7.10.2.1   Dawn raids

The Authority's functions include the carrying out of investigations, either on its own initiative or in response to a complaint made to it by any person, into any breach of the 2002 Act.

The Authority has the power, under s 45, to investigate both business premises and homes of executives where it has reasonable grounds to believe that records relating to the carrying on of a competition law offence are being kept. These on-site searches are often referred to as 'dawn raids'.

Before conducting an on-site search, the Authority must produce a copy of a District Court warrant. The warrant should only be issued where the judge is: 'satisfied from information on oath that it is appropriate to do so' (s 45(4)).

On-site investigations are carried out by 'authorised officers' appointed by the Authority under s 45(1). Members of the Garda Siochana are also authorised, under s 45(8), to assist the authorised officer in the exercise of his or her powers.

It is an offence to obstruct or impede an authorised officer in the on-site investigation. The liability for the offence, on summary conviction, is a fine of up to €3,000 and/or six months' imprisonment (s 45(10)).

According to its Annual Report, during 2004 the Authority was granted twenty-four District Court search warrants. Authorised officers of the Authority, together with the assistance of the Garda Bureau of Fraud investigation and local gardai around the country, executed the search warrants.

### 7.10.2.2   Summons

The Authority has the power, under s 31, to summon witnesses to attend before it, to examine them on oath and to require any such witness to produce to the Authority any document in his or her power or control.

A witness before the Authority in this context is entitled to the same immunities and privileges as if he or she were a witness before the High Court (s 31(2)). Any person who fails to respond to a summons, refuses to take an oath or does any other thing, which in a court would be contempt of court, is guilty of an offence and liable to a fine not exceeding €3,000 or to imprisonment for a term not exceeding six months or to both such fine and such imprisonment (s 31(3)).

According to its Annual Report, the Authority issued fifty-eight summonses during 2004.

## 7.10.3  LITIGATION

Under s 14 of the 2002 Act, any aggrieved person has a right of action in the Circuit Court or the High Court for breach of s 4 or s 5 of the 2002 Act. A successful plaintiff may be entitled to an injunction, a declaration and/or damages including exemplary damages. The Authority also has a right of action for relief by way of an injunction or a declaration.

The Authority can bring summary criminal proceedings under s 8(9) for breaches of s 4 and/or Art 81 and s 5 and/or Art 82 offences. The DPP may bring criminal proceedings on indictment. Details of proceedings instituted by the Authority and the DPP are set out in the Authority's annual reports.

The 2002 Act established a number of novel presumptions, shifting the burden of proof from the prosecution to the defendant. For hard-core offences it is presumed that the defendant's actions have the object of restricting competition unless the defendant proves otherwise (s 6(2)).

There are also certain presumptions, under s 12, in relation to the admissibility of evidence. Documents (as well as statements in the documents) can be presumed to be attributable to parties, named in the document, as having created and received those documents. In addition where an authorised officer believes that, to the best of the authorised officers' knowledge and belief, the documents found during a search belong to one person, the documents shall be presumed to belong to that person, unless the contrary is shown. There is also a presumption, in s 13, that if a document contains a statement by a person who has acted in relation to the alleged breach, then the document is admissible as if the relevant act was done by that person.

In December 2004, new court rules were adopted providing for a variety of pre-trial procedures in competition cases (SI 130/2005 Rules of the Superior Courts (Competition Proceedings) 2005, Order 63B). The rules amend the rules of the Superior Courts in order to facilitate the operation of the competition list in the High Court.

### 7.10.4    WHISTLE BLOWING

The 2002 Act offers protection for a person reporting breaches of the 2002 Act under s 50, i.e. 'whistle blowers'. Section 50 provides that whistle blowers must act in good faith in order to benefit from the provision. In order to encourage employees to report offences, s 50(3) provides that an employer may not penalise an employee for whistle blowing. The penalties for false whistle blowing are fines of up to €3,000 and/or up to six months' imprisonment.

It is also possible to obtain immunity from prosecution for cartel offences, under a cartel immunity programme adopted by the Authority and the DPP. Immunity from prosecution may be granted for reporting such illegal activity to the Authority, provided certain criteria are met. The details of the cartel immunity programme are available on the Authority's website.

## 7.11    Review of the 2002 Act

In 2007, the Minister for Enterprise, Trade and Employment began a review of the 2002 Act as it had been in force for over five years. The Minister issued a public consultation on the operation and implementation of the 2002 Act, inviting responses from the public by the end of 2007.

# CHAPTER 8

# REGULATION

## 8.1 Introduction

This chapter considers the concept of regulation. It provides an overview of the industries in Ireland that are overseen by an independent regulator and subject to a statutory regulatory regime. This overview does not include the financial services sector. The concepts governing the regulation of the financial services industry differ to the concepts governing the regulated industries discussed in this chapter.

It is important to have a general understanding of the concepts outlined in this chapter, as clients operating in a regulated industry must adhere to the statutory regulatory rules. They may also seek the assistance of the regulator in disputes with other regulated businesses. Typical issues of concern are as follows:

(a) obtaining a licence or authorisation required to operate on the market (for example, a telecoms licence);

(b) gaining access to infrastructure essential to operate on a market (for example, the electricity grid);

(c) obtaining the consent of the regulator to a change of control in the case of a merger or acquisition if required (usually where a licence contains a change of control clause);

(d) seeking the assistance of the regulator in dealing with disputes with other market operators; and

(e) challenging decisions of the regulator.

### 8.1.1 WHY REGULATE AN INDUSTRY?

The industries considered in this chapter are those industries involving a public utility (such as telecoms, transport, energy or post) that was traditionally owned by the State. Services were supplied to the public through a State company such as Telecom Eireann, the ESB and An Post. Those companies held a monopoly and there were no other businesses supplying competing services. These industries have been gradually opened up to competition through an EU 'liberalisation' programme. This programme aimed to open up certain sectors of Member State economies to competition, where previously the State had enjoyed exclusive rights conferred by national laws. These exclusive rights existed in the energy, telecoms, transport, and postal industries. The process has been achieved through a number of legislative initiatives based on Arts 2, 10 and 86 of the EC Treaty. The legislation set out a framework and timetable for the liberalisation or opening up of these markets to competition. These industries generally involve a natural monopoly. A natural monopoly exists where a single business can serve a market at a lower cost than any combination of two or more business, for example the telephone network or the electricity grid. The monopoly exists because of economies of scale. Normal forces of competition do not work in such markets, therefore regulatory intervention is necessary to enable the market to operate competitively. Regulators have therefore been established to oversee the operation of the market and facilitate competition.

## 8.1.2    THE RELATIONSHIP BETWEEN COMPETITION LAW AND REGULATION

Competition law still has a role to play in regulated industries and the prohibition on abuse of dominance and the prohibition against anti-competitive agreements still apply to regulated businesses. The independent regulators oversee the competiveness of the industry in accordance with the statutory powers set out in the legislative framework governing their industry. The Competition Authority has the power to enforce the competition rules under the Competition Act, 2002.

Under s 34 of the Competition Act, 2002 the Competition Authority is required to enter into cooperation agreements with a number of statutory bodies, most of whom are independent regulators. The purpose of cooperation agreements is to ensure consistency between the decisions of the Authority and the regulators and to avoid duplication in their activities. It is possible to complain simultaneously to the Competition Authority about an alleged abuse of dominance and to an industry regulator about a breach of the regulatory rules, however, it is likely that the complaint will be pursued by only one of them under the cooperation agreement. For example, in March 2004, the Competition Authority referred a complaint to the telecoms regulator. The complaint, from the Irish Farmers Association, concerned eircom.

## 8.2    Independent Regulators

There are a number of independent regulators in Ireland. Their functions are described briefly below. Solicitors advising clients in a regulated industry should familiarise themselves with the statutory framework for regulation in that particular industry. In most cases, there is a principal statute establishing the regulator, for example in the telecoms industry this is the Communications Regulation Act, 2002. The principal statute usually sets out the functions of the regulator, its power to licence operators in the industry, penalties for infringing the regulatory rules as well as provisions to challenge decisions of the regulator, and the establishment of an appeals panel. In most cases, the functions and duties of the regulator have been altered and expanded by European legislation.

The various regulators' websites are an invaluable source of information for solicitors advising business clients operating in regulated industries.

### 8.2.1   THE BROADCASTING COMMISSION OF IRELAND (BCI)

The BCI is an independent statutory body responsible for a number of key areas of activity with regard to television and radio services in Ireland.

The BCI derives its powers from the Broadcasting Act, 2001, the Radio and Television Act, 1988, the Broadcasting (Funding) Act, 2003 and the Broadcasting (Amendment) Act, 2007.

The BCI oversees the provision of radio and television services. It licenses independent broadcasting services with the aim of providing listener choice and diversity. The BCI's key functions are: the licensing of independent broadcasting services, including the additional licensing of television services on digital, cable, MMDS and satellite systems; the development of codes and rules in relation to programming and advertising standards; and the monitoring of licensed services to ensure that licence holders comply with their statutory obligations and terms of their contracts.

Further information is available on the BCI website: www.bci.ie.

### 8.2.2   THE COMMISSION FOR COMMUNICATIONS REGULATION (ComReg)

ComReg is responsible for the regulation of electronic communications and postal services in Ireland. Electronic communications includes telecommunications, radio communications and broadcasting transmission (i.e. broadcasting networks as opposed to broadcasting services which are regulated by the BCI).

ComReg was established by the Communications Regulation Act, 2002.

Further information is available on ComReg's website: www.comreg.ie.

### 8.2.3   THE COMMISSION FOR ENERGY REGULATION (CER)

The CER regulates the gas and electricity markets in Ireland. The CER was established as the Commission for Electricity Regulation under the Electricity Regulation Act, 1999. The CER's name was changed and its functions expanded to include the regulation of gas under the Gas (Interim) Regulation Act, 2002.

In the electricity market, the CER authorises the construction of new generating plants and licenses companies to generate and supply electricity.

The CER also regulates the process at which energy is supplied to customers.

Further information is available on the CER website: www.cer.ie.

### 8.2.4 THE COMMISSION FOR AVIATION REGULATION ('AVIATION REGULATOR')

The Aviation Regulator regulates certain aspects of the aviation and travel trade industries in Ireland. The Aviation Regulator was established under the Aviation Regulation Act, 2001.

In the aviation sector, the Aviation Regulator oversees airport charges at Dublin Airport and aviation terminal charges levied by the Irish Aviation Authority. It is responsible for setting the maximum level of airport and aviation terminal services charges. It is also responsible, under EU legislation, for the discharge of Ireland's responsibilities for schedule coordination/slot allocation and the appointment where necessary of a schedules facilitator/slot coordinator. The Aviation Regulator also licences airlines and approves ground-handling services providers.

Further information is available at: www.aviationreg.ie.

### 8.2.5 THE COMMISSION FOR TAXI REGULATION

The Commission for Taxi Regulation oversees the market for small public service vehicles and their drivers. It was established under the Taxi Regulation Act, 2003. The Commission has the function of developing and maintaining a regulatory framework for the control and operation of small public service vehicles and their drivers.

Further information is available at: www.taxireg.ie.

## 8.3 Common Concepts

There are a number of common concepts that underpin the legislation governing regulated industries. The concepts are discussed briefly below.

The various regulated industries have been liberalised as a result of various measures taken under Art 86 of the EC Treaty and harmonisation measures taken under Art 95.

Article 86 provides, inter alia, that in the case of public undertakings and undertakings to which Member States grant special or exclusive rights, Member States shall not enact or maintain in force any measures contrary to the provisions of the Treaty and in particular Art 81 to 89 (i.e. the competition rules). The various regulators have an obligation to promote competition within their respective markets. The legislation aims to open up the various markets to competition. From a competition perspective, much of the underlying objective concerns the competition rules that restrain the behaviour of dominant businesses. The rationale behind the competition law rules is that where a dominant business is present on a market, competition on that market is already weak. The concern of the competition rules is to prevent conduct by that dominant business, which risks weakening competition still further and harming consumers.

### 8.3.1 MARKET POWER

The concept of market power is central to the concept of dominance. The concept of market power is also important in regulated industries. It is necessary to determine whether a business has market power in order to apply more stringent regulatory rules to those businesses.

In a regulated industry, a business with market power usually controls some piece of essential infrastructure to which other operators require access. Market power is defined differently in different industries. For example, in the telecoms industry, it is described as 'Significant Market Power' or 'SMP'. There is a complex market analysis process for designating a telecoms operator as having SMP. The result of such a designation is that the operator is subject to various obligations, such as the obligation to provide access to its network on reasonable terms to other operators.

### 8.3.2 LICENSING

In order to operate in a regulated industry, a business will usually require a licence from the regulatory authority. When advising a business start-up or a business entering a regulated industry, it is necessary to determine the requirements for acquiring a licence.

When advising a client who wishes to purchase a regulated business it will be essential to review the terms of the target business's licence. Of particular importance are the provisions concerning the duration of the licence and whether the licence contains a change of control provision. In some cases, a change in control of the licensee requires the consent of the regulatory authority or that the regulator is notified of the change.

It is also important to determine whether the target business has fully complied with its licence conditions and to understand the consequences of breaching those conditions, as it could involve a penalty or a loss of the licence.

### 8.3.3 TRANSPARENCY AND EQUALITY

In a regulated industry, the business that controls essential infrastructure has certain obligations. Access to the infrastructure is often essential in order to compete on the market. The owner of the infrastructure must therefore grant competitors access to its infrastructure so that they can operate in the market. In order to ensure that all of the market operators can compete effectively, it is essential that they are treated equally by the owner of the infrastructure. It is also important that the owner of the infrastructure act in a transparent manner. The obligation to act in a transparent and non-discriminatory manner may be contained in statute or in the licence that permits that business to operate in the industry. For example, a telecoms business that is designated as having SMP has this obligation (see **8.3.1** above).

### 8.3.4 PUBLIC/UNIVERSAL SERVICE OBLIGATIONS

Member States must ensure that public utilities, such as telephone or postal services, are available to everyone. When a utility industry is opened up to competition, not all of the operators may wish to provide services to remote geographical locations as it would not be profitable for them to do so. From an economic perspective, the greatest revenue for that service is derived from the most densely populated areas around cities. There is therefore a need to designate a business with this public service obligation to ensure that the service is available to the public as a whole. The obligation may be imposed by statute or in the licence that permits the business to operate in the industry.

### 8.3.5 PRICING

Because the dominant operator is not controlled by the normal forces of competition with regard to the prices at which it allows access, the regulators often have some authority with regard to the method of pricing used in regulated industries. This varies from industry to industry.

## 8.4 Dispute Resolution

In a regulated industry, the regulator generally has a function to ensure compliance by regulated business with their obligations under their licence and the relevant legislation. They also have the function to investigate complaints from regulated businesses and consumers.

## 8.4.1 APPEALS

The legislation governing the regulated industries in Ireland provides for the establishment of various appeal panels. Appeals can be made to these panels against decisions of the regulator. A business might, for example, wish to challenge a regulator's decision to refuse to grant a licence, to impose onerous obligations in a licence or to impose a penalty on a regulated business for non-compliance with its obligations.

An appeals panel is generally made up of three industry experts. Appeals are generally dealt with more cheaply and quickly than if they were handled by the courts. It is still possible, however, to appeal a decision of a regulator to the courts under administrative law.

Each of the regulators described above were established by statute. The statute under which they were established provides for their respective powers and functions. It is possible to seek judicial review of a decision of a regulator if it has acted beyond the scope of its statutory powers. Judicial review may also be sought on administrative law grounds if: the regulator has acted unreasonably in the context of exercising its statutory powers; it has failed to operate fair procedures in the making of its decision; or it has discriminated between operators in an arbitrary and unjustifiable manner.

It is possible for an applicant for judicial review to claim damages as part of the relief sought, however the applicant must prove that it would have been entitled to the damages had it taken a civil claim against the decision maker (i.e. the regulator). Therefore, the applicant must provide either:

(a) that the action/decision of the regulator also constitutes a tort (e.g. negligence, false imprisonment, trespass);

(b) that the regulator was motivated by malice in the making of its decision or that the regulator knew that it did not have the legal power to make the decision that it purported to make;

(c) that the regulator committed a breach of statutory duty (e.g. on the objective justification or proportionality grounds); or

(d) that the regulator's decision amounted to an infringement of a personal constitutional right or a breach of the judicial review applicant's legitimate expectation.

In addition to the above, it should be demonstrated that the applicant suffered a reasonably foreseeable loss as a result of any of the above unlawful acts such that it should be awarded damages by the court. The latter issue can be the most difficult aspect to prove in a claim for damages in a judicial review case.

## 8.5    Conclusion

Businesses that operate in regulated industries are subject to obligations under legislation and/or an industry operating licence. In order to properly advise a business client in a regulated industry it is necessary to become familiar with the relevant legal instrument. This can often be intimidating due to both the volume of legislation involved and its reference to technical matters specific to the industry in question. The most useful starting point is usually the relevant regulator's website, as it will generally contain guides for non-lawyers as well as references to most, if not all, of the relevant legislation. It is also useful to remember the general principles outlined in this chapter as an aid to understanding the rationale underlying the relevant legislation. Finally, it may be helpful to try and obtain a guide to the technical terms and acronyms used in the industry concerned.

# CHAPTER 9

# CONSUMER LAW

## 9.1 Introduction

### 9.1.1 GENERAL

Irish consumer protection law is largely a recent development. Its standards reflect those of larger, more sophisticated economies, where the needs of consumers have been taken seriously for some time. The principal legislation in this area is discussed below.

Initially the influence for consumer law was from UK legislation but in the last twenty years or so it has been from the EU. It is predominantly a product of EU harmonisation measures in favour of the consumer in the form of Directives. However, the Consumer Protection Act, 2007 was largely a domestic inspiration, in particular Part 2 of that Act which established the National Consumer Agency. The Act transferred the powers and functions of the Director of Consumer Affairs to the National Consumer Agency. The Act also repealed the Consumer Information Act, 1978, along with more than a dozen other Acts.

## 9.2 Sale of Goods and Supply of Services Act, 1980 ('the SGSSA')

### 9.2.1 INTRODUCTORY OVERVIEW

The Sale of Goods Act, 1893 ('the 1893 Act') is still law in Ireland although it has been amended by the SGSSA. The 1893 Act defines a contract of the sale of goods as a contract whereby:

(a) the seller transfers, or agrees to transfer, the ownership of goods to the buyer;

(b) for a money consideration called the price (s 1).

### 9.2.2 IMPLIED CONTRACT TERMS

The SGSSA protects a buyer against:

(a)   the seller not being able to pass on good title to the goods;

(b)   a misdescription of the goods by the seller;

(c)   the goods purchased being of poor quality and not being fit for the purpose for which they were purchased; and

(d)   the bulk not corresponding with the sample (in a sale by sample).

#### 9.2.2.1   The seller's right to transfer ownership

In every contract for the sale of goods, there is an implied condition that the seller has a right to sell and an implied warranty that there is no undisclosed encumbrance on the goods and that the purchaser will normally enjoy quiet possession of them (s 12). Accordingly, if the goods sold turn out to have been stolen, the buyer would normally be entitled to a refund of the purchase price. A seller cannot exclude this implied contract term (see **9.2.2.7**).

#### 9.2.2.2   Description of the goods

Where there is a contract for the sale of goods by description, there is an implied condition that the goods should correspond with their description (s 13(1)). The term 'description' could cover such matters as ingredients, measurements, packing method and quantity. The selection of goods displayed on a supermarket shelf may be a sale by description and the markings on a package or label may constitute or form part of the description.

A sale of goods may still be a sale by description, even where the buyer has seen the goods if they are sold as goods answering a description.

#### 9.2.2.3   Quality of the goods

There is an implied condition of merchantable quality, except as regards:

(a)   defects specifically brought to the buyer's attention prior to the contract; or

(b)   defects which ought to have been noticed in an examination of the goods by the buyer before the contract was made (s 14(2)).

Unlike ss 12 and 13 that apply to every contract of sale, the implied term as to the quality of goods applies only if the seller is acting in the course of a business. As a result, the maxim of *caveat emptor* would still apply to private sales.

### 9.2.2.4 Merchantable quality defined

The new s 14(3) defines merchantable quality as follows:

*Goods are of merchantable quality if they are as fit for the purpose or purposes for which goods of that kind are commonly bought and as durable as it is reasonable to expect having regard to any description applied to them, the price (if relevant) and all the other relevant circumstances, and any reference in this Act to unmerchantable goods shall be construed accordingly.*

### 9.2.2.5 Fitness for purpose

Where the seller sells goods in the course of a business and the buyer, expressly or by implication, makes known to the seller any particular purpose for which the goods are being bought, there is an implied condition that the goods supplied under the contract are reasonably fit for that purpose, whether or not that is a purpose for which such goods are commonly supplied, except where the circumstances show that the buyer does not rely, or that it is unreasonable for him to rely, on the seller's skill or judgment.

Where the purpose is an obvious one (e.g. food is for eating, a car is for driving, a toy is for playing with), it is not necessary for the buyer to expressly inform the seller of the intended purpose, but where goods are required for a particular purpose which is not obvious, the seller will not be liable if not so informed.

Normally reliance will be implied, at least in the case of sales to a consumer. When a customer enters a shop, his reliance would usually be inferred, because he presumes the retailer selected his stock with skill and judgment.

### 9.2.2.6 Sale by sample

Section 15 of the 1893 Act dealing with sales by sample is re-enacted without change in the SGSSA, but for convenience is included in the table in s 10 of the SGSSA along with the new ss 13 and 14. Section 15(1) provides that a contract of sale is one by sample where there is a term in the contract, express or implied, to that effect. Section 15(2) provides that in the case of a contract for sale by sample:

(a) there is an implied condition that the bulk will correspond with the sample in quality;

(b) there is an implied condition that the buyer will have a reasonable opportunity to compare the bulk with the sample; and

(c) there is an implied condition that the goods will be free from any defect rendering them unmerchantable which would not be apparent on reasonable examination of the sample.

As regards point (c), the words 'reasonable examination' mean a normal commercial examination and not, for example, a detailed laboratory-style analysis; the term means such an examination as is usually carried out in the trade concerned.

Again, under s 55(4), as inserted by the SGSSA, the condition in s 15 may not be excluded in the case of a sale to a consumer.

### 9.2.2.7    Exclusion clauses

Section 55 of the 1893 Act had dealt with exclusion clauses and provided that where any right, duty or liability would arise under a contract of sale of goods by implication of law, it could be negatived or varied by express agreement or by the course of dealing between the parties, or by usage if the usage was such as to bind both parties to the contract. Section 22 of the SGSSA substituted a new s 55 into the 1893 Act. The new s 55 repeats this provision of the 1893 Act, but with important qualifications. The implied terms as to title and quiet possession in the 1893 Act, s 12 as amended may not now be excluded and any term of a contract purporting to exclude such terms is void.

In the case of a contract for the sale of goods, any term excluding the implied terms and conditions in ss 13, 14 and 15 will be void where the buyer deals as consumer and, in any other case, will not be enforceable unless it is shown that it is fair and reasonable. This means that any exemption clause purporting to exclude the implied terms relating to quality and fitness for purpose or conformity with description or sample are void where the buyer deals as consumer (quite apart from the application of the European Communities (Unfair Terms in Consumer Contracts) Regulations, 1995 and in any other case may not be enforced unless shown to be 'fair and reasonable'). The Schedule to the SGSSA sets out criteria to be referred to in assessing what is 'fair and reasonable'. The test is that it should be fair and reasonable having regard to the circumstances which were, or ought reasonably to have been, known to or in contemplation of the parties when the contract was made.

Regard is to be had in particular to, for example:

(a)    the strength of the bargaining positions of the parties relative to each other;

(b)    whether the customer receives an inducement to agree to the terms;

(c)    whether the customer knew or ought reasonably to have known of the existence and extent of the term, having regard to any custom of the trade and any previous course of dealing between the parties; and

(d)    whether any goods involved were manufactured to the special order of the parties.

### 9.2.2.8    Supply of services

The SGSSA is the first piece of Irish legislation to import implied terms into contracts for services. These implied terms are set out in s 39 as follows:

(a)    the supplier has the necessary skill to supply the service;

(b)    he will provide the service with due skill and diligence;

       (c)   where materials are used they will be sound and reasonably fit for their purpose; and

       (d)   where goods are supplied under the contract they will be of merchantable quality.

Under the new s 40, these implied terms may be varied or excluded by an express term of the contract or by the course of dealing between the parties or by usage but, where the recipient deals as a consumer, they may only be varied or excluded to the extent that it is fair and reasonable to do so (again by reference to the Schedule) and only if the express term is brought specifically to the consumer's attention.

### 9.2.2.9 Offence

Under s 41, it is an offence to issue in writing any statement purporting to imply that the rights given in s 39 of the SGSSA are or may be excluded or restricted in contracts for services otherwise than as provided for under s 40. Exceptions are made for particular services.

### 9.2.2.10 Minimum EU rules for sales of goods to consumers

The European Communities (Certain Aspects of the Sale of Consumer Goods and Associated Guarantees) Regulations, 2003 (SI 11/2003) (see further **9.9**) provide common minimum levels of protection to consumers in respect of consumer goods purchased by them in any Member State. The regulations are in addition to, and not in substitute for, any other enactment relating to the sale of goods or the terms of contracts concluded with consumers and in particular the 1893 Act, the SGSSA, and the EC (Unfair Terms in Consumer Contracts) Regulations, 1995. They require that consumer goods delivered under a contract of sale to a consumer be in conformity with that contract. If the goods do not conform, then the consumer has certain rights. The 2003 Regulations also provide that consumers have certain rights, with regard to guarantees by a seller or producer in respect of consumer goods. The 2003 Regulations effectively exist side by side with the SGSSA (see further **9.9**).

# 9.3    European Communities (Misleading Advertising) Regulations, 1988

## 9.3.1    INTRODUCTORY OVERVIEW

The European Communities (Misleading Advertising) Regulations, 1988 (SI 134/1988) (the '1988 Regulations') implemented EC Council Directive 84/450/EEC on the approximation of laws of the Member States relating to misleading advertising.

The 1988 Regulations give the Director the power to request any person engaged in misleading advertising to discontinue or refrain from so doing. Any person, including the Director, may seek an injunction prohibiting advertising without having to prove actual loss or damage nor to show recklessness or negligence on the part of the advertiser. The 1988 Regulations increased the powers of the Director giving him wide-ranging powers of search and inspection of companies' financial records, in order to discharge his functions under the new legislation.

## 9.3.2 THE REGULATIONS IN DETAIL

### 9.3.2.1 General

Regulation 2 states that a word or expression used in the Regulations and also used in the Directive has, unless the contrary intention appears, the meaning in these Regulations that it has in the Directive. The 1988 Regulations and the Directive must be read together; in fact, regular reference must be made to the Directive in practice in order to clarify and amplify the Regulations themselves, which are quite brief.

Article 2(2) of the Directive states:

> *Misleading advertising means any advertising which in any way, including its presentation, deceives or is likely to deceive the persons to whom it is addressed or whom it reaches and which, by reason of its deceptive nature, is likely to affect their economic behaviour or which, for those reasons, injures or is likely to injure a competitor.*

Regulation 3 provides that the National Consumer Agency, on a request being made to in that behalf or on its own initiative, may request any person engaging or proposing to engage in any advertising which is misleading advertising to discontinue or refrain from such advertising.

Regulation 4(1) provides that any person—including the National Consumer Agency—may apply to the High Court for an order prohibiting the publication (or the further publication) of advertising which constitutes misleading advertising upon giving notice of the application to any person against whom such order is sought.

Where the National Consumer Agency has made a request under reg 3 and that request has not been complied with, the National Consumer Agency may apply to the High Court for an order prohibiting the publication (or the further publication) of advertising, the publication of which is misleading advertising.

In relation to an application by either the National Consumer Agency or any other person, such applicant is not required to prove either:

(a)  actual loss or damage; or

(b)  recklessness or negligence on the part of the advertiser.

While misleading advertising was also governed until 2007 by the now repealed Consumer Information Act, 1978, the latter required loss, damage or injury to members of the public to a material degree before an offence was committed.

To eliminate the continuing effects of misleading advertising, the court may require publication of its decision in full or in part and in such form as it deems adequate and also require the publication of a corrective statement.

Where an application is made, the High Court may order an advertiser to provide evidence as to the accuracy of any factual claims made in any advertising if, taking into account the legitimate interest of the advertiser and any other party to the proceedings, this requirement appears appropriate in the particular case and the court may deem any factual claim to be inaccurate if the evidence demanded is not provided or is deemed insufficient.

In deciding on applications made under reg 4, the court is required to take account of all the interests involved and, in particular, the public interest.

Regulation 5 provides that in determining whether or not advertising is misleading, the court should take account of all its features and in particular any information it contains concerning the measures set out in para (a)–(c) of Art 3 of the Directive. These matters are:

(a) the characteristics of goods or services, such as their availability, nature, execution, composition, method and date of manufacture or provision, fitness for purpose, uses, quantity, specification, geographical or commercial origin or the results to be expected from their use, or the results and material features of tests or checks carried out on the goods or services;

(b) the price or the manner in which the price is calculated, and the conditions on which the goods are supplied or the services provided; and

(c) the nature, attributes and rights of the advertiser, such as his identity and assets, his qualifications and ownership of industrial, commercial or intellectual property rights or his awards and distinctions.

### 9.3.2.2 Authorised officers

Under reg 6(1), the term 'authorised officer' means a whole-time officer of the Minister authorised in writing by the Minister, or the National Consumer Agency to exercise the powers conferred on such an officer for the purposes of the Regulations. Every authorised officer is required to be issued with a warrant of his appointment as authorised officer and must when exercising any power conferred on him under the Regulations produce the warrant if requested to do so.

An authorised officer is given considerable powers to enable him to obtain information enabling the National Consumer Agency to discharge its functions under the 1988 Regulations, e.g. it may:

(a) enter premises in which any trade or business, or any activity in connection with the trade or business, is carried on at all reasonable times and inspect the premises and any goods on the premises and may take any of the goods on paying or making tender of payment for them;

(b) require anyone who carries on any such trade, business or activity and any employee to produce to it books, documents or records and give it such information as it reasonably requires in regard to any entries therein;

(c) inspect and take copies from such documents;

(d) require any such person to give it any information it requires in regard to the persons carrying on the business or employed in connection with it; and

(e) require any such person to give it any other information which it may reasonably require in regard to such activity.

## 9.4 European Communities (Cancellation of Contracts Negotiated Away From Business Premises) Regulations, 1989

### 9.4.1 INTRODUCTORY OVERVIEW

The European Communities (Cancellation of Contracts Negotiated Away From Business Premises) Regulations, 1989 (SI 224/1989) (the '1989 Regulations') implemented EC Council Directive 85/577/EEC to protect the consumer in respect of contracts negotiated away from business premises. The 1989 Regulations apply to contracts between a consumer and a trader when negotiations have been initiated away from business premises, e.g. by a door-to-door salesman, and offer protection to the consumer purchaser in such circumstances including the ability to withdraw from the contract during a certain period of time after entering into it.

### 9.4.2 THE 1989 REGULATIONS IN DETAIL

#### 9.4.2.1 Introduction

The 1989 Regulations deal with what are known as 'doorstep sales' so that a consumer who buys certain goods or services from traders on his own doorstep, in his home or at his place of work (unless he has expressly requested the seller's visit) must be given a minimum of seven days 'cooling-off' period within which he may withdraw from the contract without penalty.

#### 9.4.2.2 Definitions

A 'consumer' is a natural person who in transactions covered by the Regulations is acting for purposes which may be regarded as outside his trade or profession. 'Trader' means a natural or legal person who, for the transaction in question, acts in his commercial or professional capacity, and anyone acting in the name or on behalf of a trader.

This 'cooling-off' period is contrary to the traditional rules on contracts whereby persons who enter into a contract are normally bound by it immediately and may not normally escape from its terms after entry. The buyer must be given a statutory 'cancellation notice' and 'cancellation form' at the point of sale or the contract will not be enforceable against him (reg 4).

Delivery or posting of the latter form to the trader renders the contract void. When a contract is cancelled, any sums paid by the consumer become due and owing by the trader and title in any goods sold vests in the consumer three months later (reg 6).

Regulation 3 excludes certain categories of contract from the ambit of the 1989 Regulations, including insurance contracts where the consideration is less than €50, contracts for the supply of food and beverages or goods intended for current consumption in the household and supplied by regular roundsmen.

Failure to comply with certain provisions of the 1989 Regulations is an offence.

## 9.5     Liability for Defective Products Act, 1991

### 9.5.1     INTRODUCTORY OVERVIEW

The Liability for Defective Products Act, 1991 (the '1991 Act') was enacted to give effect to EC Council Directive 85/374/EEC on liability for defective products (the 'Product Liability Directive'). The 1991 Act's principal effect was to introduce into Irish law, a remedy of damages based on the principle of no-fault or strict liability so that a producer is made liable for damage caused wholly or partly by a defect in his product, regardless of whether or not he was negligent. The new remedy exists alongside the usual civil remedies on product liability in both tort and contract. Under the 1991 Act, the injured party need only prove the damage, the defect and the causal relationship between them, with no necessity to prove negligence. As it is a civil law measure, the level of proof required to be discharged in any proceedings will be that of the 'balance of probabilities', rather than 'beyond reasonable doubt'. The 1991 Act contains a prohibition on the producer excluding or limiting his liability to an injured person.

### 9.5.2     THE 1991 ACT IN DETAIL

#### 9.5.2.1     Liability for damage caused by defective products

Section 2(1) imposes liability on a producer in damages in tort for damage caused wholly or partly by a defect in his product. Causation is the main criterion: the section creates a strict liability tort with no necessity to show negligence or fault on the producer's part.

### 9.5.2.2 Definition of 'product'

'Product' was originally defined in the 1991 Act, s 1 as 'all movables with the exception of primary agricultural products which have not undergone initial processing'. The option of excepting such primary agricultural products from the definition of 'product' was offered to Member States by the Directive and Ireland chose to do so in the 1991 Act. This option has now been removed by a later Directive 99/34/EEC of 10 May 1999 amending the original Product Liability Directive so that such products are no longer outside the definition in s 1. This Directive was implemented by the European Communities (Liability for Defective Products) Regulations, 2000 (SI 401/2000).

The term 'product' includes:

    (a)    movables even though incorporated into another product or into an immovable (e.g. bricks used in building a house); and

    (b)    electricity (often deemed to be energy and not goods in other legislation) in respect of damage caused by a failure in generation.

### 9.5.2.3 Definition of 'producer'

Section 2(2) defines 'producer' as meaning:

    (a)    the manufacturer or producer of a finished product; or

    (b)    the manufacturer or producer of any raw material or the manufacturer or producer of a component part of a product; or

    (c)    in the case of products of the soil, of stock-farming and of fisheries and game, which have undergone initial processing, the person who carried out such processing; or

    (d)    any person who by putting his name, trade mark or other distinguishing feature on the product or using his name or any such mark or feature in relation to the product, has held himself out to be the producer of the product; or

    (e)    any person who has imported the product into a Member State from a place outside the European Union in order, in the course of any business of his, to supply it to another; or

    (f)    any person who is liable as producer of the product pursuant to s 2(3).

Section 2(3) deems a supplier to be a producer of a product in certain circumstances, providing that, where damage is caused wholly or partly by a defect in a product, any person who supplied the product (whether to the person who suffered the damage, to the producer of any product in which the product is comprised, or to any other person) will, where the producer of the product cannot be identified by taking reasonable steps, be liable as the producer for the damage if:

    (a)    the injured person requests the supplier to identify any person (whether still in existence or not) who comes within the definition of 'producer' in relation to the product;

(b) that request is made within a reasonable time after the damage occurs and at a time when it is not reasonably practicable for the injured person to identify all those persons; and

(c) the supplier fails within a reasonable time after receiving the request either to comply with the request or to identify the person who supplied the product to him. This means that where the retailer ('any person who supplied the product') does not or cannot identify someone above him in the chain of distribution, a plaintiff has a cause of action against the retailer as though he were the producer. There is no definition of what constitutes 'a reasonable time' so it would depend on the facts and circumstances of each particular case. Clearly the producer or manufacturer is the person to be sued in the first instance.

### 9.5.2.4 Definition of damage

'Damage' is defined as:

(a) death or personal injury; or

(b) loss of, damage to, or destruction of, any item of property other than the defective product itself provided that the item of property:

   (i) is of a type ordinarily intended for private use or consumption, and

   (ii) was used by the injured person mainly for his own private use or consumption.

### 9.5.2.5 Definition of defective product

Section 5(1) provides that a product is defective for the purposes of the 1991 Act if it fails to provide the safety which a person is entitled to expect, taking all circumstances into account, including:

(a) the presentation of the product (this could take in, e.g. advertising and labelling, presumably);

(b) the use to which it could reasonably be expected that the product will be put ('reasonably' is the operative word here); and

(c) the time when the product was put into circulation.

These criteria are not exhaustive.

### 9.5.2.6 Proof of damage and defect

The onus is on the injured person concerned to prove the damage, the defect and the causal relationship between the defect and the damage. All the injured person has to do is to prove that there was damage and that it was caused by the defect in the product, i.e. as stated earlier it is not necessary under the 1991 Act to adduce proof of fault on the producer's part.

### 9.5.2.7    Defences

Section 6 sets out several defences, which a producer may put forward in any action against him. He will not be liable under the 1991 Act if he proves:

(a)    that he did not put the product into circulation; or

(b)    that, having regard to the circumstances, it is probable that the defect which caused the damage did not exist at the time when the product was put into circulation by him or that the defect came into being afterwards; or

(c)    that the product was neither manufactured by him for sale or any form of distribution for an economic purpose nor manufactured or distributed by him in the course of his business; or

(d)    that the defect concerned is due to compliance by the product with any requirement imposed by or under any enactment or any requirement of the law of the European Communities; or

(e)    that the state of scientific and technical knowledge at the time when he put the product into circulation was not such as to enable the existence of the defect to be discovered; or

(f)    in the case of a manufacturer of a component or the producer of a raw material, that the defect is attributable entirely to the design of the product in which the component has been fitted or the raw material has been incorporated or to the instructions given by the manufacturer of the product.

The defence at point (b) above protects the producer from defects coming into being after the production process, e.g. in the course of distribution or at the hands of the injured party himself. It could create difficulties in the case of latent defects which only appear later on, e.g. the question might arise whether they were inherent in the product *ab initio* or developed later on. For instance, a particular model of a car may have a fault in the braking or steering system which only manifests itself after a year or when a certain mileage is reached but this defect may be held to have been present from the time it was put into circulation.

The defence at point (c) above protects the non-commercial producer of a product and would cover many private transactions, e.g. gifts.

The defence at point (e) above is known as the 'development risks' defence; it provides that if at the time of production a product is as safe as the current 'state of the art' permits then later improvements in safety in the production process may not be relied on to set the standard of safety.

### 9.5.2.8    Limitation of actions

An action for the recovery of damages under the 1991 Act may not be brought after the expiration of three years from the date on which the cause of action occurred, or the date (if later) on which the plaintiff became aware, or should reasonably have become aware, of the damage, the defect and the identity of the producer. A right of action under the 1991 Act will be extinguished on the expiration of the period of ten years from the date on which the actual product which caused the damage was put into circulation by the producer, unless the injured person has instituted proceedings against the producer in the meantime.

This ten-year cut-off period is a complete time bar to an action under the 1991 Act and is known as the 'long stop' provision.

### 9.5.2.9 Prohibition on exclusion clauses

A producer may not limit or exclude his liability to an injured person under the 1991 Act by any contractual term, notice or any other provision, i.e. he cannot contract out of his liability under the 1991 Act. This precludes small-print exemption clauses from being relied on by a producer against an injured person, although it says nothing about others in the chain of supply, e.g. distributors or retailers.

### 9.5.2.10 Other rights of action

Section 11 makes clear that the 1991 Act will not affect any rights which an injured person may have under any enactment or under any rule of law, i.e. other rights of action are not precluded. This means, in particular, that rights under contract law or in tort are unaffected so that the injured person may sue under the 1991 Act, i.e. on strict liability principles, or they may proceed in the alternative in contract or in tort (which may be more appropriate avenues to relief in a particular case). In practice, plaintiffs would usually sue under all these headings.

### 9.5.2.11 No retrospectivity

Under s 13, the 1991 Act will not apply to any product put into circulation in a Member State before the commencement of the 1991 Act (on 16 December 1991), i.e. there will be no retrospective application of the legislation to products put into circulation prior to that date.

## 9.6 European Communities (Unfair Terms in Consumer Contracts) Regulations, 1995 and 2000

### 9.6.1 INTRODUCTORY OVERVIEW

The European Communities (Unfair Terms in Consumer Contracts) Regulations, 1995 (SI 27/1995) (the '1995 Regulations') transposed into Irish law by EC Council Directive 93/13/EEC on unfair terms in consumer contracts. The fundamental aim of the 1995 Regulations is to invalidate terms in consumer contracts for the supply of goods and services where the terms have not been individually negotiated and are unfair according to prescribed criteria. Although they are aimed mainly at contracts in writing, they could also have an impact on oral contracts and contracts that are partly written and partly oral. The 1995 Regulations do not impose criminal liability on sellers or suppliers whose contracts with consumers contain unfair terms.

## 9.6.2    APPLICATION

Regulation 3(1) provides that the 1995 Regulations apply to any term in a contract concluded between a seller of goods or a supplier of services and a consumer which has not been individually negotiated, apart from the exceptions in Schedule 1.

Schedule 1 expressly excludes certain contracts and particular terms from the scope of the 1995 Regulations, so that they do not apply to:

(a)    contracts of employment;

(b)    contracts relating to succession rights;

(c)    contracts relating to rights under family law;

(d)    contracts relating to the incorporation and organisation of companies or partnerships;

(e)    terms reflecting mandatory statutory or regulatory provisions; and

(f)    terms reflecting the provisions or principles of international conventions to which the Member States or the EU are party.

Otherwise, the 1995 Regulations apply to terms of all consumer contracts dealing with the sale of goods or supply of services which are not individually negotiated and they thus apply to a wide range of contracts such as:

(i)    sale of goods (e.g. in shops and supermarkets);

(ii)    sale of houses to consumers by people acting in the course of a business;

(iii)    supply of services to consumers (e.g. dry cleaners, hairdressers, public transport);

(iv)    letting agreements; and

(v)    building contracts (for homes).

'Consumer' is defined in the regulations as meaning a person who is acting for purposes which are outside his business.

## 9.6.3    CORE TERMS EXCLUDED

The core terms of contracts are excluded from the application of the 1995 Regulations (regs 4 and 5). Core terms are those that define the main subject matter of a contract or concern the adequacy of the price or financial consideration payable. In order for core terms to be excluded from the application of the 1995 Regulations, they must have been drafted in plain intelligible language, otherwise, they will be treated as a non-core term.

## 9.6.4    NON-CORE TERMS IN STANDARD FORM CONTRACTS

A term will always be regarded as having not being individually negotiated where it has been drafted in advance and the consumer has therefore not been able to influence its substance (reg 3(4)). The onus of proof is on the seller or supplier who claims that a term was individually negotiated to show that it was.

## 9.6.5    UNFAIR TERMS DEFINED

Regulation 3(2) provides that for the purposes of the 1995 Regulations the contractual term will be regarded as unfair if, contrary to the requirement of good faith, it causes a significant imbalance in the parties' rights and obligations under the contract to the detriment of the consumer (taking into account the nature of the goods or services for which the contract was concluded 'and all circumstances attending the conclusion of the contract and all other terms of the contract or of another contract on which it is dependent').

The definition of the main subject matter of the contract or the adequacy of the price or remuneration are not relevant in considering whether a term is unfair in so far as those terms are in plain intelligible English. The test of unfairness is applied to particular terms and not to the contract as a whole. Schedule 3 sets out an indicative and non-exhaustive list of the terms which may be regarded as unfair, as laid out in the Directive, including terms:

- excluding or limiting the liability of a seller or supplier in the event of the death or personal injury of a consumer resulting from an act or omission of the seller or supplier;

- inappropriately excluding or limiting the legal rights of the consumer vis-à-vis the seller or supplier or another party, in the event of total or partial non-performance or inadequate performance by the seller or supplier of any of the contractual obligations, including the option of off-setting a debt owed to the seller or supplier against any claim which the consumer may have against him;

- making an agreement binding on the consumer, whereas provision of services by the seller or supplier is subject to a condition when realisation depends on his will alone;

- permitting the seller or supplier to retain sums paid by the consumer when the consumer decides not to conclude or perform the contract, without providing for the consumer to receive compensation of an equivalent amount from the seller or supplier;

- requiring any consumer who fails to fulfil his obligation to pay a disproportionately high sum in compensation;

- enabling the seller or supplier to dissolve the contract, on a discretionary basis when the same facility is not granted to the consumer, or permitting the seller or supplier to retain the sums paid for services not yet supplied by him, when it is the seller or supplier himself who dissolves the contract;

- enabling the seller or supplier to terminate a contract of indeterminate duration without reasonable notice except where there are serious grounds for doing so (a supplier of financial services is excepted from this provision, to a limited extent; moreover, the provision does not apply to transactions in transferable securities, financial instruments and other products or services where the price is linked to fluctuations in a Stock Exchange quotation or index or a financial market rate that the seller or supplier does not control);

- automatically extending a contract of fixed duration when the consumer does not indicate otherwise, when the deadline fixed for the consumer to express this wish not to extend the contract is unreasonably early;

- irrevocably binding the consumer to terms with which he had no real opportunity of becoming acquainted before the conclusion of the contract;

- enabling the seller or supplier to alter the terms of the contract unilaterally, without a valid reason, which is specified in the contract (again, there is a limited exception with regard to certain financial services contracts);

- enabling the seller or supplier to alter unilaterally without a valid reason any characteristics of the product or service to be provided;

- providing for the price of goods to be determined at the time of delivery or allowing a seller of goods or a supplier of services to increase their price without (in both cases) giving the consumer the corresponding right to cancel the contract, if the final price is too high in relation to the price agreement when the contract was concluded (again, certain financial services contracts are excepted to an extent from this provision);

- giving the seller or supplier the right to determine whether the goods or services are in conformity with the contract or giving him the exclusive right to interpret any term of the contract;

- linking the seller's or supplier's obligations to respect commitments undertaken by his agents or making his commitments subject to compliance with a particular formality;

- obliging the consumer to fulfill all his obligations where the seller or supplier does not perform his obligations;

- giving the seller or supplier the possibility of transferring his rights and obligations under the contract, when this may serve to reduce the guarantees for the consumer, without the consumer's agreement;

- excluding or hindering the consumer's right to take legal action or exercise any other legal remedy, particularly by requiring the consumer to take disputes exclusively to arbitration, unduly restricting the evidence available to him or imposing on him a burden of proof which should lie with another party to the contract.

### 9.6.6 SEVERANCE

An unfair term will not be binding on the consumer but the contract itself will continue to bind the parties if it is capable of continuing in existence without the unfair term, i.e. if the unfair term can be severed.

### 9.6.7 NATIONAL CONSUMER AGENCY

The National Consumer Agency has a role in the enforcement of the 1995 Regulations. It can apply to the High Court for an order prohibiting the use or continued use of any contractual term adjudged by the court to be unfair. This is without prejudice to the right of a consumer to rely on the 1995 Regulations in any court. The Agency's (or the Minister's) authorised officers have powers of entry and inspection.

## 9.7 Consumer Credit Act, 1995 (the '1995-Act')

### 9.7.1 INTRODUCTORY OVERVIEW

The 1995 Act applies to all credit agreements, hire purchase agreements and consumer hire agreements, to which a consumer is a party.

### 9.7.2 THE MARKETING OF CONSUMER CONTRACTS

The 1995 Act applies to any advertisement published or displayed for the purposes of a business carried on by the advertiser and offering:

(a) to provide or arrange to provide credit;

(b) to enter into a hire purchase or consumer hire purchase agreement for the letting of goods by the advertiser; or

(c) to arrange the letting of goods under a hire purchase or consumer hire agreement by another person by a consumer.

If an advertisement mentions a rate of interest or makes a claim in relation to the cost of the credit being offered it must contain a clear and prominent statement of the annual percentage rate of change (the 'APR').

In addition to the details of the APR, consumer credit arrangements must contain:

(a) a statement of any security which may be required;

(b) a clear indication of any restrictions on the availability of the credit advertised; and

(c)  in an advertisement (other than those in relation to house loans), details of any charges additional to repayment of capital and interest on the sum borrowed.

It is not an offence for credit to be provided at a lower rate than that advertised.

An advertisement may not describe credit as being without interest or any other charges, if the availability of the credit is dependent on the consumer concluding with the creditor or any other person: a maintenance contract (for any goods involved); or an insurance contract, or any other condition, compliance with which would, or would be likely in the future to, involve the consumer in any cost additional to that payable if the goods were purchased for cash.

An advertisement in which a person offers to arrange the letting of goods under a consumer hire agreement, or indicates the availability of such a letting, must include a statement to the effect that the agreement is for letting, hiring or leasing only and the goods remain the property of the owner:

(a)  which shall be afforded no less prominence than the sum of any amount payable by the hirer; and

(b)  in the case of a visual advertisement, must be enclosed by a boxed boundary line (s 23(1)).

### 9.7.3    INSERTED SELLING PROHIBITED

A person must not insert in any agreement or in any proposed form or application form used in connection with the agreement, provisions which require the consumer to indicate positively that he does not wish to obtain credit, purchase or hire any goods or avail of any services in relation to the agreement (s 138(1)).

Where any amount is due to a third party as a result of the use of such a provision, the person who inserted the provision will be liable for payment of that amount.

### 9.7.4    CIRCULARS CANNOT BE SENT TO MINORS

A person must not knowingly, with a view to financial gain, send to a minor any document inviting the minor to:

(a)  borrow credit;

(b)  obtain goods on credit or hire;

(c)  obtain services on credit; or

(d)  apply for information or advice on borrowing credit or otherwise obtaining credit or hiring goods (s 139).

### 9.7.5 CREDIT PROVIDERS CANNOT CONTRACT OUT OF LIABILITIES OR RESTRICT CONSUMERS' RIGHTS UNDER THE 1995 ACT

Except where otherwise provided for in the 1995 Act, a credit provider cannot restrict or limit any liabilities (s 140).

Any agreement in which the credit provider seeks to exclude the consumer's rights is unenforceable (s 140(4)).

### 9.7.6 STATEMENTS OR NOTICES EXCLUDING CONSUMERS' RIGHTS

A credit provider is prohibited from:

(a)   displaying on any part of any premises a notice;

(b)   publishing or causing to be published an advertisement;

(c)   supplying goods bearing a statement; or

(d)   furnishing or causing to be furnished a document,

which purports to exclude or restrict any liability imposed on any person or any right conferred on a consumer by the 1995 Act (s 141).

## 9.8 Package Holiday and Travel Trade Act, 1995 ('the PHTTA')

### 9.8.1 INTRODUCTORY OVERVIEW

Package holidays and tours are regulated by the PHTTA. The main effect of the PHTTA is to impose considerable responsibility towards consumers on organisers of package holidays which go wrong.

The PHTTA implemented Council Directive 90/314/EEC on package travel, package holidays and package tours. The PHTTA also amends the Transport (Tour Operators and Travel Agents) Act, 1982.

### 9.8.2 THE PHTTA IN DETAIL

#### 9.8.2.1 Introduction

The most significant feature of the PHTTA is that it imposes direct liability on the organiser of a holiday for the non-performance or improper performance of the obligations under the holiday contract, regardless of whether they are to be performed by the organiser or by another party involved in the provision of the holiday, i.e. the organiser is made responsible for all the elements of the package and is primarily liable for anything that goes wrong with the services, facilities or goods to be supplied as component parts of the package. It is no defence that they were supplied by other independent sub-contractors over whom it had no control, e.g. airlines, hoteliers, handling agents.

### 9.8.2.2    Definition of a 'package'

A 'package' is defined in s 2(1) of the PHTTA as being:

> *a combination of at least two of the following components pre-arranged by the organiser when sold or offered for sale at an inclusive price and when the service covers a period of more than twenty-four hours or includes overnight accommodation*
>
> *(a)    transport:*
>
> *(b)    accommodation;*
>
> *(c)    other tourist services, not ancillary to transport or accommodation, accounting for a significant proportion of the package' (e.g. golf, fishing).*

Even if the consumer has to pay separately for different components of the package, it still remains a 'package holiday', although arrangements made by a tour operator or travel agent specifically for an individual carrier's requirements are not regarded as package holidays.

### 9.8.2.3    Definition of an 'organiser'

Section 3(1) defines an 'organiser' as being:

> *a person who, otherwise than occasionally, organises packages and sells or offers them for sale to a consumer, whether directly or through a retailer.*

This could conceivably include social and sporting clubs which organise educational or sports trips or pilgrimages, in appropriate circumstances, although if organised only 'occasionally', these would usually be exempted from the ambit of the Act by virtue of the Package Holidays and Travel Trade Act (Occasional Organisers) Regulations, 1995 (SI 271/1995) which set out exemptions.

### 9.8.2.4    Definition of a 'retailer'

A 'retailer' is the person who sells or offers for sale the package put together by the organiser.

A package holiday is usually sold by a tour operator or organiser or by a retailer. The latter is almost always a travel agent and he sells the package put together by the tour operator (the organiser).

### 9.8.2.5    Definition of a 'consumer'

The PHTTA's definition of a consumer is very specific and differs considerably from that in other Irish consumer legislation such as the 1995 Act and the 1995 Regulations and from the definition of 'dealing as consumer' in the SGSSA.

A 'consumer' is defined as meaning:

(a) in relation to a contract, the person who takes or agrees to take the package (this person is referred to in the PHTTA as being 'the principal contractor'); and

(b) in any other case, where the circumstances so require:

(i) the principal contractor;

(ii) any person on whose behalf the principal contractor agrees to purchase a package (referred to as 'another beneficiary'); and

(iii) any person to whom the principal contractor, or another beneficiary, transfers the package (referred to as 'the transferee').

### 9.8.2.6    Contents of a holiday brochure

Section 10(1) requires that an organiser must not make a brochure available to a possible consumer, unless it indicates in a legible, comprehensible and accurate manner the price and adequate information about the following matters:

(a) the destination and the means, characteristics and categories of transport used;

(b) the type of accommodation, its location, category or degree of comfort, its main features and, if in a Member State of the EU, its tourist classification in that State;

(c) the meal plan;

(d) the itinerary;

(e) general information about passport and visa requirements which apply to purchase of the package and any applicable health formalities required for the journey and the stay;

(f) either the monetary amount or the percentage of the price which is to be paid on account and the timetable for payment of the balance;

(g) any tax or compulsory charge;

(h) whether a minimum number of persons is required for the package to take place and, if so, the latest time for informing the consumer in the event of cancellation;

(i) the contingency arrangements for security for money paid over in the event of the organiser's insolvency and, where applicable, repatriation of the customer; and

(j) in the case of packages offered by an organiser who has no place of business in the State, a nominated agent with an address in the State, who will accept services on behalf of and represent the organiser in any proceedings (including criminal proceedings) in respect of, or arising out of, or connected with any contract, or brought under, or in connection with, any provisions of the PHTTA.

### 9.8.2.7 Information constitutes warranties

Where a consumer enters into a contract on the basis of information which is set out in a brochure, the particulars in the brochure (whether or not they are required by the PHTTA to be included in it) will constitute warranties as to the matters to which they relate, unless the brochure contains a clear and legible statement that changes may be made in the particulars before a contract is concluded. Any such changes must be clearly communicated to, and accepted by, the other party before a contract is concluded, unless the consumer and the organiser agree, when or after the contract is made, that those particulars should not form part of the contract.

### 9.8.2.8 Liability for misleading brochures

Both the organiser and retailer may be liable to compensate a consumer for any damage resulting from the consumer's reliance on information which is false and misleading and was either contained in the brochure or given by the organiser or retailer in respect of it.

However, it will be a good defence for a retailer to show that he did not know, and had no reason to suspect, that the brochure or other descriptive matter concerned contained information which was false or misleading.

### 9.8.2.9 Compensation for misleading brochures

Where an organiser provides a brochure or other descriptive matter to a consumer (whether directly or through a retailer), he will he liable to compensate the consumer for any damage caused to him as a direct consequence of and attributable to his reliance upon information which is false or misleading where that information:

(a) is contained in the brochure or other descriptive matter; or

(b) is given by the organiser in respect of the brochure or other descriptive matter.

Arguably, this could cover misleading photographs in the brochure, e.g. of a beach or swimming pool, or of the hotel.

Section 11(4) imposes a similar liability to compensate on a retailer. The term 'compensation' is a wide one and it could include consequential loss for disappointment at the quality of the holiday as well as purely financial loss.

### 9.8.2.10 Information to be supplied before contract is concluded

A duty is imposed on the organiser, before a contract is made, to provide the intending consumer with information in writing 'or in some appropriate form' about essential matters such as:

(a) general information about passport and visa requirements related to the package;

(b) information about health formalities required by national administrations for the journey and the stay;

(c) where having insurance to cover the cost of cancellation by the consumer or the cost of assistance (including repatriation) in the event of accident or illness is compulsory under the contract, the minimum level of insurance cover stipulated by the organiser (the consumer cannot be forced to take out any specified insurance policy, e.g. the organiser's or retailer's insurance); and

(d) in the event of insolvency, the arrangements for security for the money paid over and (where applicable) for the repatriation of the consumer.

### 9.8.2.11 Information to be provided before the start of the package

In addition to supplying the consumer with certain information before a contract is concluded between the organiser and the consumer, the organiser is required to provide the consumer with certain essential information in good time before the package is due to start including:

(a) where the package includes a transport component, the times and places of intermediate stops and transport connections and details of the place to be occupied by the traveller (including cabin or berth on ship, sleeper compartment on train);

(b) the name, address and telephone number:

   (i) of the representative of the organiser in the locality where the consumer is to stay; or

   (ii) if there is no such representative, of an agency in that locality to provide assistance to a consumer in difficulty, or, if there is no such representative or agency, a telephone number or other information which will enable the consumer to contact the organiser and/or the retailer during the course of the package.

Where an organiser fails to supply such information, he will be guilty of an offence, unless the contravention is due to the failure of the retailer to pass on to the consumer, or intending consumer, the information supplied to the retailer by the organiser.

Where a retailer fails to provide the consumer, or intended consumer, with the information, he will also be guilty of an offence.

### 9.8.2.12 The essential terms of a contract

Section 14(1) sets out the essential information which the organiser (whether dealing directly with the consumer or through a retailer) must ensure is contained in the contract if relevant to the particular package. These essential terms include:

(a) the travel destination or destinations and, where periods of stay are involved, the relevant periods, with dates;

(b) the means, characteristics and categories of transport to be used and the dates, times and points of departure and return;

(c)   where the package includes accommodation, its location, its tourist category (if any) or degree of comfort and its main features;

(d)   the itinerary and meal plan and any visits or excursions included in the total price agreed for the package;

(e)   the name and address of the organiser, the retailer and, where appropriate, the insurer;

(f)   the price of the package and method of payment and, where price revisions may be made, an indication of the possibility of such price revisions and whether a minimum number of persons is required for the package to take place and, if so, the latest time for information of cancellation.

### 9.8.2.13   Form of the contract

Except in the case of a late booking, i.e. fourteen days or less before departure, the organiser is required to ensure that all the terms of the contract are set out in writing, or in such other form as is comprehensible and accessible to the intended consumer and that they are communicated to the intended consumer before the contract is made.

It is an offence for an organiser (whether dealing directly with the consumer or through a retailer) to fail to supply the consumer with a written copy of the terms of the contract, unless the contravention is due to the failure of the retailer to provide the consumer with a written copy of the terms of the contract which had been supplied to the retailer by the organiser. In the latter case the retailer is guilty of an offence.

### 9.8.2.14   Transfer of booking

Where the consumer is prevented from proceeding with the package, a term will be implied into the contract whereby the consumer may transfer the booking to a person, who satisfies all the conditions required to be satisfied by a person who takes the package, provided the consumer gives reasonable notice of his intention, to transfer, to the organiser or retailer.

Both the original purchaser and the transferee are jointly and severally liable to the organiser for payment for the package (or the balance of the payment, as the case may be) and for any other fair and reasonable costs incurred by him as a result of the transfer.

### 9.8.2.15   Contract price revision

Section 17(1) renders void a term in a contract to the effect that the prices specified in the contract may be revised, unless the contract provides for the possibility of upward or downward revision and certain conditions set out in s 17(2) are strictly observed.

No price increase may be made later than a date specified in the contract, which must be not less than twenty days before the specified departure date.

### 9.8.2.16 Alterations and cancellations

Where the organiser is compelled before departure to alter significantly an essential term of the contract, such as the price, a term will be implied that the consumer will be notified as soon as possible in order to enable him to take appropriate decisions and, in particular, to withdraw from the contract without penalty, or to accept a variation to the contract and that he will inform the organiser or retailer as soon as possible.

Where the consumer withdraws from the contract due to an alteration by the organiser of an essential term of the contract, or where the organiser, for any reason other than the fault of the consumer, cancels the package before the date when it is due to start, there is an implied term that the consumer is entitled to:

(a) take a replacement package of equivalent or superior quality if the organiser (whether directly or through a retailer) can in fact provide this; or

(b) take a replacement package of lower quality if the organiser is able to offer such a replacement and to recover from the organiser the difference in price between the two packages; or

(c) have a full refund.

In addition, there is an implied term that the consumer is entitled, without prejudice to the above, to be compensated by the organiser for non-performance of the contract except in two situations in which the organiser may cancel a package without owing any compensation, i.e. where:

(a) the package is cancelled because the number of persons who agreed to take it is less than the minimum number of persons required and the consumer is informed of the cancellation, in writing, within the period prescribed in the contract; or

(b) the package is cancelled by *force majeure*, i.e. by reason of unusual and unforeseeable circumstances beyond the control of the organiser, the retailer or the supplier of services, the consequences of which could not have been avoided even if all due care had been exercised. However, overbooking can never be considered as coming into this category.

### 9.8.2.17 Problems arising after the start of the package

Where, after departure, a significant proportion of the services contracted for is not provided, or the organiser becomes aware that a significant proportion of the services cannot be provided, there is an implied term that the organiser must make suitable alternative arrangements, at no extra cost to the consumer, for the continuation of the package and provide appropriate compensation. If such alternative arrangements cannot be made, or if they are not accepted by the consumer on reasonable grounds, there is an implied term that the organiser must, where homeward transport arrangements are a term of the contract, provide the consumer at no extra cost with equivalent transport back to the place of departure, or to another place to which the consumer has agreed. He must also compensate the consumer for the proportion of services not supplied.

### 9.8.2.18 Extent and financial limits of liability

Section 20(1) of the PHTTA imposes ultimate liability to the consumer on the organiser for the proper performance of the obligations under the contract, whether or not such obligations are to be performed by the organiser, the retailer or other suppliers of services.

This provision allows the consumer to sue the organiser for breach of contract even if the problem is with the retailer or another service provider. However, this will not affect any remedy or right of action which the organiser may have against the retailer or another supplier of services.

Section 20(2) renders the organiser liable to the consumer for any damage caused by the failure to perform the contract or the improper performance of the contract, unless the failure or the improper performance is due neither to any fault of the organiser, or the retailer, nor to that of another supplier of services, because the failures in question are attributable to:

(a) the consumer;

(b) a third party unconnected with the provision of services contracted for, and are unforeseeable or unavoidable; or

(c) *force majeure*, i.e. due to unusual and unforeseeable circumstances beyond the control of the organiser, the retailer or other supplier of services, the consequences of which could not have been avoided even if all due care had been exercised, or due to an event which the organiser, the retailer or the supplier of services, even with all due care, could not foresee or forestall.

### 9.8.2.19 Exemption or limitation clauses

A contractual term which purports to exempt the organiser from liability to the consumer under s 20(1) or (2) cannot be relied on by the organiser.

However, an organiser may rely on an exemption clause or on a limitation clause in certain limited circumstances which are set out in s 20(3), (4) and (5).

Where damage arises from the non-performance or improper performance of the services involved in the package (other than death, personal injury or damage caused by the wilful misconduct or gross negligence of the organiser), s 20(3) permits the organiser to insert a term into the contract limiting the amount of compensation payable to the consumer. Liability may be limited to not less than twice the cost of the package holiday for an adult and not less than the cost of the holiday in the case of a minor.

The contract may provide for compensation to be limited in accordance with any international conventions in force governing such services in the place where they are performed or are due to be performed.

### 9.8.2.20 Security in the event of insolvency of operator or retailer

Section 22 requires operators and retailers to have sufficient evidence of security for the refund of money paid over and for the repatriation of the consumer in the event of insolvency. The necessary evidence of security may take the form of a bond entered into by an authorised institution (defined as a person authorised under the law of a Member State to carry on the business of entering into such bonds) either under s 23 or a bond entered into pursuant to s 24, depending on whether or not an approved body (as defined) of which the package provider is a member has a reserve fund or insurance cover.

### 9.8.2.21 Complaints

Holidaymakers are required to make complaints at the earliest possible opportunity and no later than twenty-eight days from completion of the holiday, both to the person responsible for their dissatisfaction and to the organiser or local representative.

### 9.8.2.22 Prosecutions

Summary proceedings in respect of an offence under any section of the Act may be brought and prosecuted by the National Consumer Agency.

### 9.8.2.23 Role of the National Consumer Agency

The National Consumer Agency is empowered by s 8 to require that persons engaging in, or proposing to engage in practices or activities which are, or are likely to be, contrary to the obligations imposed on them by the PHTTA Act refrain from doing so.

The National Consumer Agency is also empowered to institute proceedings in the High Court for orders requiring persons engaging or proposing to engage in any such practices or activities to discontinue or refrain from doing so. The National Consumer Agency's authorised officers are given wide powers of entry and inspection and power to require information, and any failure to comply with the authorised officer's request or any obstruction of his performance of his functions will be an offence.

### 9.8.2.24 Unfair terms

It should be noted that the 1995 Regulations also apply to package holidays (as to other consumer contracts for the sale of goods or supply of services) and offer additional protection to a holidaymaker in appropriate circumstances.

## 9.9 The European Communities (Certain Aspects of the Sale of Consumer Goods and Associated Guarantees) Regulations, 2003

### 9.9.1 INTRODUCTORY OVERVIEW

The European Communities (Certain Aspects of the Sale of Consumer Goods and Associated Guarantees) Regulations, 2003 (the '2003 Regulations') (SI 11/2003) entered into force on 22 January 2003 and implement Directive 1994/44/EC on the sale of consumer goods and associated guarantees, the principle behind which is that consumers who reside in one Member State should be free to purchase goods in any other Member State based on a uniform and minimum set of fair rules governing their sale. Where the level of protection afforded to a consumer under a provision of any other legislation is greater than that afforded by a particular provision of the 2003 Regulations, then the other legislation will apply.

### 9.9.2 THE REGULATIONS IN DETAIL

The 2003 Regulations provide common minimum levels of protection to consumers in respect of consumer goods purchased by them in any Member State. 'Consumer' is defined as a natural person who, as regards a sale or associated guarantee, is acting for purposes which are outside that person's trade, business or profession. 'Consumer goods' are defined as any tangible moveable item, with the exception of goods sold by way of execution or otherwise by authority of law; water and gas where they are not put up for sale in a limited volume or set quantity; and electricity.

The 2003 Regulations exist side by side with existing domestic law comprised in the SGSSA and the EC (Unfair Terms in Consumer Contracts) Regulations, 1995 (SI 27/1995). Regulation 5(1) of the 2003 Regulations requires that consumer goods delivered to a consumer under a contract of sale be in conformity with the contract. In circumstances where the goods do not so conform, the consumer can require those goods to be repaired or replaced, unless a lesser remedy such as a reduction in the price is more appropriate (reg 7(2)–(4)).

In addition, in certain circumstances the consumer has a right to rescind. The 2003 Regulations provide as well that consumers have a right to request that guarantees provided by a seller or producer in respect of consumer goods be given in writing at the time of purchase and include details as to the duration, territorial scope and particulars to be followed to make a claim under the guarantee in question.

The 2003 Regulations do not apply where a business is selling goods to another business, nor to sales by private individuals.

## 9.10 European Communities (General Product Safety) Regulations, 2004

### 9.10.1 INTRODUCTORY OVERVIEW

The European Communities (General Product Safety) Regulations, 2004 (the '2004 Regulations') (contained in SI 199/2004) came into effect on 4 May 2004 and give effect to Directive 2001/95/EC of the European Parliament and of the Council of 3 December 2001 on general product safety. The 2004 Regulations revoked and replaced the earlier 1997 Regulations of the same name, which had implemented an earlier Directive, Council Directive 92/59/EEC on general product safety. The main objectives of that Directive were to harmonise EU product safety laws and imposing a general standard of safety in product sectors where there were no special standards already in existence, to compel producers to refrain from placing dangerous products on the market, to improve product safety monitoring and safety warnings and to permit the taking of speedy and effective action to restrict or prohibit the sale of dangerous products.

### 9.10.2 THE 2004 REGULATIONS IN DETAIL

The 2004 Regulations require that consumer products placed on the market are safe and oblige producers to place only safe products on the market. The Regulations specify the duties of producers and distributors and make it an offence to place dangerous products on the market. The National Consumer Agency is given authority to ensure that products put on the market are safe and that producers and distributors comply with their obligations under the Regulations and the Directive they implement.

### 9.10.3 DEFINITIONS

Regulation 2 sets out key definitions.

'Consumer' means any natural person who in respect of a product covered by the Directive is acting for purposes which are outside his or her trade, business or profession.

'Dangerous product' means any product which is not a safe product.

'Safe product' means any product which under normal or reasonably foreseeable conditions of use including duration and where applicable putting into service, installation and maintenance requirements, does not present any risk or only the minimum risks compatible with the product's use, considered to be acceptable and consistent with the high level of protection for the safety and health of persons.

'Distributor' and 'producer' are defined broadly—there are also specific definitions of 'recall' and 'withdrawal'.

### 9.10.4 EXCEPTIONS

The 2004 Regulations do not apply to products subject to specific safety requirements imposed by regulation or legislation, nor do they apply to second-hand
products supplied, such as antiques, nor to products to be repaired or recondi-
tioned prior to being used, provided that the supplier of such a product clearly
informs the person he supplies that such repair or reconditioning is necessary
prior to use of the product.

### 9.10.5 THE MAIN PROVISIONS OF THE 2004 REGULATIONS

Regulation 4 sets out the prohibition on the 'producer' from placing dangerous products on the market and the characteristics to be taken into account
in determining the safety of a product. Failure by a producer to comply is an
offence.

Regulation 5 sets out circumstances in which products are deemed to be safe
or presumed to be safe.

Regulation 6 sets out the duties of producers. These duties include a requirement to provide all relevant information relating to the product to consumers
to enable them to assess the risks inherent in the product throughout the normal or reasonably foreseeable period of its use, where such risks are not immediately obvious without adequate warnings, and to take precautions against
those risks.

Regulation 7 sets out the duties of distributors and states that a distributor
must act with due care to ensure that any product he supplies is a safe product.
Failure to comply with this obligation is an offence.

Regulation 8 requires a producer and/or a distributor who knows or, on the
basis of information in his possession and as a professional, ought to know
that a product he has placed on the market poses a risk to the consumer that
is incompatible with safety requirements of the 2004 Regulations or Directive,
to inform the National Consumer Agency of the risk, in accordance with the
provisions of the 2004 Regulations. Failure to comply is an offence.

Regulation 9 sets out the general functions of the National Consumer Agency
with regards to the 2004 Regulations. It is permitted by reg 14 to appoint
authorised officers. Regulation 14 also sets out the powers of such officers.

## 9.11 Miscellaneous

Apart from the principal Irish Legislative Measures in the consumer law field
set out above, there are also other more minor pieces of legislation dealing
with specific matters of relevance to consumer protection, such as: safety of

toys; labelling of footwear; names and labelling of textile products; labelling, presentation, and advertising of food stuff; and contracts on the time-sharing of world property. All these are EU led and are in the form of EU Regulations.

There is also consumer protection legislation in respect of specific sectors. Of particular note is that a considerable body of legislation now exists dealing with food safety, mostly EU driven, for example:

- Regulation EC No 178/2002: lays down general principles and requirements of food law. It defines a food business as 'any undertaking, whether for profit or not, and whether public or private, carrying out any of the activities related to any stage of production, processing and distribution of food'.

- Regulation EC No 852/2004: under this Regulation, all food businesses are obliged to have a food safety management system known as a Hazard Analysis and Critical Control Points ('HACCP') system in place, and all food businesses are required to ensure that food handlers are properly supervised and trained and are fully aware of the HACCP principles. Related to this are the European Communities (Hygiene of Food Stuff) Regulations, 2006.

- The Food Hygiene Regulations, 1950–1989: these deal with structural hygiene and general cleanliness of equipment and premises of an operator in the food business.

### 9.11.1 THE NATIONAL STANDARDS AUTHORITY OF IRELAND ACT, 1996

The Act established the National Standards Authority of Ireland (NSAI), which publishes national standards for various industries, including food and catering, which apply to all organisations involved.

## 9.12 The Consumer Protection Act, 2007

The Consumer Protection Act (CPA) came into force on 1 May 2007 and provides for the most comprehensive reform of Irish consumer legislation in almost thirty years, bringing in a range of measures to encourage compliance with consumer law through self-regulation and a number of enforcement measures. The CPA:

- established the National Consumer Agency (NCA) on a statutory basis, having being first set up on an interim basis in May 2005; and

- updated and consolidated existing consumer legislation (repealing some in the process) and transposed the EU Directive on Unfair Commercial Practices (Directive 2005/29/EC of May 2005; the Unfair Commercial Practices Directive, or UCPD) adopted in May 2005.

The NCA took over the functions and powers of the earlier office of the Director of Consumer Affairs which the CPA abolished. The new agency has even more extensive functions and powers. Its main functions are:

- to promote and protect the interests and welfare of consumers;
- to enforce the relevant consumer law;
- to encourage compliance with the relevant law;
- to investigate suspected offences under consumer law; and
- to refer to the DPP where appropriate.

The Second schedule to the CPA repealed a large number of existing enactments, including the Consumer Information Act, 1978, the Merchandise Marks Acts, 1887–1931, the Pyramid Selling Act, 1980 and the Restrictive Practices (Amendment) Act, 1987.

The objective of the UPCD is to strengthen the confidence of consumers in undertaking cross-border transactions and to achieve a higher level of consumer protection, providing the same protection against unfair practices and rogue traders to consumers, whether they are buying locally or abroad. This is the intention behind the common rules set out in the Directive.

### 9.12.1 UNFAIR PRACTICES

Part 3 of the CPA deals with commercial practices. Section 41(1) provides:

*A trader shall not engage in unfair commercial practices.*

Section 41(2) provides that a commercial practice is unfair if:

- it is contrary to one or both of 'the requirements of professional diligence'; and
- it would be likely to cause appreciable impairment of the average consumer's ability to make an informed choice in relation to the product concerned; and
- cause the average consumer to make a transactional decision that the average consumer would not otherwise make.

The 'requirements of professional diligence' are listed as:

(i)   *the general principle of good faith in the trader's field of activity*

(ii)  *the standard of skill and care that the trader may reasonably be expected to exercise in respect of consumers (s 41(2)(a)(i) and (ii)).*

In the NCA's view, a commercial practice is unfair when a breach of good faith occurs and the 'average consumer' is denied the reasonable standard of skill and care to which he is entitled.

The 'average consumer' has been interpreted by the European Court of Justice as 'reasonably well informed and reasonably observant and circumspect, taking into account social, cultural and linguistic factors'.

Under the UPCD and the CPA there are three distinct types of unfair commercial practices: misleading practices; aggressive practices; and prohibited practices.

## (1) *Misleading*

It is a misleading practice if it includes the provision of false information in relation to any matter set out in s 43(3) and that information would be likely to cause the average consumer to make a transactional decision that the average consumer would not otherwise make (s 43(1)) or if it would be likely to cause the average consumer to be deceived or misled in relation to any matter set out in s 43(3) and to make a transactional decision that the average consumer would not otherwise make (s 43(2)). It is an offence to engage in misleading practices described in s 43(1) and/or s 43(2).

Section 43(3) sets out ten matters for the purposes of s 43(1) and 43(2), listed from (a) to (j) in some detail. They include the existence or nature of a product, its main characteristics, price, the need for any part, replacement, servicing or repair in relation to it, the nature, attributes or rights of the trader and the legal rights of a consumer and when, how or in what circumstances those rights may be exercised.

Section 44 states that a practice involving marketing or advertising is misleading if it would be likely to cause the average consumer to confuse a competitor's product or trade name or trade mark with the trader's product or trade name or trade mark and to make a transactional decision that the average consumer would not otherwise make.

The tort of passing off already provides a remedy in cases of confusing similarities between products and it has been considered in a number of judgments of the Irish courts. The prohibition in s 44 is supported by the enforcement procedures set out in Part 5 of the CPA, however, an action for passing off must be taken by the aggrieved trader himself.

Section 46 provides that a commercial practice is misleading if a trader conceals material information which an average consumer would need to make an informed decision. Moreover, a trader is prohibited from giving such information in an unintelligible or ambitious way if it would lead a consumer to make a transactional decision he would not otherwise make.

## (2) *Aggressive*

A practice is aggressive if by harassment, coercion or undue influence it would be likely to:

(a) *cause significant impairment of the average consumer's freedom of choice or conduct in relation to the product concerned, and*

(b) *cause the average consumer to make a transactional decision that the average consumer would not otherwise make (s 53(1)).*

### (3) Prohibited

The CPA lists thirty-two commercial practices which are prohibited in all circumstances by s 55 and are set out in that provision. These are known as the 'black list' of prohibited commercial practices and include representations that a trader is a signatory to a code of conduct (if he is not) or is about to cease trading (if he is not), representations that a product can cure an illness (if it cannot) or that a product is available for a limited amount of time in order to elicit an immediate decision from the consumer. Other practices on the list include: promoting a product in such a way as to deliberately mislead consumers into thinking that it is that of another manufacturer, and 'cold calling'.

A trader who engages in prohibited practices set out in s 55 commits an offence and is liable to the fines and penalties provided in s 79, specifically, on a first conviction or indictment, a fine of up to €60,000 or imprisonment for up to 18 months, or both. There are stiffer penalties for subsequent convictions.

Any factual claim in a representation is presumed to be untrue unless the trader establishes its truth on the balance of probabilities.

### 9.12.2 ENFORCEMENT, SANCTIONS, AND PENALTIES

Part 5 of the CPA deals with the enforcement of its provisions, both civilly and criminally. The NCA is given a range of powers to help achieve compliance, involving:

- prosecution
- compliance notices
- undertakings
- prohibition orders, and
- fixed payment notices.

The NCA can apply for compensation orders for individual consumers in criminal proceedings. A consumer can also bring a civil action for damages.

The time limit for commencement of criminal proceedings under the CPA is set at two years after the alleged offence, rather than the previous six-months point set for summary offences in the District Court.

# CHAPTER 10

# INTELLECTUAL PROPERTY

## 10.1 Introduction

### 10.1.1 GENERAL

Intellectual property is the bedrock of the information society and has a rapidly growing importance in every area of commercial life. It impinges on every aspect of business, indeed often it is the most valuable asset a business owns. As a result, it is vital that solicitors acquire at least a general knowledge of the area so as to recognise when their clients may require advice to protect this asset and so as to be able to give pragmatic and succinct advice.

### 10.1.2 WHAT IS INTELLECTUAL PROPERTY?

Intellectual property is that area of law, which has evolved to protect what is essentially the fruit of creative endeavour. Legal rights have been introduced and developed to protect this intangible property, upon which many businesses rely and which particularly in the information technology industry, may generate enormous profits for the proprietors of those businesses.

As with any piece of property, intangible or real or personal, intellectual property may be traded. It may be sold or assigned for monetary consideration. It may be licensed or bequeathed in a will. In short it may be exploited in precisely the same way as any piece of real or personal property.

It is vital that every business knows what intellectual property rights it owns, what should be done to achieve the best possible protection of those rights, whether those rights are being exploited as well as may be and what to do if those rights are infringed. The solicitor should be in a position to advise in relation to all of these matters.

### 10.1.3 CATEGORIES OF INTELLECTUAL PROPERTY

The principal areas of intellectual property are protected by statute. These statutes make provision for a scheme of registration of various rights in order to assist in the clearer identification of those rights and of their ownership. The statutes grant the owner of an intellectual property right a clear monopoly in the property protected, which may be exploited as the owner decides. Intellectual property rights include the following categories:

(a)  patents which protect inventions;

(b)  trade marks which protect names in the course of trade and in the provision of services;

(c)  copyright and design which protect the physical form of literary, dramatic, musical and artistic endeavour;

(d)  passing-off which protects, in common law, the goodwill and reputation of a business; and

(e)  confidential information in which under common law an obligation of confidentiality exists in relation to information imparted from one party to another.

It is extremely important that, when advising clients on each occasion, the specific statute is carefully considered. Frequently, cases in this area of the law fall to be decided on the precise wording of a particular section or subsection of the relevant Act.

## 10.1.4  INTELLECTUAL PROPERTY—CONTRACTUAL CONSIDERATIONS

All of the statutes and the common law, which protect intellectual property, allow the general rules to be changed by agreement between the parties concerned. It is, in almost every situation, prudent for a solicitor to advise the client that the intention of the parties should be clearly agreed and set out in writing, prior to any dealings between the parties relating to intellectual property rights. Thus, if one party has an idea, an invention which may be parentable, it is sensible for that person, prior to discussing the invention with anyone, to enter into an agreement in writing that the parties will keep any information exchanged confidential. The parties are therefore bound by contract not to reveal any information without consent.

Similarly, all of the relevant statutes and the common law provide rules in relation to the ownership of intellectual property in an employment contract. Nonetheless, it is sensible, for the avoidance of doubt to set out in writing what has been agreed between the parties to avoid arguments in the future.

Clearly, in any case where a person has an invention, or an author has written a book, a play or a film script, and wishes to agree with a third party to exploit that work in any way, it is essential, for the avoidance of argument in the future that the terms and the basis upon which the exploitation is to take place are clearly set out in writing prior to commencement of the exploitation. It is in these situations that the solicitor may provide vital assistance to the client.

## 10.1.5  INTELLECTUAL PROPERTY AND COMPETITION LAW

As intellectual property law allows the existence of a monopoly and competition law outlaws agreements whose object or effect is to prevent, restrict or distort competition, an obvious dichotomy may arise between the two areas of law. The Competition Act, 1991, now replaced by the Competition Act, 2002 (the 'Competition Act'), introduced into Irish domestic law provisions similar to Art 81 and 82 of the EC Treaty. Unlike the EC Treaty, there is no de minimus provision in the Competition Act. The Competition Act is covered in **chapter 7**. EC Competition law is addressed in the Law Society manual on *European Law*.

Patent, know-how and research and development licences are all covered by European Commission block exemptions so that such agreements, which would generally infringe EC competition law, are permissible. There are at present no declarations (the Irish equivalent of block exemptions) for licences of intellectual property, aside from franchise agreements, under the Competition Act and so it is up to each party to assess whether an agreement complies with the Act. Care should be taken to ensure that protection under the Trade Marks Act, 1996 or other intellectual property legislation should not be used as a vehicle for the operation of an anti-competitive agreement or to abuse a dominant position as such protection may be void.

Articles 28–30 of the EC Treaty prohibit measures, which impose quantitative restrictions on imports from other Member States or have equivalent effect. The doctrine of exhaustion of rights has been developed to accommodate, on the one hand, the monopoly right granted in intellectual property law and, on the other hand, the EU rules allowing free movement of goods within the Community.

A trader applying a trade mark to and selling goods in one part of the EU cannot prevent the sale of those goods which have been placed on the market with his consent, being sold in another EU country. This is the case even when the trade mark is registered in that other EU country. The trade mark rights are exhausted when the goods have first been placed on the market for sale.

This doctrine of exhaustion of rights does not however apply to goods, which are imported from third countries outside the EU. Thus, goods which are imported from, for example, the US or the Far East, may not be sold in the EU without the unequivocal consent of the owner of the trade mark in the EU. In *Levi Strauss & Co and another v Tesco Stores Limited and another*, (2002) EWHC 1556 (Ch), the High Court in England confirmed that a trade mark owner was entitled to prevent goods bearing his trade mark from being imported into Europe without his express consent.

## 10.1.6  INFRINGEMENT REMEDIES

The remedies for infringement of intellectual property rights are in all cases damages, or an account of profits, an injunction to prohibit the infringement and delivery up and destruction of the infringing property.

Damages will be calculated by reference to a reasonable royalty rate or licence fee, but may take into account various matters in mitigation. For example, if a defendant could show that he was unaware of or had no reasonable grounds for suspecting that an intellectual property right existed, the plaintiff may be precluded from being awarded damages.

Certain of the statutes provide specific remedies for seisure of goods and orders for delivery up. Some of these remedies may be enforced by the Garda Siochána.

Further, infringement of copyright and of registered trade marks may constitute a criminal offence, the penalties for which are a fine and/or a term of imprisonment. The Directive on the Enforcement of Intellectual Property Rights (2004/48/EC) was passed on 29 April 2004 and is designed to ensure fair and equitable enforcement of intellectual property rights throughout the EU. The European Communities (Enforcement of Intellectual Property Rights) Regulations, 2006 (SI 36/2006) transpose into Irish law those aspects of Directive 2004/48/EC which had not previously been part of Irish law.

## 10.2 Patents

### 10.2.1 INTRODUCTION

The law relating to patents is governed by the Patents Act, 1992 (the '1992 Act'), the Intellectual Property (Miscellaneous Provisions) Act, 1998 and the Patents Amendment Act, 2006. The Patent Rules were also enacted in 1992 to deal with the administration of patents by the Patents Office and with the powers of the Controller of Patents in relation to the regulation of the patent regime.

A number of international conventions also exist with the objective of streamlining patent application, filing and novelty search procedures throughout the world. These are the Paris Convention of 1883, the Patent Co-operation Treaty 1970, the European Patent Convention 1973, the Community Patent Convention (not yet adopted) and the European Patent Convention 2000. Aside from licensing and transfer of patents, solicitors generally do not become involved in the area of patents until issues arise which must be decided by the courts. This is an extremely specialised area of the law and patent agents who are trained in scientific and engineering matters are expert in the drafting and processing of patents. It is important, however, for a solicitor to have some knowledge of the patent process in order to be able to advise properly when the matter reaches the stage of court proceedings.

### 10.2.2 PATENTABILITY

A patent may be obtained for any patentable invention and will grant the owner of the patent a monopoly protection in the invention for either a ten-year (short-term) or twenty-year period. An invention is patentable if it is susceptible of industrial application, is new and involves an inventive step (1992 Act, s 9(1)). In the case of a short-term patent the invention must be new, susceptible of industrial application and must not clearly lack an inventive step (1992 Act, s 63(4)). There is no definition in the 1992 Act of 'invention'. However, the following shall *not* be regarded as an invention:

(a)   a discovery;

(b)   a scientific theory;

(c)   a mathematical method;

(d)   an aesthetic creation;

(e)   a scheme, rule or method for performing a mental act, playing a game or doing business;

(f)   a computer program; and

(g)   the presentation of information.

The 1992 Act also provides that a method for treatment of the human or animal body by surgery or therapy and a diagnostic method practised on the human or animal body shall not be regarded as an invention susceptible of industrial application (1992 Act, s 9(4)). However, it is provided that this provision shall not apply to a product and, in particular, a substance or composition for use in any such method.

An invention shall be considered to be new if it does not form part of the state of the art. This comprises everything made available or disclosed to the public (whether in the State or elsewhere) in any way before the date of filling of the patent application (1992 Act, s 11). Disclosure of an invention will be discounted if it happened within six months before the filing of the patent application as a result of a breach of confidence or, because the invention was displayed at an exhibition officially recognised under the Paris Convention on International Exhibitions 1928 and the application makes a declaration to that effect when applying (1992 Act, s 12).

The invention will be considered as involving an inventive step if, having regard to the state of the art, it is not obvious to a person skilled in the art (1992 Act, s 13).

An invention is considered as susceptible of industrial application if it may be made or used in any kind of industry. Industry in this context includes agriculture (1992 Act, s 14).

There are certain exceptions to patentability under the Patents Act (1992 Act, s 10). A patent will not be granted in respect of:

(a)   an invention, the publication or exploitation of which will be contrary to public order or morality, provided that the exploitation will not be deemed to be so contrary only because it is prohibited by law; and

(b)   a plant or animal variety or an essentially biological process for the production of plants or animals other than a microbiological process or the products thereof.

The Biotechnology Directive (98/44/EC) was designed to harmonise the patenting of biotechnological inventions throughout the EU and to confirm that, inter alia, processes for cloning human beings are not patentable. The Directive was debated for some ten years before coming into force in 2000. It has been implemented in Ireland.

## 10.2.3   GRANT OF A PATENT

Patents are granted by the Patents Office to which a formal application is made. Of their nature such applications are extremely technical and the actual application will be made by a specialised patent agent. However, it is important for a solicitor to be able to give a client an idea of the procedure involved in obtaining protection.

### 10.2.3.1   Applications

A patent application may be made by any person alone or jointly with another person (1992 Act, s 15) but the right to a patent belongs to the inventor (1992 Act, s 16) who has a right to be mentioned in the application (1992 Act, s 17).

Under s 18 of the 1992 Act, a patent application for a twenty-year patent must contain:

(a)   a request for the grant of a patent;

(b)   a specification containing a description of the invention to which the application relates, one or more claims and any drawing referred to in the description or the claim; and

(c)   an abstract (a brief summary description).

The application must be accompanied by a filing fee (1992 Act, s 18), must clearly disclose the invention to which it relates (1992 Act, s 19), and the claim or claims must define the matter for which protection is sought and must be supported by the description (s 20). The application must relate to one invention only or at least to a group of inventions, which are so linked as to form a single inventive concept (s 21).

Under s 63(7) of the 1992 Act, if application is being made for a short-term (ten-year) patent, the specification must:

(a)   describe the invention and the best method of performing it, which is known to the applicant;

(b)   incorporate one or more claims, which must not exceed five, defining the matter for which protection is sought; and

(c)   be accompanied by any necessary drawings and an abstract.

A full-term (twenty-year) patent and a short-term patent may not co-exist for the same invention (1992 Act, s 64). The threshold for obtaining a short-term patent is lower than that required for obtaining a twenty-year patent (see **10.2.2**).

Under s 23 of the 1992 Act, the date of filing of a patent application is the earliest date upon which the applicant paid the filing fee and filed documents which contained:

(a) an indication that a patent is sought;

(b) information identifying the applicant; and

(c) a description of the invention even though the description does not comply with the requirements of the Act or with any requirements that may be prescribed.

If an objection is raised, at the time during which the application is being examined, that the application relates to more than one invention, the applicant may amend the specification or delete the claims. The applicant may also file another application for the extra invention. This is known as a 'divisional application' which is in respect of subject matter, which must not extend beyond the content of an earlier application as filed and complies with the relevant requirements. Such an application will be deemed to have been filed on the date of filing of the earlier application and will have the benefit of any right to priority (1992 Act, s 24).

It is also possible to file an application and claim the priority of an earlier application in respect of the same invention, which has been filed either in the State or abroad (1992 Act, s 25).

### 10.2.3.2 Priority

The date of priority is the date of filing of the patent application (1992 Act, s 27) in the State or abroad. This is an important date as it fixes the time which is to be considered for the purpose of assessing whether the invention is new. It also fixes the date from which infringement proceedings may be taken. Often an inventor will instruct his patent agent to apply for a patent at the first opportunity. This is to ensure that no rivals make application for the same invention and to obtain as early as possible a priority date. A more detailed application may then be filed within a twelve-month period. Once the application is received at the Patents Office, it is inspected by one of the Controller of Patents, Designs and Trade Marks' examiners (the 'Controller') to make sure that the application complies with the requirements of the 1992 Act. The applicant may request that a search be undertaken on behalf of the Controller in return for the appropriate fee to ensure that the invention complies with the requirement that it is new. Clearly, if the invention is not new, it is open to attack and will be invalid. The Controller must allow an applicant an opportunity to amend the application in light of the result of the search report within a prescribed period.

Alternatively, an applicant for a patent may submit a statement to the Controller to the effect that an application for a patent for the same invention has been made in a prescribed foreign State (UK or Germany) or under the provisions of any prescribed Convention or Treaty (the European Patent Convention 1973 or the Patent Cooperation Treaty 1970) (1992 Act, s 30; Patent Rules 1992, r 26).

In this case the applicant must submit evidence, either of the results of the search carried out on that application, or of the grant of a patent in pursuance of the application. Where the applicant has submitted the results of a search, the Controller shall allow an opportunity to amend the application in light of that evidence.

The patent application must then be published in the Patents Office Official Journal, which is published every fortnight and is available online on the Patents Office website, www.patentsoffice.ie. Publication must be as soon as practicable after the expiry of eighteen months from the filing date or from the priority date, if claimed. If the applicant requests it may be published earlier (1992 Act, s 28). If no objections are received, the patent proceeds to grant, it is sealed and issued.

## 10.2.4    PROTECTION CONFERRED BY A PATENT

### 10.2.4.1    Generally

While a patent is in force, it confers upon the proprietor the right to prevent all third parties not having his consent from using the invention whether directly or indirectly (1992 Act, s 40). Direct use of the invention includes, for example, making, putting on the market or using a product which is the subject matter of the patent, or importing or stocking the product for those purposes (1992 Act, s 40). The prevention of indirect use of the invention means that a proprietor may also prevent all third parties not having his consent from supplying or offering to supply in the State someone, other than a party entitled to exploit the patented invention (1992 Act, s 41).

### 10.2.4.2    Exception to monopoly

The following provisions are imported from the Community Patent Convention. The rights conferred by a patent do not extend to acts done privately for non-commercial purposes, or acts done for experimental purposes. These acts may be done without infringing the patent holder's rights. Nor do they extend to the extemporaneous preparation for individual cases in a pharmacy, of a medicine in accordance with a medical prescription. They do not extend either to use of the patented product on board vessels or aircraft or land vehicles, when such temporarily or accidentally enter territorial waters of the State or the State itself (1992 Act, s 42). This provision is presumably designed to assist in ensuring the safety of such vessels. The invention must be used exclusively for the needs of the vessel.

### 10.2.4.3    Rights on application

A patent application provisionally confers upon the applicant the same protection as that conferred on a granted patent from the date of its publication: 1992 Act, s 44. In turn, infringement proceedings may be brought after a patent has been granted in respect of infringing acts committed between the date of publication of the application and the date of grant (1992 Act, s 56).

#### 10.2.4.4　Extent of protection

The extent of the protection conferred by the patent or patent application is to be determined by the terms of the claims. A description and drawing submitted will be used to interpret the claims (1992 Act, s 45).

#### 10.2.4.5　Short-term patents

The protection conferred by a short-term patent is the same as for a twenty-year patent, subject to the provisions of the 1992 Act, s 66. This section attempts to strike a balance between the rights of a short-term patent holder and third parties. To this end it requires the holder of a short-term patent to request the Controller to establish a search report on the invention before he may initiate proceedings against a third party for alleged infringement of his patent. Any such proceedings may be brought in the Circuit Court irrespective of the amount of any claim.

### 10.2.5　OWNERSHIP

The owner of a patent is normally the inventor. In the case of joint inventors both parties may be named as the owners of the patent.

In the case of inventions made by an employee, these will belong to the employer if they are made in the course of the employee's employment. The 1992 Act does not specifically provide for this, so contracts of employment should stipulate that the inventions belong to the employer. If not stipulated in the contract, then the invention may still be deemed to belong to the employer if the court considers it should, because the invention was invented during the course of the employment of the employee or in circumstances where the employee was employed for the purposes of inventing. Section 16 of the 1992 Act states that if the inventor is an employee, the right to a patent shall be determined in accordance with the law of the State in which the employee is wholly or mainly employed.

### 10.2.6　SUPPLEMENTARY PROTECTION CERTIFICATES ('SPC')

Pharmaceuticals may not be sold to the public unless they have been granted a product authorisation. In order to obtain such an authorisation, the applicant must provide detailed technical information in relation to the testing of the product and its efficiency, all of which must be considered by the regulatory authorities, which in Ireland, is the Irish Medicines Board. The SPC was introduced at the behest of the pharmaceutical industry to compensate that industry for the lengthy regulatory delays which occur while a manufacturer of a new product is seeking approval for sale of it to the public. The European Council Regulation (EEC No 1768/92) introducing the SPC, was given effect in Irish law by the European Communities (Supplementary Protection Certificate) Regulations, 1993 (SI 125/1993). The SPC has the effect of extending the twenty-year life of a pharmaceutical patent by a period, which gives protection for fifteen years from the date upon which it first received marketing approval in the EU. The maximum extension allowed over and above the usual twenty-year patent is five years. A similar facility was introduced in respect of Plant Protection Products under Regulation (EC) No 1610/96 of the European Parliament and of the Council.

It is important to check whether an SPC exists in relation to both medicinal and plant protection products if the client is considering manufacturing the patented product, as the patent may have been extended and the client might be exposed to an infringement action.

### 10.2.7 INFRINGEMENT

A patent is infringed by anyone who, in the State without the consent of the proprietor, makes, offers or puts on the market a product which is the subject matter of a patent or uses a process which is the subject matter of a patent, knowing (or it is obvious to a reasonable person in the circumstances) that the use of the process is prohibited.

Civil proceedings may be brought by the proprietor or licensee of a patent for alleged infringement of a patent (1992 Act, s 47). He may seek:

(a) an injunction restraining the defendant from any apprehended act of infringement;

(b) an order requiring the defendant to deliver up or destroy any product protected by the patent in relation to which the patent is alleged to have been infringed or any article in which the product is inextricably comprised;

(c) damages in respect of the alleged infringement;

(d) in the alternative, an account of profits derived by the defendant from the alleged infringement; and

(e) a declaration that the patent is valid and has been infringed by the defendant.

Damages will not be awarded, nor will an order be made for an account of profits against a defendant who proves that, at the date of infringement, he was unaware of, and had no reasonable grounds for supposing that the patent in question existed.

However, he will be deemed to have been aware or to have had reasonable grounds for so supposing where the number of the relevant patent had been applied to a product (1992 Act, s 49).

### 10.2.8 GROUNDLESS THREATS

In the normal course, where a property right is being infringed the owner will instruct a solicitor to send a strong letter demanding that the infringement be stopped. This is known as a 'cease and desist' letter. In the case of patents it is important to note that a person who has been threatened with proceedings for infringement of a patent may bring his own proceedings to court for relief (1992 Act, s 53). He may seek:

(a)   a declaration to the effect that the threats complained of were unjustifiable;

(b)   an injunction against the continuance of the threats; and

(c)   such damages if any as have been suffered.

It is for these reasons that, rather than the usual form of strongly-worded cease and desist letter being sent at the commencement of a patent action, a letter is sent simply drawing the attention of the alleged infringer to the existence of the patent. This is to avoid a claim for groundless threats being made against both the client and the solicitor.

## 10.2.9   REVOCATION

Any person may apply to the court or the Controller of Patents for revocation of a patent (1992 Act, s 57). The grounds for revocation are:

(a)   the subject matter of the patent is not patentable;

(b)   the specification of the patent does not properly disclose the invention so that it may be carried out by a person skilled in the art;

(c)   the matter disclosed in the specification extends beyond that disclosed in the application which was filed;

(d)   the protection conferred by the patent has been extended by an amendment of the patent or the specification of the patent; and

(e)   the proprietor of the patent is not the person who is entitled to the patent (1992 Act, s 58).

Thus, an employee who claims that an invention is not his employer's, might apply for revocation or the owner of an existing patent might apply, if the new patent is an obvious improvement of his patent. In cases where a claim for infringement is made, one of the standard defences is to seek revocation of the plaintiff's patent on one or all of the grounds (a) to (e) above. The Controller has the power to revoke patents on his own initiative if it appears that the patent which has been granted formed part of the state of the art. In such a case, the proprietor of the patent will have an opportunity of making observations and amending this specification of the patent in order to preserve it (1992 Act, s 60). In the event that proceedings for revocation are brought before the court, the Controller must be given notice in writing by the plaintiff of those proceedings (1992 Act, s 62). Section 94 provides that a communication between a person or person acting on his behalf and a solicitor or patent agent or person acting on his behalf, or for the purpose of obtaining, or in response to a request for information which a person is seeking for the purpose of instructing the solicitor or patent agent in relation to any matter concerning the protection of an invention, patent, design or technical information, or any matter involving passing-off shall be privileged to the same extent as a communication between client and solicitor in any proceeding before a court in the State (1992 Act, s 94).

## 10.2.10 INTERNATIONAL CONVENTIONS

### 10.2.10.1 The Patent Co-operation Treaty

The main object of the Patent Co-operation Treaty 1970 (the 'PCT') is the streamlining of patent application filing and novelty search procedures for an applicant wishing to obtain patent protection in a wide number of countries around the world. It was signed by Ireland in 1970 and has been ratified as a result of the Patents Act, 1992.

Under the PCT, the applicant makes one central application, usually to their local patent office, designating the countries in which patent protection is required. A novelty search is then carried out by an international searching authority and this search is then furnished to the national office of each country in which protection is sought. Further prosecution in each country is then in the hands of the local patent office in accordance with its normal procedure.

### 10.2.10.2 European Patent Convention

The European Patent Convention 1973 (the 'EPC') is more advanced than the PCT in that searching and examination are centralised in the European Patent Office in Munich.

The EPC was made effective in Ireland by the 1992 Act. The procedure under the EPC is that anyone seeking to protect an invention in several member countries of the Convention may do so by making just one application to the European Patent Office in Munich. The applicant must designate all of the countries in which protection is desired. This means he must specifically name the countries in which he seeks patent protection for his invention. Nationals of both member and non-member countries are entitled to take advantage of this arrangement. Under the 1992 Act, a European patent designating Ireland, granted by the European Patent Office is treated as if it was granted by the Irish Patent Office (1992 Act, s 119). However, if the language of the specification of the European patent is not English, a translation in English of the specification must be filed with the Irish Patent Office and published here in order that the patent may have effect in Ireland (1992 Act, s 119(6), (7)). Similarly, in the case of a European patent application designating Ireland, such an application must be treated as having the same legal status in Ireland as an application filed with the Irish Office (1992 Act, s 120).

Section 122 of the 1992 Act permits a European patent application designating Ireland, which has been deemed to be withdrawn, to be proceeded with as a national application under the 1992 Act, subject to certain conditions.

Section 123 of the 1992 Act provides that the High Court is given jurisdiction to determine questions as to the right to be granted to a European patent and sets out the circumstances in which such jurisdiction is exercisable.

Section 124 of the 1992 Act provides for the recognition in Ireland of questions as to the right to a European patent to be determined by a court or competent authority of another Contracting State of the EPC, subject to certain conditions.

A decision as to whether to file a European patent application, specifying those European countries in which patent protection is sought or individual national applications, will depend on several factors. The European patent procedure is expensive, but if protection in several countries is required, it may still be cheaper than a corresponding series of individual country applications. The examination procedure carried out by the European Patent Office is well respected, so that if a European patent is granted, it is likely that such a patent would be subsequently upheld in the national courts. Another factor is that under Art 99 of the EPC, a European patent may be revoked in total only during the first nine months of grant; subsequently it may only be revoked country by country, by application to the appropriate national court.

Section 127 of the 1992 Act allows Ireland to be designated in an international application. This section also provides that an international application designating the State, for example, by an American client, shall be deemed to be an application for a European patent (under the EPC) designating the State. This means that functions concerning international applications, which would otherwise have to be performed by the Irish Patents Office, may instead be performed by the European Patent Office. The applicant will eventually receive a grant by the European Patent Office of a European patent designating Ireland if he has availed of this procedure.

### 10.2.10.3 Community Patent Convention

The Community Patent Convention (the 'CPC') was initially signed in 1989 but has not yet come into force. The 1992 Act does not itself mention the CPC although it includes a general provision allowing the Minister for Enterprise, Trade and Employment to make an order enabling effect to be given to 'any international treaty, convention or agreement relating to patents to which the State is or proposes to become a party' (1992 Act, s 128).

The CPC may be regarded as a further extension to the EPC with the difference that, instead of a bundle of individual patents in European countries being granted, a single patent known as a Community patent ('ComPat') is obtained throughout all those European countries which are also members of the EU. Certain difficulties arose in relation to the mechanics of the CPC and after years of debate it was completely redrafted. Unfortunately, the Council of Ministers failed to reach agreement on this new draft during 2004. There is still no consensus on the scheme for first instance jurisdiction, although there appears to be agreement on a centralised appeal system. However, the principle of the grant of a single patent remains. It is anticipated that applications will be made to the European Patent Office in Munich, in English, French or German or in any language accompanied by a translation. There are also suggestions for a Community Patent Court in Luxembourg, with power to hold hearings in Member States. The Court must be established by 2010 at the latest. It is anticipated that the ComPat will reduce the cost for two-thirds of European patent applicants. At least 30,000 European patents are granted each year.

#### 10.2.10.4 Compulsory licensing

A proposal has been made by the European Commission to allow the compulsory licensing of pharmaceuticals protected by patent rights (COM(2004)737 final). Manufacturers of pharmaceutical products will be able to apply for a licence to manufacture in the EU a pharmaceutical protected by a patent or SPC. The licensed products will be for export to countries which do not have the capacity to manufacture them and which have public health problems. This is as a result of the TRIPS Doha Declaration relating to public health in 2001.

## 10.3 Trade Marks, Counterfeit Goods, Passing-off

### 10.3.1 INTRODUCTION

This section of the law was developed to prevent the public being deceived by a trader alleging that he had an association with goods which, in fact, he did not enjoy. The first Trade Marks Act was introduced in 1875 and brought in a system of registration of trade marks. Currently, this area is governed by the Trade Marks Act, 1996 (the '1996 Act'), sections of the Patents Amendment Act, 2006 and the regulations made thereunder.

### 10.3.2 WHAT IS A TRADE MARK?

#### 10.3.2.1 Generally

Section 6 of the 1996 Act says that a 'trade mark' means:

> *any sign capable of being represented graphically which is capable of distinguishing goods or services of one undertaking from those of other undertakings.*

The 1996 Act goes on to say that a trade mark may, in particular, consist of words (including personal names), designs, letters, numerals or the shape of goods or of their packaging.

A trade mark may be something as simple as a word or name, it can be written in a particular script or with a band of colour around it, or it can be as complicated as any designer can imagine. A trade mark does not have to be a name at all. It may be three stripes, it may be the shape of a bottle, and it may even be a smell, provided that the applicant has been able to represent the smell graphically and that it is distinguishable from other smells.

Once a trade mark has been registered under the 1996 Act, it is a property right and the proprietor of a registered trade mark is entitled to all the rights and remedies provided by the 1996 Act. A trade mark may be registered in one of forty-five classes. The Nice Agreement, on the International Classification of goods and services for the purposes of the registration, provides an internationally recognised classification system of goods and services in respect of which trade marks may be registered. Ireland has signed up to the Nice Agreement and applies the classification system to the examination and registration of trade mark applications.

Under the Nice Agreement, goods and services are divided into various categories, for example food and drink, paper products, financial services etc. When a trade mark is registered, it may be registered for a particular product or service within a class or for all of the goods or services within a class or, indeed, for goods and services in several different classes. The registration of a mark, in respect of a specific product or service or class of products/services, defines the extent of the protection afforded by that registration.

The Nice Agreement consists of thirty-four classes of goods (classes 1–34 inclusive) and eleven classes of services (35–45 inclusive).

### 10.3.2.2 Marks which may be refused registration

Sections 8–10 of the 1996 Act govern marks which may be refused registration. Signs which do not satisfy the requirements described above, which are devoid of any distinctive character, or which consist of signs or indications which may serve, in trade, to designate the kind, quality, quantity, intended purpose, value, geographical origin, time of production of goods or of rendering of services, or other characteristics of goods or services which consist exclusively of signs or indications which have become customary in the practice of the trade will not be registered as trade marks.

However, if any of those trade marks has in fact acquired a distinctive character as a result of the use made of it, then registration will be permitted (for example, the Waterford Glass Mark is a mark indicating geographical origin, but is registered because of its distinctive character).

Pursuant to s 8(2) of the 1996 Act, a sign will not be registered as a trade mark if it consists exclusively of the shape which results from the nature of the goods themselves, or the shape of goods which is necessary to obtain a technical result, or the shape which gives substantial value to the goods.

Pursuant to s 8(3) of the 1996 Act, a trade mark will not be registered if it is contrary to public policy or morality or if it deceives the public, for example as to the nature, quality or geographical origin of the goods or service.

A State emblem of Ireland, or one which resembles such an emblem, will not be registered unless the consent to its registration has been given by the Minister for Communications, the Marine and Natural Resources. The national flag of the State will not be registered if it would be misleading or grossly offensive and the Controller may refuse to register a mark which consists of any emblem of a public authority unless, as provided in s 9 of the 1996 Act, 'such consent as is required by rules is obtained'.

Pursuant to s 10(2) of the 1996 Act, a trade mark will not be registered if it is identical to or similar to an earlier trade mark and the goods or services are identical, or if there exists the likelihood of confusion, including the likelihood of association of the later trade mark with the earlier trade mark. Pursuant to s 10(3) of the 1996 Act, a trade mark will not be registered if it is identical to or similar to an earlier trade mark and it is to be registered for different goods or services from those protected by the earlier trade mark if the use of the later trade mark would take unfair advantage of the earlier mark. A trade mark will not be registered if its use in the State is liable to be prevented because it is passing itself off as an unregistered mark already used in the course of trade or if it would infringe the copyright, registered design or any other law relating to a right to a name, a right of personal portrayal or an industrial property right unless the owner of the earlier trade mark consents. An 'earlier trade mark' is defined in the 1992 Act, s 11.

Pursuant to s 12 of the 1996 Act, however, if there has been what is called honest concurrent use of the trade mark, then the Controller is not allowed to refuse the application.

## 10.3.3    REGISTRATION OF A TRADE MARK

### 10.3.3.1    Application for a trade mark

Application for registration of a trade mark is made to the Controller and is made in respect of particular goods or services or in respect of particular classes of goods or services in one of the forty-five separate classes or categories of goods and services. Each class or category is defined in relation to the nature or description of the goods or services.

The Controller examines the application to make sure that the requirements of the 1996 Act have been fulfilled and once the application for registration has been accepted, it is advertised in the official Patents Office Journal which is published fortnightly and can be viewed on the Patents Office website at www.patentsoffice.ie. Any person is entitled to give notice of opposition to the registration within one month of the advertisement and that period can be extended by two months. If the Controller receives no objection then he registers the trade mark, which lasts for ten years and may be renewed for further periods of ten years on payment of the requisite fee, forever.

Section 17 of the 1996 Act provides, that a person who applies for registration of a trade mark may disclaim any right to the exclusive use of any part of the trade mark. Further, the Controller may refuse to accept the application, unless the applicant agrees to make a disclaimer in respect of a particular element of the mark. The registration which subsequently occurs therefore is restricted accordingly (s 17).

### 10.3.3.2    Non-use

Pursuant to s 51 of the 1996 Act, if a trade mark has not been put to genuine use in the State by, or with the consent of, the proprietor for a period of five years, then it may be revoked.

### 10.3.3.3 Community trade marks

The Community Trade Mark Office (Office for the Harmonisation of the Internal Market ('OHIM')) (www.OHIM.eu) opened in Alicante in Spain in April 1996 to give the applicants for trade marks the facility to apply to a Central Office for a trade mark in any European country. There is a right to claim priority for an application for a period of six months from the date of filing of the first convention application and any filing equivalent to a regular national filing shall be treated as giving rise to the right of priority (s 40).

### 10.3.3.4 Madrid Protocol

The Madrid Protocol is a system of registration of trade marks, administered by the World Intellectual Property Organization ('WIPO') which allows an applicant to apply for a trade mark in several different jurisdictions by filing one application in a single language, in one trade mark office. The Protocol became operative in Ireland on 19 October 2001. A list of countries which have joined the protocol is to be seen on the WIPO website www.wipo.int/madrid/en/index.html.

## 10.3.4 BUSINESS NAMES

It is possible to register a business name under the Business Names Act, 1963 (the '1963 Act'). However, registration does not confer an exclusive right to the name in the registered owner. The purpose of the 1963 Act is to provide a register of firms and individuals trading in the State under a name other than that of the owner or owners of the business. Thus no exclusive protection is granted to the owner of a business name by registration of it. There may be several registrations for the same name each owned by a different party.

## 10.3.5 COUNTERFEIT GOODS

There is a very useful procedure which was introduced initially by the European Communities (Counterfeit Goods) Regulations, 1990 (SI 118/1990) whereby, upon payment of a fee of £400 for each three-month period, a trade mark owner may register his trade mark with the customs section of the Revenue Commissioners.

The regulations were amended in 1996 by the European Communities (Counterfeit and Pirated Goods) Regulations, 1996 (SI 48/1996) to cover what are called 'pirated goods', which include not only infringing trade marks but also goods made without the consent of a copyright owner or owner of 'neighbouring rights' or the holder of a design right, whether or not registered under national law. A further amendment came into force in Ireland on 1 January 2004: Council Regulation (EC) No 1383/2003 and Commission Regulation (EC) No 1891/2004 introduced additional provisions which allowed the application to customs free of charge. It also abolished the requirement to provide security and instead required a rights-owner to provide an undertaking to accept liability, if the goods were ultimately found not to infringe or the procedure is discontinued. The Regulation has been further extended to include plant varieties, geographical indications and designations of origin. A streamlined procedure was also introduced to allow custom officials destroy goods, which have been abandoned without or before determining whether an intellectual property right has been infringed. Commission Regulation (EC) No 1172/2007 is the latest amendment concerning customs action against goods suspected of infringing certain intellectual property rights, and the measures to be taken against goods found to have infringed such rights came into force on 6 October 2007.

Each consignment of goods with the trade mark applied and which is imported from a third country outside the EU will be inspected to ascertain whether the goods are genuine. The trade mark owner will be requested to inspect the goods and if they are found to be counterfeit, the customs authorities will seise them and they will ultimately be destroyed.

The importer has a right to oppose a seisure and must do so within one month. The procedure is very straightforward and, in comparison with the other remedy of court application for an injunction, is from a client's point of view just as effective and much more cost effective.

## 10.3.6 WHAT IS PASSING-OFF?

### 10.3.6.1 Meaning of passing-off

Passing-off is a tort actionable at common law. It recognises the right of a person to seek to protect the goodwill of his business from unfair trading. It prohibits a third party from selling goods or carrying on business under a name, mark, description or otherwise in such a manner as is likely to mislead the public or likely to deceive or confuse them into believing that the merchandise or business is that belonging to another person. The most succinct description of passing-off is that of Lord Parker in *A. G. Spalding & Brothers v A. W. Gamage Ltd* (1915) 32 RPC 273, a case which involved a stock of the plaintiff's footballs which they had discontinued and which the defendant bought and advertised for sale at very low prices as the latest model.

Lord Parker described the tort of passing-off as follows:

> Trader A cannot without infringing the rights of Trader B represent goods which are not B's goods or B's goods of a particular class or quality to be B's goods or B's goods of that particular class or quality.

The right of protection which the plaintiff has is not just to protect a particular mark applied to goods or to protect a reputation but rather to give a trader a property right in the goodwill built up in the business. The courts have accepted that both the word 'trader' and the word 'goodwill' are very broad in meaning and whiskey and champagne makers, actors and writers have all been granted relief in passing-off. So, A cannot without infringing the rights of B represent goods, which are not B's goods, to be B's goods. This, then, is the essence of passing-off.

Passing-off is now regarded as having been categorically defined in the *Advocaat* case: *Erven Warnink BV v J. Townsend & Sons (Hull) Ltd* [1979] AC 731 where Lord Diplock decreed that there were five characteristics, which must be present in order to create a valid cause of action for passing-off:

(a) a misrepresentation;

(b) made by a trader in the course of trade;

(c) to prospective customers of his or ultimate consumers of goods or services supplied by him;

(d) which is calculated to injure the business or goodwill or another trader (in the sense that this is a reasonably foreseeable consequence); and

(e) which causes actual damage to a business or goodwill of the trader by whom the action is brought; or (in a *quia timet* action) will probably do so.

All of these characteristics have been endorsed in *Reckitt & Coleman Products Limited v Borden Int* ([1990] 1 All ER 873) and Clarke J in *Jacob Fruitfield Food Group Ltd v United Biscuits* (2007, High Court, unreported).

### 10.3.6.2 A misrepresentation

It should be understood that passing-off does not confer a monopoly right in either the name in a trade mark or in the get-up of goods. The action may only succeed if use of any of those things is calculated to mislead or may mislead. The defendant may use any part of the plaintiff's property, provided that he does not do it in a way which will deceive. The basis of the action is that a false representation is made by the defendant so that an association with another person (the plaintiff) is made in the minds of the public. This representation must be material in that there must be a proper risk of damage to the plaintiff.

### 10.3.6.3 Made by a trader in the course of trade

Although the *Advocaat* case expressly required the plaintiff to be a trader, this requirement is in fact an unnecessary one. If the plaintiff is not trading, then he cannot suffer damage to his business or to his goodwill. Having said that, what constitutes a trader is, as far as the law of passing-off is concerned, extremely wide. Basically, anyone who makes an income from the provision of goods or services may be said to be a trader. Trade associations have been successful in bringing actions for passing-off, including, for example, the BBC and the British Medical Association. Charities such as Dr Barnado's Homes have been granted injunctions. In these cases the court accepted the contention that in spite of the fact that the BBC, the British Medical Association and Dr Barnardo's are non-profit-making organisations they could nonetheless be regarded as trading. On the other hand, a political party was not considered to be a trader on the basis that it was involved in non-commercial activities: *British Medical Association v Marsh* (1931) 48 RPC 565 and *Dean v McGivan* [1982] FSR 119.

#### 10.3.6.4 To prospective customers of his

On the face of it evidence of actual deception will be useful examples to persuade a judge that a passing-off has occurred. However, at the end of the day, it is settled that the court's decision will not depend solely on the evaluation of such evidence and that 'the court must in the end trust to its own perception into the mind of the reasonable man'. This view has been approved by Laffoy J in the High Court in the interlocutory application in *Symonds Cider & English Wine Co Ltd v Showerings (Ireland) Ltd*, 10 January 1997, High Court, unreported, when she did not take into account the surveys of the opinion of the public which had been carried out by both parties as to confusion. Laffoy J was strongly of the view that she was able to decide whether a passing-off had occurred without such survey evidence and that it was more appropriate that she should do so.

#### 10.3.6.5 Business or goodwill

Goodwill is created by trading. Originally this meant that the plaintiff had to satisfy the court that his business was within the jurisdiction and that he had been trading for some time. However, over the past twenty years or so, the courts have accepted that goodwill may be created in different ways, aside from simply trading within the jurisdiction. In *C&A Modes Ltd v C&A Waterford Ltd* [1978] FSR 126, the court accepted that even though C&A had no store in the Republic of Ireland, there was a very regular custom from the south to the north of Ireland where C&A had a store in Belfast and a substantial amount of advertising was carried out by C&A in the Sunday magazine supplements and in women's magazines and on television, all of which was received in the Republic of Ireland. This was the first case where a court accepted that goodwill could be built up from foreign trading.

In *O'Neills Irish International Sports Co Ltd and Charles O'Neill & Co Ltd v O'Neill's Footwear Dryer Co Ltd*, 30 April 1997, High Court, unreported, Barron J appears to have decided in favour of the plaintiff more on the basis of their reputation than the goodwill they had built up in the name O'Neill. The defendant was a company owned by Mr John O'Neill who had obtained a patent for an electrically-operated shoe dryer. As he could not find any support from sports manufacturers, including the plaintiffs, for his invention and not having sufficient financial resources to manufacture it himself, he decided he would import a similar product from the Far East with a view to encouraging interest from manufacturers in his own product. He sold the imported product in a box similar to a normal shoe box with pictures of different types of shoe and of the dryer on it. The label on the box said that the product was an O'Neills footwear dryer and referred to Celbridge Ireland and also said 'made in China'. The plaintiffs sought an injunction on the basis of passing-off, claiming that they had a reputation in the name O'Neills and that the defendant was trading on that reputation. It was held that the defendant was deliberately trading upon the plaintiff's reputation and the court found that the defendant was wrong in the belief that he could use his own name and market his product under that name. While a person may use his own name in the course of trade, this does not entitle him to use it in such a way as is calculated to lead others to believe his goods are those of another.

#### 10.3.6.6 Damage

The plaintiff must satisfy the court that the action of a defendant has or is likely to cause the plaintiff damage. The first of these requirements, that is where the plaintiff has already suffered damage, is straightforward in that if confusion in the minds of the public may be proved as to ownership of the goods and it may be argued that the defendant's goods are inferior, then the court may be satisfied that both the goodwill and the reputation of the plaintiff are being damaged. The second category, that is that the action is likely to cause damage, is in practice generally not a difficult proof to overcome. If goodwill and reputation may be shown and if, which is almost always the case, the defendant's products or the services offered are inferior, the court will accept that damage is likely to be caused. In *Falcon Travel v Falcon Leisure Group* [1991] IHR 175 Murphy J took a novel approach to the issue of damage. The plaintiffs had been trading in Dublin for three or four years when Falcon Leisure, the UK tour operator, began trading as well. The plaintiffs were able to show that they were receiving numerous phone calls which should have been for the defendants and that they were losing business from people ringing the defendants when they intended to ring the plaintiffs. The defendants argued that there could be no likelihood of confusion to the public as they were a tour operator and the plaintiff was a travel agency. The defendant also argued that the plaintiff had actually benefited from the confusion rather than having suffered damage. Murphy J agreed that a passing-off had occurred and that the plaintiff's reputation had become entirely submerged with that of the defendant. The court found that goodwill, which was appropriated, could constitute damage in itself, without proof of loss of custom. In this case the court awarded damages to the plaintiffs rather than an injunction so that Falcon Travel could launch an advertising campaign to make sure that the public was aware of the difference between the plaintiffs and the defendants.

### 10.3.7 INFRINGEMENT

#### 10.3.7.1 Generally

The proprietor of a registered trade mark has exclusive rights in the trade mark and those rights are infringed if someone else uses an identical trade mark in relation to the same goods or services or similar goods or services so that a likelihood of confusion may arise on the part of the public (1996 Act, s 14). 'Use' includes in particular:

(a) affixing a sign to goods or the packaging thereof;

(b) offering or exposing goods for sale, putting them on the market or stocking them for those purposes under the sign or offering or supplying services under the sign;

(c) importing or exporting goods under the sign; or

(d) using the sign on business papers or in advertising.

### 10.3.7.2 Exceptions to infringement

No one is prevented from using a registered trade mark to identify goods or services as those of the proprietor or licensee of that registered trade mark, but such use must be in accordance with honest practices. Otherwise it will be treated as infringing the registered trade mark if it takes unfair advantage of, or is detrimental to, the distinctive character or reputation of the trade mark.

A trade mark is not infringed by the use of a person of his own name or address or of indications concerning the kind, quality, quantity, intended purpose, value, geographical origin, time of production of goods or of rendering of the service or other characteristics of goods or services, or where it is necessary to indicate the intended purpose of the product or service, in particular as accessories or spare parts. However, all of these uses must be in accordance with honest practices, industrial and commercial matters (1996 Act, s 15(2)).

A trade mark will not be infringed by its use on goods which have been put on the market in the European Economic Area by the proprietor of the trade mark or with his consent. This is referred to as the exhaustion of rights of a registered trade mark and stems from EU law, confirming that the owner of a trade mark has exclusive right to use the mark and protect himself against competitors wishing to take advantage of the trade mark, while at the same time prohibiting the owner of the trade mark using his mark to limit the free movement of goods.

However, there may be grounds for preventing the goods being sold, if, for example, their condition has been changed or impaired after they have been put on the market (1996 Act, s 16). Further, a trade mark owner can prevent goods from outside the European Economic Area being sold without his consent even if he has affixed his trade mark to the goods (*Levi Strauss & Co and another v Tesco Stores Limited and another*, 2002 EWHC 1556 (Ch)).

### 10.3.7.3 Remedies

When a mark is infringed, the court has the power to grant an injunction prohibiting the infringement and order the payment of damages and may require the infringer to remove the offending sign or, if that is not possible, to destroy the goods, materials or articles in question (1996 Act, ss 18, 19).

Section 20 of the 1996 Act makes provision for the owner of a trade mark to apply for an order for the delivery up to him of infringing goods, materials or articles. Section 23 of the 1996 Act says that the court may make an order destroying goods which have been seised under the 1996 Act, s 20. No rules of court have been made as to the service of notice on the infringer of this application to destroy but, in practice, the court will generally require that the infringer be notified of the application.

### 10.3.7.4 Seisure orders

Section 25 of the 1996 Act gives the district court the power to request the Garda Síochána to seise goods, materials or articles and to bring them before the court. On proof to the district court that they are infringing goods, materials or articles the court may make an order delivering them up to the owner of the registered trade mark, ordering them to be destroyed or dealt with in such other way as the court thinks fit. This is an extremely useful remedy if the client's trade marks are being infringed by the sale of counterfeit goods at, for example, a street market or concert. This section also means that an application may be made to the district court ex parte, which provides a cheap and effective remedy for the client.

### 10.3.7.5 Groundless threats

Section 24 provides that, if proceedings are threatened for an infringement of a registered trade mark when it is not in relation to the application of the mark to goods or the importation of goods to which the mark has been applied or the supply of services under the mark, then the person who receives the threat of the proceedings may seek a declaration that the threats are unjustifiable and may look for an injunction prohibiting the threat and for damages.

## 10.3.8 ASSIGNMENT AND CHARGES OF REGISTERED TRADE MARKS

Trade marks are transferable by assignment, testamentary disposition or operation of law in exactly the same way as any personal property may be transferred with either the goodwill of the business or independently. An unregistered trade mark may only be transferred with the benefit of the goodwill of a business. Any assignment must be in writing, signed by the assignor and sealed, if the assignor is a body corporate.

Registered trade marks may also be charged in the same way as any other personal property. Where a trade mark has been assigned or mortgaged, particulars of the transaction should be registered with the Controller. If this is not done then the transaction is ineffective as against a third party acquiring a conflicting interest and being unaware of the transfer or mortgage and as against anyone who is a licensee of the trade mark (1996 Act, s 29). Furthermore, unless the application for registration is made within six months of the transaction, or at least as soon as is practicable, the assignee/mortgagee will not be entitled to damages or to an account of the profits in respect of any infringement of the mark occurring after the date of the transaction and before the application for registration of the prescribed participators is made.

## 10.3.9 LICENSING

Licences of registered trade marks may be granted but they must be in writing and signed by and on behalf of the grantor to be valid. It is wise also to put a notice of the licence on the Register of Trade Marks. If this is not done the owner of the trade mark may be exposed to a claim to expunge the trade mark for non-use.

### 10.3.10 DOMAIN NAMES

A domain name or Internet protocol address is the name used to identify a website, in the same way as the address of a premises identifies it. The name corresponds to a series of numbers, but for convenience, the addresses have been converted into a more legible form and consist now of two names. Although these names often incorporate trade marks, a domain name will not necessarily become a trade mark, unless it is used to denote origin of goods or services and not merely as part of the website address. A domain name consists of two parts: the top level domain ('TLD') and the second level name. There are two types of TLDs. These are the generic TLDs which are .aero, .biz, .com, .coop, .edu, .gov, .info, .int, .mil, .museum, .name, .net, .org, and .pro plus a special top-level domain (.arpa) for Internet infrastructure and over 200 country code TLDs ('ccTLD'). The ccTLD for Ireland is ie. The second level name is a unique name chosen by its owner.

Since the Internet at its inception was completely unregulated and the Internet Corporation for Assigned Names and Numbers ('ICANN') which manages top level domains, allowed registration of any name on a first come, first served basis, numerous disputes have arisen in relation to so called 'cybersquatting'. This is the registration of well-known names of businesses of people, or of registered trade marks by third parties who do not own the names, in the hope that the owners will wish to purchase the domain names in order to protect their property right. ICANN administers, through approved dispute resolution providers, a uniform domain name dispute resolution policy, which can be used by parties as an alternative to court proceedings. If a domain name is being used in the course of business, it is sensible for the proprietor to apply to register it as a trade mark. In so doing, it is possible for a monopoly to be held in the name in those jurisdictions in which the trade mark is registered. Applications for registration of a domain name are made for the generic TLDs to an ICANN accredited registrar or to the registrar with responsibility for the relevant ccTLD. A list of accredited registrars worldwide can be viewed on the InterNIC site at www.icann.org. In Ireland, the registrar is the ie domain registry which can be found at www.iedr.ie. Fees for registration vary from registrar to registrar. In October 2004, the European Commission agreed with EURid (the European Registry for Internet Domains) that they would introduce a .eu top level domain name. This is subject to EURid entering into the necessary agreements with ICANN. .eu domain names are expected to be introduced during 2005.

## 10.4 Copyright and Designs

### 10.4.1 INTRODUCTION

Copyright subsists in the physical material of a wide variety of work. The protection does not extend to ideas or principles, which underlie any element of a work. Thus copyright is a negative right to prevent the reproduction, including copying, of physical material.

## 10.4.2 COPYRIGHT AND DESIGN PROTECTION

### 10.4.2.1 Statutory regulation

Copyright is now governed by the Copyright and Related Rights Act, 2000 (the '2000 Act'). Designs are protected by the Industrial Designs Act, 2001 (the '2001 Act'). The European Communities (Copyright and Related Rights) Regulations, 2004 were enacted on the 19 January 2004, transposing the remaining provisions of Directive 2001/29/EC on the harmonisation of certain aspects of copyright and related rights in the information society. The 2000 Act had already implemented substantially the main terms of the then draft Directive.

### 10.4.2.2 Subsistence of copyright

Copyright is a property right, like any other, which permits the owner of the copyright to authorise third parties to do certain things in relation to a work which would, except for the existence of the 2000 Act, be prohibited or, to use the word used in the 2000 Act, restricted.

Copyright subsists in:

    (a)   original literary, dramatic, musical or artistic works;

    (b)   sound recordings, films, broadcasts or cable programmes;

    (c)   the typographical arrangement of published editions; and

    (d)   original databases (s 17(2)).

### 10.4.2.3 Designs

The 2001 Act, provides that a design is registrable if it is new and has individual character. A design at s 2 'means the appearance of the whole or a part of a product resulting from the features of, in particular, the lines, contours, colour, shape, texture or materials of the product itself or its ornamentation'. Thus, any part of a product which is decorative constitutes a design. A product 'means any industrial or handicraft item, including parts intended to be assembled into a complex product, packaging, get-up, graphic symbols and typographical typefaces, but not including computer programs' (2001 Act, s 2).

A design which is new and has individual character on a worldwide basis, is registrable under the 2001 Act, in a register maintained by the Controller. However there is a provision, which allows a design to be made available to the public for a period of up to one year before filing for a design registration. The author of a design shall be treated as the first proprietor, unless the design is made in the course of employment in which case the employer is the first proprietor. The provisions for registration and rectification of the register are similar to those for registration of a trademark and designs are classified in a prescribed system of classification. There is a priority right of six months in respect of an application made in a country which is a signatory to the Paris Convention for the Protection of Industrial Property 1883.

Both an application for registration and a registered design constitute a property right. A registration lasts for a period of five years and may be renewed upon payment of a fee for four subsequent periods of five years, resulting in a total period of registration of twenty-five years (s 43). The 2000 Act, in addition, provides that copyright in a registered design expires after a period of twenty-five years (s 31A). The provisions relating to licensing, infringement, offences, remedies, search and seisure, exhaustion of rights and groundless threats are all similar to those of trademarks. Section 78 of the 2000 Act, provides that copyright in a work is not infringed by anything done pursuant to an assignment or licence from a person registered under the 2001 Act and in good faith and in reliance on such registration without notice of any proceedings for the cancellation of the registration. Council Regulation (EC) No 6/2002 on Community designs, establishes a system for registration of industrial designs providing protection throughout the Community in the same manner as the system for trade marks. The system came into operation in 2003 and is administered by OHIM. The European Communities (Community Designs) Regulations, 2003 give effect in Ireland to the provisions of the Regulations (SI 27/2003).

The Irish Court considered the Design Regulations as recently as December 2007 in *Karen Millen Ltd v Dunnes Stores and others*. The case concerned a shirt which was not a registered design but benefitted from the unregistered design right. The court found that the shirt had individual character and granted an order against *Dunnes Stores*. Damages have yet to be assessed and the matter is under appeal.

Section 79 of the 2000 Act provides that the making of any object which is in three dimensions will not be an infringement of copyright in a two-dimensional work if the object would not appear to a person who is not an expert in relation to objects of that description to be a reproduction of it.

## 10.4.3  OWNERSHIP: MEANING OF AUTHOR

Section 21 of the 2000 Act defines the term author by reference to different circumstances. Author means the person who creates a work. In the case of a sound recording, this is the producer. In the case of a film, the producer and the principal director are the authors. In the case of a broadcast, the person making the broadcast is the author. In the case of a cable program, the person providing the cable program service in which the program is included is the author. In the case of a typographical arrangement or a published edition, the publisher is the author. In the case of a work which is computer generated, the person by whom the arrangement necessary for the creation of the work is undertaken is the author. In the case of an original database, the individual or group of individuals who made the database is the author. In the case of a photograph, the photographer is the author (2000 Act, s 21).

Section 23 provides that the author of the work is the first owner of the copyright. However, there are three exceptions to this rule:

NUKMA SMURFIT LIBRARY
NATIONAL COLLEGE
OF IRELAND

(a) where the work is made by an employee in the course of employment, the employer is the first owner of any copyright in the work subject to any agreement to the contrary;

(b) where the work is the subject of Government or Oireachtas copyright then the author is not regarded as the first owner. If the work is the subject of the copyright of a prescribed international organisation or the copyright in the work is conferred on some other person by an enactment, then the author will not be the first owner of the copyright; and

(c) where a work, except a computer program, is made by an author in the course of employment by the proprietor of a newspaper or periodicals, the author may use the work for any purpose except for making it available to newspapers or periodicals without infringing the copyright.

## 10.4.4 DURATION OF COPYRIGHT

### 10.4.4.1 Literary, dramatic, musical or artistic work

Section 24 of the 2000 Act provides that copyright in a literary, dramatic, musical or artistic work or in an original database lasts for seventy years after the death of the author. In the case of such a work, which is anonymous or pseudonymous, copyright will expire seventy years after the date on which the work is first lawfully made available to the public. Where the author becomes known during that seventy-year period, copyright will expire seventy years after the death of that author.

### 10.4.4.2 Films

The 2000 Act, s 25 states that copyright in a film lasts for seventy years after the last of the following people dies: (a) the principal director of the film; (b) the author of the screenplay of the film; (c) the author of the dialogue of the film; or (d) the author of music specifically composed for use in the film.

In a case where a film is first made available to the public during the period of seventy years following the death of the last of these people, copyright will expire seventy years after the date of such making available.

### 10.4.4.3 Sound recordings

The 2000 Act, s 26 states that copyright in a sound recording lasts for fifty years after the sound recording is made or, where it is first made available to the public during that fifty year period, for fifty years from the date of such making available to the public.

### 10.4.4.4 Broadcasts

The 2000 Act, s 27 provides that copyright in a broadcast lasts for fifty years after the broadcast is first lawfully transmitted. Copyright in every repeat broadcast expires at the same time as the original broadcast.

### 10.4.4.5 Cable program

The 2000 Act, s 28 provides that copyright in a cable program will expire fifty years after the cable program is first lawfully included in a cable program service. Again, copyright in a repeat cable program expires at the same time as the original one.

### 10.4.4.6 Typographical arrangements

The 2000 Act, s 29 provides that copyright in a typographical arrangement of a published edition lasts for fifty years from the date it is first made available to the public.

### 10.4.4.7 Computer-generated works

The 2000 Act, s 30 provides that copyright in a work which is computer generated lasts for seventy years after the date on which the work is first lawfully made available.

### 10.4.4.8 Copyright in works in volumes, parts etc.

The 2000 Act, s 31 provides that where a work is made available to the public in volumes, parts, instalments, issues or episodes and the copyright subsists from the date on which the work is so made available, copyright subsists in each separate item.

### 10.4.4.9 Works not previously available

Where a work is made available to the public for the first time after the expiration of the copyright, the person who makes it available will have the same rights as the author, except for moral rights, for twenty-five years from the date the work is made available.

## 10.4.5 INFRINGEMENT

### 10.4.5.1 Rights restricted

Under the provisions of s 37 of the 2000 Act, the owner of copyright in a work has the exclusive right to undertake or authorise others to undertake all of the following acts, namely:

(a) to copy the work;

(b) to make available to the public the work; and

(c) to make an adaptation of the work.

Each of those acts is called 'acts restricted by copyright'. Copyright is infringed if any of the acts restricted is done by any person without the consent of the owner/author of a copyright. The Copyright and Related Rights (Amendment) Act, 2004 (entitled 'an act to remove doubt in relation to the lawfulness under the Copyright and Related Rights Act, 2000, of displaying certain works in public') inserted a new subsection 7(A) into s 40. The amendment provides that 'for the avoidance of doubt, no infringement of any right . . . in relation to an artistic or literary work occurs by reason of the placing on display the work, or a copy thereof, in a place or premises to which members of the public have access'. The amendment arose as a result of the centenary celebration of James Joyce's Bloomsday. An exhibition of original manuscripts of Joyce's works by the National Library was to be held as part of the celebration. However, the press reported threats of legal action for breach of copyright if the works were exhibited. The Oireachtas passed this legislation and as a result the display by the National Library of the original manuscripts, copy manuscripts and first editions of Joycean works were no longer a restricted act under s 37 of the 2000 Act and there was no infringement.

### 10.4.5.2 Secondary infringement

Secondary infringement comprises a number of dealings with a work without the permission of the copyright owner, including selling, importing, making or having in his or her possession, custody or control a copy of the work knowing it to be an infringing copy, or having an article specifically designed or adapted for making copies of that work knowing that it has been or is to be used to make infringing copies.

### 10.4.5.3 Acts permitted in relation to copyright works

Chapter 6 of the 2000 Act sets out certain acts, which are exempted from infringement (2000 Act, ss 49–106).

These include such matters as fair dealing, that is, making use of a work for a purpose and to an extent reasonably justified by the non-commercial purpose to be achieved. For example, fair dealing may be for research or for private study, for criticism or for review (2000 Act, ss 50, 51).

Copyright in a work is not infringed if it is copied in the course of educational instruction or in preparation for education and instruction (2000 Act, s 53). Librarians or archivists are permitted to make copies of a work for various purposes, again of a non-commercial nature (2000 Act, ss 61–70).

Copyright is not infringed in a work by anything done for the purpose of parliamentary or judicial proceedings or for the purpose of reporting those proceedings, nor is it infringed for the purposes of a statutory enquiry (2000 Act, s 71).

Any material comprised in records, which are open to public inspection, may be copied and a copy may be supplied to anyone without infringing copyright (2000 Act, s 73).

A back-up copy of a computer program may be made without infringing copyright (2000 Act, s 80). Copyright is not infringed when anything is done for the purposes of reconstructing a building (2000 Act, s 96).

## 10.4.6   MORAL RIGHTS

The Berne Convention on copyright requires that, independently of the author's economic rights and even after transfer of the said rights, the author shall have the right to claim authorship of the work and to object to any distortion, mutilation or other modification of or other derogatory action in relation to the said work which 'would be prejudicial to his honour or reputation'. These were introduced into Irish law for the first time in the 2000 Act.

Section 107 of the 2000 Act provides the paternity right. This is the right of the author to be identified as such. There are certain exceptions to these rules, including where copyright in the work originally vested in an employer, where the work is made for the purposes of a newspaper or periodical or where Government or Oireachtas copyright subsists in the work.

Section 109 of the 2000 Act recognises the integrity right. This is the right of the author of a work to object to any distortion, mutilation or other modification of or other derogatory action in relation to the work, which would prejudice his reputation. The integrity right does not apply to a work made for the purpose of reporting current events or of a newspaper or periodical. The integrity right is qualified in respect of works in which the copyright originally vested in the author's employer.

Pursuant to the 2000 Act, s 116 moral rights may be waived. Moral rights are not capable of assignment or alienation (2000 Act, s 118). Moral rights may be passed on the death of the person entitled to the right (s 119).

## 10.4.7   PERFORMER'S RIGHTS

A performer is granted rights by the 2000 Act for the first time in Irish law. The rights granted under s 203 are the exclusive right to authorise or to prohibit:

(a)   the making of a recording of the whole or any substantial part of a qualifying performance directly from the live performance;

(b)   the broadcasting live, or including live in a cable program service, of the whole or any substantial part of a qualifying performance; or

(c)   the making of a recording of the whole or any substantial part of a qualifying performance directly from a broadcast or a cable program including the live performance.

## 10.4.8   DATABASE RIGHT

The 2000 Act introduces for the first time in Irish law a property right in a database, which consists of the creation of a mechanical collection or arrangement of facts or information which does not require skill or judgment to compile. This is a separate or 'sui generis' right, which lasts for a period of fifteen years and exists in addition to copyright subsisting in original databases referred to at **10.4.2.2** above. The Database Right was introduced by Directive 96/9 of the European Parliament and of the Council, to ensure uniform protection throughout EU Member States. To date there has only been one significant case relating to the interpretation of this Directive. This case is the *British Horseracing Board Limited and others v William Hill Organisation Limited*. Judgment in this matter was given by Mr Justice Laddie on 9 February 2001. This case was concerned with the extent to which the plaintiffs could prevent the defendant from using, without their licence, certain data, which according to the plaintiff had been derived indirectly from them.

In this case it was argued, that the indirect capture of data (i.e. through a third party) from a database was not an extraction as it merely replicated the data. This argument was rejected. It was also argued that in the case of the database that was consistently updated, repeated and systematic taking of minor data could not be considered to be cumulative and therefore could not be considered to be an infringement, as the data was taken from different databases. This argument was also rejected. The case has been appealed and the Court of Appeal referred a number of questions to the European Court of Justice ('ECJ'). The judgment of the ECJ was handed down on 9 November 2004. The ECJ agreed that the British Horseracing Board's central database fell within the criteria for protection by Directive 96/9. The Court held that as the data extracted and used by William Hill did not involve a substantial investment, independent of the costs of creating the data, the data did not constitute a substantial part of the contents of the database. Therefore William Hill's activities did not amount to an infringement of those rights.

## 10.4.9 LICENSING

As with any property right, copyright may be licensed. A range of copyright may subsist in, for example, a song, where there is copyright in the lyrics, in the music, in the sound recording and in the performance, or in a book, where copyright may subsist in the text and in the typographical arrangement. Chapters 16 and 17 of Part II of the 2000 Act contain detailed provisions as to licensing bodies which administer schemes for the licensing of copyright in works in which rights are held by more than one owner. Section 175 of the 2000 Act provides for the establishment of a register of copyright licensing bodies who collect fees or royalty payments for use of this copyright. The Copyright and Related Rights (Register of Copyright Licensing Bodies) Regulations, 2002, set up this register and several collection agencies have been registered.

## 10.4.10 DELIVERY UP AND SEISURE

Section 256 of the 2000 Act provides, that the owner of rights in a recording of a performance may apply to the District Court for a seisure order addressed to the Garda Siochána to seise illicit recordings, articles used to make illicit recordings or protection defeating devices, where such items are being hawked, carried about or marketed and, subsequently, for such items to be destroyed or delivered up to the rights owner. Hearsay evidence will be permitted in any such application and the witness will not be required to reveal the source of his information. However, the applicant exposes himself to a claim in damages if, at the end of the day, no infringement is established or the application was made maliciously.

Section 257 of the 2000 Act introduces a novel application allowing a rights owner to seise recordings, articles or devices without the protection of a court order where it is impractical to seek an order first and subsequently to seek and order for destruction or for delivery up. Notice must first be given to the Garda Siochána for the district and the items may not be seised at a permanent or regular place of business. The section is clearly designed to assist rights owners at concerts and similar occasions.

## 10.5    Confidential Information

### 10.5.1    INTRODUCTION

This branch of intellectual property law deals with the protection of 'know-how'. Know-how may be secret formulae, secret processes as used in the manufacture of a product or something as simple as the names of customers and other sales information which, if disclosed to the competing business, would cause significant harm to the owner.

In certain cases an employer will impose an obligation of confidentiality on an employee in relation to proprietary information rather than apply for patent protection for a secret invention. This may operate as a more effective protection, since a patent has to be published and put into the public domain. This gives competitors the opportunity to improve upon the invention to such an extent that they may produce the second generation of product or a product entirely different, which is also patentable and does not infringe the first product. On the other hand, if employees are bound by contract to keep their employers' invention secret then it may never come into the public domain like, for example, the secret formula for the manufacture of Coca-Cola.

The court, in a case of confidential information, is being asked to enforce a moral obligation. An equitable principle is invoked, that a person to whom something was made known in confidence cannot use the knowledge to the detriment of the informant.

### 10.5.2    RELATIONSHIPS IMPOSING CONFIDENTIALITY

In order to assess whether a relationship is one which imposes confidentiality, the court must first decide whether there exists from the relationship between the parties an obligation of confidence regarding the information which had been imparted and it must then decide whether the information which was communicated could properly be regarded as confidential. Once it is established that an obligation of confidence exists and that the information is confidential, then the person to whom it is given has the duty to act in good faith and this means that he must use the information for the purpose for which it is imparted to him and cannot use it to the detriment of the informant. The explanation of what constitutes confidential information was given by Costello J in *House of Spring Gardens Ltd v Point Blank Ltd* [1984] IR 611. This case is the leading case in the area of confidential information in Ireland and largely follows the English dicta on the subject.

In general, the areas where an obligation of confidence would be imposed may be divided into two sections:

(a) the protection of trade secrets/confidential information in non-employment cases. Thus, for example, where a plaintiff has employed a third party company to carry out a project on the plaintiff's behalf, an obligation of confidence will be imposed upon that third party and upon the plaintiff, not to use the information without consent; and

(b) the protection of trade secrets in the master and servant situation. (In the course of employment, an employee has a duty to do nothing, which would conflict with the business interests of their employer. It is always safest, where at all possible, to avoid argument in this area and to insert in an employee's contract of employment in clear terms an obligation to keep information including trade secrets and skill and experience gained during the employment confidential.)

Once the contract of employment has concluded and an employee has left the employment, there is nonetheless a duty not to use confidential information. The leading case in this area is *Faccenda Chicken Ltd v Fowler* [1986] 1 All ER 617. In this case Neill LJ found that there were three types of information acquired by a servant in the course of employment:

(i) trivia/public information which is not protected;

(ii) skill and experience which is not protected, although it could be restricted by contract in restriction of trade clause. (This type of information is protected during the course of the employment under the duty of fidelity owed by the employee to his employer.) After the employment ends, subject to any competitive restraints, the employee is free to use his skills and experience elsewhere; and

(iii) trade secrets so confidential that, even though they have been learned by heart, cannot be used for anyone's benefit but that of the employer and are protected even after the employee leaves employment.

## 10.5.3 REMEDIES

The remedies for breach of confidential information are an injunction to restrain the breach of confidential information and damages or an account of profits. In *Nu glue Adhesives v Burgess Galvin*, 23 March 1982, High Court, unreported, McWilliam J found that if there had been an abuse of confidential information, damages would be limited to an amount equal to six weeks' salary for a chemist. He considered that the defendants could have come up with the formula themselves within a six-week period.

Where the court is asked to award an injunction, that injunction must be capable of being framed with sufficient precision to enable the enjoined party to know what it is he may not do (*Lawrence David Ltd v Ashton* [1991] 1 All ER 385).

In *Terrapin v Builders' Supply Co (Hayes) Ltd* [1960] RPC 128, Roxburgh J defined what he called the 'springboard' formula. He said:

> As I understand it, the essence of this branch of the law, whatever the origin of it may be, is that a person who has obtained information in confidence is not allowed to use it as a spring-board for activities detrimental to the person who made the confidential communication, and spring-board it remains even when all the features have been published or can be ascertained by actual inspection by members of the public. The possessor of such information must be placed under a special disability in the field of competition in order to ensure that he does not get an unfair start.

Roxburgh J granted the plaintiff an injunction.

The courts, however, have found difficulties with the 'springboard' doctrine and have in some instances suggested that rather than an injunction being granted, the correct course is to compensate the plaintiff in damages (*Coco v A. N. Clark (Engineers) Ltd* [1969] RPC 41).

In some cases, in order to overcome the advantage gained by an employee in using confidential information, the court will impose an injunction for a period of time that it considers sufficient to enable a member of the public to come up with the formula themselves.

Moreover, it should be noted that overall it is often extremely difficult to prove a plaintiff employer's case to a degree sufficient to persuade a court to grant an injunction and the importance of ensuring the employers put in place properly drafted and reasonable contractual terms dealing with confidential information cannot be over-emphasised.

# CHAPTER 11

# INFORMATION TECHNOLOGY

## 11.1 Data Protection Law and Practice

All businesses should acquaint themselves with the Data Protection Acts, 1988 and 2003. They are of general application and do not just apply to businesses involved in distance selling.

### 11.1.1 INTRODUCTION

Governments and businesses have always held and processed information about their citizens and customers respectively. The development of computers has revolutionised the processing of data. Computers allow huge amounts of personal information to be held in any one place and in relation to any one individual. The development of computer networks and the internet allows vast quantities of data to be transferred between physical locations.

One of the difficulties of modern information technology and information gathering methods is the ease with which it has become possible to interfere with the privacy of the individual. Performing daily activities, such as opening bank accounts, taking out insurance policies, using credit cards and debit cards, applying for store 'loyalty cards', all enable information to be gathered about a person's spending and leisure habits. Even browsing the Internet and particular websites may enable information to be gathered in respect of website visitors. The use of sophisticated information capturing devices, such as 'cookies', permits website owners to gather information on visitors. Individuals are also being subjected to increasing levels of 'junk mail', 'junk e-mails' and other direct marketing approaches.

In order to balance the rights of organisations to gather data with the right of the individual to control the content and use of his or her personal data, the storage and processing of personal data is now regulated. The principal Irish legislation in this regard is the Data Protection, Act 1988 (the '1988 Act') and the Data Protection (Amendment) Act, 2003 (the '2003 Act') which are construed together as one Act (the 'Acts'). The 2003 Act transposes the provisions of Directive 95/46/EC on the protection of individuals with regard to the processing of personal data and on the free movement of data into Irish law and significantly amends many of the provisions of the 1988 Act. The bulk of the 2003

Act became law by way of Ministerial Order on 1 July 2003 (SI 207/2003) while the registration provisions of the 2003 Act came into force on 1 October 2007 (SI 656/2007).

## 11.1.2 DUTIES OF DATA CONTROLLERS

Section 2 of the 1988 Act as amended by s 3 of the 2003 Act, sets out a number of data protection principles. All 'Data Controllers' are required to comply with these principles. 'Data Controllers' are defined in the Acts as persons who either alone or with others control the content and use of personal data. The Acts also impose certain obligations on data processors that are defined as persons that process data on behalf of data controllers (excluding exployees of Data Controllers).

Personal data includes automated and manual data (data that is recorded as part of a structured filing system) relating to a living individual who is or can be identified from the data or from the data in conjunction with other information which is in the Data Controller's possession or which is likely to come into such possession.

Section 23(4) of the 2003 Act contained a grace period for manual data. The data protection rules laid down in ss 2, 2A and 2B only applied to manual data existing as of 1 July 2003 from 24 October 2007. However, ss 2, 2A and 2B applied at all times to manual data created subsequent to 1 July 2003.

The data protection principles provide that a Data Controller shall comply with the obligations, set out below, in relation to personal data held by him or her.

According to guidelines issued by the Data Protection Commissioner, fairness needs to be judged by reference to the purpose for which the information was obtained. Some issues to be considered in this regard include those set out below:

(a) Individuals should be made fully aware at the time they provide personal information of:

   (i) the identity of the persons who are collecting it (though this may often be implied);

   (ii) to what use the information will be put; and

   (iii) the persons or category of persons to whom the information will be disclosed.

   The Data Protection Commissioner has suggested that by following these rules, a Data Controller will ensure 'transparency and informed consent'. These criteria are 'the touchstone of fairness in data protection'.

(b) Secondary or future uses, which might not be obvious to individuals, should be brought to their attention at the time their personal data is obtained. Individuals should be given the option of saying whether or not they wish their information to be used in these other ways.

(c) If a Data Controller has information about people and wishes to use it for a new purpose (which was not disclosed and perhaps not even contemplated at the time the information was collected), he or she is obliged to give an option to individuals to indicate whether or not they wish their information to be used for the new purpose.

It might also be noted that s 2(5)(b) of the Acts states that data shall not be regarded as having being obtained unfairly by reason only that its use for any particular purpose was not disclosed when it was obtained *provided* the data is not used in such a way that damage or distress is likely to be caused to any data subject.

Additionally, s 2D of the Acts as inserted by s 4 of the 2003 Act provides, inter alia, that in order for data to be processed fairly, the Data Controller that obtains the personal data from the data subject (defined in point (e) below) shall, as far as practicable, provide or make available to the data subject, at least the following information:

(i)   the identity of the Data Controller;

(ii)  the name of the person nominated by the Data Controller for the purposes of the Data Protection Acts;

(iii) the purpose or purposes for which the data are intended to be processed;

(iv)  certain other relevant information.

In order to ensure compliance with the fair processing requirements described in s 2D, companies regularly issue notices to their employees describing how they process employee data. Similarly website privacy policies describe how companies obtain and process personal data from web users fairly.

It should be noted that a stricter test of 'fairness' may be applied where the data subject is a minor. The Data Protection Commissioner has suggested that when dealing with the personal data of minors, the standard of fairness in the obtaining and use of the data may be more onerous than when dealing with data relating to an adult. The Article 29 Working Party (the European Commission's data protection advisory body) has made similar observations, arguing that the duty to process personal data in accordance with the principle of fairness must be interpreted strictly when the data subject is under age. As a result, Data Controllers must exercise utmost good faith when processing a child's data.

(d) Personal data shall be accurate, complete and, where necessary, kept up to date. Section 1(2) of the Acts clarifies this obligation somewhat by defining inaccurate data as data that is incorrect or misleading as to any matter of fact.

(e) Personal data shall be held only for one or more specified, explicit and legitimate purposes. Thus, collecting information about people routinely and indiscriminately, without having a sound, clear and legitimate purpose for doing so will result in a breach of this obligation. When collecting personal data, Data Controllers should clearly and explicitly specify to the person who is the subject of that data ('the Data Subject') the purpose for which the personal data is being collected and stored.

(f) Personal data shall not be further processed in a manner incompatible with that purpose or those purposes.

According to guidelines issued by the Data Protection Commissioner, a key test of compatibility is whether you use and disclose the data in a way in which those who supplied the information would expect it to be used and disclosed.

This test was failed by a leading charity in circumstances where it shared information about its donors with a financial institution. Here, it was held that the use of such data to facilitate direct marketing by financial institutions was not compatible with the purpose for which it had been obtained, and therefore this was not a legitimate use of the data (Case Study 2 of the 2001 Report of the Data Protection Commissioner).

(g) Personal data shall be adequate, relevant and not excessive in relation to that purpose or those purposes for which they were collected or further processed.

This requirement is often breached where a business seeks more information from a consumer than is strictly necessary to provide the good or service sought. For example, banks have been found in default where they seek information about consumers' personal finances (e.g. copies of P60, level of income etc.) which is not necessary for anti-money laundering or credit control reasons (Case Study 15 of the 2006 Report of the Data Protection Commissioner; Case Study 7 of the 2005 Report of the Data Protection Commissioner).

(h) Personal data shall not be kept for longer than is necessary for that purpose or those purposes.

This obligation may be broken where a business uses personal data about a former customer, acquired in the course of a previous relationship, to send direct marketing materials. For example, Sky was held to have breached this requirement where it sent marketing literature to a consumer who had terminated his subscription (Data Protection Case Study 4 of the 2006 Report of the Data Protection Commissioner).

(i) Appropriate security measures shall be taken against unauthorised access to or unauthorised alteration, disclosure or destruction of personal data, particularly where the processing involves the transmission of data over a network and against all other forms of processing.

Section 2C of the Acts as inserted by s 4 of the 2003 Act expands upon this obligation concerning security measures and provides that Data Controllers must put in place appropriate security provisions for the protection of personal data, having regard to the current state of technological development, the cost of implementing security measures, the nature of the personal data and the harm that might result from unauthorised processing or loss of the data concerned.

Data Controllers and Data Processors are also obliged to take all reasonable steps to ensure that their employees, and other persons at the place of work concerned are aware of and comply with the relevant security measures.

Section 2C goes on to provide that if a Data Controller uses a third party to process data, the processing of such data should be covered by a contract which contains certain prescribed terms. This contract should stipulate at least the following:

(a) the conditions under which data may be processed;

(b) the minimum security measures that the data processors must have in place; and

(c) some mechanism or provision that will enable the Data Controller to ensure that the data processor is compliant with the security require-ment (this might include a right of inspection or independent audit).

Since various commercial arrangements entail a personal data processing com-ponent, an increasing number of commercial contracts need to have provisions along the lines set out above.

## 11.1.3 NON-COMPLIANCE WITH DUTIES

It must be stressed that non-compliance with the principles set out in s 2(1) of the 1988 Act does not automatically constitute a criminal offence. However, it may lead to a complaint being made by a Data Subject to the Data Protec-tion Commissioner who may take action by issuing an Enforcement Notice (pursuant to s 10(2) of the Acts). However, the Data Controller may be liable under ordinary common law principles (e.g. the law of confidence, the law of contract or the law of tort), where the Data Controller fails to comply with its obligations as set in s 2 of the 1988 Act.

A Data Controller may also be in breach of its duty of care under s 7 of the Acts where it fails to adhere to its obligations in s 2 of the Acts. Section 7 of the Acts sets out the duty of care owed by Data Controllers to the Data Sub-ject. Section 7 creates a general duty of care for the Data Controller to the Data Subject. Subject to certain limitations, a person who has suffered loss as a result of non-observance of the data protection principles may recover damages in tort against the Data Controller.

## 11.1.4 WHAT DATA CONTROLLERS ARE SUBJECT TO THE DATA PROTECTION ACTS, 1988 AND 2003?

Section 1(3B)(a) of the Acts, as inserted by the 2003 Act, provides that the Acts apply only in respect of Data Controllers that process personal data if:

(a) the Data Controller is established in Ireland and the data are processed in the context of that establishment; or

(b) the Data Controller is established neither in Ireland nor in any other State that is a contracting party to the EEA Agreement but makes use of equipment in Ireland for processing the data otherwise than for the purpose of transit through the territory of the State.

Thus, the Irish data protection legislation appears to be limited in scope to Data Controllers that are established in the State or alternatively to those who are based outside the European Economic Area ('EEA') and who actively process data in the State (as opposed to merely conduiting data through the State).

### 11.1.5 THE USE OF PERSONAL DATA FOR DIRECT MARKETING PURPOSES

Section 2(7) of the 1988 Act, as amended by the 2003 Act, contains particular and detailed rules concerning the use of personal data for direct marketing purposes. These provisions are quite significant since the unrestricted use of personal data for the purposes of direct marketing gives rise to a significant degree of nuisance and inconvenience if it is not controlled.

Section 2(7) provides that where personal data is kept for the purpose of direct marketing and the relevant Data Subject requests in writing that the relevant Data Controller cease processing the data for that purpose, then generally, the Data Controller has forty days to accede to such request.

Section 2(8) creates an additional onerous burden on Data Controllers that intend to process personal data for the purposes of direct marketing. This provision provides that where a Data Controller intends to process personal data which it holds for the purposes of direct marketing, then the Data Controller shall inform the relevant Data Subjects that they may object, by means of a request in writing to the Data Controller and free of charge, to such processing. This provision appears to create a positive obligation on all Data Controllers to inform Data Subjects that are being targeted for direct marketing purposes of their right to object to such use of their personal data.

Regulation 13 of the Electronic Communications Regulations (outlined in **11.1.10** below) sets out further restrictions on the use of personal data for direct marketing purposes.

### 11.1.6 PROCESSING OF PERSONAL DATA

Section 2A and s 2B are new provisions of the Acts which were inserted by the 2003 Act. Section 2A contains the general rule that personal data shall not be processed by a Data Controller unless the Data Controller complies with its obligations under s 2 (outlined in **11.1.2** above) and provided that at least one of the pre-conditions contained in s 2A(1) is satisfied. This provision goes on to set out a series of pre-conditions to the processing of personal data.

In order to fully appreciate the importance of this provision and the potentially restrictive effects of this rule, one must consider the definition of 'processing' as set out in the Acts. In this regard, it might be noted that 'processing' is attributed a very broad definition in the Acts. It is defined as performing any operation or set of operations on the information or data, whether or not by automatic means. The definition goes on to give a non-exhaustive list of examples of processing which includes obtaining data, recording data, collecting data, storing data, altering or adapting data, retrieving data, consulting data, using data, disclosing data or blocking, erasing or destroying data. When this broad definition of processing is read in the context of the rule that processing cannot take place unless one of the pre-conditions in s 2A(1) is satisfied, it transpires that virtually no dealings in personal data can be carried out by a Data Controller unless one of the pre-conditions contained in this section is satisfied.

The first and most important pre-condition, contained in s 2A, provides that data may be processed where the Data Subject has given his or her consent to such processing. Directive 95/46/EC gives us some guidance as to the meaning of 'consent' by indicating that a Data Subject's consent must be freely given, specific and informed. The minimum age at which consent can be legitimately obtained was not defined in the Acts. Section 2A(1) of the Acts states that consent cannot be obtained from a person who, by reason of age is likely to be unable to appreciate the nature and effect of such consent. Judging maturity will vary from case to case. The Data Protection Commissioner has indicated that in the marketing area, where sensitive data is involved, including on websites, it is a matter for the Data Controller to judge if a person of a certain age can appreciate the issues surrounding consent and to be able to demonstrate that a person of that age can understand the information supplied and the implications of giving consent.

There exists an ongoing debate in the EU as to what precisely constitutes consent. From a Data Controller's perspective, it is always easier to ascertain an individual's consent by asking the individual to indicate if he or she objects to his or her data being processed (the 'opt out procedure'). On the other hand, advocates of privacy rights have argued that in order for a consent to be valid, the Data Subject is required to expressly indicate that he or she consents to his or her data being processed (the 'opt in procedure').

Certain Member States have sought to clarify this issue in transposing Directive 95/46/EC. On the other hand, the Irish legislature has not provided any particularly clear guidance in this regard. However, it is notable that the earlier drafts of the Data Protection Bill, 2002, which was ultimately enacted as the 2003 Act, did provide that the consent should be 'explicit'. This requirement was dropped from the final version of the Bill that was enacted and thus, in the absence of any requirement of 'explicit' consent in s 2A(1)(a), it can be argued that use of the 'opt out' procedure may in certain circumstances be sufficient in order to ascertain consent under the Irish legislation. However, it remains to be seen how the judiciary will interpret this requirement.

Section 2A(1) goes on to contain a number of other pre-conditions, which must be carefully considered if a Data Controller proposes to process data without the consent of the relevant Data Subjects. These pre-conditions include where the processing is necessary for the performance of a contract to which the data subject is a party, where the processing is necessary to prevent an injury or other damage to the health of the Data Subject, where the processing is necessary to protect an individual's vital interests, where the processing is necessary for the administration of justice or where the processing is necessary for the purposes of the legitimate interests pursued by a Data Controller.

## 11.1.7 THE PROCESSING OF SENSITIVE PERSONAL DATA

Section 2B contains an additional set of pre-conditions one of which must be satisfied prior to the processing of sensitive personal data. Sensitive personal data is defined in the 1988 Act, as amended by the 2003 Act, as including data concerning racial or ethnic origin, political opinion, religious belief, trade union membership, mental or physical health, sexual life or data concerning the committing of an offence or proceedings in relation to an offence.

Without going into detail in relation to the pre-conditions for the processing of sensitive data, it should be noted that one of the first of these pre-conditions is that the 'explicit' consent of the Data Subject is given, before a Data Controller can process sensitive personal data. In other words, the use of some type of an 'opt out' procedure would not appear to be adequate in these circumstances as it is unlikely to be treated as explicit consent.

## 11.1.8 RIGHTS OF DATA SUBJECTS

In parallel with setting out a series of obligations for Data Controllers, the Acts create a number of important rights for Data Subjects.

### 11.1.8.1 The right to be informed of data being kept

Section 3 of the Acts provides that where a person suspects that another is keeping personal data, he or she may write to that person requesting that he or she be informed as to whether any such data is being kept. If it is, then the individual must be given a description of the data and of the purpose for which it is kept. This must be done within twenty-one days of the request being made.

### 11.1.8.2 The right to prevent data being used for the purposes of direct marketing

This right is discussed in **11.1.5** and **11.1.10**.

### 11.1.8.3 Right of access

Section 4 of the Acts confers upon the Data Subject a right of access to the data in the Data Controller's possession. It provides that if the Data Subject makes a written request, the Data Controller must inform the Data Subject whether he or she holds personal data relating to the Data Subject and supply him or her with a detailed description of such data and additional information concerning the data.

Data Subjects should not underestimate the extent of their rights and the potential uses and value of their rights pursuant to s 4 of the Acts. Also, the Data Controller is subjected to strict time periods within which to respond to requests made pursuant to this section.

There exist a number of exceptions to this right in s 5 of the 1988 Act, as amended, which merit consideration prior to advising a client to exercise his or her s 4 rights.

In the case of *Durant v Financial Services Authority* [2003] EWCA Civ 1746, the English Court of Appeal considered the scope of a subject access request and the meaning of personal data. The court held that merely mentioning a person in a document does not make that whole document available as 'personal data' in the even of a subject access request under the UK Data Protection Act, 1998. The court adopted a narrow interpretation of the scope of 'personal data' which seems to be at odds with the concept of personal data in the national laws of other EU Member States.

The case was brought by Michael Durant, a former customer of Barclays Bank. Following an unsuccessful dispute with the Bank he asked the Financial Services Authority (the 'FSA') to investigate the Bank's conduct. The FSA did so, but did not tell Mr Durant the result, citing reasons of confidentiality. When a complaint to the FSA Complaints Commissioner failed, Mr Durant tried to exercise his access rights under the UK Data Protection Act.

Mr Durant asked the FSA to disclose manual and electronic documents containing his personal data, in a search for information with which to reopen the original case against Barclays Bank.

The FSA complied with the request as it related to electronic files, but refused to provide paper documents because, it argued, they did not fall within the statutory definition of manual data since the requested paper-based data did not form part of a relevant filing system. Mr Durant took the matter to court, with the case hinging on the meaning of 'manual data' and, in particular, the meaning of the requirement that manual data must form part of a 'relevant filing system'.

He lost his case in the District Court, the County Court and, after four months of deliberation, he lost again in the Court of Appeal. The Court of Appeal decision in this case is noteworthy for the restrictive interpretation which it ascribed to the concept of manual data. Should an Irish court adopt a similarly restrictive interpretation of manual data, then the utility value of the right to make a subject access request in Ireland would undoubtedly be diminished.

It must be stressed that the Data Protection Commissioner is of the view that CCTV footage of an individual does amount to personal data for the purposes of the Acts and can be the subject of an access request. Thus, in one case, a night-club was held to have breached this right where it failed to provide a patron, who was attacked and robbed on the premises, with footage of the incident (Case Study 11 of the 2006 Report of the Data Protection Commissioner).

### 11.1.8.4  Right of blocking of erasure

Section 6 of the 1988 Act, as amended by the 2003 Act, goes on to give the Data Subject a right to have his or her personal data in the Data Controller's possession rectified, erased or blocked if the Data Controller fails to comply with its duties under the Act and generally the Data Controller has forty days to accede to such request.

### 11.1.8.5 Right to prevent processing where it might cause damage or distress

Section 6A of the Acts, creates a new right for Data Subjects. It provides that generally an individual is entitled at any time, by notice in writing served on a Data Controller to request the Data Controller to cease or not to commence processing of that individual's personal data where such processing is likely to cause substantial damage or distress which is or would be unwarranted. There are certain public interest exceptions to this new right of Data Subjects.

### 11.1.8.6 Rights of Data Subjects concerning automatic processing of data

Section 6B of the Acts, as amended by the 2003 Act, provides that a decision which produces legal effects concerning a Data Subject or otherwise significantly affects a Data Subject may not be based solely on the processing by automatic means of personal data where such processing aims to evaluate personal matters such as work performance, credit worthiness, reliability or conduct. This right is subject to a number of exceptions.

### 11.1.8.7 The transfer of personal data outside of the State

Section 11 of the 1988 Act, as amended by the 2003 Act, contains a number of restrictions on the transfer of personal data by a Data Controller to a country or territory outside of the EEA. It provides that such a transfer may not take place, unless that particular country or territory ensures an adequate level of protection for the privacy of its Data Subjects in relation to the processing of personal data. This provision enables the European Commission to make findings as to when a particular country or territory satisfies this adequacy requirement.

There also exists a number of exceptions, to this general prohibition on the transfer of data outside of the EEA, which include where the Data Subject has consented to the transfer, where the transfer is necessary for the performance of a contract between the Data Subject and the Data Controller, where the transfer is necessary for reasons of public interest or under some international obligation of the State or where the transfer is necessary in order to prevent personal injury or damage to the health of the Data Subject. This provision gives the Data Protection Commissioner wide powers to prohibit the transfer of personal data from the State to a place outside of the State.

The European Commission has made a number of Decisions giving the all clear in relation to transfers of data to Switzerland, Canada, Argentina and the UK territories of Guernsey and the Isle of Man whose regimes are recognised by the Commission as offering adequate data protection. While these Decisions will make, inter alia, the export of personal data to Canada easier, transfers of data to the US will remain more difficult. Due to the varying standards of data protection in the US, transfers of data from the EEA to the US may only take place (in the absence of fulfilling one of the exceptions above) where the recipient in the US has signed up to the Safe Harbour Scheme which is a voluntary scheme to which US companies may sign up, whereby they adopt standards of data protection comparable to EU standards. In the absence of participation in the Safe Harbour Scheme, data exporters to the USA may need to obtain consent from the Data Subject to the data transfer or use the approved model contractual terms produced by the EU Commission.

The European Commission has recently approved a new set of standard contractual clauses which offer companies and other organisations a straightforward means of complying with their obligation to ensure 'adequate protection' for personal data transferred outside the EEA. As and from 1 April 2005, no Member State may object to the use of the new clauses by companies. The new clauses provide for a similar level of data protection as the model clauses approved by the European Commission in 2001, and give more powers to the data protection authorities to intervene and impose sanctions where necessary to prevent abuses.

While model contractual clauses may provide an acceptable approach to ad hoc international data transfers, they are a cumbersome and unappealing solution for a multinational business that wishes to transfer personal data seamlessly throughout its entire organisation. In such circumstances, a multinational corporation may seek to comply with its data protection requirements through the adoption of binding corporate rules ('BCRs'). BCRs are binding internal codes of conduct requiring that the company and its employees comply with data protection norms. Such codes of conduct are approved by a lead national data protection authority and may then be circulated to other relevant national data protection authorities, as appropriate, for comment and consideration. While a regulator ensures that the corporation complies with data protection law, the manner in which the rules operate lies at the discretion of the organisation.

## 11.1.9 REGISTRATION WITH THE DATA PROTECTION COMMISSIONER

Section 16 of the Acts and the Data Protection Act 1988 (Section 16(1)) Regulations, 2007 (the '2007 Regulations') set down who has to register with the Data Protection Commissioner. Broadly speaking, Data Controllers and Processors fall into three categories for the purpose of registration. First, certain prescribed categories of Controllers and Processors are required to register under all circumstances. Second, Data Controllers and Processors falling under expressly set out exemptions are not required to register. Third, any Data Controllers or Processors that do not fall into either of the express inclusion or exclusion categories are still required to register.

Regulation 4 of the Data Protection Act 1988 (Section 16(1)) Regulations, 2007 sets out the categories of persons who are always obliged to register with the Commissioner.

In broad terms, they include:

- banks and financial/credit institutions which are Data Controllers;

- insurance undertakings (not including brokers) which are Data Controllers;

- Data Controllers whose business consists wholly or mainly in direct marketing, providing credit references or collecting debts;

- Internet service providers which are Data Controllers;

- authorised providers of electronic communications networks or services who are Data Controllers;

- Data Controllers who process genetic data; and

- Data Processors that process personal data on behalf of any of the above Data Controllers.

In addition, reg 3 of the 2007 Regulations suggests that Data Controllers and Processors who process personal data relating to mental or physical health may be required to register.

Section 16 of the Acts and reg 3 of the 2007 Regulations set out certain categories of Data Processors and Controllers who, provided that they do not fall under one of the mandatory registration categories set out above, are excluded from the requirement to register. However, it should be noted that this exclusion will only apply where the Controller or Processor only processes data for an excluded purpose and the process is limited to that necessary for the excluded purpose.

Broadly speaking, these categories include:

- Data Controllers that are not-for-profit organisations;

- Data Controllers that only process 'manual data';

- Data Controllers who are elected representatives or candidates for electoral office;

- Data Controllers who only process data in relation to past, existing or prospective employees in the ordinary course of personnel administration;

- solicitors and barristers who are Data Controllers and process data for the purpose of providing professional legal services;

- Data Controllers who process personal data relating to their past, existing or prospective customers, suppliers, shareholders, directors or officers in the ordinary course of their business;

- Data Controllers who process personal data with a view to publishing journalistic, literary or artistic material; and

- Data Processors that only process personal data on behalf of Data Controllers falling under one of the above exceptions.

It must be stressed that any Data Controller or Data Processor who is required to register but fails to do so is guilty of an offence.

Members of the public can inspect the register free of charge and may copy entries in the register. Applications for registration can either be made in writing or online on the Commissioner's website. Registrations last for a period of one year and, at the end of the year, the entry must be renewed or removed from the register.

## 11.1.10 ELECTRONIC COMMUNICATIONS REGULATIONS, 2003

Directive 2002/58/EC concerning the processing of personal data and the protection of privacy in the electronic communications sector (known as the 'Communications Data Protection Directive' or the 'CDPD') was transposed into national law by the European Communities (Electronic Communications Networks and Services) (Data Protection and Privacy) Regulations 2003 (SI 535/2003) ('Electronic Communications Regulations') which came into effect on 6 November 2003. The CDPD replaced and updated Directive 97/66/EC concerning the processing of personal data and the protection of privacy in the telecommunications sector and, as a result, the European Community (Data Protection and Privacy in Telecommunications) Regulations, 2002 which transposed the latter Directive into national law were accordingly revoked.

The Electronic Communications Regulations strengthen the rules concerning direct marketing and accordingly have been given substantial media attention since they endeavour, inter alia, to tackle the nuisance of SPAM mail. Other issues addressed by the Regulations include the retention of telephone records, processing of location data, the creation of telephone directories, 'caller ID' and the storage and access to information on terminal equipment, i.e. 'cookies'.

Regulation 13 of the Electronic Communications Regulations restricts the ability to use publicly available electronic communications services to send unsolicited communications or to make unsolicited calls for the purpose of direct marketing. These new rules should prove to be important legal tools in tackling individuals and businesses that send unwanted and unsolicited marketing communications by SMS or by e-mail. In particular, it provides that:

(a) the use of automatic dialling machines, fax, e-mail or SMS text messaging for direct marketing to individuals is prohibited, unless the subscriber's consent has been obtained in advance; and

(b) the use of e-mail, SMS text messaging, automatic dialling machines or fax for direct marketing to non-natural persons or businesses is prohibited, if the subscriber has recorded its objection in the National Directory Database or has informed the sender that it does not consent to such messages; and

(c) the making of telephone calls for direct marketing to the line of a subscriber is prohibited if the subscriber has recorded its objection in the National Directory Database or has informed the sender that it does not consent to such messages.

Regulation 13(6) provides that the person making an unsolicited call for purposes of direct marketing shall include in the call their name and on request their address and telephone number. Similarly, the sender of an unsolicited e-mail or SMS for direct marketing purposes shall include in the message their name and a valid address at which they can be contacted.

Regulation 13(7) provides that where the subscriber's electronic contact details are obtained from a customer in the context of the sale of a product or service, e-mail and SMS text messaging can be used for direct marketing purposes if an easy to use, free of charge opportunity is given to object to these marketing messages and provided that the SMS text or e-mail concerns similar products or services.

It should be noted that the Data Protection Commissioner has taken a broad view as to what constitutes 'direct marking' for the purpose of this Regulation. Unsolicited e-mails requesting support in an election have been found to amount to unlawful direct marketing (Case Study 5 of the 2004 Report of the Data Protection Commissioner).

This broad interpretation should be noted as, unlike much of data protection law, a breach of reg 13 is a criminal offence. In a recent prosecution, the Data Protection Commissioner brought proceedings against 4's A Fortune Limited. The defendant had called 165,000 mobile phones briefly, with the intention that the recipient would not be able to answer the call and would receive a 'missed call' message. The recipient would then dial the defendant's number and would be played a pre-recorded marketing message. Notwithstanding the large number of nuisance calls made, the Commissioner was of the opinion that prosecutions could only be entered on foot of five of these. He took the view that he could only prosecute where there was no consent on the part of the recipient to receiving the call and that this could only be established where a specific complaint had been made (Case Study 11 of the 2005 Report of the Data Protection Commissioner).

Regulation 14 sets out the rules for recording subscriber's indications that they do not wish to receive unsolicited telephone calls on an 'opt-out' register in the National Directory Database. Subscribers with unlisted numbers will automatically be included on this 'opt-out' register.

Regulation 9 deals with location data. Location data created by mobile phones enables mobile phone companies and third party companies to whom they disclose such information to know the precise whereabouts of an individual in possession of a powered on mobile phone.

Regulation 9 provides that generally, location data can only be processed if made anonymous or with the consent of the individual for the provision of a value added service. Regulation 9 requires that full information must be given to users or subscribers, prior to obtaining such consent, in relation to the type of location data that will be processed and of the purposes and duration of the processing as well as the transmission of the data to any third parties. Consent to the processing of the location data can be withdrawn at any time by simply making a request that the processing be stopped. There are public interest exceptions in reg 10 with regard to the use of location data.

Regulation 5 provides that information can only be stored on or retrieved from a user or subscriber's terminal equipment, e.g. computer or phone, provided that the user is offered the right to refuse such processing and that clear and comprehensive information is provided. The information to be provided includes the purpose of storing or retrieving the information. This regulation covers the use of 'cookies' on websites among other things.

## 11.1.11 USEFUL LINKS

The Office of the Data Protection Commissioner has an excellent website which contains all the relevant legislation, reports of the Commissioner, examples of cases which the Commissioner has had to consider and guidance notes on the Acts and the responsibilities of Data Controllers and Data Processors. The website's address is www.dataprivacy.ie.

# 11.2 The Electronic Commerce Regulations, 2003

## 11.2.1 INTRODUCTION

Directive 2000/31/EC (the 'Electronic Commerce Directive') is another piece of EU legislation which aims to regulate certain aspects of electronic commerce. The Directive is quite broad in scope and tackles a number of different aspects of online and electronic commerce. This Directive was transposed into Irish law by the European Communities (Directive 2001/31/EC) Regulations, 2003 (SI 68/2003) (the 'Electronic Commerce Regulations').

The Electronic Commerce Directive relates to 'information society services' which includes any service normally provided for remuneration, at a distance, by means of electronic equipment and at the individual request of a recipient of a service. The recitals to the Directive show that this should include most online activities, including the online selling of goods.

The objective of the Directive is to create a legal framework to ensure the free movement of information society services between Member States of the EU. The Directive aims to provide a favourable legal framework for electronic commerce while ensuring that consumers are protected when transacting online.

One of the key features of the Directive is that a provider of information society services, once established in one Member State of the EU, is entitled to provide services into any other Member State. This principle, which is embodied in Art 8 of the Directive and reg 4 of the Regulations, affirms the single market principle and overrides possible national barriers to trade that could potentially inhibit the growth of electronic commerce.

Certain parts of the Electronic Commerce Directive were implemented into Irish law prior to the enactment of the Electronic Commerce Regulations. In particular, Art 9 of the Directive which obliges Member States to provide for the electronic conclusion of contracts was implemented by the Electronic Commerce Act, 2000.

At this juncture, it might also be noted that neither the Electronic Commerce Directive nor the implementing Regulations aim to harmonise Member States' laws in relation to the formation of contracts. Thus, Ireland's common law rules of offer, acceptance and consideration continue to apply notwithstanding these new rules.

## 11.2.2    COUNTRY-OF-ORIGIN PRINCIPLE

The Directive and the implementing Regulations aim to solve the problem of the multitude of applicable rules by the adoption in the Directive of the so-called 'country-of-origin rule'. This principle is embodied in Art 3 of the Directive and reg 4 of the implementing Regulations and provides that (subject to certain exceptions) information society service providers and their services will only have to comply with the rules of the country in which those service providers are established.

## 11.2.3    OBLIGATION TO PROVIDE INFORMATION PRIOR TO CONTRACT

One of the fundamental principles of the Electronic Commerce Directive and the implementing Regulations is transparency in Internet dealings. Regulation 7 of the implementing Regulations contains a requirement for businesses operating online to provide important information to users of their websites.

Regulation 7 contains a list of information which businesses operating online ('service providers') will have to provide 'in a manner which is easily, directly and permanently accessible' to the recipients of the online service and to the National Consumer Agency. The following information must be provided:

(a)    the name of the service provider;

(b)    the geographic address at which the service provider is established;

(c)    the details of the service provider, including his electronic mail address;

(d)    details of how natural persons can register their choice regarding unsolicited commercial communications and this information should be prominently displayed on the service provider's website and at every point where natural persons are asked to provide information at the service provider's website (for example, registration forms);

(e)    where the service provider is registered in a trade or similar public register, the trade register in which the service provider is entered and his registration number, or equivalent means of identification in that register;

(f)     where the activity is subject to an authorisation scheme, the particulars of the relevant supervisory authority;

(g)     where the service provider is a member of a regulated profession, certain information in relation to the relevant professional body is required;

(h)     the service provider's VAT number, if applicable; and

(i)     where the service provider refers to prices, these are to be indicated clearly and unambiguously and, in particular, must indicate whether they are inclusive of tax and delivery costs.

As a result of these provisions, service providers established in Ireland should conduct legal audits of their websites in order to ensure that they are complying with these provisions. A person who fails to comply with these information requirements shall be guilty of an offence.

## 11.2.4    RULES CONCERNING COMMERCIAL COMMUNICATIONS

Regulations 8 and 9 of the Electronic Commerce Regulations, address the issue of commercial communications and unsolicited commercial communications ('UCCs'), which are colloquially referred to as SPAM (although direct marketing companies argue that there is a distinct difference between SPAM and UCCs).

The Regulations define 'Commercial Communications' as meaning any form of communication designed to promote, directly or indirectly, the goods, services or images of a company, organisation or person pursuing a commercial, industry or craft activity or exercising a regulated profession. The definition is subject to certain exceptions. Thus, subject to the exceptions, it appears that e-mails sent for promotional or marketing purposes and pages of websites devoted to promoting or marketing a company would be caught by this definition. Regulation 8 provides that commercial communications that are part of an Information Society Service shall comply with, at least, the following conditions:

(a)     *the commercial communication shall be clearly identified as such;*

(b)     *the natural or legal person on whose behalf the commercial communication is made shall be clearly identifiable,*

(c)     *details of how natural persons can register their choice regarding unsolicited commercial communications shall be provided; these should be prominently displayed on the relevant service provider's website and at every point where natural persons are asked to provide information at the provider's website (for example a registration form);*

(d)     *promotional offers, such as discounts, premiums and gifts shall be clearly identifiable as such, shall comply with any enactment for the time being in force relating to such activities and the conditions which must be satisfied in order to qualify for them shall be easily accessible and be presented clearly and unambiguously; and*

(e)     *promotional competitions or games, where permitted under the law of the State, shall be clearly identifiable as such, and the conditions for participation shall be easily accessible and be presented clearly and unambiguously.*

This regulation aims to ensure a high level of transparency in relation to e-mails which contain or offer promotional services. However, from a business perspective, this regulation creates a further hurdle which online businesses will have to overcome in order to carry out online promotional activities. Again, any failure to comply with this regulation shall result in an offence being committed.

Regulation 9 contains provisions in relation to UCCs. It requires that an unsolicited commercial communication by a relevant service provider established within the State shall be identified clearly and unambiguously as such as soon as it is received by the recipient by stating that it is an unsolicited commercial communication. This regulation also makes it clear that the provisions of Irish data protection legislation apply in relation to UCCs.

## 11.2.5 SPECIAL RULES FOR REGULATED PROFESSIONS

Regulation 11 contains specific rules in relation to the use of commercial communications by members of a regulated profession.

## 11.2.6 ADDITIONAL INFORMATION REQUIREMENTS

Regulation 13 of the Electronic Commerce Regulations, contains further information requirements in relation to consumer contracts concluded online. Regulation 13 provides that, subject to certain exceptions, prior to the placing of an order by a consumer online, the service provider must provide the following information clearly, comprehensively and unambiguously:

(a) the different technical steps that need to be followed to conclude the contract,

(b) whether or not the concluded contract will be filed by the service provider and whether it will be accessible,

(c) the technical means for identifying and correcting input errors prior to the placing of the order, and

(d) the language or language in which the contract may be concluded.

This regulation creates yet further information requirements to which the online service provider must adhere on entering into contracts with consumers online. Regulation 13(3) also provides that the terms and conditions provided by the relevant online service provider shall be made available to recipients of the service in a way that will allow them to store and reproduce them.

It should be noted that the provisions mentioned above will not apply to contracts concluded exclusively by exchange of e-mail. Again, any failure to adhere to the provisions of this regulation will result in a criminal offence being committed.

### 11.2.7 PROCEDURES TO BE FOLLOWED WHEN CONTRACTING WITH CONSUMERS ONLINE

Regulation 14 of the Electronic Commerce Regulations provides that where a consumer of online services places his order over the Internet the following principles shall apply:

(a) the relevant service provider shall acknowledge the receipt of the order of the recipient without undue delay and by electronic means,

(b) the order and the acknowledgement of receipt are deemed to be received when the parties to whom they are addressed are able to access them.

This regulation corresponds with and qualifies s 16 of the Electronic Commerce Act, 2000, which states that, subject to any other law, where the originator of an electronic communication indicates that receipt of such a communication is required to be acknowledged but does not indicate a particular form of acknowledgement, then, unless both parties agree otherwise, the acknowledgement must be given by means of an electronic communication or any other form of communication sufficient to indicate that the electronic communication has been received.

Regulation 14(2) also requires the service provider to make available to the recipient of the service, appropriate, effective and accessible means allowing him or her to identify and correct input errors, prior to the placing of the order.

It should be noted that the provisions mentioned above will not apply to contracts concluded exclusively by exchange of e-mail. Again, any failure to adhere to the provisions of this regulation will result in a criminal offence being committed.


### 11.2.8 LIABILITY OF INTERNET SERVICE PROVIDERS

Regulations 16, 17 and 18 refer to Intermediary Service Providers ('ISPs'), which are colloquially referred to as Internet Service Providers. Regulations 16, 17 and 18 transpose Arts 12, 13 and 14 of the Directive. These provisions attempt to define the status and the limits of liability of ISPs.

Regulation 16 provides that where an ISP is acting as a mere conduit, then it shall not be liable for the information which it transmits as part of its service. Regulation 16 defines this concept of being 'a mere conduit'. It provides that an ISP will be deemed to be a mere conduit where it did not initiate a transmission, it did not select the receiver of the transmission and where it did not select or modify the information contained in the transmission. In this regard, it is critical that the ISP acts as a passive transmitter of the information only.

Regulation 16(3) indicates that the regulation shall not affect the power of any court to make an order against an ISP requiring it not to infringe or to cease to infringe, any legal rights.

Regulation 17 goes on to deal with a common practice of ISPs known as 'caching' of information. Caching can be described as the automatic, intermediate and temporary storage of information by ISPs for the sole purpose of making the onward transmission of information more efficient. Regulation 17 provides that ISPs shall not be liable for the caching of information provided that certain conditions are adhered to by the ISP.

Regulation 17 goes on to provide that the ISP shall only benefit from this exemption of liability where it acts expeditiously to remove and disable access to information, which it has stored in cache, upon obtaining knowledge of the fact that the information at the initial source of the transmission has been removed from the network, or access to it has been disabled, or that a court or an administrative authority has ordered such removal or disablement.

Regulation 17(2) indicates that the regulation shall not affect the power of any court to make an order against an ISP requiring it, not to infringe, or to cease to infringe, any legal rights.

Regulation 18 extends this exemption of liability of ISPs to the hosting of information by ISPs on behalf of third parties. This is a critical exemption from liability since one of the principal activities of ISPs is the hosting of website and web content on the internet on behalf of third parties.

Again, this exemption from liability is subject to certain conditions. For example, an ISP will not benefit from this exemption from liability where the ISP has actual knowledge that the information which is being hosted by it concerns unlawful activities.

Regulation 18(2) indicates that the regulation shall not affect the power of any court to make an order against an ISP requiring it, not to infringe, or to cease to infringe, any legal rights.

These provisions concerning the non-liability of ISPs are hugely important from the context of the goal of expanding and continuing the operation of the Internet. For example, ISPs can now take comfort and be assured that generally they may not be sued for copyright infringement, under Irish law, where they cache information which is the subject of a third party copyright. They will also be generally exempt under Irish law from liability where they transmit information which infringes copyright.

However, the scope of this general immunity may have to be reconsidered following the decision of the District Court of Brussels in *Sabam v Scarlet* (No 04/8975/A, 29 June 2007). Here, a Belgian author and composer representative body was awarded an injunction, directing the defendant ISP to install software on its network which would prevent the transmission of unauthorised copyrighted files on peer-to-peer networks. The Court considered the E-Commerce Directive in light of the Copyright Directive (Directive 2001/29/EC) and held that the 'mere conduit' defence of the E-Commerce Directive did not arise in the case. It appears that the Court relied upon the Belgian equivalent of reg 16(3), holding that the mere conduit defence would not prevent the issuing of an injunction designed to restrain copyright infringement. It is possible to read this decision as turning on the Court's interpretation of 'liable' for the purpose of Art 12 of the Directive (which was transposed into Irish law by reg 16). The Court appears to suggest that liability in this context refers to tortious liability (i.e. negligence), which was not a pre-condition to the issuing of the injunction. The Court further held that the operation of the filtering software did not amount to monitoring the network but was rather akin to the operation of anti-virus software.

It remains to be seen whether or not an Irish court would adopt the interpretation offered by the Belgian Court. In March 2008, four major record companies commenced High Court proceedings seeking orders restraining eircom from infringing copyright in their sound recordings by making available (through its network) copies of those recordings.

## 11.3 ISP and Website Owner Liability for Defamation and Obscenity

### 11.3.1 INTRODUCTION

One of the most contentious issues in relation to internet use over the last few years has been the potential liability of ISPs for transmitting and hosting information of a defamatory or obscene nature. Similarly, website owners have also been alert to the risks associated with obscene and defamatory material appearing on their websites.

### 11.3.2 DEFAMATION

Section 23 of the Electronic Commerce Act, 2000 provides that 'all provisions of existing defamation law shall apply to all electronic communications within the State including the retention of information electronically'. This provision makes it clear that the traditional rules of defamation will apply to communications made online and to information contained on websites.

While the law of defamation looks set to be reformed by the Defamation Bill, 2006, some commentators have questioned whether or not that Bill adequately considers the changes in the nature of publishing brought about by the development of the Internet. In particular, Kelleher and Murray (Kelleher and Murray, *Information Technology Law in Ireland*, 2nd edn (Tottel, 2007) at p. 639) have suggested that the Bill is unduly focused on 'old media' such as television and newspapers and fails to address the needs of 'new media' such as blogs.

This potential liability of ISPs for defamation has been the subject of proceedings in the UK in the case of *Godfrey v Demon Internet Ltd* [2000] 3 WLR 1020, [1999] 14 All ER 342. In that case, the plaintiff, Professor Godfrey, sued an

ISP for hosting an Internet bulletin board containing defamatory information. The bulletin board in question contained a posting from an unknown party in relation to the plaintiff. This posting was described by Morland J as being 'squalid, obscene and defamatory of the plaintiff'. The posting purported to have originated from the plaintiff but was in fact a forgery. On discovering the content of this posting, the plaintiff faxed the defendant informing them that the posting was a forgery and requesting them to remove it from their server. However, the posting was not removed and remained available on the defendant's news server until its expiry two weeks later. The plaintiff sued for defamation, claiming damages for libel from the date of his notification to the defendant. Rejecting the defendant's attempt to rely on its statutory defence of innocent dissemination, provided under s 1 of the Defamation Act, 1996, Morland J found that the defendant had not shown that it had taken reasonable care in relation to the publication or that it lacked the knowledge sufficient to be held liable. In other words, from the time the defendant became aware of the defamatory content, they were liable. The Court also found that the defendant could not rely on a common law defence that it did not publish the posting and that publication took place whenever a newsgroup posting was accessed by a user.

When one considers this case in light of the Electronic Commerce Regulations and their exemptions from liability for ISPs, it would appear that ISPs would generally be exempt from liability where they are unaware that the information which they are hosting and transmitting is defamatory. However, once on notice of such, the ISP ought to remove the information or else risk losing its exemption from liability. Equally website owners must be wary of information which is posted on their websites since they may be sued in the event that their website contains defamatory information. In this regard, website owners that host chat rooms or bulletin boards must be particularly wary since third parties may post defamatory information on their website. In order to avoid potential liability in these circumstances, website owners must use carefully drafted limitation and exclusion of liability clauses and incorporate these clauses into their standard terms and conditions which all users of their website should be obliged to review and agree to. While the use of disclaimers or limitation clauses can help to reduce and exclude liability of website owners and operators, it must be borne in mind that the international nature of the Internet will attract foreign visitors to the site whose local laws may differ considerably from those in this jurisdiction and may render certain exclusion clauses null and void.

The issue of website owner liability has taken on a greater impetus in recent years due to the increasing popularity of 'Web 2.0' and 'user generated content' sites such as media sharing platforms (Flicker, Youtube) and social networking sites (Facebook, Bebo). Operators of such sites need to ensure that they are not found liable for any content posted by their users. Special care should be taken to ensure that files protected by copyright are not distributed through these platforms. Ideally, website owners should require that users warrant that they own the copyright in any files uploaded or that they are otherwise permitted to upload the file.

### 11.3.3 CHILD PORNOGRAPHY AND OBSCENITY

Ireland's legal infrastructure is equipped to tackle obscenity and child pornography on the Internet. The following statutory provisions might be noted in this regard.

#### 11.3.3.1 The Child Trafficking and Pornography Act, 1998 (as amended by the Child Trafficking and Pornography (Amendment) Act, 2004)

The Child Trafficking and Pornography Act, 1998 (the '1998 Act') was drafted in full knowledge of the Internet and its potential to be used for the purposes of child pornography. Therefore, the wording of the various offences is quite broad and extends to online behaviour.

Section 5 of the 1998 Act provides that an offence will be committed by any person who:

*(a) knowingly produces, distributes, prints or publishes any child pornography,*

*(b) knowingly imports, exports, sells or shows any child pornography,*

*(c) knowingly publishes or distributes any advertisement likely to be understood as conveying that the advertiser or any other person produces, distributes, prints, publishes, imports, exports, sells or shows any child pornography,*

*(d) encourages or knowingly causes or facilitates any activity mentioned in paragraphs (a) (b) or (c); or*

*(e) knowingly possesses any child pornography for the purpose of distributing, publishing, exporting, selling or showing it.*

'Child pornography' is defined in the 1998 Act as meaning:

*(a) any visual representation—*

*(i) that shows or, in the case of a document, relates to a person who is or is depicted as being a child and who is engaged in or is depicted as being engaged in explicit sexual activity,*

*(ii) that shows or, in the case of a document, relates to a person who is or is depicted as being a child and who is or is depicted as witnessing any such activity by any person or persons, or*

*(iii) whose dominant characteristic is the depiction, for a sexual purpose, of the genital or anal region of a child,*

*(b) any audio representation of a person who is or is represented as being a child and who is engaged in or is represented as being engaged in explicit sexual activity,*

*(c) any visual or audio representation that advocates, encourages or counsels any sexual activity with children which is an offence under any enactment, or*

*(d) any visual representation or description of, or information relating to, a child that indicates or implies that the child is available to be used for the purpose of sexual exploitation within the meaning of section 3,*

*irrespective of how or through what medium the representation, description or information has been produced, transmitted or conveyed and, without prejudice to the generality of the foregoing, includes any representation, description or information produced by or from computer-graphics or by any other electronic or mechanical means . . .*

The 1998 Act's wording is very broad and extends to electronic information capable of being translated into visual images. The 1998 Act also applies to 'depictions of children' so there is no necessity to prove that the images are actually of children. The 1998 Act also extends to cover advertisements including online advertisements.

The 1998 Act does not contain any exemption for ISPs. However, in practice, the same principles as those in the Electronic Commerce Regulations will apply since a conviction under s 5 can only result if the ISP acted 'knowingly' in disseminating child pornography through its servers. In addition to the 1998 Act, there are certain other legislative provisions which might be used to tackle obscenity online.

### 11.3.3.2 Precautionary measures

In order for website owners and ISPs to avoid encountering difficulties in this area and in order to minimise potential exposure, their terms and conditions of use should be drafted to include provisions along the following lines:

   (a)   that users of the website, chat room or ISP agree not to post or publish any offensive, libellous, defamatory, illegal or unlawful material;

   (b)   that while they reserve the right to monitor the content of third party postings, they do not exercise editorial control over the material being posted;

   (c)   that they may change or remove any materials being posted which are libellous, defamatory, illegal or unlawful in nature; and

   (d)   that they do not accept liability for any linked content.

It is also extremely important that website owners and ISPs have procedures in place for dealing with complaints in relation to content. Additionally, the terms and conditions of a website owner or an ISP should be presented in such a way that users are compelled to scroll down through them and ideally users might be requested to click their acceptance of the terms and conditions. Such measures serve to avoid arguments being raised in relation to improper incorporation of the terms and conditions into the contractual relationship between user and the ISP/website owner.

On 11 January 2002, the Internet Service Providers Association of Ireland adopted a new Code of Practice and Ethics (the 'Code') applicable to its members, the principal ISPs operating in Ireland. The Code sets out broad policies and general requirements in addition to minimum practices, best practices and a number of specific provisions in relation to data protection, domain names, advertising and illegal content.

The Code requires that ISPs must have an acceptable use policy in place, prohibiting, inter alia, libellous, abusive, offensive, vulgar or obscene material.

Member ISPs are also required to register with www.hotline.ie, a notification service for the reporting of suspected breaches under the Child Trafficking and Pornography Act, 1998. In 2006, Hotline received 2,677 reports.

## 11.4    Illegal Use of the Internet

### 11.4.1    INTRODUCTION

While the Internet has led to a revolution in global communications and the creation of a new, efficient and dynamic medium in which businesses can interact, it can inevitably be used for illegal purposes and to harm individuals and companies. This part of the chapter considers certain types of illegal behaviour which take place over the Internet and considers the legal tools which have been designed and which are in place to tackle such behaviour. Illegal behaviour is not only confined to criminal behaviour, since the Internet is often used to infringe and breach intellectual property rights and to interfere with individual's privacy rights.

It is not intended to exhaustively review all types of illegal and infringing behaviour which may occur on the Internet, but rather to focus on certain types of behaviour which commonly occur on the Internet and which may infringe Irish law.

### 11.4.2    HACKING

The expression 'hacking' is not legally defined but has come to mean the application of an individual's computer skills to enable breaking into a person's computer system and/or websites in order to create damage or to steal information. Hacking, like other types of cyber crime, is often quite difficult to prosecute. However, certain legal provisions which may be used to prosecute individuals who engage in hacking currently exist.

#### 11.4.2.1    The Criminal Damage Act, 1991

The Criminal Damage Act, 1991 (the '1991 Act') creates a number of specific offences which have been designed to combat the danger of computer hackers. The 1991 Act creates four basic offences.

#### Section 2(1)

Section 2(1) of the 1991 Act criminalises damage to property. The Act defines 'property' to include 'data' and defines 'data' as including information which can be accessed by means of a computer including computer programs. The Act also defines the concept of 'damage' broadly. The concept of 'damage' includes adding to, altering, corrupting and erasing. Thus, s 2 can be used to tackle types of hacking behaviour and possibly to deal with the problem of computer viruses that alter, corrupt or erase computer data.

Section 2(2) goes on to create an offence for persons who, without lawful excuse, damage property with the intent to endanger the life of another. This type of offence would cover a situation where, for example, an individual hacked into a hospital's computer system and prescribed potentially lethal drugs for a patient.

### Section 3

Section 3 of the 1991 Act creates an offence of threatening to damage property. A person who makes a threat of hacking into another individual's computer system with a view to damaging such computer system shall be guilty of an offence irrespective of whether the person who made the threat is actually capable of carrying it out. Thus, a hacker may be charged under this section where he or she has threatened to break into a computer system even if he or she has failed to successfully access the system.

### Section 4

Section 4 of the 1991 Act is potentially the Act's most useful provision to combat hacking. It provides that, possessing anything with the intent of using it to damage property is an offence. This provision is important, as it is often difficult to prove that a hacker has actually caused criminal damage or accessed the system without authorisation. However, where it can be shown that the hacker had things in his or her possession which could be used for hacking then he or she may be convicted of an offence. Thus, a hacker who is found in possession of a computer virus which deletes information on computer systems might be prosecuted under s 4.

### Section 5(1)

Section 5(1) of the 1991 Act creates an offence of unauthorised access. It is specifically intended to apply only to computer crime and has no other application. In order to be prosecuted under this provision, the accused must access a computer system without authorisation. This offence is broadly worded and is intended to catch hackers who enter into computer systems without actually causing any damage. In order for a prosecution under this section, the accused must have 'intended to access any data'. This provision applies to hackers within Ireland accessing a computer either in Ireland or elsewhere. It also applies to a hacker who accesses data within Ireland from abroad. This provision could prove to be a useful tool in prosecuting hackers especially in the absence of evidence that a hacker has damaged data or programs.

The 1991 Act creates a comprehensive range of offences and various types of computer misuse are criminalised by the Act. It might also be noted that the 1991 Act gives the authorities very extensive powers of arrest and the ability to obtain search warrants in the District Court. The 1991 Act also provides that, where a person has been convicted of criminal damage under s 2 of the Act, the court may order him or her to compensate the injured party.

### 11.4.2.2  The Data Protection Acts, 1988 and 2003

In addition to the Criminal Damage Act, 1991, s 22 of the Data Protection Acts creates an offence of gaining unauthorised access to personal data. Any person who obtains access to personal data or information constituting such data, without prior authority of the Data Controller or Data Processor and who discloses the data or information to another is guilty of an offence. This provision appears to be aimed at hackers and others who gain access to such data without authorisation.

### 11.4.2.3  The Electronic Commerce Act, 2000

This Act creates a series of offences which are considered in more detail in **11.5** below. Some of these offences might also be used to prosecute certain hacking related fraud and theft.

### 11.4.2.4  The Copyright and Related Rights Act, 2000

This Act is also capable of being used against individuals who engage in hacking. For example, the unauthorised accessing and extracting of information from databases is prohibited by the Act.

### 11.4.2.5  Unlawful use of a computer

Section 9(1) of the Criminal Justice (Theft and Fraud Offences) Act, 2001 created a new offence for the unlawful use of a computer. It provides that a person who dishonestly, whether within or outside the State, operates or causes to be operated a computer within the State with the intention of making a gain for himself or herself or another, or of causing loss to another, is guilty of an offence. Section 9(2) provides that a person guilty of an offence under s 9(1) is liable on conviction on indictment to a fine or imprisonment for a term not exceeding ten years or both.

### 11.4.2.6  playboy.com

There have been a number of high profile hacking incidents in recent years. Perhaps the most reported incident concerned the online porn site www. playboy.com which was penetrated by hackers. The hackers gained access to credit card details of certain subscribers to the website. An e-mail to affected subscribers from a hacker going by the alias Martyn Luther Ping warned that the group of hackers had plans to use the stolen details to make purchases in excess of US$10 million.

The hackers went on to e-mail customers with their harvested details which demonstrated that they were not bluffing. The hackers also claimed to have ascertained confidential company information over a three-year period.

The number of hacking incidents in recent years including the high profile of such incidents serves to undermine the public's trust in electronic commerce. Despite having adequate laws in place to prosecute such hackers it is often extremely difficult to ascertain the identity of the people behind such activities. Had the hackers involved in the playboy.com incident been based in Ireland or had playboy.com held the data in Ireland, then the Criminal Damage Act, 1991 might have enabled prosecutions of such individuals providing their identity could be discerned.

## 11.4.3   HARVESTING

Harvesting refers to the collection of e-mail addresses for the purposes of spamming and the extracting of significant amounts of information from databases belonging to third parties without the full consent of such third parties.

Invariably, the harvesting of e-mails for the purposes of spamming will result in an infringement of s 22 of the Data Protection Acts, 1988 and 2003.

Harvesting information which does not consist of personal data may also be an offence under the Criminal Damage Act, 1991. In this regard, the following, which is a summary of a report from the *Irish Times* of 14 August 1998, might be noted:

> In 1998, Alister Kidd, managing director of Touchtel, became the first person to be charged with unauthorised access to data under the Criminal Damage Act, 1991. The prosecution followed a complaint by Kompass Ireland, which runs an online database of company information, that Mr Kidd had found a way to bypass its site's technical restrictions and download company information from the database more quickly. Mr Kidd allegedly wrote a computer program to automatically download records of company information every five seconds. He was traced via the address of the computer he used to download the records.

But the case in the Dublin District Court was dismissed following the presentation of prosecution evidence, not because Mr Kidd did not access the data in question, but because the judge ruled that the information he got was already publicly available, and there were no restrictions or limitations printed on the website saying how it should be used.

The judge held that Mr Kidd had merely found a more efficient way to download data he could already access.

The case highlights an interesting dilemma for companies like Kompass, which provide a limited amount of free online information as a sample of what they sell on a CD-Rom. The Kompass website prevents users downloading more than 100 company records at a time, and the need to complete online forms gives the company the opportunity to sell advertisements on the site. Bypassing the normal interface not only bypasses the advertisements, a dilemma for many online providers, but also allows faster access to the data than Kompass intended.

In order to combat the type of behaviour which Mr Kidd engaged in, companies need to carefully consider the terms and conditions of use of their websites. Incidentally, the Kompass site (www.kompass.ie) now indicates that users 'shall not access the Kompass Service by any means, or in any sequence, other than those provided by the Kompass Service as part of its normal user interface'.

In addition to using terms and conditions to protect information posted on a website, individuals may now have recourse to the Copyright and Related Rights Act, 2000 in an effort to combat harvesting. This Act, inter alia, implements the provisions of 96/9/EC, Directive on the legal protection of databases into Irish law. These new provisions in relation to database rights are contained in Part V of the Act and it is envisaged that they will provide a significant amount of protection to owners of information contained in electronic databases which are accessible online. These 'database rights' aim to protect the investment involved in creating and maintaining computerised collections of data.

On 10 November 2004, the European Court of Justice ('ECJ') published its decision in the long-running proceedings of *The British Horseracing Board Ltd v William Hill Organisation Ltd*, Case C–203/02. This case related to the extent of the British Horseracing Board's rights in its database of horseracing information.

The ECJ took a completely different view to the UK judge at first instance, the Court of Appeal and the ECJ's own Advocate General. The following is a summary of the case:

> In the course of its role as regulator of British horse racing, the claimant created and constantly updated a computerised collection of information on races and riders. It recouped a quarter of its annual operating cost (of STG£4 million) by charging fees to others to use the information contained in the database. This information was accessible electronically to subscribers.
>
> In early 2000, the defendant bookmaker launched a comprehensive Internet site, covering most horse racing in the United Kingdom and internationally. The public could check this site to see which horses were running and, if they wished, they could place bets electronically. The information on the website came directly from data stored on the claimant's computer.
>
> The claimant sued for infringement of its database right.

Under the Database Directive a database right is infringed if, inter alia, there is an unauthorised extraction or reutilisation of the whole or a substantial proportion of the contents of a database. This test is to be assessed quantitatively and qualitatively.

The ECJ applied the quantitative test and held that William Hill had not taken a substantial part of the database. On a qualitative analysis, the ECJ looked at whether the investment made by the BHB in obtaining, verifying or presenting the data which had been extracted or re-utilised was substantial. The BHB failed to demonstrate that this was the case, as its investment was only in creating the information on which the database was constructed rather than in the actual database. Thus, the ECJ held that no infringement of BHB's database rights had occurred.

### 11.4.4 HYPERTEXT LINKS AND 'DEEP LINKING'

Hypertext links are the means by which, at the click of a button, visitors can skip from one website to another or from one page to another within the same site.

While this practice can be perfectly legal, circumstances may arise where deep linking into websites may infringe the rights of website owners.

In this regard, the case of *Shetland Times Limited v Dr Jonathan Wills* [1997] FSR 604 might be considered. In this case the *Shetland Times* newspaper obtained a temporary injunction to prohibit its competitor, the *Shetland News*, from linking to its stories. *Shetland Times* owned and published a newspaper on its website and placed various advertisements on its home page. The *Shetland News* was a competing online newspaper and included in its website headlines from the *Shetland Times*, which were hypertext linked to news stories on the *Shetland Times* website. *Shetland Times* was unhappy that people could gain access to its news items without having to go through its front page since the advertising on its front page was being bypassed. The Scottish court granted a temporary injunction in this case prohibiting the *Shetland News* from using hyperlinks into the *Shetland Times* website on the basis that such links constituted an infringement of Scottish copyright law.

Arguably, Ireland's sophisticated copyright laws embodied in the Copyright and Related Rights Act, 2000 could be used by Irish companies to obtain similar relief against companies that engage in deep linking into their websites. Thus, it is good practice to obtain the consent of a website owner before linking into their site and it is also advised that such links are set up in such a way as not to bypass a home page if that home page contains advertising.

Needless to say, not every hyperlink from one website to another is, of itself, a breach of copyright. The facts of each particular case will have to be carefully considered before a finding of copyright infringement can occur.

Finally, it might be noted that while a plain link to a website does not automatically infringe the intellectual property rights of a target site, a link which somehow uses a registered trademark of the target site may well infringe the intellectual property rights of the proprietors of the target sites. A good illustration of this is provided in the case involving a link to the www.playboy.com website from a pornographic website. Playboy successfully argued that the use of the Playboy trademark and bunny logo as the basis of the hypertext link through to the Playboy website infringed the intellectual property rights of Playboy.

To date, there have been no reported cases in Ireland in relation to deep linking. However, in the event of such a case being taken by a target website owner, it is likely that such a case would be based on copyright infringement, breach of database rights, passing off and possibly trademark infringement.

### 11.4.5  FRAMING

Framing refers to the division of a website into real time 'frames' whereby the website owner's propriety text and material (and often advertising) is displayed next to linked third party material in the same window. This practice may infringe copyright law. For example, in the US case of *Washington Post v Total News Inc.* (No 97 CIV 1190 (PKL) (SDNY) 1997), the *Washington Post* claimed that Total News had designed its website to republish news from other websites contributing no original material of their own. Total News, through the use of framing technology, had linked to sites such as the *Washington Post* and framed material from those third party sites alongside banner advertisements which belonged to Total News. While this case settled out of court, it is understood that it was agreed that Total News was allowed to keep linking to stories but was prohibited from framing the material next to their own propriety material, logos and advertisements.

### 11.4.6  META TAGS AND TRADE MARK INFRINGEMENTS

A 'meta tag' is a piece of coding information within the HTML coding of a website that describes the website. For example, a website about electronic commerce law may include meta tags such as 'law', 'legal', 'commerce', 'copyright', and so on, to attract users that type these words into search engines. However, although meta tags are not readily apparent to the human eye their use can infringe third parties' intellectual property rights by the inclusion of, for example, a competitor's name as a meta tag within the coding of its site.

Such an infringement will invariably occur where the competitor's name is a registered trade mark. There have been a number of cases in the US which have held that use of a competitor's meta tags may result in a trade mark infringement.

## 11.5  Overview of the Electronic Commerce Act, 2000

### 11.5.1  BACKGROUND

The Electronic Commerce Act, 2000 (the '2000 Act') came into operation on 20 September 2000.

The 2000 Act implements Directive 1999/93/EC on electronic signatures, and some of the provisions of Directive 2000/31/EC on electronic commerce. The remaining provisions of the Electronic Commerce Directive were enacted in the Electronic Commerce Regulations, 2003 (see **11.2** above).

This overview should act as a guide to the legislation but you should always check the particular facts of each case carefully against the text of the legislation.

## 11.5.2  EXCLUDED LAWS

The 2000 Act, and its provisions, will not apply to the law relating to the transfer of land or to the execution of documents such as wills, trusts or enduring powers of attorney, which will still have to be evidenced in traditional forms of writing (s 10). Interestingly, a contract for the sale of land can be in electronic form while the conveyance itself must be in a traditional form of writing.

## 11.5.3  ELECTRONIC SIGNATURES AND ADVANCED ELECTRONIC SIGNATURES

The 2000 Act makes an important distinction between 'electronic signatures' and 'advanced electronic signatures'.

An 'electronic signature' means:

> *data in electronic form attached to, incorporated in or logically associated with other electronic data and which serves as a method of authenticating the purported originator, and includes on advanced electronic signature.*

This definition would seem to encompass, for example, a scanned version of a handwritten signature or, in certain cases, a typed name at the foot of an e-mail.

The issue of whether or not an e-mail address can constitute an electronic signature arose in a recent UK decision, *Nilesh Mehtha v J Pereira Fernandes SA* [2006] EWHC 813 (Ch), 7 April 2006. In this case, the defendant stated in an e-mail that he would give a personal guarantee in the amount of £25,000. The English High Court had to decide whether, for the purposes of s 4 of the Statute of Frauds 1677, the presence of an automatically inserted e-mail address at the top of the e-mail constituted a signature by, or on behalf of, the defendant.

In this case, the e-mail was not 'signed', but the header of the e-mail showed that it came from the defendant's e-mail address, which was the same e-mail address that had appeared on other e-mails sent by him to the plaintiff's solicitors, which he had signed. The wording of the e-mail in question was such that it contained an offer and contemplated that formal documents would be entered into in relation to the personal guarantee. Notwithstanding that the terms of the guarantee had been subsequently agreed orally by the defendant and the plaintiff's solicitors, the defendant argued that he was not bound to honour the terms of the guarantee on the basis that it had not been 'signed' for the purposes of s 4 of the Statute of Frauds.

The English High Court held that the contents of the e-mail constituted a sufficient note or memorandum for the purpose of s 4 of the Statute of Frauds, as it contained an offer in writing made by the guarantor which contained the essential terms of what was offered, and the offer had been accepted unconditionally by the plaintiff's solicitors (albeit orally). However, the court held that the e-mail did not bear a signature, within the meaning of s 4 of the Statute of Frauds, of either the guarantor or his authorised agent, as the automatic insertion of an e-mail address was not intended as a signature. The inclusion of the e-mail address, in the absence of contrary intention, was incidental, in that the signature or name just happened to appear somewhere rather than being inserted into the document in order to give, and with the intention of giving, authenticity to it.

As an aside, the judge stated that if a party, or a party's agent, sending an e-mail types his or his principal's name, that would be a sufficient signature, subject to other legal requirements and providing always that the name was inserted into the document in order to give, and with the intention of giving, authenticity to it.

In contrast, an 'advanced electronic signature' means an electronic signature which is:

(a) *uniquely* linked to the signatory;

(b) capable of identifying the signatory;

(c) created using means that are capable of being maintained by the signatory under his, her or its sole control; and

(d) linked to the data to which it relates in such a manner that any subsequent *change of the data is detectable.*

An example of an advanced electronic signature would be an encrypted 'digital' signature using what is called Public Key Infrastructure ('PKI'). In simple terms, the use of PKI technology allows the sender of the information to encrypt the contents of the electronic communication so that (a) the recipient can be sure that the e-mail has come from the purported sender, and (b) no other party has altered the data prior to it being received. If a sender of an e-mail encrypts his e-mail using his unique advanced electronic signature based on qualified certificate technology the e-mail can only be opened and read by the individual to whom it was sent. The recipient can be sure that it has been signed by the sender since only he has the means of encrypting the message with his advanced electronic signature based on a qualified certificate as defined in the 2000 Act.

The use of advanced electronic signatures significantly reduces the inherent confidentiality and integrity risks that are associated with an open network such as the world wide web.

Section 13 of the 2000 Act provides that, if by law or otherwise, the signature of a person or public body is required (whether the requirement is in the form of an obligation or consequences flow from there being no signature) or permitted, then, subject to meeting the requirements of s 13(2), either an electronic signature or an advanced electronic signature may be used.

In other words, in most circumstances, an electronic signature will be given functional equivalence to a hand-written signature.

However, an electronic signature does not suffice in every case. For example, where a signature is required to be witnessed, s 14 provides that, the signature to be witnessed must be an advanced electronic signature. In addition, the document must contain an indication that the signature is required to be witnessed and the witness must also sign using an advanced electronic signature which meets the requirements of Annex 1 (i.e. the advanced electronic signature both meets the definition in the 2000 Act and in addition in based on a 'qualified certificate'). The requirement to use advanced electronic signatures also applies where documents are required to be executed under seal (s 16).

## 11.5.4 CERTIFICATION SERVICE PROVIDERS

Part 3 of the 2000 Act deals with certification services. If, as we have seen, the use of an advanced electronic signature practically guarantees the identity of the sender of an electronic communication, from where does one obtain an advanced electronic signature? The PKI system depends on the integrity of trusted third parties who are prepared to effectively guarantee the identity of persons to whom they issue advanced electronic signatures. If an advanced electronic signature is not unique or is capable of being used by a third party, it will not meet the definition in the 2000 Act.

Part 3 of the 2000 Act provides for the accreditation and supervision of 'Certification Service Providers' ('CSPs') who provide certification of electronic signatures.

Section 29 provides that CSPs can operate without prior authorisation. This may seem odd. If it is so important that a CSP acts with the utmost integrity and security to protect the confidentiality of the advanced electronic signatures it issues, why are there no national or EU standards to apply to it? The answer lies in the fact that the EU does not wish to hinder the emergence of CSPs through heavy regulation. As CSPs who issue 'qualified certificates' will have liability to those who rely on any certification services they provide, then the market will determine the standards appropriate to such an emerging technology. For example, if a CSP were to lose the private keys of its customers, this would potentially ruin its business, as the fundamental trust required of a CSP would be lost and its customers would be likely to revoke their existing private keys and seek alternative CSP services elsewhere.

Notwithstanding the previous paragraph, it is open to the Minister for Enterprise, Trade and Employment to establish a scheme of voluntary accreditation of CSPs to enhance the levels of certification service provision in the State. However, no such scheme has to date been adopted.

### 11.5.5   ELECTRONIC ORIGINALS

Section 17 of the 2000 Act facilitates the retention and presentation of electronic forms of 'original' information. Information may be presented or retained in electronic form, provided:

(a) there exists a reliable assurance as to the integrity of the information from the time when it was first generated in its final form;

(b) the information is capable of being displayed in intelligible form to a person or public body to whom it is to be presented; and

(c) at the time the information was generated in its final form, it was reasonable to expect that it would be readily accessible so as to be useable for subsequent reference.

The 'consent' requirements discussed below also apply to the holding of electronic originals. In most cases, where an electronic document is stored in a secure file (e.g. a Microsoft Word file or an archived e-mail) and it can be shown that the document has not been altered since the day it was stored (e.g. by checking the 'properties' of the document), the standards listed in s 17 will be met. However, if the document was stored on an open network where many people had access to it, it may be more difficult to assert that there was a reliable assurance as to the document's integrity.

### 11.5.6   ELECTRONIC COMMUNICATIONS

Broadly speaking, the 2000 Act gives legal recognition to communications and information in electronic form. Therefore electronic communications, information, signatures and contracts cannot be denied legal effect or be discriminated against simply because they are in electronic form.

### 11.5.7   CONSENT REQUIREMENT

However, while the Act does go some way to remove some of the legal ambiguities previously associated with electronic communications, the Act does not compel people to communicate or conduct business in electronic form. Therefore, in order for an electronic communication to obtain full legal recognition, it is a requirement of the Act that the parties to the communication must consent to the information being provided in electronic form.

Where information is required or permitted to be given to a public body and the public body consents to the giving of the information in electronic form, but requires that the information be given in accordance with particular information technology and procedural requirements, or that a particular action be taken by way of verifying the receipt of the information, these requirements must be met. However, any public body which introduces IT and procedural requirements must ensure that those requirements have been made public and are objective, transparent, proportionate and non-discriminatory. For example, the Companies Registration Office ('CRO') may agree to accept the registration of certain forms on their website but the CRO will be entitled to require that the electronic forms be filled out and submitted in the manner described on the website. Another example, the Revenue Online Service (www.ROS.ie), enables the electronic filing of certain tax returns.

Where the recipient of an electronic communication is a non-public body, that person must consent to receiving the information in electronic form. The Act is not intended to force people to transact electronically (s 24).

## 11.5.8 ELECTRONIC EVIDENCE

Evidence will not be denied admissibility in legal proceedings solely because it is in electronic form (s 22). However, this is not to say that electronic evidence will always be admitted and the normal rules of evidence will continue to apply.

## 11.5.9 ELECTRONIC CONTRACTS

Section 19 confirms that an electronic contract shall not be denied legal effect, validity or enforceability solely on the grounds that it is wholly or partly in electronic form, or has been concluded wholly or partly by way of an electronic communication.

In the formation of a contract, an offer, acceptance of an offer or any related communication (including any subsequent amendment, cancellation or revocation of the offer or acceptance of the offer) may, unless otherwise agreed by the parties, be communicated by means of an electronic communication.

Section 21 deals with the time and place of dispatch and receipt of electronic communications. Under the so-called 'postal rule' acceptance is deemed by the law to occur at the time the letter of acceptance is posted by the offeree and not the time at which it is received or read by the offeror. Prior to the implementation of the Act, it was not clear whether the rule applied to electronic communications.

Section 21 provides that where an electronic communication enters an information system, or the first information system, outside the control of the originator, then, unless otherwise agreed between the originator and the addressee, it is taken to have been sent when it enters such information system or first information system. Therefore, in the case of an e-mail, an e-mailed acceptance of a contract would be deemed to be sent once it passes outside the sender's e-mail system.

Where the recipient has designated an information system for the purpose of receiving electronic communications (e.g. an e-mail address), then, unless otherwise agreed or the law otherwise provides, the electronic communication is taken to have been received when it enters that information system. Where the addressee of an electronic communication has not designated an information system the electronic communication is taken to have been received when it 'comes to the attention of the addressee'.

In practice, this would include circumstances where a recipient of an e-mail does not actually open the e-mail when he knows that it contains an acceptance of his contract offer. He will not be entitled to rely upon his failure to open the e-mail to claim that the acceptance was not received by him. Provided the sender of the acceptance has sent the e-mail to the correct e-mail address and the e-mail has been successfully sent, the fact that the recipient refuses to open the e-mail does not prevent the communication having been received by him.

The places of dispatch and receipt of an electronic communication are deemed to be the places of business of the parties or, if there is no such place of business, the place where they ordinarily reside.

Further provisions relating to electronic contracts are contained in the Electronic Commerce Regulations (see **11.2** above).

## 11.5.10 FRAUD AND MISUSE

Fraud and misuse of electronic signatures and signature creation devices are criminal offences under the 2000 Act. The 2000 Act provides that the Gardai may not require the disclosure of keys or codes that may be necessary to make information on electronic communication intelligible. This differs significantly from the approach taken in the UK where there has been much controversy surrounding its Regulation of Investigatory Powers Act. The approach in the Irish Act is consistent with the declared policy of the Irish government that the regulation of the use, import and export of encryption products should be light and flexible while respecting Ireland's obligations under international treaties such as the Wassenaar Arrangement.

## 11.5.11 .IE DOMAIN REGISTRY

Section 31 of the 2000 Act provides that the Minister for Public Enterprise may authorise, prohibit or regulate the registration and use of the .ie domain name in the State. By virtue of the Communication Regulations (Amendment) Bill, 2007, the Communications Regulator ('ComReg') has taken over most of the policy functions of IEDR. The legislation was passed by the Oireachtas and came into force on 15 May 2007 with the signing of the Communications Regulation (Amendment) Act, 2007 (Commencement) Order, 2007 (SI 224/2007).

According to the Regulatory Impact Analysis, the legislation puts in place legal instruments for the regulation of the private sector company (IEDR), which is currently administrating ccTLD.

The legislation gives ComReg complete power over .ie ccTLD policy decisions: designating the authority to register .ie domains; setting renewal periods and conditions; revoking registrations, registration conditions; pricing of .ie domains; and appeals against revocation of registrations. However, it should be noted that the IEDR still provides the day-to-day administration of .ie ccTLD.

## 11.6 European Communities (Protection of Consumers in Respect of Contracts Made by Means of Distance Communication) Regulations, 2001 (SI 207/2001)

### 11.6.1 INTRODUCTION

The European Communities (Protection of Consumers in Respect of Contracts Made by Means of Distance Communication) Regulations, 2001 (the 'Regulations') were implemented into Irish law with effect from 15 May 2001. The Regulations have substantial implications for all e-businesses or other businesses which provide goods or services to consumers by means of a distance communication such as tele-shopping, telesales or mail order.

The Regulations apply to any business supplying goods or services to consumers (i.e. persons acting for purposes which are outside their trade, business or profession) under distance contracts. Businesses covered by the Regulations must adopt terms and conditions of sale and appropriate contractual procedures to comply with the Regulations or run the risk of being guilty of one of the many offences listed under the Regulations.

The Regulations implement European Directive 97/7/EC. This Directive aims to harmonise the laws in respect of distance contracts for consumers throughout the Member States of the EU, substantially increasing protection for consumers.

This section of the materials provides an overview of the principal provisions of the Regulations. However, how the Regulations will specifically affect any business will depend on the specific nature of the goods or services being sold. Therefore, legal advice should be tailored to ascertain whether and the extent to which the Regulations apply.

### 11.6.2 WHAT BUSINESSES ARE AFFECTED?

The Regulations apply to all businesses that sell goods or services to consumers on the Internet, on interactive digital television, by mail order, by telephone, by fax and includes advertising on television or radio, in newspapers or magazines.

Financial services are not covered by the Regulations but were subsequently covered by the EC (Distance Marketing of Consumer Financial Services) Regulations, 2004.

The Regulations also do not apply to:

- vending machines and pay-phones;

- contracts for the construction and sale of property; or

- auctions (which presumably covers Internet auctions).

### 11.6.3  WHAT TYPES OF TRANSACTIONS ARE COVERED?

The Regulations apply to 'distance contracts', which are defined as:

*... a contract between a supplier and a consumer which:*

*(a)   relates to goods or services,*

*(b)   is made under an organised distance sales or service-provision scheme run by the supplier, and*

*(c)   is made by the supplier making exclusive use of one or more means of distance communication (see definition below) up to and including the moment at which the contract is made. . . .*

As it is a requirement that the distance contract be made under an organised scheme, it is probable that the Regulations do not apply if a business does not usually sell to consumers in response to letters, phone calls, faxes or e-mails. However, even one-off distance contracts may fall under the Regulations if the supplier has an organised means of responding to requests from consumers.

Further, exclusive use of a method of distance communication must be made. So if a method of non-distance communication is used at any stage prior to or at the moment of contract—for example if a sales representative speaks face to face to the contracting consumer at a showroom—the Regulations do not apply.

*'Means of distance communication'* is defined as *'any method which, without the simultaneous physical presence of the supplier and the consumer, may be used for making a contract between those parties'* and includes the following non-exhaustive examples:

- (a)   electronic mail;

- (b)   television (teleshopping);

- (c)   unaddressed printed matter;

- (d)   addressed printed matter;

- (e)   standard letter;

- (f)   press advertising with order form;

(g)   catalogue;

(h)   telephone (with or without human intervention);

(i)   telephone without human intervention (automatic calling machine, audiotext);

(j)   radio;

(k)   videophone (telephone with screen);

(l)   videotex (microcomputer and television screen) with keyboard or touch screen;

(m)   fax.

## 11.6.4   HOW WILL THE REGULATIONS AFFECT CONSUMER CONTRACTS?

### 11.6.4.1   Prior information

A contract will not be enforceable against the consumer if detailed information about the contract including the purpose of the information and the contract is not made clear in an appropriate manner to the consumer in good time prior to making of the contract. Suppliers are obliged to have due regard to principles of good faith in commercial transactions, and to any principles governing the protection of those who are unable to give their consent, such as minors. This would include for example adhering to the Advertising Standards Authority of Ireland Codes of Practice. The minimum prior information which must be provided is:

(a)   the identity of the supplier and, in the case of contracts requiring payment in advance, the supplier's address;

(b)   the main characteristics of the goods or services;

(c)   the price of the goods or services including all taxes;

(d)   delivery costs, where appropriate;

(e)   the arrangements for payment, delivery or performance;

(f)   the existence of a right of cancellation (the right of cancellation may not apply in certain circumstances, see **11.6.4.3** below);

(g)   the cost of using the means of distance communication, where it is calculated other than at the basic rate;

(h)   the period for which the offer or the price remains valid;

(i)   where appropriate, the minimum duration of the contract in the case of contracts for the supply of goods or services to be performed permanently or recurrently.

In the case of telephone communications, the identity of the supplier and the purpose of the commercial call must be made explicitly clear. Unlike the EU Directive and the UK Regulations, it is not stated that this must be achieved at the outset of the call although it would be advisable to do so.

### 11.6.4.2 Confirming the terms of the contract

A distance contract will not be enforceable against a consumer, unless the consumer has received confirmation in writing or in another accessible (to the consumer) durable medium, such as fax or e-mail, of the prior information outlined in **11.6.4.1** above, unless it has already been provided in such manner to the consumer prior to making the contract, e.g. in a catalogue or advertisement that the consumer has seen. The information confirmed must also include information on the right of cancellation, the geographical address of the place of business of the supplier to which the consumer may address any complaints, existing after-sales services and guarantees and conditions for cancelling the contract if it is of unspecified duration or longer than one year. In practice, this will require information technology operators to e-mail these details to consumers on receipt of the order for goods and services. Alternatively, the confirmation could be provided by way of a 'splash' page which appears once an order is submitted on a website.

The written confirmation must be provided during the performance of the contract and at the latest at the time of delivery of goods where goods not for delivery to third parties are concerned.

Once-off services (not goods) that are invoiced by a distance communication are exempt from the requirement of written confirmation, unless the geographical address of the place of business of the supplier to which the consumer may address complaints is not given.

### 11.6.4.3 Cooling off periods: the consumer's right to cancel the contract

The consumer has a period of seven working days in which to cancel the distance contract without giving a reason and the only cost payable by the consumer is the direct cost of returning the goods. The Regulations do not specify that the cancellation must be in writing nor that the consumer actually return the goods so it is important that these are covered in the supplier's contractual terms.

The 'cooling off' period begins as soon as the goods have been received or, for services, from the day of making the distance contract and in both cases the confirmation requirement must have been complied with before the cooling off period begins to run.

If the confirmation requirements have not been complied with, the cooling off period is extended by up to three months. For example, where the supplier fails to provide the necessary written confirmation, the cooling off period will last seven days plus the additional three months.

The consumer's right of cancellation in distance contracts, unless agreed between the supplier and the consumer, does not apply in the following contracts:

(a)    for services if performance has begun with the consumer's agreement before the cooling off period ends;

(b)    for supply of goods and services the price of which is subject to fluctuations in the financial market;

(c)    for customised or perishable goods;

(d)    for supply of audio or video recordings or computer software which was unsealed;

(e)    for the supply of newspapers, periodicals and magazines (remarkably the exception does not extend to books); and

(f)    for gaming and lottery services.

If the consumer exercises his/her right to cancel during the cooling off period, the supplier must reimburse any sums paid by the consumer, except the direct cost of returning the goods, as soon as possible after the exercise of the right of cancellation and not later than thirty days. This extends consumer protection to a right of reimbursement beyond circumstances of defective goods/services. The consumer can demand his/her money back even if the goods are in perfectly good condition. If payment for the goods and services was under a related credit agreement the cancellation notice has the effect of cancelling the credit agreement also. The supplier in limited circumstances may recover the direct cost of recovering the goods supplied, but only where the terms and conditions provide that the consumer when exercising the right of cancellation must return any goods and has failed to do so.

Provisions of the Regulations regarding prior information, confirmation, cooling off periods and reimbursement for cancellation costs do not apply to contracts for the regular supply of foodstuffs, beverages or other goods intended for everyday consumption. These select provisions also do not apply to contracts for transport, accommodation, catering or leisure services provided on specific dates.

### 11.6.4.4    Time limits on performance of the consumer contract

The supplier must execute the order within a maximum of thirty days. If goods or services are unavailable, the supplier must inform the consumer and provide a refund as soon as possible and not later than thirty days. Goods or services of equivalent quality and price may be provided to the consumer but only with notice prior to the making of the contract of such a possibility and reserving the consumer's right of cancellation and the cost of returning the goods to be paid by the supplier. The right of refund does not apply to outdoor leisure events, which by their nature cannot be rescheduled, if so agreed between the supplier and the consumer prior to making the distance contract.

### 11.6.4.5  Fraudulent credit and debit cards

Regulation 10 provides the consumer with a legal right to demand the immediate cancellation, re-credit or return of any payment as appropriate, where fraudulent use has been made of his/her credit card, charge card, debit card or store card: If a consumer's credit card has been used fraudulently, their liability cannot exceed €150 under EU Recommendation (97/489/EC) The Regulations are silent on the onus of proving whether or not the transaction was in fact fraudulent. However, one of the main commercial risks attaching to online merchants is that transactions can be subject to 'charge backs' where cardholders dispute a transaction and the merchant has no physical signature evidencing the transaction. As a result of the international rules regarding credit card payments, inevitably it is the merchant and not the banks who suffer charge backs in these circumstances. This situation is beginning to change with the emergence of new technological developments being introduced by credit card companies and banks to reduce the level of online credit card fraud.

### 11.6.4.6  Inertia selling

Inertia selling, that is, a demand for payment for an unsolicited service, is prohibited. Attempts to conclude a distance contract made by way of an automated calling system or unsolicited fax will not be enforceable against a consumer, unless the consumer's prior consent to such means being used has been obtained.

A contract made by distance communication other than by an automated calling system is not enforceable unless no clear objection has been made by the consumer to such means being used. For example, automated distance contracts require prior consent while individual distance contracts merely require that the consumer does not object. This should be read in the light of s 13 of the Electronic Commerce Act which requires each party's consent before electronic signatures will be given legal validity.

## 11.6.5  CONSEQUENCES OF NON-COMPLIANCE

A person who fails to comply with the Regulations is guilty of an offence and shall be liable on summary conviction to a fine not exceeding €3,000. Personal liability may attach to the officers of a company if they have consented or contributed to the breach.

The Director of Consumer Affairs or a consumer organisation may apply to the High Court for an order to effect compliance. Actual loss or damage or recklessness or negligence need not be proved. In particular the court will take into account the public interest.

Authorised officers of the Director of Consumer Affairs have powers of requiring information, inspection and retention of records and data and may apply to the District Court for further warrants.

A consumer may not waive the rights conferred on him/her under the Regulations and any terms and conditions which attempt to override the Regulations will be void. Similarly, if the contract has a close connection with the territory of a Member State of the EEA, any condition applying the law of a State other than a Member State of the EEA is void.

### 11.6.6   CONCLUSION

The Regulations arguably comprise the most significant consumer protection legislation for operators in Ireland. While the Electronic Commerce Act, 2000 gained much public attention, the Regulations are perhaps more important, in that they set out specific procedural obligations on website retailers who sell to consumers. The Regulations should be considered in light of other consumer protection legislation in place in Ireland such as the sale of goods, unfair contracts, misleading advertising and product liability legislation.

## 11.7   Registering and Protecting Domain Names and Trade Marks on the Web

### 11.7.1   INTRODUCTION

This section examines, in the context of the Internet, the rights and restrictions attaching to registered and unregistered trade marks and to Internet domain names. In particular, it looks at how the courts and dispute resolution bodies in various jurisdictions are interpreting the rights associated with trade marks and domain names and it explores some of the more important cases that have been decided under the ICANN Uniform Domain Name Dispute Resolution Policy ('UDRP') which has been in place since 1999, Finally, the section explores ways of adapting a commercially sensible strategy in relation to the registration and protection of trademarks and domain names on the Internet.

### 11.7.2   THE NATURE OF TRADE MARKS

Irish trade mark law is currently governed by the Trade Marks Act, 1996. The full title of the Act illustrates its scope:

> *An Act to make new provision for registered trade marks, implementing Council Directive No 89/104/EEC of 21 December 1988, to approximate the laws of the Member States relating to trade marks; to make provision in connection with Council Regulation (EC) No 40/94 of 20 December 1993, on the Community Trade Mark; to give effect to the Madrid Protocol relating to the international registration of marks of 27 June 1989, and to certain provisions of the Paris Convention for the Protection of Industrial Property of 20 March 1883, as revised and amended; to permit the registration of trade marks in relation to services and for connected purposes.*

The Act deals primarily with registered trade marks but also makes reference to unregistered trade marks. In particular, s 7(2) provides that nothing in the Act shall affect the law relating to passing off. Trade marks are covered more fully in the intellectual property module.

Trade marks have traditionally been registered by reference to:

(a)    their ability to distinguish goods or services;

(b)    use in the course of trade;

(c)    specific territories, such as Ireland for an Irish trade mark or the EU for a Community Trade Mark; and

(d)    an international class system (currently the Nice Classification, 7th edn) in relation to categories of goods or services.

Unregistered trade marks traditionally derive protection on the basis of:

(a)    use in the course of trade;

(b)    reputation within a territory; and

(c)    a prejudicial exploitation of the goodwill which has been generated in the mark by the owner of the unregistered right.

Section 8 of the Act lists grounds for refusal of registration of a trade mark. These can be summarised as follows:

(a)    the trade mark is not distinctive;

(b)    the trade mark is purely descriptive and has not acquired distinctiveness through use;

(c)    the trade mark is contrary to public policy or morality;

(d)    the trade mark is deceptive; and

(e)    the application for registration is made in bad faith by the applicant.

Under s 10 of the Act, a trade mark will not be registered if there exists an earlier trade mark which is identical with the trade mark in question and is identical to the goods or services for which the earlier trade mark is protected. Section 10 also protects identical trade marks registered in relation to similar goods or services and similar trade marks registered for similar goods or services where there exists a likelihood of confusion on the part of the public. If there is unfair advantage or detriment to the distinctive character or reputation of an earlier mark, an application to register an identical or similar trade mark for dissimilar goods or services will also be rejected.

In light of the legislative requirements outlined above, the successful registration of a trade mark usually requires professional advice and significant expense.

## 11.7.3    THE NATURE OF DOMAIN NAMES

Unlike trade marks, domain names can usually be registered quickly and with little expense. Before looking at how domain name disputes are resolved, it is worth examining the nature of domain names and how they contrast with trade marks.

The term 'Top Level Domain' ('TLD') is used to describe the suffix attaching to the end of a domain name. So for example, .ie is the TLD for Ireland while .uk is the TLD for the United Kingdom.

Broadly speaking, TLDs fall into two categories:

(a)   generic TLDs ('gTLDs'), and

(b)   country code TLDs ('ccTLDs').

gTLD domain names are issued on a first come first served basis. They do not indicate geographic origin and the applicant need not prove any use or trade within any particular class of goods or services to acquire a gTLD domain name. The most widely used gTLDs are .com, .net and .org. Other gTDLs include .biz, .info, .name, .pro, .museum and .coop.

The market for domain names is such that a domain name with the gTLD '.com' can be extremely valuable. At the height of the dot com economy, domain names such as business.com attracted values as high as US$7 million.

In contrast with registered trade marks, a gTLD domain name need not be distinctive and indeed some of the most valuable gTLD domain names are purely descriptive. Personal names are registrable as domain names, but are not necessarily registrable as trade marks. In contrast with registered trade marks, domain names can usually be registered without professional advice or significant expense.

While trade mark law allows concurrent use of the same or similar marks in relation to different industries or different geographic regions, the unique character strings that comprise a domain name means that no two identical domain names can exist. Conversely, while a name containing a minor variation of a registered trade mark, for example amazom.com (note the 'm'), would be unlikely to be registered as a trade mark on grounds of confusing similarity with the registered trade mark amazon.com, the confusing similarity of the trade marks will not prevent registration of both domain names. (In fact, the domain name amazom.com was owned by 'Amazombooks.com' in the US, although the website, which previously sold books online, no longer trades.)

Originally, the gTLDs .com, .net and .org were administered by Network Solutions Inc. ('NSI') but there are now several other domain registries offering gTLD domain registration services.

ccTLDs are administered by the domain registry of the applicable country. So, for example, the Irish domain registry which administers domain names with the ccTLD '.ie' is IE Domain Registry Limited (www.IEDR.ie) ('IEDR').

Each ccTLD administrator applies its own rules in relation to registrability of its domains. All applicants applying for an .ie domain name who are not situated in the thirty-two counties of Ireland must demonstrate a 'real, and substantive connection with Ireland' (with the exception of those applying with a registered Community trade mark), before the IEDR will approve the registration of a domain name with the ccTLD .ie. The IEDR rules are available at www.iedr. ie. Some other ccTLD registries operate on an open basis without the need to prove a connection to the particular country or to prove intellectual property rights in the domain being acquired.

In Ireland and in the UK, domain names are not regarded as property rights, rather they are rights obtained by contract. However, in the United States, domain names are regarded as property rights. For this reason, the registrant of the domain name sex.com, which received some 25 million hits per day, was awarded US$65 million in damages by a US court when his domain name was allegedly fraudulently transferred. (However, unfortunately for the plaintiff, the domain thief has absconded and the plaintiff appears unlikely to actually receive any damages.)

## 11.7.4   TRADE MARK DISPUTES

Having briefly examined some of the contrasting features of trade marks and domain names above, it is worth looking at the ingredients of a typical trade mark dispute before contrasting it with a typical domain name dispute. Typically in the course of trade mark litigation, the following issues would be likely to arise:

### (a) Jurisdiction

The plaintiff would typically rely upon a registered trade mark which is applicable to the jurisdiction in question.

### (b) Use in the course of trade

In order to establish infringement, the plaintiff will ordinarily demonstrate use by the plaintiff in the course of trade and infringing use by the defendant. The issue of honest concurrent use can arise where the defendant can indicate use within the State with the plaintiff's consent or prior bona fide prior commercial use within the State.

### (c) Confusion/likelihood of association

In relation to non-identical trade marks or identical trade marks registered in relation to different classes, the plaintiff may be required to establish a likelihood of confusion on the part of the public, which includes the likelihood of association of the defendant's sign with the plaintiff's trade mark.

### (d) Remedies

Typically the remedies sought in an action for trade mark infringement would include injunctive relief, damages and/or an account of profits. The plaintiff may also seek remedies in tort, such as inducing a breach of contract or conspiracy. Other issues which can arise include whether the trade mark was a 'well known' trade mark under the Paris Convention and whether there has been fraudulent application or use of the trade mark in relation to goods.

For unregistered trade marks, Lord Diplock in *Erven Warnink BV v Townend & Sons (Hull) Ltd* [1979] AC 731 identified, from the cases decided before 1980, five characteristics which had to be present in order to create a valid cause of action for passing off:

(a)   a misrepresentation;

(b)   made by a trader in the course of trade;

(c)   to prospective customers of his or ultimate consumers of goods or services supplied by him;

(d)   which is calculated to injure the business or goodwill of another trader (in the sense that this is a reasonably foreseeable consequence); and

(e)   which causes actual damage to a business or goodwill of the trader by whom the action is brought or (in a *quia timet* action) will probably do so.

Usually, therefore, it is more difficult to establish a case for the protection of unregistered rights compared to the more 'automatic' redress available for registered trade marks.

### 11.7.5   DOMAIN NAME DISPUTES

Domain name disputes have typically been resolved by way of either litigation based on trade mark rights or unfair competition or, alternatively, by alternative dispute resolution ('ADR') procedures based on the terms of the registration agreement between the owner of the domain name and the domain name registry. Frequently, the parties to the dispute and the domain registry in question would reside in different countries.

In light of the logistical, jurisdictional and expense issues which trade mark holders were facing in actions to recover domain names from so called cybersquatters, the International Corporation for Assigned Names and Numbers ('ICANN') adopted a Uniform Domain Name Dispute Resolution Policy ('UDRP') in October 1999. The UDRP applies to gTLD domain disputes although some ccTLD administrators have opted to incorporate the ICANN UDRP into their registration agreements. The UDRP has been a tremendous success with many thousands of cases having been decided by this means. The success of the UDRP was originally based largely upon its global application, efficiency and low cost which contrasts sharply with the position in relation to traditional multi-jurisdictional trade mark litigation.

If the UDRP applies to a particular registry, in accordance with the terms of the Domain Registration Agreement, a domain name holder is required to submit to a mandatory UDRP administrative proceeding in the event that a third party (a 'Complainant') asserts to the arbitration body, in compliance with its rules, that:

(a)   the domain name is identical or confusingly similar to a trade mark or service mark in which the Complainant has rights; and

(b)   the domain name holder has no rights or legitimate interests in respect of the domain name; and

(c)   the domain name has been registered and is being used in bad faith.

The UDRP provides a non-exhaustive list of factors which shall be prima facie evidence of bad faith and also includes a non-exhaustive list of suggested ways in which the respondent can demonstrate rights to and legitimate interests in the domain name. A more detailed consideration of the UDRP is available at www.icann.org.

In deciding whether or not to avail of the UDRP, an aggrieved party would have to consider whether it can establish bad faith on the part of the respondent. This is a different standard to that imposed by the courts in trade mark or passing off cases. If a trade mark owner requires immediate redress, the UDRP may not be appropriate as, although cases are typically resolved within forty-five days, a trade mark owner may need to seek an emergency injunction to prevent damage being caused by the cybersquatter. In contrast to court litigation, the UDRP does not provide for damages and a successful complainant will only be entitled to the transfer of the domain name in question.

The UDRP does not address the standard of proof to be applied by dispute panellists. Panellists may however refer to local laws but are not bound to follow previous decisions of other panels.

ccTLD domain disputes can be litigated before the appropriate courts. Alternatively, most ccTLDs (there are around 250) will provide some form of alternative dispute resolution procedure. The IEDR launched a dispute policy, based on the UDRP which came into effect on 31 July 2003.

In general, ccTLD registries will require some indication of trade mark infringement or passing off before they will suspend, cancel or transfer a domain name the subject of a dispute.

## 11.7.6 THE THREE ELEMENTS OF THE UDRP

Before looking at some of the UDRP cases, it is worth considering each of the three elements of the UDRP individually.

### (a) 'The domain name is identical or confusingly similar to a trade mark or service mark in which the complainant has rights.'

As shown above, the Complainant must show that the domain name is identical or confusingly similar to a mark in which the Complainant has rights. Generally, this is relatively easy to show and there is no requirement that the trade mark or service mark be registered with any trade mark registry.

Curiously, the UDRP does not cover 'trade names' but does cover trade marks although the meaning and rationale behind the distinction is not clear so, for example, in the case of manchesterairport.com (WIPO D2000–0638), the majority of the three member Panel deciding the case held that Manchester Airport plc had no relevant rights in the name 'Manchester Airport' as it was not a trade mark or service mark. Despite the fact that the respondent offered to sell the domain name to the complainant for £10,000, the majority of the Panel was satisfied that before the respondent had any notice of the dispute, it was using or had demonstrated that it was preparing to use the domain name in connection with a bona fide offering of goods or services. The minority panellist has since voiced his disapproval of the distinction between trade marks and trade names.

### (b) 'The domain name holder has no rights or legitimate interests in respect of the domain name.'

The second element of the UDRP provides that the Complainant must show that the domain name registrant has no rights or legitimate interest in the domain name. The UDRP is not designed to arbitrate disputes between parties with competing rights in good faith in identical or similar trade marks. The WIPO Report which preceded the UDRP and the Policy itself makes it clear that the UDRP is designed to addressed flagrant cybersquatting cases. Notwithstanding this, some of the decided cases have purported to interpret national trade mark and intellectual property law notwithstanding the international nature of the process, the differing standards of proof required in different jurisdictions and the variations in trade mark law and practice in the jurisdictions of complainants and respondents.

### (c) 'The domain name has been registered and is being used in bad faith.'

The third element of the UDRP is for the Complainant to establish that the domain name has been registered and is being used in bad faith. This is the main element of the UDRP process.

In light of para 4(b) of the UDRP and the extensive reported case law to date, the following is a non-exhaustive list of examples of prima facie bad faith:

(a)   an attempt to transfer the domain name to the trade mark owner or a competitor for valuable consideration in excess of registration costs;

(b)   evidence of an intent to profit through domain speculation;

(c)   evidence of a history of blocking access to trade marks in which others have rights;

(d)   evidence of an intent to disrupt a competitor's business;

(e)   evidence of an intent to cause confusion;

(f)   the respondent hiding his contact details;

(g)   where the respondent is an ex-employee or distributor for the Complainant; and

(h)   'typosquatting' (deliberate misspelling of a well-known name).

In defence to an allegation of bad faith, para 4(c) of the UDRP illustrates some grounds for the respondent to rebut allegations of bad faith. These include:

(a)   bona fide use of the name prior to receiving notification of the dispute;

(b)   bona fide use of one's own name (although in the case of oxford-university.com (WIPO D2000–0308), where the respondent alleged, without providing evidence, that he had changed his name to Mr Oxford University after becoming aware of the complaint, this was not sufficient to rebut the bad faith allegation);

(c)  non-commercial or fair use of the domain without intent to profit; and

(d)  evidence that the respondent is commonly known by the domain name.

The UDRP also provides for what it calls 'Reverse Domain Name Hijacking' which is where the complainant uses the policy in bad faith to attempt to deprive a registered domain name holder of a domain name. In k2r.com (WIPO D2000–0622), the complainant made wild allegations of bad faith which the respondent disproved to the satisfaction of the Panel. The Panel therefore upheld the respondent's claim of Reverse Domain Name Hijacking. However, the UDRP provides no penalty for Reverse Domain Name Hijacking unlike in many jurisdictions where unjustified allegations of infringement can amount to an offence or a civil wrong entitling the subject of the ungrounded claims to damages.

## 11.7.7  UDRP CASE LAW

All UDRP cases are published on the Internet and readers can go to www. icann.org/udrp for a full list of the decided UDRP cases.

A typical and recent Irish example involved the domain name facebook.ie. In *Facebook Inc. v Talkbeans Media Limited*, Case No DIE2007–0009, Talkbeans Media registered the domain name facebook.ie in February 2007. Facebook Inc. filed a complaint with the WIPO Arbitration and Mediation Center on the basis that it has rights in the Community-registered trade mark FACEBOOK, and, further, has rights in the mark FACEBOOK as an unregistered website protected by Irish common law due to the substantial goodwill that it has acquired in the use of the FACEBOOK mark in relation to the provision of social networking services. The Administrative Panel concluded that Facebook Inc. has established rights in the unregistered service mark FACEBOOK at common law in Ireland and that Talkbeans Media sought to take predatory advantage of Facebook Inc.'s goodwill by registering a domain name intending to intercept Internet traffic intended for facebook.com and diverting it to its own social networking site. Consequently, the Administrative Panel directed that the domain name facebook.ie be transferred to Facebook Inc.

## 11.7.8  DOMAIN NAME LITIGATION OUTSIDE OF THE UDRP

It is beyond the scope of this chapter to examine the vast amount of reported court cases involving disputed domain names. However, some examples from home and abroad offer guidance as to how the courts in various jurisdictions approach domain name disputes.

### (a) Ireland

*LK Shields v Engefield Management Consulting Limited, Irish Times*, 30 May 2000
(see htttp://scripts.ireland.com/search/highlight.plx?TextRes=LK%20Shields&
Path=/newspaper/ finance/2000/0530/fin10.htm)

In these proceedings, the Irish law firm, LK Shields, sought, inter alia, an interlocutory injunction from the Irish High Court against the Irish registered owner
of the domain name lkshields.com. The case was settled and the settlement
terms were made a rule of court with each side bearing its own costs.

*Local-Ireland Limited and Another v Local Ireland On-Line Limited and Another*, 2
October [2000] 4 IR 567

In this case, Herbert J granted the plaintiffs an interlocutory injunction stating
that he was satisfied that the plaintiffs had established a bona fide case that the
use of the domain name locallyirish.com was so close to the business name
and domain name of the plaintiff (localireland.com) that no sufficient or real
distinction could reasonably be said to exist between them, particularly having
regard to the similarity of the services being offered by the parties. Unfortunately, this matter did not go to full trial.

### (b) United Kingdom

*British Telecommunications plc v One in a Million* [1999] FSR 1

In this case before the English Court of Appeal, the plaintiffs succeeded in
establishing passing off and threatened passing off by the defendant. The
defendant had registered a series of well-known trade marks such as *Marks and
Spencer, Ladbrokes, Sainsbury, Virgin, BT* and *Cellnet* in domain names. The Court
of Appeal found that the registrations of the domain names were 'instruments
of fraud' and that any future use would be passing off. The Court found that
there was a clear intention to fraudulently use the names and that even if such
use was in relation to dissimilar goods or services, such use without due cause
would be detrimental to the reputation of the plaintiff. The Court of Appeal
found that the warehousing of domain names could amount to use for the
purposes of passing off as internet users would be confused when consulting
with the 'WHOIS' directory to find that the domain names are not registered
with the plaintiff.

This approach has come in for some criticism. If an Internet user was to enter
the website and find material that made it clear that the website was in no
way related to the trade mark holder, it is possible that confusion could be
avoided. The Court of Appeal, however, took the view that a user would be
likely to visit the 'WHOIS' directory for the domain name to ascertain who the
owner would be. While the decision was a welcome one in terms of policy, the
Court of Appeal's rationale behind the decision may be open to further scrutiny. Interestingly, the domain names in this case were a mixture of both gTLDs
and the ccTLD 'co.uk'.

### *Efax.com Inc v Oglesby* [2000] Masons CLR 28

This case concerned an application for an interlocutory injunction by efax.com against efax.co.uk. Efax provided a service to subscribers, which involved the conversion of fax messages to e-mail. The defendant provided the same services, with the difference being that he charged subscribers for the service. After an offer by the claimant to purchase the domain name was rejected, it brought proceedings for an interlocutory injunction. The defendant cross claimed for strike out and summary judgment, claiming that the word 'efax' was descriptive of and generic when used in relation to any service offering fax to e-mail services.

The court held that there was 'considerable force' in the submission that the word 'efax' was essentially descriptive in nature but it did not mean that the claim would inevitably fail at trial and therefore refused the defendant's application for strike out or summary judgment. In relation to the interim injunction, the court held that there was a serious issue to be tried and when weighing the balance of convenience, considered the extent to which confusion would occur if the injunction was not granted. Parker J held that any confusion which was likely to take place would be as a result of the descriptive nature of the domain name, as opposed to any misrepresentation by the defendant.

### *Easyjet Airline Co Ltd v Dainty (t/a easyRealestate)* [2001] EBLR 104

In this case, the claimant was the well-known, low-cost airline in the UK. The advertising for easyJet and its associated companies is a distinctive bright orange background with white lettering, with 'easy' appearing in lower case and the first letter of the next part of the word appearing in upper case. The defendant claimed he chose the domain name easyrealestate.co.uk as the domain name for a cut-price Internet estate agency he planned to run.

The defendant argued that the claimant should not be entitled to appropriate the word 'easy', and although the court agreed with this position, found for the claimant on the basis of the overall look of the website, which mirrored that of the claimant's. Given that the only company the defendant appeared to have approached in relation to his estate agency proposal was the claimant, the court did not find credible his claim that he was not aware of the claimant's design. Therefore, following the same approach as the Court of Appeal in One in a Million, the court concluded that although the name easyrealestate. co.uk was not inherently liable to lead to passing off, the overall appearance of the site was such that its use would probably lead to passing off and therefore ordered the transfer of the domain name to the plaintiff.

### *Phones4u Ltd v Phone4u.co.uk and others* [2006] EWHC 2355 (Ch), para 132

Here, the plaintiff operated a chain of shops in the UK called 'Phones4u' and they also operated a website phones4u.co.uk. The defendant registered a website with the address phone4u.co.uk. The only difference between the two addresses being the absence of an 's' from the defendant's address. Thus, the Court could not see how there could be any realistic use of phone4u.co.uk without causing deception.

*Tesco Stores Ltd v Elogicom Ltd and another* [2006] EWHC 403 (Ch)

In this case before the English High Court, the plaintiffs succeeded in establishing that the use of domain names similar to their trade marks constituted trademark infringement. The plaintiff entered into an arrangement with an organisation called TradeDoubler under which other websites would sign up as affiliates and display an advertisement or panel on their sites as a direct link to the plaintiff's sites. Affiliated websites get a commission for each successful click-through. This commission is paid by the plaintiff to TradeDoubler and is then passed on to the affiliate.

The defendant was one such affiliate who registered over a dozen domain names similar to those of the plaintiff's. Therefore, if a potential shopper guessed the Internet address of the plaintiff, but the address was actually one of the defendant's registered domains, the browser would link the user to the plaintiff's real site but the TradeDoubler software would register the user as coming via the affiliated domains, triggering a commission payment to the defendant.

Although this meant that potential customers were not being diverted from the plaintiff's sites, it did mean that the defendant was getting paid commissions for domain names it had not registered through the Trade Doubler program. The UK High Court found that the defendant used in the course of trade, a series of signs (being the domain names), each being similar to the trade marks registered by the plaintiff and each being used in relation to services identical with or similar to those for which the trade marks were registered. Furthermore, the signs were used in circumstances where there existed a likelihood of confusion on the part of the public, including the likelihood of association of the defendant's services with the plaintiff's registered trade marks.

### (c) United States

*e-cards.com v ecards.com* (reported in *E-Commerce Law and Policy*, Vol. 2, Issue 5, May 2000)

In this case, e-cards.com was awarded US$4 million against the Canadian company ecards.com even though the defendant had a US trade mark. The case was based on unfair competition and was decided by a jury in the US District Court in San Francisco. The plaintiff had launched its website in 1995 and the Canadian defendant had launched its website in 1998. Both websites provided online greeting cards.

## 11.7.9   ADOPTING A STRATEGY

While prevention might well be better than cure, the infinite permutations and combinations of domain names which may be registered by a potential cybersquatter make it commercially unrealistic to register all domain names that could be relevant to a business. Similarly, the intellectual property portfolio and budgets of companies will vary widely so no one trade mark and domain name strategy fits all. However, all organisations should put in place a portfolio of its trade marks and domain names which should be updated regularly.

Renewal fees should be paid, and to this end it is important to maintain up to date contact details with each registry.

In light of this, an organisation should identify particular brand and company names which are strategically important to its business. The organisation should conduct appropriate trade mark and Internet searches for identical and similar names before committing expenditure to marketing the brand name.

Where infringement is identified, it may be commercially sensible to reach an early settlement with the owner of the domain name. Any such settlement should be based on an undertaking agreeing not to register similar names and any settlement should be confidential. If the organisation decides to pursue a cybersquatter, it should be aware of the potential public relations issues which can arise when the dispute becomes public. For example, when the proprietor of the children's character *Pokemon* pursued the registrant of the domain name pokey.org, it received negative publicity as the domain was held by a young child running a fan site. Organisations should monitor the Internet for obvious exploitation of their trademarks or domain names without necessarily pursuing every possible infringer.

Once a domain name has been registered, the registrant should establish a legitimate right to use the name and commence use as soon as possible.

If a decision is taken to pursue a cybersquatter, the trade mark owner should take advice on the following issues:

(a) Who are the parties to the dispute? For example, can the registrant be identified and should the domain registry be joined as a party to the proceedings?

(b) What is the appropriate forum? Court, UDRP or another alternative dispute resolution mechanism?

(c) What is the potential damage to the organisation? Will litigation dispose of such potential damage or merely raise publicity in favour of the respondent?

(d) In correspondence with the cybersquatter, any evidence of an attempt to sell the domain name by the registrant can assist in establishing bad faith under the UDRP.

(e) Groundless threats should be avoided. For example, under s 24 of the Trade Marks Act, 1996, where a person threatens another with proceedings for infringement of a registered trademark and the threats are found to be unjustifiable, a court may award damages in respect of any loss sustained by the threat.

## 11.7.10 CONCLUSION

While domain names and trade marks share many of the same characteristics, it is important not to presuppose that existing trade mark rights will prevail in the event of a dispute with a domain name holder. A separate domain name jurisprudence is emerging which, while containing many of the ingredients of traditional trade mark and passing off disputes, does present new challenges for those competing for a unique Internet address.

## 11.8 Managing Employee and Contractor Use of E-mail, Internet and Computer Systems

As a result of the proliferation of e-mail and Internet as essential business tools, it is becoming increasingly common for solicitors to receive instructions in respect of a variety of related legal issues. Typically, you may be asked to advise a company who has uncovered an employee abusing the company's e-mail system for personal gain, such as e-mailing confidential information out of the organisation. Other common examples would include on-site computer contractors who make unauthorised use of the company's computer software or employees viewing or disseminating unsuitable content over the Internet. This section looks at the legal remedies available in the most common situations.

### 11.8.1 E-MAIL

Companies, who provide e-mail access to employees face a difficult decision in balancing a number of competing interests. In the same way as few companies would prohibit limited personal use of the office telephone system, most employers similarly do not wish to appear to be draconian in their views regarding personal use of e-mail. However, unlike telephone communications, the ease and global reach of e-mail does create added legal risk to the organisation. This has to be balanced against the commercial value that e-mail communications brings to the organisation and the need for employers to trust that their employees will act responsibly.

E-mails sent by employees, whether internally or externally, can often cause offence. Jokes, inappropriate material and graphic pictures are easily transmitted to multiple recipients and these can cause offence and possibly result in litigation between employees or, more frequently, against the employer.

In this context, it is worth pointing out that under the provisions of the Employment Equality Acts, 1998–2004 sexual harassment is broadly defined to include any act or conduct including 'the production, display or circulation of written words, pictures or other material'. Under the Act an employer is liable for acts done by employees, including sexual harassment. Furthermore, harassment on a number of other grounds is prohibited under the Act. For example, the sending of an e-mail that is construed by the recipient as blasphemous could amount to discrimination under the 1998–2004 Acts for which an employer could be liable.

All employers should have an Acceptable Usage Policy in respect of e-mail and Internet use and access to computer systems and inappropriate use of e-mail should be specified to lead to activation of the organisations' disciplinary procedures.

## 11.8.2 INTERNET ACCESS

Most companies provide some level of Internet access to staff for business purposes. In addition, the Internet can be a useful time-saving device for employees who, for example, wish to do their banking online rather than leave the office for this purpose. The commercial reality is that the Internet is widely used for web surfing unrelated to business, for example, searching for cheap holiday deals or finding accommodation. Excessive web surfing during working hours can represent a significant difficulty for employers and leads to loss of productivity.

There has been no shortage of reported cases in relation to employee and contractor misuse of Internet and e-mail facilities. While the issues here can be complex, employers should ensure that their Acceptable Usage Policy in relation to internet and e-mail is properly incorporated into the employment relationship with employees. Technical safeguards should complement any legal policies which should be implemented fairly. Internal and remote access to systems by employees, contractors and tele-workers should be monitored so as to ensure that company policies are being maintained.

It is unlikely that the use of the Internet for unauthorised purposes will amount to a sufficient reason for dismissing an employee without notice and prior warning in the absence of a clear written statement to this effect in the company's policy. An exception to this perhaps would be a situation where an employee was using the company's facilities to download obscene material such as pornography. The penalties in the Child Trafficking and Pornography Act, 1998 are severe and where an employer suspects or becomes aware of any access to child pornography (which is very widely defined) via the organisation's computer systems, the matter should be referred to the computer crimes division of the Garda Siochána in Harcourt Street.

## 11.8.3 VIRUS DISSEMINATION

The primary source of computer viruses arises where certain types of files are downloaded from the Internet or attached to e-mails. The more deadly viruses have a dramatic global effect causing temporary loss of business and profitability within a very short time. Apart from the necessity of having virus checking software packages installed on a computer system, employees should be reminded in the Acceptable Usage Policy that they should exercise caution in opening e-mails from unknown sources, particularly if they have any suspicion over the integrity of the source.

## 11.8.4 CONFIDENTIALITY

E-mails can be sent with relative ease compared to other means of correspondence such as letter and fax. As a result, there is greater scope for sending confidential information to persons other than the intended recipient. To protect against the situation where sensitive information ends up in the wrong hands, the Acceptable Usage Policy should point out to employees that they should always double-check the addresses of their external e-mails.

Furthermore, it is commonplace now for external e-mails to have a template added which provides that the information being transmitted is confidential and if received in error by a person other than the intended recipient its contents should not be disclosed.

## 11.8.5   DISCOVERY

In the context of litigation, all forms of electronically stored information (ESI) are now discoverable. ESI includes material held on e-mail, data held on a storage system, and even data stored in text messages and personal digital assistants. In a recent case, *Dome Telecom v Eircom* [2007] IESC 59, the Supreme Court held that the courts, as part of the discovery process, have the power to order a party to analyse data in their possession (in this case on a database) and to produce a report containing that information. In light of the increased burden on those from whom discovery is sought, companies would be well advised to adopt a document storage and retention policy to cover both hard copy and electronic documents.

## 11.8.6   INTELLECTUAL PROPERTY RIGHTS

Files downloaded by employees from the internet or received as an attachment to e-mails will usually have some level of intellectual property rights ('IPRs') attaching to them. As a result, employees can easily unlawfully copy software or copyrighted material and use it or transmit it in contravention of the holder of the IPRs' legal rights. Once again, employers could become liable for such actions on the part of their employees.

## 11.8.7   DISCRIMINATION

The Employment Equality Acts, 1998–2004 contain a prohibition on discrimination which is defined as less favourable treatment of an individual based on one of the following grounds:

(a)   gender;

(b)   marital status;

(c)   family status;

(d)   sexual orientation;

(e)   religion;

(f)   age;

(g)   disability;

(h)   race; and

(i)   membership of the travelling community.

The Acts provide for the vicarious liability of employers in relation to breaches by employees. The Law Society manual on *Employment Law*, deals in greater detail with this legislation.

## 11.8.8  MONITORING STAFF

In order to eliminate, or at least reduce, unauthorised e-mail use and Internet activity in the workplace, it is obviously desirable for companies to have facilities in place to monitor staff use of company equipment. Monitoring also has the effect that it enables employers to effectively deal with misuse by staff through the disciplinary procedures. In this regard it is possible to randomly review a company's e-mail traffic and also to log Internet activity for the purpose of detecting excessive use or whether employees are visiting inappropriate sites.

In examining the legality of monitoring and surveillance by employers, it is important to acknowledge two competing rights. These are the implied right of an employee to privacy and the right of an employer to protect its legitimate business interests.

Any attempt to introduce a form of covert monitoring or surveillance in the workplace is likely to encounter resistance from trade unions and/or employees. It is therefore vital that any monitoring of e-mail and Internet usage is done in a fair and reasonable manner. The most effective way of achieving this is by implementing a clearly worded workplace policy.

Employees should be required to consent to the introduction of such a policy by acknowledging their consent to and understanding of the contents of the policy. In light of the Electronic Commerce Act, 2000, this consent can be given electronically.

There is no legislation applicable in Ireland that deals with the area of e-mail/ Internet monitoring. However, the provisions of the Data Protection Acts, 1988 and 2003 do have application in this area. One of the principles contained in s 2 of the Act is that data must be obtained and processed fairly. Therefore, unless employees have a clear understanding that e-mail is for business use only, to displace an employee's right to privacy the Office of the Data Protection Commissioner takes the view that it is necessary to obtain express consent to monitoring e-mails.

## 11.8.9  EUROPEAN CONVENTION FOR THE PROTECTION OF HUMAN RIGHTS AND FUNDAMENTAL FREEDOMS (THE 'CONVENTION')

In the recent case of *Copland v United Kingdom* ([2007] ECHR 253) the European Court of Human Rights ('ECHR') ruled that a college had violated an employee's right to respect for her private life and correspondence under Art 8 of the Convention, by the way in which it monitored her telephone calls, e-mail correspondence and Internet use. Case law has established that telephone calls from business premises attract rights of privacy and fall within the recognised notions of 'private life' and 'correspondence'. It followed logically that e-mails and Internet usage should also be similarly protected.

The ECHR found it to be of particular significance here that the employee had been given no warning that her communications and Internet usage would be monitored. The Court concluded that the collection and storage of personal information relating to her telephone, e-mail and Internet usage, without her knowledge, amounted to an interference with her right to respect for her private life and correspondence, in breach of the Convention.

The Court reasoned that:

- the fact that the data might have been legitimately obtained by her employer (in the form of telephone bills) was no bar to finding an interference with rights guaranteed under the Convention; and

- the storage of personal data relating to the private life of an individual also fell within the application of the Convention.

It was irrelevant that the data held by her employer was not disclosed or used against her in disciplinary or other proceedings.

The Convention was implemented in Ireland in the form of the European Convention on Human Rights Act 2003 (the 'HRA'). Therefore, employees can now pursue actions for alleged breaches of the HRA through the Irish courts. In light of this case, employers wishing to monitor their employees should be clear about the purpose for so doing and be satisfied that the particular monitoring arrangement is justified by real benefits that will be delivered. Furthermore, employees should be made aware of the nature, extent and reasons for any monitoring, unless (exceptionally) covert monitoring is justified.

## 11.8.10 DRAFTING AN ACCEPTABLE USAGE POLICY

Most businesses in Ireland that have a human resources section have a wide range of workplace policies to deal with all aspects of the employment relationship, for example, disciplinary procedure; grievance procedure; equal opportunities policy and confidentiality policy.

Organisations take varying approaches to the use of company e-mail and Internet facilities. However, some of the key points to be contained in a typical Acceptable Usage Policy might be summarised as follows:

(a) The extent (if any) to which e-mail may be used for private purposes. Some companies tolerate limited personal use or allow personal e-mail accounts so that the company's name is not associated with personal messages. However, the company's technical ability to monitor such accounts is limited.

(b) E-mail may be accessed and intercepted by company managers and the IT department to review all messages which are sent and received on the e-mail system for whatever purposes.

(c)    Internet use is only for business-related activities and web-surfing for personal use is prohibited. If limited personal use of e-mail and Internet is tolerated by the company, the policy should lay down the ground rules as to the extent of permitted use, prohibited categories of sites etc.

(d)    Do not send e-mails which are obscene or may cause offence or annoyance to others. The downloading of certain types of pornographic or obscene material from the Internet is a criminal offence for which one may be prosecuted.

(e)    Staff should be careful to ensure that any software, files or any other documentation is not copied or retransmitted in breach of copyright or other intellectual property rights.

(f)    By sending an e-mail message the company may be contractually bound and therefore it should always be ensured that the sending of information via e-mail is authorised by the appropriate senior personnel.

(g)    Always double check the addressees of external e-mails.

(h)    Personal data contained in e-mails and by which a person may be identified may be accessed as of right by those persons under the Data Protection Acts, 1988 and 2003, the Freedom of Information Act, 1997 and in the context of discovery.

(i)    Never open an e-mail or an e-mail attachment from an unknown source unless certain as to the integrity of the source.

(j)    Any breaches of the e-mail or Internet policy may lead to disciplinary action up to and including dismissal.

## 11.8.11  CONCLUSION

This chapter merely outlines of some of the issues that arise in the area of Internet and e-mail use and abuse. The Law Society manual on *Employment Law* contains a more detailed consideration of much of the relevant legislation. Similarly a company's ability to obtain injunctive relief is be covered in the Law Society manual on *Litigation*.

# CHAPTER 12

# COMMERCIAL LENDING

## 12.1    Introduction

The array of legal issues which could arise in the giving of money on a temporary basis between businesses is potentially vast, but the issues which arise on a day-to-day basis tend to be predictable, if not always capable of precise determination. This chapter endeavours to highlight these common issues, some of the pitfalls for those unfamiliar with the lending process and the main registration matters without which the taking of security may become, in a legal sense, meaningless. The main focus is on companies borrowing from, and granting security to lending institutions.

The chapter confines itself to situations where the lender of the money is a financial institution. Intra-group lending is common, but tends to be surrounded by such informality that solicitors are often not part of the process. Nevertheless, issues of permissible borrowing (particularly in the context of financial assistance) may arise in the intra-group situation. Practitioners need to be alert to the legal consequences of proposed structures, even or perhaps particularly, when the client regards the matter as straightforward and internal.

The first part of this chapter deals with different types of borrower and a selection of financial facilities. The second part analyses different forms of security and the usual checks to be carried out when the borrower is a company incorporated under the Companies Acts, 1963–2006 (the 'Companies Acts'). The third part deals with registration issues. The fourth part examines the minefields of financial assistance and transactions, which may come within Part III of the Companies Act, 1990 ('CA 1990'). Finally, the fifth part outlines how company law may change.

## 12.2    Who is the Borrower?

It may seem trite to emphasise that the legal characterisation of the borrower will be crucial in deciphering the legal requirements to ensure that effective security is achieved. This review examines individuals, partnerships, companies, corporate entities and State boards. Each is examined in terms of capacity, authorisation and applicable legislation.

## 12.2.1 INDIVIDUALS

### 12.2.1.1 Capacity

An individual may do anything unless prohibited by law. If the borrower is an individual, the issues which may affect capacity are as follows:

(a) Is the person eighteen or older? (If not, the law relating to infant contracts will have to be analysed to make sure that the terms of the loan agreement will be enforceable);

(b) Is the person a bankrupt or capable of being made a bankrupt? (A search in the Bankruptcy Office and the Judgments Office will assist. If the transaction which is being funded is at less than market value, a declaration of solvency may be useful); and

(c) Is the person of sound mind? (As individuals become more asset rich and live longer, dementia and related matters are becoming factors in more cases.)

### 12.2.1.2 Authorisation

Individuals may authorise others to act on their behalf. A power of attorney is usually required to prove the authorisation in any borrowing transaction. Some matters are peculiarly within the knowledge of the individual. Because of this, most solicitors advising lenders would be very reluctant to accept, for example, a family home declaration made by an attorney.

### 12.2.1.3 Applicable law

As individuals may do anything unless prohibited by law, until recently, there was little to concern lenders in general applicable law. However, consumer legislation now means that dealing with individuals may often require more legal due diligence than needed when lending to a company.

The European Communities (Unfair Terms In Consumer Contracts) Regulations, 1995 (SI 27/1995) and the Consumer Credit Act, 1995 both circumscribe freedom of contract by imposing procedural and substantive obligations on a party dealing with a consumer, namely a person acting outside his trade, profession or business. Legal advisers to financial institutions lending to individuals constantly face the question of whether the individual borrower is a consumer. The Consumer Protection Code may also be relevant.

If so, the consequences for the documentation are fundamental. Most financial institutions have standard consumer credit documents, but some which only deal with business lending (as they see it) may not be aware of the possible impact of the consumer legislation and rely on their legal advisers to highlight any difficulties.

General domestic legislation, such as the Family Home Protection Act, 1976, may impact on commercial lending. Many sole traders live on the business premises, be it a farm, pub or shop. If the entire premises is given as security, then issues of spousal prior informed consent, guarantees, independent legal advice and value on any forced sale will have to be considered. Splitting the premises so that only the business portion is captured is not always feasible. The Consumer Credit Act, 1995 provisions in relation to housing loans would also require careful scrutiny in such a situation.

Given the reference to 'curtilage' in the Family Home Protection Act, any division of the property aimed at excluding the family home from the security is not guaranteed to be successful. If the loan is revolving (being drawn, repaid and drawn again), as will often be the case in small businesses where the loan is really filling cashflow gaps, the Supreme Court decision in *Bank of Ireland v Purcell* [1989] IR 327 necessitates ensuring family home and related legislation compliance each time the redrawing takes place. Each event is a new loan with new security amounting to a new conveyance for the purpose of this societal legislation.

There is one area where special rules have been created for individual borrowers. Floating charges are generally only available to companies. However, the Agricultural Credit Act, 1978 allows individual farmers to create floating charges on agricultural stock. Farming income tends to be seasonal with a high capital requirement to acquire stock or buy seed and then income coming in during another part of the year. The stocking and restocking in particular would be cumbersome if security had to be taken each time, so the floating charge is useful.

## 12.2.2 PARTNERSHIPS

### 12.2.2.1 Capacity

While the partnership legislation provides a framework for entities to come together with a view to profit, the law does not recognise the partnership as having any legal personality which is separate from the partners. Therefore, questions of capacity of partnerships are really questions about the capacity of each partner.

### 12.2.2.2 Authorisation

An analysis of the partnership deed and the partnership legislation will disclose who may act for the partnership. Often, one partner may bind all, but in some circumstances the lender requires all partners to sign regardless, so that there is no possibility of any subsequent dispute about authority.

### 12.2.2.3 Applicable law

The Partnership Act, 1890 is enabling, not mandatory. Parties are free to depart from the parameters set out. No separate legal entity is created and limited liability is not granted, so the law is comfortable with the partners deciding themselves how to regulate their venture. The Partnership Act, 1890 has provided a useful set of non-mandatory parameters for partnership activity.

Limited partnerships (under the Limited Partnerships Act, 1907) may give rise to limited liability, but only for passive partners. The 1907 Act is in addition to the general partnership law. The Investment Limited Partnerships Act, 1994 made some further changes, primarily to encourage collective investment schemes.

To avail of tax reliefs, partnerships became popular vehicles for investments in items as diverse as hotels, car parks, life policies and equipment. Successive Finance Acts have limited the tax efficacy of partnerships and so the frequency with which partnership structures will appear in financing transactions in the future has been substantially reduced.

## 12.2.3  COMPANIES

### 12.2.3.1  Capacity

Most commercial lending transactions involve companies borrowing. Most companies have been incorporated under the Companies Acts. As an artificial legal entity, a company may only do what the law permits. Before deciding what a company may do, the first question to answer is whether the company exists. In this regard, the following issues should be considered.

(a) The certificate of incorporation proves that the company was incorporated on a particular day—it does not guarantee ongoing existence. However, sometimes the promoters of a company seek to borrow before the company is incorporated, so checking that there is a certificate can be useful. The certificate will also confirm the company number. As a company may change its name, using the company number in documents such as a guarantee and a mortgage may assist in identifying the corporate borrower in spite of any subsequent name change.

(b) A company might be in legal limbo due to being struck off the register. The Companies Registration Office has been using its powers of strike off to encourage companies to file annual returns and accounts. Under the State Property Act, 1954 the assets of a company which has been dissolved by strike off vest in the Minister for Finance. Section 12(6) of the Companies (Amendment) Act, 1982 ('C(A)A 1982') permits the company, or indeed a creditor, to apply to the High Court for reinstatement of the company to the register. Once restored, the company is deemed by s 12(6) to have continued in existence as if it had never been struck off. The Registrar may restore the company if application is made within one year of strike off.

(c) A company may have been placed in receivership, under the protection of the court (examinership), or in liquidation.

A search in the Companies Registration Office is an important first step when dealing with a borrower which is a company. The information is not exhaustive or necessarily conclusive, but it may avoid subsequent embarrassment at completion if, for example, the company has been struck off.

The objects of the company are set out in the memorandum of association. Generally, borrowing and granting security are not regarded as objects, but rather as powers to be used to further the objects of the company. Therefore, matching the borrowing to a permissible business objective is important. Often, the objects will have been sourced from standard company memoranda, which as a matter of luck may or may not have objects which match the actual business. It is a simple matter to amend the memorandum to introduce appropriate objects, but if the deficiency is not spotted, the borrowing may be invalid and consequently the lender may be unable to recover the money lent.

Because incorporation as a limited company provides not only a separate legal entity but also limited liability, the legislation contains various protections so that this special privilege is not abused to the detriment of third parties. Two of the major issues which arise in this area, namely financial assistance and dealings with directors or connected persons, are considered in more detail below.

### 12.2.3.2 Authorisation

Because a company is an artificial entity, it necessarily has to deal with the world through others. The articles of association set out how the internal management is regulated. Usually, the board of directors will have day-to-day control. Sometimes the shareholders/members will have to consent, either because of a specific legislative requirement (e.g. CA 1990, s 29 for substantial property transactions) or because of bank policy (e.g. where there is a potential conflict of interest between a director's own affairs and those of the company). It is vitally important in the lending context to ensure that article 79 of Table A has been excluded from the articles of association of the borrowing company (article 79 is dealt with in more detail at **12.6.5**) as otherwise the directors' authorisation to borrow will be rendered practically worthless.

In addition, a company may appoint an attorney, although this usually only arises for transactions abroad.

### 12.2.3.3 Applicable law

The Companies Acts are undergoing extensive review. The Company Law Review Group continues its work. Its website, www.clrg.org, is worth checking from time to time to track progress of proposed legislative changes.

## 12.2.4 OTHER CORPORATE ENTITIES

While much commercial activity is carried on through companies, partnerships and sole traders, other legal forms of business organisation also exist. Specific legislation deals with friendly societies and cooperatives. Foreign corporates may operate branches in Ireland rather than establishing separate subsidiaries. The cooperative movement has been particularly successful in Ireland in the agriculture and agribusiness areas.

MURMA SMURFIT LIBRARY NATIONAL COLLEGE IRELAND

#### 12.2.4.1 Capacity

Sometimes the question of whether the co-op has the power to borrow, never mind how much it may borrow, may arise. As co-ops tend to have a large membership, changing the rules can be difficult and time consuming. Establishing the basic capacity of a co-op to enter into the proposed transaction has to be the first priority when dealing with a co-op borrower.

#### 12.2.4.2 Authorisation

Likewise, on authorisation the committee may have to go to the members to approve borrowing or the granting of security. If this is needed, there may be substantial notice periods required to convene a meeting of the members.

#### 12.2.4.3 Applicable law

Currently, the government is overhauling the legislation affecting cooperatives, and not before time. The Industrial and Provident Societies Acts and the Friendly Societies Acts belong to a different era, both temporally and commercially.

### 12.2.5 STATE BOARDS

Many State commercial enterprises are incorporated under the Companies Acts, e.g. Bórd na Móna plc. However, others which have separate legal personality(ies) are creatures of a tailor-made statute, e.g. the Electricity Supply Board. In the latter category, one must check the specific legislation to ascertain whether the body may borrow, what protection third parties are given in relying on a decision of the board or whatever the body is called, and whether any third party consent (often that of the Minister for Finance) is needed for the transaction to be effective.

## 12.3 Lending to a Company

### 12.3.1 DOCUMENTS

The certificate of incorporation, the memorandum and articles of association, a list of directors and a search in the Companies Registration Office provide the starting point. A discussion with the lender about the purpose of the loan from the bank's perspective helps clarify whether the reason is a legitimate object of the company.

The facility letter/letter of offer is checked to make sure that the security is capable of being put in place. Issues of independent legal advice may arise if a spousal guarantee is needed to take effective security. For example, a small business may not be able to offer sufficient security to satisfy the bank's requirements. The owner may be asked to give a personal guarantee backed by security on some personal assets, some of which may be in the joint names of that person and their spouse.

## 12.3.2 TYPES OF SECURITY

A company may create a fixed charge on property. A company may also create a floating charge on its general assets or a category of assets. A fixed charge would be the usual security on a building. A floating charge would be used for ancillary items or for categories where the items constantly change (e.g. the stock of the business). A fixed charge gives the best position to the bank as regards any consequences of enforcement. The main distinction with a floating charge is that the preferential creditors such as the Revenue Commissioners have priority before the floating charge but after the fixed charge.

Cashflow, the money being paid into a company by its customers, is very important to the financial health of a company. But these debts, which are due to the company, are constantly changing with new debts being created and old ones being paid off. Until the 1980s it was doubted whether a fixed charge could be taken on such receivables. In *Re Keenan Brothers Ltd (in receivership)* [1985] IR 401, the Supreme Court decided that an appropriately worded security on receivables could qualify as fixed. The Revenue Commissioners responded by getting special priority status inserted into the following year's Finance Act (Finance Act, 1986, s 115). Subsequent Supreme Court decisions are difficult to reconcile, with practitioners being left with the unsatisfactory and dangerous task of trying to anticipate the conclusions of a court which is reluctant to overrule its previous decisions and yet which does not always seem to adhere to *stare decisis*.

## 12.3.3 ASSETS AVAILABLE FOR SECURITY

Title documents are needed for property security. Sometimes banks will accept certificates of title from the solicitor acting for the borrower. This may raise difficult questions of responsibility. If the solicitor knows something which might be relevant to a decision on credit rating, must he disclose it to the bank? Few solicitors endeavour to clarify the nature of the task they are performing when giving certificates, even though arguably a duty of care is owed to the bank. As well as dealing with title and access matters, the identity of the property and the status of any authorisations, not just for the buildings and use but also for the business activity (such as an EPA integrated pollution prevention control licence), are relevant to the bank. After all, there is little point in getting the title right if the business cannot function because of failure to comply with applicable regulatory requirements.

If stocks and shares are being given then the nature of the security should be clarified. Will the shares be transferred into the name of a nominee company of the bank? Who will have the benefit of dividends, bonus shares and voting rights? Are the shares represented by a share certificate or have they been 'dematerialised' as part of the CREST paperless trading system? If the shares are not quoted on a Stock Exchange how does the bank expect to trade them? If there are restrictions in the articles of association on trading shares, can these be amended to enable the bank to sell without reference to the board of the company?

Sometimes confusion arises as to who is checking the insurance position. Banks will normally want their interest noted on property insurance policies and to ensure that appropriate levels of business risk insurance (e.g. for employer liability and public liability) are in place. Some banks insist on being named as recipients of any insurance proceeds in property policies to be certain that the proceeds of any claim come to the bank. The business risk policies may not seem relevant but a claim could wreck the financial viability of the borrower. The bank would prefer that the loan was repaid rather than having to enforce the security.

If any life policy is to be put in place, then early application by the assured is advisable. Occasionally, the due diligence, which the life assurance company does, turns up some factor requiring further investigation (e.g. a family history of a medical problem). Even having to do a medical examination may lead to unforeseen delays and tension if this is the only matter holding up drawdown of the facility.

A life policy in simple terms is a promise by the life assurance company to pay if a death occurs. The bank takes security by having the person entitled to the policy (not necessarily but usually the life assured) execute a security assignment to the bank. The bank (or its legal adviser) should:

(a)   notify the life company of the security interest; and

(b)   seek confirmation that no prior notices have been received, that the life company does not have any claim and that the policy will not be terminated without giving the bank notice (between fourteen and thirty days) so that the bank could try to keep the policy in force (e.g. by paying outstanding premiums).

## 12.4   Types of Facilities

### 12.4.1   OVERDRAFTS

Overdrafts are usually negotiated for a period of up to one year and are repayable on demand. These facilities are most suitable for customers with frequent fluctuation between debit and credit balances. Often the bank will require that an account with the benefit of an overdraft nevertheless has a credit balance for a minimum aggregate period (e.g. a month) during the year. If the customer cannot achieve this, then a longer term loan may be more appropriate.

### 12.4.2   TERM LOAN

Term loans comprise loans which are repayable by negotiated amounts over a period. As these loans are not repayable on demand (unlike overdrafts), the events of default which enable the bank to require early repayment are important. Term loan facilities usually require regular disclosure of financial information (whether in the form of management accounts or audited accounts or both), as well as ongoing covenants to ensure that the business continues to be run on a sound financial basis.

### 12.4.3   REVOLVING CREDIT FACILITIES

Revolving loans comprise loans which are rolled over after specified periods with an original or renegotiated maturity. Loans which are repaid may be drawn again. A typical money market revolving credit facility envisages the borrowing/rolling over of borrowings by a company for interest periods to be selected by the company subject to a bank veto. For example, a company will elect to borrow €1,000,000 for a period of six months. At the end of that period, the company may renew the loan for another period as selected by the company and agreed by the bank.

The bank borrows the money on the inter-bank market and then lends it on to the company with a margin for its profit together with certain expenses. These revolving credit facilities may be quasi-overdrafts or may be term loans. They may be demand facilities, without events of default, or may be term loans with events of default.

### 12.4.4   PROVISION OF GUARANTEES TO THIRD PARTIES

Financial institutions may provide guarantees, indemnities or undertakings to third parties at the request of a company. A typical example of such a guarantee would be a performance bond on a building contract or on a planning permission condition. The bank issues an undertaking to a third party such as the employer of the builder on a building contract or the local authority imposing conditions in a planning permission. If specified events occur (e.g. failure to complete the development permitted by a planning permission), then the bank must pay the specified sum of money. The bank will require a counter-indemnity from the company so that the bank can clearly recover from the company any such payments.

### 12.4.5   FACTORING

Factoring, strictly speaking, does not constitute a lending service by banks. However, companies that factor their debts to banks usually see factoring as a financial facility comparable to borrowing. Factoring, in practical terms, constitutes the offering by a company to a lender of an option whereby the lender may acquire the debts invoiced by the company for particular sums of money and those debts are paid to the lender rather than to the company. Effectively, the debts are sold in advance of their being paid. Factoring in the ordinary course of business is exempt from stamp duty.

### 12.4.6 LEASING

Leasing, again, whilst not constituting the giving by a bank of a loan, nonetheless enables companies to acquire assets by making periodic payments tapering down to nominal payments. The bank buys an asset and leases it for a primary leasing period which may be anything from two to eight years. After the expiry of the primary leasing period, a secondary leasing period for an indeterminate time proceeds, at the start of which the rental payment is reduced to a nominal amount. To all commercial intents and purposes (and from an accounting point of view), the asset then becomes the property of the lessee/company. Legally, however, it remains the property of the lender.

With the deregulation of commercial hire purchase on the enactment of the Consumer Credit Act, 1995, the legal need to avoid the option to purchase on the completion of the primary leasing period disappeared. As a result, many such transactions are now characterised as commercial hire purchases, with the lessee having the option to buy the asset for a nominal amount at the end of the primary period.

## 12.5 Types of Security

Why do banks require security? What do the buzzwords mean? What types of security are sought?

### 12.5.1 PURPOSE-PRIORITY ON INSOLVENCY

The purpose of a bank taking security is to ensure a quicker and more assured payout in the event that a company goes into receivership, examinership or liquidation. The priority set by CA 1963, ss 285 and 98 as amended is as follows:

(a) creditors secured by a fixed charge;

(b) preferential creditors (e.g. certain taxes, rates, redundancy payments, payments due to employees which rank *pari passu*);

(c) creditors secured by a floating charge;

(d) ordinary creditors;

(e) subordinated creditors (e.g. participators' loans specifically subordinated, e.g. for the purpose of obtaining an IDA grant);

(f)    (sometimes) preferential shareholders;

(g)    ordinary shareholders; and

(h)    (occasionally) deferred shareholders.

## 12.5.2    LEGAL TERMINOLOGY

### 12.5.2.1    Debenture

The term debenture has three meanings set out below:

(a)    'An instrument usually under seal, issued by a company or public body as evidence of a debt or as a security for a loan of a fixed sum of money, at interest. It contains a promise to pay the amount mentioned in it and is usually called a debenture on the face of it' (*Osborn's Concise Law Dictionary*).

(b)    In the context of borrowing by a company, the word debenture usually means a document which contains a covenant by the company to pay all sums due or to become due by the company to the lender and which contains a charge (fixed and/or floating) in favour of the lender.

(c)    On the money markets, a debenture usually means a debt security (whether secured or unsecured). Section 2(1) of CA 1963 states that 'debenture' includes debenture stock, bonds and other securities of a company whether constituting a charge on the assets of the company or not.

### 12.5.2.2    Mortgage

There is a distinction between a legal and an equitable mortgage:

(a)    A legal mortgage is a transfer of a legal estate or interest in land or other property for the purpose of securing the repayment of a debt. In the real property context, a mortgage transfers the land interest to the mortgagee. Mortgages are used for Registry of Deeds property.

(b)    An equitable mortgage is one which passes only an equitable estate or interest, either because the form of transfer or conveyance used is an equitable one, i.e. operates only as between the parties to it and those who have notice of it (such as an equitable mortgage by deposit of title deeds or an equitable mortgage of shares by deposit of the share certificates), or because the mortgagor's estate or interest is equitable, that is, it consists merely of the right to obtain a conveyance of the legal estate.

### 12.5.2.3    Charge

A charge is the form of security for the repayment of a debt or performance of an obligation consisting of the right of a creditor to receive payment out of some specific fund or out of the proceeds of the realisation of specific property.

In the real property context, a charge is taken on Land Registry property and is registered as a burden on the folio.

#### 12.5.2.4 Pledge

A pledge arises where goods or documents of title for goods are delivered by the pledgor to the pledgee to be held as security for the payment of a debt, or for the discharge of some other obligation. The subject matter of the pledge will be restored to the pledgor as soon as the debt or other obligation is discharged. Where a definite time for payment has been fixed, the pledgee has an implied power of sale upon default. If there is no stipulated time for payment, the pledgee may demand payment and in default thereof may exercise the power of sale after giving notice to the pledgor.

In the case of a pledge, delivery of possession may be actual or constructive. A pledgor of goods has only a 'special property' in them while a mortgagee has an absolute title to the goods subject to the right of redemption. A further distinction between a pledge and a mortgage is that a pledgee (unlike a mortgagee) cannot obtain a foreclosure but only has a right to sell the goods. A pledge is the transfer of possession—but not ownership—of a chattel as security for the payment of a debt or performance of an obligation. The chattel may be sold if the owner defaults.

This form of security is relevant in the case of items the ownership of which may be transferred by delivery.

#### 12.5.2.5 Hypothecation

Hypothecation is the creation of a charge on a chattel as security for payment of a sum of money where the property remains in the possession of the debtor.

#### 12.5.2.6 Lien

A possessory lien is the right to retain that which is in the possession of the person claiming the lien until the claim is satisfied. Possession is essential to the effective creation of a lien. The person claiming the lien must have acquired possession rightfully and possession must be continuous.

A lien is the right to hold the property of another as security for the performance of an obligation. A particular lien exists only as a security for the particular debt incurred (e.g. a garage holding on to a car pending payment of a repair bill), while a general lien is available as a security for all debts arising out of similar transactions between the parties (e.g. a solicitor having a lien on his client's papers to secure his costs).

A possessory lien (whether particular or general) is lost where the claimant loses possession of the goods, the amount claimed is paid, alternative security is taken or the lien is abandoned. A lien may be enforced only by right of retention. No claim may be made for storage or for any other expense to which the person exercising the lien may be put. There is no general right of sale.

Notwithstanding the old law that solicitors have a general lien, there has been an increasing tendency for solicitors being required to prove a particular lien. Sections 125 and 180 of CA 1990 have removed a solicitor's lien in so far as it relates to corporate books, documents and records, if the company is in liquidation or under court protection.

Common carriers have a lien in respect of the freight on goods carried. Innkeepers have a lien on most of the luggage and other property brought in to the inn. A person who, at the request of the owner, has done work and expended money on a chattel has a particular lien in respect of his claim.

### 12.5.2.7 Principal securities delivered by companies

*Floating charge over undertaking*

A floating charge usually constitutes a charge over all the assets of the borrower company as acquired from time to time. The company remains free to deal with its assets in the ordinary course of its business. The charge only becomes a fixed charge upon crystallisation. On the appointment of a receiver or liquidator, the floating charge is fixed on all assets in the ownership of the company at that time.

The main elements of floating charges include those set out below:

(a) *The covenant to pay.* This usually extends to cover all sums due or to become due whether as principal or as surety, whether alone or jointly with any person, company or other entity.

(b) *The charging clause or provision.* This will usually be a charge on 'all the undertaking property and assets of the company whatsoever and wheresoever present and future including its uncalled capital for the time being and goodwill'.

(c) *Negative pledge/restrictions on other charges.* There will usually be a restriction on the company creating any other charge ranking *pari passu* (equal) with or in priority to the floating charge. In the absence of such a provision, the company could create a fixed mortgage or charge on particular property in favour of another lender. This negative pledge restriction should be included on the Form C1 so that any subsequent lender searching in the Companies Registration Office would be made aware, not only of the existing floating charge, but also of the negative pledge restriction.

(d) *Continuing security/the rule in Clayton's Case.* The rule in *Clayton's Case* (1816) 1 Mer 572, stated that sums paid into a borrower's account go to reduce or extinguish the liability on foot of a security whilst subsequent payments out of the account create new advances not caught by the security. Therefore, this rule is specifically excluded if the charge is to constitute continuing security and is not to be satisfied by any interim repayments.

(e) *Further assurance and power of attorney*. The company will undertake to deliver such further documents as the lender may require to ensure that the charge created continues to be valid. It is usual also for the security document to contain a power of attorney by way of security, whereby the lender is authorised to do whatever is necessary in order to perfect the security and do other things in the name of the company.

(f) *Events of default and power to appoint receiver*. Events of default are essential in a term facility. The power to appoint a receiver is the most important practical power that a lender has to enforce its security.

### Mortgage/charge/equitable mortgage over land

A mortgage is created on unregistered property subject to the Registry of Deeds and a charge is created on registered property which is registered in the Land Registry. A charge on registered land constitutes a mortgage by deed for the purposes of the Conveyancing and Law of Property Act, 1881 (by virtue of the Registration of Title Act, 1964). Therefore, the holder of such a charge is entitled to exercise the statutory powers of sale set out in the Conveyancing Acts.

An equitable mortgage is created by the deposit on behalf of the company of relevant documents of title to property. Unusually, an equitable mortgage may be created by deed if the interest being mortgaged by the borrower company is an equitable interest only.

### Mortgage of plant and machinery

It is possible for a company to create a specific mortgage over its plant and machinery (as well as charging such plant and machinery in the general sense by way of floating charge). Frequently, such a document is described as a 'chattel mortgage'. This expression should not be confused with a chattel mortgage under the Agricultural Credit Act, 1978.

### Chattel mortgage under Agricultural Credit Act, 1978

It is possible for an individual, a company or for that matter any other entity to create a chattel mortgage in favour of a 'recognised lender' (most of the Irish licensed banks are recognised lenders) of 'stock' under the Agricultural Credit Act, 1978. Stock is agricultural produce or machinery used in processing or distributing it. This is dealt with in greater detail below. The chattel mortgage may include fixed and/or floating charges over such stock.

## 12.5.3 PARTICULAR ASSETS

### 12.5.3.1 Land including licensed premises

When taking security over land, it is usual for the memorandum of association of the company to be checked to see that the company has authority in its objects clause to acquire, hold, mortgage and dispose of land. The conveyancing procedures involved in taking a mortgage of land from a company do not differ greatly from those followed when an individual is creating a mortgage over land although there are extra registration requirements per the Form C1 which is referred to later. Formalities required for the purpose of taking mortgages over land are dealt with in the Conveyancing module of the Professional Practice Course to which you should cross-refer for necessary materials.

A company is entitled to hold a licence for the sale of intoxicating liquor although it has to be said that many district judges are happier to see a company's licence held in the name of an individual nominee of a company. The licence to sell intoxicating liquor is not a transferable asset.

Instead, it is usual for a collateral deed of covenant to be delivered to the bank by the licence holder, be it the company or the individual nominee. The covenantor undertakes to do everything to preserve the licence and to do everything necessary so as to vest the licence in the bank's nominee should the occasion arise on an enforcement of security.

### 12.5.3.2 Stock-in-trade

It is usual for the stock-in-trade to be charged by the floating charge in a debenture but not by any fixed charge. It is technically possible for stock to be charged by way of fixed charge, but then such assets would cease to be 'stock-in-trade' in the accepted sense as a specific release would be required every time the particular stock was sold. When representing a lender, it is worth finding out how much stock-in-trade is subject to reservation of title. Any receiver put in by the lender could not dispose of such property for the benefit of the company unless agreed by the owner retaining title.

### 12.5.3.3 Plant and machinery

Plant and machinery, if they are movable or if they are not substantial, will often be charged simply by the floating charge provisions of a debenture. However, in addition in cases of substantial machinery, e.g. valuable printing machines or packing machines, fixed charges, sometimes security in the form of a chattel mortgage, will be taken. It is important that details of the make or the manufacturer or supplier are obtained, together with a precise description of the items and details of the serial numbers. Sufficient information should be included in the mortgage clearly to identify the property.

Most importantly, a lender will have to satisfy itself that the items are not subject to any hire purchase or leasing agreements and that any reservation of title clauses in the contracts of supply have been waived. Alternatively, an auditor's certificate to this effect will be sought, or a letter from the supplier.

### 12.5.3.4 Ships

Ship mortgages are a particular discipline and art form in themselves. These must conform to a particular format and, when delivered, there is usually a collateral deed of covenant between mortgagor and lender. Fishing vessels are frequently mortgaged as security and appropriate specific covenants should be included in the deed of covenant.

### 12.5.3.5 Aircraft

Aircraft may be mortgaged by chattel mortgage in the same way as plant and machinery save that such chattel mortgages are likelier to be more 'big ticket' (in other words, of greater monetary value) than plant and machinery chattel mortgages. Section 122 of CA 1990 clarified that mortgages of aircraft or shares in an aircraft and ships must be registered under CA 1963, s 99. Charges on ships or shares in a ship were registrable under s 99. Section 122 of CA 1990 included, for the first time, an aircraft or share in an aircraft.

### 12.5.3.6 'Stock' (Agricultural Credit Act, 1978)

Stock is defined by the Agricultural Credit Act, 1978 (the 'Agricultural Credit Act'), as including:

- (a) animals and birds of every kind and the progeny and produce of such animals and birds;

- (b) insects and fish of every kind and the progeny and produce of such insects and fish;

- (c) agricultural crops (whether growing on or severed from the land);

- (d) trees (whether growing on or severed from the land);

- (e) any product derived from any of the foregoing; and

- (f) machinery, implements, vehicles, fixtures, fittings and materials used in or for the production, manufacture, processing, preparation for sale or marketing of any agricultural or fishery produce.

Agribusiness is exceedingly important in Ireland and it is conceivable that all of the assets of a company, other than its land, could constitute 'stock' within the meaning of the Agricultural Credit Act. It may be worthwhile for a lender to put in place this form of security rather than a standard debenture and charge. There are certain powers given to a chattel mortgagee, such as the right of inspection, the making of an inventory and the possibility of crystallising a floating charge before the appointment of a receiver, specifically under the terms of the Agricultural Credit Act.

### 12.5.3.7 Shares and debentures

It is common for lenders to take security over stocks and shares. More often than not, security will be taken over quoted shares and debentures which are securities of public companies. Security over shares in unquoted companies is less attractive because of the lack of a ready market for sale and, in private companies, restrictions on transferability. However, share security may be taken to enable a subsidiary (and not just its assets) to be sold on an enforcement. Shares may be fully or partly paid up but it is unusual for partly-paid shares to be offered as security for a loan or for that matter to be accepted by lenders as security. The three principal categories of shares and debentures to be considered in the context of taking security are set out below.

### (a) Bearer shares/debentures

The title to bearer securities passes by delivery and share warrants can be fully negotiable instruments.

### (b) Registered shares/debentures

Most securities are 'registered', i.e. the names and addresses of the holders are entered in a register which shows the amount of stock or the number of shares which they hold. As proof of such registration, a share certificate or stock certificate is issued. However, the advent of the CREST system of dematerialised shares has changed this for certain quoted companies.

### (c) Inscribed shares/debentures

Inscribed stock involves the persons named being entered in the inscription books of the registration authority. No certificate is supplied but instead a stock receipt or certificate of inscription is issued. This stock receipt (unlike a stock certificate) does not have to be produced when the stock is sold. The stock is transferable in the books of the registration authority on the personal attendance of the holder or of a duly appointed attorney, who is normally a solicitor or banker.

Therefore, the transfer of inscribed stock to a lending institution would require personal attendance with the registration authority. This kind of stock is common enough on the continent but is rare in Ireland. However, the advent of the CREST system of dematerialised shares has changed this. CREST allows for the paperless ownership and trading of shares, which are listed on certain Stock Exchanges.

The usual forms of securities offered as security to lenders are as follows:

    (a)    debenture stock (a loan to the company which may or may not be secured on the assets);

    (b)    preference shares/stock (these will usually rank before the ordinary shares with regard to payment of dividend and capital);

    (c)    ordinary shares/equity capital (these shares constitute the 'real' ownership of a company); and

    (d)    deferred shares (these are rarely issued these days and would rank last for payment of dividend and capital).

Stocks and shares in quoted companies have certain advantages as security:

    (a)    these are easy to value;

    (b)    there are few formalities when transferring them;

    (c)    these may easily be sold; and

    (d)    there is full negotiability in the case of bearer securities.

Unquoted shares have their own disadvantages. There may be difficulty in valuing the shares or in finding a purchaser. Even if the bank finds a purchaser, it may be that the directors in the exercise of the power conferred on them by the articles may decline to register a transfer in the lender's favour or in favour of the lender's nominee or purchaser. In certain cases, the articles of association may prevent the bank taking a legal mortgage over the shares in the first place.

### CREST (uncertified securities)

The Companies Act 1990 (Uncertified Securities) Regulations, 1996 (SI 68/1996) came into effect on 24 January 1997. The Regulations provide for the holding of shares of a class in uncertificated form if they are to be a 'participating security' for the purposes of the Regulations. On a voluntary basis, publicly quoted companies may apply to CRESTCO Limited (a company established under the Regulations to operate the CREST system in Ireland) for admission of their shares as participating security. It is not possible to take an equitable deposit over uncertificated marketable shares (because there are no share certificates).

### 12.5.3.8 Cash, debts receivable

It is possible to take a fixed charge over credit balances at a bank or to take fixed charges over debts receivable.

In the case of charges over cash, the House of Lords in *Morris v Agrichemicals* [1997] 3 WLR 909 has confirmed that it is possible for a bank to obtain a charge over a credit balance of a borrower with itself. The bank will often look to obtain rights of set off against that deposit in addition to the banker's right of set off. As to fixed charges on book debts, the provisions of the Taxes Consolidation Act, 1997, s 1001 require careful consideration. The section was introduced to defeat the priority that fixed charges over book debts were obtaining, ahead of the Revenue Commissioners as a preferential creditor. The provisions enable the Revenue Commissioners to serve notice on the holder of a fixed charge over book debts requiring that holder to pay to the Revenue sums received on foot of any security subject to certain rules. There is limited protection to lenders if a copy of the Form C1 is sent to the Collector General (currently at Sarsfield House, Limerick) within twenty-one days of the creation of the charge.

### 12.5.3.9 Goods and bills of lading

In the case of exports of goods, a bank may be required to open a letter of credit to facilitate the transaction. The bank will take a pledge of the relevant goods upon receipt of the documents of title to those goods which, in certain contracts, will typically be an invoice, an insurance policy and a bill of lading.

A bill of lading is a document signed by the ship's owner or by the master or other agent of the ship's owner which states that certain goods have been shipped on a particular ship and sets out the terms on which those goods have been delivered to and received by the ship's owner. It is generally used when the goods shipped form part only of the intended cargo of the ship (a charterparty being employed if the goods form the complete cargo). On its being signed, it is handed to the shipper. A bill of lading has three purposes which are that:

(a) it is a receipt for the goods shipped containing the terms on which these have been received;

(b) it is evidence of the contract for the carriage of the goods; and

(c) it is a document of title to the goods.

Therefore, security over such goods would be created by a pledge of the bill of lading.

From a strict legal point of view, there is no necessity for any written evidence of a pledge. In practice, however, a pledgee usually obtains the pledgor's signature to a document called a 'letter of pledge'. A separate letter of pledge may be executed in respect of each transaction of a pledgor or the pledgor may be asked to execute a general letter of pledge. A general letter of pledge will contain provisions such as those set out below:

(a) The pledgee will have a pledge upon all goods delivered by the pledgor, or by his agents, into the possession of the pledgee and upon all bills of lading and other documents of title deposited by the pledgor, or his agents, with the pledgee or its agents.

(b) The pledgor will agree that the goods and documents of title are pledged as a continuing security for the payment of all sums owed by the pledgor either solely or jointly with any other person or persons, whether on balance of account or on guarantees or in respect of bills of exchange and including interest and other banking charges.

(c) The pledgor will agree that in the case of a default on demand, the pledgee may sell the goods or any part thereof.

(d) The pledgor will agree to keep the goods fully insured in such office as the bank may approve.

(e) The pledgor will undertake to pay all rent and other expenses incidental to the warehousing of the goods.

(f) The pledgee will look for an indemnity from the pledgor in respect of any default or neglect by any agent of the pledgor.

## 12.5.4 SUPPORTING SECURITY

### 12.5.4.1 Guarantee

*Meaning*

A contract of guarantee is a contract by one person to be answerable for the debt or default of another. Under the Statute of Frauds (Ireland), 1695, a guarantee must be in writing.

There are three parties concerned and two contracts:

(a)   the first contract involves the principal creditor ('lender') and the principal debtor ('borrower');

(b)   the contract of guarantee involves the principal creditor (lender) and the guarantor or surety. The guarantee is a collateral security and there must be primary liability in some person other than the guarantor, the guarantor being liable only secondarily, i.e. if the principal debtor (borrower) does not pay.

An indemnity is different from a guarantee in that the person giving the indemnity is primarily liable on foot of the indemnity and there is no secondary liability. An indemnity is a more onerous obligation than a guarantee. Even though the principal may escape, the indemnifier remains liable. One distinction between a guarantee and indemnity is that, whereas a guarantee must be in writing, an indemnity need not be. In practice, frequently in a guarantee document, there is an indemnity to require payment by the guarantor if the guarantee provisions in the guarantee fail. As with other contracts, the guarantee must be supported by consideration, unless under seal, but the consideration does not have to be expressed in the guarantee. Invariably, however, consideration is expressed in the guarantee and lenders are generally not happy to accept a guarantee without some consideration being expressed in it, even if it is under seal.

### Termination of liability of guarantor

The guarantor is a favoured debtor and may insist on rigid adherence to the terms of the guarantee. A guarantor's liability does not arise until the principal debtor has made default. Although only secondarily liable for the debt, it is not necessary for the creditor to request the debtor to pay or to sue the debtor before taking proceedings against the guarantor. It has been held that, in the absence of a specific provision to the contrary, a guarantor is discharged from liability under a guarantee in the following circumstances:

(a)   if the transaction is void as between the principal debtor and the creditor;

(b)   if the principal debtor is discharged or if the creditor releases the principal debtor from liability;

(c)   if there is any material variation of the terms of the contract between the creditor and the principal, e.g. allowing the principal debtor extra time to pay;

(d)   if there is any change in the consitution of the persons to or for whom the guarantee was given (e.g. changes in partnerships). This rule was embodied as far as partnerships were concerned in the Partnership Act 1890, s 18.

### Usual clauses found in guarantees

Most guarantees contain a clause permitting the creditor, without the consent of the guarantor, to vary the form of security, which it has in respect of the principal debtor's debt, and to grant the principal debtor extra time for payment.

The guarantee will also contain a clause whereby the guarantor undertakes not to protect himself by taking security from the principal debtor. The reason for this is to ensure that if the debtor becomes bankrupt and part of his liability is unsecured, his free assets will not be depleted to the detriment of the creditor as a result of charges created in favour of the guarantor.

The guarantee should also contain a clause indicating that the security will be a continuing security and that it will remain in full force until all obligations of the principal debtor have been discharged. This is inserted in order to exclude the operation of the rule in *Clayton's Case* (1816) 1 Mer 572. If the rule was not excluded, each sum paid into the principal debtor's account, in the case of a bank after the execution of the guarantee, would reduce the guarantor's liability, while each debit to the account would create a fresh advance for which the guarantor would not be liable.

The guarantor will be prohibited from suing the debtor in respect of any money paid on foot of the guarantee, until such time as the entire debt due to the creditor has been discharged in full. If this clause were not included, it could prejudicially affect the creditor.

The operative clause whereby the guarantor agrees to guarantee the debt usually contains a provision that the guarantor will pay the principal debt on demand. By inserting this provision, one may avoid the Statute of Limitations, 1957 running until such time as demand is made. For example, where a debtor has a running account with the bank for a number of years, this could be relevant. The guarantee should also contain a provision as to what will constitute the service of the demand and this will usually be contained in a notice clause.

As stated above, it is usual for provisions to be incorporated into the guarantee permitting the creditor and the principal debtor to vary the contract, even if the liability of the guarantor is thereby increased.

### Guarantees by partnerships

Unless it may be shown that the giving of guarantees is necessary for the carrying on of the business of a particular partnership in the ordinary way, one partner has no implied authority to bind the firm by executing a guarantee (Partnership Act 1890, s 5.) Therefore, unless it clearly appears from the partnership agreement that the giving of guarantee is part of the ordinary business of the firm, a creditor should either have the guarantees signed by all the partners on behalf of the firm or, alternatively, have a guarantee executed by one partner with the express written authority of the others.

*Guarantees by limited companies*

A company may not execute a guarantee unless it has the power to do so by virtue of its memorandum of association. In general, unless the company is a finance house, the guarantee will have to be in furtherance of some other objects of the company. One should look at the articles to check the provisions for proper execution. Unless there are provisions to the contrary, the guarantee may be executed under seal or under hand. Whichever method is followed, at the very least, a board resolution should be passed.

### 12.5.4.2 Assignment of life policy

Life assurance policies are frequently taken out by companies on key personnel. These life policies may be mortgaged by the company that has taken out the insurance. More usually the particular key individuals take out policies for the purpose of a financial transaction. The life policies are assigned to the lender by means of a deed of assignment. Failure to get a life policy organised is often a cause of delays in completing a lending transaction. If there is a life policy requirement, it should be acted on immediately to avoid delays arising for instance, due to the non availability of the medical report by the date the loan is due to be drawn down. A lender will require to be satisfied that the policy details are in order. The main relevant points would include:

(a) the life assured;

(b) the beneficiary under the policy—often the same as the life assured, but may be the borrower company or a spouse of the life assured. The assignment of the policy must come from the beneficiary of the policy;

(c) the amount of the policy; and

(d) the term of years of the assurance.

A life policy is a chose in action (property which cannot be reduced to physical possession). As with all charges over choses in action, the creditor/bank must protect its priority by giving notice of its security to the obligor, in this case the assurance company.

However, the rule that priority of an assignment is governed by the order of notice to the debtor is subject to the variation that the policy of assurance is equivalent to the title deeds of real property. Therefore, if the chargor is unable to produce the policy, this is a circumstance which puts the creditor/bank on enquiry. If the policy is held by an existing mortgagee, then failure to produce it would be constructive notice of the prior charge. A chargee with notice of a prior charge does not obtain priority even if he is the first to give notice to the debtor.

Just as in the case of stocks and shares, the charge over the policy may be either legal or equitable. However, notice to the assurance company is necessary in either case to preserve priority and protect the efficacy of the charge.

Life policies have certain advantages as security:

(a) After a number of years certain life policies will generally acquire what is called a surrender value which value will increase from year-to-year.

(b) A life policy may be easily realised, if the bank takes a legal mortgage of the policy. In this situation, the creditor is in a position to surrender the policy and obtain payment at the surrender value.

(c) The policy retains a relatively stable and generally increasing value provided the premiums are paid.

As against this, certain disadvantages should be borne in mind:

(a) the risk that the policy holder may be unable to pay future premiums;

(b) the risk that the policy may be vitiated by the assured's non-disclosure of all facts and circumstances affecting the risk;

(c) the risk that the policy holder may not have an insurable interest in the life assured (unlikely if the individual himself/herself has taken out the policy);

(d) the terms of the policy, e.g. medical exceptions on certain policies. Certain life assurance policies constitute accident policies only. Other types to be alert to include those which provide death benefit cover, and cover which reduces over time, e.g. mortgage protection policies.

A legal mortgage of a life policy is effected invariably by an assignment of the life policy. It is possible for an absolute assignment to be made of a life policy in favour of a lender. This may happen from time to time where the insurance policy itself has no surrender value. On completion of the relevant borrowing relationship the policy may simply be allowed to lapse.

However, usually there is a conditional assignment of the life policy, i.e. an assignment subject to redemption or repayment of the secured obligation. The deed of assignment contains an assignment of the assured's right to recover the policy money and notice of assignment is served on the assurance company. The notice to the assurance company binds the assurance company to pay the money on foot of the policy to the assignee. Notice also enables the creditor to acquire priority over earlier assignees who have not given notice to the assurance company, provided that the creditor had not received actual or constructive notice of the earlier assignment at the time when the creditor made the advance.

Non-production of the policy may amount to constructive notice of an earlier assignment and therefore the creditor should always insist upon production of the policy. The notice must be in writing. The notice must give the date and purport of the assignment and it must be addressed to the assurance company's principal place of business. It is usual practice to request the assurance company to acknowledge receipt of the notice by signing a duplicate notice and returning it to the lender.

An equitable mortgage of a life policy is also possible, but is not particularly common. Being a chose in action, no particular formality is necessary to create a mortgage of it. An equitable mortgage of a life policy may be created by an oral agreement between the parties or by a deposit of the policy accompanied by a written memorandum. A mortgage of this nature is perfectly valid as against the mortgagor's assignee or trustee in bankruptcy but it gives the mortgagee an equitable interest only. When the policy money becomes payable, the borrower company will require a discharge from the assured as well as from the mortgagee.

Equitable mortgages of life policies are rare, but if a creditor is content with this security, the debtor's signature to a memorandum of deposit should be obtained containing clauses to the effect that the security will be a continuing security, that he/she will pay the premiums when they become due, and that he/she will execute a legal mortgage when called upon.

Notice should be made to the assurance company of the equitable mortgage to protect the mortgagee's priority. If equitable mortgagees fail to give notice, their priorities are determined by the order of the dates of their respective equitable mortgages.

It will be unlikely that a second charge will be created over a life policy where the creditor holds the policy in its possession. However, where a second assignment is executed, the assignee should give notice thereof to the creditor/bank.

### 12.5.4.3 Collateral issues

Frequently, the controller of a company will create a charge over his/her individual property to support a guarantee or indemnity obligation. In these circumstances, it is important that the provisions of relevant family and consumer credit legislation are considered.

For example, if the managing director of a company is guaranteeing the company's borrowings and granting security over the family home his wife should obtain independent legal advice with regard to the transaction. The bank will need advice on whether this security amounts to a housing loan within the Consumer Credit Act, 1995.

### 12.5.4.4 Set-off

We discussed earlier the matter of set-off in the context of the ability of a company to create a charge over a cash deposit with a bank in favour of that bank. It is usual, in conjunction with the taking of security over companies (or for that matter on the opening of accounts of the companies in the case of certain banks), for 'Letters of Lien, Appropriation and Combination' to be signed on behalf of a borrowing company entitling the bank to combine accounts at will so that, particularly in the event of insolvency, it will be the net sum due by the company to the bank that must be repaid only, with any other sums due being written off against credit balances. CA 1990 amended C(A)A 1990 to provide that in the case of court examinations, banks were not entitled to exercise rights of set-off. C(A)(No 2)A 1999 restored the former position so that exercise of set-off between accounts of the same company is allowed again.

# 12.6 Secretarial Considerations and Requirements

Set out below are company documents and procedures which a lender's adviser will examine concerning a borrowing company.

## 12.6.1 INCORPORATION

The fact of incorporation of the company must always be proven. 'Does the company (still) exist (under its supposed name)' may seem a very basic question, but it is one which must always be addressed. Frequently, an anticipated change of name may not have occurred, and occasionally an intending borrowing company has been struck off the register for failure to deliver annual returns. In view of the practice of the Companies Registration Office, whereby companies that do not deliver annual returns are struck off the Register, the fact of nondissolution proved by an up-to-date company search will be required.

## 12.6.2 POWER OF THE COMPANY TO BORROW

A certified copy of the memorandum of association will be required, first so as to establish what the company's objects are and, second to ensure that there is a specific enabling power set out in the objects clause permitting the company to borrow money and, where relevant, to deliver security and/or to give guarantees in respect of the obligations of third parties such as subsidiary companies. A typical sub-clause in the objects clause permitting borrowing would be:

> To raise or borrow or secure the payment of money in such manner and on such terms as the directors may deem expedient and in particular by the issue of bonds, debentures or debenture stock, perpetual or redeemable, or by mortgage, charge, lien or pledge upon the whole or any part of the undertaking, property, assets and rights of the company, present or future, including its uncalled capital for the time being and goodwill and generally in any other manner as the directors shall from time to time determine and any such debentures, debenture stock or other securities may be issued at a discount, premium or otherwise, and with any special privileges as to redemption, surrender, transfer, drawings, allotments of shares, attending and voting at general meetings of the company, appointment of directors or otherwise.

### 12.6.3 POWER OF THE COMPANY TO DELIVER SECURITY

It is usual for the sub-clause in the objects clause of the memorandum of association which authorises borrowing to deal also with the delivery of security, as in the above example.

### 12.6.4 POWER OF THE COMPANY TO GIVE GUARANTEES

It is usual for there to be a separate sub-clause in the objects clause of the memorandum of association which authorises the giving of guarantees. The following is a typical example:

> To become surety for and to guarantee, support or secure whether by personal covenant or indemnity or by mortgaging or charging all or any part of the undertaking property and assets (present and future) uncalled capital and goodwill of the Company or all or any of such methods, and either with or without the Company receiving any consideration therefor, the performance of the obligations or the repayment or payment of the principal amounts of and premiums interest and dividends on any loans, stocks, shares, debentures, debenture stocks, notes, bonds or other securities of any person, authority (whether supreme, local, municipal or otherwise), firm or company, including (without prejudice to the generality of the foregoing) any body corporate which is for the time being the Company's holding company as defined by Section 155 of the Companies Act, 1963, or any statutory modification or re-enactment thereof or another subsidiary, as defined by the said Section, of the company's holding company or otherwise associated with the Company in business, including suppliers of goods to the Company, its holding company or any subsidiary thereof, as defined by the said Section.

### 12.6.5 DIRECTORS' POWERS TO EXERCISE THE COMPANY'S POWERS

The articles of association of the borrower company will be looked at especially to see if any amendment has been made to article 79 of Table A. Article 79 of Table A limits the amount that the directors may borrow to an amount equal to the nominal value of the issued share capital of the company, unless the company in general meeting authorises a higher amount of borrowing.

A typical article found in the articles of association of a private company, excluding article 79, would be as follows:

> The Directors may exercise all the powers of the Company to borrow money, and to guarantee, support or secure (whether by guarantee indemnity or otherwise) the obligations of third parties, and to mortgage or charge all or any part of its undertaking, property and assets (present and future), uncalled capital and goodwill in connection with such borrowing or guaranteeing,

and, subject to Section 20 of the Companies (Amendment) Act, 1983, to issue debentures, debenture stock and other securities whether outright or as security for any debt, liability or obligation of the Company or of any third party. Debentures, debenture stock and other securities may be made assignable free of any equities between the Company and the person to whom the same may be issued. Any debentures or debenture stock may be issued at a discount, premium or otherwise and with any special rights as to redemption, surrender, drawings, allotment of shares, attending and voting at general meetings of the Company, appointment of directors or otherwise.

In the case of public limited companies with a quote on one of the Stock Exchange markets, the articles disapply the provisions of Table A. There is, however, an article enabling the directors to borrow money, but limiting the amount to a particular multiple (usually three times) of the aggregate of the nominal share capital of the company and the consolidated reserves of the company and its subsidiaries. Occasionally a public limited company's auditors will be asked to confirm that such borrowing limits have not been exceeded in a particular transaction.

### 12.6.6 REQUIREMENT FOR ORDINARY OR SPECIAL RESOLUTION OF THE COMPANY IN GENERAL MEETING

An ordinary resolution approving borrowing, delivery of security or the giving of a guarantee is mandatory if the company's articles include regulation 79 of Table A and the amount to be borrowed or liability to be incurred exceeds the limits set out in that regulation, or if there is any similar restriction on the borrowing powers of the directors.

A special resolution approving borrowing, delivery of security or the giving of a guarantee needs to be passed by the company in general meeting if the provisions of CA 1963, s 60 apply to the proposed borrowing, delivery of security or giving of a guarantee. The provisions of s 60 are dealt with in **12.8.1–12.8.5**.

An ordinary resolution is usually required if CA 1990, s 29 dealing with substantial non-cash asset transactions is relevant. Section 29 is dealt with in **12.8.6.7**. Sometimes, in the case of transactions where a company is guaranteeing the obligations of third parties, lenders will seek the passing of a resolution of the company in general meeting noting that the giving of the guarantee is bona fide in the best interests of the company, noting some consideration received by the company for the giving of the guarantee, and resolving that the board of directors be authorised and directed to attend to the delivery of a guarantee. A typical resolution doing this would be as follows:

> A form of guarantee was produced to the meeting whereby the company would guarantee all sums due or to become due from [*holding company*] to [*bank*] without limitation. It was resolved that the giving of such guarantee by the company would be bona fide in the best interests of the company as a whole, the company receiving administration services from [*holding*

*company*] and for this and other reasons the meeting being unanimously of the opinion that the company would derive a benefit from the giving of the guarantee and such guarantee would be in connection with the obligations of [*its holding company*] and it was resolved that such guarantee as may be required by [*Bank*] be given and that the board of directors be and they are hereby authorised and directed to arrange for the execution and delivery of the proposed guarantee and any other matters arising in connection therewith.

## 12.6.7 RESOLUTION OF THE BOARD OF DIRECTORS

As a general rule, it may be said that in transactions where a company is borrowing itself and the objects clause and directors' powers permit it to do so, a lender will look for a resolution of the board of directors whereby the directors resolve to borrow the money and, if relevant, deliver the relevant security in accordance with their powers.

Where a document is to be a deed, it will be sealed in accordance with the provisions of the articles of association. Most companies either adopt regulation 115 of Table A or an article in similar terms whereby the seal is to be affixed on documents only by the authority of a resolution of the board of directors with the relevant document being signed by a director and countersigned by another director, the secretary or some other person appointed by the directors for the purpose.

## 12.6.8 COMPLETION OF A BORROWING TRANSACTION— DOCUMENTS TABLED/HANDED OVER TO LENDER'S SOLICITOR

### 12.6.8.1 Certificate of incorporation

The original certificate of incorporation, any certificate(s) of incorporation on change of name and an up-to-date Companies Registration Office search will be required so as the continued incorporation of the company under its purported name is seen to subsist.

The original certificate of incorporation and any certificates of incorporation on change of name will be required in connection with delivery of any charge document to the Land Registry.

### 12.6.8.2 Memorandum of association

A copy of the memorandum and articles of association certified as being a true copy of the current document incorporating all amendments will be required. Authentication of such a document under the Companies Acts may be effected by a director or the secretary.

### 12.6.8.3    Members' resolutions

If CA 1963, s 60 applies, a certified copy of the special resolution will be required together with evidence that the resolution has been delivered to the Companies Registration Office for filing. Most importantly, a copy of the relevant statutory declaration made under the provisions of CA 1963, s 60 must be furnished. A copy of the declaration must be delivered within twenty-one days of the giving of the financial assistance for filing to the Companies Registration Office.

In the event that reg 79 or a comparable article applies, a certified copy of the ordinary resolution approving the borrowing will be required. Likewise, if an ordinary resolution is obtained for general purposes only, for example, in the case of a guarantee by a company with a minority shareholder.

If CA 1990, s 29 is relevant, then a certified copy of the requisite resolution will be needed.

If CA 1990, s 34 is relevant, then a certified copy of the requisite resolution and proof of compliance with all other elements of s 34 (as revised by the Company Law Enforcement Act, 2001 (CLEA 2001)) will be required.

### 12.6.8.4    Directors' resolution

A certified copy of the resolution of the meeting of the board of directors approving borrowing/delivery of security/giving of guarantee will be required. As a general rule, a certified copy resolution will be signed by either the chairman or the secretary although the chairman should be the signatory in view of CA 1963, s 145(2).

### 12.6.8.5    Security documents

The following additional documents may be needed, depending on the security:

| | |
|---|---|
| Mortgage of land | All documents of title to land |
| Mortgage over plant and machinery | Auditors' certificate as to no reservation of title/HP or leasing |
| Charge over shares | Share warrant or share certificate memorandum of deposit executed incomplete stock transfer form |
| Assignment of life policy | Original life policy, letter confirming no lapse or cancellation of life policy, birth certificate of life assured (if age not admitted on the policy) |

### 12.6.8.6 Form C1 for security documents containing charges

Prescribed particulars of charges must be delivered to the Registrar of Companies (Companies Registration Office) within twenty-one days of the creation of a charge. If the security includes a fixed charge on book debts, then a copy should also be sent to the Collector General within the same twenty-one-day period.

### 12.6.8.7 Memorial of any security documents affecting any interest in land

If a mortgage of unregistered land is being created by a company, then a memorial of that mortgage will be needed. From July 2008, the memorial is being replaced with an application form. Even if a debenture contains merely a floating charge in general terms over the undertaking property and assets of the company, a memorial (or application form) of that debenture may be registered in the Registry of Deeds provided there is general charge wording.

### 12.6.8.8 Certificate of company secretary as to certain corporate details

It is common, on completion, to obtain a certificate from the company secretary certifying the identity of the directors, the secretary, the location of the registered office, including confirmation that no other charges have been executed, that no resolution has been circulated to put the company into receivership, liquidation or court examination and that no petition is pending to put the company into receivership, liquidation or court examination, that no judgment has been obtained capable of being converted into a judgment mortgage and that the company is not subject to any agreement, order or trust whereby its powers of borrowing or delivering security are in any way impaired. It is unclear what redress a lender will obtain from a secretary who misstated any of these facts, but it does at least provide some comfort that these matters have in fact been looked into.

### 12.6.8.9 Particulars of insurance

Frequently, lenders will look for evidence of non-life insurance, which is relevant for a borrower's business, e.g. insurance of particular key assets or buildings.

Generally, lenders will require that their interest be noted on the insurance policies. At the very least, a letter is sought from the insurers undertaking that they will not let the policies lapse or be cancelled without prior written notice to the lender. This will be so as to enable the lender to pay the premiums to preserve the insurance if the lender believes that that is important. Increasingly, lenders are requiring that they be joint beneficiaries or sole loss payee.

### 12.6.8.10 Searches

Searches with satisfactory explanations of acts appearing will be required to be handed over by the borrowing company.

| Office | Will disclose |
| --- | --- |
| Companies Registration Office | Charges, insolvency, dissolution of company, restriction and disqualification of directors, timing of annual returns |
| Judgments Office | Registered money judgments |
| Sheriffs Office | Unexecuted execution orders against goods, rates certificates |
| Revenue Sheriffs Office | Unexecuted Revenue certificates |
| Registry of Deeds | Documents affecting any interest in heritable property |
| Land Registry | Burdens on registered property, pending dealings, registered owner |

In certain cases searches on overseas registers will be required.

## 12.7    Post-completion Procedures

### 12.7.1    STAMP ALL STAMPABLE DOCUMENTS

Stamp duty ceased to be payable on security documents such as mortgages on 7 December 2006. Prior to this, the rate was €1 per €1,000 secured, subject to a maximum of €630 on a document. Where the amount secured was more than €250,000, collateral and counterpart documents were stamped at €12.50 each. Note that documents transferring an interest in real or leasehold property and certain asset sale agreements must be stamped at various rates depending on the nature of the property and other factors. As stamp duty law in the residential sector is regularly amended, practitioners must be particularly careful to ensure documents have the relevant statutory certificates and sufficient money is held to pay applicable stamp duty.

If a promissory note is taken as part of the security package, an adhesive stamp of 10c is affixed.

### 12.7.2    REGISTRATION OF A CHARGE

#### 12.7.2.1    Companies Registration Office

When a company executes a charge, particulars of the charge must be delivered to the Registrar within twenty-one days from the date of its creation. Failure to do so renders the charge void against the company, any liquidator or creditor.

Registration of a charge on an Irish company's property is undertaken by lodging a Form C1. In the case of a foreign company, a similar procedure using a Form 8E is required, whether or not the company has registered on the External Register. If the applicant for registration is the company itself, the form must be verified by some person interested in the charge otherwise than on behalf of the company, setting out such interest. Generally, the solicitor for the lending institution will verify the particulars. If particulars are not filed within the appropriate period, application may be made to court under CA 1963, s 106 for an order extending the time for registration or rectifying the error in the application. The court must be satisfied that the omission to register was accidental.

If the charge becomes void under s 99 by failure to register on time, the money secured immediately becomes payable and the lender may immediately sue for the debt. A new security document may be executed and the appropriate particulars filed within the appropriate time. The difficulty which could arise here is in respect of CA 1963, s 288 in that in the case of a floating charge, the charge could be rendered invalid if the borrower is wound up within twelve months of the creation of the charge as no cash is paid to the company at the time of, or in consideration for, the granting of the charge. It should be noted that if a property subject to an existing mortgage is acquired by a company, the new purchasing company must file a Form C1(b), as the existing charge now represents a charge on its property. It should also be noted that the Irish Companies Registration Office practice is to reject any Forms C1/Forms 8E delivered outside the twenty-one-day period even if the Form C1/8E had been delivered originally within the period with inadvertent errors only.

Certain charges created by non-Irish companies over assets in Ireland are registered on the 'Slavenburg Register'. This has arisen because of the mismatch between CA 1963, s 111 and Part XI of that Act. External companies having an established place of business in Ireland should have delivered appropriate particulars to the Companies Registration Office so that a file may be opened in their name in the Companies Registration Office to register charges. Section 111 applies the rules as to registration of charges to companies having an established place of business in Ireland whether or not they have so registered. The practice has developed, therefore, of delivering Forms 8E to the Companies Registration Office of such companies and they are put on a (non-indexed) 'Slavenburg Register' (named after the case of that name which highlighted the issue in England).

### 12.7.2.2 Land registry/registry of deeds

Normal registration in the Registry of Deeds and Land Registry proceeds where title is unregistered and registered land respectively.

In the case of registered land, debentures incorporating floating charges only are not ordinarily registered against folios although it should be noted that in 1986 an amendment to the Land Registry Rules, 1972 (SI 230/1972) was enacted making crystallised floating charges registrable charges under the provisions of the Registration of Title Act, 1964.

### 12.7.2.3 County Registrar (Agricultural Credit Act chattel mortgages)

A charge over stock must be registered with the appropriate County Registrar under the Agricultural Credit Act, 1978, within one month from the date of its creation. It should be noted that the registration requirement arises wherever the 'land' of the borrower is situate. Land is defined as any land used for the purpose of the business of the company. Frequently registration has to be effected in more than one county. If more than one registration is to be effected, careful checking of each registrar's requirements is advisable. For example, is a stamped original required to be presented?

### 12.7.2.4 Port of ship

A mortgage on a ship must be registered at the port of registration of the ship.

### 12.7.2.5 Notification to other lending institutions

If there is a prior mortgage or charge and the security is to rank second, notice should be served on the first mortgagee that a second mortgage or charge is being created.

If there is a sharing arrangement between two or more banks, it should be evidenced in writing and agreed on by the various lenders setting out the sum of money in respect of each lender for which the security will be shared. Priority may be regulated in a priority agreement.

### 12.7.2.6 Notice to assurance company

When a life policy is assigned as security, notice must be served on the assurance company that the policy has been assigned. The notice should also request particulars of any prior notice of charge to the insurance company. A statutory fee of 32c may be payable but is rarely if ever required.

### 12.7.2.7 Obligations of company-filing requirements

*Section 60 declaration*

A copy s 60 declaration of solvency by the directors must be delivered to the Companies Registration Office for filing within twenty-one days after 'financial assistance' within the meaning of s 60 has been given.

*Section 34 declaration and certificate*

A copy of a s 34 declaration of solvency by the directors must be delivered to the Companies Registration Office within twenty-one days after the giving of the guarantee or the granting of security. The declaration must be accompanied by a report from a person qualified to be the auditor of the company confirming that the declaration was made on reasonable grounds.

*Special resolutions*

Generally, under s 141 special resolutions must be filed in the Companies Registration Office within fifteen days.

Where a charge document charges assets situated in a foreign jurisdiction (e.g. Northern Ireland or the UK), filing on a foreign companies or commercial register may be needed. If there is any element of foreign law to be considered, whether because of the location of assets or the place of incorporation of the borrower, appropriate legal advice should be obtained from a lawyer qualified to practise in that jurisdiction.

*Write up register of debenture holders*

Section 91 of CA 1963 requires a company to keep a register of debenture holders. The register should be written up by the company secretary.

*Have copy charge document available under s 109*

Section 109 of CA 1963 requires a company to have copies of documents creating charges available for inspection by creditors.

***Put members'/directors' resolution in minute book pursuant to s 145***

Section 145 of CA 1963 requires the keeping of minute books. Appropriate minutes should be put in the appropriate books.

## 12.7.3   RELEASE OF SECURITY

### 12.7.3.1   Floating charge

A release of a floating charge may be effected by deed or by letter returning the original floating charge. If the floating charge has been registered in the Registry of Deeds, then it is usual for there to be a deed of release and for a memorial (after July 2008, an application for release) to be furnished. In a conveyancing transaction, a non-crystallisation letter is handed over.

### 12.7.3.2   Mortgage on real/leasehold property

A mortgage is released by a deed of release or by receipt under the Housing Act, 1988.

### 12.7.3.3   Charge registered in the land registry

A charge registered in the Land Registry is released by means of a deed of discharge in the appropriate Land Registry Form 71A or B.

### 12.7.3.4 Equitable mortgage by deposit of title deeds

An equitable mortgage by deposit of title deeds is released by a simple letter of release.

### 12.7.3.5 Notification of release

Unusually, it is the company which notifies the Companies Registration Office that a charge has ceased to affect the company's property or that it has been discharged. A Form C6 or a Form C7, as appropriate, is submitted to the Companies Registration Office. The Registrar serves notice on the relevant lending institution that a form has been filed and that the charge will be struck off within a certain period, unless notice to the contrary is served by the lending institution on the Companies Registration Office.

## 12.8 Financial Assistance in Connection with Purchases of and Subscriptions for Shares

### 12.8.1 THE LEGAL PROVISIONS

One of the most troublesome provisions of Irish company law is CA 1963, s 60. The origins of this section go back to the English Companies Act, 1929, s 45 which was introduced on the recommendation of the Greene Committee which had reviewed English legislation. It outlawed the giving by a company of assistance for the purpose of, or in connection with, the purchase of (but not subscription for) its shares. The Committee's example of the sort of transaction that the section was ultimately aimed at was where a group of individuals acquired control of a company by buying shares out of borrowed money which, when they were appointed directors to the company, they would procure that the company would repay from its own assets. The company therefore provided money for the purchase of its shares.

The 1929 provision was re-enacted with amendments as in the English Companies Act, 1948, s 54, which prohibited financial assistance for the purpose of, or in connection with, the subscription for, as well as the purchase of, shares in the company concerned. This provision was enacted into Irish law by CA 1959, s 3. The Jenkins Committee, which reported on the operation of the English Companies Acts in June 1962, proposed certain amendments and, as often happens in these circumstances, Ireland took heed of deliberations overseas. When consolidating companies legislation, the Oireachtas enacted the provisions of the Companies Act, 1959, s 3, with some of the amendments as proposed in the Jenkins Committee Report, as CA 1963, s 60.

The motivation for the provision is to prevent the reduction of the share capital of the company and asset stripping. However, as we will see later, it has a wider effect than that anticipated. The Jenkins Committee had described the previous unqualified provision as 'an occasional embarrassment to the honest without being a serious inconvenience to the unscrupulous'. The same may be said of our s 60.

The European Communities (Public Limited Companies Subsidiaries) Regulations, 1997 (SI 67/1997) prohibit a subsidiary of a public limited company from financially assisting in the purchase of, or subscription for, shares in its parent public company.

Directive 2006/68/EC allowed Member States some flexibility with regard to plcs giving financial assistance. However, our implementing statutory instrument (SI 89/2008) did not avail of the opportunity.

## 12.8.2 WHAT IS FORBIDDEN BY S 60

### 12.8.2.1 General

Section 60 prohibits financial assistance:

– directly or indirectly

– by means of a loan

– by means of a guarantee

– by means of the provision of security

– or otherwise

for the purpose of or in connection with:

– a purchase made

– a purchase to be made

– a subscription made

– or subscription to be made

by any person of shares:

– in the company

– or in the company's holding company.

The following are examples of transactions that would be affected by s 60:

| | |
|---|---|
| 'directly or indirectly' | If buyer company wishes to buy shares in a target company, the target company cannot lend money to the subsidiary of the buyer company so as the buyer company may be put in funds. |
| 'by means of a loan' | A target company cannot lend money to a buyer company to enable it to buy the shares. |

| | |
|---|---|
| 'by means of a guarantee' | A target company cannot guarantee the borrowings of a buyer of its shares. |
| 'by means of . . . the provision of, security' | This would be a corollary of the previous example where, for example, a target company would give security to a bank by way of a charge over its assets and a guarantee to secure borrowings of a buyer of its shares. |
| 'otherwise' | Examples of other forms of financial assistance could include the purchase by a target company of an asset belonging to a subscriber or purchaser of its shares, a similar purchase by that company's subsidiary, or the placing of the target company's trading opportunities in the hands of a subscriber or purchaser of shares. |

### 12.8.2.2 Has there been financial assistance?

Has the target company or any of its subsidiaries helped a buyer of shares in any way directly or indirectly?

Has the company whose shares are being subscribed for or transferred or any of its subsidiaries done anything to help the share subscription or share transfer happen?

### 12.8.2.3 Is there a connection?

While it is easy to establish where assistance has been given 'for the purpose of a share purchase or subscription', it is less easy to establish where assistance has been given 'in connection with' such a transaction.

(a) Would the share purchase or subscription have proceeded in the absence of the transaction whose connection with the share purchase or subscription is in doubt?

(b) Would that transaction whose connection is in doubt have proceeded in the absence of the share purchase or subscription?

### 12.8.2.4 A word of warning

The extremely restrictive provisions of the English Companies Act 1948, s 54 generated a jurisprudence which could be said to rely on benevolent interpretation of that section. The view of certain legal authors in relation to the replacement of those provisions which are now in the English Companies Act, 1985, ss 151–158, is that those replacement provisions will be construed more widely, as the sections provide a way out of the difficulties in certain circumstances, as does the Irish s 60. Therefore, one cannot rely completely on cases interpreting the previous English law. In particular, many of the UK s 54 cases are concerned with the legality or otherwise of the transactions being considered. In Ireland, s 60(14) is specifically concerned with this point.

The current English law refers to the 'acquisition' of shares, rather than a 'purchase' or 'subscription'. This, along with the precedents (one pre-1948, interpreting their 1929 legislation, and another post-1948 but interpreting a section to do with prospectuses), has led some UK commentators to suggest that the previous law would not apply on a share-for-share exchange. However, it may be argued that if, but for this technicality, there was financial assistance, the directors would be in breach of their fiduciary duties if they were to enter into a transaction in which such financial assistance was present. There is no guarantee that an Irish court would not include a share exchange in the definition of 'purchase' or 'subscription'.

In the case of *Belmont Finance Corporation v Williams Furniture (No 2)* [1980] 1 All ER 393 a company bought an asset at a fair market price from a purchaser of its shares so as to put the purchaser in funds to purchase the shares. The corresponding UK provisions were stated to have been breached. An arm's length transaction in the ordinary course of a company's business which serves to finance an acquisition of a company's shares may be caught by this section. However, in the English case of *Charterhouse Investment Trust Ltd v Tempest Diesels* [1986] BCLC 1 it is suggested that one should look at the commercial realities of the circumstances.

## 12.8.3   CONSEQUENCES OF CONTRAVENING S 60

Making the statutory declaration without reasonable grounds for the opinion that the company will be able to pay its debts as they fall due may result in a fine and imprisonment on conviction. If a company acts in contravention of s 60, every officer in default is liable to a fine and imprisonment.

Any transaction in breach of s 60 is voidable at the instance of the company against any person (whether a party to the transaction or not) with notice of the facts which constitute the breach. In *Bank of Ireland Finance Ltd v Rockfield Ltd* [1979] IR 21 the Supreme Court held that the notice required was actual notice.

## 12.8.4   WHAT S 60 DOES NOT PROHIBIT

The s 60 prohibition does not apply to financial assistance given by a company (other than a public limited company or in relation to plc shares) under the authority of a special resolution where the procedures set out in s 60(2)–(11) are complied with. Other transactions which are exempted include the payment of a dividend properly declared by a company (s 60(12)(a)), the discharge of a liability lawfully incurred by a company (s 60(12)(b)), the lending by a company of money in the ordinary course of its lending business (s 60(12)(d)), the provision by a company of funding for an employee share scheme (s 60(12)(e)) and the making by a company of loans to employees (other than directors) (s 60(12)(f)) to enable such persons to purchase or subscribe for shares in the company. Section 60 does not apply to the acquisition of non-convertible debentures or loan stock.

Section 56 of the Investment Funds, Companies and Miscellaneous Provisions Act, 2005 inserted new wording in subsections (12) and (13), clarifying that a company giving warranties to its purchaser was not financial assistance (s 60(12)(g)) and that refinancing a previously validated transaction is excluded (s 60(12)(c)) from the prohibition.

## 12.8.5   FINANCIAL ASSISTANCE COMPLIANCE

As the reason for the capital maintenance rules is to preserve the share capital of the company for the benefit of creditors and shareholders, it is not surprising that the procedure available to private companies under s 60(2)–(11) to give financial assistance requires the safeguarding of these interests.

### 12.8.5.1   Creditor protection

Creditors are protected through a declaration of solvency by a majority of the directors of the company. This statutory declaration must be made at a meeting of the directors held not more than twenty-four days before a meeting of shareholders. Section 60(4) of CA 1963 is very specific about what the statutory declaration must contain. The declaration must state:

(a)   the form the assistance will take;

(b)   the persons to whom the assistance is to be given;

(c)   the purpose for which the company intends those persons to use the assistance; and

(d)   that the directors making the declaration have made full enquiries as to the affairs of the company and that having done so they have formed the opinion that the company, having carried out the transaction whereby such assistance is to be given, will be able to pay its debts in full as they become due.

The equivalent English legislation requires all the directors to make the declaration and also requires that an auditor's report reinforcing the opinion of the directors be obtained. Neither requirement exists under Irish law. However, in practice, directors often seek professional advice from the company's auditors so that they will be able to confirm that they have made full enquiry into the financial condition of the company.

Under s 60(5), the penalty for making a declaration without having reasonable grounds for the stated opinion is a criminal offence leading on conviction to the possibility of imprisonment and/or a fine. If the company is wound up within twelve months after the making of the declaration, and if the debts of the company are not paid within twelve months of the commencement of the winding-up, then there is a statutory presumption that directors did not have reasonable grounds for making the statutory declaration of solvency.

### 12.8.5.2 Shareholder protection

The shareholders are protected through being notified about the transaction in advance and being given the opportunity of considering it. Notice of the extraordinary general meeting at which the matter will be considered must be accompanied by a copy of the statutory declaration of solvency. Notice must be given to all shareholders, regardless of whether or not under the articles of association they have the right to receive notice and to attend the special resolution meetings. Since the introduction of CLEA 2001, it is possible for a company to avail of s 141(8) CA 1963 and pass this members' resolution by way of written resolution of all the members. Where all the members are agreeable to the financial assistance, this makes organising matters easier.

If all of those entitled to vote do actually vote in favour, the transaction may proceed. Otherwise, if because of absence, abstention or opposition, there is not unanimity, there is a waiting period of thirty days during which a shareholder may apply to court to have the transaction blocked. Those who voted in favour of the resolution may not subsequently object (s 60(10)). Shareholders wishing to challenge the decision must have at least 10 per cent of the nominal value of the issued share capital or any class of issued share capital (s 60(9)). Any court challenge must be launched within twenty-eight days after the day on which the special resolution was passed (s 60(11)).

Often the validation procedure will be organised so that all members are consenting and, therefore, the extraordinary general meeting may be held on the same day as notices are issued. This may be achieved if all the members consent to the meeting being held at short notice and the auditors consent as well, or, alternatively, if all members entitled to attend and vote at an annual general meeting sign a written resolution pursuant to s 141(8), the matter can proceed.

### 12.8.5.3 Filing requirements

It is of crucial importance that s 60(2)(b) is strictly adhered to. A copy of the directors' declaration of solvency must be filed in the Companies Registration Office within twenty-one days after the giving of the financial assistance. Failure to comply with this requirement means that the validation procedure is not applicable and the transaction is voidable (s 60(14)).

Strict compliance with the various procedural requirements of the section is necessary. For example in the case of *Re Northside Motor Co Ltd*, 24 June 1985, High Court (unreported), efforts to comply with s 60 were not made until after the financial assistance had been granted and the court held that the attempt by the company to retrospectively comply with the s 60 validation procedure was unlawful and to no avail. In addition, Costello J considered that the special resolution which was in fact passed was inaccurate. On either ground the section would not have been complied with. Subsequently, in the case of *Lombard & Ulster Banking Ltd v Bank of Ireland*, 2 June 1987, High Court (unreported), Costello J emphasised that 'if the procedural requirements were not adopted the transaction is an illegal one'.

#### 12.8.5.4 Consequences of breach

Any transaction in breach of s 60 is voidable at the instance of the company against any person with notice of the facts which constitute the breach. It is important to note that it is notice of the facts, and not notice of the legal consequence of the facts, that is important here. Therefore, if anyone in the relevant organisation knows the circumstances but fails to appreciate the legal significance that will still constitute adequate notice to that organisation.

The most likely situation in which a company will endeavour to avoid such a transaction, is where the company has been wound up and the liquidator is endeavouring to set aside security granted to a bank in relation to the transaction.

The Supreme Court has decided in *Bank of Ireland Finance Ltd v Rockfield Ltd* [1979] IR 21 that notice in this context means actual knowledge and not constructive notice. In the circumstances of that case, even though s 60 had not been complied with, the bank security survived because the bank did not have actual notice of the relevant facts. Costello J went into further detail in the *Lombard & Ulster* case (on p. 11 of the unreported judgment) referred to in **12.8.5.3**:

> It must be shown that [the party] had 'actual notice' of the facts which constitute the breach, that is (a) that they or their officials actually knew that the required procedures were not adopted or that they knew facts from which they must have inferred that the company had failed to adopt the required procedures or (b) that an agent of theirs actually knew of the failure or knew facts from which he must have inferred that a failure had occurred.

If a company contravenes s 60, then every officer who is in default is liable on conviction to a fine or imprisonment or both (s 60(15)).

#### 12.8.5.5 Exceptions

Section 60(12) specifically states that s 60 does not prohibit the payment of a dividend or the making of a distribution out of distributable profits or the discharge of a liability lawfully incurred (see **12.8.4**). Regulation 116 of Table A states that the company in general meeting may declare dividends. Under regulation 117 the directors may pay interim dividends. The exception given by s 60(12) as amended in 2005 applies now to all dividends whether final or interim.

There has been some debate about the limits on the concept of a liability lawfully incurred. In particular, from time to time, questions arise as to whether a transaction at an inflated value or on unusual terms would qualify. In the British case of *Belmont Finance Corporation v Williams Furniture Ltd (No 2)* [1980] 1 All ER 393 the company acquired an asset at a fair price from a third party. The case was rather an extreme example because it seemed clear that the company had no need for the asset bought and that the sole reason for entering into the transaction was to put the other party in funds to buy the shares. The court decided that this was not a lawfully-incurred liability within the meaning of the equivalent English legislation. Specifically, the court refused to give a view on a hypothetical situation where there was some commercial reason for the transaction and funding the potential shareholder was another reason.

In the case of *Charterhouse Investment Trust Ltd v Tempest Diesels Limited* [1986] BCLC 1 the transaction under consideration was a management buyout. As the target company was in financial difficulties the vendor parent company agreed to improve the financial state of the company, including, for example, injecting €750,000 in cash into the company, making redundancy payments and rearranging intra-group debt terms all in exchange for the target company surrendering tax losses.

Hoffmann J (now Lord Hoffmann) decided that the transaction did not constitute financial assistance within the meaning of the equivalent English section. He stated that the transaction should be looked at as a whole to decide whether it constituted the giving of financial assistance. In this case, the target company was substantially better off after the transaction. The judge decided that the surrendering of the tax losses did not amount to financial assistance.

Various provisions of the judgment have been cited with approval by McCracken J in the case of *Re CH (Ireland) Inc, in Liquidation v Credit Suisse Canada* [1999] 4 IR 542. However, the focus on the purpose and overall effect of the transaction does not seem to give sufficient weight to the wording of the section which also allows for financial assistance to arise where the transaction is not for the purpose of, but is in connection with, a subscription or purchase of shares. Given that breach of the section may result in a criminal sanction, it is understandable that the judges have given narrow interpretations where there is room for doubt. McCracken J endorsed Hoffmann J's common sense approach that:

> The words have no technical meaning and their frame of reference is in my judgment the language of ordinary commerce. One must examine the commercial realities of the transaction and decide whether it can properly be described as the giving of financial assistance by the company, bearing in mind that the section is a penal one and should not be strained to cover transactions which are not fairly within it.

The difficulty for the practitioner is forecasting whether, in a subsequent case, a judge will adopt a similarly purposive approach rather than a literal interpretation of how the section applies. Until the position is clarified by further legislation, a cautious approach is probably the more prudent route to take.

### 12.8.5.6 Public company subsidiaries

A public limited company may only lend money, assist employees, and share schemes under s 60(12)(d)–(f) if its assets are not reduced, or else it must fund out of distributable profits (s 60(13)). The European Communities (Public Limited Companies Subsidiaries) Regulations, 1997 (SI 67/1997) restricted the circumstances in which certain companies could, among other things, provide financial assistance for the purchase of, or subscription for, shares in a parent public company. Until these regulations were introduced, the restrictions on public limited companies providing financial assistance could be avoided by having a subsidiary provide the assistance instead. While the provisions of the statutory instrument are quite difficult to decipher, in so far as they relate to subsidiaries giving financial assistance, the starting point should always be to ascertain whether regulation 5 applies if assistance is being given in connection with a purchase of or subscription for shares in a plc.

#### 12.8.5.7　Restricted director

If a director of the company is the subject of a restriction order pursuant to CA 1990, s 150 then CA 1990, s 155(2) stipulates that the company cannot avail of the validation procedures set out in CA 1963, s 60(2)–(11). Therefore, if a company has a restricted director, the only financial assistance which may be given by that company is assistance within s 60(12) and (13), which relate to properly declared dividends, lawfully incurred liabilities, lending money in the ordinary course of business and assisting employee share schemes.

### 12.8.6　TRANSACTIONS WITH DIRECTORS

Part III of CA 1990 placed extensive restrictions on transactions, which could take place between the company, on the one hand, and directors or connected persons on the other hand. There was a concern that persons in positions of power could siphon off company assets, thereby depriving creditors and shareholders of items which should rightfully be kept by the company. In a sense, the legislation was an extension of the capital maintenance rules, and in some ways created an asset maintenance rule. In practice, the legislation has been difficult to interpret, has increased the costs of doing business and has not necessarily resulted in those disposed to improper activity refraining from such activity.

#### 12.8.6.1　Transactions

The legislation relates to loans, quasi-loans and credit transactions, as well as guarantees and security given in relation to loans, quasi-loans and credit transactions. Section 25(1) of CA 1990 confirms that the word 'guarantee' includes 'indemnity'. A quasi-loan is defined by CA 1990, s 25(2) as being a transaction under which the creditor pays a sum for the borrower or reimburses expenditure incurred on behalf of the borrower in circumstances where the borrower is to reimburse the creditor. Therefore, if the company pays a director's personal credit card bill, the company is acting as creditor and the director is a borrower from the company.

A credit transaction is defined by CA 1990, s 25(3) as one in which the creditor supplies any goods or sells any land, enters into a hire purchase agreement or conditional sale agreement, leases or licenses the use of land, hires goods in return for periodical payments or otherwise disposes of land, or supplies goods or services on the understanding that payment is to be deferred. If a company leases a car to a director, the company is a creditor in a credit transaction.

### 12.8.6.2 Prohibitions on a company

Section 31 of CA 1990 provides that a company may not:

(a) make a loan or a quasi-loan to a director of a company or of its holding company or to a person connected with such a director;

(b) enter into a credit transaction as creditor for such a director or a person so connected; or

(c) enter into a guarantee or grant security in connection with a loan, quasi-loan or credit transaction to any other person for such a director or a person so connected.

### 12.8.6.3 Who are directors?

Section 27 of CA 1990 extends the meaning of 'director' to include shadow directors. These are persons in accordance with whose directions or instructions the appointed directors of the company are accustomed to act. There is an exception for professional advisers. Section 2(1) of CA 1963 defines a 'director' as including any person occupying the position of director by whatever name called.

### 12.8.6.4 Who is a connected person?

It is far more difficult to determine who is a connected person. Section 26 of CA 1990 lists relevant persons as including the spouse, parent, brother, sister or child of the director. Note that there is no age limitation in relation to the child. A person acting in his capacity as the trustee of any trust, the principal beneficiaries of which are the director, his spouse or any of his children or any corporate body which he controls is also a connected person. A partner of the director (in the sense of a partner within the meaning of s 1(1) of the Partnership Act, 1890) is also a connected person.

A body corporate is deemed to be connected with a director, if it is controlled by that director. The section (in s 26(3)) goes on to provide that a director is deemed to control a body corporate if, but only if, he is alone or together with any director, directors or the persons previously mentioned, interested in one half or more of the equity share capital of that body or entitled to exercise or control the exercise of one half or more of the voting power at any general meeting of that body.

Under CA 1963, s 155, equity capital means the issued share capital of the company excluding any part thereof which neither as respects dividends nor as respects capital carries any right to participate beyond a specified amount on a distribution. Therefore, to be excluded, the share capital must have participation rights, both in relation to dividends and capital, which are capped.

There has been some debate about the interaction of s 26(2), which deems a body corporate to be connected with the director if it is controlled by that director, and s 26(3) which sets out situations in which the body corporate is deemed to be controlled. Subsection (2) makes the body corporate a connected person if it is controlled by a director. Section 26(3) deems specified circumstances to amount to control. It is possible that a situation could arise where the facts do not amount to deemed control within s 26(3) but could be equated with actual control, thereby falling within s 26(2).

### 12.8.6.5 Exceptions

#### *Minor transactions*

Because various day-to-day transactions, such as the payment of personal expenses to be reimbursed in due course by the director, come within the s 31 prohibition, s 32 provides a threshold below which transactions do not infringe. If the net value of arrangements between a company and a director or a connected person are worth less than 10 per cent of the relevant assets of the company, then the exception applies.

Section 29(2) of CA 1990 defines 'relevant assets' as either the value of net assets determined by reference to the last set of statutory accounts laid before an annual general meeting or, if that has not happened, the amount of the called-up share capital. The range of the exception is further limited because it only applies where the company makes a loan or quasi-loan or enters into a credit transaction for the director or connected person. Granting a guarantee or providing security in respect of a loan, quasi-loan or credit transaction made for a director or connected person by a third party do not appear to be covered.

Furthermore, the utility of the s 32 exception is further eroded because if the actual value of arrangements availing of s 32 exceeds 10 per cent of the relevant assets for any reason, the arrangements must be reorganised within two months so that the 10 per cent level is not exceeded. Therefore, if the relevant asset value falls, for example, because the company is making losses, reorganisation of these arrangements may be needed. Because of this, s 32 is only really of use for temporary arrangements.

A further impediment to s 32 having any effective use is that s 39 allows for unlimited personal liability to be imposed on a person who benefited from a s 32 arrangement where a company being wound up is insolvent, if the court concludes that the arrangements made a material contribution to the company's inability to pay its debts if they fell due. It is for the court to decide the extent of any personal liability on the basis of all the circumstances.

#### *Guarantees and security*

Section 34 (as inserted by CLEA 2001, s 78) allows for the guaranteeing of, or the giving of security in connection with, loans, quasi-loans and credit transactions for directors if the provisions of s 34 are adhered to. In essence, this involves a process akin to that required for s 60 compliance with some important additions. It is important to note that the scope of this exception is limited to guarantees and security—any other prohibited transaction, e.g. giving a loan to a director, is outside s 34.

An independent person, categorised as being a person who is qualified to be the auditor of the company, must certify in a statutory form report that the declaration of solvency of the directors is based on reasonable grounds. Concerns about the scope of responsibility which a person giving this report is thereby assuming have resulted in many accountants refusing to give the report.

The declaration must set out the benefit which the company is getting by entering into the transaction. The benefit may be direct or indirect.

### Intra group transaction

Section 35 allows a company to enter into a loan, quasi-loan or credit trans-action and to guarantee and give security in relation to loans, quasi-loans or credit transactions in respect of any company in the same group as it (given the amendment made by CLEA 2001, s 79).

### Ordinary course of business

Section 37 enables transactions in the ordinary course of business on arm's length terms to take place without coming within the prohibitions set out in s 31. The value of the transaction must not be greater, and the terms in which it is entered into must not be more beneficial for the person for whom the transaction is made, than that or those which the company ordinarily offers or it is reasonable to expect the company to have offered to a person of the same financial standing as the director or connected person. However, while the exception relates to loans, quasi-loans and credit transactions, it does not mention guarantees or security in relation to loans, quasi-loans and credit transactions.

### 12.8.6.6  Consequences of breach

Section 38 sets out civil remedies. The transaction is voidable at the instance of the company (which will include any liquidator). Purchasers for value without actual notice take precedence. The transaction will not be avoided if restitution is no longer possible or if the company has been indemnified for the loss or damage suffered by it. Furthermore, the benefiting director or connected person, along with every director who approved the transaction, is liable to the company for any gain made and must indemnify the company for any loss suffered by the company. Lack of actual notice of the circumstances which constitute the contravention is a good defence but, as with s 60, the defence is lack of actual knowledge of the facts which give rise to the contravention rather than lack of actual knowledge of the legal consequences of those facts.

An offence is committed by an officer of the company who permits the contravention of s 31. Likewise, a person who procures a company to enter into a transaction prohibited by s 31 is also guilty of an offence.

### 12.8.6.7  Substantial property transactions

Less severe restrictions are placed on substantial property transactions. Nevertheless, compliance with the relevant provisions of CA 1990, s 29 is equally important because the consequences of non-compliance result in the transaction being voidable. If a director, or connected person, is acquiring a non-cash asset of a certain value, then the transaction must be approved by an ordinary resolution of the company in general meeting and if the person is a director, or a person connected to a director, of the holding company a resolution in general meeting of the holding company.

Breach of s 29 results in the transaction being voidable at the instance of the company (which would include a liquidator). Purchasers for value without notice, the provision of an indemnity for loss or damage suffered by the company, ratification by the company in general meeting within a reasonable period or the impossibility of restitution prevent avoidance being used.

However, the director, connected person and any director authorising the transaction will be made liable to account for any gain made and to indemnify the company for any loss or damage suffered by the company.

No ordinary resolution is required for substantial property transactions between a holding company and a wholly-owned subsidiary or between two wholly-owned subsidiaries of the one holding company.

### 12.8.6.8  Proposed changes

The combined efforts of the Director of Corporate Enforcement, the relevant government Departments and the Company Law Review Group are likely to lead to a dramatic recasting of Irish company law in the coming years. This will have consequences for security taking and enforcement, although it is too early to judge whether the alterations will be cosmetic or substantive. Amendments effected by the CLEA 2001 have improved matters somewhat for practitioners, particularly in relation to transactions with directors and the filing period for s 60 declarations.

397

# CHAPTER 13

# INSOLVENCY

## 13.1 Introduction

The purpose of this chapter is to discuss the main principles of corporate insolvency law in Ireland. The chapter is divided into four parts. The first part deals with receivership; the second part deals with rescue procedures available to companies in financial difficulties; the third part is concerned with the winding up of companies; and the final part deals with the consequences of insolvent liquidation.

## 13.2 Insolvency and Winding-up Procedures Applicable to Companies

The insolvency and winding-up procedures applicable to companies are:

    (a)   receiverships;

    (b)   restructuring and reorganisations;

    (c)   examinerships;

    (d)   members' voluntary winding up;

    (e)   creditors' voluntary winding up; and

    (f)   compulsory liquidations.

The application of these procedures is governed by the Companies Acts, 1963–2003 (the 'Companies Acts'), the Rules of the Superior Courts and case law.

## 13.3 Receivership

The appointment of a receiver is a remedy available to a secured creditor for the enforcement of a security. In practice, it is treated as an insolvency procedure. A receiver is appointed on foot of a debenture that creates a legal mortgage or charge, wherein the secured creditor is entitled to appoint its own receiver for the purposes of taking possession of and realising the assets secured by the debenture. A receiver is usually appointed where the company has defaulted in the repayments on the loan, which was secured.

Irish law provides for different types of receivership (including the appointment of a receiver by the court). However, the most common type occurs where a secured creditor (usually a lending institution) appoints a receiver under contractual powers granted by the company in a debenture. Where there is no such contractual power contained in the debenture, the creditor can apply to the High Court for the appointment of a receiver. The debenture is a contractual document, all the powers of the debenture holder and of the receiver depend on this document, except for a small number of statutory provisions, which are contained in Part VII of the Companies Act, 1963 (ss 314–323).

A receiver can be appointed only over those assets which have been charged. The appointment of the receiver does not change the status of the company. Although the directors cease to control the assets over which the receiver has been appointed, their normal powers and duties continue in respect of other assets and liabilities of the company.

A receivership can be a temporary condition affecting a company, which unlike liquidation does not necessarily lead to the company's dissolution. After a receiver has been discharged, the directors resume their normal functions in relation to all of the company's affairs, unless a liquidator has been appointed in the meantime.

In practice, most receiverships do result in the dissolution of the company's business. A receiver and liquidator may act concurrently in respect of the same company but a liquidator is unable to deal with those assets under a receiver's control.

## 13.4　Examination

The examination procedure is a procedure for the rescue of companies in financial difficulties.

Examinerships are governed by the Companies (Amendment) Act, 1990, as amended by the Companies (Amendment) (No 2) Act, 1999. A summary of the main provisions of the examination process is set out below.

### 13.4.1　APPOINTMENT OF AN EXAMINER

Where a company is, or is likely to be, unable to pay its debts and has not been wound up, a petition may be presented to the High Court seeking the protection of the court and the appointment of an examiner. Such a petition may be presented by any of the following:

   (a)   the company;

   (b)   the directors;

      (c)    any creditor, secured, unsecured or contingent creditor (including an employee); or

      (d)    shareholders representing 10 per cent or more of the paid-up capital of the company.

In making an order to appoint an examiner, the court must be satisfied that there is a reasonable prospect of the survival of the company and the whole or any part of its undertaking as a going concern.

### 13.4.2 EFFECT OF COURT PROTECTION

For a period of seventy days from the date of the petition (which period can be extended in certain circumstances by a further thirty days), the creditors of the company are prevented from taking action to enforce their securities. During the period of protection, no winding-up proceedings may be commenced, no receiver can be appointed, no attachment or execution against assets or no attempt to repossess goods under a hire purchase or retention of title agreement will be allowed. No steps can be taken against any third party who has guaranteed the liabilities of the company.

### 13.4.3 DUTY OF AN EXAMINER

The principal duty of an examiner is to prepare a report for the court on the viability of the company. As part of this report, the examiner formulates proposals for a compromise or scheme of arrangement in respect of the company. The proposals are then put to the shareholders and to the different classes of creditors and shall be deemed to be accepted by the creditors if passed by a majority in number and value of any class.

Once the examiner's proposals have been voted upon by the members and creditors, he must again report to the court on the outcome of those meetings. At this hearing, any creditor or member whose claim or interest would be impaired if the proposals were implemented may appear and be heard. The court has a discretion to confirm, confirm subject to modifications or refuse to confirm the proposals subject to the proviso that it cannot confirm the proposals unless at least one class of creditors, whose interests or claims would be impaired by implementation of the proposals, has accepted the proposals.

If the court decides to confirm the proposals, it can fix a date for the implementation of the proposals, which will not be later than twenty-one days from the date of its confirmation. The date of the implementation of the proposals will be the date on which the company comes out of court protection and the role of the examiner ceases.

If the proposals are not confirmed by the court, then it can make such order as it deems fit which is likely to be an order for the winding up of the company.

### 13.4.4 ARRANGEMENTS AND RECONSTRUCTIONS

Section 201 Companies Act, 1963 provides, inter alia, that, where a compromise or arrangement is proposed between a company and its creditors, the court may, on the application of the company, or of any creditor or member of the company order a meeting of the creditors or members, as the case may be, to be summoned in such manner as the court directs.

If the majority of the creditors or members representing at least three-quarters in value of that class, vote in favour of the resolution agreeing to any compromise arrangement, the compromise shall, if sanctioned by the court, be binding on all the creditors.

This section is a very rarely used provision and has effectively been superseded by the process of examinership.

## 13.5 Winding Up

There are three forms of winding-up procedure available under Irish law discussed below.

### 13.5.1 MEMBERS' VOLUNTARY WINDING UP

The provisions applicable to members' voluntary winding up are contained in ss 256–264 Companies Act, 1963 as amended. A members' voluntary winding up is a form of winding up of a solvent company. The members of the company pass a special resolution that the company be wound up. Strictly speaking, it is not an insolvency procedure because the company must be solvent.

#### 13.5.1.1 Declaration of solvency (s 256 Companies Act, 1963)

To avail of the members' voluntary winding-up procedure, the directors of the company (or where the company has more than two directors, a majority of them) must meet and make a statutory declaration that they have made a full enquiry into the affairs of the company and that, having done so, they have formed the opinion that the company will be able to pay its debts (including any contingent or prospective liabilities) in full within a period not exceeding twelve months from the commencement of the winding up. The declaration must be sworn at a meeting of directors before a commissioner for oaths or practising solicitor.

#### 13.5.1.2 Statement of assets and liabilities

The statutory declaration must embody a statement of the company's assets and liabilities as at the latest practicable date before the making of the declaration, and in any event at a date not later than three months before the making of the declaration.

### 13.5.1.3 Report of independent person

The declaration must be accompanied by a report made by an independent person (usually the company's auditor), stating whether in his opinion and to the best of his information and according to the explanations given to him:

(a) the opinions of the directors in the declaration; and

(b) the statement of the company's assets and liabilities embodied in the declaration are reasonable.

### 13.5.1.4 Statement of independent person

The declaration must also be accompanied by a statement by the independent person that he has given and has not withdrawn his written consent to the issue of the declaration with his report attached thereto.

### 13.5.1.5 Personal liability

It is important that the directors be advised that if it is subsequently proved that the company (for whatever reason) is unable to pay its debts within the period specified in the declaration of solvency, a court may declare that any director who is party to the declaration without having reasonable grounds for the opinion that it would be able to pay its debts in full within the twelve-month period specified will be personally liable, without any limitation of liability, for all or any of the debts or the liabilities of the company.

### 13.5.1.6 Extraordinary General Meeting of the members of the company

After the directors of the company have made their declaration of solvency, and the independent person has given his report, the directors should then call an Extraordinary General Meeting (EGM). This must be held within twenty-eight days of the date of the Declaration of Solvency. Unless consent to short notice of the EGM can be obtained from all members and the auditors of the company, the minimum notice periods provided for in the company's articles of association should be adhered to.

At the EGM, the members must pass a special resolution that the company be wound up voluntarily as a members' voluntary winding up. Within fourteen days from the passing of the winding-up resolution, notice of the resolution must be published in *Iris Oifigiuil*.

### 13.5.1.7 Matters following commencement of winding up

A voluntary winding up is deemed to commence at the time of the passing of the members' winding-up resolution. The company will then cease to carry on business, except in so far as is necessary to facilitate the liquidation.

The liquidator's function is to wind up the affairs and distribute the assets of the company. The appointment of the liquidator usually puts an end to the directors' powers.

Where a members' voluntary winding up continues for a period in excess of one year, the voluntary liquidator must, within three months of the end of that year and in each succeeding year, summon a general meeting of the company.

If at any time the liquidator forms the opinion that, contrary to the directors' declaration, the company is unable to pay its debts in full, he must publicly advertise and call a meeting of the company's creditors. The liquidation will then no longer be a members' voluntary winding up, but will proceed as a creditors' voluntary winding up. It would be in these circumstances that the question of directors' personal liability would arise.

### 13.5.1.8    Final meeting of members

When the company's assets have been collected and all creditors and shareholders are paid off, the liquidator convenes a final meeting of members and provides an account of the winding up, showing the receipts and disbursements in the period of the liquidation and showing how the property of the company has been disposed of, either by realisation for cash or by way of distribution *in specie* to the shareholders.

This meeting must be called by advertisement in two daily newspapers circulating in the district where the registered office of the company is situated, and must be published twenty-eight days before the meeting is held.

Once the meeting is held, a copy of the liquidator's account, together with a return of the holding of the final meeting, must be sent to the Registrar of Companies. The company is deemed to be dissolved three months following the Registrar receiving these documents.

### 13.5.2    CREDITORS' VOLUNTARY WINDING UP

This is a liquidation, which is commenced by resolution of the shareholders. The procedure is used for companies that are insolvent or where a Declaration of Solvency has not been sworn. It is also the procedure which applies where a members' voluntary winding up is converted to a creditors' voluntary winding up, where the company could not discharge its liabilities in full.

The procedure to implement a creditors' winding up is summarised as follows:

1.    The board of directors of the company decide that steps should be taken to implement a creditors' voluntary liquidation and to appoint a liquidator.

2.    The board instructs the secretary to convene a meeting of shareholders for the purpose of passing an ordinary resolution pursuant to s 251 Companies Act, 1963. The most common resolution passed

for a creditors' voluntary winding up is that 'the company cannot, by reason of its liabilities, continue to trade and ought to be wound up voluntarily'.

3.   The shareholders' meeting can be held on such notice as the articles of association permit, and obviously can be held on short notice by the consent of all shareholders entitled to attend and vote and the auditors. As to the timing of such meeting, see below.

4.   At the meeting of members, the members must pass the resolution for the winding up of the company and for the appointment of a liquidator.

5.   Section 266 Companies Act, 1963, states that a meeting must be convened of all creditors of the company, to be held on the same day or the day immediately following the day on which the shareholders' meeting is held. The purpose and agenda of the creditors' meeting is as follows:

   (a)   to inform the creditors of the winding-up resolution passed by the shareholders;

   (b)   pursuant to s 266(3) Companies Act, 1963, to present the directors' statement of affairs to the creditors;

   (c)   to confirm the appointment of a liquidator. (If creditors representing a majority in value of those attending and voting at the creditors' meeting, vote for a liquidator other than the liquidator nominated by the shareholders, that liquidator shall prevail. Otherwise, the liquidator nominated by the shareholders stands confirmed (s 267(3) Companies Act, 1963, as inserted by s 47 Company Law Enforcement Act, 2001)); and

   (d)   the election, if required, of a committee of inspection. (There is no mandatory requirement to elect a committee of inspection and its function, if elected, is typically to supervise the liquidation and to be available for consultation by the liquidator.)

6.   All creditors must be given at least ten days' notice in writing of the creditors' meeting. The holding of the creditors' meeting must be advertised in two daily newspapers circulating in the district in which the company carried on business. This timetable cannot be shortened.

7.   The function of the liquidator once appointed is to realise all of the assets of the company. The liquidator will then distribute the proceeds of sale of the assets to creditors, in accordance with the priorities contained in the Companies Acts.

   The liquidator conducts the liquidation independently of all parties and reports on the conduct of the liquidation to meetings of the members and creditors held at the end of each year following his appointment.

### 13.5.3 COMPULSORY WINDING UP

Under s 213 Companies Act, 1963, the High Court has power to order the winding up of a company and appoint a liquidator. The parties who may petition the Court for such an order include creditors, members or the company itself. The most common petitioner is the creditors' petition.

If a creditor presents a petition to the High Court to wind up a company, the Court must determine that the company is insolvent and unable to pay its debts as they fall due or that it is just and equitable that the company be wound up.

The grounds upon which a petition may be presented are listed in s 213 Companies Act, 1963. The two most common grounds are:

(a)    that a company is unable to pay its debts (para (e) of s 213), the circumstances in which a company is deemed to be unable to pay its debts are set out in s 214; and

(b)    that it is just and equitable that the company should be wound up (in the opinion of the Court) (para (f) of s 213).

On hearing the petition, the Court may dismiss it, adjourn it or make a winding-up order. This order places the company into liquidation and appoints the *official liquidator* who becomes its sole officer. The directors' powers cease on the appointment of the official liquidator.

The Court can, on sufficient urgency being shown, appoint a provisional liquidator prior to the winding up order for the purpose of continuing the company's business or protecting its assets up until the appointment of an official liquidator.

The procedure in a compulsory liquidation is broadly similar to that outlined above in relation to the conduct of a voluntary liquidation, save that the appointment arises, not from meetings of members and creditors, but by order of the High Court.

Court liquidations are more time consuming and cumbersome than voluntary liquidations and it would certainly be expected that the costs, fees, and expenses associated with the process would be significantly higher than those incurred in a voluntary liquidation.

The obligations of the liquidator, in both cases, is to take control of all the property and assets of the company, to realise the assets in such a way as to discharge all the company's liabilities and to pay all the creditors, if possible. If it is not possible to pay all the creditors, there are statutory provisions setting out the priorities to be applied. In summary, those priorities are as follows:

(a)    fixed charges in order of priority of their creation;

(b)    costs and expenses of the winding up;

(c)    fees, costs and expenses of an examiner;

(d)    fees due to the liquidator;

(e)    claims under the Social Welfare Consolidation Act, 1981;

(f)    preferential debts pursuant to s 285 Companies Act, 1963, ranking *pari passu* with each other;

(g)    uncrystallised floating charges in order of their creation;

(h)    unsecured debts ranking *pari passu* with each other; and

(i)    deferred debts ranking *pari passu* with each other.

The liquidator is charged with certain statutory duties and powers, including carrying on the business of the company as far as may be necessary for the beneficial winding up. To that end, he is empowered to continue contracts to which the company is a party, but only insofar as it is for the benefit of the winding up.

## 13.6    Consequences of Insolvent Liquidation

### 13.6.1    FUNCTIONS OF A LIQUIDATOR

#### 13.6.1.1    Functions

A liquidator is appointed to wind up the affairs of a company. This involves the realisation and distribution of assets. His duties include examining the affairs of a company to establish if these are assets which were improperly transerred by the company. In exceptional circumstances, directors can be held personally liable for the debts of the company.

The following is an introduction to the provisions of the Companies Acts, 1963–2003, which are commonly invoked in practice in the context of an insolvent liquidation of a company.

#### 13.6.1.2    Post-commencement dispositions

Section 218 Companies Act, 1963 provides that:

> *in a winding up by the court, any disposition of the property, including things in action and any transfer of shares or alteration in the status of the members of the company, made after the commencement of the winding up, shall be void.*

Accordingly, payments out of a company's bank account after the appointment of a liquidator will be void.

#### 13.6.1.3    Fraudulent dispositions of property (s 139 Companies Act, 1990)

A liquidator may apply to the High Court for the return of property disposed of by the company if the liquidator is of the opinion that the *effect* of such a disposal was to perpetrate a fraud on the company, its members or creditors. Where the court is satisfied of this, it may order the return of the proceeds of sale on such terms as it sees fit.

#### 13.6.1.4    Fraudulent preference (s 286(1) Companies Act), 1963

Section 286(1) Companies Act, 1963, provides, inter alia, that any payment or disposal of property of a company, which at the time is unable to pay its debts as they fall due, in favour of any creditor, within six months of the commencement of the winding up, with a view to giving the creditor a preference over the other creditors, shall be deemed to be a fraudulent preference of its creditors and will be invalid. Where a payment or disposal of the asset was made in favour of a connected person, the period of six months is replaced with a period of two years and there is a presumption that an intent to prefer existed.

#### 13.6.1.5    Invalidating floating charges (s 288 Companies Act, 1963)

Section 288(1) of the Companies Act, 1963, provides that:

> where a company is being wound up, a floating charge on the undertaking or property of the company created within 12 months before the commencement of the winding up shall, unless it is proved that the company, immediately after the creation of the charge was solvent, be invalid, except as to money actually advanced or paid, or the actual price or value of goods or services sold or supplied to the company at the time of or subsequent to the creation of, and in consideration for the charge.

If a floating charge is declared to be invalid, the creditor becomes an unsecured creditor in the liquidation of the company.

#### 13.6.1.6    Fraudulent trading (s 297 Companies Act, 1963)

Section 297 of the Companies Act, 1963, provides that:

> Where a person is knowingly a party to the carrying on of a business with intent to defraud creditors of the company, or creditors of any other person or for any fraudulent purpose, that person shall be guilty of an offence.

The section provides for a maximum penalty of imprisonment for a term not exceeding seven years or a fine not exceeding €63,487.00 (IR£50,000), or both.

Under s 297(A), any person found guilty of fraudulent trading can also be held personally liable without limitation of liability for all or any part of the debts or other liabilities of the company as the court may direct. In order to impose this civil liability, it is necessary to show *fraudulent intent* on the part of directors. There have been only a limited number of reported cases, the most important ones being: *Kellys Carpetdrome Limited (In Liquidation)* [1984] ILRM 418, *Hunting Lodges Limited* [1985] ILRM 75, *Re Aluminium Fabricators Limited* [1984] ILRM 399 and *Corran Building Services Limited (In Liquidation)* 18 March 2004, District Court, unreported.

#### 13.6.1.7    Reckless trading

Section 297(A) of the Companies Act, 1963 (as amended by the Companies Act, 1990), provides that personal liability can be imposed where it appears that a person was, when an officer of the company, 'knowingly a party to the carrying on of any business of the company in a reckless manner'.

Without prejudice to the general concept of recklessness, the section contains a deeming provision, so that the following are deemed instances of recklessness:

(a) where a person was a party to the carrying on of the business and having regard to the general knowledge, skill and experience that may reasonably be expected of a person in his position, he ought to have known that his actions or those of the company would cause loss to the creditors of the company or any of them; or

(b) he was a party to the contracting of a debt by the company and did not honestly believe on reasonable grounds that the company would be able to pay the debt when it fell due for payment, as well as all its other debts (taking into account the contingent and prospective liabilities).

The test is an objective test and accordingly any director who assumes such a position must meet certain standards of knowledge, skill and experience.

Since the introduction of the concept of reckless trading, there have been very few reserved judgments on this section. The leading case is the case of *Re Hefferon Kearns Limited* [1992] ILRM 51. In this case, there was evidence that the directors were aware of the fact that the company was insolvent, but continued to trade and incur certain debts in an effort to rescue the company. On the facts, the court found in favour of the defendant directors, but the judgment contains a number of important statements about the concept of reckless trading:

(a) The section does not impose collective responsibility. It operates independently, individually and personally against the officers and the onus is on a claimant to prove in relation to each director and officer that his conduct falls within the ambit of conduct prohibited.

(b) The inclusion of the word 'knowingly' in the section requires that the director is a party to the carrying on of the business in a manner which the director *knows very well* involves an obvious and serious risk of loss or damage to others and yet ignores that risk because he does not really care whether others suffer loss or damage, or because his selfish desire to keep his own company alive overrides any concern he might have for others.

This judgment is the main Irish judgment on the section. The critical feature of reckless trading, and the most common basis for proving such conduct, is if it can be shown that the directors have caused or permitted the company to continue to incur liabilities without having reasonable grounds to believe that the company would be able to pay its debts so incurred as they fall due.

### 13.6.1.8 Failure to keep proper books of account (s 202 Companies Act, 1990)

Section 202 Companies Act, 1990, requires that every company shall cause to be kept proper books of account. Sections 203 and 204 prescribe the liability of officers of the company where proper books of account are not kept. If the company is being wound up and is unable to pay all its debts and has contravened s 202 and the court considers that such contravention has contributed to the company's inability to pay all of its debts, or has resulted in substantial uncertainty as to the assets and liabilities of the company, or has substantially impeded the orderly winding up thereof, then under s 203 criminal liability can be imposed, including a fine of up to €12,697 (IR£10,000) or a term of imprisonment of up to five years or both. Under s 204, in an insolvent liquidation, the court has power to declare that any officer so in default shall be personally liable without limitation of liability for all or such part as may be specified by the court of the debts of the company.

Each of these sections provides for a defence that where a director took all reasonable steps to secure compliance by the company with s 202 or had reasonable grounds for believing and did believe that a competent and reliable person acting under the supervision or control of a director of the company who has been formally allocated such responsibility was charged with the duty of ensuring that that section was complied with and was in a position to discharge that duty.

The leading case on this remedy is the case of *Mantruck Services Limited: Mehigan v Duignan* [1997] 1 ILRM 171. In that case, the court held there would have to be established a casual link between the failure complained of, in this case the failure to keep proper books of account, and the loss suffered by the creditors. The court held that the director concerned should be held personally liable for that portion of the costs, fees and expenses associated with the winding up of the company, which was directly attributable to the failure to maintain proper books and records.

### 13.6.1.9 Misfeasance (s 298 Companies Act, 1963)

Section 298 Companies Act, 1963, has not frequently been invoked. This section provides that where it appears that an officer or other party has misapplied assets of the company or been guilty of 'misfeasance or breach of duty or breach of trust', the court may make an order compelling him to restore the property or assets concerned or to contribute to the assets of the company by way of compensation in respect of the misapplication of assets. The section is not confined to directors and officers, but applies to any person who has taken part in the formation or promotion of the company.

## 13.6.2 CONSEQUENCES OF INSOLVENT LIQUIDATION FOR DIRECTORS OF A COMPANY

### 13.6.2.1 Restriction (s 150 Companies Act, 1990, as amended by s 56 of the Company Law Enforcement Act, 2001)

Section 150 Companies Act, 1990, provides that where a person has been a director of a company at any time within twelve months prior to the commencement of the winding up and the company is placed in insolvent liquidation, he shall be liable to be restricted from acting as a director of another company for a period of five years.

Section 56 Company Law Enforcement Act, 2001, provides that the liquidators of all insolvent companies are obliged to bring an application under s 150 Companies Act, 1990, unless the liquidator is relieved of this obligation by the Director of Corporate Enforcement.

A restriction order means that any company to which the director is subsequently appointed must meet capital requirements such as the nominal value of the allotted share capital of the company shall:

(a)   in the case of a public limited company, be at least €317,434.32; and

(b)   in the case of any other company, be at least €63,486.90.

There are also specific rules regarding the maintenance of share capital. To defend a restriction application, the respondent must demonstrate that they acted honestly and responsibly in relation to the conduct of the affairs of the company and that there is no other reason why it would be equitable that a restriction order be made. The onus of establishing that the person has acted honestly and responsibly is on the director concerned. There have been numerous judgments on the provisions of s 150 and the meaning of the terms 'acting honestly and responsibly'.

Most of the decided cases concerning this section have focused on the question of what is meant by acting 'responsibly', it having been accepted that there was no evidence of dishonesty. However, there have been some reported judgments where the courts have considered whether the directors of a company have acted honestly. In the case of *Re Outdoor Advertising Services Limited* [1997] IEHC 201, Costello J held that the directors had not acted honestly or responsibly as they had consciously and deliberately sought to benefit themselves personally at the expense of the insolvent company's creditors.

In *La Moselle Clothing Limited* [1998] ILRM 345, the court held that the simple fact that the business failed is not evidence of a lack of responsibility or of dishonesty. The court identified the considerations which should be taken into account in determining whether a director has acted 'responsibly'. These considerations were approved by the Supreme Court in *Re Squash (Ireland) Limited*, and are as follows:

(a)   The extent to which the director has or has not complied with any obligation imposed by the Companies Acts.

(b)   The extent to which his conduct could be regarded as so incompetent as to amount to irresponsibility.

(c)   The extent of the director's responsibility for the insolvency itself.

(d)   The extent of the director's responsibility for the net deficiency in the assets disclosed at the date of the winding up.

(e)   The extent to which the director has in his conduct of the affairs of the company displayed a lack of commercial probity or want of proper standard.

The court also considered that it may take into account any relevant conduct after the commencement of the winding up such as failure to cooperate with the liquidator.

In *Re Tralee Beef & Lamb Limited* (20 July 2004), it was held that the court should also have regard to the duties imposed on a director at common law. This judgment has been overturned by the Supreme Court in a judgment that was critical of the legislation governing restriction orders. However, in considering the conduct of directors, it is possible in future cases that the court will have regard to the common law duties of directors.

# 13.7    Disqualification

Under s 160 Companies Act, 1990, the grounds for the making of a disqualification order include the following:

(a)    that the person has been convicted of an indictable offence or has been guilty of any fraud or dishonesty in relation to a company, its members or creditors;

(b)    breach of duty;

(c)    having a declaration of personal liability made under s 297(A) Companies Act, 1963 (i.e. fraudulent or reckless trading);

(d)    conduct making him unfit to be concerned in the management of a company;

(e)    persistent default in relation to the 'relevant requirements'. These are primarily requirements concerning the filing of company returns, but they now include having been found guilty of two or more offences under s 202 Companies Act, 1990;

(f)    being a person disqualified under the law of another state from being appointed to act as a director or officer in cases where the court is satisfied that if the conduct concerned had arisen in this state, it would have been proper to make a disqualification order; and

(g)    being a director of a company that is struck off the register pursuant to s 12 Companies (Amendment) Act, 1982.

## 13.7.1    SHADOW DIRECTORS

The remedies and sanctions discussed in this section apply to 'shadow directors'. There are a number of cases arising from s 150 in which the court has had to consider whether persons have become shadow directors and as such should be the subject of restriction or disqualification orders. Section 27 of the

Companies Act, 1990, defines a shadow director as '*a person in accordance with whose directions or instructions the directors of a company are accustomed to act*'.

In the case of *Re Vehicle Imports Limited,* 23 November 2000, High Court, unreported, the court held that the company's accountant and auditor was in the particular circumstances a shadow director. There was evidence that the accountant advised the client as to which cheques to write and which payments to make from time to time. He advised the client to sign blank cheques, which were then left with the accountant to determine, *as part of his auditing role,* which suppliers of the company were to be paid. As such, the accountant/auditor was in substantial control of all of the financial lodgements. Finally, the accountant concerned had also given advice to the directors concerning the signing of personal guarantees.

Section 27 specifically provides that if the directors are accustomed to acting on the advice or directions of a person by reason only that they are doing so on advice given by him in a professional capacity, this will not constitute the person concerned a shadow director.

The case of *Gasca Limited* [2001] IEHC 20 concerned a company in which the only two directors had resigned some time prior to the liquidation. The shareholder appointed two persons to act as managers of the company and to run the company's affairs on a day-to-day basis. They were not appointed directors. Mr Justice McCracken considered that there was sufficient evidence to show that the principal shareholder of the company was in effect controlling the affairs of the company by giving direct instructions to the managers concerned. As such, he had become a shadow director and a restriction order was made in respect of him.

## 13.7.2 DE FACTO DIRECTORS

The issues discussed in this chapter can also apply to persons who have not been formally appointed to the board of directors of a company. Section 2 Companies Act, 1963, defines a director to '*include any person occupying the position of director by whatever named called*'.

The question of a person, other than a shadow director, being deemed to be a de facto director, was considered for the first time in the case of *Re Lynrowan Enterprises Limited (In Liquidation)* [2002] IEHC 90, which arose from an application by the liquidator of the company for restriction orders pursuant to s 150 Companies Act, 1990. In this case, the liquidator named as a respondent to the application a person, Mr James V. Mealy, who had never been validly appointed a director of the company. The court held that:

> a person although not validly appointed a director of a company may nonetheless be said to be a *de facto* director and thus deemed to be a 'a director' within the meaning of s 2 (1) Companies Act, 1963 and thus amenable to the restriction contained in s 150 Companies Act, 1990 in the following circumstances:

(a)   where there is clear evidence that that person has been either the sale person directing the affairs of the company, or

(b)   is directing the affairs of the company with others equally lacking in valid appointment, or

(c)   where there were other validly appointed directors that he was acting on an equal or more influential footing with the true directors in directing the affairs of the company.

## 13.8   Recent Developments Affecting Insolvency Law and Practice

In the last number of years, there have been far-reaching developments in the field of insolvency law, which have the aim of improving both the conduct of directors and officers of companies and the manner in which their conduct is supervised.

The developments have come in two principal forms:

(a)   the Company Law Enforcement Act, 2001; and

(b)   the EU Insolvency Regulation No 1346/2000.

### 13.8.1   COMPANY LAW ENFORCEMENT ACT, 2001

The main function of the Company Law Enforcement Act, 2001 (the '2001 Act') was to establish the office of the Director of Corporate Enforcement. The Director, whose principal function is to ensure compliance with the Companies Acts and other corporate regulations, has a number of powers conferred upon him by the 2001 Act, including investigative powers that were previously held by the Minister for Enterprise, Trade and Employment and powers to supervise the conduct of liquidations and receiverships.

#### 13.8.1.1   Reporting of liquidators

The 2001 Act, with the aim of reforming the way in which the accountancy profession is regulated, also imposes a positive obligation on bodies regulating the profession to report certain matters to the Director. Section 58 provides that where a disciplinary committee of a prescribed professional body finds that one of its members conducted a liquidation or receivership and did not maintain appropriate records, that body must report the finding, and details of same, to the Director. Similar obligations apply where the body has reasonable grounds for believing that a member has committed an indictable offence under the Companies Acts during the course of a liquidation or receivership.

While the 2001 Act had the aim of improving the manner in which persons who act as liquidators or receivers are supervised, it did not introduce a system for the licensing of insolvency practitioners, as exists in the UK. At present, the only provision which makes stipulations in relation to the qualifications of liquidators is s 300 Companies Act, 1963, which merely stipulates the parties who are not qualified to act as liquidator of a company. They include a body corporate or a person who has been within twelve months from the commencement of the company an officer or servant of the company, or persons connected to such an officer or servant.

### 13.8.1.2 Other powers of Director

The 2001 Act also enables the Director of Corporate Enforcement to initiate actions, which previously were only available to liquidators and individual creditors, such as misfeasance proceedings against directors, promoters, liquidators, receivers or examiners under s 298 Companies Act, 1963.

Finally, the 2001 Act also granted the Director the power to initiate certain proceedings that could previously only be initiated by directors. Section 251 Companies Act, 1990, provided that where a company which is insolvent and is not being wound up and the only reason why it is not being wound up is the insufficiency of its assets, the liquidator of the company could bring a number of applications such as proceedings to hold directors personally liable for fraudulent or reckless trading or misfeasance proceedings or proceedings to hold directors personally liable for failure to keep proper books of account of the company. The 2001 Act extends the power to commence such proceedings to the Director of Corporate Enforcement.

## 13.8.2 EU COUNCIL REGULATION NO 1346/2000 ON INSOLVENCY PROCEEDINGS

Before this Regulation was enacted, liquidators who were appointed to companies that operated across the EU encountered difficulties in ensuring that their appointment and powers were recognised in other Member States. The Brussels Convention on Jurisdiction of Courts and Enforcement of Judgments in Civil and Commercial Matters expressly exempted bankruptcies, the winding up of insolvent companies, judicial arrangements, compositions and analogous proceedings from its operation. Consequently, courts of different Member States were forced to adopt an ad hoc and frequently inconsistent approach towards the recognition of liquidators on a cross-border basis.

These problems were addressed by Regulation No 1346/2000, which came into force on 31 May 2002 and which applies where the company concerned has its main centre of interests within a Member State of the EU. While the Regulation does not attempt to harmonise substantive bankruptcy and insolvency laws across the EU, it does establish a regime for improving the efficiency of the conduct of cross-border insolvencies. The Regulation creates a system whereby basic orders relating to the appointment of liquidators and other officials, or the invocation of remedies typically available to them, that are made in one Member State may be recognised and enforced across all other Member States. The Regulation also establishes a regime for the management of asset realisation and processing of creditor claims.

One of the most important decisions relating to the interpretation of the Regulation is the Irish case of *Eurofood IFSC Limited*. Any students interested in cross-border insolvency matters should read the judgment in that case.

As a regulation passed at EU level, the position was only altered in so far as Member States were concerned. Denmark has opted out of the Regulation and accordingly the rules for recognition and enforcement, which previously applied to that State and to non-EU Member States, remain unchanged.

# CHAPTER 14

# DISPUTE RESOLUTION

## 14.1 Introduction

There are many ways in which a commercial dispute can be settled. The ideal is that the disputing parties settle their dispute without reference to anyone else. If they are unable to settle their differences on their own, then, unless they are prepared to agree to some other way of determining their dispute, their only recourse is to the courts. Litigation can be slow, expensive and unpredictable and for that reason, in both common law and civil law jurisdictions, there has been a growing focus over the last twenty years or so on finding ways whereby parties to a commercial contract can resolve their disputes in a more productive, efficient, and cost-effective way.

### 14.1.1 METHODS OF DISPUTE RESOLUTION

The methods of dispute resolution fall into two categories.

#### 14.1.1.1 Final determination procedures

Under these procedures, the parties have failed to resolve the disputes which have arisen between them and now require the disputes to be resolved by a third party. The principal procedures under this heading are the following:

(a) litigation;

(b) arbitration; and

(c) expert determination.

These procedures essentially involve an analysis of the legal obligations of the parties, both under the terms of the contract which the parties have signed and under the law applicable to it. Because this analysis is generally an historical analysis of who has abided by the terms of the contract and who has not, a determination under one of these three procedures generally results in one party being a winner and the other a loser.

### 14.1.1.2 Preliminary determination procedures

These procedures are designed to give to the parties greater control over the resolution of their disputes and to offer potentially more flexible, creative, and more future-orientated outcomes. The principal procedures are as follows:

(a) mediation;

(b) conciliation;

(c) mini-trial;

(d) med-arb; and

(e) Dispute Boards.

These procedures are in effect preliminary processes which give the parties a realistic opportunity to resolve their disputes on terms acceptable to them but on the basis that if the adopted procedure fails, they may be left with no alternative but to have their dispute determined by one of the Final Determination Procedures, the choice of which will depend on the terms of the applicable contract.

These procedures have been welcomed and adopted widely, both in Ireland and abroad. They are entirely market driven, with the construction industry being in the vanguard of their development.

The enormous increase in international trade has seen a comparable growth in the international character of all modes of dispute resolution. This has led to a desire, both nationally and internationally, to simplify and standardise dispute resolution procedures, which has resulted in an overhaul of many procedural codes.

## 14.1.2 AGREEMENT OF PARTIES

An important point to bear in mind, is that if the parties to a contract wish to avail of any of the procedures for determining disputes other than litigation, they have to agree to do so. The reality is that if that agreement is not reached when the contract is being negotiated, it may prove difficult, if not impossible, to do so once the dispute has arisen.

## 14.1.3 ADR

All methods of dispute resolution other than litigation and arbitration are commonly referred to as 'ADR' (Alternative Dispute Resolution).

## 14.2    Final Determination Procedures

### 14.2.1    LITIGATION

Litigation is the fallback for resolving disputes if the parties cannot agree on an alternative. That said, something in the order of 90 per cent of litigation proceedings which are commenced do not proceed to a full trial and court judgment, either because for one reason or another they are not pursued, or because they are settled before or during the trial.

Court delays and the general costs of litigation continue to be the main frustration of practitioners. However, the following developments should be noted:

(a)    both common law and civil law jurisdictions are increasingly seeking ways to improve the efficiency, speed and cost of access to the courts. This will have some impact on the use of alternatives;

(b)    courts and legal systems are increasingly adopting active case management systems, such as have been established by the Woolf reforms in England and in the Commercial Court in Ireland; and

(c)    courts are increasingly attempting to integrate ADR methods into court procedures, in that the parties may be advised by the court to try to resolve their disputes by some method of alternative dispute resolution in the first instance, with any party failing to participate in such ADR process other than for good reason being subject to sanction by the court.

Parties involved in international business do need to be aware that both the laws and court procedures vary from country to country and a party should not enter into a contract with a party from another country or a foreign subject matter without being clear as to what law applies to the contract and any dispute arising under it.

### 14.2.2.    ARBITRATION

#### 14.2.2.1    General

With the exception of certain statutory arbitrations (see **14.2.2.5** below), the basis of all arbitration is the agreement to arbitrate. If the parties to a dispute do not agree to arbitrate there can be no arbitration.

#### 14.2.2.2    Examples

Arbitration is not a speciality. It can arise in a variety of agreements, for example:

• Law Society Conditions of Sale

• RIAI Building Contract

- Rent Review Clause
- Holiday Booking Conditions
- Trade Associations

### 14.2.2.3 Possible advantages

Arbitration is often chosen by parties to commercial agreements because of the potential advantages of arbitration over litigation. The advantages can be the following.

#### (a)  Privacy

Arbitration proceedings are held in private and remain private, unless there is an issue in the proceedings which becomes the subject of a reference to the courts.

#### (b)  Specialist knowledge of arbitrator

Where the dispute requires specialist knowledge or experience to understand, the parties may feel more comfortable having the dispute adjudicated by a person with the particular specialist knowledge or experience. In arbitration, the parties can choose the person whom they wish to act as arbitrator or alternatively the method by which the arbitrator will be appointed.

#### (c)  Flexibility of procedure

The conduct of the arbitration is not tied to any defined procedure. The parties, if they agree, are able to choose whatever procedure they feel is best suited to the resolution of their dispute.

#### (d)  Costs

Because they have a considerable measure of control over how the arbitration is to be conducted, the parties have control over the costs of the arbitration proceedings. The arbitration costs will, of course, include those of the arbitrator, unlike in litigation where the parties are not responsible for the costs of the judge.

#### (e)  Speed

Because the parties have control over the arbitration procedure, they have control, subject to the cooperation of the arbitrator, over the speed at which the arbitration will be conducted and the time within which they can have a ruling on their dispute.

### (f) Finality of the arbitrator's award

An arbitrator's award is final and binding on the parties. It cannot be the subject of an appeal, other than under one of the limited headings for appeal permitted by the Arbitration Acts (as defined in **14.2.2.5** below).

### (g) Enforcement abroad

The enforcement of court judgments abroad can be difficult. Certain international conventions make arbitration awards much easier to enforce in countries which have subscribed to the conventions.

### 14.2.2.4 Possible disadvantages

The possible advantages have, however, to be weighed against the following:

### (a) Costs

The costs for which the parties are responsible in an arbitration will include the fees and expenses of the arbitrator. This is a cost not borne by parties in litigation who are not responsible for the costs of the judge.

### (b) Collteral disputes

An arbitrator does not have any jurisdiction, either over persons who are not parties to the arbitration agreement, or over issues which are not the subject of the reference to arbitration. Disputes between the parties involving other issues or involving third parties will, unless all of the parties concerned agree otherwise, have to be the subject of separate proceedings.

### (c) Sanctions

An arbitrator does not have all the powers of a judge to impose sanctions on a defaulting party. An arbitrator does not, for example, have power to strike out arbitration proceedings for want of prosecution.

### 14.2.2.5 Irish arbitration law

Irish arbitration law is governed by the Arbitration Act, 1954 (the '1954 Act'), the Arbitration Act, 1980 (the '1980 Act') and the Arbitration (International Commercial) Act, 1998 (the '1998 Act') (together referred to as 'the Arbitration Acts').

Certain kinds of dispute may, however, be governed by the provisions of a particular statute which requires the dispute to be resolved in accordance with the provisions of an arbitration system established by the statute. This is commonly known as statutory arbitration. An example is the arbitration system established by the Acquisition of Land (Assessment of Compensation) Act, 1919, which provides for the compensation payable to a landowner, whose land has been acquired under a compulsory purchase order, to be determined by arbitration by one of two statutory arbitrators appointed for the purpose under the Act.

Two kinds of arbitration are specifically excluded from the application of the Arbitration Acts; namely, unwritten arbitration agreements and arbitrations relating to employment.

### (a) Unwritten arbitration agreements

An arbitration agreement is defined by s 2(1) of the 1954 Act as meaning 'a written agreement to refer present or future differences to arbitration, whether an arbitrator is named therein or not'. Although arbitration agreements are almost always in writing, this does not mean that an oral arbitration agreement is invalid but rather that it will not be governed by the provisions of the Arbitration Acts. This could be very important when it comes to the enforcement of the arbitration award, because an award under the Arbitration Acts may be enforced, by leave of the High Court, in the same manner as a court judgment or order to the same effect.

### (b) Arbitrations relating to employment

Section 5 of the 1954 Act states that notwithstanding anything contained in the 1954 Act, the 1954 Act does not apply to:

    *(a)   an arbitration under an agreement providing for the reference to, or the settlement by, arbitration of any question relating to the terms or conditions of employment or the remuneration of any employees, including persons employed by or under the State or Local Authorities, or*

    *(b)   an arbitration under s 70 of the Industrial Relations Act, 1946 (No 26 of 1946).*

The purpose of excluding such employment arbitrations from the provisions of the Arbitration Acts was to allow these to be dealt with by tribunals established to deal specifically with employment disputes (e.g. the Employment Appeals Tribunal).

### 14.2.2.6   Matters which can be referred to arbitration

There is no clear distinction to be drawn between disputes which may be settled by arbitration and those which may not.

The general rule is that any dispute or claim concerning legal rights, which can be the subject of an enforceable award, is capable of being settled by arbitration. This general principle must be qualified as follows:

    (a)   under Art 34.3.1 of the Constitution, the High Court has original jurisdiction in and power to determine all matters and questions, whether of law or of fact, civil or criminal;

    (b)   certain kinds of arbitration are governed by special statute (see **14.2.2.5** above);

    (c)   public policy requires that certain issues be dealt with by the courts or some other statutory tribunal;

(d)    illegality may render an arbitration agreement unenforceable;

(e)    by virtue of s 26 of the 1954 Act, an arbitrator does not have power to order specific performance of any contract relating to land or any interest in land; and

(f)    an arbitration clause may not be enforceable where the claimant is a child.

> In *Brenton Dewick (a Minor) v Falcon Group Overseas Limited* (High Court, Johnson J, 22 October 2001, unwritten and unreported), the defendant applied to the court under s 5 of the 1980 Act for a stay on the court proceedings, arguing that the original holiday booking form signed by the claimant's mother provided for any disputes or claims arising in connection with the holiday to be determined in the absence of agreement by arbitration. The court refused to grant the stay, on the grounds that s 5 did not override the court's jurisdiction in cases involving children conferred by Ord 22, rule 10 of the Rules of the Superior Courts, 1986.

### 14.2.2.7    Arbitration agreements

There are two basic types of arbitration agreement:

(a)    the first is the agreement to submit existing disputes to arbitration which is often referred to as a 'submission agreement'; and

(b)    the second is the agreement to submit future disputes to arbitration which usually takes the form of an arbitration clause in a more substantial agreement.

While a submission agreement has the same basic objective as an arbitration clause, there is nevertheless a fundamental difference in the way a submission agreement and an arbtration clause are approached.

When a submission agreement is being drafted, the dispute has actually arisen. The parties are in a position to tailor the submission agreement to fit the particular dispute. This, of course, necessitates cooperation between the parties which may not be achievable.

This situation is quite different from the friendly relationship which normally exists when the parties are entering into a contract and are simply providing for the resolution of a possible dispute in the future. The arbitration provisions in such a contract do not normally go into too much detail, as the parties do not know at the time what kind of disputes (if any) are likely to arise, and, if they do, how best they should be handled.

Arbitration clauses can be found in a wide variety of contracts ranging from the once-off commercial contract which has been the subject of detailed paragraph by paragraph negotiation to the Law Society's General Conditions of Sale and the standard conditions of many building contracts, insurance policies and travel booking forms.

### 14.2.2.8 Drafting the arbitration clause

The importance of a properly worded arbitration clause cannot be over empha-sised. All too often agreements contain arbitration clauses, which are poorly drafted and are either inadequate as a basis for the intended arbitration or are ill-suited to the kind of dispute which the arbitration is intended to resolve.

The following specimen arbitration clauses are set out at the end of the chapter:

| | |
|---|---|
| Schedule 1 | Short form arbitration clause recommended by the Law Society |
| Schedule 2 | Submission agreement |
| Schedule 3 | Agreed arbitration clause for arbitration scheme arranged by the Chartered Institute of Arbitrators—Irish Branch on behalf of Tour Operators who are members of the Irish Travel Agents Association and which is to be included in their Booking Conditions |
| Schedule 4 | Arbitration Clause in Agreement and Schedule of Conditions of Building Contract issued by the Royal Institute of the Architects of Ireland—2002 Edition with pre-condition for prior reference to conciliation |
| Schedule 5 | Recommended Arbitration Clause—International Chamber of Commerce |
| Schedule 6 | Model Arbitration Clause—United Nations Commission on International Trade Law (UNCITRAL) |

There are many issues to be taken into account by the parties when drafting the arbitration agreement. Issues in relation to disputes arising in the future are more difficult to determine than issues in relation to disputes already in existence.

The following are issues to be considered.

#### Number of arbitrators

It is a matter for the parties to decide, when drawing up their arbitration agree-ment, whether they wish to have one or more arbitrators. The general practice in Ireland is for arbitration clauses, in relation to commercial disputes, to pro-vide for the appointment of one arbitrator.

#### Qualifications of arbitrator

Generally speaking, any person may be chosen to act as an arbitrator if he has legal capacity.

Unless it is very clear what the nature of the dispute is going to be, it is often best left to those empowered to appoint the arbitrator, when the dispute has arisen, to choose an arbitrator appropriately qualified to deal with the dispute.

The arbitration rules of some institutions stipulate specific criteria and qualifications for the arbitrator and accordingly, if these rules apply to the arbitration, the arbitrator appointed will have to meet the criteria and qualifications required.

### *Replacement of arbitrator*

If the original arbitrator dies, refuses or is unable to act or if he becomes disqualified as a result of a successful challenge, the parties may wish to appoint a substitute. If the arbitration clause does not provide for the appointment of a substitute, then application will have to be made to the High Court for a substitute to be appointed.

### 14.2.2.9 Staying litigation proceedings

Section 5(1) of the 1980 Act provides that if any party to an arbitration agreement commences legal proceedings against another party to the agreement in respect of any matter agreed to be referred to arbitration, any party to those proceedings may at any time after an appearance has been entered, but before delivering any pleadings or taking any other steps in the proceedings, apply to the court for the proceedings to be stayed. The court is bound to grant the stay, unless it is satisfied that the arbitration agreement is null and void, inoperative or incapable of being performed or that there is not in fact any dispute between the parties with regard to the matter agreed to be referred.

The following points should be noted.

(a) An application for a stay may only be made after an appearance to the litigation proceedings has been entered. A premature application for a stay will be refused.

(b) 'Taking any other steps in the proceedings' has been held to mean conduct by the applicant which shows a decision on his part to use the proceedings already commenced to advance his case against the other party. In *O'Flynn v An Bord Gais Eireann* [1982] ILRM 324, Finlay P reviewed the question of what was or was not a step in the proceedings and stated the criterion to be whether the step taken involved costs which would be lost were the stay to be granted and the matter referred to arbitration. In that case, the defendant's solicitor wrote to the plaintiff's solicitor seeking an extension of time to file the defence. The Court held that that was not a step in the proceedings which would preclude a stay. In *Gleeson v Grimes and McQuillan* unreported, High Court, 1 November 2002, Record No 2001 16198P, the second-named defendant, in the affidavit grounding his application for a stay, argued inter alia that he was not a party to the contract but consented to the Court determining that issue if it wished to do so.

The plaintiffs opposed the application on the grounds that the submission of this argument to the court constituted a step in the proceedings by the second-named defendant. Finlay Geoghegan J ruled that two requirements must be satisfied for conduct to constitute a step in the proceedings:

(i) the conduct of the applicant must be such as to demonstrate an election to abandon his right to a stay in favour of allowing the litigation to proceed; and

(ii) the act in question must have the effect of invoking the jurisdiction of the court.

As the learned judge held that the second-named defendant in making the averments in his affidavit could not be considered to have elected to abandon his rights to a stay, she granted the stay sought by him.

(c) In *Administratia Asigurarilor de Stat and others v Insurance Corporation of Ireland plc* [1990] ILRM 159, the High Court held that it has an overriding jurisdiction to refuse a stay where there are bona fide allegations of fraud.

(d) In *Brenton Dewick (a Minor) v Falcon Group Overseas Limited*, 22 October 2001, High Court, Johnson J (unwritten and unreported) the High Court held that s 5 cannot be availed of to oust the jurisdiction conferred on the High Court by Ord 22, r 10 of the Rules of the Superior Courts, 1986 in relation to cases involving children.

(e) The comments of Keane CJ in *Re Via Net Works (Ireland) Limited* [2002] 2 IR 47 seem to suggest the application of a principle in the context of staying litigation proceedings that not only will parties to an arbitration agreement be bound to adhere to it, but so, too, will those who have agreed to a certain and defined mechanism of ADR.

(f) Section 18 of the 1998 Act amended s 5 of the 1980 Act where small claims are concerned. It provides that nothing in s 5 of the 1980 Act shall prevent any party to an arbitration agreement from bringing civil proceedings under the Small Claims Procedure of the District Court as provided by the Rules of Court. The Small Claims Procedure in the District Court deals with consumer claims where the judgment sought does not exceed €1,269 (formerly IR£1,000).

### 14.2.2.10 Appointing the arbitrator

It is very much in the claimant's interest, when a dispute arises and there is an agreement to arbitrate, to ensure that the arbitrator is appointed without delay. This is because:

(a) no orders can be made or other procedural steps taken until the arbitrator has been appointed;

(b) most claims must be made within certain time limits and failure to adhere to the time limits may be fatal; and

(c)   although a successful party may be awarded the costs which he has incurred in having to arbitrate a dispute, it is unlikely that he will recover legal or other costs incurred before the arbitration proceedings are commenced.

Arbitrators may be appointed in a number of different ways. The most usual are the following.

### Agreement of the parties

Most arbitration clauses require the parties to try to agree on an arbitrator before any other method of appointing an arbitrator is adopted. Generally, the claimant will suggest a few names to the respondent who will either accept one of them or suggest some alternatives. If agreement cannot be reached, then the procedure for the appointment of an arbitrator in default of agreement, which will be set out in the arbitration clause if properly drafted, will have to be invoked. This, for example, may require the arbitrator to be appointed by the President of some named institution. If there is no specified procedure, the party seeking the appointment will have to consider whether the High Court has the power under the 1954 Act to make the appointment.

Naming a specific arbitrator in an arbitration clause relating to a possible future dispute, where there is no guarantee that the person designated in the agreement to act as arbitrator will be willing and able to do so, is to be avoided.

Naming a specific arbitrator in a submission agreement entered into after the dispute has arisen, when the kind of person required as arbitrator is readily identifiable, makes sense if there is provision for a substitute arbitrator to be appointed if the appointed arbitrator refuses or is unable to act or dies.

It is not, of course, sufficient for the parties merely to agree on the arbitrator. The person chosen must be prepared to accept the appointment.

### Professional institutions

Many arbitration agreements provide that if the parties cannot agree on an arbitrator, the appointment may be made on the application of either party by the President for the time being of a named institution.

Most institutions nowadays have established their own guidelines for such appointments.As a general rule, they will charge an administration fee before considering any application for an appointment and will require the following basic information to be submitted to the President before any appointment is made:

(a)   a copy of the arbitration agreement;

(b)   the names and addresses of the parties involved;

(c)   details of the nature of the dispute;

(d)   an estimate of the value of the claim in dispute;

(e)   the names and addresses of any parties who for one reason or another should not be considered for appointment as arbitrator; and

(f)    evidence that the parties have failed to agree upon the appointment of an arbitrator.

The purpose of obtaining this information is because the President, before he can make the appointment, will have to:

(a)    satisfy himself that he has the power to make the appointment and that any preconditions to the making of the appointment have been complied with; and

(b)    have sufficient information about the nature of the dispute and the parties to enable him to choose an appropriate arbitrator.

Normally, once he has made his appointment, the President will have no further powers in relation to the arbitration. Accordingly, if the arbitrator appointed by him subsequently refuses to act or is incapable of acting or dies, the parties, in the absence of any special provision in the arbitration clause, may be left with no alternative but to consider an application to the High Court under the Arbitration Acts for a substitute appointment to be made.

For this reason, it is recommended that an arbitration clause which gives a third party the power to appoint an arbitrator in the event of a dispute should also give him the power to nominate a substitute arbitrator, if circumstances require it.

### Arbitration institutions

Institutions have been established nationally and internationally to promote arbitration. These institutions invariably have model clauses which they recommend to parties whose wish it is, when entering into an arbitration agreement, to have the arbitration governed by their rules.

It is, however, always open to the parties to expand or modify the clauses to meet their own requirements. Some arbitration institutions (for example, The Chartered Institute of Arbitrators and The International Chamber of Commerce) have their own specific rules dealing with the conduct of the arbitration while others may adopt a standard set of rules with or without ammendment.

### Trade associations

Many arbitrations are governed by the regulations of trade associations, whose standard conditions of trade provide for all disputes arising with members of the trade to be resolved by an arbitration system established by the particular trade.

### High Court

Section 18 of the 1954 Act confers on the High Court the power to appoint an arbitrator in cases where the parties have chosen arbitration as the method by which they wish their dispute to be resolved and have either not agreed on the manner in which the arbitrator is to be appointed or the arbitrator, or the authority chosen by them to appoint the arbitrator, is for whatever reason unwilling or unable to act.

### 14.2.2.11 Limitation periods

The Statute of Limitations, 1957, applies to arbitrations as it applies to actions in the High Court. Accordingly, an arbitration may be time-barred if the arbitration proceedings are not initiated in time.

Section 74 of the statute deems an arbitration to have commenced:

> *when one party to the arbitration agreement serves on the other party or parties a written notice requiring him or them to appoint or concur in appointing an arbitrator or, where the arbitration agreement provides that the reference shall be to a person named or designated in the agreement, requiring him or them to submit the dispute to the person so named or designated.*

Quite apart from the limitation period imposed by the statute, the arbitration agreement itself may impose a limitation period for the commencement of any arbitration proceedings, the conduct of the arbitration or the publication of the arbitrator's award.

However, s 45 of the 1954 Act empowers the court to extend any time limit for such period as it thinks proper, if it is of opinion that in the circumstances of the case undue hardship would otherwise be caused. The matters that should be taken into account in determining if there would be undue hardship were considered in *Walsh v Shield Insurance Company Limited* [1977] ILRM 218, where the Court held that while there had been inexcusable delay on the part of the applicant in commencing arbitration proceedings under the terms of an insurance policy, the respondent had not been prejudiced by such delay and accordingly the Court agreed to extend the time limit for appointing the arbitrator beyond that specified in the policy.

### 14.2.2.12 Preliminary meeting

Except in the case of arbitrations involving small claims, a preliminary meeting is probably the most important procedural step if the potential advantages of arbitration are to be achieved. The preliminary meeting should be convened by the arbitrator as soon as possible after his appointment. The primary objective of the preliminary meeting is to establish the future conduct of the arbitration, with a view to having the dispute resolved in the most efficient and economical way. On this, the arbitrator should seek to get the agreement of the parties but, in the absence of agreement, he is fully empowered to fix the procedure subject to any special provisions in the arbitration clause and subject to the general principles of natural justice.

A draft agenda of matters, to be discussed at the preliminary meeting, is included in Schedule 7. The arbitrator may, however, decide to exclude from the agenda matters relating to the conduct of the arbitration hearing and postpone these for consideration to another meeting, to be convened when the exchange of pleadings has been concluded.

As a general rule, before an arbitrator will agree to proceed with the arbitration, he will require one, or preferably both, of the parties to sign a Form of Appointment of Arbitrator on the lines of the draft set out in Schedule 8. The arbitrator's purpose in requiring such a form to be completed is to give him a contractual right against at least one of the parties to recover any fees or expenses incurred by him in relation to the arbitration. An arbitrator can be left high and dry, having done a considerable amount of work in relation to the arbitration, if the parties settle their dispute and do so without reference to him.

Immediately following the preliminary meeting, the arbitrator will normally issue an Order for Directions, which will encompass formal directions from the arbitrator on the future conduct of the arbitration by reference to what has been agreed or fixed at the preliminary meeting.

### 14.2.2.13 Powers of the arbitrator

An arbitrator is appointed to determine a dispute which has arisen between the parties. It is important that the arbitrator identifies all of the elements of the dispute and that he takes all reasonable steps to conduct the arbitration, having at all times regard to the wishes and interests of both parties, in a fair, efficient and economic way.

Subject to any terms contained in the arbitration agreement, an arbitrator has a wide discretion as to how the arbitration is to be conducted. He must, however, have regard at all times to the overriding principles of natural justice.

Apart from any specific powers conferred upon him by the arbitration agreement, an arbitrator has powers conferred upon him by statute. The principal statutory powers are the following.

(a) Section 19 of the 1954 Act provides that every arbitration agreement (unless a contrary intention is expressed in the agreement and subject to any legal objection) shall be deemed to contain the following provisions:

   (i) that the parties to the reference and all persons claiming through them shall submit to be examined by the arbitrator on oath or affirmation;

   (ii) that any witnesses shall, if the arbitrator thinks fit, be examined on oath or affirmation;

   (iii) that the arbitrator will have power to administer oaths or to take the affirmation of any such person;

   (iv) that the parties to the reference and all persons claiming through them shall produce before the arbitrator or umpire all documents (other than documents the production of which could not be compelled on the trial of an action) within their possession or power respectively which may be required or called for; and

   (v) that the parties to the reference and all persons claiming through them shall do all such other things which during the arbitration proceedings the arbitrator may require.

(b) Section 23 of the 1954 Act gives the arbitrator power to make an award at any time.

(c) Section 25 of the 1954 Act gives the arbitrator power to make an interim award.

(d) Section 26 of the 1954 Act gives the arbitrator the same power as the High Court to order specific performance of any contract other than a contract relating to land or any interest in land.

(e) Section 28 of the 1954 Act gives the arbitrator power to correct in an award any clerical mistake or error arising from any accidental slip or omission.

(f) Section 29 of the 1954 Act gives the arbitrator power to order to and by whom and in what manner the costs of the reference and of the award are to be paid including, with the consent of the parties, power to tax or settle the amount of those costs.

(g) Section 35 of the 1954 Act gives the arbitrator power to state any question of law arising in the course of the reference or any award or any part of the award in the form of a special case for the decision of the High Court. (See **14.2.2.15** below.)

(h) Section 17 of the Arbitration (International Commercial) Act, 1998 amends s 34 of the 1954 Act and gives the arbitrator power to award interest at whatever rate he feels meets the justice of the case on all or part of any amount awarded by him both up to the date of the award and from the date of the award up to the date of actual payment. (See **14.2.2.21** below.)

Unless the arbitration agreement provides otherwise, an arbitrator does not have the following powers:

(a) power to order security for the amount claimed;

(b) power to order security for costs;

(c) power to grant injunctions; or

(d) power to strike out arbitration proceedings for want of prosecution.

### 14.2.2.14 Protective measures

Section 22 of the 1954 Act gives the High Court, in relation to arbitration proceedings, the same power as it has in relation to court proceedings of making orders in respect of the following:

(a) security for costs;

(b) discovery and inspection of documents and interrogatories;

(c) the giving of evidence by affidavit;

(d) examination on oath of any witness before an Officer of the Court;

(e)   the preservation, interim custody or sale of any goods which are the subject matter of the arbitration;

(f)   securing the amount in dispute;

(g)   the detention, preservation or inspection of any property or thing which is the subject of the reference; and

(h)   interim injunctions or the appointment of a receiver.

Section 22, however, states that the fact that the High Court is given these specific powers is not to be taken to prejudice any power which may be vested in an arbitrator to make such an order.

**14.2.2.15   Special case**

If an arbitrator is in doubt about the law, he is empowered under s 35 of the 1954 Act to refer any question of law arising in the course of the reference in the form of a special case for the decision of the High Court. Further, if one of the parties in the course of the proceedings, but before the award has been published, requests the arbitrator to state a case to the High Court on a point of law, the arbitrator is obliged, in the absence of good reason, to do so.

In *Stillorgan Orchard Limited v McLoughlin & Harvey* (1978) ILRM 128 the plaintiff sought to have the arbitrator's award set aside on the grounds that the arbitrator had failed to state a case on a question of law for the decision of the High Court. The High Court refused the plaintiff's application on the grounds that:

(a)   no formal request appeared to have been made by the plaintiff to the arbitrator for a special case to be stated;

(b)   there was no suggestion that the arbitrator attempted to preclude the plaintiff from stating a case;

(c)   the failure of the arbitrator to state any question of law in the form of a special case is not of itself misconduct because s 35 is permissible and not mandatory; and

(d)   the arbitrator was not guilty of misconduct.

In *Corporation of Dublin v MacGinley and another*, the plaintiff requested the arbitrator to state a case on a point of law. The arbitrator declined on the grounds that the point of law had been clearly decided in a number of recent High Court cases. The plaintiff applied to the High Court for an order compelling the arbitrator to state a case, but the High Court held that the arbitrator was correct in taking the view that he did not require the further guidance of the courts and the plaintiff's application failed.

In *Re Mizen Hotel Company* 1980 No 511 SS, the Court held that the power of the arbitrator under s 35 extends to questions of law only and not to questions of fact.

In *J. J. Jennings v O'Leary and Midland Construction and Engineering, Limited* [2004] IRLHC 318 (High Court Commercial List ex tempore, 27 May 2004, unreported,

Finlay Geoghegan J followed earlier court decisions that the question as to whether or not the court would direct a case to be stated would depend, inter alia, on the point of law in question and ruled, rejecting the claim of one of the parties that the arbitrator was obliged to state a case, that under s 35 of the 1954 Act, the court itself has a discretion as to whether or not a case should be stated, even where the question of law arises in the course of an arbitration.

In *Kevin Byrne v Edward Byrne* [2005] IEHC 55, the High Court was asked to consider whether an award made under the Dispute Resolution Clause which provided for a choice between arbitration and mediation, would be binding on the parties. Macken J held that once the parties had chosen arbitration over mediation or once an arbitration had been imposed on them in default of agreement as to one or the other, any award made pursuant to such an arbitration was binding on both parties.

### 14.2.2.16 Removal of the arbitrator

Section 24 of the 1954 Act empowers the High Court to remove an arbitrator who fails to use all reasonable dispatch in entering and proceeding with the reference in making an award. An arbitrator who is removed by the High Court in such circumstances is not entitled to receive any remuneration for his services.

The High Court may also remove an arbitrator, under s 37 of the 1954 Act, where the arbitrator has been guilty of misconduct. In the context of arbitration, the word 'misconduct' has been held to mean that the arbitrator exceeded his jurisdiction, or did not act impartially or has acted in a way which might 'reasonably give rise in the mind of an unprejudiced onlooker to the suspicion that justice was not being done'. It does not necessarily mean that the arbitrator has acted in any dishonest way.

In *State (Hegarty) v Winters* (1956) IR 320, where the arbitrator inspected the property which was the subject of the reference accompanied by an employee of one of the parties, the arbitrator was held to be guilty of misconduct and his award was set aside.

### 14.2.2.17 Documents-only arbitrations

While the general practice is for a formal arbitration hearing to be convened, the parties may agree that the matter in dispute can be satisfactorily determined by the arbitrator on the basis of written submissions being made to him. This could involve a substantial saving in costs.

In Ireland, the vast majority of arbitrations involve an arbitration hearing but in small straightforward arbitrations, having the dispute determined by written submission may make more economic sense. The general principle is that if all parties to the arbitration wish the arbitrator to proceed by way of written submission only then the arbitrator should accede to this request but if any party objects, then an oral hearing should be held.

### 14.2.2.18 Arbitration hearing

#### Pre-hearing review

If there is to be an arbitration hearing, the arbitrator may well decide, unless the arbitration is very straightforward, to hold a further meeting with the parties or their representatives when the pleadings have been closed. The purpose of such a meeting would be:

(a) to check whether all of the directions given at the preliminary meeting have been complied with and whether any further directions are required;

(b) to review the issues in dispute and to encourage the parties, where possible, to agree figures, documents, photographs, plans or other exhibits with a view to avoiding unnecessary proofs at the hearing;

(c) to review and fix the format of the arbitration hearing;

(d) to check that the facilities and other requirements necessary for the proper conduct of the arbitration hearing are in order; and

(e) to confirm the date of the arbitration hearing and the availability of all necessary parties.

#### Arbitration hearing

When all of the pleadings have been exchanged and any pre-hearing review has taken place, the arbitrator will, in consultation with the parties, seek to fix a mutually convenient date, time and place for the hearing. If he cannot agree these with the parties, then he is at liberty to fix them himself. In fixing them, he must, of course, have regard to any reasonable representations made by any party.

The arbitrator must conduct the arbitration hearing in accordance with the arbitration agreement. Within the constraints of natural justice, he has full power to decide on how the case will be heard and what procedure will be followed. This is, however, likely to have been agreed or fixed at the preliminary meeting or the pre-hearing review. It is a matter for the parties whether they wish to conduct their own case or be represented by solicitors or counsel. However, where one party is being represented by a solicitor or counsel, it is proper for the arbitrator to ensure that the other party is given an equal opportunity to be so represented.

The conduct of the hearing, depending on the nature and size of the arbitration involved, can vary from being a mirror image of a court hearing on the one hand to extreme informality on the other. Whatever is agreed or determined, the underlying principle is that each party should be treated fairly and should have a reasonable opportunity to present his own case and to oppose his opponent's case.

An arbitrator is entitled to proceed with a hearing without one of the parties being in attendance if he has given that party a reasonable opportunity to attend (*Grangeford Structures Limited (in liquidation) v S. H. Limited* 1990 ILRM 277).

### Evidence

Evidence can either be written or oral (unless, of course, it is a documents-only arbitration when all submissions will be written).

Unless the parties have agreed otherwise, the arbitrator is bound by the same rules of evidence as are the courts. He must allow each party a reasonable opportunity to present all his evidence and, if he fails to do so, his award may be set aside.

It is also important that the arbitrator decide only on the evidence before him and not on any knowledge or expertise of his own, unless he openly expresses his views arising from that knowledge or expertise and allows the parties ample opportunity to comment on them.

As far as witnesses are concerned, an arbitrator has power under s 19(1) of the 1954 Act, unless the arbitration agreement provides otherwise, to examine on oath or affirmation the parties and witnesses to the reference. A witness who refuses to attend and give evidence at the hearing can be summoned to do so by the issue of a subpoena. The arbitrator has also an implied power under s 19 to order discovery.

Where there are expert witnesses who have produced written reports, it is recommended that these be exchanged before the arbitration hearing. The arbitrator will frequently encourage the expert witnesses to distil their reports in advance of the hearing with a view to establishing the exact differences between them and thereby helping to identify for the arbitrator the precise issues in dispute.

### 14.2.2.19  Sealed offers

Because there is no equivalent in arbitration to the lodgment system which exists in litigation, offers which have been made by one party to the other prior to the arbitration hearing, and which the party making the offer wishes the arbitrator to take into account in any award which he is making on costs, are normally communicated to the arbitrator in a sealed envelope prior to the conclusion of the arbitration hearing. In case it influences his decision, the arbitrator should not open the sealed envelope until he has made his award on the substantive issue in dispute. The arbitrator will then make his award on costs having regard to whether or not the amount of the offer exceeds the amount of the award.

### 14.2.2.20  The award

There are two kinds of award:

(a)  an interim award; and

(b)  a final award.

An arbitrator can only make one final award. Accordingly, once he has made that award, his jurisdiction in relation to the arbitration to all intents and purposes ends.

Section 25 of the 1954 Act provides that, unless a contrary intention is expressed in the arbitration agreement, the arbitration agreement shall be deemed to contain a provision that the arbitrator may, if he thinks fit, make an interim award. The right to make an interim award allows the arbitrator to deal initially with some issues without having to deal with others. This can be very important if there is a preliminary issue involved, a decision on which may determine the outcome of the whole dispute without any other issues having to be decided upon.

If an issue of law arises on which the arbitrator requires a decision of the High Court, the arbitrator may give his award in the form of a special case. In such circumstances, the arbitrator will generally issue two or more alternative awards to cover the possible decisions which the High Court may give.

Unless the arbitration agreement provides otherwise, an award is not required to be in any particular form. If, however, it is to be enforceable, it should be in writing, signed by the arbitrator and dated.

As far as the contents of the award are concerned, the High Court will not enforce an award by an arbitrator, unless it contains a clear and unambiguous adjudication on all of the matters referred to him. In this regard, it is not essential that each and every issue in dispute is dealt with separately but simply that the arbitrator has not left any issues referred to him, and over which he has jurisdiction, outstanding.

The practice in Ireland is for the arbitrator not to give reasons for his award unless he is specifically required by the parties to do so. That practice was endorsed by the Supreme Court in *Manning v Shackleton and Cork County Council* [1994] I IR 397 where the applicant instituted High Court proceedings by way of judicial review seeking, inter alia, reasons for the arbitrator's award. On appeal, the Supreme Court dismissed the applicant's claim holding that the requirement that justice should appear to be done does not require that an arbitrator's award should incorporate anything in the nature of a reasoned judgment.

### 14.2.2.21  Interest

Under s 34 of the 1954 Act, a sum directed to be paid by an award, unless the award otherwise directs, carries interest from the date of the award at the same rate as a judgment debt. Section 34 did not, however, confer on an arbitrator power to award interest on any sums due up to the date of the arbitrator's award.

Section 17 of the 1998 Act amends s 34 and gives the arbitrator power to award interest at whatever rate he feels meets the justice of the case on all or part of any amount awarded by him both up to the date of the award and from the date of the award up to the date of actual payment.

Section 17 applies only to arbitration agreements entered into after the day on which the 1998 Act came into operation (20 May 1998), unless the parties to the arbitration agreement agree otherwise.

### 14.2.2.22  Costs

In arbitration, costs are divided into two categories:

(a)  the costs of the reference which are all the costs and expenses which a party has incurred in bringing his case to arbitration; and

(b)  the costs of the award which are the arbitrator's own fees and expenses.

Section 29 of the 1954 Act states that, unless the arbitration agreement provides otherwise, it shall be deemed to include a provision that the costs of both the reference and the award shall be in the discretion of the arbitrator who may direct to and by whom and in what manner those costs or any part of them shall be paid. The arbitrator is also empowered with the consent of the parties to tax and settle the amount of costs to be so paid.

Section 29 goes on to state that where an award directs any costs to be paid then, unless the arbitrator, with the consent of the parties, taxes or settles the amount to be paid by each party then the costs shall in default of agreement between the parties be taxed and ascertained by a taxing master of the High Court.

Section 33 of the 1954 Act provides that if an arbitrator refuses to deliver his award until the fees demanded by him have been paid, the High Court may order that the arbitrator deliver the award to the applicant on payment into the High Court by the applicant of the fees demanded and the arbitrator's entitlement shall be such as the Taxing Master may in due course determine on taxation.

The following points should, however, be noted.

#### (a) Agreement as to costs

In dealing with the issue of costs, the arbitrator must observe the provisions of the arbitration agreement. Under s 30 of the 1954 Act, any provision in an arbitration agreement to the effect that any party shall pay all or any part of his own costs of the reference or award shall be void. This provision, however, does not apply to an agreement to submit to arbitration a dispute which has arisen before the making of that agreement.

#### (b) Award of costs

If the arbitrator does not deal in his award with the liability for costs, any party to the reference may, within fourteen days of the publication of the award or such extended time as the High Court may allow, apply to the arbitrator for an order directing by and to whom those costs shall be paid. In such event, the arbitrator shall, after hearing any party who may desire to be heard, amend his award by adding such directions as he may think proper in relation to the payment of costs.

### (c) Arbitrator's discretion

While an arbitrator has a discretion over who shall bear the costs of both the award and the reference and the manner in which those costs shall be paid, it has been held that that discretion must be exercised judicially. It is, therefore, unwise for an arbitrator to depart without good reason from the well-established judicial principle that 'costs follow the event'.

### 14.2.2.23 Payment of costs of the award

As a matter of practice, an arbitrator will not issue his award until he has been paid his fees and expenses in full. The party who believes himself to be the successful party is more likely to be taking up the award. It is frequently the party who is ultimately not liable for the arbitrator's fees and expenses who therefore pays them in the first instance. Accordingly, while it may be self-evident, the award will often provide that in the event that the costs of the award are paid by the party not responsible for them, that party is entitled to recover those costs from the other.

### 14.2.2.24 Publication of award

When an arbitrator has made his award, it is generally said to be 'published'. However, the time limits for challenging the award are usually determined by reference to the date when there was publication or delivery of the award to the parties.

### 14.2.2.25 Challenging the award

The High Court has power under the 1954 Act to remit or to set aside an award. The distinction between remission and setting aside is that in the case of remission the award is referred back to the arbitrator for his reconsideration, whereas when an award is set aside the whole arbitration is made null and void.

Section 36 of the 1954 Act gives the High Court power to refer to an arbitrator for reconsideration any issues on which he has made an award and provides that, unless the court order directs otherwise, the arbitrator shall make his further award within three months after the date of the order.

In *Catherine McCarrick v The Gaiety (Sligo) Limited* (2000 552SP, High Court, Herbert J, 2 April 2001), the Court held that through a procedural mishap which was no fault of the arbitrator or of the respondent, the claimant had not received a fair hearing and that because the possible injustice which the claimant might suffer in the future should the award not be remitted exceeded any risk of detriment to the respondent the Court remitted the award to the arbitrator for his reconsideration.

Section 38 of the 1954 Act enables the High Court to set aside the award where:

(a)  the arbitrator has been guilty of misconduct; or

(b)  the arbitration or award has been improperly procured.

The High Court also has a general power under s 39 of the 1954 Act to give relief where the arbitrator is not impartial or the dispute referred to arbitration involves a question of fraud.

In *McCarthy v Keane and others*, 24 June 2003, High Court, unreported, Mr Justice Lavan, the Court considered the issues to which a Court should have regard in assessing whether to interfere with an arbitrator's award. Lavan J upheld the arbitrator's award on the basis that:

(a)  no mistake of law appeared on the face of the award;

(b)  the arbitrator had conducted himself correctly within the terms of his appointment and made the award accordingly; and

(c)  any perceived bias on the part of the arbitrator should have been asserted during the course of the arbitration and not subsequent to the award having been made.

In *G.L.C. Construction Limited v the County Council of the County of Laois* [2005] IEHC 53, Laffoy J remitted the award to the arbitrator, as she was satisfied that there was an error of law patent on the face of the award to the extent that the arbitrator was not entitled to determine that any damages to which the plaintiff was entitled would be set off against any damages to which the respondent was entitled without first assessing the damages, if any, due to each party against the other, having regard to the evidence adduced before him.

Overall the grounds on which an award can be challenged are limited.

An application to the High Court to remit or set aside an award must be made within six weeks after the award has been made and published to the parties or within such further time as the High Court may allow.

### 14.2.2.26  Enforcing the award

Under s 41 of the 1954 Act, an award on an arbitration agreement may, by leave of the High Court, be enforced in the same manner as a judgment or order to the same effect.

While a High Court judgment is directly enforceable, application has to be made to the High Court for the enforcement of an arbitration award. This is done by way of special summons pursuant to the provisions of r 4 of Ord 56 of the Rules of the Superior Courts (SI 15/1986).

### 14.2.2.27 International arbitrations

*International arbitrations generally*

International arbitration arises from disputes in international trade and as international trade increases so does international arbitration.

The facts which give rise to local or national disputes are normally no different from those which give rise to international disputes save for the fact that the disputing parties are of different nationalities or the subject matter of the dispute or the place where the obligation of the parties is to be performed is outside the State in which the parties have their places of business.

With the enormous increase in trade between Ireland and other members of the European Union, more and more disputes are falling within the category of international dispute.

Because litigation in an international contract is, in most cases, complex, slow, expensive and unpredictable and because the New York Convention 1958 on the Recognition and Enforcement of Foreign Arbitral Awards provides the means for enforcing awards in countries who have subscribed to the Convention, arbitration has become a primary method of resolving international commercial disputes.

*New York Convention 1958*

A successful award is essentially valueless, unless there is a means of enforcing it and a claimant, before embarking on any arbitration proceedings, should always consider whether, if his claim in the arbitration is successful, it can be readily enforced against the respondent.

The enforcement of an arbitration award is the prerogative of the courts in the country where enforcement is being sought. While in general their power to review awards is limited, the courts will only assist an enforcement if they are satisfied that the award has been made in a proper way. This applies as much in domestic arbitrations as it does in international arbitrations.

The 1958 New York Convention on the Recognition and Enforcement of Foreign Arbitral Awards was drafted with a view to simplifying the enforcement procedure. Essentially, this Convention sets out internationally accepted rules for the recognition and enforcement of arbitral awards but while the Convention has considerably simplified the procedure for enforcement, the enforcement procedure is only available in those countries which have adopted the Convention. By 2002, it had been adopted by more than 130 countries which means that it has almost universal recognition. It was given legislative effect in Ireland by the 1980 Act.

Section 8 of the 1980 Act requires any person seeking to enforce an award to which the New York Convention applies to produce the duly authenticated original award or a duly certified copy, the original arbitration agreement or a duly certified copy and a certified translation if either of these is in a language other than English or Irish.

**439**

Section 9 of the 1980 Act details the limited grounds on which enforcement may be refused.

### International arbitration institutions

There are many international arbitration institutions. The principal institutions as far as Ireland is concerned are the following.

### The International Chamber of Commerce

The ICC was founded in 1919 and is based in Paris where it established its Court of Arbitration in 1923. The court does not itself settle disputes. This is the task of the arbitrators appointed. It does, however, supervise each case, including the appointment of the arbitral tribunal, the conduct of the proceedings and the validity of the award. The arbitration clause recommended for adoption by the ICC is set out in Schedule 5.

### The London Court of International Arbitration

The LCIA was originally founded in 1892 as the London Chamber of Arbitration. It provides rules and facilities for international arbitrations and is supervised by a joint committee of management composed of representatives of the Chartered Institute of Arbitrators, the Corporation of the City of London and the London Chamber of Commerce and Industry. The membership of the Court comprises twenty-four leading international arbitrators drawn from different countries throughout the world.

### American Arbitration Association/International Centre for Dispute Resolution

The AAA was established in 1926. It administers both domestic and international arbitrations. It has different sets of rules for different kinds of arbitration. Its international Arbitration Rules were revised with effect from 1 September 2000. The AAA's international arbitration section moved its headquarters to Dublin in 2001 and now operates under the name International Centre for Dispute Resolution ('ICDR'). The AAA is also actively involved in the promotion of mediation and other forms of ADR.

### WIPO Arbitration Centre

The WIPO Arbitration Centre was established in 1994 under the auspices of the World Intellectual Property Organisation. It was established due to the growing importance of intellectual property and the need to have an arbitration system and a panel of arbitrators capable of dealing with the highly technical nature of intellectual property disputes.

The WIPO Arbitration Centre is based in Geneva.

### The International Centre for the Settlement of Investment Disputes

The ICSID was established in 1966 pursuant to the 1965 Washington Convention on the Settlement of Investment Disputes between States and Nationals of Other States and was given effect in Ireland by the 1980 Act. It operates under the auspices of the World Bank and is based in Washington.

ICSID arbitration is applicable only where at least one party to the dispute is a State which has ratified the Convention.

Most international institutions charge substantial fees for the services they provide.

### *The UNCITRAL Model Law*

In 1985 the United Nations Commission on International Trade Law ('UNCITRAL') published a draft law on International Commercial Arbitration. The draft law known as the UNCITRAL Model Law was drafted by UNCITRAL in an effort to bring some harmony to the settlement of disputes in international trade, on the basis that it would be adopted by countries interested in the promotion of arbitration as a means of resolving such disputes. Since its adoption, many countries have enacted legislation based on the Model Law.

### *The 1998 Act*

The 1954 Act and the 1980 Act did not draw any distinction between domestic arbitrations and international arbitrations. This was regarded as unsatisfactory in the context of international commercial arbitration. Parties involved in international commercial transactions who choose arbitration as a means of resolving their disputes do so as a general rule to avoid the difficulties which might otherwise be involved in litigation. The fact that the 1954 Act allowed for reference to the courts under the special case procedure was accordingly unattractive in the context of international commercial arbitration.

The 1998 Act adopted, with a few amendments, the UNCITRAL Model Law on International Commercial Arbitration.

The effect of the 1998 Act is that Irish law now draws a distinction between domestic arbitrations and international arbitrations.

### *Attitude of Irish courts to arbitration*

Recent decisions of the superior courts confirm that, apart from providing procedural assistance in arbitrations or dealing with points of law specifically referred to them for determination, the courts will not interfere with the arbitral process unless patent injustice or error requires them to do so. In the case of *Noel Hogan and others v St Kevin's Company and Owen Purcell* 1986 IR 80, Murphy J expressed the law as follows at p. 88:

It seems to me that where parties refer disputes between them to the decision of an arbitrator chosen by them, perhaps for his particular qualification in comprehending technical issues involved in the dispute or perhaps for reasons relating to expedition, privacy or costs, it is obviously and manifestly their intention that the issue between them should be decided and decided finally by the person selected by them to adjudicate upon the matter . . . and it seems to me that at the end of the day both parties were content to have the important point of law determined not by the courts but by the arbitrator and that notwithstanding the fact that he himself possessed no legal qualifications. Having adopted that course it seems to me that it would be unfair and unjust to permit the unsuccessful party to assert a right to have a decision of the High Court substituted for that of the arbitrator.

That view was endorsed unanimously by the five judges of the Supreme Court in *Keenan v Shield Insurance Company Limited* 1988 IR 89, all of whom subscribed to the views expressed in recent years by different High Court judges in many cases that arbitral awards ought to be regarded as final in all respects and should only be interfered with if they involve an error in law which is so fundamental that it cannot be allowed to stand.

## 14.2.3 EXPERT DETERMINATION

### 14.2.3.1 Differences between arbitration and expert adjudication

The traditional role of an expert lies in the areas of valuation and assessment. In litigation or arbitration proceedings, he has normally been employed by one of the parties to act as an expert witness in support of the case of that party. However, where issues of valuation or assessment only are involved, the employment of one independent expert agreed by both parties (or in default of agreement nominated by a third party) to make a final determination is becoming more frequent.

The following are some of the principal differences between arbitration and expert adjudication:

(a) In arbitration, the powers and rights of the arbitrator are governed, not only by the arbitration clause, but normally also by statute and judicial precedent. Expert adjudication is governed specifically by the terms of the clause referring the matter to the expert.

(b) An arbitrator, in reaching his conclusion, is normally only entitled to take into account the evidence presented by both parties to him. He is not, therefore, entitled to draw on his own knowledge without making it clear to the parties that he is doing so and allowing the parties time to make any appropriate representations to him.

(c) An arbitrator can be challenged on the grounds of misconduct, which in the context of arbitration means that his award can be set aside or remitted by the court if it can be shown that the arbitrator has conducted the arbitration proceedings in some way which is not totally fair and impartial. An expert is generally immune from such a challenge. Accordingly, there are in general less safeguards for the parties where an expert adjudicator is appointed.

(d) In many jurisdictions, arbitrators enjoy statutory immunity for their acts and omissions, except where bad faith is shown. An expert adjudicator, on the other hand, can be open to claims of negligence.

(e) The decision of an expert adjudicator, while binding, cannot be enforced in the same way as an arbitration award.

### 14.2.3.2 Why a party might choose expert adjudication

The reasons why a party might choose expert adjudication over arbitration are as follows:

(a) subject to the terms of the contract under which he is appointed, an expert adjudicator may make his determination without receiving evidence or arguments from the parties, provided that in general terms he conducts the proceedings fairly. He is not, however, obliged to follow any set procedure and in most jurisdictions there is no entitlement for a party to have an expert's decision set aside for failing to observe due process as there normally is with an arbitrator's award. Accordingly, determination by an expert adjudicator is likely to be obtained much more quickly than that by an arbitrator; and

(b) as an expert adjudicator may not require detailed submissions or the involvement of lawyers or other experts, the procedure for obtaining a determination by an expert adjudicator is likely to be considerably cheaper.

The question of whether an accountant who was asked to value a shareholding in a company was acting as an arbitrator or an expert was considered by Laffoy J in *Collis Lee v Millar* (2004/45SP 30/7/2004).

### 14.2.3.3 Sample clause

A sample clause for the appointment of an expert adjudicator is contained in Schedule 9.

## 14.3 Preliminary Determination Procedures

### 14.3.1 MEDIATION

A mediator is someone who helps the parties to reach their own agreement. Unlike the judge or the arbitrator, the mediator does not decide the dispute. He simply acts as a go-between, assisting the parties as best he can to reach a settlement. He expresses no views and remains impartial throughout. It also differs from arbitration and expert adjudication in that, although the adoption of all three procedures is based on the agreement of the parties, the decision of the mediator, unlike that of the arbitrator and the expert adjudicator, is non-binding.

In recent years, there has been a growing interest in the mediation of civil and commercial disputes. Various organisations have been founded which offer mediation services to the private sector. In the UK, the best known is CEDR (Centre for Effective Dispute Resolution).

A particular feature of mediation is that the entire process is confidential. It operates on a 'without prejudice' basis, so that any documentation or information furnished by one party to the other in the course of the mediation cannot be used in subsequent litigation. Mediation can also be speedy and thereby cost effective.

A further feature of mediation is that any party can get up and walk away from the mediation at any time, unless and until the terms of settlement have been agreed and signed.

### 14.3.1.1   Advantages of mediation

The advantages of mediation over litigation or arbitration are the following:

(a)   the parties have control over the outcome;

(b)   any continuing relationship between the parties is normally not jeopardised (unlike in litigation and arbitration, where the adversarial nature of the proceedings forces the parties to be confrontational and can seriously damage, or indeed make impossible, any future working relationship between them);

(c)   the parties can introduce any issues into their discussions, with a view to finding a consensus and are not limited by the rights and wrongs of the particular dispute; and

(d)   implementation of an agreement reached through consensus is more likely to be achieved than where a unilateral judgment or award is imposed.

### 14.3.1.2   Consensual settlement

The mediation process aims for a consensual settlement so an outcome from the process is not guaranteed. As a result, the mediation clause will normally specify a deadline date by which agreement is to be reached. If agreement has not been reached by the deadline date or by such extended time as the parties may agree, the parties are left to pursue their remedies through litigation or arbitration.

### 14.3.1.3 English Civil Procedure Rules

In England, under the new Civil Procedure Rules, parties have a duty to consider seriously the possibility of using mediation or some other ADR procedure for the purpose of resolving their dispute, or particular issues within it, when encouraged by the court to do so. This has meant that the English courts now take a particular interest in whether or not ADR has been used in a case and will penalise parties who do not avail of it.

### 14.3.1.4 EU

The European Union has also recognised the advantages of ADR and has issued a draft Directive on alternative dispute resolution in civil and commercial matters.

### 14.3.1.5 Draft clause

A draft clause for the appointment of a mediator under the CEDR Procedures is contained in Schedule 10.

### 14.3.1.6 International disputes

In relation to international commercial disputes, the International Chamber of Commerce, for example, has published with effect from 1 July 2001, its ADR Rules for the use of parties who wish to settle their disputes or differences amicably with the assistance of a third party. One of the clauses recommended by the ICC for the adoption of its ADR Rules is contained in Schedule 11. Other international institutions have also published ADR Rules.

## 14.3.2 CONCILIATION

While mediation and conciliation are often used as if they are interchangeable terms, traditionally in the construction industry in Ireland, a conciliator is a little more proactive than the mediator and goes one step further than the mediator by proposing terms of settlement which may become binding on the parties if the parties do not reject them within a specified period of time.

## 14.3.3 MINI-TRIAL

This is a more formal type of mediation procedure. It essentially involves the lawyers or other advisers for each party presenting a mini version of their case to a panel consisting of senior executives from each company with (usually) a neutral chairman to manage the proceedings. It therefore allows the decision makers in the company the opportunity to listen more objectively to an overview of the available evidence before they enter into negotiations for the settlement of the dispute. The neutral chairman will also be available to facilitate any negotiation and to act as a mediator or conciliator would do.

### 14.3.4   MED-ARB

Parties may wish, for reasons of cost or time, to avoid the possibility that mediation may not achieve final determination of a dispute if the parties fail to agree. They therefore contract to give the mediator power to convert to an arbitrator role and make a legally binding award in the event that the mediation does not lead to settlement of all issues.

As far as any combination of arbitration and mediation is concerned, it has been the conventional wisdom in some jurisdictions that arbitration is quite distinct from mediation and that the functions of arbitrator and mediator should never be combined. In other jurisdictions (e.g. USA, South Africa, China), rules and schemes have existed for many years whereby the same person can fulfil the two functions. This system, which is often referred to as 'med-arb', appears to be growing in popularity.

### 14.3.5   DISPUTE BOARDS

Dispute Boards are designed to nip problems in the bud before they escalate into a dispute. They have been established with some of the major international construction projects in recent times. In the Channel Tunnel project, for example, any dispute had to be referred to the Panel of Experts and then, if either party so requested, to arbitration under the ICC rules. A similar system was established in the Boston Central Artery/Tunnel project. Again, in the Hong Kong Airport project there was a four-step process. First, the dispute was submitted for a decision by the engineer, followed (if either party was dissatisfied at any stage) by mediation, adjudication and then arbitration.

The types of Dispute Boards are varied. A Dispute Board which makes a non-binding 'recommendation' is generally referred to as 'Dispute Review Boards' (DRBs), while those making a more binding decision are referred to as 'Dispute Adjudication Boards' (DABs).

Many international institutions (e.g. ICC, LCIA, ICDR) have established Dispute Board procedures which can be adopted by interested parties.

One of the problems involved in setting up a Panel or a Committee of Experts is that of knowing what specialist qualifications are required of the experts who are to constitute the Panel.

## 14.4   Trade and Maritime Associations

Many disputes are governed by the regulations of trade associations whose standard conditions of trade provide for all disputes arising with members of the trade to be resolved by arbitration or other dispute resolution system established by the particular trade.

## 14.5    Consumer Contracts

Some agreements which people routinely sign (e.g. holiday booking forms) also provide for disputes to be resolved by arbitration or other dispute resolution system.

## 14.6    Online Dispute Resolution ('ODR')

Not only have there been developments in the methods of resolving disputes but there is now much better use of technology. An example of this is ICC NetCase, which is a service established by the ICC to allow arbitration to be conducted online. NetCase enables the participants to communicate through a secure website hosted by the ICC and offers participants the advantages of instantaneous and efficient communication, round-the-clock access, security and confidentiality, and organised handling and storage of documents.

The ICDR also has procedures for online arbitration to permit arbitration proceedings to be conducted and resolved exclusively via the Internet. They provide for all parties' submissions to be made online and for the arbitrator to render an award and to communicate it to the parties via the Internet.

## 14.7    Conclusion

Interest in the Preliminary Determination Procedures is growing at a fast pace and with many successful outcomes resulting from the use of such procedures, interest is likely to grow substantially. That said, what may be a good way to resolve a dispute in one case may be quite inappropriate or not suit another. Each case has to be assessed on its own merits.

## 14.8    Specimen Arbitration Clauses

### 14.8.1                    SCHEDULE 1

#### Short Form Arbitration Clause Recommended by the Law Society

'All disputes which arise between the parties in connection with this Agreement, or the subject matter of this Agreement, shall be decided by an arbitrator agreed by the parties or, in default of agreement, appointed by the President for the time being of the Law Society of Ireland or in the event of his being unwilling or unable to do so by the next senior officer of the Society who is willing and able to make the appointment provided always that these provisions shall apply also to the appointment (whether by agreement or otherwise) of any replacement arbitrator where the original arbitrator (or any replacement) has been removed by order of the High Court, or refuses to act, or is incapable of acting or dies'.

**14.8.2**                              **SCHEDULE 2**

### Submission Agreement

This Agreement is made the       day of       20       between

[

                                                                                        ]

of [

                                                                ] ('the Claimant') of the one part and

[

                                                                ]

of [

                                                    ] ('the Respondent') of the other part.

WHEREAS:-

1.      [*Recital of Agreement between Claimant and Respondent*]

2.      Disputes have arisen between the Claimant and the Respondent arising out of the said Agreement and the Claimant and the Respondent wish to resolve all such disputes by arbitration.

Accordingly, the Claimant and the Respondent hereby agree to refer all of the said disputes to [*named arbitrator*] or should he be unable or unwilling to accept the appointment, to an arbitrator to be agreed by the Claimant and the Respondent or, in default of agreement, to be appointed by the President for the time being of the Law Society of Ireland or, in the event of his being unwilling or unable to do so, by the next Senior Officer of the Society who is willing and able to make the appointment **PROVIDED ALWAYS** that these provisions shall apply also to the appointment (whether by agreement or otherwise) of any replacement arbitrator where the original arbitrator (or any replacement) has been removed by order of the High Court or refuses to act, or is incapable of acting or dies.

**14.8.3**                 **SCHEDULE 3**

### Agreed Arbitration Clause for Arbitration Scheme arranged by the Chartered Institute of Arbitrators—Irish Branch on behalf of Tour Operators who are members of the Irish Travel Agents Association and which is to be included in their Booking Conditions

'Any dispute or difference of any kind whatsoever which arises or occurs between any of the parties hereto in relation to any thing or matter arising under, out of or in connection with this Contract shall be referred to arbitration under the Arbitration Rules of the Chartered Institute of Arbitrators—Irish Branch'.

**14.8.4**                 **SCHEDULE 4**

### Arbitration Clause in Agreement and Schedule of Conditions of Building Contract issued by the Royal Institute of the Architects of Ireland (2002 Edition) with pre-condition for prior reference to conciliation

'Clause 38(a)—If a dispute arises between the parties with regard to any of the provisions of the contract such dispute shall be referred to conciliation in accordance with the Conciliation Procedures published by the Royal Institute of the Architects of Ireland in agreement with the Society of Chartered Surveyors and the Construction Industry Federation.

If a settlement of the dispute is not reached under the conciliation procedures either party may refer the dispute to arbitration in accordance with Clause 38(b).

Clause 38(b)—Provided always that in case any dispute or difference shall arise between the Employer or the Architect on his behalf and the Contractor, either during the progress of the Works or after the determination of the employment of the Contractor under the Contract or the abandonment or breach of the Contract, as to the construction of the Contract or as to any matter or thing arising thereunder or as to the withholding by the Architect of any certificate to which the Contractor may claim to be entitled, then either party shall forthwith give to the other notice of such dispute or difference and such dispute or difference shall be and is hereby referred to the arbitration and final decision of such person as the parties hereunto may agree to appoint as Arbitrator or, failing agreement, as may be nominated on the request of either party by the President for the time being of the Royal Institute of the Architects of Ireland after consultation with the President of the Construction Industry Federation and the award of such Arbitrator shall be final and binding on the parties. Such reference, except on Article 3 or Article 4 of the Articles of Agreement or on the question of certificates, shall not be opened until after the Practical Completion or alleged Practical Completion of the Works or determination or alleged determination of the Contractor's employment under this Contract, unless with the written consent of the Employer or of the Architect on his behalf and the Contractor. The Arbitrator shall have power to open up, review and revise any opinion, decision, requisition or notice, and to determine all matters in dispute which shall be submitted to him and of which notice shall have been given as aforesaid in the same manner as if no such opinion, decision, requisition or notice had been given. Every or any such reference shall be deemed to be a submission to arbitration within the meaning of the Arbitration Act 1954 (No. 26 of 1954), or the Arbitration Act (Northern Ireland) 1957 (as the case may be) or any act amending the same or either of them'.

**14.8.5**                           **SCHEDULE 5**

### Recommended Arbitration Clause—International Chamber of Commerce

'All disputes arising out of or in connection with the present contract shall be finally settled under the Rules of Arbitration of the International Chamber of Commerce by one or more arbitrators appointed in accordance with the said Rules'.

**14.8.6**                           **SCHEDULE 6**

### Model Arbitration Clause—United Nations Commission on International Trade Law (UNCITRAL)

'Any dispute, controversy or claim arising out of or relating to this Contract or the breach, termination or invalidity thereof, shall be settled by arbitration in accordance with the UNCITRAL Arbitration Rules as at present in force'.

[NOTE: The Rules state that the parties may wish to consider adding:—

(a)   the appointing authority shall be .............................. (name of institution or person);

(b)   the number of arbitrators shall be .................................................. (one or three);

(c)   the place of arbitration shall be ...................................... (town or country);

(d)   the language(s) to be used in the arbitral proceedings shall be ...

**14.8.7**                    **SCHEDULE 7**

### Draft Agenda for Preliminary Meeting

[NOTE: **If the arbitrator intends to have a pre-hearing review with the parties, he may well confine the Agenda for the Preliminary Meeting to matters dealing with the conduct of the arbitration other than the hearing on the basis that the Agenda for the pre-hearing review will cover all matters pertaining to the conduct of the hearing.]**

1. Review of Arbitration Agreement.

2. Check on any pre-conditions to be complied with before commencement of arbitration proceedings or appointment of arbitrator.

3. Validity of appointment of arbitrator.

4. Identification of parties in dispute.

5. Outline of dispute:

    (i)    subject matter of dispute;

    (ii)   approximate amount of claim;

    (iii)  details of any counterclaim;

    (iv)   approximate amount of any counterclaim.

6. Representatives of the parties and whether Counsel are being briefed.

7. Rules of procedure.

8. Any preliminary issues to be determined.

9. Pleadings:

    (i)    points of claim;

    (ii)   points of defence (and counterclaim, if any);

    (iii)  points of reply (and defence to counterclaim);

    (iv)   reply to defence to counterclaim;

    (v)    close of pleadings.

10. Evidence:

    (i)    witnesses of fact;

    (ii)   expert witnesses;

    (iii)  extent to which expert reports and other evidence can be exchanged and agreed.

11. Discovery:

    (i)    extent to which discovery is required;

    (ii)   arrangements to be made.

12. Hearing:

    (i)    need for hearing;

    (ii)   estimated duration of hearing;

    (iii)  venue;

    (iv)  provisional date;

    (v)   need for transcript;

    (vi)  arrangements to be made and responsibility therefor.

13. Inspection:

    (i)    need for inspection of any property or items involved in the dispute;

    (ii)   date of inspection;

    (iii)  arrangements to be made;

    (iv)  persons to be present.

14. Award:

    (i)    need for any interim award;

    (ii)   final award;

    (iii)  procedure in relation to sealed offer.

15. Costs of the award:

    (i)    basis of arbitrator's charges;

    (ii)   joint and several liability;

    (iii)  time and method of payment.

16. General directions:

    (i)    all communications by any party to the arbitrator (except for the purpose of fixing dates) to be simultaneously copied to the other party and to be noted on the correspondence accordingly;

    (ii)   exhibits, photographs and plans to be agreed where possible;

    (iii)  reports and other evidence to be agreed where possible;

    (iv)  figures to be agreed as figures where possible;

    (v)   what documents to be submitted to the arbitrator and when;

    (vi)  liberty to apply.

17. Any other business.

**14.8.8**

# SCHEDULE 8

## Draft Form of Appointment of Arbitrator

### IN THE MATTER OF THE ARBITRATION ACTS 1954–1998 AND IN THE MATTER OF AN ARBITRATION

**BETWEEN/**

_____      **Claimant**

_____      **Respondent**

**TO: [The Arbitrator]**

In consideration of your agreement to act as Arbitrator in the disputes or differences which have arisen between us relating to the matter detailed in the First Schedule hereto, which disputes and differences are hereby referred to you, we jointly and severally agree:

(i)     to pay your fees, costs and expenses in connection with the Arbitration on demand and if so required by you by interim payments, whether in one final account or in one or more interim accounts and whether or not the arbitration shall be brought to a conclusion and an award made or published, such fees, costs and expenses to be charged in accordance with the schedule of charges set out in the Second Schedule hereto; and

(ii)    to take up any award within ten days of receipt of notification from you of the making of any such award.

### First Schedule

### (Details of Contract in Dispute)

### Second Schedule

### (Fees, Costs and Expenses)

(a)     Minimum fee (for up to 2 hours)      €

(b)     Fee for each hour or part hour in
excess of 2 hours (subject to
annual review)      €

(c)   Expenses incurred (eg hire of
      room, hotel and travelling expenses,
      document copying)                        at cost

(d)   Fees and costs of Advisers or
      Assessors (if any)                       at cost

(e)   Value Added Tax on the above items    rate current at time of charge.

**DATED THIS**    **DAY OF** [*Month*] [*Year*]


**SIGNED** for and on behalf of
the Claimant in the presence of:



**SIGNED** for and on behalf
of the Respondent in the presence of:


## 14.8.9                    SCHEDULE 9

### Sample Clause for appointment of Expert Adjudicator to determine disputes relating to Completion Accounts in Share Purchase Agreement

*In the event of a dispute arising between the Vendor and the Purchaser in relation to the Completion Accounts as defined in this Agreement then either party may refer the dispute to an independent firm of Chartered Accountants of national repute agreed by the parties or in default of agreement appointed by the President for the time being of [INSTITUTE] or in the event of his being unable or unwilling to act by the next senior officer of [INSTITUTE] who is willing and able to make the appointment with the request that the said independent firm of Chartered Accountants (the 'Expert') rule on the dispute and if necessary prepare a set of Completion Accounts and determine the Completion Net Assets Figure. In any reference the Expert shall act an as expert and not as an arbitrator. The decision of the Expert shall, in the absence of manifest error, be final and binding on both paries.*

*Both parties will give and the Purchaser will procure that the Company will give all reasonable assistance to the Expert to enable it to resolve the dispute. The costs of the Expert shall be borne by the party against whom the Expert rules. In the event that the Expert does not clearly rule in favour of either the Vendor or the Purchaser, the Vendor and the Purchaser shall bear the costs of the Expert equally.*

**14.8.10**

## SCHEDULE 10

### ADR Clause for mediation under CEDR Procedures

This Agreement shall be governed by the laws of [                    ]. The parties will attempt in good faith to negotiate a settlement to any claim or dispute between them arising out of or in connection with this Agreement. If the matter is not resolved by negotiation the parties will refer the dispute to mediation in accordance with CEDR (Centre for Effective Dispute Resolution) Procedures. If the parties fail to agree within [  ] days of the commencement of the procedures the dispute shall be referred to [INSERT EITHER ARBITRATION OR LITIGATION]. [If arbitration is chosen the procedure for the appointment of the arbitrator and the application of any arbitration rules will have to be specified.]

**14.8.11**

## SCHEDULE 11

### Suggested Clause requiring parties to submit dispute for resolution under the ADR Rules of the International Chamber of Commerce with an automatic expiration mechanism

'In the event of any dispute arising out of or in connection with the present contract, the parties agree to submit the matter to settlement proceedings under the ICC ADR Rules. If the dispute has not been settled pursuant to the said Rules within 45 days following the filing of a Request for ADR or within such period as the parties may agree in writing, the parties shall have no further obligations under this paragraph'.

# PART 4
# BUSINESS AGREEMENTS

# CHAPTER 15

# VERTICAL AGREEMENTS (AGENCY, DISTRIBUTION, FRANCHISING)

## 15.1    Introduction

The agreements considered in this chapter are: distribution agreements, franchising agreements and agency agreements. The competition law term used to describe these agreements is 'vertical agreements'. At one end of the supply chain is the business that makes or wholesales a product, while at the other end is the business that distributes or retails the product to the end consumer. The relationship between the businesses at either end of the supply chain is considered to be vertical as the product is supplied from the manufacturer down to the end consumer.

The relationship between these businesses is governed by the ordinary principles of contract law. The restrictions in the agreements are governed by competition law. In addition, agency agreements need to be considered under legislation relating specifically to 'commercial agents'.

## 15.2    Distribution Agreements

Distribution agreements are agreements between suppliers and resellers (referred to as 'distributors') of goods and/or services. In general, distribution agreements fall into one of three categories: 'non-exclusive; exclusive'; and 'selective'.

### 15.2.1    EXCLUSIVE AND NON-EXCLUSIVE DISTRIBUTION AGREEMENTS

A 'non-exclusive' distribution agreement is an agreement between a supplier and distributor where the supplier is not restricted from supplying other distributors. In other words, the supplier does not sell exclusively to one distributor, he may sell to others.

An 'exclusive' distribution agreement is an agreement between a supplier and distributor where the supplier is restricted from selling to other distributors. The contract will usually define a territory which is to be kept exclusive to the distributor and the supplier will not supply other distributors in that territory. For example, if John Murphy is granted an exclusive distribution agreement by the manufacturer of 'Cool Freezers' for the distribution of 'Cool Freezers' in Ireland, then the manufacturer agrees not to sell 'Cool Freezers' to any other distributor in Ireland. This type of contractual restriction is considered further at **15.5** below.

## 15.2.2 SELECTIVE DISTRIBUTION AGREEMENTS

A 'selective' distribution agreement is an agreement between a supplier and a distributor where the distributor has been appointed on the basis of his having met certain selection criteria laid down by the supplier. Selective distribution agreements are usually used by manufacturers of technically advanced or luxury products who want to have some control over the manner in which the product is sold. The distributor is therefore required to adhere to certain standards set by the supplier and is restricted from selling the goods to unauthorised distributors.

## 15.2.3 COMMERCIAL CONSIDERATIONS

In addition to the usual contractual considerations concerning any business agreement (see further **chapter 16** on Commercial Drafting), the issues outlined below require consideration when drafting, or advising on, a distribution agreement:

(a) the appointment of the distributor;

(b) the definition of the resale territory;

(c) in exclusive distribution agreements:

- restrictions on the supplier from selling to other distributors in the defined exclusive territory

- obligations on the distributor to focus its sales efforts on the exclusive territory

- restrictions on the distributor opening retail outlets outside the territory and 'actively selling' to customers outside the exclusive territory;

(d) in selective distribution agreements:

- selection criteria

- sales criteria

- training and support to be provided by the supplier to the distributor

- restrictions on the distributor from selling to unauthorised distributors;

(e) the terms and conditions concerning the sale and purchase of the goods including:

  - orders

  - when title to the goods pass from the supplier to the distributor

  - price, payment and discounts;

(f) the distributor's use of the supplier's intellectual property rights in the sale of the property. The distributor is typically granted a non-exclusive licence to the supplier's trademarks for the purpose of re-selling the products.

The application of competition law to restrictions in distribution agreements is considered at **15.5** below.


## 15.3    Franchise Agreements

A franchise agreement involves the grant by one party (the franchisor) of the right to another party (the franchisee) to sell goods or services under intellectual property rights granted by the franchisor. The agreement confers certain rights and obligations in relation to the franchisor's trade mark and know-how. In addition, a franchisor will typically supply the franchisee with an operating manual in accordance with which the franchised business should be operated.

Franchise agreements are described in the European Commission guidelines on Vertical Restraints (the 'Vertical Restraints Guidelines') ((2000) OJ C291/1) as follows:

> Franchise agreements contain licences of intellectual property rights relating in particular to trade marks or signs and know-how for the use and distribution of goods or services. In addition to the licence of IPRs, the franchisor usually provides the franchisee during the life of the agreement with commercial or technical assistance. The licence and assistance are integral components of the business method being franchised. The franchisor is in general paid a franchise fee by the franchisee for the use of the particular business method. Franchising may enable the franchisor to establish, with limited investments, a uniform network for the distribution of his products. In addition to the provision of the business method, franchise agreements usually contain a combination of different vertical restraints concerning the products being distributed, in particular selective distribution and/or non-compete and/or exclusive distribution or weaker forms thereof. (para 199)

A typical example of this type of agreement would be a situation where a company had successfully developed a pizza restaurant called, for example, 'Pizzaworks'. In order to expand the business, the owner decides to license the method of running the business to someone (i.e. the franchisee) who will set up an identical 'Pizzaworks' restaurant in accordance with the 'Pizzaworks' business formula. The franchisee will operate the business in accordance with the owner's (i.e. the franchisor's) requirements set out in the contract and an operating manual supplied by the franchisor. The franchisee will pay the franchisor a fee for the use of the formula and intellectual rights concerning the 'Pizzaworks' brand or otherwise.

## 15.3.1   COMMERCIAL CONSIDERATIONS

In addition to the usual contractual considerations concerning any business agreement (see further **chapter 16** on Commercial Drafting), the following issues require consideration when drafting, or advising on, a franchise agreement:

(a)   licensing intellectual property rights concerning the franchisor's brand name, trade marks, and know-how;

(b)   the fee that will be paid by the franchisee to the franchisor and how it will be calculated;

(c)   the franchisor's obligations with regard to business support, training and specifications regarding the product and the layout of the premises;

(d)   the franchisee's obligations in adhering to the business method set out in the agreement and an operating manual provided by the franchisor to the franchisee; and

(e)   the franchisee's exclusive right to operate the franchise within a defined territory (if applicable) and a definition of that territory.

The application of competition law to restrictions in franchise agreements is considered at **15.5** below.

The Irish Franchise Association's website contains useful information about franchising in Ireland, including the Association's code of ethics. The code of ethics requires, among other things, that:

(a)   franchised members will not sell products or services that will mislead prospective purchasers;

(b)   franchised members will not use trade marks or brand names in a manner that would mislead or deceive;

(c)   written disclosure of all information material to the franchise relationship shall be given to prospective franchisees prior to the execution of any binding contract; and

(d)   franchise agreements should be clear, unambiguous and in writing.

The Irish Franchise Association's website address is: www.irishfranchiseassociation.com.

## 15.4     Agency Agreements

Agency agreements involve a principal and an agent. The agent sells goods or services on behalf of the principal in return for the payment of commission. Agency agreements are described in the Vertical Restraints Guidelines as follows:

> Agency agreements cover the situation in which a legal or physical person (the agent) is vested with the power to negotiate and/or conclude contracts on behalf of another person (the principal), either in the agent's own name or in the name of the principal for:
>
> – purchase of goods or services by the principal, or
>
> – sale of goods or services supplied by the principal (para 12).

A typical example of this type of agreement is one between a travel agent and a hotel or airline.

Agency agreements are governed by general principles of contract law. They also require consideration under both competition law and the Commercial Agents Directive (Council Directive 86/653/EEC) as implemented in Ireland by the Commercial Agents Regulations (SI 33/1994 and SI 31/1997).

### 15.4.1     COMPETITION LAW

In order to determine the application of competition law to an agency contract, it is necessary to determine whether the contract is between two separate businesses within the meaning of the competition law term 'undertakings' (see **chapter 7** for a discussion on the competition law concept of 'undertakings').

An agent is generally considered to be independent economically from his principal as he is acting on behalf of the principal and usually bears little commercial risk. In other words, the agent is considered to be integrated with the principal, therefore together they form one 'undertaking'. The agreement between them is not an agreement between two or more separate 'undertakings'. The agreement between them does not therefore come within the scope of the prohibition on anti-competitive agreements contained in s 4 of the Competition Act, 2002 (the '2002 Act') and Art 81 of the EC Treaty.

Whether or not the principal and agent are considered to be one undertaking depends on the commercial risk borne by the agent. The situation is described in the Vertical Restraints Guidelines as follows:

> In the case of genuine agency agreements, the obligations imposed on the agent as to the contracts negotiated and/or concluded on behalf of the principal do not fall within the scope of application of Article 81(1). The determining factor in assessing whether Article 81(1) is applicable is the financial or commercial risk borne by the agent in relation to the activities for which he has been appointed as an agent by the principal. In this respect it is not

material for the assessment whether the agent acts for one or several principals. Non genuine agency agreements may be caught by Article 81 (1), in which case the Block Exemption Regulation and the other sections of these Guidelines will apply (para 13).

In other words, if the agreement is between two or more undertakings, then the normal rules of competition law apply and the agreement is treated like other vertical agreements (considered at **15.5** below).

Detailed guidance on this issue is contained in the Vertical Restraints Guidelines (paras 12–20).

## 15.4.2  COMMERCIAL AGENTS DIRECTIVE

The principal is generally the stronger contractual party involved in an agency agreement. Certain legislative safeguards have therefore been created to protect so-called 'commercial agents' in the form of the Commercial Agents Directive (Council Directive 86/653/EEC on the coordination of the laws of the Member States relating to self-employed Commercial Agents). The Directive was implemented in Ireland by the Commercial Agents Regulations (SI 33/1994 and SI 31/1997)). It is important to assess whether an agency agreement comes within the scope of this legislation, as its application will have consequences for the relationship between the parties, regardless of what is written in the contract or whether it is even described as an 'agency' contract.

Of particular concern to business clients is the fact that the legislation imposes conditions into the contract concerning: remuneration of the commercial agent; the notice to be given in order to terminate the contract; and the compensation that an agent may receive for damage incurred as a result of the contract terminating.

### 15.4.2.1  Definition of a commercial agent

In order to determine whether this legislation applies to the agreement, it is necessary to first determine whether the agent is a 'commercial agent' as defined in the legislation. The Commercial Agents Regulations provide that where an agent comes within the scope of the definition of a 'commercial agent', then the provisions of the Directive apply to the relationship between the agent and the principal.

A commercial agent is defined in the Commercial Agents Regulations as:

*A self-employed intermediary who has continuing authority to negotiate the sale or purchase of goods on behalf of another person, hereinafter called the 'principal' or to negotiate and conclude such transactions on behalf of and in the name of the principal (reg (2)(1) (SI 33/1994)).*

There are a number of exclusions to this definition (listed at **15.4.2.2** below).

The definition of 'commercial agent' in essence means that there are three tests to be satisfied in order for an agent to be a 'commercial agent'. The first two elements of this test are relatively straightforward. First, the agent must be self-employed and second, the agent must have continuing authority to act on behalf of the principal. The third element of the test can be more difficult to interpret, namely that the agent negotiate or negotiate and conclude a transaction on behalf of the principal.

The Irish High Court provided guidance on this issue in the case of *Michael Kenny v Ireland ROC Limited* ([2007] 1 IR 448). The High Court held that active bargaining is not required to qualify as 'negotiate'. The test is to ascertain whether the agent 'brought a material level of skill or consideration to conducting, managing or otherwise dealing with the sale or purchase of products on behalf of [the principal]' (para 6.2).

### 15.4.2.2 Exclusions

The definition of a commercial agent does not include the following listed in reg 2(1) (SI 33/1994):

(a) *A person who, in the capacity of an officer of a company or association, is empowered to enter into commitments binding on that company or association;*

(b) *A partner who is lawfully authorised to enter into commitments binding on the partners;*

(c) *A receiver, a receiver and manager, a liquidator or an examiner, as defined in the Companies Acts, 1963 to 1990, or a trustee in bankruptcy;*

(d) *A commercial agent whose activities are unpaid;*

(e) *A commercial agent operating on commodity exchanges or in the commodity market; or*

(f) *A consumer credit agent or a mail order catalogue agent for consumer goods, whose activities, [are presumed] to be secondary.*

### 15.4.2.3 Evidenced in writing

The Directive gave Member States the option to decide that an agency contract would not be valid unless evidenced in writing. Ireland exercised this option (reg 5 (SI 33/1994)).

### 15.4.2.4 Obligations of the parties

The Commercial Agents Directive sets out various rights and obligations of both the commercial agent and the principal (Art 3).

Both parties are required to act dutifully and in good faith.

In his relations with his principal, a commercial agent is required to:

(a) look after his principal's interests;

(b) make efforts to negotiate and where appropriate conclude the transactions he is instructed to take care of; and

(c) communicate necessary information to his principal and comply with reasonable instructions given by his principal.

In his relations with his commercial agent, a principal is required to:

(a) provide the commercial agent with the necessary documentation relating to the goods concerned;

(b) obtain information for the commercial agent necessary for the performance of the contract and to notify him, within a reasonable period, if he anticipates that the volume of commercial transactions will be significantly lower than that which the commercial agent could normally have expected; and

(c) inform the agent within a reasonable period of his acceptance, refusal, and non-execution of a commercial transaction which the commercial agent has procured for the principal.

### 15.4.2.5 Remuneration

The Commercial Agents Directive contains various provisions concerning remuneration.

In the absence of agreement between the parties concerning the level of remuneration, a commercial agent is entitled to the remuneration that commercial agents, in the place where he carries out his activities, appointed for the goods forming the subject of the contract are customarily allowed. If there is no such customary practice, a commercial agent is entitled to reasonable remuneration, taking into account all aspects of the transaction (Art 6).

Commercial agents are typically remunerated by receiving a commission on the goods that they sell on behalf of the principal. If the contract provides that the commercial agent shall be remunerated by way of commission, then he has certain entitlements under the Commercial Agents Directive (Art 7). 'Any part of the remuneration which varies with the number or value of business transactions' is deemed to be commission within the meaning of the Commercial Agents Directive (Art 6(2)).

A commercial agent is entitled to commission in the following circumstances during the term of the contract:

(a) where the transaction has been concluded as a result of his action; or

(b) where the transaction is concluded with a third party whom he has previously acquired as a customer for transactions of the same kind (Art 7(1)).

In Ireland, a commercial agent is also entitled to commission *during* the term of the contract, where he has an exclusive right to a specific geographical area or group of customers and where the transaction has been entered into with a customer belonging to that area or group (reg 4 (SI 33/1994)). The Commercial

Agents Directive gave Member States a choice regarding the implementation of this aspect of the Directive (Art 7(2)).

A commercial agent is not entitled to commission during the term of the contract if it is due to the previous commercial agent (pursuant to Art 8 of the Commercial Agents Directive), unless it is equitable in the circumstances for the commission to be shared between the commercial agents.

A commercial agent is entitled to commission in the following circumstances *after* the contract has terminated:

(a)   if the transaction is mainly attributable to the commercial agent's efforts during the period covered by the contract and it was entered into within a reasonable period after that contract terminated; or

(b)   if in accordance with the conditions in Art 17, the third party's order reached the principal or the commercial agent before the contract terminated (Art 8).

The commission becomes due as soon as either:

(a)   the principal has executed the transaction; or

(b)   the principal should, according to his agreement with the third party, have executed the transaction; or

(c)   the third party has executed the transaction.

The commission becomes due at the latest when the third party has executed his part of the transaction or should have done so if the principal had executed his part of the transaction as he should have. The commission must be paid no later than the last day of the month following the quarter in which it became due (Art 10). There must be no derogation from this contractual provision to the detriment of the commercial agent.

The right to commission can only be extinguished if it is established that the contract between the third party and the principal will not be executed and that fact is due to a reason for which the principal is not to blame.

Any commission which the commercial agent has already received is to be refunded if the right to it is extinguished (Art 11). There must be no derogation from this contractual provision to the detriment of the commercial agent.

The principal must supply his commercial agent with a statement of the commission due, not later than the last day of the month following the quarter in which the commission has become due. This statement must set out the main components used in calculating the amount of commission.

The commercial agent is entitled to demand all necessary information and in particular an extract from the books, in order to check the amount of commission due to him (Art 12). There must be no derogation from this contractual provision to the detriment of the commercial agent.

### 15.4.2.6 Termination

The Commercial Agents Directive contains certain provisions regarding:

(a) the period of notice which must be given to an agent in order to terminate a contract; and

(b) the level of compensation to which an agent is entitled on termination of the contract.

#### Notice periods

Where an agency contract is concluded for an indefinite period, either party may terminate it by notice. The period of notice to terminate the contract is as follows (Art 15):

– one month for the first year of the contract;

– two months for the second year; and

– three months for the third year and subsequent years.

The parties may not agree on shorter periods of notice. If the parties agree on longer periods, then the notice period for the principal may not be shorter than that for the agent. The end of the period of notice coincides with the end of a calendar month, unless otherwise agreed by the parties.

Where an agency contract for a fixed period continues to be performed after that period has expired, then it is deemed to be a contract for an indefinite period and the notice periods above apply to the termination of the contract. The earlier fixed period must be taken into account in the calculation of the period of notice.

#### Compensation for damage

The Commercial Agents Directive provides that when the contract terminates, an agent shall either be indemnified or compensated for damage (Art 17). In Ireland, a commercial agent is entitled to be compensated for the damage he suffers as a result of the termination of his relations with the principal.

Damage is deemed to have occurred in particular when the termination takes place in circumstances:

(a) that deprive the commercial agent of the commission which proper performance of the agency contract would have procured him whilst providing the principal with substantial benefits linked to the commercial agent's activities; and/or

(b) which have not enabled the commercial agent to amortise the cost and expenses that he had incurred for the performance of the agency contract on the principal's advice.

Entitlement to damage also arises where the agency contract is terminated as a result of the commercial agent's death.

The commercial agent loses his entitlement to damage if he has not notified the principal, within one year following termination, that he intends to pursue his entitlement.

The compensation is not payable in the following circumstances (Art 18):

(a) where the principal has terminated the contract because of default by the commercial agent which would justify immediate termination of the contract under Irish law;

(b) where the commercial agent has terminated the contract, unless such termination is justified by circumstances attributable to the principal or on grounds of age, infirmity or illness of the commercial agent, as a result of which he cannot reasonably be required to continue his activities; and

(c) where with the agreement of the principal, the commercial agent assigns his rights and duties under the contract to another person.

The parties may not derogate from these compensation provisions to the detriment of the agent, before the contract expires.

### 15.4.2.7   Restraint of trade

The Commercial Agents Directive provides that a restraint of trade clause (i.e. a non-compete provision) in a commercial agency contract may be valid if: it is in writing; if it relates to the geographical area or group of customers and goods covered by the contract; and if it does not exceed two years (Art 20). For the application of competition law to agency agreements see **15.4.1** above.

## 15.4.3   COMMERCIAL CONSIDERATIONS

In addition to the usual contractual considerations concerning any business agreement (see further **chapter 16** on Commercial Drafting), the following issues require consideration when drafting or advising on an agency agreement:

(a) consider whether the agent is a commercial agent within the meaning of the Commercial Agents Directive and implementing regulations discussed above. If the agent does come within the scope of this definition, then certain terms will apply to the contract from which the parties may not derogate;

(b) consider how the agent will be paid, if it is by way commission then the method of calculating the commission will need to be determined; and

(c) consider the degree of financial risk borne by the agent, as this will impact on the application of competition law to the restrictions in the agreement.

## 15.5 The Application of Competition Law to Vertical Agreements

From a competition law perspective, agreements are often categorised as either 'horizontal' or 'vertical' agreements. Horizontal agreements are agreements between undertakings (see **chapter 7** for a discussion on the concept of 'undertakings') at the same end of the supply and distribution chain, i.e. competitors. Vertical agreements are agreements between undertakings at different ends of the supply and distribution chain, such as suppliers and distributors.

The rationale for the distinction between horizontal and vertical agreements is that, in general, vertical agreements pose a low risk of impacting negatively on competition, unless one of the undertakings involved has a high degree of market power (see **chapter 7** for a discussion on the concept of 'market power'). On the contrary, horizontal agreements involve cooperation between competitors, therefore they pose a high risk of impacting negatively on competition, unless they are limited to issues that are unlikely to have such an impact. European legislation has evolved to accommodate this fact.

Section 4 of the Competition Act 2002 and/or Art 81 of the EC Treaty may apply to restrictions in vertical agreements. In order to analyse a vertical agreement under s 4 or Art 81, it may be helpful to adopt the approach outlined below. Vertical agreements are generally compatible with s 4/Art 81 provided that:

(a)   the parties involved do not hold market power;

(b)   the agreement does not contain any 'hard-core' restrictions detailed in the legislation (such as price fixing, market sharing or output limitation);

(c)   the agreement does not contain restrictions which, although not hard-core restrictions, go beyond that which is necessary to attain the commercial objectives of the agreement (for example, post-termination non-compete restrictions).

There is a general exemption for vertical agreements under both EC and Irish competition law. There are also exemptions which take into consideration the specific nature of agreements in certain industries. The general exemption is considered in some detail below, as it is relevant to the review of the majority of vertical agreements. The industry specific exemptions are considered in general terms. The Competition Authority's general declaration on vertical agreements is modelled on a European Commission block exemption regulation.

### 15.5.1 EUROPEAN VERTICAL RESTRAINTS BLOCK EXEMPTION REGULATION

Commission Regulation (EC) No 2790/1999 on the application of Article 81(3) to categories of vertical agreements and concerted practices ((1999) OJ

L336/21) (the 'Block Exemption') exempts certain vertical agreements from the prohibition in Art 81(1), provided they comply with certain conditions.

It is not necessary that the agreement be structured to conform to the Block Exemption, it is only necessary that the agreement does not contain any provisions that are prohibited by the Block Exemption. The Block Exemption should be interpreted together with the Vertical Restraints Guidelines.

There is no presumption of illegality where an agreement falls outside the scope of the Block Exemption, however, businesses must make their own assessment. If the Commission, the Competition Authority or the Irish courts examine the case, they will have the burden of proving that the agreement infringes Art 81(1). By way of defence, a business may substantiate efficiency claims and explain why a certain agreement is likely to bring about benefits which are relevant to the conditions for exemption under Art 81(3) (see further para 63, Vertical Restraints Guidelines).

## 15.5.2 IRISH VERTICAL RESTRAINTS DECLARATION

On 1 January 2004, a declaration (the 'Declaration') and notice (the 'Notice') issued by the Competition Authority, in respect of vertical agreements, came into force (D/03/001 and N/03/002).

The Declaration is modelled on the Block Exemption. The Declaration applies to vertical agreements, which fall under s 4(1) of the 2002 Act but in the Competition Authority's opinion generally comply with the conditions set out in s 4(5). The Declaration provides exemption for those agreements falling within its scope.

The Competition Authority has stated its intention to publish a guidance note on the Declaration and Notice. In the meantime, the Vertical Restraints Guidelines should be relied upon for guidance.

Similar to the Block Exemption, there is no presumption of illegality where an agreement falls outside the scope of the Declaration, however, businesses must make their own assessment. If the Competition Authority/Irish courts examine the case, they will have the burden of proving that the agreement is contrary to s 4(1). By way of defence, a business may substantiate efficiency claims and explain why a certain agreement is likely to bring about benefits which are relevant to the conditions for exemption under s 4(5).

## 15.5.3 APPLICATION OF THE BLOCK EXEMPTION AND THE DECLARATION

The Block Exemption only relates to Art 81 and the Declaration only relates to s 4 of the 2002 Act. Neither legal instrument contains an exemption from the prohibition on abuse of dominance in Art 82 of the EC Treaty, and s 5 of the 2002 Act.

Both the Block Exemption and the Declaration are subject to certain limitations set out in Art 2. The limitations concern:

(a) agreements between an association of undertakings;

(b) agreements concerning intellectual property rights;

(c) agreements between competing undertakings; and

(d) agreements covered by sector specific exemptions or regulations.

If the agreement is between an association of undertakings, the Block Exemption will only apply where all members of the association are retailers of goods and no member of the association (together with its connected undertakings) has a total annual turnover exceeding €50 million. This is without prejudice to the application of Art 81 to horizontal agreements, concluded between the members of the association or decisions adopted by the association. There is no such provision in the Declaration.

Both the Block Exemption and the Declaration concern the distribution of goods and services but not pure licences of intellectual property rights. Both the Block Exemption and the Declaration apply to vertical agreements, which involve the assignment of intellectual property rights, provided that such rights are secondary in the manner described in Art 2.

As a general principle, the Block Exemption and Declaration do not cover vertical arrangements between competing undertakings but, as a limited exception, there may be non-reciprocal vertical arrangements where certain conditions set out in Art 2 are satisfied.

Finally, neither the Block Exemption nor the Declaration will apply to a vertical agreement where the arrangement falls within the scope of any other block exemption or declaration, as the case may be (see below for exemptions and declarations relating to certain sectors). It is sufficient that the arrangement falls within the scope of another block exemption or declaration (i.e. falls within its subject matter) to preclude the application of the Block Exemption or declaration. It is irrelevant whether the arrangement benefits from the other block exemption or declaration.

### 15.5.3.1 Market share pre-conditions

In general, and provided the agreement does not contain 'hard-core restrictions' (discussed below), then it is only vertical agreements between businesses with market power that are likely to raise competition concerns. The Block Exemption creates a presumption of legality for certain vertical agreements, depending on the market share of the supplier or the buyer (subject to the exclusion of certain prohibited clauses from the agreement). The market share threshold is 30 per cent. Article 3 of the Block Exemption and Declaration set out the market share pre-conditions for the application of the exemption.

In general, it is the market share of the supplier on the market where it sells the contract goods or services which determines the applicability of the exemption. Where the agreement contains an exclusive supply obligation as defined in

Art 1, it is the buyer's market share which may not exceed the 30 per cent threshold. The 30 per cent threshold is not an absolute barrier to the application of the exemption. Arrangements between undertakings with market shares above 30 per cent should be analysed in accordance with the Vertical Restraints Guidelines to determine their compatibility with Art 81(3) of the EC Treaty or s 4(5) of the 2002 Act (by analogy to Art 81(3) of the EC Treaty).

### 15.5.3.2 Calculation of market share

Article 9 of the Block Exemption and Art 8 of the Declaration set out the means of calculating market share, including the applicable rules where the market share rises up to 35 per cent. The market share is calculated on the basis of the market sales value of the contract goods or services and other goods or services sold by the supplier, which are regarded as interchangeable or substitutable by the buyer, by reason of the products' characteristics, their prices and their intended use. If market sales value data are not available, estimates based on other reliable market information, including market sales volumes, may be used to establish the market share of the undertaking concerned. Where the market share of the buyer and not the supplier is concerned, it is either the market purchase value or estimates thereof which are used to calculate the market share.

### 15.5.3.3 Hard-core restrictions

Article 4 of both legal instruments describes the vertical agreements, which do not benefit from the exemption. The presence of any of these restrictions in an agreement denies the agreement the benefit of the exemption. The restrictions are as follows:

(a) Resale price maintenance, i.e. direct or indirect obligations on the buyer to set its retail price in accordance with the supplier's instructions (without prejudice to the possibility of the supplier imposing a maximum sale price or recommending a sale price);

(b) Territorial restrictions on the buyer other than:

- the restriction of active sales into the exclusive territory or to an exclusive customer group reserved to the supplier or allocated by the supplier to another buyer, where such a restriction does not limit sales by the customers of the buyer;

- the restriction of sales to end users by a buyer operating at the wholesale level of trade;

- the restriction of sales to unauthorised distributors by the members of a selective distribution system; and

- the restriction of the buyer's ability to sell components, supplied for the purposes of incorporation, to customers who would use them to manufacture the same type of goods as those produced by the supplier

(c) the restriction of active or passive sales to end users by members of a selective distribution system operating at the retail level of trade, without prejudice to the possibility of prohibiting a member of the system from operating out of an unauthorised place of establishment;

(d) the restriction of cross-supplies between distributors within a selective distribution system;

(e) the restriction agreed between a supplier of components and a buyer who incorporates those components, which limits the supplier to selling the components as spare parts to end-users or to repairers or other service providers not entrusted by the buyer with the repair or servicing of its goods.

Internet sales are considered to be passive sales, therefore every distributor must be free to use the Internet to advertise or to sell products (Vertical Restraints Guidelines, para 51).

### 15.5.3.4 Provisions resulting in the loss of the exemption

The Block Exemption and Declaration both provide (Art 5) that the following restrictions are not exempted:

(a) any direct or indirect non-compete obligation (see below for a definition of 'non-compete'), the duration of which is indefinite or exceeds five years (there is an exception where the contract goods or services are sold by the buyer from premises owned/leased by the supplier (or unconnected third parties)); and

(b) any post-termination restriction on the buyer (other than a one-year non-compete restriction limited to the premises from which the buyer has operated during the contract period), which is indispensable to protect know-how transferred by the supplier to the buyer. This is without prejudice to the possibility of imposing a restriction, which is unlimited in time on the use and disclosure of know-how, which has not entered the public domain.

The first type of restriction, a non-compete obligation, is typical in most vertical agreements, whereas the second restriction concerning know-how is typically found in franchise agreements.

A 'non-compete obligation' is defined as follows:

*any direct or indirect obligation causing the buyer not to manufacture, purchase, sell or resell goods or services which compete with the contract goods or services, or any direct or indirect obligations on the buyer to purchase from the supplier, or from another undertaking designated by the supplier, more than 80% of the buyer's total purchases of the contract goods or services and their substitutes on the relevant market, calculated on the basis of the value of its purchases in the preceding calendar year. (Article 1(b) of the Block Exemption and Art 1(c) of the Declaration)*

The legality of vertical agreements containing these restrictions differs under the Block Exemption and the Declaration.

The general principle under the Block Exemption is that the agreement infringes Art 81(1) if it contains any of the hard-core restrictions listed in Art 4. The agreement does not benefit from Art 81(3); therefore, the agreement is void under Art 81(2). If the agreement contains the prohibited restrictions listed in Art 5, then the restrictions rather than the agreement are void (see further paras 66–67 of the Vertical Restraints Guidelines).

The Competition Authority has curiously taken a slightly different approach. If the agreement contains the prohibited restrictions listed in both Art 4 and Art 5 of the Declaration, then the agreement does not benefit from the Declaration. In essence, this means that the whole agreement may be void under s 4.

Where variations or divergences occur between the Block Exemption and the Declaration, the Declaration should ultimately be relied upon for guidance in the application of s 4 of the 2002 Act to vertical agreements.

### 15.5.3.5  Industry specific block exemptions and declarations

The Block Exemption and Declaration apply to agreements concerning the sale and resale of goods or services. They do not apply to agreements that are the subject of another block exemption (in the case of EC competition law) or declaration (in the case of Irish competition law).

The following Competition Authority declarations are currently in force:

(a)  exclusive purchasing agreements for the sale of motor fuels (Decision No 25); and

(b)  exclusive agreements for the purchase of cylinder liquefied petroleum gas (D/05/001).

The following Commission block exemption regulations (and related guidelines) are currently in force:

(a)  motor vehicle distribution (Commission Regulation (EC) No 1400/2002 (2002) OJ L203); and

(b)  technology transfer agreements (Commission Regulation (EC) No 772/2004 (2004) OJ L123).

#### *Motor Fuels Declaration*

Category licenses issued by the Competition Authority and still existing at 30 June 2002 continued for the rest of their term, unless revoked, as though they were Declarations. The Motor Fuels Category Licence (Decision No 25) was one such licence. It expired in June 2008 and the Competition Authority proposed to extend its term to 2010. It concerns long-term exclusive purchasing arrangements for the resale of petroleum products in service stations. The Category Licence was based on a Commission Regulation, which has since expired.

The Category Licence permits exclusive obligations in relation to the sale of motor fuels for up to ten years, provided there is no provision for any first option to renew upon termination and provided the agreement only applies to company-owned outlets operated under licence or in accordance with a lease. It should be noted that this sector-specific licence addresses long-term agreements in the same way as the Block Exemption (see Art 5(b)).

### Cylinder liquid petroleum gas

The Competition Authority issued a Declaration (as amended) concerning exclusive purchasing agreement in the cylinder liquid petroleum gas ('LPG') market on 31 March 2005. The declaration concerns exclusive purchasing agreements for LPG. It will be reviewed in 2010 and it will expire in 2015.

The Declaration applies to agreements where a reseller agrees to purchase cylinder LPG exclusively from the supplier or another undertaking specified by the supplier. The Declaration only applies where there are two undertakings involved in the agreement and the exclusive purchasing obligation does not exceed two years. The Declaration outlines a number of restrictions which may be imposed on the reseller (Art 3) and a black list of prohibited restrictions (Arts 4 and 5).

The Declaration has been criticised, largely on the basis that two suppliers who have a combined market share of 98 per cent dominate the market (see Competition Press, 'The curious case of the dog that didn't bark', p. 161, Vol. 13, edn 8). Having regard to the general principle that restrictions in vertical agreements are more likely to restrict competition in a market where the supplier has market power, it is surprising that this Declaration was issued.

### Motor vehicle block exemption regulation

The motor vehicle sector is an important one, both from the point of view of the economy as a whole and of the individual consumer. The European Commission regularly publishes car price reports and monitors competition in the industry. It has taken several cases against manufacturers for infringing Art 81. Many of the decisions have resulted in car manufacturers being fined for impeding parallel trade in cars and limiting competition in the leasing and sale of motor vehicles. The aim of the block exemption regulation, which came into force in October 2002, was to improve competition in the industry (Commission Regulation (EC) No 1400/2002 of 31 July 202 on the application of Article 81(3) of the Treaty to categories of vertical agreements and concerted practices in the motor vehicle sector).

The motor vehicle block exemption regulation governs the relationships between car suppliers (which in Ireland comprise wholesalers rather than manufacturers) and their dealers throughout the EU. The Regulation aims to reduce the control which suppliers have over their dealers. The most important aspects of the Regulation concern:

(a)    multi-branding;

(b)    a prohibition on the link between sales and after-sales services; and

(c)    a choice between exclusive and selective distribution.

In other words, car suppliers must appoint dealers, either on the basis of an exlusive distribution system or a selective distribution system. Previously, suppliers could appoint their dealers using a combination of both. The type of restrictions which a car supplier may place on his dealers depends on the type of distribution system which he chooses. This choice is determined by a market share test. The Commission has also issued detailed guidelines which explain how the competition rules are applied in individual cases.

The Competition Authority has not issued a declaration in relation to motor vehicles. When analysing a vertical agreement concerning the sale, distribution and servicing of motor vehicles in Ireland, reference should be made to the Commission's block exemption regulation on motor vehicle distribution. This is because the regulation places more onerous obligations on car suppliers and car service providers than the Declaration. Where national competition rules are more liberal than the EC competition rules, the EC competition rules take precedence (see further Case 14/68, *Walt Wilhelm* [1969] ECR 1 and Arts 3(2), 15 Regulation 1/2003).

### Technology transfer agreements

A business that holds intellectual property rights may prevent any unauthorised use of its intellectual property. It may also exploit its intellectual property rights by licensing them to third parties. Technology transfer agreements concern the licensing of technology. Such agreements may be considered to be pro-competitive as they can reduce the duplication of research and development, strengthen the incentive for the initial research and development, increase innovation, facilitate diffusion and generate product market competition. However, licensing agreements may also be used for anti-competitive purposes, for example where two competitors use a licensing agreement to share out markets between themselves or where an important licence holder excludes competing technologies from the market. The block exemption Regulation (Commission Regulation (EC) No 772/2004 on the application of Article 81(3) to categories of technology transfer agreements (2004) OJ L123) aims to strike a balance between the protection of intellectual property rights and the protection of competition. The regulation sets out the parameters for restrictions in technology transfer agreements. The definition of a technology transfer agreement includes a patent licensing agreement, a know-how licensing agreement and a software copyright licensing agreement (Art 1(b)). The guidelines specify how Art 81 of the Treaty should be applied to agreements not falling within the scope of the regulation.

## 15.6    Conclusion

In summary, vertical agreements are agreements between businesses that operate at different ends of the supply and distribution chain. The usual rules of contract law apply to vertical agreements. In addition, it is important to remember that:

(a)    competition legislation provides that restrictions in vertical agreements must not exceed certain parameters. The parameters are set out in block exemptions under EC law and Declarations under Irish law; and

(b)    contracts between commercial agents and their principals are subject to the Commercial Agents Directive, which imposes certain terms in the contract, regardless of what is agreed between the parties.

**CHAPTER 16**

# COMMERCIAL DRAFTING

The difficult task, after one learns how to think like a lawyer, is relearning how to write like a human being.

(Floyd Abrams)

## 16.1   Introduction

The purpose of good drafting is the same in commercial law as in any field. It is to set out as clearly as possible the rights and duties of the parties. Your clients may be as technically proficient as any legal expert in reviewing these agreements, or they may be entering into a commercial contract which is more complex than any they have negotiated before. Irrespective of who your client is, whether a large multinational corporation with a team of in-house lawyers, or a small family-owned business, many of them will believe that most lawyers simply are not capable of reducing their agreement to writing.

They may well be right. Many lawyers cannot write well. Simple ideas get lost in a fog of over-complex drafting and poor grammar. If the lawyer drafting the agreement cannot reduce it concisely to writing then what chance have the parties of finding it useful in their ongoing relationship? What happens when one of the parties has a different interpretation of the terms of the agreement to the other and seeks the aid of the courts as a result of a disagreement?

The purpose of this chapter is to provide some useful tips to ensure clarity in your commercial drafting. Drafting is one of the primary skills you will develop as a lawyer. You should not expect that your first piece of drafting gets reviewed by the senior partner you work for without amendment. Retain early drafts if you believe that the comments noted on them may be of use to you in future similar exercises.

## 16.2   Instructions and Objectives

It is critically important that you receive clear instructions from a client on what the purpose of an agreement is before you commence drafting. You may have a very clear e-mail from the client setting out the background, timing requirements etc. but it is often useful to call a client to elicit additional information. People are often more candid in a telephone call than in an e-mail. Has the client, for example, found that a previous agreement had certain weaknesses that it would like addressed in the new draft? Perhaps the earlier agreement was drafted in another jurisdiction and needs to be localised in greater depth than before. Are there commercial reasons why the agreement needs to be changed—your client may be moving to a different business model (for example franchising) and all of this information may not have been included in the original set of instructions. Nevertheless, it may enable you to prepare a draft which is more precisely tailored to the business needs of your client.

There may be changes outside your client's business which may have an impact on the draft. For example, including a certain kind of provision may be becoming more widespread in the industry in which the client operates and, while not yet legally required, your client may wish their contracts to be more in tune with those trends.

If your client has an in-house lawyer, then instructions will be likely to come from him or her. The in-house lawyer's area of work may be different from yours and so you are being engaged to provide specialist advice. If the instructions are coming from a non-lawyer, you need to take care that you do not assume that their understanding of legal terms is the same as yours—there may be cultural differences if you are in two different jurisdictions, or a word may have a slightly different nuance of meaning in their industry to the strict legal interpretation.

Do not be afraid to ask the client to clarify what a term means in their industry. Many professions, other than law, use jargon and some of it may be highly technical, though second-nature to your client. You, however, may not know what they are talking about. Most people are quite happy to give a short explanation to you or e-mail over a chart or memo which gives you more background. This is especially so in the scientific, medical and technological fields.

## 16.3    Legal and Other Constraints

A client may ask you to prepare a document which, unbeknown to the client, is illegal. This is extremely rare and most people are well aware that for example, one cannot enter into an agreement with competitors to fix prices or selling conditions. If you suspect that there may be legal constraints on what your client wishes to achieve, then you should alert him or her to the nature of these constraints as soon as possible. There is an increasingly strong compliance culture across the globe and most organisations are extremely risk-averse and do not wish there to be the slightest doubt about the enforceability of their agreements. In the unlikely even of a client insisting on the preparation of a document which you know to be illegal, then you should decline to act.

Similarly, you may be of the view that entering into an agreement, no matter how clear the instructions, seems not to be in the best interests of your client. You can (diplomatically of course) query the purpose of the agreement and draft it so as to best protect your client's interests if he or she wants to proceed. You should ensure that your reservations as to the commercial terms are noted by the client so put them in writing if you remain concerned.

## 16.4    Organisation

If you find you write better with a tidy desk, clear it and begin. If you have a complex structure in terms of numbers of parties, draw up a structure chart and have it to hand when drafting. Get the mechanics out of the way—how will each party sign—under seal? By hand? Under a power of attorney? Insert the appropriate signing clauses, names, addresses, and then begin with the recitals. The recitals should express in three or four paragraphs why the agreement is being entered into.

## 16.5    Format

Place 'discussion draft' on the front of your draft and if you do not wish your client to send it to the other side, tell him or her so. Often business people believe that they are speeding things up (especially in the age of e-mail) by sending first drafts to all concerned. This is rarely efficient especially if you need your client's input on technical and business issues in the agreement before providing him with a more advanced second draft. Explain to your client what you think is best in terms of who processes changes to the document. Should you meet after the first draft has been sent out or make a call if meeting is not possible? Decide these things with your client before you begin drafting and it will give you more time to complete your task and you will both be aware of when the client can expect to receive the draft.

## 16.6    Precedents

You will rarely come across an agreement that no one else has had to draft before. If your office does not have a good set of precedents, you should consider investing in a loose-leaf set from reputable local legal publishers. There are many available and while they will not provide wording for every eventuality they will cover very many areas and will save you time. Do not use them slavishly, non-Irish precedents may not work in Irish law or there may be reasons, particular to your transaction, why they are inappropriate.

Ensure consistency between your own document and the precedent. For example, if the precedent uses the word 'factory' and you use the word 'premises', then you should use only one of those terms to avoid confusion.

Has the client ever done a transaction like this before? He may have prepared working notes or an internal memorandum which will greatly assist your drafting. A client will rarely object to his lawyer asking him for more background information in order to ensure that the first draft is as close to the client's needs as possible, so do not be afraid to ask.

## 16.7 Audience

Will your drafting be reviewed by an in-house lawyer or a non-lawyer What? jurisdiction are they based in? Bear this in mind when drafting.

Once your have determined the above information, you can proceed to the detail of the drafting.

## 16.8 Expertise

Does the contract relate in part to aspects of the law with which you are not familiar? If yes, then, if possible, have it reviewed by a colleague who is familiar with that area of law.

## 16.9 Timing

You will need to estimate, in advance, for the client how long it will take for you to send him a first draft. This will have implications for cost and practicality and your client will need to communicate this to their opposite number in the company with which they are contracting.

Sometimes unforeseen complications arise, which make the deadline impossible to reach. However, estimating the time needed is a drafting skill in itself with which you will become more accurate.

You should remember that not all drafting is actually writing and time can be spent on initial research, precedent hunting and considering the structure. All these are an integral part of the drafting process so try not to underestimate the time you will need for these tasks. Also, the time taken will to a large degree depend on how many of these types of agreements you have prepared before. Most clients understand that larger-value agreements will involve negotiation with the other party at every stage at which they may have a lawyer's input. More simple or lower-value arrangements may be signed after one or two drafts.

## 16.10  External Experts

It may be necessary for you to brief an external expert such as an environmental consultant before finalising your draft. Factor this into your time estimate if needed.

## 16.11  Legal Research

The law relating to the contract may be unclear or changing. You may need to factor this into timing estimates also.

## 16.12  Plain English

Try to use clear and plain English in your drafting. You may need to use a Latin term for which there is no short English equivalent, but keep Latinisms to a minimum as they can be off-putting. If you are writing a set of terms and conditions for use in dealings with consumers then you should take special care to use readable, immediately clear language. Short sentences and the use of the word 'you' rather than 'the hirer' or 'the consumer' will add greatly to the clarity of your drafting.

## 16.13  Cross-references

Check cross-references to ensure that they are correct before sending the draft out. If possible, minimise the use of cross-references as checking and rechecking that they remain accurate through several drafts is time-consuming and therefore expensive for the client.

## 16.14 Outline

Prepare an outline agreement based on your structure chart, if you have used one. It will make the drafting seem less daunting if the agreement is complex. Insert your boilerplate provisions, such as choice of law etc., in square brackets so that you can fine-tune them later on if needed.

## 16.15 Structure

The structure of an agreement is critical to its clarity.

It should include the items detailed below.

### 16.15.1 TITLE

What is the name of the agreement to be? You should include a drafting date on all drafts to assist you if the agreement goes through a large number of drafts.

### 16.15.2 DATE

The date of the agreement is the date on which it is entered into. If your client wants to include an earlier effective date there is generally nothing wrong with that (for example an agreement may have in practice been assigned to another company and they are only now getting around to formalising that transfer). Nonetheless, you will still need your agreement to be dated when it is signed, in case of disputes as to its validity. For clarity, write dates and numbers in digits and in words and have your clients check them.

### 16.15.3 PARTIES

Are both entities companies as we understand that term in Irish law? If an agreement is entered into by a company before it is properly incorporated, the promoter will be personally liable for the contract. Will the parent or subsidiary be entering into the agreement if your client forms part of a group? Will anyone else be guaranteeing the obligations of one of the parties under the agreement? If so, then they need to be included as a party. Do searches against the parties. People often believe their registered business name to be a legal entity in its own right.

### 16.15.4 PRE-CONDITIONS

Are there any conditions precedent to be satisfied before the agreement comes into effect? If so they need to be included. For example, the agreement may be subject to regulatory approval (such as that of the Competition Authority or the Financial Services Regulator). Alternatively, your client may want to ensure that certain consents are obtained first—for example shareholder consents, environmental licences or planning permissions may be required.

### 16.15.5 SCHEDULES

You may wish maps, drawings, lists and technical descriptions to be included in a schedule to the agreement. If these are technical in nature (a common example is the specification for a computer system) then you as the lawyer may not be involved in drafting them. You should ensure, if they are being prepared in parallel, that those drafting them are aware of the deadlines to avoid any last-minute delays. You should read these schedules, when produced, to ensure that nothing in them is at odds with what you have drafted in the main agreement.

### 16.15.6 BLANKS

You may be asked to produce a first draft while there are terms still being negotiated and there will therefore be blanks in your agreement. These should be square-bracketed and closed off with your client as the negotiations progress.

### 16.15.7 DEFINITIONS

If you are using certain terms repeatedly, then having a list of definitions will shorten and simplify your agreement. If a term is only used once, it may not be necessary to include it in a definitions list. Many Acts have cumbersome titles and it may be simpler to define the Act to which you refer as the 'Principal Act' rather than repeating its full title each time it is referred to.

It is a matter of personal or firm style as to where the list of definitions is placed. Generally, they appear at the front of the document and are always alphabetical.

## 16.16 Execution Clauses

Decide in what way each party will execute the agreement and provide for that in the execution clause. It may be necessary to execute the agreement under seal in certain instances (for example, if there is no consideration in the contract or if local law requires it). If the contract is being entered into by a company, it is important to refer to the articles of association for details as to how the contract should be executed.

## 16.17 Style

Whether or not we write well, we all write with a particular style. Try to develop your own voice in drafting and keep it constant. You may find that reading your drafting aloud helps you pick up errors. Absorb as much as possible from your colleagues—war stories may make it easier for you to avoid drafting errors than any chapter on drafting ever will.

## 16.18 Boilerplate Provisions

The term 'boilerplate' refers to frequently used provisions in agreements that do not vary much from agreement to agreement. As with precedents, you need to take care that you are not just dropping such clauses into your agreement without any thought as to whether they fit in well to the rest of the agreement. You should constantly review other lawyers' boilerplate terms to see whether they include useful provisions. Legal developments may mean a boilerplate term becomes obsolete, so they should be read by you fully each time you draft.

Boilerplate provisions can deal with interpretation issues. For example, you may have a clause saying the male includes the female, headings are for reference only, schedules form part of the agreements, reference to an Act mean that Act as it is amended etc.

Commonly used boilerplate provisions include those detailed below.

### 16.18.1 TERMINATION

The parties set out detailed provisions dealing with how the agreement is to be terminated. You may need to provide for fault-based as well as no-fault termination.

### 16.18.2 NO PARTNERSHIP

You may wish it to be explicit that the parties are not carrying on a partnership. Be careful of dropping in long lists of boilerplate clauses—'no partnership' clauses have been dropped into partnership agreements where they are plainly inappropriate!

### 16.18.3 FURTHER ASSURANCES

The parties agree to execute anything additional requested by the other party to give effect to the agreement.

### 16.18.4 WAIVER AND FORBEARANCE

The parties may wish to provide in the agreement that if they decide, once, to give a concession to the other party, that does not compel them to continue to do so in the future.

### 16.18.5 SEVERABILITY

The parties may wish to provide that if a clause is unenforceable then it can be dropped without the entire agreement failing, unless it goes to the root of the contract. A court may or may not choose to follow this, but such terms are common and may be useful.

### 16.18.6 COUNTERPARTS

If an agreement is to be executed in several counterparts, this should be stated and the clause should confirm that any one of those counterparts shall be an original.

### 16.18.7 NOTICES

The parties should provide how notices should be given to each other under the contract and to whom. If an organisation has job titles for its senior roles, then those should be used, not the name of individuals in case those persons move on and their post is not passed quickly to their successor.

### 16.18.8 GOVERNING LAW/JURISDICTION/ARBITRATION

These are separate fields of law in their own right but you should check their desirability before finalising your contract. You also need to ensure you take the governing law into account—for example, there is no point providing for Irish governing law if your client's customers are located all across Europe and may, under the Rome Convention, have the protection of their own mandatory rules. Irish law may still be, for the most part, the governing law, but your clients may need to brief lawyers in the other jurisdictions in which consumer customers reside to brief the client on what protections they will have there.

### 16.18.9 NO DEDUCTIONS

Many agreements provide that any payments made under them are to be made without deduction for or withholding tax or any other charges. You should either check the taxation aspects of the contract yourself or ask your clients to ensure that their own in-house or external tax experts approve the drafting. Make sure that if you are advising on tax that you are being paid for that separate advice.

### 16.18.10 JOINT AND SEVERAL OBLIGATIONS

You may wish to provide that any warranties, indemnities and obligations given or entered into by more than one person are given jointly and severally.

## 16.19 The Second Draft

After your client has reviewed the first draft, it is usual, assuming no great travel is involved, to have a meeting to 'turn the pages' on it together before proceeding to the next draft. The agreement can then be fine-tuned and resent to the client. You should emphasise to your client that generally a first draft should not be sent to the other side's lawyers if it is in very rough form. Both sides do not need to spend legal fees until the draft is more advanced. Often, time constraints may mean that this is not possible, but you should aim for it if at all practicable, as it will save time and money all round in the long run.

## 16.20 Problems in Drafting

### 16.20.1 ERRORS

Spelling errors and other typos may cause confusion—do not rely on computer spellcheck programs to catch errors—the typo may itself be a proper word and so may not be caught. Reread—if possible the next day—as you may pick up errors more easily after a rest. Have someone else read your draft if you think this will help pick up either errors or ambiguities in what you have drafted.

### 16.20.2 INCONSISTENCIES

Reread what you have drafted to ensure that where you use a term, that its use is consistent throughout. Any reader who picks up inconsistencies will find your draft difficult to read and will doubt the accuracy of what is there.

A common error is to have excellent definitions and then use those defined words in the agreement as if they were undefined. Capitalise defined words if possible to minimise the risk of this happening.

Have you used the wrong word—for example, if you wish to convey an obligation to do something as opposed to the option to do it, then use the word 'must' not 'may'.

### 16.20.3 UNUSUAL USE OF WORDS

A key to clear drafting is to use words in their normal meaning. If a term has become outdated (all the more so if it now may cause offence and may not have in the past) then you should use an alternative word or expression.

### 16.20.4 POOR GRAMMAR

If the grammar you use in the document is inaccurate your client may not trust the rest of the content! The rules of grammar are there to ensure readability and accuracy and your should ensure that you use of English is correct at all times.

Good punctuation will mean that when you cannot avoid a long sentence now and then, at least it will be readable. Use grammar and structure to your advantage. Break out complex ideas into paragraphs to make them more readable. Do not use more than one idea per paragraph or clarity will be lost. Use sub-paragraphs if necessary. Use headings to signpost ideas.

## 16.21 The Negotiation Process

Now that your draft is prepared, you will need to take your client through the process of getting it finalised with the other side. If you think that there will be a lengthy time gap between this and your client's original negotiations, then there should be a letter of intent in place to govern the gap period or at least a confidentiality agreement to protect your client if negotiations break down. The letter of intent (sometimes called a memorandum of understanding) may be binding or non-binding as provided for in the letter and may have a short exclusivity period built into it. If it is binding then you should endeavour to finalise the written contract as quickly as possible and try to ensure that your client does not commence performance under the contract until it is signed.

When the other side's lawyers have reviewed the contract, they will invariably send you comments for you and your client to discuss. Part of the negotiation process will be for you and your client to accept what changes you can, while maximising your client's protection under the agreement. Not all of the other side's changes will be unreasonable so you should try at all times to ensure good relations with the other lawyers. Many clients fear 'over-lawyering' in business, so you should represent your profession as being commercial, helpful and expert and remain aloof from any petty squabbling that you may be drawn into. Indeed it may suit the respective parties to the deal to portray the lawyers as the 'bad guys', as a justification for making certain contractual demands on one another. Within limits this can be unavoidable; however, you should make sure that your position is represented accurately.

A common bone of contention in the negotiation of commercial agreements is risk allocation. Your client may be investing a great deal of money in the purchase of a business in which it has a limited chance to carry out due diligence enquiries. In that scenario, it would be usual to expect the sellers of the business to provide extensive warranties to your client, the purchaser. These will naturally be contested by the seller's lawyers and so the extent of the risk allocation should be made clear to all parties at initial meetings.

Before negotiations begin, you should take the opportunity to discuss alternative plans with you client should negotiations fail. If negotiations become heated, and you want you client to have the benefit of your advice at an all-parties meeting without the others being present, you should ask to park certain points and revert to them at the end of the meeting after a short chat with the client. Often other points will by then have been negotiated and the parties will be more willing to compromise as they can see that progress is being made towards concluding the agreement.

## 16.22 Conclusion

Keep up to date with case law in the meaning of contractual terms, both in Ireland and abroad. These terms are often the subject of high-value litigation and an awareness of the legal trends is part of what your client is paying for. Learn from your colleagues' good drafting where you notice it, but respect copyright laws, your client is not paying for your 'cutting-and-pasting' skills! Conversely, protect your own intellectual property and recognise the financial worth of what you write for your clients. Many firms now have a policy of sending out documents only in PDF format for this reason (and others); however, this practice is not yet widespread.

# INDEX

**491**

# INDEX